# Routledge Handbook of Public Policy



This *Handbook* pr[...] n by an outstanding line-u[...] spects of the policy process[...]

- theory – from [...]
- frameworks – [...] ilibrium models and in[...]
- key stages in [...] entation and evaluation[...]
- the roles of k[...]
- policy learnin[...]

This is an invalua[...] ic policy and policy analys[...]

**Eduardo Arara**[...] Policy, National Univers[...]

**Scott Fritzen** is [...] National University of Sin[...]

**Michael Howle**[...] at Simon Fraser University [...]

**M Ramesh** is C[...] stitute of Education and [...] National University of Singapore.

**Xun Wu** is Associate Professor at the Lee Kuan Yew School of Public Policy, National University of Singapore.

# Routledge Handbook of Public Policy

*Edited by*
*Eduardo Araral Jr.*
*Scott Fritzen*
*Michael Howlett*
*M Ramesh*
*Xun Wu*

Routledge
Taylor & Francis Group
LONDON AND NEW YORK

First published in paperback in 2015

First published 2013
by Routledge
2 Park Square, Milton Park, Abingdon, Oxon OX14 4RN

Simultaneously published in the USA and Canada
by Routledge
711 Third Avenue, New York, NY 10017

*Routledge is an imprint of the Taylor & Francis Group, an informa business*



*British Library Cataloguing in Publication Data*
A catalogue record for this book is available from the British Library

*Library of Congress Cataloging in Publication Data*
Routledge Handbook of Public Policy / edited by E. Araral ... [et al.].
p. cm.
Includes bibliographical references and index.
1. Policy sciences. I. Araral, Eduardo. II. Title: Handbook of Public Policy.
H97.R68 2013
320.6–dc23
2012008846

ISBN: 978-0-415-78245-6 (hbk)
ISBN: 978-1-138-90888-8 (pbk)
ISBN: 978-0-203-09757-1 (ebk)

Typeset in Bembo
by Taylor & Francis Books

Printed and bound in Great Britain by
TJ International Ltd, Padstow, Cornwall

# Contents

# Illustrations

## Figures



## Tables

## Box

# Contributors

**Camilla Adelle** is a Senior Research Associate in the Science, Society and Sustainability Research Group, School of Environmental Sciences, University of East Anglia, Norwich, UK.

**Robert Agranoff** is an Emeritus Professor in the School of Public and Environmental Affairs, Indiana University, Bloomington, USA and Catedrático in the Government and Public Administration Program, Instituto Universitario Ortega y Gasset, Madrid, Spain. He joined Indiana University in 1980 from Northern Illinois University and started at Ortega y Gasset in 1990. He continues to be professionally active, specializing in public administration, intergovernmental relations and management, and public network studies.

**Paul Dragos Aligica** is a Senior Research Fellow at the Mercatus Center, a Senior Fellow on the F.A. Hayek Program for Advanced Study in Philosophy, Politics and Economics, a Faculty Fellow at the James Buchanan Center for Political Economy at George Mason University, USA, and an Adjunct Fellow at the Hudson Institute, Washington DC, USA. He studies institutional analysis and institutional theory.

**Eduardo Araral Jr.** is an Assistant Professor at the Lee Kuan Yew School of Public Policy, National University of Singapore. He is interested in the study of institutions for collective action from local to international levels and covering a variety of areas from the commons, international security, climate adaptation, bureaucracy and aid and water resources management.

**Thomas A. Birkland** is William T. Kretzer Distinguished Professor at the School of International and Public Affairs, North Carolina State University, USA where he teaches courses on the public policy process, environmental politics and policy, and disaster policy and management. His research has focused on how and to what extent major 'focusing events' influence policy agendas. His current research seeks to connect focusing events and policy failure to policy change and learning. He is the author of *An Introduction to the Policy Process* (2nd edn, M.E. Sharpe), and *After Disaster* and *Lessons of Disaster* (both Georgetown University Press), and is co-editor with Todd Schaefer of *The Encyclopedia of Mass Media* (CQ Press).

**Pieter Bots** is an Associate Professor in the Faculty of Technology, Policy and Management (TPM), Delft University of Technology, Netherlands. His expertise lies mainly in conceptual models and computer-based tools to support problem formulation and multi-actor systems analysis, preferably in combination with serious gaming/simulation.

**Graeme Boushey** is an Assistant Professor in the Department of Political Science at the University of California, Irvine, USA, where he teaches courses in American politics, Californian and state politics, public policy, and research methodology. His research focuses on public policy processes and political decision-making in American federalism. His teaching and research are organized around practical and theoretical questions of state and federal policy-making.

**Derick W. Brinkerhoff** is a Distinguished Fellow in International Public Management, at the Research Triangle Institute and has more than 30 years of experience with public management issues in developing and transitioning countries, focusing on policy analysis, programme implementation and evaluation, participation, institutional development, democratic governance, and change management. He is co-editor of the journal *Public Administration and Development*, and serves on the editorial boards of *Public Administration Review* and *International Review of Administrative Sciences*. He also holds an associate faculty appointment at the Trachtenberg School of Public Policy and Public Administration, George Washington University, USA.

**Jennifer M. Brinkerhoff** is Professor of Public Administration and International Affairs and Co-Director, GW Diaspora Program at the Elliott School of International Affairs at George Washington University, USA. She teaches courses on public service, international development policy and administration, development management and organizational behaviour. She is particularly keen on encouraging people to pursue service careers thoughtfully, grounding their commitment to change in self-awareness and working in community. She is the author of *Digital Diasporas: Identity and Transnational Engagement* (Cambridge University Press, 2009) and *Partnership for International Development: Rhetoric or Results?* (Lynne Rienner, 2002); the editor of *Diasporas and Development: Exploring the Potential* (Lynne Rienner, 2008); and co-editor of *NGOs and the Millennium Development Goals: Citizen Action to Reduce Poverty* (Palgrave Macmillan, 2007).

**Giliberto Capano** is Professor of Political Science and Public Policy at the University of Bologna, Italy. He specializes in comparative higher education, public administration and theories of policy-making. He has recently edited (with Elisabetta Gualmini) *La Pubblica amministrazione* in Italy (Il Mulino, 2011) and *European and North American Policy Change* (Routledge, 2009) with Michael Howlett.

**Carsten Daugbjerg** is a Professor at the Institute of Food and Resource Economics, University of Copenhagen, Denmark. His research area is comparative public policy with a particular interest in historical institutitionalism, policy networks, policy instruments and ideas in public policy. His empirical research has focused on agricultural policy reform, trade negotiations in the World Trade Organization, global food regulation, government interest group relations and environmental policy.

**Sarah E. DeYoung** is a doctoral student at North Carolina State University, USA, in the Psychology in the Public Interest programme. Her research interests are disaster policy and community disaster preparedness.

**Kevin P. Donnelly** is Assistant Professor of Political Science and Public Administration at Bridgewater State University, USA. His previous work includes *Foreign Remedies: What the Experience of Other Nations Can Tell Us about Next Steps in Reforming U.S. Health Care* (2012), co-authored with David A. Rochefort.

**Claire A. Dunlop** teaches politics and administration at the University of Exeter, UK. Previously she worked for the Scottish Consumer Council and the Scottish Executive. She has worked and published widely on issues related to knowledge use in governments and policy appraisal. Her recent work has appeared in *Political Studies*, *Public Management Review* and *Regulation and Governance*.

**Stephen J. Farnsworth** is Professor of Political Science and International Affairs at the University of Mary Washington, USA, where he directs the university's Center for Leadership and Media Studies. He is the author or co-author of four books on media and politics and a former Fulbright Scholar at McGill University, Canada.

**David Fuente** is a PhD student in the Department of City and Regional Planning at the University of North Carolina at Chapel Hill, USA.

**Boyd Fuller** is an Assistant Professor in the Lee Kuan Yew School of Public Policy at the National University of Singapore. His research focuses on the resolution of difficult water, environmental and land conflicts when stakeholders have apparently irreconcilable differences in values, identities or culture. He is currently researching the use of traditional and innovative dispute resolution techniques for public disputes in post-conflict areas of Southeast Asia. His previous research examined the mediation of intractable environmental conflicts in the United States. He has eight years' experience designing and implementing water supply projects in developing countries.

**Sarah Giest** is a PhD student in the Department of Political Science at Simon Fraser University in Burnaby, BC, Canada. She works on innovation systems and networks with special reference to comparative biotechnology clusters.

**Christoffer Green-Pedersen** is Professor of Political Science at Aarhus University, Denmark. His research focuses on agenda-setting dynamics and party competition.

**Michael Hayes** is Professor of Political Science at Colgate University, USA, specializing in interest group theory, incrementalism and policymaking, effects of public opinion on the legislative process. He has taught at Lawrence University and Rutgers University and published *Incrementalism and Public Policy*; *Lobbyists and Legislators*; various book chapters and articles (*Journal of Politics, Polity*) on the influence of interest groups and public opinion on policy-making.

**Carolyn M. Hendriks**'s work examines the democratic practices of contemporary governance, particularly with respect to public deliberation, inclusion and political representation. She has taught and published widely on the application and politics of inclusive and deliberative forms of citizen engagement. With a background in both political science and environmental engineering, Carolyn has a particular interest in the governance of the environment, as well as science and technology issues. She has recently published a book on the practice of deliberative democracy entitled *The Politics of Public Deliberation: Citizen Engagement and Interest Advocacy* (Palgrave Macmillan, 2011).

**Ruth Schuyler House** is a PhD student in the Lee Kuan Yew School of Public Policy at the National University of Singapore. Her research concentrates on the fields of water and sanitation policy. She is also interested in the changing face of governance and emerging opportunities for the private sector to assume responsibility for and lend valuable knowledge and resources to addressing poverty alleviation.

**Michael Howlett** is Burnaby Mountain Professor in the Department of Political Science at Simon Fraser University in Vancouver, Canada. He has published widely, most recently *Designing Public Policies: Principles and Instruments* (Routledge, 2011) and is co-editing with David Laycock *Regulating Next Generation Agri-Food Biotechnologies, Lessons from European, North American and Asian Experiences* (Routledge, 2012)

**Darryl S.L. Jarvis** is Vice-Dean of Academic Affairs and Associate Professor at the Lee Kuan Yew School of Public Policy, National University of Singapore and specializes in risk analysis and the study of political and economic risk in Asia, including investment, regulatory and institutional risk analysis. He has been a consultant to various government bodies and business organizations, and for two years was a member of the investigating team and then chief researcher on the Building Institutional Capacity in Asia (BICA) project commissioned by the Japanese Ministry of Finance.

**Bryan D. Jones**'s research interests centre on the study of public policy processes, American governing institutions, and the connection between human decision-making and organizational behaviour. Before joining the Department of Government at the University of Texas, Austin, USA, in 2008, Professor Jones was the Donald R. Matthews Distinguished Professor of American Politics at the University of Washington. Previously, he was Distinguished Professor and head of department at Texas A&M University, and also taught at Wayne State University. His books include *Politics and the Architecture of Choice* (2001) and *Reconceiving Decision-Making in Democratic Politics* (1994), both winners of the APSA Political Psychology Section Robert Lane Award; *The Politics of Attention* (co-authored with Frank Baumgartner, 2005); *Agendas and Instability in American Politics* (co-authored with Frank Baumgartner, 1993), winner of the 2001 Aaron Wildavsky Award for Enduring Contribution to the Study of Public Policy of the American Political Science Association's Public Policy Section and *The Politics of Bad Ideas* (co-authored with Walt Williams).

**Andrew Jordan** is Professor of Environmental Politics at the University of East Anglia, Norwich, UK. He is interested in the governance of environmental problems in many different contexts, but especially that of the European Union.

**Adrian Kay** is an Associate Professor in the Crawford School at the Australian National University and Director of its Policy and Governance Program. His current research interests are in the relationships between international and domestic policy processes, with a particular empirical focus on health and agriculture.

**David Knoke** is a Professor in the Department of Sociology at University of Minnesota, USA, where he teaches a graduate network analysis seminar that attracts students from diverse disciplines. He co-authored *Network Analysis* (1982) and has published 15 books and more than 100 articles and book chapters, primarily on organizations, networks, politics and social statistics. He was principal co-investigator on several National Science Foundation-funded projects on voluntary associations, lobbying organizations in national policy domains, and organizational surveys of diverse establishments.

**Andrea Lawlor** is a PhD student the Department of Political Science McGill University, Canada specializing in media and public policy. Other research interests include political parties, party financing and Quebec politics. Her research can be found in *Canadian Public Administration*.

**Raul Perez Lejano** is an Associate Professor of Planning, Policy and Design in the School of Social Ecology at the University of California, Irvine, USA. His research is currently in environmental planning, new decision models for explaining non-state/non-market institutions, relational models of collective action, planning theory, institutional models of care and justice research.

**Patrik Marier** holds a Tier-II Canada Research Chair (CRC) in Comparative Public Policy. His research focuses broadly on the impact of changing demographic structures on reforms to the welfare state in comparative contexts. His earlier work examined the politics of pension reform in a number of countries including Sweden, Canada, Mexico and the United States. His current research looks more broadly at the impact of ageing populations on a number of public policy fields including education, health care and labour policy across comparative cases.

**Igor S. Mayer** is a Senior Associate Professor in the Faculty of Technology, Policy and Management (TPM) at Delft University of Technology, Netherlands. He is also the director of the TU-Delft Centre for Serious Gaming.

**Allan McConnell** is Professor in the Department of Government and International Relations, University of Sydney, Australia. He has published extensively on policy and political issues surrounding crises, disasters, failures and fiascoes, as well as the more upbeat topic of policy success.

**Michael D. McGinnis** is Professor and Director of Graduate Studies in the Department of Political Science at Indiana University, Bloomington, USA. He studies the unique contributions that faith-based organizations make to the design and implementation of public policy related to humanitarian relief, development assistance, peace-building and reconciliation in troubled regions of the world, as well as standard public services in education, health care and welfare assistance in societies less directly challenged by the ravages of war.

**Michael McGuire** is Professor in the School of Public and Environmental Affairs, Indiana University, Bloomington, USA. He works on intergovernmental and interorganizational collaboration and networks and has published widely on public management topics. His recent publications on the subject have appeared in *Public Administration Review* and *Public Administration* among others.

**Michael Mintrom** is Professor of Public Sector Management at Monash University and the Australia and New Zealand School of Government. He is the author of *Contemporary Policy Analysis* (Oxford University Press, 2012), *People Skills for Policy Analysts* (Georgetown University Press, 2003), and *Policy Entrepreneurs and School Choice* (Georgetown University Press, 2000).

**Peter B. Mortensen** is Associate Professor of Political Science at Aarhus University. His research focuses on agenda-setting and public policy.

**Gary Mucciaroni** is a member of the Political Science Department at Temple University, USA and was Department Chair between 2005 and 2010. The focus of his research and publication is the politics of public policy-making in the United States – examining the forces and actors that impinge upon the policy choices of government. He has published *The Political Failure of Employment Policy, 1945–1982*, *Reversals of Fortune: Private Interests and Public Policy*, *Deliberative Choices: Debating Public Policy in Congress* and *Same Sex, Different Politics: Issues and Institutions in the Struggle for Gay and Lesbian Rights*.

**Daniel Nohrstedt** is an Associate Professor of Political Science at the Department of Government, Uppsala University, Sweden. His research is primarily focused on crisis and learning, intelligence issues, counter-terrorism policy and the public policy process.

**Anthony Perl** is Professor and Director of the Urban Studies Program and a member of the Department of Political Science at Simon Fraser University in Vancouver, Canada. His current research crosses disciplinary and national boundaries to explore the policy decisions that affect transportation, cities and the environment. His latest book, co-authored with Richard Gilbert, is *Transport Revolutions: Moving People and Freight Without Oil* published by New Society Publishers in 2010.

**Ora-orn Poocharoen** is an Assistant Professor at the Lee Kuan Yew School of Public Policy at the National University of Singapore. Her research interests include public management reform, public administration theory, organization theory, comparative public administration and public policy analysis.

**David A. Rochefort** is Arts and Sciences Distinguished Professor of Political Science at Northeastern University, USA. His previous works include *Foreign Remedies: What the Experience of Other Nations Can Tell Us about Next Steps in Reforming U.S. Health Care* (2012), written with Kevin P. Donnelly, and co-editor with Roger W. Cobb of *The Politics of Problem Definition* (1994), among other titles.

**Sophie Schmitt** is an Assistant Professor in the Department of Comparative Public Policy and Administration, University of Konstanz, Germany, and specializes in comparative public policy with a particular focus on environmental and social policy and regulation. She has recently published articles in the *Journal of European Public Policy* and *European Integration Online Papers*.

**Anne Schneider** is a Professor in the School of Justice at the University of Arizona, USA and specializes in public policy and the role of policy in democracy. She and long-time co-author Helen Ingram are the authors of *Policy Design for Democracy* (Kansas University Press), and *Deserving and Entitled* (SUNY Press), and 'The social construction of target populations,' *American Political Science Review*, June 1993.

**Chris Silvia** looks at interorganizational approaches to service delivery through the lens of emergency management. His research aims to help public managers, who are more accustomed to leading in hierarchical organizations, successfully contribute to leading networks. His recent research has appeared in *Journal of Public Affairs Education*, *State and Local Government Review* and *Public Administration Review*.

**Stuart Soroka** is an Associate Professor in the Department of Political Sciences, McGill University, Montreal, Canada.

**Geert R. Teisman** is currently Professor of Public Administration and Complex Decision Making and Process Management at the Erasmus University Rotterdam, Netherlands, and was previously Professor of Spatial Planning at the University of Nijmegen. He is member of the board of Habiforum, a joint venture between science, private sector and public authorities which explores possibilities of multiple land use. He is Scientific Director of Living with Water, a foundation which governs a variety of projects in which water system improvement is one of its important aims. He is member of the executive board of Netlipse, a European knowledge exchange network in the field of infrastructure project management. He regularly advises governments and private organizations on complex decision-making, strategic planning, public-private partnerships, process management, intergovernmental co-operation in metropolitan areas and policy evaluation.

**H.F. Thomas III** is a PhD student at Pennsylvania State University, USA, working on information, science and technology policy issues.

**John Turnpenny** is a Senior Research Associate at the University of East Anglia, Norwich, UK. His research focuses on the relationship between science, evidence and public policy-making.

**Arwin van Buuren** is an Associate Professor at the Department of Public Administration at the Erasmus University Rotterdam, Netherlands. His research focuses on the domain of water and climate governance. He is especially interested in the way in which complex governance processes are organized and how the relationship between knowledge and governance can be optimized. He combines fundamental with applied research. His recent articles have been published in *International Journal of Project Management, International Journal of Public Management, Public Management Review, Climatic Change and Environmental Impact Assessment Review.*

**Els van Daalen** is an Associate Professor at the Faculty of Technology, Policy and Management (TPM), Delft University of Technology, Netherlands. Her research interests include system dynamics modelling and the use of models in policy-making.

**Evert Vedung** is an Emeritus Professor of Political Science and a specialist in housing policy at Uppsala University, Sweden. He has held posts at Mälardalen University College and the University of Uppsala. He has been a board member of the Swedish Evaluation Society since its foundation.

**Christopher M. Weible** is an Assistant Professor in the School of Public Affairs at the University of Colorado Denver, USA. He teaches courses in environmental policy and politics, public policy, policy processes, policy analysis, and research methods and design. His area of research is in policy change, learning, political behaviour, coalitions and networks, institutions and collective action, collaborative governance, and the role of scientific and technical information in the policy process.

**Andy Whitford** is a Professor of Public Administration and Policy in the School of Public and International Affairs at the University of Georgia, USA. He concentrates on research and teaching in organizational studies and public policy, with specific interest in organization theory, models of decision-making and adaptation, and the political control of the bureaucracy. His interests in public policy include environmental, regulation and public health policy. He has particularly strong interest in the use of simulation and experimental methods for understanding organizational behaviour and individual choice.

**Dale Whittington** is a Professor of Environmental Sciences and Engineering, City and Regional Planning, and Public Policy, at the University of North Carolina at Chapel Hill, USA. Since 1986 he has worked for the World Bank and other international agencies on the development and application of techniques for estimating the economic value of environmental resources in developing countries, with a particular focus on water and sanitation and vaccine policy issues.

**Claire Williams** is a policy advisor at Victoria University of Wellington, New Zealand. She has previously published in *Policy and Society*.

**Chen-Yu Wu** is a graduate student in the Department of Sociology at the University of Minnesota, USA, and was a Teaching Assistant for the courses 'Introduction to Sociology' and 'Basic Social Statistics.'

**Lori Young** is a PhD student in the Annenberg School of Communication at the University of Pennsylvania, USA. Her published work includes studies of foreign news reporting in Canada and the United States and has appeared in journals such as *The International Journal of Press/Politics*.

# Part I

# Introduction to the study of the public policy process

## History and method

# 1

# Public policy debate and the rise of policy analysis

*Michael Mintrom and Claire Williams*

Since the mid-1960s, an increasingly large number of people, trained in the humanities and social sciences, have come to devote their professional lives to producing policy advice. This is a global phenomenon, although until recently the intensification of activities associated with policy advising has been most pronounced in the United States. As government demand for well-trained policy analysts and advisors has risen, universities have sought to provide relevant graduate-level training.

The rise of policy analysis is usefully construed as a movement. Use of this term implies a deliberate effort on the part of many people to reconceive the role of government in society and renegotiate aspects of the relationships that exist between individuals, collectivities and governments. However, the claim that there is a policy analysis movement should not be taken to imply either consistency of purpose or a deliberate striving for coordination among producers of policy analysis. While not directly comparable in a political sense with other social movements, the policy analysis movement has been highly influential. It has served to transform the advice-giving systems of governments, altered the nature of policy debate, and, as a consequence, challenged informal yet long-established advising practices through which power and influence flow. The profundity of this transformation has often eluded the attention of social and political commentators. That is because the relevant changes have caused few immediate or obvious ruptures in the processes and administrative structures typically associated with government or, more broadly speaking, public governance.

Early representations of policy analysis tended to cast it as a subset of policy advising. As such, policy analysis was seen primarily as an activity conducted inside government agencies with the purpose of informing the choices of a few key people, principally elected decision-makers (Lindblom 1968; Wildavsky 1979). Today, the potential purposes of policy analysis are understood to be much broader. Many more audiences are seen as holding interests in policy and as being open to – indeed demanding of – appropriately presented analytical work (Radin 2000). Beyond people in government, people in business, members of non-profit organizations, and informed citizens all constitute audiences for policy analysis. While policy analysts were once thought to be mainly located within government agencies, today policy analysts also can be found in most organizations that have direct dealings with governments, and in many organizations where government actions significantly influence the operating environment. In addition, many university-based researchers, who tend to treat their peers and their students as their primary audience, conduct studies that ask questions about government policies and that answer them using forms of policy analysis. Given this, an appropriately encompassing definition of contemporary policy analysis needs to recognize the range of topics and issue areas policy analysts work on, the range of analytical and research strategies they employ, and the range of audiences they seek to address. In recognizing the contemporary breadth of applications and styles of policy analysis, it becomes clear that effective policy analysis calls for not only the application of sound technical skills (Mintrom 2012), but also deep substantive knowledge, political perceptiveness and well-developed interpersonal skills (Mintrom 2003). Although producing high-quality, reliable advice remains a core expectation for many policy analysts, advising now appears as a subset of the broader policy analysis category. The transition from policy analysis as a subset of advising to advising as a subset of analysis represents a significant shift in orientation and priorities from earlier times.

In what follows, we first review the sources of increasing demand for policy analysis. We then review the growth and adaptation in the supply of policy analysis that has occurred in response to this demand. We conclude by discussing the current state of public policy debate and the likely future trajectory of both the practice of policy advising and the training of policy analysts. Throughout, we take the United States as our main point of reference. However, we have also sought to demonstrate the comparative relevance of our argument. We have done this by discussing the international embrace of New Public Management orthodoxy (from the late 1970s to the mid-1990s) and government responses to the global financial crisis (from 2007 into 2012).

Before proceeding, it is useful to define terms. For the purposes of this discussion, *public policies* are considered to be any actions taken by governments that represent previously agreed responses to specified circumstances. Governments design public policies with the broad purpose of expanding the public good (Howlett 2011; Mintrom 2012). *Policy studies* refers to research on policy topics and analytical work conducted primarily by university-based researchers with the goal of critically assessing past, present and proposed policy settings. Policy studies can be undertaken by researchers in many disciplinary or cross-disciplinary settings. They can draw upon a range of analytical and interpretative methodologies. Policy studies may be historical and comparative in their scope. The term *policy sciences* refers to the subset of analytical techniques devised in the social sciences that have been applied to understanding the design, implementation and evaluation of public policies. *Policy analysis* is here discussed as work intended to advance knowledge of the causes of public problems, alternative approaches to addressing them, the likely impacts of those alternatives, and trade-offs that might emerge when considering appropriate governmental responses to those public problems. *Policy advising* is defined here as the practice of providing information to decision-makers in government, with the intention of improving the base of knowledge upon which decisions are made. While policy advising need not be based upon rigorous policy analysis, over recent decades such policy analysis has come to play a more central part in the development of advice for decision-makers.

## The evolving demand for policy analysis

Demand for policy analysis has been driven mostly by the emergence of problems and by political conditions that have made those problems salient. Early in the development of policy analysis techniques, the people who identified the problems that needed to be addressed tended to be government officials. They turned to academics for help. Frequently, those academics deemed to be most useful, given the problems at hand, were economists with strong technical skills, who had the ability to estimate the magnitude of problems, undertake statistical analyses, and determine the costs of various government actions. During the twentieth century, as transportation, electrification and telecommunications opened up new opportunities for market exchange, problems associated with decentralized decision-making became more apparent (McCraw 1984). Meanwhile, as awareness grew of the causes of many natural and social phenomena, calls emerged for governments to establish mechanisms that might effectively manage various natural and social processes. Many matters once treated as social conditions, or facts of life to be suffered, were transformed into policy problems (Cobb and Elder 1983). Together, the increasing scope of the marketplace, the increasing complexity of social interactions, and expanding knowledge of social conditions created pressures from a variety of quarters for governments to take the lead in structuring and regulating individual and collective action. Tools of policy analysis, such as the analysis of market failures and the identification of feasible government responses, were developed to guide this expanding scope of government. Yet as the reach of policy analysis grew, questions were raised about the biases inherent in some of the analytical tools being applied. In response, new efforts were made to account for the effects of policy changes, and new voices began to contribute in significant ways to policy development. To explore the factors prompting demand for policy analysis, it is useful to work with a model of the policy-making process. A number of conceptions of policy-making have been developed in recent decades. Here, we apply the 'stages model', where five stages are typically posited: problem definition, agenda setting, policy adoption, implementation, and evaluation (Eyestone 1978).

Initial demands for policy analysis were prompted by growing awareness of problems that governments could potentially address. Questions inevitably arose concerning the appropriateness of alternative policy solutions. Thus, in the United States in the 1930s, as the federal government took on major new roles in the areas of regulation, redistribution and the financing of infrastructural development, the need arose for high quality policy analysis. With respect to regulatory policy, concerns about the threat to the railroads of the emerging trucking industry prompted the expansion of the Interstate Commerce Commission (Eisner 1993). This body employed lawyers and economists who helped to devise an expanding set of regulations that eventually covered many industries. Although the American welfare state has always been limited compared with welfare states elsewhere, especially those within Europe, its development still required concerted policy analysis and development work on the part of a cadre of bureaucrats (Derthick 1979). Initially, much of the talent needed to fill these positions was drawn from states like Wisconsin, where welfare policies had been pioneered by Robert LaFollette. As the role of the United States government in redistribution expanded, policy analysts swelled the ranks of career bureaucrats in the Treasury, the Office of Management and Budget, and the Department of Health and Human Services. Meanwhile, benefit-cost analysis, a cornerstone of modern policy analysis and a core component of public economics, was developed to help in the planning of dam construction in the Tennessee Valley in the 1930s. Politicians at the time worried that some dams were being built mainly to perpetuate the flow of cash to construction companies rather than to meet growing demand for electricity and flood control (Eckstein 1958). The broad applicability of the technique soon became clear and its use has continually expanded. At the same time, efforts to improve the sophistication of the technique, and to develop variations on it that are best suited to different sets of circumstances have also continued to occur (Boardman *et al.* 2006; Carlson 2011).

Several features of policy development, the politics of agenda setting, and the policymaking process have served over time to increase demand for policy analysts. The dynamics at work have been similar to those through which an arms race generates ongoing and often expanding demand for military procurements. In Washington, DC, the growing population of policy analysts employed in the federal government bureaucracy led to demand elsewhere around town for policy analysts who could verify or contest the analysis and advice emanating from government agencies. A classic example is given by the creation of the Congressional Budget Office (CBO). This office was established as an independent resource for Congress that would generate analysis and advice as a check on the veracity of the analyses prepared and disseminated by the executive-controlled Office of Management and Budget (Wildavsky 1992). The General Accounting Office – renamed in 2004 the Government Accountability Office – was also developed to provide independent advice for Congress. The purview of this Office has always been broader than that of the Congressional Budget Office.

As the analytical capabilities available to elected politicians grew, groups of people outside government but with significant interests in the direction of government policy began devoting resources to the production of high-quality, independent advice. Think tanks, like the Brookings Institution and the American Enterprise Institute, established in the 1920s and 1940s respectively, and both still going strong, represent archetypes of many independent policy shops now located in Washington, DC (Smith 1991).

Today, due to the knowledge base of think tanks and their entrepreneurial capacity, their staff and affiliates are often regarded as members of a select few who dominate policy. Networks between non-governmental policy experts and politicians in the United States are strengthened through appointments into government departments – often described as a "revolving door" – in which policy experts frequently move into and out of key positions in the government over successive presidential elections. Therefore, United States think tanks are often viewed as trustworthy sources of advice to the administration because of their deep connections, the star status of some of their people, and their sophisticated influence efforts.

It is useful to note that the roles, character, and effectiveness of think tanks are shaped by country-specific institutional and political factors. In the United States, most think tanks tend to serve both as 'watch dogs' and as 'idea brokers'; how much they exhibit either characteristic depends largely on their alignment or lack of alignment with the political colours of the current Administration. In contrast, most think tanks operating in Asian countries tend to view their role as 'regime-enhancing' (Stone 2000; Stone and Denham 2004; Abelson 2004).

Parliamentary systems, found most conspicuously in Commonwealth countries, tend to exhibit greater centralization of legislative power and accountability than systems like that of the United States where the separation of powers is a fundamental characteristic of governance. Centralization of power gives those in leadership positions greater control over policy. The electoral system can serve to either enhance or diminish the power that those in government exercise over policy development. This has been clearly exhibited in the case of New Zealand, where a switch in 1996 from first-past-the-post to mixed member proportional representation in parliament changed the political landscape. Due to the increased diversity and number of actors in the policy-making process, policy deliberation now tends to be longer and more consultative, requiring greater input from a wider range of political actors and interest groups (Boston *et al.* 2003). This change in the electoral system has resulted in greater demand for policy analysis. The potential for influence among political parties, members of parliament and interest groups outside the government has led them to build analytical strengths that had previously been almost the exclusive preserve of government departments.

The American constitution has an enshrined checks and balances system including a federal and presidential system which is highly decentralized and fragmented. Establishment of the Congressional Policy Advisory Board in 1998 has provided a further channel for experts to share their advice with members of Congress as three-quarters of the policy experts on the board are from think tanks. Combined with weak parties and considerable employee turnover, the United States government is open to a host of government and non-government experts engaging in policy-making (McGann and Johnson 2006).

Although policy analysis is often understood as work that occurs before a new policy or programme is adopted, demand for policy analysis has also been driven by interest in the effectiveness of government programmes. The question of what happens once a policy idea has been adopted and passed into law could be construed as too operational to deserve the attention of policy analysts. Yet, during the past few decades, elements of implementation have become recognized as vital for study by policy analysts (Bardach 1977; Lipsky 1984; Pressman and Wildavsky 1973). In part, this has been led by results of programme evaluations, which have often found policies not producing their intended outcomes, or worse, creating whole sets of unintended and negative consequences. One important strain of the work devoted to assessing implementation has contributed to what is now known as the 'government failure' literature (Niskanen 1971; Weimer and Vining 2005; Wolf 1979). The possibility that public policies designed to address market failures might themselves create problems led to a greater respect for market processes and a degree of scepticism on the part of policy analysts towards the remedial abilities of government (Rhoads 1985). In turn, this required policy analysts to develop more nuanced understandings of the workings of particular markets. The government failure literature has led to greater interest in government efforts to simulate market processes, or to reform government and contract out aspects of government supply that could be taken up by private firms operating in the competitive marketplace (Osborne and Gaebler 1993). Where efforts to reform government have been thorough-going, an interesting dynamic has developed. As the core public sector has shrunk in size, the number of policy analysts employed in the sector has increased, both in relative and in absolute terms. This dynamic is indicative of governments developing their capacities in the management of contracts rather than in the management of services (Savas 1987). In these new environments, people exhibiting skills in mechanism design and benefit-cost analysis have been in demand. Therefore, employment opportunities for policy analysts have tended to expand, even as the scope of government has been curtailed. Fiscal conservatism, which was a hallmark of governments in many jurisdictions that embraced the New Public Management practices added to this trend (Yergin and Stanislaw 1998; Williamson 1993). When budgets are squeezed, it becomes critical for all possible efficiency gains to be realized. More than any other trained professionals, policy analysts working in government are well-placed to undertake the kind of analytical work needed to identify cost-saving measures and to persuade elected decision-makers to adopt them.

The exact influence policy advisors have been able to exert over political decision-makers is difficult to measure because of the range of factors that influence policy outcomes. Moreover, the changing nature of political and institutional environments throughout periods in history have meant that not only has the definition of policy analyst changed over time but the extent of their influence has also fluctuated. 'Windows of opportunity' for policy influence appear more frequently in some circumstances than in others (Kingdon 1995). For example, the move towards addressing large national debts led to wide-scale reform of government policy settings in many jurisdictions during the 1980s and 1990s.

By the 1980s the world had become intensely global: economically, socially and politically. Global problems often resulted in similar policy outcomes. In New Zealand at that time, political leaders became aware that the country's economic position was deteriorating. Faced with economic stagnation, social disruption and ideological shifts away from dependence upon government for the allocation of many resources in society, the New Zealand government became open to the influence of institutions and agencies with perceived expertise in the dominant problems of the day (Oliver 1989).

The strength of central agencies, endowed with economic expertise, such as the New Zealand Treasury and organizations such as the New Zealand Business Round Table (NZBRT), were intensified by individual networks intertwining ministers with key bureaucrats and non-elected political actors. Not unlike other countries such as Norway, Sweden, Britain and France, in the 1980s, a single economics ministry in New Zealand meant that there were few opportunities for countervailing power. The system in New Zealand at that time was thus described by one commentator as an 'elective dictatorship' (Boston 1989).

In New Zealand the Treasury was the Government's most important advisory body. By recruiting a senior manager from the Treasury, Roger Kerr, to lead the NZBRT in 1986, business leaders recognized the value of networks and the strength of the Treasury department (Mintrom 2006). The NZBRT ensured that the views of business leaders were fully articulated in policy discussions. The Minister of Finance was reported at the time to have a relationship with the Round Table that was 'so close you couldn't slide a Treasury paper between them' (Murray and Pacheco 2001).

The conditions that allowed a few advisors broad influence over political decision-makers can partly explain why the economic restructuring undertaken in New Zealand in the 1980s and 1990s was so extensive. As with 'Reaganism' in the United States, and at least the early days of 'Thatcherism' in Britain, 'Rogernomics' in New Zealand followed a pattern of international policy transfer which included commercialization, liberalization and deregulation. These ideas were not new. They began in North America and Europe a decade earlier and 'represented a global spread of neo-liberal politics' (Dolowitz and Marsh 2000; Heffernan 1999).

Over the past few decades, technological advances have improved communication and made it easier for policy advisers and decision-makers to assess different policy decisions, thus increasing the occurrences of policy transfer. While it is relatively simple to spot broad trends in policy development, individual countries always exhibit specific, even idiosyncratic, policy design elements. Liberalization in New Zealand, the United States and Britain during the 1980s and 1990s included rescission of the existing regulatory regime and a reduction in protectionist legislation aimed at instituting competitiveness through a free market. In New Zealand, it was carried out extensively at an unprecedented speed and has largely been unparalleled (Goldfinch 1998). In the United States the focus on monetary policy as a prime instrument to shape the economy represented a comprehensive change in policies which were up to that time not politically viable. In contrast, liberalization and deregulation in Britain were not as quick, nor were they a radical departure from ideas already in train, and were thus seen as more path dependant and incremental (Niskanen 1988; Heffernan 1999).

The global financial crisis emerged rapidly in mid-2007. This saw governments around the world intervene in the operation of financial markets in a manner that would have been shunned during the 1980s and 1990s. The degree to which public policy settings undergird the effective workings of markets has become salient again. As a consequence, the current period has entrenched the pervasive role of government in capitalist societies. At its best, this new era of policy-making has seen efforts being made to carefully balance responses to market failures against risks of government failure. At its worst, the new era has offered instances of those who contributed to the crisis being cushioned, with those most harmed by the crisis receiving no governmental relief. In short, the current period has opened space for extensive debate about public policy and the role of government in society. The developmental role of governments in promoting economic advancement – observed most starkly in the Asian tiger economies over recent decades – has been eyed by some observers as a sound prescription, even for the most advanced economies in the world. Sceptics have been much more concerned about extensive government interventions into economic activities. Frequent voice has been given to the worry of government failure – exhibited most obviously by special interest capture of government subsidies.

Discussions during the 1960s and 1970s of the role of policy analysts in society often portrayed them as 'whiz kids' or 'econocrats' on a quest to imbue public decision-making with high degrees of rigour and rationality (Self 1977; Stevens 1993). Certainly, proponents of benefit-cost analysis considered themselves to have a technique for assessing the relative merits of alternative policy proposals that, on theoretical grounds, trumped any others on offer. Likewise, proponents of programme evaluation employing quasi-experimental research designs considered their approach to be superior to other approaches that might be used to determine programme effectiveness (Cook and Campbell 1979). That the application of both benefit-cost analysis and quantitative evaluation techniques has continued unabated for several decades speaks to their perceived value for generating usable knowledge. However, the limitations of such techniques have not been lost on critics. In the case of benefit-cost analysis, features of the technique that make it so appealing – such as the reduction of all impacts to a common metric and the calculation of net social benefits – have also attracted criticism. In response, alternative methods for assessing the impacts of new policies, such as environmental impact assessments, social impact assessments and health impact assessments have gained currency (Barrow 2000; Lock 2000; Wood 1995). Similarly, widespread efforts have been made to promote the integration of gender and race analysis into policy development (Mintrom 2012; Myers 2002; True and Mintrom 2001). In the case of evaluation studies, fundamental and drawn-out debates have occurred covering the validity of various research methods and the appropriate scope and purpose of evaluation efforts. Significantly for the present discussion, these debates have actually served to expand demand for policy analysis. Indeed, government agencies designed especially to audit the impacts of policies on the family, children, women and racial minorities have now been established in many jurisdictions. Further, evaluation of organizational processes, which often scrutinize the nature of the interactions between organizations and their clients are now accorded equivalent status among evaluators as more traditional efforts to measure programme outcomes (Patton 1997; Weiss 1998). Yet these process evaluations are motivated by very different questions and draw upon very different methodologies than traditional evaluation studies that assessed programme impacts narrowly.

This review of the evolving demand for policy analysis has identified several trends that have served both to embed policy analysts at the core of government operations and to expand demand for policy analysts both inside and outside government. These trends have much to do with the growing complexity of economic and social relations and knowledge generation. Yet there is also a sense in which policy analysis itself generates demand for more policy analysis. While these trends have been most observable in national capitals, where a large amount of policy development occurs, they have played out in related ways in other venues as well. For instance, in federal systems, expanding cadres of well-trained policy analysts have become engaged in sophisticated, evidence-based policy debates in state and provincial capitals.

Cities, too, are increasingly making extensive use of policy analysts in their strategy and planning departments. At the global level, key coordinating organizations, such as the World Bank, the International Monetary Fund, the World Trade Organization, and the Organization for Economic Cooperation and Development have made extensive use of the skills of policy analysts to monitor various transnational developments and national-level activities of particular relevance and interest.

Today, the demand for policy analysis is considerable, and it comes both from inside and outside governments. This demand is likely to keep growing as calls emerge for governments to tackle emerging, unfamiliar problems. On the one hand, we should expect to see ongoing efforts to harness technical procedures drawn from the social sciences and natural sciences for the purposes of improving the quality of policy analysis. On the other hand, more people are likely to apply these techniques, reinvent them, or develop whole new approaches to counteract them, all with the purpose of gaining greater voice in policy-making at all levels of government from the local to the global.

## The evolving supply of policy analysis

To meet the growing demand for policy analysis, since the mid-1960s supply has greatly expanded. But this expansion has been accompanied, at least around the edges of the enterprise, by a transformation in the very nature of the products on offer. Consequently it is now commonplace to find policy analysts who question the questions of the past, who are politically motivated, or who seek to satisfy intellectual curiosity rather than to offer solutions to immediate problems. Thus, the apparently straightforward question of what constitutes policy analysis cannot be addressed in a straightforward manner. Answers given will be highly contingent on context. For example, an answer offered in the mid-1970s would be narrower in scope than an answer offered now. Likewise, the question of who produces policy analysis is also contingent. Economists have always been well represented in the ranks of policy analysts. People from other disciplines have also contributed to policy analysis, although there has often been a sense that other disciplines have less to contribute to policy design and the weighing of alternatives. Today, practitioners and scholars heralding from an array of disciplines are engaged in this kind of work, and the relevance of disciplines other than economics is well understood. In this review of the evolving supply of policy analysis, we consider both the development of a mainstream and the growing diversity of work that now constitutes policy analysis.

There has always been a mainstream style of conducting policy analysis. That style is more prevalent today than it has ever been. The style is portrayed by practitioners and critics alike as the application of a basic, yet continually expanding, set of technical practices (Stokey and Zeckhauser 1978). Most of those practices derive from microeconomic analysis. They include the analysis of individual choice and trade-offs, the analysis of markets and market failure, and the application of benefit-cost analysis. Contemporary policy analysis textbooks tend to build on this notion of policy analysis as a technical exercise (Bardach 2000; Mintrom 2012; Munger 2000; Weimer and Vining 2005). For example, in his practical guide to policy analysis, Eugene Bardach (2000) contends that a basic, 'eightfold' approach can be applied to analysing most policy problems. The approach requires us to define the problem, assemble some evidence, construct the alternatives, select the criteria, project the outcomes, confront the trade-offs, decide, and tell our story. As with Stokey and Zeckhauser's approach, Bardach's approach clearly derives from microeconomic analysis, and benefit-cost analysis in particular. None of this should surprise us since, to the extent that a discipline called policy analysis exists at all, it is a discipline that grew directly out of microeconomic analysis. That disciplinary linkage remains strong. Economists comprise the majority of members of the United States-based Association for Public Policy Analysis and Management (APPAM), the largest such association in the world. Likewise, contributions to the Association's *Journal of Policy Analysis and Management* are authored predominantly, although certainly not exclusively, by economists.

Viewed positively, we might note that the basic approach to policy analysis derived from microeconomics is extremely serviceable. As scholars have continued to apply and expand this style of analysis, a rich body of technical practices has been created. Extensive efforts have been made to ensure that university students interested in careers in policy analysis gain appropriate exposure to these approaches and receive opportunities to apply them. Most Masters programmes in public policy analysis or public administration require students to take a core set of courses that expose them to microeconomic analysis, public economics, benefit-cost analysis, descriptive and inferential statistics, and evaluation methods. Sometimes the core is augmented by courses on topics such as strategic decision-making, the nature of the policy process, and organizational behaviour. Students are usually also given opportunities to augment their core course selections with a range of elective courses from several disciplines. Without doubt, graduates of these programmes emerge well-equipped to immediately begin contributing in useful ways to the development of public policy. Over recent decades, many universities in the United States have introduced Masters programmes designed to train policy analysts along the lines suggested here. More recently, similar programmes have been established in many other countries around the globe. Those establishing them know that there is strong demand for the kind of training they seek to provide. These professional courses create opportunities for people who have already been trained in other disciplines to acquire valuable skills for supporting the development of policy analyses. Graduates end up being placed in many organizations in the public, private and non-profit sectors.

Viewed more negatively, the mainstream approach to teaching and practising policy analysis can be critiqued for its narrowness and the privileging of techniques derived from economic theory over analytical approaches that draw upon political and social theory. Suppose we again describe the policy-making process as a series of stages: problem definition; agenda setting; policy adoption; implementation; and evaluation. The mainstream approach to policy analysis has little to contribute to our understanding of agenda setting, or the politics of policy adoption, implementation and evaluation. Steeped as it is in the rational choice or utilitarian perspective, mainstream policy analysis is poorly suited to helping us to understand why particular problems might manifest themselves at given times, why some policy alternatives might appear politically palatable while others will not, and why adopted policies often go through significant transformations during the implementation stage. In addition, technical approaches to programme evaluation, while obviously necessary for guiding the measurement of programme effectiveness, typically prescribe narrow data collection procedures that can leave highly relevant information unexamined. Studies that dwell on assessing programme outcomes are unlikely to reveal the multiple, and perhaps conflicting, ways that programme personnel and programme participants often make sense of programmes. In turn, this might cause analysts to misinterpret the motivations that lead programme personnel and participants to redefine programme goals from those originally intended by policy-makers. Problems of programme design or programme theory might end up being ignored in favour of interpretations that place the blame on faulty implementation (Chen 1990). More generally, mainstream approaches to policy analysis can encourage practitioners to hold tightly to assumptions about individual and collective behaviour that are contradicted by the evidence. In the worst cases, this can lead to inappropriate specification of proposals for policy change.

The foregoing observations might cause us to worry that mainstream training in policy analysis does not sufficiently equip junior analysts to become reflective practitioners or practitioners who listen closely to the voices of people who are most likely to be affected by policy change (Forrester 1999; Schön 1983). Certainly, strong critiques of mainstream analytical approaches have led to some rethinking of the questions that policy analysts should ask when working on policy problems (Stone 2002). Yet it is a fact that many people who have gone on to become excellent policy managers and leaders of government agencies began their careers as junior policy analysts fresh out of mainstream policy programmes. This suggests that, within professional settings, heavy reliance is placed on mechanisms of tacit knowledge transfer, whereby narrowly trained junior analysts come to acquire skills and insight that serve them well as policy managers. Our sense is that the key components of this professional socialization can be codified and are teachable (Mintrom 2003). But much of what it takes to be an effective policy analyst is not captured in the curricula of the many university programmes that now exist to train future practitioners.

Beyond mainstream efforts to expand the supply of policy analysts, all of which place heavy emphasis on the development of technical skills informed primarily by microeconomic theory, other disciplines also contribute in significant ways to the preparation of people who eventually become engaged in policy analysis. In these cases, the pathway from formal study to the practice of policy analysis is often circuitous. People with substantive training in law, engineering, natural sciences and the liberal arts might begin their careers in closely related fields, only to migrate into policy work later. For example, individuals trained initially as sociologists might gain professional qualifications as social workers and, after years in the field, assume managerial roles that require them to devote most of their energies to policy development. People pursuing these alternative professional routes towards working as policy analysts can bring rich experiences and diverse insights to policy discussions. The resulting multidisciplinary contributions to policy discussions have been known to generate their share of intractable policy controversies (Schön and Rein 1994). Yet, when disagreements that emerge from differences in training and analytical perspectives are well managed, these multidisciplinary forums can produce effective policy design. Indeed, increasing efforts are now being made to address significant problems through 'joined-up government' initiatives (Perri 6: 2004). Through these, individuals with diverse professional backgrounds who are known to have been working on similar problems are brought together to work out cohesive policy strategies to address those problems. For example, pediatricians, police officers, social workers and educators might be asked to work together to devise policies for effective detection and prevention of child abuse.

Two somewhat contradictory trends in the evolving supply of policy analysis have been noted here. On the one hand, the growth of university-based professional programmes designed to train policy analysts has contributed to a significant degree of analytical isomorphism. No matter which university or country such programmes are based, the students are required to study much the same set of topics and to read from a growing canon of articles and books covering aspects of policy analysis. These programmes promote ways of thinking about public policy that owe heavy debts to the discipline of economics. On the other hand, researchers and practitioners working out of other disciplines have increasingly become involved in the production of policy analysis. These contributions from outside the mainstream have tended to promote analytical diversity. Taken together, these contradictory trends define the contemporary field of policy analysis. Often, the differences are downplayed. For example, while the *Journal of Policy Analysis and Management* publishes research articles and shorter pieces on teaching practice, all of which can be informed by a variety of disciplinary perspectives, the overall impression given is that of a journal devoted to the furtherance of mainstream methods of policy analysis. In contrast, controversies in the interdisciplinary field of evaluation studies have left a distinctly different impression. As a result, courses on policy evaluation, when taught in professional public policy programmes, can introduce perspectives that sit uncomfortably with those taught in other core courses. Similarly, the eclecticism of contributions to organizational studies can transform otherwise staid courses on public management and administration into eye-opening explorations of organizational behaviour that present perspectives and analyses differing starkly from mainstream economic interpretations.

The evolving supply of policy analysis is likely to continue to be defined by a mixture of mainstream and alternative analytical perspectives. New policy problems generated by changing social conditions, technologies and political agendas cannot be expected to readily lend themselves to mainstream policy analysis. Indeed, although policy analysis textbooks present specific forms of market failure or government failure as defensible rationales for policy action, many contemporary problems defy such categorization. For example, changing understandings of morally appropriate behaviour (Mooney 2000) and differing perspectives on the degree to which parents and the state should be trusted to act in the best interests of children (Nelson 1984; Shapiro 1999) have provided impetus for a range of recent policy disputes. Mainstream approaches to policy analysis are not well suited to assessing the relative merits of competing arguments and perspectives in these areas. This suggests that, for any headway to be made in addressing disputes of this sort, the comparative strengths of alternative disciplinary perspectives must be drawn upon to guide policy analysis. The frontiers of policy analysis are also being advanced by a growing awareness of the degree to which national policies hold implications for international relations, transnational norms, and global trade or environmental concerns (Sandler 2004; Tabb 2004). These developments will require further innovation in the design and application of policy analysis techniques. In many instances, the mainstream perspective will need to be augmented by alternative perspectives that offer sound analytical traction on otherwise difficult conceptual and practical problems. Thus, definitions of policy analysis are likely to keep expanding and the set of actors having relevant and important contributions to make will remain dynamic.

## Prospects for the policy analysis movement

The policy analysis movement began to emerge in the mid-1960s. Today, it is large, diverse and global. The phenomenon of many people generating policy analysis for consumption by an array of audiences can be claimed to be a movement for several reasons. First, policy analysts, no matter where they are located within society, all focus their energies in one way or another on identifying, understanding and confronting public problems. As techniques of policy analysis have been more routinely applied to investigating public problems, new problems and new approaches to addressing them have been revealed. While a finite set of known policy problems might exist at any given time, that set is continually being revised, as particular problems are resolved and as others become salient. Second, while people engaged in policy analysis work out of a variety of perspectives and often make contradictory and conflicting arguments, there is a widely shared recognition that knowledge of public problems and how they can best be addressed requires thorough, theory-driven, and evidence-based investigation. This is highly significant, because changing perceptions of what kind of claims should guide public deliberations have made it harder for long-entrenched groups to use their informal, quiet power to influence government actions. Third, the increasing reliance placed on this style of policy analysis has required a core of people to routinely apply a well-established set of analytical and research methods. The result has been the clear definition of a mainstream of policy analysis, and many university programmes have been established to professionalize budding analysts. Fourth, the development of policy analysis has not been restricted to those people applying mainstream techniques. Indeed, there has been a level of openness to people from various disciplines offering alternative theoretical and empirical arguments concerning particular policy matters. Critique of mainstream methods has often resulted in significant efforts to improve the analytical approaches employed. Finally, people engaged in policy analysis, regardless of their substantive interests or their immediate purposes, have shared an understanding that they are engaged in important, socially relevant work. They share a common understanding that, at base, public policy involves systematic efforts to change social institutions. The seriousness of this work helps to explain why policy disputes are often prolonged and heated. Taken together, these various features of contemporary policy work clearly represent markers of a policy analysis movement. Those associated with it are, in their many particular ways, contributing to the ongoing task of defining the appropriate role of government in society, and how governments can best mediate social and economic relations.

What are the future prospects of this movement? How might it continue to evolve? Internal and external dynamics are likely to ensure further expansion of the movement. With respect to internal dynamics, a clear lesson of the foregoing discussion is that good policy analysis creates its own demand. This happens because, in competitive settings like debates over policy choices, opposing parties face strong incentives to find ways to outsmart their opponents. If one party's arguments are consistently supported by strong policy analysis and this appears to give them an edge in debate, then other parties will soon see the merit in upping their own game. This can involve emulating, revising or critiquing the methods of opponents. But, no matter what, the result is further production of policy analysis. Aside from this, careful policy studies, especially evaluations of existing programmes, often reveal aspects of policy design or implementation that require further attention. When we are forced to return to the drawing board, further policy analysis occurs. The lesson that good policy analysis creates its own demand suggests that the currently observed momentum and vibrancy of that movement will continue.

The external dynamics that drive expansion of the policy analysis movement derive from changing social, economic and political conditions. In the future, the increasing integration of economies and societies, referred to generally as globalization, can be expected to generate new sets of policy problems. In this regard, the changes associated with globalization echo the dynamics that were observed from the late nineteenth century well into the twentieth century in federal systems. During that period, increasing commerce across state and provincial borders, and the emergence of intensive inter-jurisdictional competition prompted new considerations of the role of government in society. Extensive effort also went into determining what levels of government were best suited to performing different functions. New times introduce new problems and questions. Drawing lessons from the past, it seems clear that many new policy problems will arise on government agendas and be the focus of extensive debates in the coming decades. While globalizing forces will be responsible for generating many of these challenges, the challenges themselves will be manifested at all levels of government, from the local upwards. As in the past, people both inside and outside government can be expected to show intense interest in these policy challenges, and they will call for further supply of innovative and high-quality policy analysis to build their knowledge and strengthen their debating points.

## Bibliography


Abelson, Donald. 2004. 'The think tank industry in the USA', in Diane Stone and Andrew Denham. *Think Tank Traditions: Policy Research and the Politics of Ideas*. Manchester: Manchester University Press.

Bardach, Eugene. 1977. *The Implementation Game: What Happens After a Bill Becomes a Law*. Cambridge, MA: MIT Press.

—— 2000. *A Practical Guide for Policy Analysis: The Eightfold Path to More Effective Problem Solving*. New York: Seven Bridges Press/Chatham House.

Barrow, C.J. 2000. *Social Impact Assessment: An Introduction*. New York: Oxford University Press.

Boardman, Anthony E., David H. Greenberg, Aidan R. Vining and David L. Weimer. 2006. *Cost-benefit Analysis: Concepts and Practice*. Englewood Cliffs, NJ: Pearson/Prentice Hall.

Boston, Jonathan. 1989. 'The Treasury and the organisation of economic advice: Some international comparisons', in Brian Easton (ed.) *The Making of Rogernomics*. Auckland: Auckland University Press, 68–91.

—— Stephen Church and Tim Bale. 2003. 'The impact of proportional representation on government effectiveness: The New Zealand experience', *Australian Journal of Public Administration* 62(21).

Carlson, Deven. 2011. 'Trends and innovations in public policy analysis', *Policy Studies Journal* 39: 13–26.

Chen, Huey-Tsyh. 1990. *Theory-Driven Evaluations*. Newbury Park, CA: Sage.

Cobb, Roger W. and Charles W. Elder. 1983. *Participation in American Politics: The Dynamics of Agenda-Building*, 2nd edn. Boston, MA: Allyn and Bacon.

Cook, Thomas D. and Donald T. Campbell. 1979. *Quasi-Experimentation: Design and Analysis Issues for Field Settings*. Boston, MA: Houghton Mifflin Company.

Dahl, Robert A. 1998. *On Democracy*. New Haven, CT: Yale University Press.

Derthick, Martha. 1979. *Policymaking for Social Security*. Washington, DC: Brookings Institution.

Dolowitz, D. and D. Marsh. 2000. 'Learning from abroad: The role of policy transfer in contemporary policy-making', *Governance* 13: 5–24.

Eckstein, Otto. 1958. *Water Resource Development*. Cambridge, MA: Harvard University Press.

Eisner, Marc Allen. 1993. *Regulatory Politics in Transition*. Baltimore, MD: Johns Hopkins University Press.

Eyestone, Robert. 1978. *From Social Issues to Public Policy*. New York: John Wiley & Sons.

Forester, John. 1999. *The Deliberative Practitioner: Encouraging Participatory Planning Processes*. Cambridge, MA: MIT Press.

Goldfinch, Shaun. 1998. 'Remaking New Zealand's economic policy: Institutional elites as radical innovators', *Governance* 11, 177–207.

Heffernan, Richard. 1999. *New Labour and Thatcherism: Political Change in Britain*. New York: St. Martin's Press.

Howlett, Michael. 2011. *Designing Public Policies: Principles and Instruments*. Abingdon: Routledge.

Kingdon, John W. 1995. *Agendas, Alternatives, and Public Policies*. New York: HarperCollins College Publishers.

Lindblom, Charles E. 1968. *The Policymaking Process*. Englewood Cliffs, NJ: Prentice-Hall.

Lipsky, Michael. 1980. *Street-Level Bureaucracy: The Dilemmas of the Individual in Public Services*. New York: Russell Sage Foundation.

—— 1984. 'Bureaucratic disentitlement in social welfare programs', *Social Service Review* 58(1): 3–27.

Lock, Karen. 2000. 'Health impact assessment', *British Medical Journal* 320: 1395–8.

McCraw, Thomas K. 1984. *Prophets of Regulation*. Cambridge, MA: Belknap Press.

McGann, James and Erik Johnson. 2006. *Comparative Think Tanks, Politics and Public Policy*. Cheltenham: Edward Elgar Publishing.

Mintrom, Michael. 2003. *People Skills for Policy Analysts*. Washington, DC: Georgetown University Press.

—— 2006. 'Policy entrepreneurs, think tanks, and trusts', in Raymond Miller (ed.) *New Zealand Government and Politics*, 4th edn, Melbourne: Oxford University Press, 536–46.

—— 2012. *Contemporary Policy Analysis*. New York: Oxford University Press.

——and Sandra Vergari. 1996. 'Advocacy coalitions, policy entrepreneurs, and policy change', *Policy Studies Journal* 24: 420–35.

Mooney, Christopher Z. (ed.) 2000. *The Public Clash of Private Values: The Politics of Morality Policy*. New York: Chatham House Publishers of Seven Bridges Press.

Munger, Michael C. 2000. *Analyzing Policy: Choices, Conflicts, and Practices*. New York: W.W. Norton.

Murray, Georgina and Douglas Pacheco. 2001. 'Think tanks in the 1990s', The Australian National University.

Myers, Samuel L. Jr. 2002. 'Presidential address - analysis of race as policy analysis', *Journal of Policy Analysis and Management* 21: 169–90.

Nelson, Barbara. 1984. *Making an Issue of Child Abuse*. Chicago: University of Chicago Press.

Niskanen, William A., Jr. 1971. *Bureaucracy and Representative Government*. Chicago: Aldine-Atherton.

—— 1988. *Reaganomics: An Insider's Account of the Policies and the People*. New York: Oxford University Press.

Oliver, W. Hugh. 1989. 'The labour caucus and economic policy formation, 1981-1984', in Brian Easton (ed.) *The Making of Rogernomics*. Auckland: Auckland University Press, 11–52.

Osborne, David and Ted Gaebler. 1993. *Reinventing Government: How the Entrepreneurial Spirit is Transforming the Public Sector*. New York: Penguin Books.

Patton, Michael Quinn. 1997. *Utilization-Focused Evaluation: The New Century Text*. Thousand Oaks, CA: Sage.

Perri 2004. 'Joined-up government in the western world in comparative perspective: A preliminary literature review and exploration', *Journal of Public Administration Research and Theory* 14: 103–38. Available at: http://en.wikipedia.org/wiki/Perri_6

Pressman, Jeffrey L. and Aaron Wildavsky. 1973. *Implementation*. Berkeley, CA: University of California Press.

Radin, Beryl A. 2000. *Beyond Machiavelli: Policy Analysis Comes of Age*. Washington, DC: Georgetown University Press.

Rhoads, Steven E. 1985. *The Economist's View of the World: Government, Markets, and Public Policy*. New York: Cambridge University Press.

Rochefort, David A. and Roger W. Cobb (eds). 1994. *The Politics of Problem Definition: Shaping the Policy Agenda*. Lawrence, KS: University Press of Kansas.

Sabatier, Paul A. 1988. 'An advocacy coalition framework of policy change and the role of policy-oriented learning therein', *Policy Sciences* 21: 129–68.

Sandler, Todd. 2004. *Global Collective Action*. New York: Cambridge University Press.
Savas, E.S. 1987. *Privatization: The Key to Better Government*. Chatham, NJ: Chatham House.
Schön, Donald A. 1983. *The Reflective Practitioner: How Professionals Think in Action*. New York: Basic Books.
——and Martin Rein. 1994. *Frame Reflection: Toward the Resolution of Intractable Policy Controversies*. New York: Basic Books.
Self, Peter. 1977. *Econocrats and the Policy Process: The Politics and Philosophy of Cost-Benefit Analysis*. Boulder, CO: Westview Press.
Shapiro, Ian. 1999. *Democratic Justice*. New Haven, CT: Yale University Press.
Smith, James A. 1991. *The Idea Brokers: Think Tanks and the Rise of the New Policy Elite*. New York: The Free Press.
Stevens, Joe B. 1993. *The Economics of Collective Choice*. Boulder, CO: Westview Press.
Stokey, Edith and Richard Zeckhauser. 1978. *A Primer for Policy Analysis*. New York: W.W. Norton.
Stone, Deborah. 2002. *Policy Paradox: The Art of Political Decision Making*, revised edn. New York: W.W. Norton.
Stone, Diane 2000. 'Non-governmental policy transfer: The strategies of independent policy institutes', *Governance* 13: 65.
——and Andrew Denham. 2004. *Think Tank Traditions: Policy Research and the Politics of Ideas*. Manchester: Manchester University Press.
Tabb, William K. 2004. *Economic Governance in the Age of Globalization*. New York: Columbia University Press.
True, Jacqui and Michael Mintrom. 2001. 'Transnational networks and policy diffusion: The case of gender mainstreaming,' *International Studies Quarterly* 45: 27–57.
Weimer, David L. and Aidan R. Vining. 2005. *Policy Analysis: Concepts and Practice*, 4th edn. Upper Saddle River, NJ: Prentice Hall.
Weiss, Carol H. 1998. *Evaluation*, 2nd edn. Upper Saddle River, NJ: Prentice Hall.
Wildavsky, Aaron. 1979. *Speaking Truth to Power: The Art and Craft of Policy Analysis*. Boston, MA: Little-Brown.
—— 1992. *The New Politics of the Budgetary Process*, 2nd edn. New York: Harper Collins Publishers.
Williamson, John (ed.). 1993. *The Political Economy of Policy Reform*. Washington, DC: Institute for International Economics.
Wolf, Charles, Jr. 1979. 'A theory of nonmarket failures', *Journal of Law and Economics* 22: 107–39.
Wood, Christopher. 1995. *Environmental Impact Assessment: A Comparative Review*. Burnt Mill: Longman Scientific and Technical.
Yergin, Daniel and Joseph Stanislaw. 1998. *The Commanding Heights: The Battle Between Government and the Marketplace that Is Remaking the Modern World*. New York: Touchstone.

# 2

# The policy-making process

*Michael Howlett and Sarah Giest*

## The policy cycle model of the policy process

The idea that policy development can be thought of as a series of steps in a decision-making process was first broached systematically in the work of Harold Lasswell, a pioneer in the field of policy research (Lasswell 1956, 1971). In most recent work, a five-stage model of the policy process has been most commonly used. In this model, "agenda-setting" refers to the first stage in the process when a problem is initially sensed by policy actors and a variety of solutions put forward. "Policy formulation" refers to the development of specific policy options within government when the range of possible choices is narrowed by excluding infeasible ones, and efforts are made by various actors to have their favored solution ranked highly among the remaining few. "Decision-making" refers to the third stage in which governments adopt a particular course of action. In the fourth stage of "policy implementation" governments put their decisions into effect using some combination of the tools of public administration in order to alter the distribution of goods and services in society in a way that is broadly compatible with the sentiments and values of affected parties. Finally "policy evaluation" refers to the fifth stage in the process in which the results of policies are monitored by both state and societal actors, often leading to the reconceptualization of policy problems and solutions in the light of experiences encountered with the policy in question (Howlett *et al.* 2009).

This idea of policy-making existing as a set of interrelated stages provides a general "framework" for understanding the policy development process and points to several of the key temporal activities and relationships that should be examined in furthering study of the issue. However, it does not answer several key questions such as the actual substance of policy, the number and type of relevant actors involved in the process and what motivates them, the exact manner and sequence in which actual policy development processes occur, and whether there exist basic patterns of development in different issues areas, sectors or jurisdictions (Sabatier 1991). Empirical studies aimed at answering these questions and generating more detailed models of the policy-making process, however, have developed some knowledge about the activities of policy actors at each stage of the cycle, summarized below, which draw attention to the limited number of common modes, or *styles*, which characterize policy processes throughout the world and the factors which drive policy-making through the various stages.

## Styles of policy behavior in the policy cycle

### *Agenda-setting*

In the scholarly literature on agenda-setting, for example, a useful distinction is often drawn between the *systemic* or unofficial public agenda and the *institutional* or formal, official, agenda which helps to conceptualize policy-making dynamics at this stage of the process. The systemic agenda "consists of all issues that are commonly perceived by members of the political community as meriting public attention and as involving matters within the legitimate jurisdiction of existing governmental authority" (Cobb and Elder 1972). This is essentially a society's agenda for discussion of public problems, such as crime or health care, water quality or wilderness preservation. The formal or institutional agenda, on the other hand, consists of only a limited number of issues or problems to which attention is devoted by policy elites (Baumgartner and Jones 1991; Kingdon 1984). Each society has literally hundreds of issues which some citizens find to be matters of concern and would have the government do something about. However, only a small proportion of the problems on the public or systemic agenda are actually taken up by policy actors actively involved in policy development and understanding how and why this movement occurs is key to understanding process dynamics at the 'front-end' of the policy process.

Almost 40 years ago the American political scientists Cobb, Ross and Ross developed a model of typical agenda-setting styles based on this insight. In their analysis, they argued that three basic patterns of agenda-setting could be discerned, distinguished by the origins of the issue as well as the resources utilized to facilitate its inclusion on the agenda. In the *outside initiation* pattern "issues arise in nongovernmental groups and are then expanded sufficiently to reach, first, the public [systemic] agenda and, finally, the formal [institutional] agenda" (Cobb *et al.* 1976). The *mobilization* case is quite different and describes "decision-makers trying to expand an issue from a formal to a public agenda." In this model, issues are simply placed on the formal agenda by the government with no necessary preliminary expansion from a publicly recognized grievance. In the third type of agenda-setting, *inside initiation*, influential groups with special access to decision-makers initiate a policy and do not necessarily want it to be expanded and contested in public. This can be due to technical as well as political reasons. Entrance is virtually automatic due to the privileged place of those desiring a decision.

Further research conducted by John Kingdon into the dynamics of agenda-setting in the US Congress in the early 1980s focused on the timing of these processes of agenda entrance. In his work, he focused on the role played by policy entrepreneurs both inside and outside government in taking advantage of agenda-setting opportunities—policy windows—to move items onto formal government agendas (Kingdon 1984). Kingdon argued that the characteristics of issues (the problem stream) combined with the characteristics of political institutions and circumstances (the politics stream) and the development of policy solutions (the policy stream), lead to the opening and closing of opportunities for agenda entrance. Such opportunities can be seized upon or not, as the case may be, by policy entrepreneurs who are able to recognize and act upon them. The policy window types which can lead to issue entrance include routine, spill-over, discretionary and random types (Kingdon 1984; Howlett 1998). Empirical evidence suggests that the frequency of occurrence of the window types varies by level of institutionalization—with the most institutionalized types occurring much more frequently than the least institutionalized (Howlett 1998).

### Policy formulation

Studies of the second stage of the policy cycle, policy formulation, have also emphasized the importance of specific kinds of actors interacting to develop and refine policy options for government

(Freeman 1965; Linder and Peters 1990) and the resulting small number of styles of policy formulation. But unlike agenda-setting, where the public is often actively involved, in policy formulation, the relevant policy actors are restricted to those who not only have an opinion on a subject, but also have some minimal level of knowledge of the subject area, allowing them to comment, at least hypothetically, on the feasibility of options put forward to resolve policy problems.

The power of the ideas held by these actors and their stability in policy subsystems, in particular, has been a subject of much attention in studies of policy formulation in recent years. Carstensen (2011), for example, has suggested that ideas change incrementally, when new elements of meaning are added to them, resulting in a characteristic process of policy formulation in which similar ideas inform similar policy options over long periods of time. This shifts the focus of the analysis towards the influence of discourses within certain institutional settings as a key factor affecting the nature of the kinds of policy alternatives put forward in the policy formulation (Schmidt 2006, 2010, 2011). Focusing on the information or knowledge available to decision-makers has led policy research in this vein to focus on concepts such as epistemic communities (ECs) in policy formulation. These are loose groupings of experts or knowledge "providers" for the decision-making process—opening up new opportunities for influence on policy alternatives. The suggested mechanism underlying this is their "ability to transfer policy by assuming control over knowledge production and in doing so guiding decision-maker learning" (Dunlop 2009: 290; Haas 1992).

Scholars over the years have developed a variety of such concepts in order to help identify who are the key actors in these *policy subsystems,* what brings them together, how they interact, and what effect their interaction has on policy development (Jordan 1990a, 1990b; Jordan and Schubert 1992). Most of these distinguish between a large set of actors with some knowledge of the policy issue in question, such as an epistemic community and a smaller set in which actors not only have the requisite knowledge, but also have established patterns of more or less routine interactions with each other and with decision-makers to allow them to influence alternative formation (Knoke 1993).

Membership in knowledge-based *policy communities* extends to actors such as state policy-makers (administrative, political, and judicial), members of non-governmental organizations (NGOs) concerned with the subject, members of the media who report on the subject, academics who follow or research the area, and members of the general public who, for whatever reason, have taken an interest in the subject (Sabatier 1987, 1988). In many issue areas, the policy community also involves members of other organizations such as businesses, labor unions, or various formalized interest groups or professional associations concerned with government actions in the sector concerned. In some cases, international actors such as multinational corporations, international governmental or NGOs, or the governments of foreign states, can also be members of sectoral policy communities (Haas 1992). The subset of these actors who interact within more formalized institutions and procedures of government are defined as members of *policy networks* (Coleman and Skogstad 1990; Marin and Mayntz 1991; Pross 1992). These policy networks include representatives from the community, but are "inner circles" of actors, who effectively hold the power to veto many policy options as untenable or unfeasible.

In this view, the likely results of policy formulation are contingent upon the nature and configuration of the policy community and network in the specific sector concerned. A key variable that many observers have argued affects the structure and behavior of policy networks, for example, is their number of members, which influences their level of integration and the types of interactions they undertake (van Waarden 1992; Atkinson and Coleman 1989, 1992; Coleman and Skogstad 1990). What is important for policy communities, on the other hand, is not the number of participants in the community but the number of relatively distinct "idea sets" which exist within it. This affects the nature of conflict and consensus which exists in the community and, as a result, affects the behavior of community actors (Schulman 1988; MacRae 1993; Smith 1993).

Taken together, these configurations can define a policy formulation style, one which can be quite long-lasting and resistant to change. In open subsystems where networks have many members and communities share many idea sets, for example, it can be expected that a propensity for new, radical, alternatives to the status quo may be generated in the policy formulation process. In closed subsystems, where networks have few members and communities are dominated by a single idea set, on the other hand, a status quo orientation will emerge in the policy options developed and put before decision-makers. In subsystems where only a few actors make up the network but communities are open to new ideas, significant alternatives to the status quo may emerge from the formulation process, but usually over the opposition of network members. In subsystems where many actors deal with few ideas, marginal or incremental options tend to develop.

Although the network framework has been criticized as being a descriptive metaphor, due to the fact that "the independent variables, (of policy-making) are not network characteristics per se but rather characteristics of components within the networks" (Dowding 1995: 137), it remains helpful in that it provides a general mechanism to help organize the complex reality of multiple actors, institutions, and ideas found in the policy formulation process (Howlett *et al.* 2009; Smith 1994; Howlett and Ramesh 1998; Howlett 2002a).

## Decision-making

Similar styles have been identified at the decision-making stage of the policy process. Many early studies of policy-making in companies, governments, and organizations conducted largely by students of public and business administration, for example, argued that decision-makers attempt to follow a systematic method for arriving at logical, efficient decisions. They argued that policy-makers achieved superior results when they first established a goal; explored alternative strategies for achieving it; attempted to predict its consequences and the likelihood of each occurring; and then chose the option which maximized potential benefits at least cost or risk (Gawthrop 1971; Carley 1980; Cahill and Overman 1990).

This model was "rational" in the sense that it prescribed a standard set of procedures for policy-making which were expected to lead in all circumstances to the choice of the most efficient means of achieving policy goals (Jennings 1987; Torgerson 1986). Pure "rational" models of decision-making thought of policy-makers as neutral "technicians" or "managers," who identify a problem and then find the most effective or efficient way of solving it (Elster 1991). Many of the latest efforts to enhance the efficiency and effectiveness of public policy decision-making, such as, for example, the "evidence-based policy movement" (Pawson 2006), focuses on the application of a systemic evaluative rationality to policy problems (Sanderson 2006; Mintrom 2007) in classic rational style.

Empirical research into decision-making processes, however, has discovered that political processes of bargaining and negotiation often outweigh "rational" deliberations and calculations of costs and benefits are subject to substantive and procedural limitations. Policy-makers were often found to be neither necessarily neutral nor competent and other models of the public policy decision-making processes have argued that this is not an accidental situation but rather an inherent and unavoidable characteristic of the policy-making exercise.

Perhaps the most noted critic of the rational model of decision-making was the American behavioral scientist Herbert Simon. In a series of books and articles beginning in the early 1950s, he argued that there were several hurdles that prevented decision-makers from attaining "pure" comprehensive rationality in their decisions (Simon 1955, 1957). Simon noted definite cognitive limits to the decision-makers' ability to consider all possible options, which forces them to selectively consider alternatives. He concluded from his assessment of the rational model that public decisions in practice did not maximize benefits over costs, but merely tended to satisfy whatever criteria decision-makers set for themselves in the instance in question. This *"satisficing"* criterion, as he put it, was a realistic one given the "*bounded rationality*" with which human beings are endowed. This analysis did not rule out the use of rationality-forcing techniques but pointed out that rational models would only result in optimal decisions in very specific situations where full information on options existed and could be mobilized by key decision-makers (Smith and May 1980).

The well-known *incremental model* of policy-making developed by Yale University political scientist Charles Lindblom incorporated these insights into limited or "bounded" rationality into a general model of public policy decision-making (Dahl and Lindblom 1953; Lindblom 1955, 1958, 1959; Hayes 1992). Lindblom summarized the elements of his model as consisting of the following a "mutually supporting set of simplifying and focusing stratagems":

- limitation of analysis to a few somewhat familiar policy alternatives ... differing only marginally from the status quo;
- an intertwining of analysis of policy goals and other values with the empirical aspects of the problem (that is, no requirement that values be specified first with means subsequently found to promote them);
- a greater analytical preoccupation with ills to be remedied than positive goals to be sought;
- a sequence of trials, errors, and revised trials;
- analysis that explores only some, not all, of the important possible consequences of a considered alternative;
- fragmentation of analytical work to many (partisan) participants in policymaking (each attending to their piece of the overall problem domain).

*(Lindblom 1979)*

This resulted, as he put it in his oft-cited 1959 article on "The Science of 'Muddling Through'," in decision-makers working through a process of "continually building out from the current situation, step-by-step and by small degrees" or "increments" in which policies were invariably developed through a process of "successive limited comparisons" with earlier ones with which decision-makers were already familiar (Lindblom 1959).

Braybrooke and Lindblom (1963) argued that different styles of decision-making could be discerned depending upon the amount of knowledge at the disposal of decision-makers, and the amount of change the decision involved from earlier decisions. Other authors, like Graham Allison, also developed similar models of distinct decision-making styles (Allison 1969, 1971), but did not specify in any detail the variables which led to the adoption of a particular style (Bendor and Hammond 1992).

Attempting to improve upon these models, John Forester (1984, 1989) suggested that decision-making is affected by the number of agents involved in a decision, their organizational setting, how well a problem is defined, the information available on the problem, its causes and consequences, and the amount of time available to decision-makers to consider possible contingencies and their present and anticipated consequences. The number of agents can expand and multiply almost to infinity. The setting can include many different organizations and can be more or less open to external influences. The problem can be ambiguous or susceptible to multiple competing interpretations. Information can be incomplete, misleading or purposefully withheld or manipulated, and time can be limited or artificially constrained and manipulated. In this model, decision-makers situated in complex subsystems are expected to undertake adjustment strategies while those dealing with simple configurations of actors and ideas will be more prone to undertake search-type strategies. The nature of the decision criteria, on the other hand, varies with the severity of the informational, time and other resource constraints under which decision-makers operate. Hence decision-makers faced with high constraints will tend to favor satisficing over optimization, itself an outcome more likely to occur in situations of low constraint. Overall this would lead to a pattern in which most decisions would be incremental except in specific circumstances where other kinds of decisions could emerge.

## Policy implementation styles

Generally speaking, comparative implementation studies have also shown that governments tend to develop specific implementation styles (Knill 1998; Hawkins and Thomas 1989; Kagan 1991; Howlett 2002b) which combine various kinds of instruments into a more or less coherent whole which is then applied in particular sectors (Howlett 2011; Wu *et al.* 2010). Linked to implementation, policy tools provide the substance or content to what was planned in the formulation stage and decided upon afterwards in the decision-making stage of the policy process (Howlett 2011).

These tools fall into two types. *Substantive instruments* are those directly providing goods and services to members of the public or governments. They include a variety of tools or instruments relying on different types of governing resources for their effectiveness (Tupper and Doern 1981; Vedung 1997; Woodside 1986; Peters and Van Nispen 1998; Salamon 1989). A useful way to classify these (see Table 2.1) is according to the type of governing resource upon which they rely: nodality or information; authority, treasure or financial resources, or administrative or organizations ones (Hood 1986).

*Procedural instruments* are different from substantive ones in that their impact on policy outcomes is less direct. Rather than affect the delivery of goods and services, their principal intent is to modify or alter the nature of policy processes at work in the implementation process (Howlett 2000; in't Veld, 1998). A list of these instruments is provided in Table 2.2.

Why a particular combination of procedural and substantive instruments is utilized in particular policy issue areas is a key question (Gunningham and Young 1997; Dunsire 1993; Howlett 2000; Salamon 2002; Clark and Russell 2009; McGoldrick and Boonn 2010). Some studies suggest that policy mixes can be designed. Studies such as Gunningham, Grabosky and Young's work on "smart regulation," for example, led to the development of efforts to identify complementaries and conflicts within instrument mixes or tool "portfolios" involved in more complex and sophisticated policy designs (Barnett *et al.* 2009; Buckman and Diesendorf 2010).

Each tool mix decision combines advantages and disadvantages of each tool in its relationship to other tools as well as the effect it has on costs and benefits for government (Howlett 2011).

*Table 2.1* A taxonomy of substantive policy instruments

| *Principal use* | *Governing resource* | | | |
|---|---|---|---|---|
| | *Nodality* | *Authority* | *Authority* | *Organization* |
| *Effectors* | • Advice<br>training | • Licences<br>• Certification<br>regulation<br>user charges | • Grants<br>• Loans<br>• Tax expenditures | • Bureaucratic administration<br>• Public enterprises |
| *Detectors* | • Reporting<br>registration | • Census-taking<br>consultants | • Polling<br>policing | • Record-keeping<br>surveys |

Source: Howlett, Michael. *Designing Public Policies: Principles and Instruments.* New York: Routledge, 2011. Available at: www.routledge.com/books/details/9780415781336/

*Table 2.2* A resource-based taxonomy of procedural policy instruments

| *Principal use* | *Governing resource* | | | |
|---|---|---|---|---|
| | *Nodality* | *Authority* | *Treasure* | *Organization* |
| *Positive* | • Education | • Agreements | • Interest-group funding | • Hearings |
| | • Exhortation | • Treaties | • Research | • Evaluations |
| | • Advertising | • Advisory-group creation | • Intervenor-funding | • Institutional-bureaucratic reform |
| | • Training | | | |
| *Negative* | • Misleading information/ propaganda | • Banning groups and associations | • Eliminating funding | • Administrative delay |
| | | | | • Information suppression |

Source: Howlett, Michael. *Designing Public Policies: Principles and Instruments.* New York: Routledge, 2011. Available at: www.routledge.com/books/details/9780415781336/

The preferences of state decision-makers and the nature of the constraints within which they operate are key factors which many studies have highlighted as affecting instrument choices and policy implementation styles (Bressers and O'Toole 1998). A state must have a high level of administrative capacity, for example, in order to utilize authority, treasure, and organization-based instruments in situations in which they wish to affect significant numbers of policy targets. When it has few of these resources, it will tend to utilize instruments such as incentives or propaganda, or to rely on existing voluntary, community or family-based instruments (Howlett *et al.* 2009). Similarly a key feature of procedural instrument choice is a government's capacity to manipulate policy subsystems. Undertaken in order to retain the political trust or legitimacy required for substantive policy instruments to be effective (Beetham 1991; Stillman 1974), procedural policy instrument choice is also affected by the size of the policy target. Whether a government faces sectoral delegitimation or widespread systemic delegitimation affects the types of procedural instruments a government will employ (Habermas 1973, 1975; Mayntz 1975).

## Policy evaluation styles

The last stage of the cycle is policy evaluation. For many early observers, policy evaluation was expected to consist of assessing if a public policy was achieving its stated objectives and, if not, what could be done to eliminate impediments to their attainment. Thus David Nachmias (1979) defined policy evaluation as "the objective, systematic, empirical examination of the effects ongoing policies and public programs have on their targets in terms of the goals they are meant to achieve." However, while analysts often resorted to concepts such as "success" or "failure" to conclude their evaluation, as Ingram and Mann cautioned:

> [T]he phenomenon of policy failure is neither so simple nor certain as many contemporary critics of policy and politics would have us believe. Success and failure are slippery concepts, often highly subjective and reflective of an individual's goals, perception of need, and perhaps even psychological disposition toward life.
>
> *(Ingram and Mann 1980)*

That is, public policy goals are often not stated clearly enough to find out if and to what extent they are being achieved, nor are they shared by all key policy actors. Moreover, the possibilities for objective analysis are also limited because of the difficulties involved in the attempt to develop objective standards by which to evaluate a government's level of success in dealing with subjective claims and socially constructed problems.

What is significant in the evaluative process is thus not so much ultimate success and failure, but that policy actors and the organizations and institutions they represent can *learn* from the formal and informal evaluation of policies in which they are engaged. This can lead them to modify their positions in the direction of greater substantive or procedural policy change, or it can lead them to resist any alteration to the status quo (Majone 1989). And, like with other stages of the policy process, a few common or typical styles of learning have been identified in the literature on the subject.

A significant variable in this regard is the capacity of an organization to absorb new information (Cohen and Levinthal 1990). Only when state administrative capacity is high, for example, would one expect any kind of learning to occur. If a relatively closed network dominates the subsystem, then this learning is likely to be restricted to some form of "lesson-drawing," in which policy-makers draw lessons from past uses of policy instruments (Rose 1991; Bennett and Howlett 1992). Open subsystems allow for "social learning" when administrative capacity is high and more informal evaluation where the ability to adapt is rather low. "Social learning" occurs when ideas and events in the larger policy community penetrate into policy evaluations. If the policy subsystem is dominated by closed networks, one would expect to find formal types of evaluation with little substantive impact on either policy instruments or goals and lesson-drawing attempts (Howlett *et al.* 2009).

Policy evaluations do not necessarily result in major policy change. That is, while the concept of evaluation suggests that an implicit "feedback loop" is an inherent part of the policy cycle, in many cases this loop may not be operationalized (Pierson 1993). Path dependence, in which policies are set on "trajectories" following some "critical juncture" can hinder policy change and learning (Pierson 2000). Organizational-institutional properties (Eising 2004; Olsen and Peters 1996) are also often seen as barriers to learning from policy evaluations.

## Conclusion: policy development as policy style

As Lasswell noted in the 1950s, envisioning policy development as a staged, sequential, and iterative process is a useful analytical and methodological device. Methodologically such an approach reduces the complexity of public policy-making by breaking down that complexity into a small number of stages and substages, each of which can be investigated alone, or in terms of its relationship to any or all the other stages of the cycle. The policy cycle idea also helps to answer many key questions about public policy-making regarding the effectiveness of different tools and the identification of bottlenecks in policy processes. The stages allow for the identification of typical actors and actions in different phases of tackling a problem which makes it easier to identify independent and dependent variables in the study of policy processes and behaviour and moves thinking forward by helping to identify the relatively limited range of styles of activity possible at each stage of the cycle (Freeman 1985; Coleman 1994; Tuohy 1992; Vogel 1986).

## Bibliography

Allison, G. 1969. 'Conceptual models and the Cuban missile crisis', *American Political Science Review* 63(3): 689–718.

—— (1971) *Essence of Decision: Explaining the Cuban Missile Crisis.* Boston: Little Brown.

Atkinson, M. and W. Coleman. 1989. 'Strong states and weak states: Sectoral policy networks in advanced capitalist economies', *British Journal of Political Science* 19(1): 47–67.

——and W. Coleman. 1992. 'Policy networks, policy communities and the problems of governance', *Governance* 5(2): 154–80.

Barnett, Pauline, Tim Tenbensel, Jacqueline Cuming, Clare Alyden, Toni Ashton, Megan Pledger and Mili Burnette. 2009. 'Implementing new modes of governance in the New Zealand health system: An empirical study', *Health Policy* 93: 118–27.

Baumgartner, Frank R. and Bryan D. Jones. 1991. 'Agenda dynamics and policy subsystems', *Journal of Politics* 53(4): 1044–74.

Beetham, D. 1991. *The Legitimation of Power*. London: Macmillan.

Bendor, Jonathan and Thomas H. Hammond. 1992. 'Re-thinking Allison's models', *American Political Science Review* 86(2): 301–22.

Bennett, Colin J. and Michael Howlett. 1992. 'The lessons of learning: Reconciling theories of policy learning and policy change', *Policy Sciences* 25(3): 275–94.

Braybrooke, David and Charles E. Lindblom. 1963. *A Strategy of Decision: Policy Evaluation as a Social Process*. New York: Free Press of Glencoe.

Bressers, Hans Th.A. and Laurence J. O'Toole. 1998. 'The selection of policy instruments: A network-based perspective', *Journal of Public Policy* 18(3): 213–39.

Buckman, Greg and Mark Diesendorf. 2010. 'Design limitations in Australian renewable electricity policies', *Energy Policy* 38(7): 3365–76.

Cahill, Anthony G. and E. Sam Overman. 1990. 'The evolution of rationality in policy analysis', in S.S. Nagel (ed.) *Policy Theory and Policy Evaluation: Concepts, Knowledge, Causes, and Norms*. New York: Greenwood Press.

Carley, Michael. 1980. *Rational Techniques in Policy Analysis*. London: Heinemann Educational Books.

Carstensen, Martin B. 2011. 'Ideas are not as stable as political scientists want them to be: A theory of incremental ideational change', *Political Studies* 59(3): 596–615.

Clark, C.D. and C.S. Russell. 2009. 'Ecological conservation: The problems of targeting policies and designing instruments', *Journal of Natural Resources Policy Research* (1): 21–34.

Cobb, Roger W. and Charles D. Elder. 1972. *Participation in American Politics: The Dynamics of Agenda-Building*. Boston: Allyn and Bacon.

—— J.K. Ross and M.H. Ross. 1976. 'Agenda building as a comparative political process', *American Political Science Review* 70(1): 126–38.

Cohen, Wesley M. and Daniel A. Levinthal. 1990. 'Absorptive capacity: A new perspective on learning and innovation', *Administrative Science Quarterly* 35: 128–52.

Coleman, William D. 1994. 'Policy convergence in banking: A comparative study', *Political Studies* 42: 274–92.

——and Grace Skogstad (eds). 1990. *Policy Communities and Public Policy Canada: A Structural Approach*. Mississauga, ON: Copp Clark Pitman.

Dahl, Robert A. and Charles E. Lindblom. 1953. *Politics, Economics and Welfare: Planning and Politico-economic Systems Resolved into Basic Social Processes*. New York: Harper and Row.

Dowding, K. 1995. 'Model or metaphor? A critical review of the policy network approach', *Political Studies* 43(1): 136–58.

Dunlop, Claire A. 2009. 'Policy transfer as learning: Capturing variation in what decision-makers learn from epistemic communities', *Policy Studies* 30(3): 289–311.

Dunsire, Andrew. 1993. *Manipulating Social Tensions: Collaboration as an Alternative Mode of Government Intervention*. Cologne: Max Plank Institute.

Eising, R. 2004. 'Multilevel governance and business interests in the European Union', *Governance* 17(2): 211–45.

Elster, Jon. 1991. 'The possibility of rational politics', in D. Held (ed.) *Political Theory Today*. Oxford: Polity.

Forester, John. 1984. 'Bounded rationality and the politics of muddling through', *Public Administration Review* 44(1): 23–31.

—— 1989. *Planning in the Face of Power*. Berkeley, CA: University of California Press.

Freeman, Gary P. 1985. 'National styles and policy sectors: Explaining structured variation', *Journal of Public Policy* 5(4): 467–96.

Freeman, J. Leiper. 1965. *The Political Process: Executive - Bureaucratic - Legislative Relations*, revised edn. New York: Random House.

Gawthrop, Louis C. 1971. *Administrative Politics and Social Change*. New York: St. Martin's Press.

Gunningham, N., P. Grabosky and D. Sinclair. 1998. *Smart Regulation: Designing Environmental Policy*. Oxford: Clarendon Press.
——and M.D. Young. 1997. 'Toward optimal environmental policy: The case of biodiversity conservation', *Ecology Law Quarterly* 24: 243–8.
Haas, Peter M. 1992. 'Introduction: Epistemic communities and international policy coordination', *International Organization* 46(1): 1–36.
Habermas, Jürgen. 1973. 'What does a legitimation crisis mean today? Legitimation problems in late capitalism', *Social Research* 40(4): 643–67.
—— 1975. *Legitimation Crisis*. Boston, MA: Beacon Press.
Hawkins, Keith and John M. Thomas (eds). 1989. *Making Regulatory Policy*. Pittsburgh, PA: University of Pittsburgh Press.
Hayes, Michael T. 1992. *Incrementalism and Public Policy*. New York: Longmans.
Hood, Christopher. 1986. *The Tools of Government*. Chatham, NJ: Chatham House.
Howlett, Michael. 1998. 'Predictable and unpredictable policy windows: Institutional and exogenous correlates of Canadian federal agenda-setting', *Canadian Journal of Political Science* 3(3): 495–524.
—— 2000. 'Managing the "hollow state": Procedural policy instruments and modern governance', *Canadian Public Administration* 43(4): 412–31.
—— 2002a. 'Do networks matter? Linking policy network structure to policy outcomes: Evidence from four Canadian policy sectors, 1990–2000', *Canadian Journal of Political Science* 35(2): 235–68.
—— 2002b. 'Policy instruments and implementation styles: The evolution of instrument choice in Canadian environmental policy', in D.L. Van Nijnatten and R. Boardman (eds) *Canadian Environmental Policy: Context and Cases*. Toronto: Oxford University Press, 25–45.
—— 2009. 'Governance modes, policy regimes and operational plans: A multi-level nested model of policy instrument choice and policy design', *Policy Sciences* 42(1): 73–89.
—— 2011. *Designing Public Policies: Principles and Instruments*. London and New York: Routledge.
——and M. Ramesh. 1998. 'Policy subsystem configurations and policy change: Operationalizing the postpositivist analysis of the politics of the policy process', *Policy Studies Journal* 26(3): 466–82
——M Ramesh and Anthony Perl. 2009. *Studying Public Policy: Policy Cycles and Policy Subsystems*. Toronto: Oxford University Press.
Ingram, Helen M. and Dean E. Mann. 1980. *Why Policies Succeed or Fail*. Beverly Hills, CA: Sage.
in't Veld, Roeland J. 1998. 'The dynamics of instruments', in B. Guy Peters and F. K. M. Van Nispen (eds) *Public Policy Instruments: Evaluating the Tools of Public Administration*. New York: Edward Elgar, 153–62.
Jennings, B. 1987. 'Interpretation and the practice of policy analysis', in F. Fischer and J. Forester (eds) *Confronting Values in Policy Analysis: The Politics of Criteria*. Newbury Park, CA: Sage: 128–52.
Jordan, A. Grant. 1990a. 'Policy community realism versus "new" institutionalist ambiguity', *Political Studies* 38(3): 470–84.
—— 1990b. 'Sub-governments, policy communities and networks: Refilling the old bottles?', *Journal of Theoretical Politics* 2(3): 319–38.
Jordan, G. and K. Schubert. 1992. 'A preliminary ordering of policy network labels', *European Journal of Political Research* 21(1/2): 7–27.
Kagan, Robert A. 1991. 'Adversial legalism and American government', *Journal of Policy Analysis and Management* 10(3): 369–406.
Kingdon, John. 1984. *Agendas, Alternatives and Public Policies*. Boston: Little, Brown.
Knill, Christoph. 1998. 'European policies: The impact of national administrative traditions', *Journal of Public Policy* 18(1): 1–28.
Knoke, David. 1993. 'Networks as political glue: Explaining public policy-making', in W.J. Wilson (ed.) *Sociology and Public Agenda*. London: Sage, 164–84.
Lasswell, H.D. 1956. *The Decision Process: Seven Categories of Functional Analysis*. College Park, MD: University of Maryland.
—— 1971. *A Pre-View of Policy Sciences*. New York: American Elsevier.
Lindblom, C.E. 1995. *Bargaining: The Hidden Hand in Government*. Los Angeles, CA: Rand Corporation.
—— 1958. 'Policy analysis', *American Economic Review* 48(3): 298–312.
—— 1959. 'The science of muddling through', *Public Administration Review* 19(2): 79–88.
—— 1979. 'Still muddling, not yet through', *Public Administration Review* 39(6): 517–26.
Linder, Stephen H. and B. Guy Peters. 1990. 'Research perspectives on the design of public policy: Implementation, formulation, and design', in Dennis J. Palumbo and D.J. Calista. *Implementation and the Policy Process: Opening Up the Black Box*. New York: Greenwood Press.

McGoldrick, Daniel E. and Ann V. Boonn. 2010. 'Public policy to maximize tobacco cessation', *American Journal of Preventive Medicine* 38(3) Supplement 1: S327–S32.
MacRae, Duncan, Jr. 1993. 'Guidelines for policy discourse: Consensual versus adversarial', in Frank Fischer and John Forester (eds) *The Argumentative Turn in Policy Analysis and Planning*. Durham, NC: Duke University Press: 291–318.
Majone, Giandomenico. 1989. *Evidence, Argument, and Persuasion in the Policy Process*. New Haven, CT: Yale University Press.
Marin, Bernd and Renate Mayntz (eds). 1991. *Policy Networks: Empirical Evidence and Theoretical Considerations*. Frankfurt-am-Main: Campus.
Mayntz, Renate. 1975. 'Legitimacy and the directive capacity of the political system', in Leon N. Lindberg, Robert Alford, Colin Crouch, and Claus Offe (eds) *Stress and Contradiction in Modern Capitalism*. Lexington, MA: Lexington Books: 261–74.
Mintrom, Michael. 2007. 'The policy analysis movement.', in L. Dobuzinskis, M. Howlett and D. Laycock (eds) *Policy Analysis in Canada: The State of the Art*. Toronto: University of Toronto Press: 7–84.
Nachmias, David. 1979. *Public Policy Evaluation: Approaches and Methods*. New York: St. Martin's Press.
Olsen, Johan P. and B. Guy Peters (eds). 1996. *Lessons from Experience: Experiential Learning in Administrative Reforms in Eight Democracies*. Oslo: Scandinavian University Press.
Pawson, Ray. 2006. *Evidence-Based Policy: A Realist Perspective*. London: Sage.
Peters, B. Guy and F.K.M. Van Nispen (eds). 1998. *Public Policy Instruments: Evaluating the Tools of Public Administration*. New York: Edward Elgar.
Pierson, Paul. 1993. 'When effect becomes cause: Policy feedback and political change', *World Politics* 45: 595–628.
—— 2000. 'Increasing returns, path dependence, and the study of politics', *American Political Science Review* 94(2): 251–67.
Pross, A. Paul. 1992. *Group Politics and Public Policy*, Toronto: Oxford University Press.
Rose, Richard. 1991. 'What is lesson-drawing?', *Journal of Public Policy* 11(1): 3–30.
Sabatier, Paul A. 1987. 'Knowledge, policy-oriented learning, and policy change', *Knowledge: Creation, Diffusion, Utilization* 8(4): 649–92.
—— 1988. 'An advocacy coalition framework of policy change and the role of policy-oriented learning therein', *Policy Sciences* 21(2 & 3): 129–68.
—— 1991. 'Toward better theories of the policy process', *PS: Political Science and Politics* 24(2): 144–56.
Salamon, Lester M. (ed.) 1989. *Beyond Privatization: The Tools of Government Action*. Washington, DC: Urban Institute.
—— 2002. 'The new governance and the tools of public action', in L.M. Salamon (eds) *The Tools of Government: A Guide to the New Governance*. New York: Oxford University Press: 117–55.
Sanderson, I. 2006. 'Complexity, "practical rationality" and evidence-based policy making', *Policy and Politics* 34(1): 115–32.
Schulman, Paul R. 1988. 'The politics of "ideational policy"', *Journal of Politics* 50: 263–91.
Schmidt, Vivien A. 2006. 'Discursive institutionalism: The explanatory power of ideas and discourse', *Annual Review of Political Science* 1: 303–26.
—— 2010. 'Taking ideas and discourse seriously: Explaining change through discursive institutionalism as the fourth new institutionalism?', *European Political Science Review* 2(1): 1–25.
—— 2011. 'Speaking of change: Why discourse is key to the dynamics of policy transformation', *Critical Policy Studies* 5: 106–26.
Simon, Herbert A. 1955. 'A behavioral model of rational choice', *Quarterly Journal of Economics* 69(1): 99–118.
—— 1957. *Administrative Behavior: A Study of Decision-Making Processes in Administrative Organization*, 2nd edn. New York: Macmillan.
Smith, Gilbert. 1994. 'Policy networks and state autonomy', in S. Brooks and A.-G. Gagnon (eds) *The Political Influence of Ideas: Policy Communities and the Social Sciences*. New York: Praeger.
——and David May. 1980. 'The artificial debate between rationalist and incrementalist models of decision-making', *Policy and Politics* 8(2): 147–61.
Smith, Martin J. 1993. *Pressure, Power and Policy: State Autonomy and Policy Networks in Britain and the United States*. Aldershot: Harvester Wheatsheaf.
Stillman, Peter G. 1974. 'The concept of legitimacy', *Polity* 7(1): 32–56.
Torgerson, Douglas. 1986. 'Between knowledge and politics: Three faces of policy analysis', *Policy Sciences* 19(1): 33–59.

Tuohy, Caroline. 1992. *Policy and Politics in Canada: Institutionalized Ambivalence*. Philadelphia, PA: Temple University Press.

Tupper, Allan and G.B. Doern. 1981. 'Public corporations and public policy in Canada', in Allan Tupper and G.B. Doern (eds) *Public Corporations and Public Policy in Canada*. Montreal: Institute for Research on Public Policy: 1–50.

van Waarden, F. 1992. 'Dimensions and types of policy networks', *European Journal of Political Research* 21(1/2): 29–52.

Vedung, Evert. 1997. 'Policy instruments: Typologies and theories', in M.L. Bemelmans-Videc, R.C. Rist and E. Vedung (eds). *Carrots, Sticks and Sermons: Policy Instruments and Their Evaluation*. New Brunswick, NJ: Transaction Publishers: 21–58.

Vogel, David. 1986. *National Styles of Regulation: Environmental Policy in Great Britain and the United States*. Ithaca, NY: Cornell University Press.

Weiss, Carol H. 1977. *Using Social Research in Public Policy Making*. Lexington, MA: Lexington Books.

Woodside, K. 1986. 'Policy instruments and the study of public policy', *Canadian Journal of Political Science* 19(4): 775–93.

Wu, Xun, M. Ramesh, Michael Howlett and Scott Fritzen. 2010. *The Public Policy Primer: Managing Public Policy*. London: Routledge.

# 3

# Comparative approaches to the study of public policy-making

*Sophie Schmitt*

## Introduction: what is comparative public policy analysis?

Scholars of comparative public policy are interested in systematically studying public policies and their origins in order to gain a better understanding of the causes, factors and institutional or actor constellations that bring about different kinds of policy decisions. They try to advance our understanding of the processes and determinants of public policy-making by comparing the situations and contexts that lead policy-makers to agree on similar or diverging policies. In this vein, these analyses include comparisons over time and/or over units (comparing, for example, national, state or local governments). In a nutshell, comparative policy researchers seek to explain why and under what conditions policy-makers agree on what policies (see, for example, Lerner and Lasswell 1951; Windhoff-Héritier 1987; Howlett and Ramesh 2003). In an oft-cited definition, Dye describes public policy as "whatever governments choose to do or not to do" (1976: 1). A review of a number of subdisciplines of comparative public policy analysis shows that scholars of different research traditions employ different strategies in order to probe this inclusive and vast definition of "public policy" in both theoretical and empirical respects. While policy science covers a broad field that includes analyses of actors, institutions, instruments, programs, decision-making processes, policy implementation or evaluation from various theoretical perspectives (cf. Mayntz 1983; Howlett and Ramesh 2003), the analytical focus of the literature on comparative policy analysis is on the policy decisions themselves and the explanatory factors.

Research on comparative policy-making can be classified into three groups according to its analytical focus. First, while a number of approaches aim to compare *public policies* as such, other subdisciplines address the *patterns* of policy-making or the decision-making *processes* from a comparative perspective. In this context, the first category covers the entire policy change literature, which is rather fragmented with regard to the different approaches for conceptualizing and defining the subject of study (public policy).

Second, the patterns of policy-making are at the focus of scholars of policy diffusion, policy convergence, policy termination or policy dismantling. Whereas the policy diffusion perspective departs from the patterns of spread and the mechanisms of policy change, the policy convergence literature does not try to explain the individual policy-making behavior of governments but focuses on the degree of similarity their policy decisions reach over time. Scholars of

policy termination and of policy dismantling compare decisions to completely or partially revoke policies introduced in the past.

Third, the process-oriented strands of comparative policy research focus on particular explanatory factors or causes that determine the decision-making of governments. In this context, research on policy learning or lesson-drawing analyzes how policy actors perceive and process policy experiences made elsewhere, while the policy transfer perspective describes and explains how policies travel from one unit (e.g. nation-state) to another. Institutional analysis is a useful strategy to assess the impact of institutional constraints (e.g. veto players) on the actors' policy decision.

However, the broad field of comparative policy research also diverges with respect to the underlying methodological choices and to the range of causal explanations taken into account. This has led to contradictory results and a variety of identified factors and constellations that determine policy-making, its direction, extent and implications. Thus, in order to advance this field of research as a whole and to conceptually locate related research within the broader field, it is essential to have an overview of its different strands of research, approaches and analytical foci.

This chapter provides a systematic review of the field of comparative public policy research with regard to the fields of environmental and social policy. The following sections address first, different ways of conceptualizing and operationalizing the subject of study (public policy), second, different analytical perspectives of the patterns of public policies, and third, literature with distinct foci on the processes and explanatory factors of public policy-making. Next, I will provide a short review of the methods used to compare and analyze decision-making in the fields of social and environmental policy. I will then conclude with a short discussion of the main strengths and shortcomings of current approaches to comparing public policy-making over space and time along with an outlook on the challenges for further research.

## Varieties of comparative public policy research: policies, patterns or processes

The broad field of comparative public policy research comprises of research perspectives or traditions, theoretical approaches, empirical scopes and research methods. Numerous sub-disciplines and perspectives have emerged over the last decades. This development reflects the variety—and probably also limited commensurability—of the different paradigms guiding scholars of comparative public policy. So far, no dominant approach has emerged. In the following sections, I identify and discuss four dimensions along which studies of comparative public policy diverge.

## Comparing public policies

There is a variety of different approaches in the literature to depict and measure the subject of study, namely "public policy." This conceptual heterogeneity delimits the comparability and consolidation of the findings.

Scholars of comparative public policy analysis seek to systematically describe and explain the decisions of different governments, their timing and content. To this end, several strategies have emerged to determine governmental behavior and decisional output—including for instance legislative acts, executive decrees or administrative circulars. A first group of scholars measures the *impact* of policies by analyzing the policies' effects on the target of regulation. A second group of researchers focuses on policy *outcomes*, namely the immediate consequences of a policy decision, while the third approach refers to policy *outputs*, namely the content of the decision. As an example from the social policy field, one might consider unemployment protection policies. In this context, the decision to introduce monetary unemployment benefits at a certain level reflects the immediate policy output. The same decision could also be approximated by referring to total government spending on this particular social protection scheme (i.e. the outcome) or by measuring the effects of the policy decision on the regulatory target, such as, for instance, the number or the quality of life of unemployed persons (i.e. the impact). In the field of environmental policy-making one could consider emission standards for industrial plants. The definition of the standard itself, such as a limit value for the emission of sulfur dioxide, connotes the policy output, whereas the policy impact would be measured by the associated change in industrial emissions and air quality with respect to this particular substance. These brief examples illustrate the considerable risk of incomparability and incommensurability that result from the conceptualization and operationalization of the dependent variable (government policy decisions). From a policy cycle perspective, policy output on the one hand and policy outcome or impact on the other refer to different stages of the policy process. While the former is more a part of the policy formulation stage, the latter concepts pertain to the implementation phase (see Windhoff-Héritier 1987: 18f; cf. Sabatier and Mazmanian 1980, Howlett and Ramesh 2003: 143ff.). There is, however, a divide between policy outputs and their consequences (outcome and impact) not only with respect to the temporal patterns but also with regard to the potentially high number of intervening factors that influence the effects of policy decisions. It is almost impossible to infer governmental decisions and intentions based on indirect outcome and impact measures. Jänicke (1992) for instance finds that environmental policy performance and success crucially depend on institutional arrangements, economic structures and international dynamics. Esty and Porter (2005) conducted an extensive study in which a variety of different factors were analyzed to examine their influence on environmental performance (outcome data). The authors find other factors besides institutional arrangements to have an impact on the policy outcome in addition to the policy outputs themselves including socio-economic and infrastructure-related factors. Thus, as this example shows, selecting indicators for the subject of analysis or the dependent variable is far from trivial.

The literature on both social and environmental policy shows that the majority of large-n comparative studies rely on outcome or impact instead of output measures due to eased data availability. Wälti (2004), for instance, approximates the different nation-states' prioritization of environmental protection by using air quality data on nitrogen and sulfur oxides levels. Others argue that policy outcomes are the more appropriate and feasible way to measure a government's commitment toward environmental protection since its willingness to reduce air pollution is not only reflected in single policy decisions (e.g. to lower limit values). It is rather the result of a series of decisions including institutional ones that cannot be comprehensively assessed by comparing single policy outputs (see Scruggs 2003: 20ff.). As a consequence, many scholars have opted for environmental performance indices that are designed to reflect the policy-makers' overall commitment for protecting the environment. These indices are compiled from various outcome measures. They differ in their breadth in terms of the number of included pollutants (cf. Crepaz 1995; Jänicke 1996; Jahn 1998; Scruggs 1999, 2003).

Impact and outcome measures are also common in the literature on social policy. This might also be due to the conceptual and notional focus given that most scientists belonging to this area of research focus on the analysis of the *welfare state* as a whole rather than the explanation of single social policies. Analogously to the field of environmental policy research, policy output studies are uncommon. Nevertheless, scholars of social policies are usually more careful to distinguish between approaches focusing on outcome measures and those addressing the policies' impact. The former branch of research usually seeks to indirectly measure the politicians' commitment with respect to certain policy fields while the latter research takes more the form of program evaluation studies. Outcome indicators in the field of social policy differ with regard to their conceptual closeness to the underlying policy decision.

On rather abstract levels, data on public expenditure allow for the comparison of public commitment to policies, governments or time. Expenditure data are usually easily available proxies for policy decisions. They are often used in quantitative comparative studies (cf. Stephens *et al.* 1999; Huber and Stephens 2001; Castles 2004, 2009; Clasen and Siegel 2007). However, as with the case of environmental policy the direct linkage between policy outputs and outcomes is questionable. A number of authors find alternative factors that have an impact on public spending levels (Wilensky 1974; Castles and Mitchell 1992; Pierson 1996; Castles 1999; Kitschelt 2001; Allan and Scruggs 2004). The comparison between the politics of pension reform and unemployment protection, for instance, illustrates the complex interplay between socio-economic conditions, government action and welfare expenditure and the risk of endogeneity for the resulting analyses. On the one hand, demographic change and aging of the population are likely to trigger policy-making by governments which then translates into (expected) expenditure levels for this specific social policy program (Bonoli 2000). On the other hand, socio-economic conditions might also lead decision-makers to adapt unemployment protection policies. This is quite evident in the field of unemployment policies, where altered rates of unemployment directly impact on the resulting expenditure levels of the protection scheme (Allan and Scruggs 2004). Again, these developments might motivate policymakers to take action (Vis 2009). As these brief examples show, multidirectional effects cause problems of endogeneity which in turn pose serious risks for the validity of the findings obtained from such analyses. Furthermore, expenditure analyses entail the risk of omissions, as stable outcome levels of social policy might obscure underlying changes due to altered contexts (e.g. higher unemployment replacement rates that coincide with lower unemployment rates, cf. Knill *et al.* 2010).

As a consequence of these problems and the goal to more closely reflect actual political decisions, scholars have turned toward the measurement of replacement rates instead of cumulated expenditure levels (Martin 1996; Green-Pedersen 2004; Swank 2005; Clasen and Clegg 2007; Kühner 2007). Replacement rates refer to the amount of monetary compensation paid to retirees, unemployed persons or those unable to work because of illness. Social generosity from this perspective is operationalized through the benefit levels (e.g. pension, unemployment or child allowances) for such people, usually industrial workers (Allan and Scruggs 2004). This strategy allows for consistent cross-country or cross-time comparisons for certain sub-aspects of policy-making. A major problem with this approach is that available data on replacement levels cover only few aspects of the policy. On the one hand, the use of replacement rates is biased toward policy decisions with monetary implications. On the other hand, by focusing on the benefits for representative standard employees, such studies often also neglect the full range of policy decisions with regard to the different levels of benefits. Thus, cross-country comparisons on the basis of replacement rate indicators only incur serious risk of biased results due the systematic focus on the monetary implications of social policies (Whiteford 1995; Lynch 2001; Bonoli 2007; Scruggs 2007; Knill *et al.* 2010).

The recent literature on social policy-making, however, shows a number of more sophisticated fine-grained analytical frames to study and compare policy-making in different countries. Immergut *et al.* (2007) as well as Häusermann (2010) systematically analyze and compare policy decisions in the field of pension politics in different countries. Altogether, the decision of how to conceptualize and measure the subject of study (i.e. public policy) is of crucial relevance as it impacts on the ability to describe and explain public policy-making. The comparative approach often requires a certain degree of pragmatism and simplification with respect to the operationalization of the underlying concepts—particularly when it comes to designing quantitative large-n studies. However, as this brief overview of different ways of conceptualizing and operationalizing the dependent variables in comparisons of public policy-making illustrates, these decisions might considerably influence the validity of the findings due to the choice of variables and indicators.

In this context, policy (change) analyses with a direct focus on policy output are one way to assess the underlying decision-making of governments—hence covering various stages of the policy cycle including agenda-setting, policy formulation and decision-making (see Howlett and Ramesh 2003: 162). They represent the eventual consensus that has been reached by the group of involved policy actors. Policy outcome studies are based on rather indirect measures of the underlying policy decisions. These include performance indices or pollution data for certain substances and expenditure data for the fields of environmental and social policy, respectively. Given the supposedly complex processes that account for the outcomes, the direction of causal mechanisms is far from evident, which again creates risks of endogeneity. Scholars of quantitative comparative environmental policy research have partly acknowledged this challenge by including certain policy outputs (e.g. limit values for emission) as only one set of explanatory factors for predicting policy outcomes (see above; cf. in particular Esty and Porter 2005). Nevertheless, given the bi-directional causation between policy output and outcome, one could argue that policy outcomes are crucial in explaining follow-up policy-making. As outcomes reflect the effectiveness of previous policy decisions (through records of either financial expenditure or pollution) they might also create incentives for future policy-making.

Furthermore, the heterogeneity of the different approaches found in the literature impacts on the degree of comparability of the results of different studies themselves. Even within the subfield of outcome studies, there are currently many different strategies to design environmental performance indices or to compile expenditure indicators for social policies. This arbitrariness might explain the limited comparability and inconsistency of the findings.

## Comparing patterns of public policy-making

The above discussion on the different ways to conceptualize and operationalize "public policies" in comparative research on environmental and social policy-making illustrates that governmental behavior and decision-making can be measured at different levels of abstraction depending on the scientific aim of the research endeavor. As a consequence of the difficulty in comparing the policy-making behavior of governments in its entirety, various research traditions have emerged to analyze and compare public policies from distinct perspectives. In this section, I present and discuss three different research traditions that analyze public policy-making from a comparative perspective by taking a particular analytical lens and focusing on the observed patterns of policy change or adoption.

First, studies of public policy can be classified according to the direction or range of policy change that follows from a government's choices. While the majority of scholars include positive as well as negative decisions in the analysis, scholars of *policy termination or dismantling* focus exclusively on decisions that are of reductive nature through the partial or complete abolishment of policies.

Research on policy termination was initiated by Brewer in the early 1970s with the objective directing scientific attention toward this final stage of the policy cycle process. He defined this type of policy choice as those adjusting "policies and programs that have become dysfunctional, redundant, outmoded, and/or unnecessary" (Brewer 1978: 338). His initiative led to a vital but short-lived scholarly reaction to analytically advance research into this aspect of policy-making (cf. Bardach 1976; Biller 1976; Behn 1978; deLeon 1978; Hogwood and Peters 1982). Despite persistent theoretical problems and inconsistencies, a number of empirical studies followed (e.g. Frantz 1992; Daniels 1995, 2001; deLeon and Hernández-Quezada 2001; Geva-May 2001; Harris 2001; Graddy and Ye 2008). The policy termination approach develops types or forms of policy termination that are of different scope and that are debated between groups of opponents and proponents of different strengths (cf. in particular Bardach 1976).

Policy dismantling is a related concept in that it focuses on policy decisions to reduce public generosity (distributive policies like social policy) or water down the rigidity of regulatory policies (e.g. environmental policies). Policy dismantling has initially been studied in the context of welfare state analyses. Scholarly attention has continuously been at a high level since Pierson's seminal book (1994). So far, various methods have been applied to analyze such policy decisions mainly in the field of social or welfare state policy (e.g. Esping-Andersen 1996; Clayton and Pontusson 1998; Bonoli 2001; Kitschelt 2001; Green-Pedersen 2002; Korpi and Palme 2003; Hacker 2004; Starke 2006, Starke *et al.* 2008).

A second criterion for case selection is based on the empirically observed patterns of spread of certain policy innovations. The broad literature of *policy diffusion* seeks to explain the dissemination of certain policies among units at different levels (i.e. nation-states, states or local entities) by identifying causes and factors that promote policy diffusion. In order to reduce complexity in comparing public policy-making over cases or units, policy diffusion scholars analyze single policies or policy innovations by describing the underlying adoption patterns over time and units. Assuming that policy choices are "interdependent" (e.g. Braun and Gilardi 2006: 299), diffusion scholars try to explain the spread of policies by identifying the relevant domestic and international factors at work. This way, diffusion scholars seek to estimate the international influence on domestic policy decisions (cf. Frank *et al.* 2000; Busch *et al.* 2005; Elkins and Simmons 2005; Elkins *et al.* 2006). Since its emergence in the 1970s (Gray 1973; Collier and Messick 1975), policy diffusion research has become ever more sophisticated especially with respect to the development of ambitious research methods to detect diffusion channels (cf. Tyran and Sausgruber 2005; Brooks 2007; Volden *et al.* 2008; Marsh and Sharman 2009; Plümper and Neumayer 2010).

Third, the *policy convergence* perspective is another way of comparing the patterns of policy-making of different nation-states, states or local entities by focusing on and explaining the degree of similarity they reach over time as a consequence of passing policies of similar contents (Bennett 1991; Knill 2005). This rather indirect analysis of public policies does not seek to explain the actual decision of a government but how it changes the status quo in relation to other cases (e.g. nation-states). There are a number of studies dealing with the degree of transnational convergence in the fields of environmental and social policy (cf. Heichel *et al.* 2005; Jordan 2005; cf. Overbye 1994; Howlett 2000; Starke *et al.* 2008). The analytical motivation of convergence scholars has often been twofold: to describe the dynamics of policy change over time and in relation to other units, and to explain the observed patterns. This way, they address the question of whether and under which conditions globalization leads to "races to the top" or "races to the bottom" in for instance the adoption of environmental policies (see e.g. Holzinger *et al.* 2008; cf. Drezner 2001, 2005; Busch and Jörgens 2005; Holzinger and Knill 2005).

This brief summary of different analytical strands, that each address certain sub-aspects of policy-making from a comparative perspective, highlights the complexity of the subject of investigation. Comparing public policies over space and time often requires narrowing the analytical lens in favor of a more selective focus on policy-making. As a consequence of this conceptual simplification the above approaches suffer from certain theoretical limitations that impede on the generalizability of the results with respect to public policy-making in general.

First, the risk of biased results cannot be excluded due to the one-directional analysis of policy-making that is inherent to, for instance, the subdisciplines of policy dismantling, policy termination and policy diffusion research. While the former two perspectives make statements about government decisions of reductive nature, the latter have traditionally exclusively dealt with expansion policies (although this does not occur by definition).

Second, biases are likely to affect those studies that select their subject of study (i.e. the policy) based on its empirically observed distribution. In other words, results from diffusion studies might only allow for valid inference with respect to policies that have reached a certain degree of dissemination. Policies that do not reach the stage of a "best practice" are *ex ante* excluded from analysis, which is why large-n diffusion studies are most likely to overestimate the impact of international factors, such as harmonization (for a critical analysis of the limitations of this particular research perspective cf. Howlett and Rayner 2008).

## Comparing processes of public policy-making

In the following paragraphs, I will provide a further criterion along which to classify the literature on comparative public policy: the processes and factors of public policy-making. While the conceptualization and operationalization of the dependent variable (see above) crucially influences the validity of the findings, the selection of policies according to their patterns of spread (see above) primarily impacts on the generalizability of the results toward public policy-making in general.

There are several subdisciplines of comparative research on public policies that explain policy decisions or outputs by focusing on selective explanatory factors or processes. These include scholars of policy learning and policy transfer as well as research on political institutions. One common feature of these studies is the objective to analyze and compare the respective processes of the decision-making and the behavior of the involved actors. As a consequence, the results of these studies are often *ex ante* focused on specific explanations.

One way of narrowing down the empirical focus of comparative public policy analysis can be found within the literatures on *policy learning, policy transfer* or *emulation*. Scholars belonging to these research traditions identify certain mechanisms or factors that cause the dissemination of policies with the aim of tracing and explaining the underlying processes. Similarly to the diffusion perspective, they describe the way in which policies travel from one unit (e.g. nation-state) to another by focusing on distinct mechanisms or ways of communication. As opposed to the previously discussed research perspective, policy transfer, learning or emulation take a process orientation. In this context, policy learning (or lesson-drawing) refers to instances in which governments adopt a certain policy based on the evaluation of a policy in place elsewhere (for a thorough discussion of different forms of horizontal and vertical learning see Bennett and Howlett 1992; cf. Sabatier 1987; Rose 1991, 1993; Hall 1993; Meseguer 2006, 2009; Radaelli 2008).

Further, lesson-drawing may cause governments to decide on policies found elsewhere as "transfers can be voluntary or coercive or combinations thereof" (Stone 2001: 9). Thus, the policy transfer literature analyzes the role of actors by pointing to the importance of interest groups, NGOs, think tanks, non-state policy entrepreneurs (as transfer agents) and the role of policy networks in promoting the diffusion of ideas and their intersubjective perceptions of solutions as well as in providing social learning and building up epistemic communities (cf. Dolowitz and Marsh 1996, 2000, Radaelli 2000; Stone 2000, 2001, 2004). Cases of negative lesson-drawing, in turn, might also lead governments to deliberately exclude policy options found elsewhere (cf. Rose 1991, 1993).

The literature subsumed under the label of *institutionalism* provides another framework for the analysis of government choices by explaining policies and their content based on the institutional conditions that channel the decision-making processes. The point of departure of this approach is veto players, "individual or collective decision-makers whose agreement is required for the change of the status quo" (Tsebelis 2000: 442). According to this view, policy-making is best explained by the systematic analysis of the institutional rules that delimit the actors' leeway and influence on the eventual policy decision (cf. Tsebelis 1995; Hall and Taylor 1996; Scharpf 1997; Jupille and Caporaso 1999). Veto player (Bonoli 2001; Immergut and Anderson 2007) and institution-centered analysis (Swank 2001; Streeck and Thelen 2005) are common approaches in the comparative analysis of, for instance, social policy change. As the "veto players approach emphasizes the ways in which political decision-making institutions structure attempts to change the legislative status quo" (Immergut and Anderson 2007: 7), it allows for explaining policy differences between units (e.g. nation-states) for a range of issues. There are a number of studies that illustrate the role of the fragmentation of political power (horizontal or vertical) for reforming the pension systems of Western democracies (cf. Bonoli 2001, 2004; Swank 2001; Baccaro 2002; Ferrera 2007; Baccaro and Simoni 2008; Häusermann 2010).

Research of comparative public policies that belong to the sub-disciplines of policy learning, policy transfer or institutional analysis puts the analytical focus on understanding and describing the processes that impact on and shape the policy decisions. As a consequence, the empirical results of these studies might be of limited generalizability to policy-making in its complexity. Given the individual conceptual points of departure, scholars belonging to these research traditions are at risk to overestimate the influence of certain explanatory concepts either through potentially biased case selection (policy learning or transfer) or by the analytical focus on one explanation only (institutionalism). As studies pertaining to these research traditions tend to select their cases according to specific causal processes, their findings might not hold for explaining policy-making in general.

Altogether, the degree of specificity of the dependent variable differs over the analytical perspectives discussed in the previous two sections, which furthermore reduces the generalizability of the results for public policy-making.

While transfer and diffusion studies solely explain whether a certain policy has been passed or not, policy learning studies allow for a more detailed conceptual calibration. Similarly, the analytical precision of policy termination studies is rather low; dismantling or retrenchment studies in turn apply refined conceptual approaches by considering different sub-aspects of policy outputs. Policy convergence in this context, also allows for a multidimensional perspective on the dependent variable (i.e. a government's decisions with respect to a range of regulatory aspects; e.g. the emission standards designed to assess a country's prioritization of regulating air quality). Nevertheless, they provide only indirect and selective accounts of the governments' actual decisions because they measure policy-making not in absolute terms but with respect to a certain threshold (i.e. the average policy output of the sample included in the analysis).

## Research methods and causal explanations in comparative public policy

There is a large number of empirical studies that analyze social and environmental policies based on different methodologies (qualitative versus quantitative) and levels of analysis (micro versus macro). Interestingly, the methodological lines of division are almost identical to the ones separating the various research traditions discussed above.

More precisely, the question of whether to study policy outcomes instead of policy outputs is predominantly an issue for scholars of quantitative research. Given the difficulty of constructing and obtaining comparable measures for policy-making over large numbers of cases, macro-quantitative studies often switch to outcome indicators due to improved data availability. However, authors of case studies (e.g. Weidner and Jänicke 2002; Jordan *et al.* 2003; Jordan and Liefferink 2004; Busch and Jörgens 2005; Hall 1993; Kersbergen 1995; Huber and Stephens 2001; Taylor-Gooby 2004) seem to be less affected by the "dependent variable" problem (Green-Pedersen 2004; Clasen and Siegel 2007; cf. Howlett and Cashore 2009) by taking a micro-analytical perspective.

The division between quantitative and qualitative studies continues also within the different subdisciplines of comparative public policy research as discussed earlier in this chapter. In this context, policy learning and lesson-drawing are mostly addressed through comparative case study designs (for an exception see Sommerer 2010), while diffusion is often analyzed through large-n designs (but see, for example, Tews *et al.* 2003).

The policy change literature also reflects the methodological divide. While the policy termination literature almost exclusively consists of comparative case studies, welfare state retrenchment research of policy outcomes (comprising studies based on expenditure or replacement rate data) usually involves large-n studies. In this context, analyses of the dismantling or termination of environmental policies are still in general the exception (but see, for example, Knill *et al.* 2008). While research on policy dismantling or termination tends to overestimate the factors that lead to negative policy choices, the diffusion and transfer literature is biased toward policy innovations and positive policy decisions, respectively. In spite of this potential bias, there have been hardly any efforts in comparative analyses of social or environmental policies to systematically compare policy outputs of both directions, with the possible exception of the literature on policy convergence. As already mentioned, output studies that provide in-depth analyses of policies or policy change in social or environmental policy are almost exclusively limited to qualitative case studies due to their conceptual and empirical complexity.

The literature on comparative social and environmental policy shows biases with respect to the explanatory factors taken into account. Policy diffusion, convergence or welfare- state retrenchment studies in these policy fields, for instance, tend to take a macro perspective focusing particularly on the effects of globalization and economic pressure (Castles 1998; Drezner 2001; Sykes *et al.* 2001; Weidner and Jänicke 2002; Korpi and Palme 2003; Stone 2004; Swank 2005; Holzinger *et al.* 2008). Looking at the role of political parties for public policy-making (from a meso perspective), for instance, there is an interesting fragmentation between the literatures on environmental and social policy. While this factor has received abundant attention in research on the welfare state in general and welfare state retrenchment in particular (e.g. Huber and Stephens 2001; Kitschelt 2001; Green-Pedersen 2002, 2007; Korpi and Palme 2003; Allan and Scruggs 2004; Vis and Kersbergen 2007; Vis 2009), it has less frequently been studied in the context of environmental policy-making (but see Shipan and Lowry 2001; Knill *et al.* 2010). Similarly, the two fields of research differ with respect to the incorporation of institutional explanations for policy-making. The concept of veto players is often applied to analyze reforms of the welfare state and to explain the feasibility of cutbacks in public generosity (Bonoli 2001; Crepaz 2001; Ganghof 2003; Immergut *et al.* 2007; Ha 2008). However, it is a concept scarcely addressed in comparative analyses of environmental policy research (for an exception see Jahn and Müller-Rommel 2010). In addition, institutional factors have received limited attention in this field of research (but see Dryzek *et al.* 2003).

This brief overview on the methods used and causal explanations tested in the analysis of social and environmental policy-making points to systematic differences between the approaches used in the two policy fields. Choices of methods and explanatory factors, which determine the comparability of results, seem to be related to both the analytical perspective on the dependent variable and the field of research (e.g. social or environmental policy). These patterns of comparative policy research illustrate the internal fragmentation of this scientific discipline and the limits of generalizability of its findings.

## Discussion and outlook

This brief presentation and discussion of different approaches toward the study of public policies from the comparative perspective shows that we are still far from academic consensus with respect to the meaning of the term "public policy" itself and in view of the range of explanatory factors to be considered. Scholars of comparative public policy usually make an implicit statement through either the conceptualization of the dependent variable, case selection based on certain policy patterns, by focusing on certain processes or by choosing specific explanatory concepts. These choices entail fundamental consequences for the expected degree of generalizability of the results and the scope of explanation (see below Table 3.1).

On the one hand, process-oriented approaches toward public policy-making reveal a tendency to focus on the explanatory factors (i.e. lesson-drawing, transfer or institutional determinants in this context). On the other hand, pattern-oriented studies (termination, dismantling, and diffusion) tend to put more analytical emphasis on explaining and comparing certain types of public policies themselves. Both subdisciplines share the narrow perspective on the subject of study, i.e. public policy-making. As a consequence, the approaches are limited to policies with certain characteristics or policy aspects. In this context, the literatures on policy learning, transfer or institutional change consider policies that are influenced by distinct explanatory factors. Policy termination and policy dismantling studies incorporate exclusively negative policy decisions, while research on policy diffusion is biased toward policy innovations that have reached a certain degree of dissemination.

These features might limit the generalizability of all these approaches. The policy change literature claims to broaden the analysis of policy-making—at least theoretically—by means of an inclusive conceptualization of the dependent variable and explanatory processes and factors (for a discussion of the deficits in current policy change research, see Howlett and Cashore 2009). As shown, however, in the discussion on the different ways to conceptualize

*Table 3.1* Subdisciplines of comparative public policy research

| | | *Focus on generalizability* | |
|---|---|---|---|
| | | *Low* | *High* |
| ***Focus on*** | *Explanans* | Policy termination<br>Policy dismantling<br>Policy diffusion | Policy change (outcome/impact analyses) |
| | *Explanandum* | Policy learning<br>Policy transfer<br>Institutionalism | Policy change (output analyses) |

Source: Author

and measure public policies in practice, the policy change perspective also has its limits of comparability.

This fragmentation in current public policy analysis illustrates the potential benefits of more integrated approaches that on the one hand, give primary attention to a more careful conceptualization of the subject of research and comparison. On the other hand, the findings call for more flexible combinations of research perspectives, methods, and different explanatory factors in both fields of research. This would enhance the generalizability and the validity of the findings and enable theoretical progress to be made based on the consolidation of the different approaches.

## Bibliography

Allan, J.P. and L. Scruggs. 2004. 'Political partisanship and welfare state reform in advanced industrial societies', *American Journal of Political Science* 48(3): 496–512.

Baccaro, L. 2002. 'Negotiating the Italian pension reform with the unions: Lessons for corporatist theory' *Industrial and Labor Relations Review* 55(3): 413–31.

——and M. Simoni. 2008. 'Policy concertation in Europe: Understanding government choice', *Comparative Political Studies* 41(10): 1323–48.

Bardach, E. 1976. 'Policy termination as a political process', *Policy Sciences* 7(2): 123–31.

Behn, R.D. 1978. 'How to terminate a public policy: A dozen hints for the would-be terminate', *Policy Analyses* 4(3): 393-413.

Bennett, C.J. 1991. 'What is policy convergence and what causes it?', *British Journal of Political Science* 21(2): 215–33.

——and M. Howlett. 1992. 'The lessons of learning: Reconciling theories of policy learning and policy change', *Policy Sciences* 25(3): 275–94.

Biller, R.P. 1976. 'On tolerating policy and organizational termination: Some design considerations', *Policy Sciences* 7(2): 133–49.

Bonoli, G. 2000. *The Politics of Pension Reform: Institutions and Policy Change in Western Europe.* Cambridge: Cambridge University Press.

—— 2001. 'Political institutions, veto points, and the process of welfare state adaptation', in P. Pierson (ed.) *The New Politics of the Welfare State.* Oxford and New York: Oxford University Press, 238–64.

—— 2004. 'The institutionalization of the Swiss multi-pillar pension system', in M. Rein and W. Schmähl (eds) *Rethinking the Welfare State: The Political Economy of Pension Reform.* Northampton, MA: Edward Elgar, 102–21.

—— 2007. 'Too narrow and too wide at once: The "welfare state" as dependent variable in policy analysis', in J. Clasen and N.A. Siegel (eds) *Investigating Welfare State Change: The 'Dependent Variable Problem' in Comparative Analysis.* Cheltenham: Edward Elgar, 24–42.

Braun, D. and F. Gilardi. 2006. 'Taking "Galton's problem" seriously: Towards a theory of Policy diffusion. *Journal of Theoretical Politics* 18(3): 298–322.

Brewer, G.D. 1978. 'Termination: Hard choices—harder questions', *Public Administration Review* 38(4): 338–44.

Brooks, S.M. 2007. 'When does diffusion matter? Explaining the spread of structural pension reforms across nations', *The Journal of Politics* 69(3): 701–15.

Busch, P.-O. and H. Jörgens. 2005. 'International patterns of environmental policy change and convergence', *European Environment* 15(2): 80–101.

—— H. Jörgens and K. Tews. 2005. 'The global diffusion of regulatory instruments: The making of a new international environmental regime', *The Annals of the American Academy of Political and Social Science* 598(1): 146–67.

Castles, F.G. 1998. *Comparative Public Policy: Patterns of Post-war Transformation.* Cheltenham: Edward Elgar.

—— 1999. 'Decentralisation and the post-war political economy', *European Journal of Political Research* 36(1): 27–53.

—— 2004. *The Future of the Welfare State: Crisis Myths and Crisis Realities.* Oxford: Oxford University Press.

—— 2009. 'What welfare states do: A disaggregated expenditure approach', *Journal of Social Policy* 38, 45–62.

——and D. Mitchell. 1992. 'Identifying welfare state regimes: The links between politics, instruments and outcomes', *Governance: An International Journal of Policy and Administration* 5(1): 1–26.

Clasen, J. and D. Clegg. 2007. 'Levels and levers of conditionality: Measuring change within welfare states', in J. Clasen and N.A. Siegel (eds) *Investigating Welfare State Change: The 'Dependent Variable Problem' in Comparative Analysis.* Cheltenham: Edward Elgar, 166–97.

——and N.A. Siegel (eds). 2007. *Investigating Welfare State Change: The 'Dependent Variable Problem' in Comparative Analysis.* Cheltenham: Edward Elgar.

Clayton, R. and J. Pontusson. 1998. 'Welfare-state retrenchment revisited: Entitlement cuts, public sector restructuring, and inegalitarian trends in advanced capitalist societies', *World Politics* 51(1): 67–98.

Collier, D. and R.E. Messick. 1975. 'Prerequisites versus diffusion: Testing alternative explanations of social security adoption', *The American Political Science Review* 69(4): 1299–315.

Crepaz, M.M.L. 1995. 'Explaining national variations of air pollution levels: Political institutions and their impact on environmental policy-making', *Environmental Politics* 4(3): 391–414.

—— 2001. 'Veto players, globalization and the redistributive capacity of the state: A panel study of 15 OECD countries', *Journal of Public Policy* 21(1): 1–22.

Daniels, M.R. 1995. 'Organizational termination and policy continuation: Closing the Oklahoma public training schools', *Policy Sciences* 28(3): 301–16.

—— 2001. 'Policy and organizational termination', *International Journal of Public Administration* 24(3): 249–62.

deLeon, P. 1978. 'Public policy termination: An end and a beginning', *Policy Analyses* 4(3): 369–92.

——and J.M. Hernández-Quezada. 2001. 'The case of the national solidarity program in Mexico. A study in comparative public policy termination', *International Journal of Public Administration* 24(3): 289–309.

Dolowitz, D.P. and D. Marsh. 1996. 'Who learns what from whom: A review of the policy transfer literature', *Political Studies* 44(2): 343–57.

—— 2000. 'Learning from abroad: The role of policy transfer in contemporary policy making', *Governance: An International Journal of Policy and Administration* 13(1): 5–24.

Drezner, D.W. 2001. 'Globalization and policy convergence', *International Studies Review* 3(1): 53–78.

—— 2005. 'Globalization, harmonization, and competition: The different pathways to policy convergence', *Journal of European Public Policy* 12(5): 841–59.

Dryzek, J.S., D. Downes, C. Hunold and D. Schlosberg. 2003. *Green States and Social Movements: Environmentalism in the United States, United Kingdom, Germany, and Norway.* Oxford and New York: Oxford University Press.

Dye, T.R. 1976. *Policy Analysis: What Governments Do, Why They Do it, and What Difference it Makes.* Tuscaloosa, AL: University of Alabama Press.

Elkins, Z., A.T. Guzman and B.A. Simmons. 2006. 'Competing for capital: The diffusion of bilateral investment treaties, 1960–2000', *International Organization* 60(4): 811–46.

—— and B. Simmons 2005. 'On waves, clusters, and diffusion: A conceptual framework', *The Annals of the American Academy of Political and Social Science* 598(1): 33–51.

EspingAndersen, G. (ed.). 1996. *Welfare States in Transition: National Adaptations in Global Economies.* London and Thousand Oaks, CA: Sage.

Esty, D.C. and M.E. Porter. 2005. 'National environmental performance: An empirical analysis of policy results and determinants', *Environment and Development Economics* 10(4): 391–434.

Ferrera, M. 2007. 'The European welfare state. Golden achievements and silver prospects', URGE working paper, 4/07.

——and M. Jessoul. 2007. 'Italy: A narrow gate for path-shift', in E.M. Immergut, K.M. Anderson and I. Schulze (eds) *The Handbook of West European Pension Politics.* Oxford, New York: Oxford University Press, 396–453.

Frank, D.J., A. Hironaka and E. Schofer. 2000. 'The nation-state and the natural environment over the twentieth century', *American Sociological Review* 65(1): 96–116.

Frantz, J.E. 1992. 'Reviving and revising a termination model', *Policy Sciences* 25(2): 175–89.

Ganghof, S. 2003. 'Promises and pitfalls of veto player analysis', *Swiss Political Science Review* 9(2): 1–25.

Geva-May, I. 2001. 'When the motto is "till death do us part": The conceptualization and the craft of termination in the public policy cycle', *International Journal of Public Administration* 24(3): 263–88.

Graddy, E.A. and K. Ye. 2008. 'When do we "just say no"? Policy termination decisions in local hospital services', *Policy Studies Journal* 36(2): 219–42.

Gray, V. 1973. 'Innovation in the states: A diffusion study', *The American Political Science Review* 67(4): 1174–85.

Green-Pedersen, C. 2002. *The Politics of Justification: Party Competition and Welfare-state Retrenchment in Denmark and the Netherlands from 1982 to 1998.* Amsterdam: Amsterdam University Press.

—— 2004. 'The dependent variable problem within the study of welfare state retrenchment: defining the problem and looking for solutions', *Journal of Comparative Policy Analysis* 6(1): 3–14.

—— 2007. 'More than data questions and methodological issues: Theoretical conceptualization and the dependent variable "problem" in the study of welfare reform', in J. Clasen and N.A. Siegel (eds)

*Investigating Welfare State Change: The 'Dependent Variable Problem' in Comparative Analysis*. Cheltenham: Edward Elgar, 13–23.

Ha, E. 2008. 'Globalization, veto players, and welfare spending', *Comparative Political Studies* 41(6): 783–813.

Hacker, J.S. 2004. 'Privatizing risk without privatizing the welfare state: The hidden politics of social policy retrenchment in the United States', *American Political Science Review* 98(2): 243–60.

Hall, P.A. 1993. 'Policy paradigms, social learning, and the state: The case of economic policymaking in Britain', *Comparative Politics* 25(3): 275–96.

——and R.C.R. Taylor. 1996. 'Political science and the three new institutionalisms', *Political Studies* 44(5): 936–57.

Harris, M. 2001. 'Policy termination: The case of term limits in Michigan', *International Journal of Public Administration* 24(3): 165–80.

Häusermann, S. 2010. *The Politics of Welfare State Reform in Continental Europe: Modernization in Hard Times*. Cambridge: Cambridge University Press.

Heichel, S., J. Pape and T. Sommerer. 2005. 'Is there convergence in convergence research? An overview of empirical studies on policy convergence', *Journal of European Public Policy* 12(5): 817–40.

Hogwood, B.W. and G.B. Peters. 1982. 'The dynamics of policy change: policy succession', *Policy Sciences* 14(3): 225–45.

Holzinger, K. and C. Knill. 2005. 'Causes and conditions of cross-national policy convergence', *Journal of European Public Policy* 12(5): 775–96.

——, C. Knill and T. Sommerer. 2008. 'Environmental policy convergence: The impact of international harmonization, transnational communication, and regulatory competition', *International Organization* 62 (4): 553–87.

Howlett, M. 2000. 'Beyond legalism? Policy ideas, implementation styles and emulation-based convergence in Canadian and US environmental policy', *Journal of Public Policy* 20(3): 305–29.

——and B. Cashore. 2009. 'The dependent variable problem in the study of policy change: Understanding policy change as a methodological problem', *Journal of Comparative Policy Analysis* 11(1): 33–46.

——and M. Ramesh. 2003. *Studying Public Policy: Policy Cycles and Policy Subsystems*. Toronto: Oxford University Press.

——and J. Rayner. 2008. 'Third generation policy diffusion studies and the analysis of policy mixes: Two steps forward and one step back?', *Journal of Comparative Policy Analysis* 10(4): 385–402.

Huber, E. and J.D. Stephens. 2001. *Development and Crisis of the Welfare State Parties and Policies in Global Markets*. Chicago: University of Chicago Press.

Immergut, E.M. and K.M. Anderson 2007. 'Editors' introduction: the dynamics of pension politics', in E.M. Immergut, K.M. Anderson and I. Schulze (eds) *The Handbook of West European Pension Politics*. Oxford, New York: Oxford University Press, 1–45.

——, K.M. Anderson and I. Schulze (eds). 2007. *The Handbook of West European Pension Politics*. Oxford, New York: Oxford University Press.

Jahn, D. 1998. 'Environmental performance and policy regimes: Explaining variations in 18 OECD-countries', *Policy Sciences* 31: 107–31.

——and F. Müller-Rommel. 2010. 'Political institutions and policy performance: A comparative analysis of Central and Eastern Europe', *Journal of Public Policy* 30(1): 23–44.

Jänicke, M. 1992. 'Conditions for environmental policy success: An international comparison', *The Environmentalist* 12(1): 47–58.

——(ed.). 1996. *Umweltpolitik der Industrieländer: Entwicklung–Bilanz–Erfolgsbedingungen*. Berlin: Sigma.

Jordan, A. 2005. 'Policy convergence: A passing fad or a new integrating focus in European Union studies?', *Journal of European Public Policy* 12(5): 944–53.

Jordan, A. and D. Liefferink (eds). 2004. *Environmental Policy in Europe: The Europeanization of National Environmental Policy*. London and New York: Routledge.

——, R.K.W. Wurzel and A.R. Zito (eds). 2003. *'"New" Instruments of Environmental Governance? National Experiences and Prospects*. London and Portland, OR: Frank Cass.

Jupille, J. and J. Caporaso. 1999. 'Institutionalism and the European Union: Beyond international relations and comparative politics', *Annual Review of Political Science* 2: 429–44.

Kersbergen, K. van 1995. *Social Capitalism: A Study of Christian Democracy and the Welfare State*. London and New York: Routledge.

Kitschelt, H. 2001. 'Partisan competition and welfare state retrenchment: When do politicians choose unpopular policies?', in P. Pierson (ed.) *The New Politics of the Welfare State*. Oxford, New York: Oxford University Press, pp. 265–302.

Knill, C. 2005. 'Introduction: Cross-national policy convergence: Concepts, approaches and explanatory factors', *Journal of European Public Policy* 12(5): 764–74.

——, J. Tosun and S. Heichel. 2008. 'Balancing competitiveness and conditionality: Environmental policy making in low-regulating countries', *Journal of European Public Policy* 15(7): 1019–40.

——, M. Debus and S. Heichel. 2010. 'Do parties matter in internationalised policy areas? The impact of political parties on environmental policy outputs in 18 OECD countries, 1970–2000', *European Journal of Political Research* 49(3): 301–36.

——, K. Schulze and J. Tosun. 2010. 'Politikwandel und seine Messung in der vergleichenden Staatstätigkeitsforschung: Konzeptionelle Probleme und mögliche Alternativen', *Politische Vierteljahresschrift* 51 (3): 409–32.

Korpi, W. and J. Palme. 2003. 'New politics and class politics in the context of austerity and globalization: Welfare state regress in 18 countries, 1975–95', *American Political Science Review* 97(3): 425–46.

Kühner, S. 2007. 'Country-level comparisons of welfare state change measures: Another facet of the dependent variable problem within the comparative analysis of the welfare state', *Journal of European Social Policy* 17(1): 5–18.

Lerner, D. and H.D. Lasswell (eds). 1951. *The Policy Sciences: Recent Developments in Scope and Method.* Stanford, CA: Stanford University Press.

Lynch, J. 2001. 'The age-orientation of social policy regimes in OECD countries, *Journal of Social Policy* 30 (3): 411–36.

Marsh, D. and J.C. Sharman. 2009. 'Policy diffusion and policy transfer', *Policy Studies* 30(3): 269–88.

Martin, J.P. 1996. 'Measures of replacement rates for the purpose of international comparisons: A note', *OECD Economic Studies* 26(1): 99–115.

Mayntz, R. 1983. 'The conditions of effective public policy: A new challenge for policy analysis', *Policy and Politics* 11(2): 123–43.

Meseguer, C. 2006. 'Rational learning and bounded learning in the diffusion of policy innovations', *Rationality and Society* 18(1): 35–66.

—— 2009. *Learning, Policy Making, and Market Reforms.* Cambridge and New York: Cambridge University Press.

Overbye, E. 1994. 'Convergence in policy outcomes: Social security systems in perspective', *Journal of Public Policy* 14(2): 147–74.

Pierson, P. 1994. *Dismantling the Welfare State? Reagan, Thatcher, and the Politics of Retrenchment.* Cambridge and New York: Cambridge University Press.

—— 1996. 'The new politics of the welfare state, *World Politics* 48(2): 143–79.

Plümper, T. and E. Neumayer. (2010. 'Model specification in the analysis of spatial dependence', *European Journal of Political Research* 49(3): 418–42.

Radaelli, C.M. 2000. 'Policy transfer in the European Union: Institutional isomorphism as a source of legitimacy', *Governance: An International Journal of Policy and Administration* 13(1): 25–43.

—— 2008. 'Europeanization, policy learning, and new modes of governance', *Journal of Comparative Policy Analysis* 10(3): 239–54.

Rose, R. 1991. 'What is lesson-drawing?' *Journal of Public Policy* 11(1): 3–30.

—— 1993. *Lesson-Drawing in Public Policy: A Guide to Learning Across Time and Space.* Chatham, NJ: Chatham House.

Sabatier, P.A. 1987. 'Knowledge, policy-oriented learning, and policy change: An advocacy coalition framework', *Science Communication* 8(4): 649–92.

——and D. Mazmanian. 1980. 'The implementation of public policy: A framework of analysis', *Policy Studies Journal* 8(4): 538–60.

Scharpf, F.W. 1997. *Games Real Actors Play: Actor-Centered Institutionalism in Policy Research.* Boulder, CO: Westview Press.

Scruggs, L. 1999. 'Institutions and environmental performance in seventeen Western democracies', *British Journal of Political Science* 29: 1–31.

—— 2003. *Sustaining Abundance: Environmental Performance in Industrial Democracies.* Cambridge: Cambridge University Press.

—— 2007. 'Welfare state generosity across space and time', in J. Clasen and N.A. Siegel (eds) *Investigating Welfare State Change: The 'Dependent Variable Problem' in Comparative Analysis.* Cheltenham: Edward Elgar, 133–65.

Shipan, C.R. and W.R. Lowry. 2001. 'Environmental policy and party divergence in Congress', *Political Research Quarterly* 54(2): 245–63.

Sommerer, T. 2010. *Transnationales Lernen als Faktor von Policy-Wandel: Eine vergleichende Analyse der Umweltpolitik in 24 OECD-Staaten*. Wiesbaden: VS Verlag für Sozialwissenschaften.

Starke, P. 2006. 'The politics of welfare state retrenchment: A literature review', *Social Policy and Administration* 40(1): 104–20.

——, Obinger, H. and F.G. Castles. 2008. 'Convergence towards where: In what ways, if any, are welfare states becoming more similar?' *Journal of European Public Policy* 15(7): 975–1000.

Stephens, J.D., E. Huber and L. Ray, L. 1999. 'The welfare state in hard times', in H. Kitschelt, P. Lange, G. Marks and J.D. Stephens (eds) *Continuity and Change in Contemporary Capitalism*. Cambridge: Cambridge University Press.

Stone, D.L. 2000. 'Non-governmental policy transfer: The strategies of independent policy institutes', *Governance: An International Journal of Policy and Administration* 13(1): 45–62.

—— 2001. 'Learning lessons, policy transfer and the international diffusion of policy ideas' (Electronic Version). Warwick Centre for the Study of Globalisation and Regionalisation (CSGR) Working Paper No. 69/01. Available at www2.warwick.ac.uk/fac/soc/csgr/research/workingpapers/2001/wp6901.pdf

—— 2004. 'Transfer agents and global networks in the "transnationalisation" of policy', *Journal of European Public Policy* 11(3): 545–66.

Streeck, W. and K.A. Thelen (eds). 2005. *Beyond Continuity: Institutional Change in Advanced Political Economies*. Oxford and New York: Oxford University Press.

Swank, D. 2001. 'Political institutions and welfare state restructuring: The impact of institutions on social policy change in developed democracies', in P. Pierson (ed.) *The New Politics of the Welfare State*. Oxford and New York: Oxford University Press, pp. 197–237.

—— 2005. 'Globalisation, domestic politics, and welfare state retrenchment in capitalist democracies', *Social Policy and Society* 4(2): 183–95.

Sykes, R., B. Palier and P.M. Prior (eds). 2001. *Globalisation and European Welfare States: Challenges and Change*. Basingstoke and New York: Palgrave MacMillan.

Taylor-Gooby, P. (ed.). 2004. *New Risks, New Welfare: The Transformation of the European Welfare State*. Oxford and New York: Oxford University Press.

Tews, K., P.-O. Buschand and H. Jörgens. 2003. 'The diffusion of new environmental policy instruments', *European Journal of Political Research* 42(4): 569–600.

Tsebelis, G. 1995. 'Decision making in political systems: Veto players in presidentialism, parliamentarism, multicameralism and multipartyism', *British Journal of Political Science* 25(3): 289–325.

—— 2000. 'Veto players and institutional analysis', *Governance: An International Journal of Policy and Administration* 13(4): 441–74.

Tyran, J.-R. and R. Sausgruber. 2005. 'The diffusion of policy innovations: An experimental investigation', *Journal of Evolutionary Economics* 15(4): 423–42.

Vis, B. 2009. 'Governments and unpopular social policy reform: Biting the bullet or steering clear?', *European Journal of Political Research* 48(1): 31–57.

——and K. van Kersbergen. 2007. 'Why and how do political actors pursue risky reforms?' *Journal of Theoretical Politics* 19(2): 153–72.

Volden, C., M.M. Ting and D.P. Carpenter. 2008. 'A formal model of learning and policy diffusion', *The American Political Science Review* 102(3): 319–32.

Wälti, S. 2004. 'How multilevel structures affect environmental policy in industrialized countries', *European Journal of Political Research* 43(4): 599–634.

Weidner, H. and M. Jänicke (eds). 2002. *Capacity Building in National Environmental Policy: A Comparative Study of 17 Countries*. Berlin: Springer-Verlag.

Whiteford, P. 1995. 'The use of replacement rates in international comparisons of benefit systems', *International Social Security Review* 48(2): 3–30.

Wilensky, H.L. 1974. *The Welfare State and Equality: Structural and Ideological Roots of Public Expenditures*. Berkeley, CA: University of California Press.

Windhoff-Héritier, A. 1987. *Policy-Analyse: Eine Einführung*. Frankfurt and New York: Campus Verlag.

# 4
# International dimensions and dynamics of policy-making

*Anthony Perl*

The days when policy researchers could count upon domestic politics and society to contribute sufficient data for a satisfactory analysis are now a memory. Whether policy researchers are prepared to enter another analytical universe or not, the accelerating flow of ideas, information, goods and money across national borders has affected the nature of policy problems, reshaped the attempts to engage these problems and thus reoriented the way in which explanations of policy-making can be productively pursued. The big questions that animate policy studies may not have changed, but the available data and the concepts needed to analyze them have been shifting. This chapter will seek to connect these emerging global dynamics to long recognized drivers of policy-making and present a conceptual framework that can help in understanding the resulting interactions. Enhancing the linkage between theoretical frameworks that have informed international relations and public policy concepts promises a better understanding of policy-making in a volatile universe.

Despite the growing awareness of globalization as an influence on many aspects of policy-making, there remains a knowledge gap among the findings produced by those who seek to explain policy-making on its own terms, and those who are more interested in interrogating the transnational forces that have evolved in recent years. While international relations scholars are perhaps more experienced in assessing how interactions across boundaries affect politics, they are also less inclined to extend these efforts to elucidating the internal workings of a policy subsystem. Such sectoral interpretations can appear mundane to those who are focused on matters of global conflict and governance.

Conversely, students of public policy may be quite motivated to consider how global dynamics affect policy-making within a subsystem, in search of a better understanding about how exogenous influences can shape the authoritative dynamics within that domain. But researchers who have been trained to explore policy-making in a single government or administration, or perhaps compare those efforts, are likely to lack the conceptual tools that are required to integrate a global interplay of policy inputs into the workings of a particular subsystem. The most promising approach to taking the measure of global influences on policy subsystems thus appears to extend the policy researcher's ability to assess these exogenous forces from an international perspective. Extending the capacity of policy researchers to better interpret international interactions could enhance the prospects for a fruitful dialogue between policy studies and international relations. As policy studies have more to say about the increasing global influences and interactions, those engaged in international political research could become more attracted to engaging such findings about how global forces influence policy subsystems.

This examination of how to account for international forces in policy studies will draw upon concepts that have been developed to examine meso-level political relationships between the state and society. This tradition includes identifying configurations of actors and classifying them into a typology of policy communities (i.e. ranging from the collaborative partnerships of corporatism to the competitive advocacy of pluralism). More sophisticated classifications of authority can be found in the literature on policy networks, and as the scope of such relations has broadened, the term governance network has been put forward. These approaches to analyzing policy dynamics that cross organizational and jurisdictional boundaries can be particularly effective in assessing global influences on policy-making because they draw upon relational measures of authority. Assessing these relationships in the international arena is a natural conceptual progression. Furthermore, the analytical skills that are developed through analyzing policy networks and communities could be readily scaled up to examining global forces affecting policy, unlike some conceptual approaches.

We will consider the value of applying a network perspective on understanding global influences through four stages of consideration. Initially the chapter will examine the concept of globalization and briefly assess the implications that it raises for studying policy-making. Next, we will turn to the literature on policy communities and policy networks to highlight tools that can be used in assessing global influences on policy subsystems. Then, the chapter will consider the concept of policy paradigms and contemplate the role that ideational influences play in modulating global impacts on policy. Finally, a fourfold typology of internationalized policy environments will be presented, in order to illuminate how particular configurations of policy communities and networks can refract the global influences on governance. In conclusion, the dynamic role of policy community mediators in trying to steer subsystem responses to global forces will briefly be considered.

## Seeking policy explanations in a time of increasingly permeable political boundaries

The political boundaries that have structured many examinations of policy-making are less definitive than at any time since the mid-twentieth century. And as a result, political factors and forces that could once be safely ruled out of bounds in studying policy, because they were seen to have little impact on the policy subsystems within a given jurisdiction, have to be considered in ways that take account of contemporary reality without hopelessly cluttering the scope of a given investigation. Cerny (1995) contended that global forces have reshaped the way that states function when they make policy by providing policy actors with cues of equal or greater influence than the domestic interests and institutions which previously determined both the political calculus and the substantive assessment of policy options. His claims were provocative when first asserted, but appear increasingly self-evident in the early twenty-first century.

For example, American auto manufacturers had successfully resisted changes to fuel economy regulations for decades when the US surface transportation subsystem was governed by a cohesive domestic cluster of interests and institutions (Perl and Dunn 2007). It is not a coincidence that the US government has established a much higher fuel economy standard for motor vehicles following the 2008 global financial crisis. A multi-billion dollar bailout that saved both Chrysler and General Motors from liquidation opened the window for changing technical standards in ways that had previously been anathema to industry leaders in the domestic subsystem. In this instance, the international drivers of policy change dramatically, obviously because the influence of these forces was concentrated in a global financial crisis, but many subsystems have been reshaped by international influences in a less dramatic fashion.

Even cultural characteristics which once informed the values behind distinct traditions of the state in policy-making (Dyson 1980) have become harder to operationalize as independent variables. From the social welfare traditions of Scandinavian states to the neoliberalism embraced by Anglo-American polities, state-specific ideas on the role of government no longer provide a clear and consistent policy orientation. Instead, virtual communities of interest spread ideas and values across social networks that span the globe at the same time that supranational institutions develop explicitly global values that foster convergence in policy-making.

Not surprisingly, scholars in international relations have been drawing attention to the global influences on policy-making for some time already. During the 1970s, Keohane and Nye (1977) had identified "interdependence" as a driving force behind international economic and political relationships. Gourevitch (1978) proposed an explanation of how these international forces could directly affect domestic politics, which would then reverberate by influencing foreign policies in a formulation that he labeled the "second image-reversed." This dynamic was shown to extend from domestic politics into policy-making by Robert Putnam (1998) through his "two-level games" perspective on policy negotiations in the international arena. While this attention to international policy influences grew out of a focus on the workings of formal governing arrangements across political boundaries, another stream of thinking that is closer to home in policy studies has sought to understand how societal forces can influence policy when they cross organizational boundaries.

In this broader consideration of transnational political forces, "globalization" has become a commonly used term to encompass economic, political and cultural influences that cut across borders, not only those of formal state structures but also societal organizations from corporations to virtual networks. Held has characterized such globalization as

> the stretching and deepening of social relations and institutions across space and time such that, on the one hand, day-to-day activities are increasingly influenced by events happening on the other side of the globe and, on the other, the practices and decisions of local groups or communities can have significant global reverberations.
>
> *(1995: 20)*

The effects of such globalization have reshaped the roles and routines of policy subsystems. Policy inputs from subnational, national, regional, and international levels are likely to expand the range of ideas and interests that are interacting within the subsystem, yielding less stable relationships among actors and less predictable actions at different stages of the policy cycle.

This expansion of global influences can be seen following the liberalization of capital movements in the 1980s and the subsequent impact of global financial considerations that has played out within just about every policy subsystem. Facing the need to engage with these global financial dynamics, most governments have sought to cooperate at scales ranging from informal dialogue and information sharing (e.g. the Asia-Pacific Economic Cooperation) to creating supra-national currencies and reserve banks (e.g. the Euro and European Central Bank). These initiatives have further amplified global influences on policy subsystems, since the economic "fundamentals" shaping many policy contexts have become increasingly transnational.

And while the effects of globalization vary across subsystems, there are few, if any, domains that have been left unaffected by this erosion of political boundaries. Even subsystems supporting "core" areas of state sovereignty, such as the military and national security, have been affected by the globalization of combat and terrorism. The multinational military intervention that determined the outcome of Libya's civil war in 2011 illustrates the influence of global forces on at least two different levels. On the one hand, global communications and social networks sparked rebellions in autocratic regimes across the Arab world. And on the other hand, nations that had not previously allied in Middle East military intervention jointly took a side in the Libyan conflict, responding partly to domestic appeals that democratic ambitions and human rights must not be extinguished by the Qaddafi counteroffensive.

Other policy subsystems have experienced less dramatic, but no less important, changes from beyond their borders as states have more or less explicitly pooled their sovereignty to address environmental, financial, trade, and other policy challenges. The common characteristic in each of these diverse instances where global forces have modified the interaction of ideas and interests within a policy subsystem is that more permeable political boundaries have let in ideas, information, and interests that had not previously exerted a direct affect on the actors and organizations.

This augmenting encroachment of global influences into a policy subsystem, mirrors and often stimulates another kind of change that has impacted the nature of policy-making in recent years. The rules and norms that once demarcated the duties of public officials from the actions of civil society participants in a policy subsystem have also changed, with a tendency toward blurring the distinction between public and private spheres of responsibility. The relationship between the public realm and the private sector can no longer be counted upon to conform to Weberian administrative norms. Scholars in public policy have thus had to develop their own concepts and analytical tools that could better interpret this reconfiguration of activities and relationships between the public realm and the private sector, leading into a post-Weberian universe where states make policy through governance (Kooiman 2003).

Assessing the potentials and the pitfalls of policy-making that unfold beyond the bureaucracy's formal accountability for translating democratically attained decisions into policy outcomes has taken policy studies into the more interactive and contingent deliberations occurring in governance networks. Scholars such as Rhodes (1996) claimed that societies were experiencing a new mode of policy-making in which governance provided the capacity for "governing without government". Examining political dynamics that span the boundary between the state and society is thus increasingly familiar to scholars who look at how policy communities and policy networks have changed the way that policy gets developed. This approach can develop the skills needed to extend such analysis to explain the political effects of globalization on policy.

When the interactions between state and society have grown more convoluted as their boundaries have blurred, the analysis of how these relationships are managed requires some robust guiding principles. Coleman and Perl (1999) proposed two conceptual axes that can orient navigation through the many intricacies of governance and globalization. First, they draw attention to the *degree and patterns of integration* of relationships among policy actors. Next, they highlight the extent and manner in which *public power is shared* between state and civil society actors. Since these dimensions are interdependent, the potential for confusion is best avoided by linking each axis to an established analytical viewpoint in the study of meso-level policy-making. By focusing on participants, the policy community perspective can capture the interaction of actors and organizations within a given governance structure. (Coleman and Skogstad 1990) And similar to van Waarden's (1992) usage, the concept of policy network will characterize the institutional dimension in which public power can be shared by members of the policy community.

Policy communities can be conceptualized as the cognitive and discursive space where issues are problematized as appropriate, or inappropriate, objects of public engagement. Where such debates used to emphasize the merits and disadvantages of placing a problem onto the public policy agenda, thus triggering a government's subsequent engagement with formulating and implementing a course of action, the trend toward governance has led policy communities to remain continuously, although variably, engaged in efforts to pursue policy options. The degree of integration within policy communities is determined by their boundary rules, and represents one of two defining characteristics. Boundaries can be more or less restrictive depending on the nature and enforcement of rules that specify size (Jordan and Schubert 1992), openness (Hassenteufel 1995) and stability of membership (Le Gales 1995). These rules also have a bearing on the quantity and nature of information that is exchanged (Laumann and Knoke 1987).

Another significant aspect of the boundary defining a policy community is the extent of shared values and norms among its membership. The most well developed conceptualization of such ideational ties can be found in Sabatier and Jenkins-Smith's (1993) "Advocacy Coalition Framework" in which core beliefs about the causes and effects of policy intervention focus participants on a common understanding of problems and draw them into shared political pursuit of a preferred solution. The number of advocacy coalitions and the relationship between their preferred policy solutions can greatly affect the character of a policy community. A similar concept has been put forward from international relations scholarship, the "epistemic community" (Haas 1992). Here, it is ostensibly objective expertise, rather than more subjective beliefs, that draw policy actors together into shared knowledge and cooperative action that can transcend national boundaries.

By specifying the boundaries of policy communities, and then analyzing what goes on inside these spaces, policy scholars have been able to link the participants' state of mind to their interactions both within and outside the policy community, and then correlate these relationships with actual policy orientations. One important finding from this line of analysis has been that the greater the degree of integration of actors within a policy community, the higher the likelihood of collaborative approaches to policy-making. Scharpf (1997) claims that instead of a short-term focus, and zero sum calculus of competition, more integrated policy communities can pursue policy options which go beyond the lowest common denominator and address the needs of a broader cross-section of policy actors than would be able to work together in less integrated contexts. Another finding has been that once a particular advocacy coalition or epistemic community has become widely recognized for its influence or expertise, then that group's values and norms will convey legitimacy on some actors while denying it to others (Smith 1995). Some policy preferences will thus become more legitimate than others for the time that consensus on values persists. But when consensus within a policy community erodes, political conflict over options at each stage of policy-making can be expected.

When it comes to assessing the ways in which political authority plays out in a policy subsystem, the policy network perspective looks beyond the cognitive and discursive attributes of policy community participants and focuses on a scarce resource that is essential to overcoming the policy-making constraints that are posed by organizational interdependencies, technical complexities, and factual uncertainties. That resource is power, in particular the power that flows either directly or indirectly from state sovereignty.

During the strategic manoeuvring of policy actors, the sharing of information and ideas, and the negotiation of competing interests and perspectives, outcomes will be shaped considerably by who has the power to make decisions binding across all of society based on the sovereign authority of government. This authority may well be delegated and shared across the policy community, but in one form or another, power influences the outcome of policy-making. And it is through those different configurations of power that influence how particularly configured policy networks can make a significant impact on the policy process.

Policy network typologies have made it possible to move analysis of governance beyond the blunt distinction between pluralism and corporatism (van Waarden 1992: 30). With the blending of public and private roles in policy formulation and delivery, more precise network configurations such as "state corporatism" and "clientelism" are able to capture the effects of delegation of public authority to coalitions or to particular entities within the policy community. This precision can be even more helpful in sorting out the authoritative dynamics of transnational policy communities in which public actors operating at multiple levels of government interact and share their authority over policy-making, either with one another or with a subset of societal actors and organizations. The more hybridized such relationships become, and the further that policy-making dynamics blur the distinction between public and private spheres of accountability, the greater value that more nuanced policy network categories can offer in highlighting both the efficacy and the accountability of particular governance modes.

In a world where some of the boundaries that used to matter most for policy-making—those between government and the private sector, and those demarcating one state's sovereignty from another—are no longer preeminent, other structures that can integrate the ideas and interests of policy communities with the influence and power deployed in policy networks merit greater analytical attention. Instead of concentrating on the forces of cohesion within policy subsystems that emanate from formal state structures, the influence of ideas that cut across state and societal boundaries need to be given greater weight in attempts to explain policy-making.

These ideas about what is to be done, and how it is to be done, comprise the essence of a policy paradigm. As Peter Hall has illustrated, such globally established paradigms as the role of monetary policy and the financial institutions that implement it can be more influential than any government's formal economic policy capacity. Policy paradigms thus offer an intellectual center of gravity that can serve some of the role that state actors and structures have traditionally played in shaping the dynamics of policy subsystems. The following section will consider the policy paradigm as a conceptual construct that can offer guidance in interpreting a policy universe containing more varied international forces than ever before.

## How policy paradigms guide governance networks through an accelerating policy universe

The growing permeability of boundaries, both among nations and between the state and society, has increased the volume and velocity of forces from the policy universe that are transmitted into policy communities, raising the level of instability in policy-making. But this growing exposure to exogenous forces has also enhanced the dissemination of a particular type of ideas that can bring, or return, coherence to volatile governance networks by fashioning a common point of view among policy actors. Numerous scholars have noted the influence that a coherent set of ideas can exert in aligning the vision of policy actors toward a shared set of goals (Jobert and Muller 1987; Hall 1993; Shon and Rein 1994). Offering advice on which problems are critical and which ones are less important, which policy instruments provide appropriate means to address these problems and which do not, and what instrument settings could best resolve a problem, are the stock in trade of policy practitioners' work. Hall has labeled the guiding principles that support such deliberations as a "policy paradigm." Shon and Rein characterize these ideas as "policy frames," while Jobert and Muller speak of a reference system that guides French policy-making. Each of these concepts highlights the shared vision that can be created by a set of norms which focus policy communities on commensurate goals and build confidence in the causal relationships that will guide actors within those communities to agree that particular instruments should be deployed in specific ways. These policy paradigms exert influence by evoking "images" or "generative metaphors" that help policy actors to make sense of a complex and contingent policy universe. Examples of such influential images have included "Energy Security," "Universal Health Care," and "Free Trade." These ideas and images provide certain actors in the policy community, and their beliefs, with greater legitimacy in the policy process than other groups and individuals can muster.

The acceleration in speed and volume of communication across boundaries has often aided the dissemination of consistent, if not always convergent, policy paradigms. One such vector has been the rise of a global cadre of policy consultants who perceive material incentives to sell similar solutions across a range of policy jurisdictions (Perl and White 2002). Another driving force for consistent thinking about how to approach problems has been the role of public and private financial institutions from the International Monetary Fund to financial rating agencies that apply analogous measures of risk and efficacy to public policies and programs across the globe. These and other inputs present policy actors with consistent signals, along with incentives to follow them and potential penalties for straying too far from the global consensus on appropriate policy options and effective solutions.

When these transmission mechanisms are working well, a policy paradigm will be widely accepted, and the policy subsystem settles into a period of political quiescence. Policy communities abridge the discourse and engagement in their given policy domain, often corresponding with a delegation of power from state actors to certain policy community participants. These terms of engagement can enable a particular policy community to dominate all stages of the policy cycle, from agenda-setting through policy evaluation. More often than not, the actors or advocacy coalitions granted legitimacy by the policy paradigm become the principal civil society actors who participate in key decisions, conduct informal or formal oversight, and even deliver program outputs. Policy discourse becomes more technical as issues of day-to-day management and fine tuning of policy instruments are deemed relevant subjects for discourse.

But the same transmission of ideas and information that can encourage consistency in outlook across political boundaries, and among a critical mass of policy actors throughout civil society, can also undermine the consensus that had been fostered by a policy paradigm. From the sudden revelation of confidential information through sources disseminated by Wikileaks through the flash mobs that are mobilized to protest policy options on Facebook and Twitter, experiences and ideas that challenge conventional wisdom can be shared more immediately, and more extensively, than ever before. When faced with such challenges, policy-makers' first instinct is to turn inward toward the policy community participants they know best and seek a modest revision of the recipes that are most familiar to them. The second level of response to a global perturbation would see the state changing its relationship with actors in the policy community. Such reconfiguration could go in either of two directions. Either new actors could be admitted into the corridors of power and with them, the range of outcomes that could be considered acceptable would expand. Or the number of actors with a recognized role in the governance network could be pruned back in order to make space for a new paradigm to emerge eventually. Such a redefinition of boundary rules and a reallocation of influence may reequip the policy community to better "manage" the process of policy change.

When neither of these tactics to adjust the policy paradigm from within the policy community succeeds, the debate is likely to shift from resolvable differences to deeper disputes where an existing policy paradigm is called into question, and directly challenged with a contending paradigm. Faced with conflicting opinions, political leaders will have to choose who to recognize as authoritative, especially on matters of technical credibility. Under these circumstances, the policy community is most likely to engage in a political contest over the issues at hand (Hall 1993: 281). In such times of widespread contention over goals and values, engagement spreads beyond the policy community itself engaging political actors from unfamiliar, and less predictable, corners of the policy universe. Contributions from unfamiliar sources of expertise, among them the "sub-elites" that Etzioni-Halevy (1993: 194) has identified as playing an influential role by developing alternative policy options in between points of political decision-making (e.g. elections), will broaden the discourse to include new approaches and ideas. And without the paradigmatic consensus established to screen out nonconforming perspectives, the policy community will experience more wide-ranging debates about what is to be done. At such times, political ideologies—explicit meaning systems that profess universal principles to guide policy-making (Swidler 1986)—will contend to sway the hearts and minds in the policy community, and the wider engaged public, toward embracing a new paradigm.

During periods of such widespread conflict over policy, changes in policy communities and networks will be more profound. Levels of integration within policy communities will decline as the rules for appropriate discourse and action become relaxed, if not entirely suspended. As conflict levels increase, state actors may pull back their delegation of authority to societal actors, or they may shift such a delegation of authority from one set of actors to another. Corporatist policy networks would thus be most susceptible to restructuring, while more loosely organized issue networks would see less change in their structure, as the content of their discourse shifted. In the event that the level of conflict surpasses some threshold, which might vary across jurisdictions, the state may take the lead in reorganizing a policy community, creating a state-directed policy network.

Broadly speaking, the more unsettled the differences of opinion regarding policy options, the less likely it is that the policy community will be capable of managing the entire spectrum of change. Multiple sources of input into policy formulation, implementation and evaluation will arise, with growing potential for transnational engagement in the stages of policy development. There may even be an international ratification of policy, such as when the European Central Bank prescribes and proscribes fiscal options for countries like Greece, Portugal and Ireland that are struggling to refinance their public debt. Jobert's (1995) analysis of French policy paradigm shifts suggested that during times of heightened conflict, the deference to expert consensus in a policy community evaporates and competing interests and ideologies tend to pull policy actors apart. When this happens, the disjointed inputs and unpredictable combinations of ideas and interests can take on the character of Cohen, March and Olsen's (1972) "garbage can" model of policy-making.

As the velocity and volume of global communication accelerates, policy paradigms can thus provide a structure for managing the flood of ideas and information that inundates policy domains around the clock, 365 days a year. But the same channels of discourse and sources of expertise that often manage to interpret and filter the policy inputs in a way that focuses policy communities on a common approach, can also transmit information and interpretations that will undermine the consensus behind a policy paradigm. In this schizophrenic twist to policy formulation in an unpredictable world, the same policy actors who have embraced open borders and global norms can suddenly be disrupted by these same sources of input. Structures such as policy communities, and modes of governance practiced in policy networks, which had appeared fully functional within a particular policy paradigm will quickly degenerate into confusion and conflict under the influence of transnational ideas and information. An explicit focus on supranational governance arrangements, or lack thereof, can better make sense of tendencies and trajectories when the global influences on policy-making shift from promoting consensus to destabilizing it. The following section will offer such a schema for considering the influence of supranational governance forces.

## The mediating influence of internationalized policy environments

The relational focus of policy community and policy network analytical approaches make them well suited to examining the forces that cross the borders between states as well as traversing the boundary between state and society. Whether policy paradigms are in force or in flux, the levels of shared understanding, common discourse and the locus and distribution of authority that are gauged by taking account of policy communities and networks enables an appreciation of how policy-making now occurs in open environments where exogenous influences can flow freely.

Some have expressed skepticism about the utility of scaling up concepts that were developed to examine policy-making at the national and subnational levels to gain insight into the policy dynamics of supranational governance (Kassim 1994). Policies made in the European Union or efforts by the United Nations to develop binding agreements on climate change, for example, can pose challenges for meso-level analysis because of their transnational dynamics. When exogenous sources give rise to borderless bursts of disruptive information, the functioning of policy communities and networks can be affected in unpredictable ways. But analogous instabilities within state–society relations have not undermined policy community and network analyses of volatile political contexts. Risse-Kappen (1995) has suggested that contemporary transnational governance arrangements include the same type of horizontal coordinating networks that cross national borders, as well as bridging the boundaries between state and society.

In extending the utility of policy community and network concepts into policy-making contexts that experience high levels of global influence, Coleman and Perl (1999) advanced the concept of internationalized politics to explore a context in which at least some stages of the policy cycle take place at a more encompassing level than the nation-state. Thus defined, and illustrated in Table 4.1, internationalized policy environments may be differentiated according to their level of public sector activism and by the degree to which supranational governing arrangements are institutionalized. Public sector activism refers to the direct involvement of politicians and senior civil servants in managing governance dynamics within and among policy communities. Societal actors will take on a dominant role in managing governance through policy communities and networks when public sector activism is low, and politicians and senior civil servants will steer such governance when public sector activism is high.

The second dimension of internalized politics is expressed in the degree to which international institutions have a developed role in policy-making. In some policy domains, international institutions play a role that is mandated in supranational law. With a legal mandate, international institutions gain a capacity to manage governance in policy communities and networks. Where supranational laws do not establish an explicit role for international institutions, national policy actors will maintain greater autonomy in responding to international influences. Applying these two dimensions of internationalized politics to the ways in which policy communities and networks are affected by global influences, one can distinguish between the four ideal-typical internationalized policy environments which are depicted in Table 4.1. These are briefly described below.

When the levels of public sector activism and institutionalization of supranational governing arrangements are both high, policy-making will be characterized by a dynamic of *multilevel governance* (MLG). In places where MLG is common, like the European Union, both national and supranational governments are well developed institutionally. As a result, politicians, bureaucrats, and

*Table 4.1* Supranational governance dynamics

| | *Public sector activism in governance* | |
|---|---|---|
| *Institutionalization of supranational governing arrangements* | *High* | *Low* |
| High | Multilevel governance | Self-regulatory and private regimes |
| Low | Intergovernmental negotiations | Loose couplings |

Source: Adapted from Coleman and Perl (1999)

civil society actors and organizations engage in a multitude of cooperative working arrangements that cross organizational boundaries and lead to well-integrated policy communities. Public authority for policy-making is more likely to be delegated under such conditions. While MLG is most advanced in Europe, the activity of international institutions in trade, finance, and the environment extends well beyond Europe and has advanced the conditions in which this mode of internationalized politics is influential in the workings of policy communities and networks.

When they are well integrated, national level policy communities are likely to take on considerable responsibilities in multilevel policy implementation. There are also likely to support transnational policy communities, composed of actors from both national and international levels that link these different national policy communities while connecting them to international institutions. Transnational policy communities can be very influential in the formulation of policy options, and transnational experts are likely to work closely with national policy communities during the implementation stage. Over time, the relative level of integration in domestic and transnational policy communities will shape the trajectory of how MLG adapts to global drivers of change.

The more integrated that the transnational policy community is, the more it will be able to focus inputs entering the domestic policy arena, as well as the more coherent its proposals for policy options to address those inputs are likely to be. The more integrated the domestic policy community is, the more discretion it will exert in filtering those inputs and (re)interpreting those policy prescriptions. Given the diversity of interests and the fluidity of participation, transnational policy communities are often likely to be less integrated than their domestic counterparts. Considering the ways in which these different layers interact to either reinforce a policy paradigm or to undermine it is a research area that promises interesting findings as examinations of the 2008 global financial crisis and its ongoing effects begin to unravel the intricacies of transnational policy community activity and influence.

When governments remain active in steering policy communities, but do so in an international environment that is lacking in supranational governance structures, policy effects will likely be seen through the mode of *intergovernmental negotiations*. This is the well-explored domain of international relations scholarship, and one of the most influential models of how such negotiations relate to domestic policy can be found in Putnam's (1988) "two-level games metaphor," as elaborated by Evans *et al.* (1993). Here, heads of state or their delegated negotiators work to craft agreements at the international level that can be accepted, either through formal ratification or some other form of political enactment, at the domestic level. The anticipated degree of difficulty in such ratification, or acceptance, creates smaller or larger win sets (i.e. possible agreements that can be accepted) for the negotiators.

Intergovernmental negotiations will thus reinforce a strong role for national policy communities in the agenda-setting, ratification, and implementation stages of policy-making. When intergovernmental negotiations become regularized, as in the regularly scheduled conferences of parties to the United Nations Framework Convention on Climate Change or meetings of the Group of Eight (G8) heads of state, *ad hoc* coalitions of political actors will be drawn beyond domestic policy communities to participate in "people's summits" that are held alongside, yet outside, the official negotiations. Here, opposition groups define and publicize policy alternatives to the options being discussed in official negotiations. These alternatives are not envisioned as replacing the options being considered by authorized negotiators. But they are expected to influence these options by building support back home for alternative positions, or stirring up opposition to the negotiations, and thus narrowing the set of what the official negotiators can expect to be accepted by their respective domestic political jurisdictions.

In many policy subsystems, the rules of the game were established by private actors who have maintained a prominent role in both elaborating norms and enforcing them. A prime example of such a regime can be found in markets for equities, bonds, and the arcane derivative instruments that have weighed so heavily on the global financial system since 2008. These privately led governance systems emerged for various reasons. In some circumstances, private organizations held a monopoly, or oligopoly, over the technical knowledge needed to design and operate the policy subsystem. In other situations, jurisdictional or fiscal constraints (i.e. federalism) fostered gaps in public sector capacity that private organizations moved in to fill. These self-regulating policy communities rarely remained purely private.

States would give assent to these privately established rules and practices by incorporating them into law or by delegating the authority to pursue self-regulation in the public interest. Private entities, usually non-profit industry associations, would police a policy sector under such delegated authority, leading to the evolution of "private interest governments" (Streeck and Schmitter 1985). Such *self-regulatory and private regimes* have played important roles in policy domains that experienced the greatest volume and velocity of global interchange. These formal and informal institutions have become the epicentre of governance in important elements of the architecture of globalization, such as financial transactions that reach beyond the borders of most states and create new norms of behavior and obligation.

In the context of self-regulatory and private regimes, transnational policy communities are likely to be much more tightly integrated than those operating in multilevel governance or intergovernmental negotiations contexts. The leading role played by private actors in the domestic nodes of these transnational policy communities (e.g. domestic financial organizations) will favor the establishment and maintenance of clientelist policy network relationships. Private regimes will derive authority from the imbalance of resources, especially knowledge, between state and private actors, giving them strong incentives to avoid transparency in their activities.

The internationalized policy environment that gives rise to a context of *loose couplings* is defined largely by the absence of institutionalized structures and the lack of any obvious delegation of public authority. High levels of scientific and technical uncertainty associated with new domains of innovation (e.g. social networks) may discourage state actors from intervention, while no stable private organization exists to support a privately led policy regime. In some cases, physical or political crises can undermine previous structures, leading to new configurations of global and local initiative to restructure rogue states (e.g. Bosnia, Iraq) or rebuild devastated local jurisdictions (e.g. New Orleans, Port-au-Prince).

Implementing policy under conditions of pragmatic alliances among policy actors can bring about what Browne (1990) has termed "issue niches" in which a transient policy community coalesces around particular understandings of an issue and the options to address it. The venerable "garbage can model" of Cohen *et al.* (1972) can be helpful in conceptualizing the arbitrary outcomes that arise from such unstructured interaction between policy problems, solutions, participants, and choice opportunities. Under such circumstances, policy community structure will be quite fluid, with state and societal actors drifting in and out of different stages of policy-making. The configuration of authority will resemble an issue network in which participants are more likely to share information and ideas, as opposed to values and interests.

## Conclusion

In seeking to better understand the dynamic effects of global influences on public policy, policy researchers and international relations scholars can cumulate their insights by focusing on the relational dynamics of authority found in policy community and policy network analytical perspectives. Both fields have pursued such relational measures in drawing attention to the importance of horizontal coordination efforts in decision-making. From international accords to impromptu "coalitions of the willing," these policy actor groupings can generate rules and norms that flow across boundaries in the wake of information and resources that move beyond borders ever more quickly.

As further research is pursued on the governance of globalized policy domains, insights will accumulate about various configurations of transnational policy communities from both the policy studies and international relations avenues of enquiry. These findings can be expected to illuminate the role of policy community mediators who are active in several transnational policy communities and could thus be expected to influence the interactions between global and national, or local, politics at their points of intersection and overlap. Such mediators could function as pragmatic policy brokers, akin to Sabatier and Jenkins-Smith's (1993) understanding of a "policy broker" or Kingdon's (2003) conceptualization of a "policy entrepreneur" who connects problems with solutions by opening windows of political opportunity.

Another mode of mediation that may be even more significant in an expanding policy universe occurs through the translation of policy paradigms between policy communities that become connected through flows of information or interests that cross established boundaries. Kuhn anticipated that in situations where scientific paradigms conflict, some experts would function as translators between the different linguistic communities. Schön and Rein (1994) posit that such translation can offer the key to resolving conflict between different paradigms or frames. To overcome such conflict, the policy community mediator must construct a view of the world that can engage the ideas and interests of multiple policy communities and open a dialogue among them. Such transversal policy deliberations may provide a means to accommodate the disruptive forces generated by unfamiliar, and often unintelligible, information and ideas that flow freely across the boundaries of contemporary policy subsystems.

## Bibliography


Browne, William P. 1990. 'Organized interests and their issue niches: A search for pluralism in a policy domain', *Journal of Politics* 52(2): 477–509.

Cerny, Philip. 1995. 'Globalization and the changing logic of collective action,' *International Organization* 49(4): 595–625.

Cohen, Michael James March, and Johan Olsen. 1972. 'A garbage can model of organizational choice', *Administrative Science Quarterly* 17(1): 1–25.

Coleman, William and Anthony Perl. 1999. 'Internationalized policy network environments and policy network analysis', *Political Studies* 47(4): 69–709.

——and Grace Skogstad (eds). 1990. *Policy Communities and Public Policy in Canada: A Structural Approach*, Toronto: Copp Clark Pittman.

Dyson, Kenneth. 1980. *The State Tradition in Western Europe: A Study of An Idea and an Institution*. Oxford: M. Robertson.

Etzioni-Halevy, Eva. 1993. *The Elite Connection: Problems and Potentials of Western Democracy*. Cambridge, MA: Polity Press.

Evans, Peter, Harold Jacobson and Robert Putnam. 1993. *Double-edged Diplomacy: International Bargaining and Domestic Politics*. Berkeley, CA: University of California Press.

Gourevitch, Peter. 1978. 'The second image reversed: The international sources of domestic politics', *International Organization* 32(4): 881–912.

Haas, Peter. 1992. 'Introduction: epistemic communities and international policy coordination,' *International Organization* 46(1): 1–35.

Hall, Peter, 1993. 'Policy paradigms, social learning and the state: The case of economic policymaking in Britain', *Comparative Politics* 25(3): 275–96.

Hassenteufel, Patrick. 1995. 'Do policy networks matter?', in P. Le Gales and M. Thatcher (eds) *Les réseaux de politique publique: Débat autour des policy networks*. Paris: L'Harmattan, 91–108.

Held, David. 1995. *Democracy and the Global Order: From the Modern State to Cosmopolitan Governance*, Stanford, CA: Stanford University Press.

Jobert, B. 1995 'Rhétorique politique, Controverses scientifiques et construction des normes institutionelles: Esquisse d'un parcours de recherche', in A. Faure, G. Pollet and R. Warin (eds) *La construction du sens dans les politiques: Débats autour de la notion de référentiel*. Paris: L'Harmattan, 13–24.

——and Pierre Muller. 1987. *L'État en action: Politiques publiques et corporatismes*. Paris: Presses Universités de France.

Jordan, G. and K. Schubert. 1992. 'A preliminary ordering of policy network labels', *European Journal of Political Research* 21(1–2): 7–27.

Kassim, Hussein. 1994. 'Policy networks and European Union policy making: A skeptical view', *West European Politics* 17(4): 15–27.

Keohane, Robert and Joseph Nye. 1977. *Power and Interdependence: World politics in transition*. Boston: Little, Brown.

Kingdon, John. 2003. *Agendas, Alternatives, and Public Policies*. New York: Longman.

Kooiman, Jan 2003. *Governing as Governance*. Thousand Oaks, CA: Sage.

Laumann, Edward. and David Knoke. 1987. *The Organizational State: Social Choice in National Policy Domains*. Madison, WI: University of Wisconsin Press, 226–48.

Le Gales, P. and M. Thatcher. 1995. *Les réseaux de politique publique*. Paris: Editions L'Harmattan.

Perl, Anthony and Donald White. 2002. 'The changing role of consultants in Canadian policy analysis', *Policy, Organisation and Society* 21(4): 49–73.

Perl, Anthony and James A. Dunn Jr. 2007. 'Reframing automobile fuel economy policy in North America: The politics of punctuating a policy equilibrium,' *Transport Reviews* 27(1): 1–35.

Putnam, Robert. 1998. 'Diplomacy and domestic politics: The logic of two-level games', *International Organization* 42(3): 427–60.

Rhodes, R.A.W. 1996. 'The new governance: Governing without government', *Political Studies* 44(3): 652–67.

Risse-Kappen, T. 1995. 'Bringing transnational relations back in: Introduction' and 'Governance and transnational relations: What have we learned,' in Thomsa Risse-Kappen (ed.) *Bringing Transnational Relations Back In*. Cambridge: Cambridge University Press, 3–36, 280–313.

Sabatier, Paul A. and Hank C. Jenkins-Smith. 1993. *Polity Change and Learning: An Advocacy Coalition Approach*. Boulder: CO: Westview Press.

Scharpf, Fritz W. 1997. *Games Real Actors Play: Actor Centred Institutionalism in Policy Research*. Boulder, CO: Westview Press.

Schön, D and M. Rein, 1994. *Frame Reflection, Toward the Resolution of Intractable Policy Controversies*. New York: Basic Books.

Smith, A. 1995. 'Réintroduire la question du sens dans les réseaux d'action publique', in P. Le Gales and M. Thatcher (eds) *Les réseaux de politique publique: Débat autour des policy networks*. Paris: L'Harmmattan, 109–20.

Streeck, Wolfgang and Philippe Schmitter. 1985. 'Community, market and state associations?', in Wolfgang Streeck and Philippe Schmitter (eds) *Private Interest Government*, London: Sage, 1–29.

Swidler, Ann. 1986. 'Culture in action: Symbols and strategies', *American Sociological Review* 51(2): 273–86.

van Waarden, Frans 1992. 'Dimensions and types of policy networks', *European Journal of Political Science* 21(1): 29–52.

# Part II

# Conceptualizing public policy-making

# 5

# State theory and the rise of the regulatory state

*Darryl S.L. Jarvis*

Theories in the social sciences fall into different types or orders depending upon the type and range of social phenomena they attempt to explain and the basic method they use to derive their insights and hypotheses. That is, social scientific theories differ according to their '*level of analysis,*' '*method of analysis*' and '*unit of analysis*' (Almond and Genco 1977: 489–522). With respect to their level of analysis, some social scientific theories are 'general' or *macro*-level social theories that attempt to explain all phenomena within their purview. Others are less wide-ranging and focus only on a few very specific subsets of social life, either at a *micro*- or *meso*-level of analysis (Ray 2001: 355–88). Similarly, social theories also differ according to their method of analysis: some are '*deductive*' theories developed largely on the basis of the application of general presuppositions, concepts or principles to specific phenomena. Others are less deductive and more '*inductive*', developing generalizations only on the basis of careful observation of empirical phenomena and subsequent testing of these generalizations against other cases (Lundquist 1987; Przeworski 1987: 31–49; Hawkesworth 1992: 291–392). And, with respect to their units of analysis, some social theories focus attention on *individuals* as the basic social actor whose behaviour and actions must be explained, while some view aggregate collections of individuals, or *groups*, as the relevant analytical unit. Still, others consider larger social *structures* to have an independent impact on individual and collective actions (Hay and Wincott 1998: 951–7; Clark 1998: 245–70; Tilly 1984).

If all the permutations within these three variations are considered, the list of policy-relevant social theories would be almost infinite. However, for most purposes, this task can be simplified somewhat by focusing only on general, or macro-level, social theories. This is acceptable because policy-relevant academic disciplines such as economics and political science are interested in all social behaviour and activities and tend to view public policy-making as only a subset of such behaviour, amenable to the general theories and explanations prevalent in each field. As such, only a few representative cases exist, therefore, based on differences in the characteristic basic unit of analysis they employ and their method of theory construction (see Table 5.1) (Dessler 1999: 123–37).

'State theory' focuses on the impact and evolution of social structures and political institutions on policy-making. Many analyses in this mould focus solely on the state, seeing it as the leading institution in society and the key agent in the political process. Others, however, attribute explanatory significance to other organized social actors, such as business or labour, in addition

*Table 5.1* General approaches to political phenomena and illustrative theoretical examples

| | | *Method of theory construction* | |
|---|---|---|---|
| | | *Deductive* | *Inductive* |
| *Unit of Analysis* | *Individual* | Rational choice theories (Public choice) | Sociological individualism (Welfare economics) |
| | *Collectivity* | Class analysis (Marxism) | Group theories (pluralism/corporatism) |
| | *Structure* | Actor-centred Institutionalism (Transaction cost analysis) | Socio-historical neo-institutionalism (Statism) |

Source: Howlett, Michael, M. Ramesh, and Anthony Perl. *Studying Public Policy: Policy Cycles and Policy Subsystems.* Oxford University Press (2009)

to the state. Both interpretations have their origin in the works of late nineteenth-century German historical sociologists and legal theorists who highlighted the effects of the development of modern state institutions on the development of society. Rather than argue that the state reflected the nature of a nation's populace or social structure, theorists such as Max Weber and Otto Hintze noted how the state's monopoly on the use of force allowed it to re-order and structure social relations and institutions (Hintze 1975; Nettl 1968: 559–92; Weber 1978).

Sociological or historical 'neo-institutionalism' which focuses on the role of the state in policy-making has been summarized by Stephen Krasner as follows:

> An institutionalist perspective regards enduring institutional structures as the building blocks of social and political life. The preferences, capabilities, and basic self-identities of individuals are conditioned by these institutional structures. Historical developments are path dependent; once certain choices are made, they constrain future possibilities. The range of options available to policymakers at any given time is a function of institutional capabilities that were put in place at some earlier period, possibly in response to very different environmental pressures.
> *(1988: 67)*

This perspective explicitly acknowledges that policy preferences and capacities are usually understood in the context of the society in which the state is embedded (Nettl 1968: 559–92; Przeworski 1990; Therborn 1986: 204–31). Like its more deductive counterpart, the kinds of actor-centred institutionalism found in the work of scholars such as Elinor Ostrom, Peter Hall described a statist 'institutionalist' analysis as one focused on the impact of large-scale structures on individuals and vice versa. As he put it (Hall 1986: 19):

> The concept of institutions … refer[s] to the formal rules, compliance procedures, and standard operating practices that structure the relationship between individuals in various units of the polity and economy. As such, they have a more formal status than cultural norms but one that does not necessarily derive from legal, as opposed to conventional, standing. Throughout, the emphasis is on the relational character of institutions; that is to say, on the way in which they structure the interactions of individuals. In this sense it is the organizational qualities of institutions that are being emphasized.

This form of historical or sociological neo-institutionalism differs from its deductive counterpart in several critical areas. First, there is no effort made in this approach to reduce institutions to less organized forms of social interaction, such as norms, rules or conventions. Second, there is no attempt made to reduce institutions to the level of individuals and individual activities such as economic or social transactions. And, third, institutions are simply taken as 'givens', that is, as observable social entities in themselves, with little effort made to derive the reasons for their origins from a priori principles of human cognition or existence (March and Olsen 1994).

Using such a socio-historical line of analysis yields, to use Theda Skocpol's terms, a 'state-centric' as opposed to 'society-centric' explanation of political life, including public policy-making (Skocpol 1985: 343). In a 'strong' version of the statist approach, as Adam Przeworski put it in a pioneering book:

> states create, organize and regulate societies. States dominate other organizations within a particular territory, they mould the culture and shape the economy. Thus the problem of the autonomy of the state with regard to society has no sense within this perspective. It should not even appear. The concept of 'autonomy' is a useful instrument of analysis only if the domination by the state over society is a contingent situation, that is, if the state derives its efficacy from private property, societal values, or some other sources located outside it. Within a true 'state-centric' approach this concept has nothing to contribute.
> *(1990: 47–8)*

In the statist version of neo-institutional analysis the state is viewed as an autonomous actor with the capacity to devise and implement its own objectives, not necessarily just to respond to pressure imposed upon it by dominant social groups or classes. Its autonomy and capacity are based on its staffing by officials with personal and agency interests and ambitions and the fact that it is a sovereign organization with unparalleled financial, personnel, and – in the final instance – coercive resources. The proponents of this perspective claim that this emphasis on the centrality of the state as an explanatory variable enables it to offer more plausible explanations of long-term patterns of policy development in many countries than do other types of political theory (Krasner 1984: 223–46; Skowronek 1982; Orren and Skowronek 1998–9: 689–702).

It is difficult to accept statism in the 'strong' form described above, however. It cannot easily account for the existence of social liberties and freedoms or explain why states cannot always enforce their will, as in times of rebellion, revolution, or civil disobedience. In fact, even the most autocratic governments make some attempt to respond to what they believe to be the population's preferences. It is, of course, especially impossible for a democratic state to be entirely autonomous from a society with voting rights. And, as Lindblom and others pointed out, in addition to efforts to maintain and nurture support for the regime among the population, capitalist states, both democratic and autocratic, need to accommodate the imperatives of the marketplace in their policies. Second, the statist view suggests implicitly that all 'strong' states respond to the same problem in the same manner because of their similar organizational features. This is obviously not the case, as different states (both 'strong' and 'weak') often have different policies dealing with the same problem. To explain the differences, we will need to take factors into account other than the features of the state (Przeworski 1990).

To be fair, however, few subscribe to statism in the 'strong' form described above. Instead of replacing the pluralist notion of the societal direction of the state with the statist notion of the state's direction of society, most inductively oriented institutionalist theorists merely want to point out the need to take both sets of factors into consideration in their analyses of political phenomenon (Hall and Ikenberry 1989; McLennan 1991). As Skocpol herself has conceded:

> In this perspective, the state certainly does not become everything. Other organizations and agents also pattern social relationships and politics, and the analyst must explore the state's structure in relation to them. But this Weberian view of the state does require us to see it as much more than a mere arena in which social groups make demands and engage in political struggles or compromises.
>
> *(1985: 7–8)*

This milder version of statism thus concentrates on the links between the state and society in the context of the former's pre-eminence in pluralist group theory. To that extent, statism complements rather than replaces society-centredness and restores some balance to social and political theorizing which had lost its equilibrium (Orren and Skowronek 1993; Almond 1988: 853–901; Cortell and Peterson 2001: 768–99).

## Theorizing the regulatory state: power, structural orientations, capacities – towards a typology

Many more specific policy-related theories find their basis in statist thinking. One such contemporary mode of thinking is the theory of the 'regulatory state'. The rise of the regulatory state is more often asserted than theorized. What precisely constitutes a regulatory state remains a vexed question, and what forms, functions, modalities, operational and institutional mechanisms define its parameters tend to be inferred rather than systematically outlined.

Part of the explanation for this state of affairs rests in the multiple discourses that have contributed to conceptions of the regulatory state. Rather than a singular school of thought or a compact literature, the regulatory state emerges from a conflation of debates as much about the rise of transnational capital, globalization, and perceptions of the decline of the state as it does concerns with regulation and the growth of state power. Liberal internationalist perspectives on foreign policy, for example, conflate the emergence of the regulatory state with the rise of a neo-liberal order, seeing the regulatory state as part reaction to the loss of fiscal authority, and part reaction to the rising power of markets. Waves of tomes since the 1970s have thus declared the decline of the state. Susan Strange, for example, proclaims that the state is in full retreat, its authority and absolute power shrinking. Heads of governments, she notes, 'may be the last to recognize that they and their ministers have lost the authority over national societies and economies that they used to have' (Strange 2000: 3). For Strange, this 'progressive loss of real authority' masks the emergence of transnational actors, international finance, and the rise of market dominance, each of which are evolving non-state authority and legitimacy over their functional domains (ibid., 91–9; see also van Creveld 1999: 336–414).

More consequential for many theorists has been the ascent of markets combined with globalization. As markets have become transnational and capital mobility heightened through financial liberalization, the power of the state to tax and control its economic domain has been seen as increasingly imperiled, imposing fiscal constraints on the state or, at worse, 'hollowing out' the state and its capacity for governance (see Rhodes 1994: 138–40; Holliday 2000: 167–8). In this view, states are now disciplined by market sentiment and neo-liberal rationalism, forcing nation-states to conform to the demands of capital lest capital migrates to more attractive jurisdictions. The decline of the welfare state is thus explained as a combination of diminishing state fiscal capacity due to the pressures of globalization, mobile capital and labour migration – too high a tax regime and mobile, highly qualified labour will migrate (see Razin and Sada 2005). Similarly for Ulrich Beck, the advent of increasing capital mobility forces Western nation-states to abandon the very tools that for so long made them successful: the ability to pool economic, social and individual risk through state-provisioned health and unemployment insurance, state ownership of key resources and utilities, and state-guaranteed entitlements in respect of education and social security (see Beck 1999; Jarvis 2007; Strange 2000; 83). For Beck, the absolute power of the state relative to capital is now inverted, forcing nation-states in a 'race to the bottom' (one of the few exceptions to the 'decline of the state' thesis is the work of Linda Weiss (1999)). The regulatory state thus represents the triumph of capital, with the state forced to retreat to managerialism – a hollow shadow of its former self.

Still others proffer the decline of the state as a process of the globalization of regulatory norms and standards as power is transferred between agential actors. Cobden *et al.*, along with other liberal internationalists, see the power of the state being systematically transferred to international organizations and global rule regimes, depriving the state of absolute political and economic sovereignty because of the exigencies of globalization and the transnationalization of an increasing spectrum of economic, political and social activity – everything from growing international trade, investment and the movement of people that require the formation of global standards, codes and practices to facilitate a global political-economy (Cobden *et al.* 2005; see also Braithwaite and Draos 2000; Scott 2004). Global governance thus transposes the functional imperatives of state-based governance, systematically diminishing the propinquity of state agential authority and the *raison d'être* of the state itself.

All these approaches share a common conceptual framework, assuming state power to be predominantly located in the fiscal capabilities of the state and derived from its taxing authority over markets, where the power of each is inversely related to the other; a kind of zero-sum continuum – as markets rise, states decline, and vice versa. Such approaches have a particularly narrow conceptualization of the sources of state power, however, perhaps unfairly characterizing the regulatory state as weak, eviscerated and powerless. But as Majone (1996: 54) observes, the sources of state power are more diffuse and spread across several functional domains:

1 *Redistributive function* where resources are transferred between groups to correct social inequalities, or public goods provisioned to groups who are then compelled to consume them (elementary education, public transportation, public health care, for example), and financed through taxation, borrowing and the spending power of the state.
2 *Stabilization function* in which the state manages employment, inflation and interest rates through a determination of industrial and labour policy and the manipulation of fiscal and monetary policy.
3 *Regulatory function* in which the state sets rules that define the allocative and settlement mechanisms of markets and the requirements for market participation; define standards, procedures and practices, and enunciate codes that order social, economic and political engagement.

In this schema, state power is essentially dichotomized between *fiscal authority*; that is the ability of the state to tax, borrow and spend, and between *regulatory authority*; that is the ability of the state to set and make rules, enforce compliance and delegate authority (Majone 1997: 13; Majone 1999: 4–6). The importance of this distinction for the state is that fiscal constraints or a diminished legitimacy to tax and spend does not imply a diminished capacity to make rules and regulate. Rather than a reduction in state power the means by which the state exercises its authority is simply transposed from direct to indirect forms of government. More importantly, as Majone observes, rule-making is largely free and imposes few fiscal burdens on the state apart from the time, effort and paper needed to make and print rules: 'the public budget is a soft constraint on rule makers because the real cost of regulatory programs is borne not by the regulators but by those who have to comply with the regulation' (Majone 1997: 13). Measuring the extent, reach or impact of the state simply in terms of its interventionist or fiscal capacities is thus a poor proxy of state power since states can govern and exercise authority equally as effectively through rule making and regulation. As the US Office of Management and Budget observes:

> Budget and revenue figures are good summaries of what is happening in welfare, defence or tax policy, and can be used to communicate effectively with the general public over the fray of program-by-program interest group contention … In the world of regulation, however, where the government commands but nearly all the rest takes place in the private economy, we generally lack aggregate numbers to describe what is being 'taxed' and 'spent' in pursuit of public policies.
>
> *(quoted in Majone 1997: 13)*

These twin sources of state power, however, are not always reconciled. For Susan Strange, it represents a paradox; what she observed as an obvious 'decline of state power' but at the same time the increasing 'intrusion of governments into our daily lives' in a quantum that is palpably greater than at any time before in history:

> Statutory or administrative law now rules on the hours of work, the conditions of safety in the work-place and in the home, the behavior of citizens on the roads. Schools and universities are subject to more and more decisions taken in ministries of education. Planning officials have to be consulted before the smallest building is started or a tree is cut down. The government inspector … has become a familiar and even fearful figure.
>
> *(Strange 2000: xi)*

Yet for theorists like Majone this paradox lies at the heart of the rise of the regulatory (rule-making) state and the decline of the interventionist (tax and spend) state. It produces both a reduction in the size of government while expanding its powers of governance. At one and the same time we thus observe the implementation of a neo-liberal agenda ('downsizing' the state, shedding bureaucracies, cutting taxes, reducing fiscal expenditures) simultaneously with the emergence of greater regulatory authority (more rule-making, and more indirect forms of state control). In the United Kingdom this transpired into a 25 per cent reduction in the number of civil servants between 1976 and the early 1990s, but a relative explosion in staffing levels in regulatory bodies, growing by over 90 per cent (Hood *et al.* 1999: 29–31; Levi–Faur 2005: 20). Indeed, a casual glance at the composition of the unified civil service in the UK in the late 1980s compared to the mid-1990s might indeed lead one to assume government and the state had shrunk. The 'Next Steps' programme commenced in 1988, for example, announced a rationalization of the number of civil servants in ministerial departments, preserving only a small 'core engaged in the function of servicing ministers and managing departments' (quoted in Dowding 1995: 72). By 1994, ministerial departments had staffing levels only about a third of levels at the commencement of the programme. Yet the sense in which government shrank or its power to govern diminished is problematic. The profusion of statutory bodies and regulatory agencies witnessed fully 62 per cent of civil servants in ministerial departments transfer directly into statutory and delegated agencies charged with regulatory oversight (Dowding 1995: 72–3; Majone 1997: 10). At the same time, rule-making and the depth of regulatory direction over domain specific areas, increased enormously. In the last year of its administration, for example, the Brown government issued 2,500 pages of directives to the UK police forces concerning protocols of conduct, governance, and directives about policing, without any changes to the fiscal expenditures on policing (BBC 15 September 2010).

For Majone, the regulatory state is thus not necessarily a weaker, less powerful state, but a reconfigured state that uses alternative modalities of governance to effect its power. Indeed, for many proponents the regulatory state strikes the right balance and modality of governance. In the UK, the regulatory state became synonymous with the Third Way, New Labour and the premiership of Tony Blair, and was constructed around a 'range of governance programs' that relied on managerial and institutional arrangements to enhance market operation and efficiency for the broader social good (Jayasuriya 2005: 12).

## Towards a typology of the regulatory state: modalities of governance

These images of the regulatory state produce mutually reinforcing and contradictory theorizations as to its rise. On the one hand, the regulatory state is seen as an outcome of the decline of traditional forms of statist power amid the rise of markets, and on the other, the outcome of changing modalities of governance that preserve the centrality of the state but in ways that confine it to new, less interventionist instruments of government. Both acknowledge the rise of markets, the globalization of rule-governed behaviour and the formation of global rule regimes, and thus both accept these new modalities as legitimate and, in a sense, optimal given the new political economy of markets. For these theorists, the adoption of regulatory modes of governance is thus seen as a 'necessary condition for the functioning of markets' and not just a 'compromise between economic imperatives and political and social values' (Levi-Faur 2005: 19).

As a typology of the composite elements of the regulatory state, however, 'rule-making' does not get us very far. So governments are making rules, and perhaps more of them, and exercise power through the issue of rules and directives. But governments have always made rules, issued decrees and directives, and exerted power through doing so (Hood and Scott 1996: 323). How does this constitute the emergence of a fundamentally new state entity – the regulatory state? Again, the answer to this question lies across multiple literatures, suggesting a composite set of images. For Majone, one of the major theorists of regulatory governance, its distinctive modalities are situated in increasing levels of administrative decentralization, the break-up of unified forms of administrative control (central bureaucracies), the creation of single-purpose regulatory units with budget autonomy, delegation of public service delivery to profit/not-for profit agencies, competitive tendering and the introduction of contractual/quasi-contractual relationships where 'budgets and decision-making powers are devolved to purchasers who, on behalf of their client group, buy services from the supplier offering the best value for money' (Majone 1997: 10, 1999: 3–9; Levi–Faur 2010). Essentially, the regulatory state is thus distinctive because of the reorganization of how the state does business: who provides services, how tendering, contracts and quality assurance is administered, and through what instrumentalities this is achieved. It is this latter element that is perhaps most important: 'the rise of a new breed of specialized agencies and commissioners operating at arm's length from central government' that represents the 'most obvious structural consequence of the shift to a regulatory mode of governance' (Majone 1999: 17). The delegation of authority to statutory, independent agencies marks a fundamental change in how rules are made, and, in turn, a fundamental reallocation of power among government instrumentalities, moving it progressively towards decentralized administrative units (Majone 1997: 21; Blankart 1990: 230–6; Legaspi 2006: 139).

For proponents, the agency model offers a series of distinctive advantages over previous modalities of governance. First, it allows specialized agencies to develop domain-specific expert knowledge, improving governance capacity especially in domains where technical complexities operate (financial services, for example). Second, it depoliticizes governance, moving decision-making to technical and expert domains, where decisions are more likely to be rendered via evidence-based assessment and determination, balancing social and economic objectives. Third, it provides technical-expert decision-makers with autonomy, creating technocratic policy spaces that are not subject to short-termism or political pressures, but able to plan and design policy in support of the longer-term sustainability of the sector. Fourth, freed of short-termism or political pressures, the agency model improves the prospects for policy continuity, increasing policy certainty and the efficiency of governance in the sector. Fifth, the agency model enhances the credibility of regulatory commitments, reducing uncertainty by removing the prospects for 'devastating ministerial interference' and thus, in turn, helping to mobilize private capital into the sector. Finally, agency-based modalities of governance are seen to engineer high levels of legitimacy: '[F]aith in the power of expertise as an engine of social improvement', notes Majone, which 'neither legislators, courts nor bureaucratic generalists' possess provides 'an important source of legitimization for regulators' (Majone 1997: 17, 1999: 12; see also Cook and Mosedale 2007: 45–8). The twin pillars of *expertise* combined with *independence* thus provide the cornerstone that cements regulatory governance as an effective, if not superior modality of governance.

For others, the regulatory state is more than just a modality of governance: it is also a means of reform and suggests an alternative, depoliticized agency through which to achieve market operation, efficiency and thus development. Indeed, for many it represents a modality able to overcome obstacles to reform, reform blockages and transform the whole of government incentive structures in developing countries, where reforms have historically been 'bogged down' by the operation of perverse incentives, inefficient bureaucracies, poor institutional design, accountability and oversight systems. For such proponents, while the regulatory state is thus about the design and construction of new regulatory institutions and regulatory instruments, more fundamentally it is also about the realization of state-market outcomes (International Finance Corporation 2010: 21–2; see also Hira *et al.* 2005; United Nations 2006: 128–9). As the IFC observes, 'Reforms that increase quality in regulatory procedures and requirements – and more importantly, in regulatory institutions, capacities and incentives – can simultaneously improve a country's quality of social life and the conditions for economic activity' (2010: 1). In the eyes of the IFC, the regulatory state model is thus seen as a means to:

- making public policy more efficient by allocating national resources to higher value users, by reducing the risk of policy failures, and by finding effective policy designs that respect market principles;
- lowering policy costs and barriers to market entry for firms, goods, and services, which in turn boosts foreign direct investment (FDI) and trade, increases the returns on participation in formal markets, speeds the uptake of new technologies and other innovations, and frees resources for other uses;
- reducing policy risks for market actors by increasing transparency in the design and use of policy and by involvement of stakeholders in shaping policies important to them;
- improving business security and market neutrality of policy by increasing accountability for policy implementation and results, and lowering corruption and vulnerability to capture government functions.

*(International Finance Corporation 2010: 13)*

## Conclusion

Clearly, this image of the regulatory state is laden with objectives that go beyond a modality of governance and encompass forms of policy transfer designed to construct markets and a series of specific institutional types defined by neo-liberal market rationalism. The regulatory state thus assumes a larger political project, one designed to embed developing states in a specific economic and political order. As Julia Black notes, the focus on regulatory techniques (agency-based regulation, stakeholder engagement and transparency practices, etc.) 'can result in a radical rethinking of the ways in which societal ends can be achieved. However, it can [also] divert attention from the issue of how those ends should be defined, and by whom' (Black 2000: 598). The danger, as Black observes, is that in pursuit of an increasingly 'proceduralized' approach to regulation, the literature and practices of regulation become 'technicized'; the predominant concern being the implementation of regulation rather than the values that are pursued: that the focus on the epistemological character of regulation is obscuring issues of its moral form (ibid.; see also Levi-Faur 2005: 14; North 1990).

While Black is correct to suggest that 'technicized' discourses can conceal the values that underlie them, it remains the case that constructing regulatory states in the global South of whatever 'moral form' rests on a series of technical instrumentalities. These fall into three main areas: first, design of regulatory instruments, including institutional composition, functional structure and rule deployment; second, capacity and operational requirements, including resource, technical, administrative and analytical capacities; and third, institutional technologies for normalizing and proceduralizing the various dimensions of regulation, including the instantiation of legitimacy, trust, and compliance regimes. In the most visceral sense, these requirements speak to the displacement and redesign of entire institutional landscapes in a process that involves new rules, new ways of making and enforcing rules, new incentive systems for engendering compliance and distributing costs and economic gains among sectoral actors, and new accountability, participation, and transparency instruments that serve as functional mechanisms to sustain governance and efficiency in the sector. While, of course, much attention focuses on the institutional design elements of regulatory governance, the greater and more significant quantum rests in evolving a series of highly complex reflexive relationships between agential actors, formal institutions, procedural authority and norms that instantiate the new institutional and rule environment (Cook and Mosedale 2007: 45). It is this latter series of institutional–socio-political technologies that suggests a much greater, more complicated, problematic, and costly set of relationships to construct and a political space where, potentially, errors, possibilities for maleficence, regulatory capture, corruption and less than optimal sector outcomes, ultimately rest. Constructing governance regimes that are legitimate and perceived to be so, that are observed to be transparent and free from special interest capture, and function in a way that is seen to balance public and private sector interests while delivering enhanced social and economic outcomes, is a highly complex regulatory exercise. These dimensions of regulatory governance thus suggest a much greater series of costs, capacities and institutional technologies across a wide spectrum of socio-political sites (the judiciary, administrative review systems, tribunals and appeals processes, enforcement and compliance regimes, consultation and engagement systems, etc.), than might first appear to be the case. Indeed, while proponents of regulatory modes of governance launder their cost-effectiveness and suggest they impose few fiscal burdens on the state, in reality the acquisition and realization of the soft-institutional technologies necessary to ensure their efficient functioning represent extensive acquisition, set up, implementation, and maintenance costs (see Minogue 2004).

*Table 5.2* A comparative typology of the interventionist and regulatory state

| *Attributes* | *Quasi-patrimonial state* | *Interventionist state* | *Regulatory state* | *Required capacities and attributes* |
|---|---|---|---|---|
| Functional roles | Reproduction and maintenance of social, political and economic order | Redistribution | Constructing markets | Institutional technologies for the collection, ordering and dissemination of information |
| | Servicing socio-political-economic networks | Macroeconomic stabilization (economic growth, employment, inflation and interest rates) | Enhancing market efficiency | Technical and institutional platforms to overcome information asymmetries |
| | Preserving and enhancing existing authority structures | Enhancing access to social, economic and political resources | Facilitating capital mobilization | Access to information provisions and state-based information mechanisms of disclosure |
| | Protecting vested interests | | Providing credible commitments | Participatory processes in decision-making |
| | Controlling dissent | | | Consultative and review mechanisms |
| | | | | Effective accountability mechanisms |
| | | | | Institutional capacity for third parties to enforce/seek redress to enforce government commitments |
| | | | | Market-based clearing and settlement systems across various sectors |
| | | | | Institutional/market design capacity |

*Table 5.2* (continued)

| *Attributes* | *Quasi-patrimonial state* | *Interventionist state* | *Regulatory state* | *Required capacities and attributes* |
|---|---|---|---|---|
| Instruments | Patron-client-based access to/distribution of resources | Taxation | Rule-making | Institutional mechanisms to ensure information transparencies |
| | Indirect coercion through access/denial of patronage | Borrowing | Compliance and enforcement | Effective, functioning and impartial judiciary |
| | Dispensation of access/denial to state resources/revenue streams | Fiscal expenditures | Administrative review and adjudication | Judicial legitimacy and recognized authority |
| | Control and access to markets/business/governance domains | Budget allocations and resource transfers between groups | Competitive tendering | Negligible to low levels of judicial corruption |
| | | Monetary policy | Issuance of contracts | Adequate judicial capacity |
| | | Fiscal policy | Licenses | Administrative review/tribunals proceduralization |
| | | Industrial policy | Setting standards and codes | Compliance and audit capacities across various institutional spectrums |
| | | | Defining and controlling procedural mechanisms | Functional property rights |
| | | | | Enforcement and punitive mechanisms across various institutional spectrums |
| | | | | Probity monitoring and enforcement mechanisms |

*(Continued on next page)*

*Table 5.2* (continued)

| *Attributes* | *Quasi-patrimonial state* | *Interventionist state* | *Regulatory state* | *Required capacities and attributes* |
|---|---|---|---|---|
| Key actors | Oligarchs | Political parties | Regulators | Adequate and independent resources for regulators and regulatory affairs |
| | Political elites | Civil servants | Industry/private sector groups | Platform capacity for stakeholder engagement/review in decision-making |
| | Business/economic elites | Corporate groups | Civil society groups | Sufficient analytical and human capacity to populate regulator |
| | Nominated mandarins | Trade unions | Technocrats and experts | Adequate compensation to attract and retain personnel with sufficient analytical and expert knowledge capacity |
| | | | Administrative tribunals | Sufficient capacity and resources to operationalize transparent administrative review processes |
| | | | Judiciary/Judges | Operational accountability mechanisms to ensure regulator is held accountable for decisions |
| | | | | Disclosure, transparency and freedom of information mechanisms to ensure against regulatory capture by sectional interests |
| | | | | Realized legitimacy of the regulator in discharge of regulatory mandate |

*Table 5.2* (continued)

| *Attributes* | *Quasi-patrimonial state* | *Interventionist state* | *Regulatory state* | *Required capacities and attributes* |
|---|---|---|---|---|
| Conflict arenas | Relationships between oligarchs | Budgetary allocations | Competition for control over rule-making | Review and disputation procedures are in place and operative |
| | Elite competition for access to oligarchs | Entitlements | Disputes/inter-agency competition for rule ownership | Enforcement mechanisms for compensation |
| | Competition/disputes over patronage entitlements | Budget transfers | Disputes over domain authority, reach and extensity | High-capacity administrative review |
| | Factionalism and disputes between political and social networks | Ministerial control over resource allocation<br>Inter-ministerial/ministry competition | Disputes over rule interpretation | Compliance to and respect for administrative proceduralism |
| Key Institutions and governance modalities | Oligarch/elite control of key decision-making institutions/apparatus | Parliament | Parliamentary committees | Ability to reallocate power from centralized bureaucracies to independent administrative units |
| | Nominated senior political mandarins | Civil service/bureaucracy | Independent agencies | Ability to mediate inter-agency resource competition |
| | Elite-controlled executive branch | Ministerial departments | Commissions | Ability to coordinate among polycentric nodes of governance |
| | | State-owned enterprises<br>Command and control | Tribunals<br>Public hearings<br>Polycentric decision-making structures | |
| Policy style | Top-down, elite-dominated, command and control, low levels of accountability or transparency | Discretionary, populist, political | Rule-bound, mandated, legalistic | |

*(Continued on next page)*

*Table 5.2* (continued)

| *Attributes* | *Quasi-patrimonial state* | *Interventionist state* | *Regulatory state* | *Required capacities and attributes* |
|---|---|---|---|---|
| Political culture | Oligarch/elite-based power | Corporatist, hierarchical, centralized, top-down; statist | Pluralist, diffuse, administrative, technical, specialist, domain specific, market-orientated | |
| | personal/family power networks<br>Dominance of oligarchic/elite political/social/economic networks<br>Circulation of power positions among elites | | | |
| Political accountability | Nominal accountability | Direct/representative democracy | Indirect/agency-based | |
| | Intra-elite informal accountability through patron-client networked based consent | | | |

Source: Adapted from Majone 1997: 12–15. Jarvis, D. S. L., Regulatory states in the South: Can they exist and do we want them? The case of the Indonesian power sector (1 December 2010). Lee Kuan Yew School of Public Policy Research Paper No. LKYSPP10-11. Available at: http://ssrn.com/abstract=1738189 or http://dx.doi.org/10.2139/ssrn.1738189

## Bibliography


Almond, Gabriel A. 1988. 'The return of the state', *American Political Science Review* 82(3): 853–74.

Almond, Gabriel A. and Stephen J. Genco. 1977. 'Clouds, clocks, and the study of politics', *World Politics* 29 (4): 489–522.

Ananta, Aris and Yohanes Eko Riyanto. 2006. 'Riding along a bumpy road: Indonesian economy in an emerging democratic era', *ASEAN Economic Bulletin* 23(1): 1–10.

BBC World Service, September 15, 2010.

Besant-Jones, John E. 2006. 'Reforming power markets in developing countries: What have we learned?' Energy and Mining Sector Board Discussion Paper no. 19, World Bank, Washington, DC.

Beck, Ulrich. 1999. *World Risk Society*. Cambridge: Polity Press.

Black, Julia. 2000. 'Prodecuralizing regulation: part 1, *Oxford Journal of Legal Studies* 20(4): 597–614.

Blankart, Charles B. 1990. 'Strategies of regulatory reform: An economic analysis with some remarks on Germany', in Giandomenico Mojone (ed.) *Deregulation or Reregulation? Regulatory Reform in Europe and the United States*. London: Pinter Press, 211–22.

Braithwaite, John and Peter Draos (eds). 2000. *Global Business Regulation*. Cambridge: Cambridge University Press.

Carroll, Toby. 2010. *Delusions of Development: The World Bank and the Post-Washington Consensus in Southeast Asia*. London: Palgrave Macmillan.

Clark, William Roberts. 1998. 'Agents and structures: Two views of preferences, two views of institutions, *International Studies Quarterly* 42(2): 245–70.

Cobden, Richard, David Mitrany and Kenichi Ohmae. 2005. *Liberal Internationalism and the Decline of the State*. London: Palgrave Macmillan.

Cook, Paul and Sarah Mosedale. 2007. *Regulation, Markets and Poverty*. Cheltenham: Edward Elgar.

Cortell, Andrew P. and Susan Peterson. 2001. 'Limiting the unintended consequences of institutional change', *Comparative Political Studies* 34(7): 768–99.

Dessler, David. 1999. 'Constructivism within a positivist social science', *Review of International Studies* 25: 123–37.

Dowding, Keith. 1995. *The Civil Service*. London: Routledge.

Hall, John A. and G. John Ikenberry. 1989. *The State*. Milton Keynes: Open University Press.

Hall, Peter. 1986. *Governing the Economy: The Politics of State Intervention in Britain and France*. New York: Oxford University Press.

Hawkesworth, Mary. 1992. 'Epistemology and policy analysis', in William N. Dunn and Rita M. Kelly (eds) *Advances in Policy Studies since 1950*. New Brunswick, NJ: Transaction Publishers.

Hay, Colin and Daniel Wincott. 1998. 'Structure, agency and historical institutionalism', *Political Studies* 46(5): 951–7.

Held, David. 1995. *Democracy and the Global Order: From the Modern State to Cosmopolitan Governance*. Stanford, CA: Stanford University Press.

Hintze, Otto. 1975. *The Historical Essays of Otto Hintze*. New York: Oxford University Press.

Hira, A., D. Huxtable, and A. Leger. 2005. 'Deregulation and participation: An international survey of participation in electricity regulation', *Governance* 18(1): 53–88.

Holliday, Ian. 2000. 'Is the British state hollowing out?', *The Political Quarterly* 71(2): 167–76.

Hood, Christopher and Colin Scott. 1996. 'Bureaucratic regulation and new public management in the United Kingdom: Mirror-image developments?, *Journal of Law and Society* 23(3): 321–45.

——, Colin Scott, Oliver James, George Jones and Tony Travers. 1999. *Regulation Inside Government*. Oxford, Oxford University Press.

International Finance Corporation. 2010. 'Regulatory governance in developing countries', Investment Climate Advisory Services, Washington, DC, World Bank.

Jarvis, Darryl S.L. 2007. 'Risk, globalization and the state: A critical appraisal of Ulrich Beck and the world risk society thesis', *Global Society*, 21(1): 23–46.

—— 2010. 'Institutional processes and regulatory risk: A case study of the Thai energy sector', *Regulation and Governance* 4: 175–202.

Jaswal, Pragya and Mitali Das Gupta. 2006. 'Energy demands and sustaining growth in Southeast Asia', Asia 2015: Promoting Growth, Ending Poverty. Available at: www.asia2015conference.org

Jayasuriya, Kanishka. 2005. Economic constitutionalism, liberalism and the new welfare governance', Working Paper no. 121, June, Asia Research Centre, Murdoch University, Perth, Western Australia.

Jordana, Jacint, David Levi-Faur and Xavier Fernandez Marin. 2009. 'The global diffusion of regulatory agencies: Channels of transfer and stages of diffusion', *IBEI Working Papers*, 2009/28, Barcelona.

Kapur, Devash, John P. Lewis and Richard Webb, 1997. *The World Bank: Its First Half Century*. Washington, DC: The Bookings Institution.

Krasner, Stephen D. 1984. 'Approaches to the state: Alternative conceptions and historical dynamics, *Comparative Politics* 16(2): 23–246.

—— 1988. 'Sovereignty: An institutional perspective', *Comparative Political Studies* 21(1): 66–94.

Legaspi, Perla E. 2006. 'Reform and practices in local regulatory governance: The case of the Philippines', in Martin Minogue and Ledivina Cariño (eds) *Regulatory Governance in Developing Countries*. Cheltenham: Edward Elgar, 138–56.

Levi-Faur, David. 2005. 'The global diffusion of regulatory capitalism', *Annals of the American Academy of Political and Social Science* 598: 12–32.

—— 2010. 'Regulation and regulatory governance', Jerusalem Papers in Regulation and Governance, Working Paper 10, February, Jerusalem Forum on Regulation and Governance, Hebrew University, Israel.

——and Jacint Jordana. 2005. 'Regulatory capitalism: Policy irritants and convergent divergence', *Annals of the American Academy of Political and Social Science* 598: 191–7.

Lundquist. 1987. *Implementation Steering: An Actor-Structure Approach.*

McLennan, Gregor. 1991. *Marxism, Pluralism and Beyond: Classic Debates and New Departures*. Cambridge: Polity Press.

Majone, Giandomenico. 1996 'The rise of statutory regulation in Europe', in Giandomenico Majone and Jeremy Richardson (eds) *Regulating Europe*. London: Routledge, 47–60.

—— 1997 'From the positive to the regulatory state: Causes and consequences of changes in the mode of governance', Estudio/Working paper 1997/93, Centro de Estudios Avanzados en Ciencias Socales, Instituto Juan, Madrid, Spain.

—— 1999 'The regulatory state and its legitimacy problems. *West European Politics* 22(1): 1–24.

—— 2006 'The internationalization of regulation: Implications for developing countries', in Martin Minogue and Ledivina Cariño (eds) *Regulatory Governance in Developing Countries*. Cheltenham: Edward Elgar, 39–60.

March, J.G. and J.P. Olsen. 1979a. 'Organizational choice under ambiguity', in J.G. March and J.P. Olsen (eds) *Ambiguity and Choice in Organizations*. Bergen: Universitetsforlaget, 10–23.

——and J.P. Olsen. 1979b. *Ambiguity and Choice in Organizations*. Bergen: Universitetsforlaget.

——and Johan P. Olsen. 1994. *Institutional Perspectives on Political Institutions*.

Mason, Edward S. and Robert E. Asher. 1973. *The World Bank since Bretton Woods*. Washington, DC: The Bookings Institution.

Minogue, Martin. 2004. 'Public management and regulatory governance: Problems of policy transfer to developing countries', in Paul Cook, Colin Kirkpatrick, Martin Minogue and David Parker (eds) *Leading Issues in Competition, Regulation and Development*. Cheltenham: Edward Elgar, 165–81.

—— 2006. 'Apples and oranges: Comparing international experiences in regulatory reform', in Martin Minogue and Ledivina Cariño (eds) *Regulatory Governance in Developing Countries*. Cheltenham: Edward Elgar, 61–81.

Nettl, J.P. 1968. 'The state as a conceptual variable', *World Politics* 20(4): 559–92.

North, Douglas. 1990. *Institutions, Institutional Change and Economic Performance*. Cambridge: Cambridge University Press.

Orren, K. and S. Skowronek (eds). 1993. *The Dynamics of American Politics: Approaches and Interpretations*. Boulder, CO: Westview Press.

——and S. Skowronek. 1994. 'Beyond the iconography of order: Notes for a "new2 institutionalism', in L. Dodd and C. Jillson (ed.) *Dynamics of American Politics*. Boulder, CO: Westview Press.

——and Stephen Skowronek. 1998–1999. 'Regimes and regime building in American government: A review of literature on the 1940s', *Political Science Quarterly* 113(4): 689–702.

Phillips, Nicola. 2006. 'States and modes of regulatory governance in the global political economy', in Martin Minogue and Ledivina Cariño (eds) *Regulatory Governance in Developing Countries*. Cheltenham: Edward Elgar, 17–38.

Przeworski, Adam. 1987a. *Methods of Cross-National Research, 1970–83: An Overview*, 31–49.

——(ed.). 1987b. *Comparative Policy Research: Learning from Experience*. Aldershot: Gower.

—— 1990. *The State and the Economy under Capitalism*. London: Routledge.

Ray, James Lee. 2001. 'Integrating levels of analysis in world politics', *Journal of Theoretical Politics* 13: 355–88.

Razin, Assaf and Efraim Sadka. 2005. *The Decline of the Welfare State*. Cambridge, MA: MIT Press.

Rhodes, R.A.W. 1994. 'The hollowing out of the state: The changing nature of the public service in Britain', *The Political Quarterly* 65(2): 138–51.

Robison, Richard and Andrew Rosser. 2000. 'Surviving the meltdown: Liberal reform and political oligarchy in Indonesia', in Richard Robison, Mark Beeson, Kanishka Jayasuriya and Hyuk-Rae Kim (eds) *Politics and Markets in the Wake of the Asian Crisis*. London and New York: Routledge, 171–91.

Sari, Agus P. n.d. 'Power sector restructuring and public benefits', World Resources Institute. Available at: http://pdf.wri.org/power_politics/indonesia.pdf

Scott, Colin. 2004. 'Regulation in the age of governance: the rise of the post regulatory state', in Jacint Jordana and Davi Levi-Faur, (eds) *The Politics of Regulation: Institutions and Regulatory Reforms for the Age of Governance*. Cheltenham: Edward Elgar, 145–74.

Skocpol, Theda. 1985. 'Bringing the state back in: Strategies of analysis in current research', in Peter B. Evans, Dietrich Rueschemeyer and Theda Skocpol (eds) *Bringing the State Back In*. Cambridge: Cambridge University Press, 3–43.

Skowronek, Stephen. 1982. *Building a New American State: The Expansion of National Administrative Capacities 1877–1920*. Cambridge: Cambridge University Press.

Smith, David. 1999. *Will Europe Work?* London: Profile Books.

Spiller, Pablo T. 1996. 'Institutions and commitment', *Industrial & Corporate Change* 5(2): 421–52.

——and Mariano Tommasi. 2005. 'The institutions of regulation: An application to public utilities', in C. Menard and M.M. Shirley (eds) *Handbook of New Institutional Economics*. Dordrecht: Springer, 515–43.

Stern, Jon. 1997. 'What makes an independent regulator independent', *Business Strategy Review* 8(2): 67–74.

—— 2000. 'Electricity and telecommunications regulatory institutions in small and developing countries', *Utilities Policy* 9: 131–57.

——and Stuart Holder. 1999. 'Regulatory governance: Criteria for assessing the performance of regulatory systems. An application to infrastructure industries in the developing countries of Asia', *Utilities Policy* 8: 33–50.

Strange, Susan. 2000. *The Retreat of the State: The Diffusion of Power in the World Economy*. Cambridge: Cambridge University Press.

Thomas, Steve, David Hall and Violeta Corral. 2009. 'Electricity privatization and restructuring in Asia-Pacific'. Available at: www.psiru.org (accessed 14 June 2010).

Therborn, Göran. 1986. 'Neo-Marxist, pluralist, corporatist, statist theories and the welfare state', in A. Kazancigil (ed.) *The State in Global Perspective*, Northampton, NH: Gower, 204–31.

Tilly, Charles. 1984. *Big Structures, Large Processes, Huge Comparisons*. New York: Russell Sage Foundation.

United Nations. 2006. 'Diverging growth and development: World economic survey 2006', Department of Economic and Social Affairs, United Nations, New York.

van Creveld, Martin. 1999. *The Rise and Decline of the State*. Cambridge: Cambridge University Press.

Weber, Max. 1978. *Economy and Society: An Outline of Interpretive Sociology*. Berkeley, CA: University of California Press.

Weiss, Linda. 1999. *The Myth of the Powerless State*. Ithaca, NY: Cornell University Press.

Williams, J.H and N.K. Dubash. 2004. 'Asian electricity reform in historical perspective', *Pacific Affairs* 77: 411–36.

Wu, Xun and Priyambudi Sulistiyanto. 2006. 'Independent power producer (IPP) in Indonesia and the Philippines', in Michael Howlett M Ramesh (eds) *De-regulation and Its Discontents: Rewriting the Rules in Asia*. Cheltenham: Edward Elgar, 109–23.

Yoo, S.H. 2006. 'The casual relationship between electricity consumption and economic growth in the ASEAN countries', *Energy Policy* 34: 3575–82.

Zhang, Yin-Fang and Margo Thomas. 2009. 'Regulatory reform and governance: A survey of selected developing and transition economies', *Public Administration and Development* 29(4): 330–9.

# 6
# The public choice perspective

*Andy Whitford*

## Introduction

Over the last five decades, few research agendas in the social sciences have brought about more controversy about the "proper" role of government than public choice theory. On the one hand, public choice researchers have built theories and empirical studies that start with the core intuitions of economics but extend from that to describe a range of activities in government. On the other hand, political scientists and those working in the policy sciences often point to public choice theory as a primary example of the excesses and pathologies of the rational choice paradigm.

This chapter describes some of the contributions to the study of public policy processes of those who have helped build that agenda. I start with two assumptions: that public choice offers some fundamental insights about how policy is made and implemented, and that some of the insights drawn from public choice theory are fundamentally flawed. Public choice, like many other research agendas, is a collection of imperfect attempts to understand complex and dynamic phenomena. One reason for this imperfection is that unlike in physics where the particles rarely learn from the researchers, those who make or implement policy—or at least want to bend policy for their own purposes—have often used public choice as a way of justifying those purposes. Public choice is an important argument about the proper role of government (Majone 1989).

In brief, public choice theory uses the tools of economics to understand why politicians and the people who elect them do what they do when they make decisions about what governments will or should do. The fingerprints of economists are all over public choice theory, and this is for good reason: many of those who founded public choice theory have gone on to receive great acclaim for their contributions, including winning the Nobel Prize. Names like Kenneth Arrow, Duncan Black, James Buchanan, Gordon Tullock, Anthony Downs, and Mancur Olson are known largely in economics because of the contributions they made to the theoretical infrastructure of this field. Other names like William Riker and Elinor Ostrom are known—even though most of their footprints have been in political science—because of their contributions to public choice theory.

Specifically, public choice has changed how we understand the inner workings of democratic decision-making. For scholars like James Buchanan, who as much as (and probably more) than any other person put public choice on the intellectual map, public choice is different from how political science (at least political science pre-public choice) sees the world, because public choice is "politics without romance." For many people, public choice is largely associated with one set of people and in fact one state of the Union: Virginia. What public choice brought to the table was a willingness to ignore most of what we thought we knew about politics by situating every analysis in a logical framework built on the assumption that officials (either elected or unelected) are not public-spirited: that they do not necessarily pursue the "public interest" as "servants of the people." Indeed, many debates in public choice have raged around the question of whether we can ever know what "the people" want—whether there is a knowable "social welfare function."

In traditional economics, a person wants to maximize his or her own utility, and while one of the signature results of public choice is that this assumption does not require that people fail to care about others, outsiders often see it as a restrictive assumption that people are mostly guided by their own self-interest. Of course, people outside government, living in markets, sometimes seem to follow their own interests, so public choice theorists did not see much of a problem assuming the same about people in government—that they are just like the rational actors that populate traditional economic theories of markets.

Economists see the world through the lens of "methodological individualism" (a focus on individuals over groups), which is different from how political science circa the 1950s largely saw politics. But another signature contribution of public choice—one not always recognized in either political science or the policy sciences—is that the agenda changed how economists saw the world: that in government, the costs and benefits of choice are often collective, rather than individual. So public choice theorists had to throw out many of the intuitions of the traditional economic model because this means that an individual is affected by the decisions they make in complicated ways.

This chapter will tell the story of public choice theory by walking through the canon: the insights that most people who have added to the literature would count among the foremost contributions, the things that they can "hang their hats on." I engage these insights by considering six basic questions that public choice theory has sought to answer about the electors, the elected, and the governments they create and maintain. I want to be clear that there are other ways to recount these insights. For instance, Shughart sees the contributions as revolving around the different ways political preferences are aggregated and/or expressed—of how theorists have come to understand elections, legislatures, bureaucracies, and other institutions such as the courts (Shughart 2008). Many people have tried to summarize the field, with varying degrees of thick description for example (Mueller 2003; Rowley and Schneider 2004; Shughart and Razzolini 2001). The approach taken in this chapter has as its inspiration Mueller (1976).

Public choice tells us that:

> electing better people will not, by itself, lead to much better government. Adopting the assumption that all individuals, be they voters, politicians, or bureaucrats, are motivated more by self-interest than by public interest evokes a Madisonian perspective on the problems of democratic governance. Like that founding father of the American constitutional republic, public choice recognizes that men are not angels and focuses on the importance of institutional rules under which people pursue their own objectives.
>
> *(Shughart 2008)*

As such, the agenda is similar to other, affiliated theories in economics, such as new institutional economics, that also worry about institutional design and effectiveness in a variety of economic and political settings. That topic is the focus of the next chapter in this volume.

## Six questions and the canon

This overview of public choice theory centers on six important questions this literature has sought to answer over the past five decades. The first question can be written as "why is there collective choice?" One way we can write the second question is "do we need politicians?" The third question follows from the second: "what happens when we have politicians?" While the fourth question is narrower than the first three, it shows how important public choice theory has been to the evolution of both economics and the policy sciences. The fourth question is "what we do about those pesky public goods?" While the fifth question is not unique to public choice theory, public choice theory has helped to answer this question in ways that are both unique and novel. The fifth question this review will discuss is "what should society want?" While the sixth question has involved only a select subgroup of public choice theorists and researchers, this question is particularly important for a review that describes the importance of public choice theory for those interested in public policy processes. The sixth question is "what about those who implement public policy?"

One reason to evaluate the canon of public choice theory from the perspective of these six questions is that those outside the canon often see it as a monolith. Specifically, readers often see public choice theory as solely centered on not using the state to improve public policy outcomes. This is understandable if only because of the aforementioned conservative bias sometimes expressed by those who founded and have continued to expand the field. Yet, as this review hopefully will make clear, public choice is sometimes less a well-constructed and synthetic paradigm than it is a starting point for evaluating a wide array of institutions we observe every day in governments around the world. Together these questions show the breadth, reach, and even internal disputes that are hallmarks of public choice theory.

It is abundantly clear that a full review of these questions is beyond the scope of this chapter. Interested readers are directed to the other reviews noted above, and those interested in a full discussion of certain topics are directed to classics such as (Arrow 1963; Black 1958; Buchanan and Tullock 1962; Downs 1957; Niskanen 1971; Olson 1965; Riker 1962). For instance, Shughart and Razzolini (2001) provide a range of perspectives—including showing public choice theory's fractures.

*Why is there collective choice?* As noted above, public choice theory builds on the axioms of traditional microeconomic theory (e.g. atomistic competition, having many buyers and sellers, particular information conditions, and other attributes of perfect competition), which build on simple assumptions about individuals being both rational and self-interested. In markets, while all the attributes of traditional microeconomic theory lead to outcomes that economists would call socially preferable (namely, Pareto efficient outcomes), that is not the case in some important situations.

The simplest context to see this is the well-known prisoner's dilemma, which shows that two individuals, both pursuing their self-interest and acting rationally, may achieve outcomes that benefit neither one. As Dennis Mueller puts it in his classic survey of public choice theory, "problems of collective choice exist in all but a purely Hobbesian, anarchistic society and are coterminous with the existence of recognizable groups and communities" (Mueller 1976: 397). For public choice theorists, these situations happen when people debate and select different levels or attributes of the provision of public goods. Examples include national defense, public safety, and other attributes of free and civilized societies. Theorists and empiricists have debated different solutions to the problem of public goods provision. Because of these efforts, we now know that how society solves these kinds of problems depends in part on the size of the group and how long individuals expect to interact (Buchanan 1965; Olson 1965).

As Mueller puts it, "Thus, democracy, formal voting procedures for making and enforcing collective choices, is needed by communities of only a certain size and impersonality" (Mueller 1976: 398). This shows that in some situations individuals choose to make decisions collectively and these decisions must be governed by "rules of the game," the purpose of which is to regularize the interactions to reduce the chance that people will make decisions individually that lead to socially suboptimal outcomes.

In one sense, public choice theory became an attempt inside the discipline of economics to understand and perhaps formulate different rules, given that individuals are rational, self-serving, and cognizant of the need for collective choice. This was different from what political scientists were doing at that time because of a modeling technology that flowed from traditional microeconomics. Essentially, public choice theory had "pure" microfoundations. Yet, inside economics, those foundations had led most economists to ignore collective choice. An example of this is the Keynesian approach to macroeconomic analysis, which included government as almost an omniscient and pure dictator/planner. Other views, such as those expressed within "rational expectations theory," also modeled the politician and/or bureaucrat in naïve ways—in this case, the planner is largely inept (Mitchell 2001).

In sum, public choice theory sees a need for collective choice but also envisions collective choice as fraught with opportunities for individuals to subvert the collective process for their own ends.

*Do we need politicians?* Recognizing the need for collective choice does not answer the question of what kind of collective choice we need. For this, public choice theorists turned to the tools of formal modeling, and in doing so they encountered an array of subsidiary questions. First, what happens if people try to make decisions under unanimity rule? The answer largely has been "it isn't easy." Specifically, public choice theory asked whether people, making decisions under a unanimity rule, could decide to support the provision of public goods. Writers argued for processes that essentially auctioned off goods (using a variant of Walrasian tâtonnement, with prices "discovered" through a series of bids) (the so-called Lindahl equilibrium) (Lindahl 1919; Milleron 1972). The difficulty with this outcome is that it must be discovered, over time, through interactions that are themselves costly (Black 1958; Buchanan and Tullock 1962). Also, the process is susceptible to strategic behavior.

A consequence is that theorists then tried to understand optimal decision rules in a democratic society. If unanimity increased costs, was another rule less costly? For Mueller, studies like Buchanan and Tullock (1962) and Breton (1974) show us that "the optimal rule is thus the one for which the expected gain in utility from redefining the bill to gain one more supporter just equals the expected loss in time from doing so" (Mueller 1976: 402). Mueller goes on to say that the problem is that the optimal rule will vary across issues.

Many societies use majority rule, and while a full discussion of its advantages and disadvantages is beyond the scope of this chapter, a few key aspects warrant emphasis. Essentially, Rae (1969) and Taylor (1969) show that majority rule is the only rule that reduces the potential bad outcomes, or what we might call regret, that a supporter would feel if her proposal does not pass (or one that she opposes does pass). The difficulty with majority rule, though, is the prospect of cycling. Discussing cycling can be particularly technical but the intuition is quite straightforward. In some cases, when individuals have certain types of preferences, there is a chance that no one proposal can gain a majority that is impervious to the introduction or consideration of an alternative proposal. Debates have raged over what this means in practice, even though the technical literature is fairly consistent on this possibility. A reason for this consistency is that we have studied cycling for at least 200 years, and technical work has confirmed long-held intuitions (McKelvey 1976; Satterthwaite 1975; Schofield 1978). Some models suggest cycling is less likely to happen in some situations, usually involving large numbers of voters or unusual decision rules (Saari 2006; Tovey 2010).

Of course, political scientists have also helped us to extend our early understanding of the difficulties of direct representation. Economists contributed much of the early legwork in this area, but political scientists and others working in "positive political theory" have helped to broaden those early intuitions. This is now mostly associated with the arena of "social choice and welfare" than with public choice theory, although the roots are similar. Instead, public choice theorists are associated with their development of the consequences of cycling such as logrolling. Buchanan and Tullock described some of the issues involved in logrolling extensively in their classic 1962 book. Essentially, logrolling flows from different individuals finding issues differently salient. Views vary on logrolling and its usefulness in voting systems, partly due to some beliefs that logrolls may reduce efficiency rather than increase it. Commonly cited examples include tax policy and pork barreling.

*What happens when we have politicians?* Most people think of logrolling in the context of legislatures, and since we have elected politicians in most democracies, public choice theorists sought to understand how individuals, considering their own preferences and their options, choose representatives. Moreover, how do politicians, given those preferences and options, compete for votes?

The central result in this area is the "median voter theorem," which says that if preferences lie in a single (liberal-conservative) dimension, and if people vote for the candidate closest to their own position on that dimension, then the winning candidate will pick the position of the median voter. This result, first offered in Hotelling (1929) but elaborated most notably by Downs (1957) and Black (1958), is considered "the pioneering contribution in public choice" (Mueller 1976: 408, fn. 22). The power of the theorem has led to a host of refinements, some of which are particularly important for understanding public policy processes. For instance, when candidates are elected in stages (e.g. primaries followed by general elections), the candidates are pulled apart in terms of the policy positions they select (e.g., Aronson and Ordeshook 1972). When the model moves to two policy dimensions, the situation becomes even more complicated, if only because of the importance of the cycling theorems noted above.

The literature on the median voter theorem then moved on to even more refined versions. For instance, what happens when some voters are alienated? What happens when the distributions of policy preferences are multi-modal? What happens when we take into account logrolling (especially when a group with minority policy preferences supports a candidate)? In all of these and other situations, the constant worry about cycling remains. As Downs (1957) notes, there are real implications of cycling if it leads to the regular defeat of incumbents since policy is essentially "swinging" in the two-dimensional space. While in some systems (like the US) incumbents seem to enjoy regular advantages at the point of re-election, in other situations (e.g. municipal elections, school boards) incumbents often lose.

In Hotelling's original model, voters choose from among two candidates, but this is not so for much of the world since multiple parties often compete for votes. The canonical position in public choice theory recognizes that single-member plurality, first-past-the-post (SMP) systems are a specific rule chosen to govern the operation of democratic systems, and that other systems, such as proportional representation (PR) can lead to qualitatively different outcomes. Following pioneering work by political scientists like Riker (1962), which showed that different systems converged to coalitions of roughly the same sizes, scholars like Schofield added numerous wrinkles to the study of multiparty democracies. Much of this follows from the search for stability in systems where there are two policy dimensions.

The public choice canon also sought to understand what happens to voters when politicians are asked to represent constituents. For instance, Mueller describes how public choice studies broke the vote decision into components that depended on comparing the costs (of voting), with the potential benefits (e.g. the risky public benefits and the expected private benefits). This focus, found in writings like Downs (1957) and Tullock (1967), is important if only because it led to one of the classic statements about politics held by those working in public choice theory: that the costs of gathering political information or voting, as they grow, will swamp the benefits of information acquisition or voting—with the effect that people may not vote or acquire information. This "rational ignorance" or "rational abstention" argument is particularly attractive because it helps to explain the lack of attention or involvement by some people in (what others may consider) important policy decisions. The upshot: "For most people the outcome of an election is a public good and political participation is vulnerable to free-riding" (Mueller 1976: 411).

Another important contribution is a statement about how politicians try to control those who implement public policy. Below, I will briefly discuss one position in this literature (the "budget-maximizing bureaucrat"), but much of the work in the public choice canon contributed to what we know now as the "Congressional dominance" perspective. As Shughart notes:

> In that model, government bureaucracies are not free to pursue their own agendas. On the contrary, agency policy preferences mirror those of the members of key legislative committees that oversee particular areas of public policy … that constrain bureaucratic discretion by exercising their powers to confirm political appointees to senior agency positions, to mark up bureau budget requests, and to hold public hearings.
>
> *(2008)*

The congressional dominance model has received serious challenge in political science (Miller 2005), but remains significantly influential in public choice theory.

*What do we do about those pesky public goods?* As is apparent above, public choice theorists have made significant contributions to the study of public goods. The purpose of this discussion is to describe three important basic findings that economists have discovered about public goods in practice. Recent advances in the theory of public goods provision—theoretically, empirically, and (especially) experimentally—are also relevant here, although space constraints limit thorough coverage (Scotchmer 2002).

In 1956 Tiebout described a key point in public choice theory about public goods provision (Tiebout 1956). Note that there are many different kinds of goods and that many variations in publicness are possible. On the one hand, markets are efficient at delivering private goods; on the other hand, pure public goods require true collective choice. Tiebout essentially showed that individuals could select from different levels of public goods provision by "voting with their feet" and moving from one community to another. In this decentralized model, individuals compare and select, and Pareto optimality is achieved "by grouping individuals together in politics of homogenous tastes" (Mueller 1976: 412), though having a large number of public goods necessitates having a large number of communities to select from. It is hard to overstate the impact of the Tiebout paradigm (Mieszkowski and Zodrow 1989). Increasingly, we understand Tiebout sorting as part of a broader, more complex dynamic process.

If we can exclude people from partaking in the public good, then a host of other strategies are available for figuring out what goods people want, how much they want, and how to get them to reveal their demand for the goods. In the public choice canon, these situations are treated as access to "club goods." The basic issue here is how, as we add individuals to the club, the average cost of providing the good changes. When the average cost falls throughout, the optimal group size is the entire population. However, if at some point in adding individuals the cost of provision starts to rise, then the club will be smaller.

Buchanan (1965) laid the groundwork for understanding situations involving club goods with the result that a host of studies have followed trying to understand settings as diverse as social clubs and churches. One of the early issues encountered in the canon was how homogenous the preferences were of those who wanted to join the club. In those situations, it is easier to form the club and decide the optimal level of membership. The key is the size of the population compared to the optimal size of the clubs, because we could see optimal provision through a series of clubs as people select one from a set, and perhaps leave existing ones to start new ones with people more like themselves (Mueller 1976). The real advantage of club goods, presumably, is that Tiebout-type solutions require some sort of geographic colocation to allow people to "vote with their feet."

Since the advent of the Tiebout and club goods perspectives on the public goods problem, a whole host of studies have sought to extend and enrich our understanding of these situations in which traditional microeconomic perspectives rooted in perfect competition seem deficient. Some have been theoretical, while others have been empirical or experimental techniques. For the purposes of this chapter, the reader is pointed to broader treatments of the development of this literature. However, it is important to describe the impact of one strand of this literature for understanding public policy processes generally.

Elinor Ostrom was awarded the Nobel Prize in Economics in 2009 (jointly with Oliver Williamson, the progenitor of transactions costs economics), largely for her studies in new institutional economics and other new flavors of political economy. Her signature contributions have come from providing a uniquely political science-influenced view of how people manage common pool resources (CPRs) (which is one way the public goods literature has evolved). CPRs are public goods involving natural or human-made resource systems (e.g. fisheries or water sources) for which it is either too difficult or costly to exclude individuals, so club goods theory mostly does not apply. CPRs can suffer from congestion because adding an additional user will damage the current or future usage of this good by others. In her *Governing the Commons: The Evolution of Institutions for Collective Action*, Ostrom identified "design principles" that societies (perhaps governments but often autonomous collectivities of individuals) might use to manage access to the CPR and reduce damage from congestion (Ostrom 1991). Widely known as the Institutional Analysis and Design (IAD) framework, her approach is different from traditional public choice theory, but can be seen as a logical continuation of debates central to the public choice canon. Two themes warrant emphasis. First, individuals often select the solutions; they are not imposed from outside (sometimes referred to as "covenants without the sword" (Ostrom *et al.* 1992). Second, this research stream is different from broader public choice because it relies heavily on thousands of case studies gleaned from CPRs around the world, along with traditional theory and experimental research.

*What should society want?* As is apparent from the above discussion, it is an open question whether public choice is mostly positive or mostly normative. It is impossible to discern this—and silly to group normative approaches as a separate question in this chapter—mainly because contributors to any research paradigm bring their own concerns and preferences whenever they focus on a specific research question. Many associate the public choice paradigm with conservative movements and think tanks (Cato or the Liberty Fund) if only because many active researchers are also policy commentators.

Consider public goods research. The Tiebout model is a positive statement of mobility and goods selection by individuals in a geographic space populated by competing political jurisdictions; the club goods model also makes positive statements. Yet, both have normative implications. Likewise, researchers use Ostrom's IAD framework to understand how people provide and manage CPRs. But Ostrom herself refers to distilled "rules" in this paradigm, especially in the case of irrigation systems, as "design principles." Physics is useful for studying machines, just as the positive tools of public choice theory help us to understand public goods. But just as the use of machines implies engineers, the public choice paradigm has spawned normative claims about "what society should do." In this section, I briefly review three important strands that have helped us better to understand policy processes. Outsiders may not associate these with public choice but the canon itself claims them as "founding debates" that have framed the field's evolution. The three are the study of justice, the construction of constitutions, and the qualities of social welfare functions.

First, the public choice canon claims Rawls' theory of justice as an example of how theorists could engage normative analysis from "first principles" (Rawls 1971). Specifically, Rawls starts with ideas present in public choice theory: rational, egoistic individuals, who are not altruistic. He then overlays a game of chance on this participation: people find themselves in segments of society that determine their happiness, but individuals can imagine what their location in these segments might have been had the game of chance turned out differently. Stepping behind the "veil of ignorance," individuals stand in the "original position" and choose the rules of the social contract. For Rawls, justice is fairness.

Extensions, refinements, and reassessments followed Rawls, but the main point—the game of chance—appears in other normative theories in the public choice paradigm. As Mueller notes, "What is important to the theory of public choice, however, is not the principles Rawls arrives at, but the process by which he gets there" (Mueller 1976). For instance, Mueller points to similarity between Rawls and Buchanan and Tullock's theory of the constitution as a social contract (Buchanan and Tullock 1962). If an individual is uncertain about who he will be in the future, he will select a constitution that affects his welfare over a long period of time by "placing themselves in the envisaged positions of all future citizens" (Mueller 1976). People are uncertain about future circumstances, to the end that "actual constitutions formed under unanimity rules become just political contracts" (ibid.). Uncertainty also shows up in Harsanyi's view of constitutions as social welfare functions, because individuals assume that they might be any other person in the society in the future (that they might have a different person's preferences) (Harsanyi 1953).

Justice and constitutions clearly have normative aspects, but economists have long taken a positive approach to social choice, like how they study individual choice. Individuals choose to do the best they can with reference to their own utility functions. For over 70 years, economists have considered the possibility of a "social welfare function," but working with them seemed to require making interpersonal comparisons of utility. In the case of a system of justice or a constitution, the problem was deciding what we wanted from society: this debate also arises with regard to a social welfare function. It is easier if people share an ethical belief. Arrow's Impossibility Theorem helps us to understand this better (Arrow 1963).

Given five basic attributes of a society, Arrow argued that no social welfare function always satisfies all five. The five are values that show up regularly in the public choice literature as well as literatures on democratic theory. The first is that the welfare function should allow for any possible set of individual preferences. The second is that the welfare function should be Pareto efficient. The third is that function should be consistent (transitive). The fourth is that it should be non-dictatorial (no person should be able to overrule all other preferences). The last is that preferences over irrelevant options should not be able to affect the choice between two other alternatives. Public choice theorists want society to have a decision rule that would never violate these postulates.

The public choice and social choice and welfare literatures have debated which postulate to relax to make it possible to get a social welfare function. Many theorists who have refined or elaborated on Arrow's theorem think a way out of this trap is to relax the assumption of "universal domain": that individual preferences should not be able to take any possible ordering. But this means people cannot be "free to choose" as they are in markets because allowing that makes it difficult for us to know what society as a whole wants. Or we could relax the independence assumption. As Mueller notes:

> Each in turn raises questions of what issues are to be decided, who is to decide, and of those who decide, which preferences shall be weighted. Such choices directly or indirectly involve interpersonal utility comparisons and must rest on some additional value postulates, which if explicitly introduced would imply specific interpersonal utility comparisons. The latter cannot be avoided.
>
> *(1976: 421)*

*What about those who implement public policy?* One of the most persistent external perceptions of the public choice canon is "bureaucrat bashing." Specifically, Niskanen (1971) argued that those who implement policy—the elected and (especially) the career bureaucrats—would use advantages they hold from their positions (expertise and information) to extract the largest possible budgets. Public choice theory fears the "budget-maximizing bureaucrat."

In many ways, the problem was one of competition. Niskanen argues that competition would allow the comparison of the relative prices of competing bureaus and shift power from bureaucrats to politicians—that under competition spending on services would fall and technical efficiency increase. Refinements argued that Niskanen inaccurately characterized the interaction between bureaucrats and legislators (e.g. Blais and Dion 1991). Migué, Bélanger, and Niskanen (1974) note that bureaucrats may maximize other goals instead of the supply of public services. Conybeare (1984) argues that Niskanen implicitly assumes perfect price discrimination (see also Bendor *et al.* 1985; Breton and Wintrobe 1975). Miller and Moe (1983) model the legislature, which changes the Niskanen prediction. Empirical studies are mixed at best on the Niskanen proposal (Boyne 1998; Conybeare 1984; Higgins *et al.* 1987). Conybeare (1984) notes that even if multiple, competitive bureaus are competing for funding, rather than producing equivalent goods (as in McGuire *et al.* (1979)), there may be negative side effects such as high monitoring costs. What, then, is the value of competition? Miller and Moe (1983) show that competition for the public supply of a good is valuable when it reveals information about actual supply costs, and thus places monitors in better decisional positions and enhances their power. The advantage of competition is how it reveals information by allowing comparison.

## Conclusion

These six questions have helped to shape the public choice theory canon. The answers that have been given for these questions—the positions taken, the theorems offered—are arguments about the rules of the game that underlie the operation of democratic systems around the world. Public choice is an important strand in the diverse theories developed by social scientists to study policy processes if only because the canon has changed how economists see the state. Rather than as a benevolent dictator or a dolt, economists mostly see the state as a collection of actors, each working for their own ends, sometimes working within the rules of the game and sometimes changing those rules. At a minimum, economics is a richer discipline because of public choice. The policy sciences and political science have also moved forward, if only because public choice provides a foil against which to argue when building new theories of the policy processes.

It is important to reiterate that public choice is not a monolith, and there is an argument to be made that public choice itself has been eclipsed by other rigorous and insightful views of the state that also have come from within economics. One is the competing "Chicago School" of political economy, in which work by Gary Becker, George Stigler, Sam Peltzman and others has fundamentally reshaped our understanding of what is eligible for formalization in terms of economic theory. Mitchell notes that the different approaches taken by the Virginia and Chicago schools have led to qualitatively different inferences about politics (e.g. as in the case of the literature on regulatory politics). He notes: "Most Virginians believe that politics is rarely efficient while Chicagoans, apparently, believe that political institutions routinely achieve efficient results. The contending arguments are both powerful and subtle" (Mitchell 2001).

The second "new school" is that of "political economics," whose leaders are economists like Alberto Alesina, Torsten Persson, and Guido Tabellini (Blankart and Koester 2006). The main thrust of the movement is to join important schools of thought, several of which were made more important specifically because of the public choice movement. Political economics joins together the work of public choice with that of Lucas' rational expectations macroeconomics, and the game theory that has become omnipresent in all of economics. Specifically, political economics is different from the naïve view of macroeconomics because it builds in roles for rational politicians, voters, and parties.

The final assessment of the public choice paradigm is not in its narrow application to the policy processes but its overall contribution to the way social scientists study policy: enriching political science, challenging the policy sciences, reshaping economics, and even giving politicians and voters something to talk about.

## Bibliography


Aronson, P.H. and P.C. Ordeshook. 1972. 'Spatial strategies for sequential elections', in R.G. Niemi and H.F. Weiseberg (eds) *Probability Models of Collective Decision-Making*. Columbus, OH: Merrill.

Arrow, Kenneth Joseph. 1963. *Social Choice and Individual Values* 2nd edn. New York: Wiley.

Bendor, Jonathon, Serge Taylor and Roland van Gaalen. 1985. 'Bureaucratic expertise versus legislative authority: A model of deception and monitoring in budgeting'. *American Political Science Review* 79(4): 1041–60.

Black, Duncan. 1958. *The Theory of Committees and Elections*. Cambridge: Cambridge University Press.

Blais, André and Stéphane Dion. 1991. *The Budget-Maximizing Bureaucrat*. Pittsburgh, PA: University of Pittsburgh Press.

Blankart, C.B. and G.B. Koester. 2006. 'Political economics versus public choice', *Kyklos* 59(2): 171–200.

Boyne, George A. 1998. 'Competitive tendering in local government: A review of theory and evidence, *Public Administration* 76(4): 695–712.

Breton, Albert. 1974. *The Economic Theory of Representative Government*. Chicago: Aldine Publishing.

——and R. Wintrobe. 1975. 'The equilibrium size of a budget-maximizing bureau: A note on Niskanen's theory of bureaucracy', *The Journal of Political Economy* 83(1): 195–207.

Buchanan, James M. 1965. 'An economic theory of clubs, *Economica* 32(125): 1–14.

——, and Gordon Tullock. 1962. *The Calculus of Consent: Logical Foundations of Constitutional Democracy*. Ann Arbor, MI: University of Michigan Press.

Conybeare, John A.C. 1984. 'Bureaucracy, monopoly and competition: A critical analysis of the budget-maximizing model of bureaucracy', *American Journal of Political Science* 28(3): 479–502.

Downs, Anthony. 1957. *An Economic Theory of Democracy*. New York: Harper.

Harsanyi, John C. 1953. 'Cardinal utility in welfare economics and in the theory of risk-taking', *Journal of Political Economy* 61(5): 434–5.

Higgins, Richard S., William F. Shughart II and Robert D. Tollison. 1987. 'Dual enforcement of the antitrust laws', in Robert J. Mackay, James Clifford Miller and Bruce Yandle (eds) *Public Choice and Regulation: A View from Inside the Federal Trade Commission*. Stanford, CA: Hoover Institution Press.

Hotelling, Harold. 1929. 'Stability in competition', *The Economic Journal* 39(153): 41–57.

Lindahl, Erik. 1919. 'Just taxation – a positive solution', *Classics in the Theory of Public Finance* (134): 168–76.

McGuire, Thomas, Michael Coiner and Larry Spancake. 1979. 'Budget-maximizing agencies and efficiency in government', *Public Choice* 34(3): 333–57.

McKelvey, Richard D. 1976. 'Intransitivities in multidimensional voting models and some implications for agenda control', *Journal of Economic Theory* 12(3): 472–82.
Majone, Giandomenico. 1989. *Evidence, Argument and Persuasion in the Policy Process*. New Haven, CT: Yale University Press.
Mieszkowski, P. and G.R. Zodrow. 1989. 'Taxation and the Tiebout model: The differential effects of head taxes, taxes on land rents and property taxes', *Journal of Economic Literature* 27(3): 1098–146.
Migué, Jean-Luc, Gérard Bélanger and William A. Niskanen. 1974. 'Toward a general theory of managerial discretion', *Public Choice* 17(1): 27–47.
Miller, Gary J. 2005. 'The political evolution of principal-agent models', *Annual Review of Political Science* 8: 203–25.
——and Terry M. Moe. 1983. 'Bureaucrats, legislators, and the size of government', *American Political Science Review* 77(2): 297–322.
Milleron, J.C. 1972. 'Theory of value with public goods: a survey article, *Journal of Economic Theory* 5(3): 419–77.
Mitchell, William C. 2001. 'The old and new public choice: Chicago versus Virginia', in William F. Shughart II and Laura Razzolini (eds) *The Elgar Companion to Public Choice*, Northampton, MA: Edward Elgar, 3–32.
Mueller, Dennis C. 1976. 'Public choice: A survey', *Journal of Economic Literature* 14(2): 395–433.
—— 2003. *Public Choice III*. Cambridge: Cambridge University Press.
Niskanen, William A. 1971. *Bureaucracy and Representative Government*. Chicago: Aldine.
Olson, Mancur. 1965. *The Logic of Collective Action: Public Goods and the Theory of Groups*. Cambridge, MA: Harvard University Press.
Ostrom, Elinor. 1991. *Governing the Commons: The Evolution of Institutions for Collective Action*. Cambridge: Cambridge University Press.
Ostrom, E., J. Walker and R. Gardner. 1992. 'Covenants with and without a sword: Self-governance is possible', *American Political Science Review* 86(2): 404–17.
Rae, Douglas W. 1969. 'Decision-rules and individual values in constitutional choice', *The American Political Science Review* 63(1): 40–56.
Rawls, John. 1971. *A Theory of Justice*. Cambridge, MA: Belknap Press of Harvard University Press.
Riker, William H. 1962. *The Theory of Political Coalitions*. New Haven, CT: Yale University Press.
Rowley, Charles Kershaw and Friedrich Schneider. 2004. *The Encyclopedia of Public Choice*, 2 vols. Boston: Kluwer Academic Publishers.
Saari, Donald G. 2006. 'Which is better: The Condorcet or Borda winner?', *Social Choice and Welfare* 26(1): 107–29.
Satterthwaite, Mark A. 1975. 'Strategy-proofness and Arrow's conditions: Existence and correspondence theorems for voting procedures and social welfare functions', *Journal of Economic Theory* 10(2): 187–217.
Schofield, Norman. 1978. 'Instability of simple dynamic games', *The Review of Economic Studies* 45(3): 575–94.
Scotchmer, S. 2002. 'Local public goods and clubs', *Handbook of Public Economics* 4: 1997–2042.
Shughart, William F. 2008. 'Public Choice', in David R. Henderson (ed.) *The Concise Encyclopedia of Economics*. Indianapolis, IN: Liberty Fund, 427–30.
——and Laura Razzolini. 2001. *The Elgar Companion to Public Choice*. Northampton, MA: Edward Elgar.
Taylor, M. 1969. 'Critique and comment: Proof of a theorem on majority rule', *Behavioral Science* 14(3): 228–31.
Tiebout, C.M. 1956. 'A pure theory of local expenditures', *The Journal of Political Economy*: 416–24.
Tovey, Craig A. 2010. 'The almost surely shrinking yolk', *Mathematical Social Sciences* 59(1): 74–87.
Tullock, Gordon. 1967. *Toward a Mathematics of Politics*. Ann Arbor, MI: University of Michigan Press.

# 7

# Institutional analysis and political economy

*Michael D. McGinnis and Paul Dragos Aligica*

## Political economy[1] and the analysis of non-market decision settings

The foundational idea of the Ostroms' institutionalism is simple but powerful in its implications: analysis of the public sector should be no different in its basic assumptions from studies of the market-oriented private sector. The focus of analysis is in both cases the individuals and their actions in various institutional arrangements. Methods used to understand complex economic industries involving large and small profit-seeking enterprises competing within more or less efficient and competitive markets, should be expected to be equally functional for the study of equally complex public structures. The large number of public enterprises operating in a modern society (at the national level or at local, metropolitan levels) could be studied using tools transferable from one domain to another. Although the standard framework needs special adjustments in order to get adapted to a phenomenon that is in the end different from the market-based phenomena, the analysis of public governance issues requires an approach that is fundamentally similar to the analysis of private industries (Ostrom and Ostrom 1965, 1977; E. Ostrom 1972, 1983, 1996).

The key is that public enterprises should be seen as organizations that produce goods and services for a variety of consumers and groups of consumers. Public goods and services have different characteristics and require a variety of arrangements and processes to be delivered. As in the case of private enterprises, these features determine the nature of the institutions, strategies and policies needed. The functional problems of production, acquisition, distribution, and consumption of public and common goods lead to the emergence of complex institutional arrangements.

Once one starts to look at the public sector through the lens of competitive public economies, the reality will never be the same again. For instance, the observation that most private enterprises purchase many of the goods and services that they need from other enterprises, draws attention to the notion that production (physical rendering) of public services may be considered separately from the provision of such services (i.e. the decision how to produce goods or services, or decisions concerning the quantity and quality of these products) and there remains the separate question of deciding on billing and other financial details). Issues of scale and efficiency, concerned mainly with production, can be analytically considered separately from questions of what public goods and services should be made available to members of the group that will collectively consume them, and from questions about how producers will be paid and their products evaluated (Ostrom and Ostrom 1965; E. Ostrom *et al.* 1994).

Distinctions among production, provision, financing, and evaluation were laid out quite explicitly in a classic article on the organization of metropolitan governance in the United States (Ostrom *et al.* 1961). Urban public economies are micro-universes that display, on a small scale, governance problems and processes that are ubiquitous at larger scales. This perspective considers local government officials as *service providers* responsible "for making taxing and spending decisions, determining appropriate types of service and levels of supply, and arranging for and monitoring production." As providers, these public officials face several options in arranging for the actual production of public goods, including creating its own production unit, contracting for services with an external producer or creating a joint venture with other provision units in order to have the services produced.

To sum up, the implication is that the organization of provision and the organization of production have different principles of operation and should be institutionalized in different ways. A local government may, on the one hand, be organizing service financing through collective consumption units and, on the other hand, be purchasing services from alternative public or private suppliers. Institutional diversity is thus the natural pattern in the public sector, while centralization and uniformity may be more of an exception.

The political economy institutionalism approach has thus more than just a methodological value. One of its important consequences is that it introduces the notion of optimum scale of performance. A crucial question in public administration and public policy is addressed frontally: is there "some special characteristic of governmental functions that makes large units necessary to efficiency?" In the light of the above, one cannot avoid the answer that efficiency depends on the nature and type of service that a governmental agency is meant to produce and not on some special characteristics of governmental functions associated to the scale of the activity. The question of the validity of the notion that efficiency is a function of large-scale centralization is thus confronted. The thesis advanced is that the optimum scale of production is not the same for all public goods and services and that some services may be produced "more efficiently on a large scale while other services may be produced more efficiently on a small scale (E. Ostrom [1972] in McGinnis 1999b; Oakerson 1999; V. Ostrom *et al.* 1988). Implications questioning the basic postulates of centralized governance in the modern public system are even today perceived by many as counterintuitive and paradoxical.

It is clear why political economy institutionalism suggests that the existence of multiple agencies interacting and overlapping should not be considered a priori and by definition dysfunctional. This overlapping and duplication is the result of the fact that different services require a different scale for efficient provision and that the principles of division of labor, cooperation and exchange function in the public sector, too. In traditional bureaucratic theory, duplication of functions is assumed to be wasteful and inefficient. But in a market economy multiple firms serve the same market. Overlapping service areas and duplicate facilities do not lead to inefficiency. Can we expect similar forces to operate in a public economy? The Ostroms' answer is positive. The public sector includes not only "bureaucratic command structures controlled by chief executives" but also "interorganizational arrangements" with self-regulating tendencies with efficiency-inducing and error-correcting behavior (Ostrom and Ostrom 1965: 3).

The discussion leads sooner or later to the very notion of competition. In what measure and how does the public policy process incorporate the competition process? There is no presumption that competition among public agencies is necessarily efficient or inefficient in all settings, but only that such competiton need not take the same forms as market competition (V. Ostrom *et al.* 1961; Bish 1971).

The bottom line is that the presence of more than a single producer of public goods within a certain area enables citizens to make more effective choices about the mix of services they prefer to receive while enabling citizens to "vote with their feet" or by enabling individuals residing within an existing community to choose among alternative producers of public services. Furthermore, multiple producers of some public goods may nullify each other's actions and lead to a reduction in the net output of public goods. In other words, political economy institutionalism considers the practical effect of competition among public agencies as an empirical question depending upon the type of urban public good being considered and the specific circumstances of the case (E. Ostrom [1972] in McGinnis 1999b: 148)

Toonen (1998) argues that the 1961 Ostrom, Tiebout and Warren article synthesized all of the following components of New Public Management and related visions of network governance: entrepreneurial leadership, contracts for service delivery, deregulation, devolution of authority to market actors, the important contributions made by professional associations and community groups, and an emphasis on evaluating the performance of public officials and the quality of the products they produce or procure. Each of these topics has attracted substantial interest in recent years, and, to be fair, the authors did not systematically lay out any of these implications in detail. In effect, these same ideas were later rediscovered and elaborated upon by other scholars, who were in effect following a path initially laid out by these founders of the Bloomington School of Institutional Analysis.

To sum up, the Bloomington School not only offers a specific set of theoretical lenses and a new perception of the public and policy arena but also questions the assumption deeply ingrained in the traditional view that large bureaucracies are more efficient in solving problems and in providing public goods and services than the systems based on competition or bargaining. In doing that, this approach challenges our perspective on the very nature of the policy process. Complexity, scale and scope, levels and diversity, overlapping institutions and functional differentiation invite us to rethink the public governance system. Sooner or later we are forced to reconsider the criteria we are using in policy evaluation in all its aspects: policy theory, policy implementation, and policy impact.[2]

## Polycentricity and monocentrism

Political economy institutionalism is an effort to change the paradigm. A new domain of institutional complexity and diversity needed to be charted and that requires an entirely new framework. The concept of polycentricity lies at the heart of this new paradigm. As initially defined, the term "polycentric" connotes many centers of decision-making which are formally independent of each other.

> To the extent that they take each other into account in competitive relationships, enter into various contractual and cooperative undertakings or have recourse to central mechanisms to resolve conflicts, the various political jurisdictions in a metropolitan area may function in a coherent manner with consistent and predictable patterns of interacting behavior.
>
> *(Ostrom* et al. *1961: 831)*

Subsequently, Ostrom further clarified his vision of polycentricity as constituting a "highly federalized system" that required all of the following component parts: "a rich structure of overlapping jurisdictions with substantial autonomy among jurisdictions, substantial degrees of democratic control within jurisdictions, and subject to an enforceable system of constitutional law" (V. Ostrom 1973: 229).

The alternative, and still much more influential paradigm, is to presume that effective governance requires a single ultimate authority exercising control through a unified command and control structure. Conversely, in a polycentric order, the elements of a complex system are allowed to make mutual adjustments to each other "within a general system of rules where each element acts with independence of other elements" (V. Ostrom 1972). The conceptual spaces defined by the two notions are interlinked. "The possibility that a polycentric political system can exist does not preclude the possibility that a monocentric political system can exist" (ibid.).

Above and beyond the theoretical problems and debates, is a practical issue. The key question is whether there is any prima facie ground for expecting less efficient performance from polycentric arrangements than from a centralized system. As we have seen, before the work of the Ostroms and their associates started to have an impact, the duplication of services (one of the main features of polycentric systems) was assumed to be wasteful and to generate disorder.

To compare these two paradigms, an extensive empirical research agenda focused on governance in municipal areas was initiated (Oakerson 1999; McGinnis 1999b). That empirical work "started to identify and chart the patterns of order looming underneath the apparent chaos intrinsically associated to the experience of polycentricity" as well as specified conditions for efficient performance (V. Ostrom 1972). Polycentricity raises fundamental challenges to social and political theory that have broader ramifications that go beyond the issue of the governance of metropolitan areas. An analysis of the class of phenomena displaying a multiplicity of decision centers shows that there are many forms of organization that might seem analogous to a polycentric order. However, not all of them had the attributes associated to polycentricity. For instance, a breakdown of order and rules may lead to situations where multiple decision centers coexist. Political corruption leads to situations where various forms of bosses divide "territories" and "jurisdictions." Could that be called polycentric order? Therefore, it is important to specify the conditions that could create a system of government organized in a polycentric manner. In this respect, five features are pivotal: the legitimate exercise of coercive capabilities; an overarching system of rules; freedom to enter and exit; freedom to orderly change the rules; and incentives alignment.[3]

A mere review of polycentricity reveals that the problem of whether the government of a political system can be organized in a polycentric manner has a considerable history. As V. Ostrom (1971, 1997) argued, Alexis de Tocqueville's classic study *Democracy in America* is an exploration in polycentric governance. The challenge faced by the founding fathers of the American constitution was in fact to design a polycentric order. *The Federalist* did not use the term polycentricity. However, Alexander Hamilton and James Madison's conception of the "principles of federalism and separation of powers within a system of limited constitutions meets the defining conditions for polycentricity" (V. Ostrom 1972, 1973, 1971). The federal system, argues V. Ostrom, assumes a fragmentation of authority in many centers of decision-making that implies a separation of powers. In other words, designing the American constitution could be viewed as an experiment in polycentricity. Federalism itself could be seen as one way to capture the meaning and operationalize one aspect of this type of order.

Last but not least, it is important to highlight the normative dimensions of polycentric forms of organization. Polycentricity seems to be a necessary condition for political objectives such as "liberty" and "justice." The dispersion of decision-making capabilities and the checks and balances defining polycentricity allows for "substantial discretion or freedom to individuals and for effective and regular constraint upon the actions of governmental officials." As such, is an essential characteristic of democratic societies. Last but not least, a polycentric arrangement has a built-in system of self-correction. While opportunistic behavior and malfeasance are a problem for any institutional arrangements, "a political system that has multiple centers of power at differing scales provides more opportunity for citizens and their officials to innovate and to intervene so as to correct maldistributions of authority and outcomes." Thus, "polycentric systems are more likely than monocentric systems to provide incentives leading to self-organized, self-corrective institutional change" (E. Ostrom 1998b). To conclude, one of the strong theses put forward by students of polycentrism is that the very nature and existence of democratic societies depends on the presence of sizable elements of polycentricity in their governance systems (Aligica and Boettke, 2009: 22–23).

## Coproduction: consumer producers

The perspective opened up by the political economy and polycentricity theoretical lenses has led to a series of important empirical and theoretical insights regarding the problem of public policies and governance in the public sector. To illustrate this point, let us use as an example the concept of coproduction.

Empirical research of Bloomington scholars identified a series of cases in which the collaboration between those who supplied a service and those who used it was the key factor in determining the effective delivery of the service. For instance, the health of a community depends not only on the professional quality of health care personnel but also on the informed efforts of individuals, while the quality of an "educational product" is largely determined by the efforts of the "users of educational services," namely the efforts students make. Similarly, the quality and supply of neighborhood security depends on the joint efforts of citizens as well of the professional police officers. These are cases in which the users of services also function as coproducers, in the sense that the production process cannot be totally separated from consumption. Without the informed and motivated efforts of service users, "the service may deteriorate into an indifferent product with insignificant value." Under co-production, "the resources, motivations, and skills brought to bear by the client or consumer are much more intimately connected with the *level* of achieved output than in the case of goods production." Coproduction means more than the existence of at least two producers" (Ostrom and Ostrom [1977] in McGinnis 1999b: 93; Aligica and Boettke, 2009: 32–33).

This phenomenon is far from marginal. It appears to be characteristic of much public service production (Parks 1993; Parks and Oakerson 1989). Appreciation of the role of coproduction in public service delivery requires a change of focus in our approach to public administration and public policy. Instead of focusing exclusively on bureaucratic structures or public organizations, it highlights the critical importance of consumer input. Many public policy puzzles may be solved if the productive roles of consumers as *coproducers* of the services they receive is taken into account (Kiser and Percy 1980; E. Ostrom 1996; Ostrom and Ostrom 1977; Whitaker 1980).

Once clearly defined, coproduction problems could be identified in many areas of the service in public sectors. A typical example is the so-called "service paradox."

> When professional personnel presume to know what is good for people rather than providing people with opportunities to express their own preferences, we should not be surprised to find that increasing professionalization of public services is accompanied by a serious erosion in the quality of those services.
>
> *(Aligica and Boettke 2009: 33)*

The better services are, as defined by professional criteria, and as supplied exclusively by "highly trained professionals, the less satisfied citizens are with those services." Satisfaction and effectiveness is in the end a function of citizens "functioning as essential co-producers" (Ostrom and Ostrom [1977] in McGinnis 1999b: 93–4).

While usually the attention in public services management and evaluation is primarily on the production side, the strategies of consumption are as important as the strategies of production.

Coproduction requires that "both production and consumption go hand in hand to yield optimal results." One should try to take into account both the "economies of consumption as well as of production and provides for the co-ordination of the two" (Ostrom and Ostrom [1977] in McGinnis 1999b: 94).

Political economy institutionalism from the Bloomington School demonstrates that despite the absence of the level of flexibility found in fully competitive markets, the search for solutions in the public arena is not blind. A notion like coproduction could be used as a diagnostic tool and with it an entire battery of concepts and theories could be developed for institutional design, policy analysis and assessment. The particular nature of each good and service plus the technological and economic conditions of its production and consumption require a complex institutional system in which public and private, markets and hierarchies combine to generate an institutional architecture with diverse patterns of organization and diversely organized systems of governance. To cope with this challenge new methodological tools needed to be developed.

## The IAD framework

The Institutional Analysis and Development (IAD) Framework encapsulates the collective efforts of the Bloomington School to understand the ways in which institutions operate and change over time. The IAD framework assigns all relevant explanatory factors and variables to categories and locates these categories within a foundational structure of logical relationships.[4]

The IAD framework serves as a tool to simplify the analytical task confronting anyone trying to understand policies and institutions in their full complexity. At the heart of the IAD framework is the action situation, in which individuals (acting on their own or as agents of formal organizations) observe information, select actions, engage in patterns of interaction, and evaluate outcomes. As is typical in strategic interactions, potential outcomes are differentially valued by those actors with partial control over the determination of actual results. The IAD framework highlights the social-cultural, institutional, and biophysical context within which strategic decisions are made. Specifically, the IAD framework helps to organize the task confronting a scholar or policy analyst approaching a policy issue by directing their attention to first, the rules-in-use, rather than the rules on paper, second, the underlying biophysical nature of the good under consideration, in terms of it being a private, public, or toll/club good or a common-pool resource (CPR), as well as third, the most relevant attributes of the community, especially ambient levels of trust and shared norms of reciprocity.

Systems typically look very different depending on the level of aggregation being used, and the IAD framework explicitly distinguishes three levels of analysis in which different types of choice processes take place: first, operational level choices (regarding policy implementation); second, collective level choices involving the determination of which strategies, norms and rules are or should be available to actors fulfilling the specific roles defined by that group (as well as specifying who is assigned to fill these roles); and third, constitutional level choices relating to who is or should be empowered to participate in the making of collective and operational-level decisions. The critical insight behind this framework is that the outcomes of interactions in these different arenas of choice are explicitly connected to each other.

The actors in any action situation are presumed to be boundedly rational. They seek to achieve goals for themselves and for the communities with which they identify but do so within the context of ubiquitous social dilemmas and biophysical constraints, as well as cognitive limitations and cultural predispositions. Within this broad framework, a range of theoretical perspectives may be employed to develop and analyze models of specific situations.

Rational choice theory, grounded in methodological individualism, provides the general inspiration for the IAD framework, but different decision models are relevant for different situations. For example, the same individual might follow Simon's (1955) satisficing procedure in one decision context while engaging in more extensive information search and evaluation in other situations. There is no reason to presume that any one individual acts in exactly the same way in all circumstances; still, there is merit in trying to locate the relevant range of decisional procedures within the context of a common explanation.

In the IAD framework analysts must incorporate, in some manner, the actors' self-understanding of their roles and their conceptions of proper or acceptable behavior in particular contexts. By incorporating factors not typically considered by rational choice theorists, the IAD framework can encompass approaches to analysis that many of them would no longer recognize as rational choice. Indeed, Ostrom (1998a) has called for a "second-generation" of rational choice theory more firmly grounded in behavioral regularities, many of which have been discovered by critics of the rational choice tradition.

The IAD framework is implicitly grounded in a dynamic view of policy processes. Social, institutional, and biophysical factors are inputs to processes of individual decisions (with those decisions presumed to be influenced by their preexisting cognitive capabilities and cultural presuppositions), and these decisions are then aggregated to constitute policy outputs that would then interact with exogenous factors to produce observable outcomes, with actors' evaluations of these outcomes by these actors (or by other observers) feeding back into all of the previous components of this never-ending process.

Institutional arrangements shape and constrain the behavior of individuals, but there is no need to presume that individuals will always follow the rules. In the IAD framework considerable importance is attached to the means by which actors (at all levels) monitor each other's activities and sanction undesirable or inappropriate behavior. In empirical research it often turns out that those systems which involve local participants in monitoring and sanctioning are more likely to be sustainable than those in which those functions are instead fulfilled by agents of the national government (E. Ostrom 1990).

The IAD framework bears a family relationship to game models (E. Ostrom 1986), but it is essential to keep in mind the extent to which actors' preferences as well as the choice options available to them are determined by the institutional arrangements that define their position or that shape their perceptions and options. Concurrent games in other arenas of choice interact in subtle ways with any ongoing process of interaction (McGinnis 2011b). The payoffs and menu of choices available to participants in operational games have been defined by collective choice processes. Games over collective deliberations are in turn shaped by the positions and interests defined or manifested in the constitutional choice arena. In a strict sense, this may be no different from a complete specification of a game model, but in practice this concern with simultaneous consideration of multiple choice arenas inspires Workshop-affiliated scholars toward a more inductive mode of analysis (Mitchell 1988). Yet all this research remains inspired by a common vision of the critical importance of polycentricity in the policy world, and how critical it is for analysts to realize the complexities inherent in the systems they are studying.

## Conclusions: public policy analysis

Irrespective of school of thought, knowledge base, or analytical sophistication, most forms of policy analysis are by their very nature dealing with a single fundamental problem: collective action.[5] Slowly, an interdisciplinary theory uniting all the many factors that influence collective action is emerging, and members of the Bloomington School are playing critical roles in its emergence (E. Ostrom 2010a).

A defining feature of the political economy institutionalism advanced by the Ostroms and their associates is that this general theory of collective action requires realization through very specific and problem-oriented analyses. It refers to concrete, public affairs problems confronting specific communities or groups. Its objectives are not abstract and theoretical but applied and aimed at problem solving (V. Ostrom 1991: 21). Policy analysis "is variable with problematical situations" and "any diagnostic assessment must necessarily be conjectural." Without knowledge well grounded in the *problematic circumstances* of a collective action "policy analyses are likely to be misspecified." That may seem commonsensical. However a common source of policy failure lies in efforts to formulate and implement general solutions in total ignorance of the local conditions. A diagnostic assessment "is complexly linked to the institutional facts," that is to say knowledge of the institutional environment is crucial (V. Ostrom 1991: 25–6).[6]

We have examined a few ways in which the Bloomington School has analyzed links between institutional diversity and the complexity of polycentric systems of governance. Conversely, policy analysts committed to the monocentric alternative often reveal a surprising lack of interest in real-world institutions. In other words, the way policy analysis was thought about for most of the twentiethth century resulted in misguided effort to implement universal solutions, typically centered in national level public officials (V. Ostrom 1991: 2).[7]

This logic and its implications are not accidental but a basic paradigmatic problem. As such, it is prone to persist as long as policy analysts continue to conceptualize social order using just two ideal types—markets and hierarchies—and believe that all societies could be described by reference to them, thus ignoring the "diverse nestings of institutional arrangements in time and place specificities." But once the theoretical lenses of polycentricity are used, policy analysis is forced to give more attention to institutional analysis driven by analytical methods and to problem-solving using "variable policy formulations" based upon "different presuppositions" (V. Ostrom 1997: 104).

In his writing on public policy Vincent Ostrom tried to rescue the study of public policy from the trap of intellectual triviality. Policy is not a purely technical exercise of adjusting means to given ends fixed in function of "obvious" problems. By their very nature, social scientists are deeply involved in clarifying the meaning and place of values and norms in the development of human institutions. An understanding of values, or a normative inquiry, is a prerequisite to performing the tasks of policy design and evaluation. Moreover, if one wants to design or assess decision rules, one needs criteria. Then the question is: what kind of criteria for those rules? How we construct (or for that matter assess) those rules depends on the criteria used. The task of the policy analyst is not only to use values as entry points or vehicles for analysis but to apply them. These values are not "given." In a word, the very notion of a "policy problem" is infused by deeper philosophical or normative speculations related to human nature and the human condition. The full dimensions and the complexity of the problems are fully revealed when normative concepts "collide with natural conditions of human beings" (V. Ostrom 1991: 25). The world of policy analysis is in the end the world of implementation—namely the world of action and decision, and therefore is the world of normative commitments.

## Notes

1 As might be expected for scholars whose work extends over several decades, the terms the Ostroms used to define their approach to the study of political institutions has undergone several changes, and these changes can generate some confusion. For example, in Ostrom and Ostrom (1971) they use the term "public choice" to refer to their proposed new mode of analysis, but later developments in public choice gave a much different meaning to that term. At the time, they were key participants in what Vincent Ostrom famously labeled the "no-name" conference at Charlottesville, Virginia, organized by James Buchanan in 1964 (V. Ostrom 1965). They have also used "public economy" as a generalization

of market economy, intended to incorporate all relevant public, private, voluntary, and community-based organizations active in a given area of public policy, and "public service industry" or "public enterprise" to generalize the concept of a market sector to include non-explicitly commercial organizations. The term "behavioral approach" (Ostrom and Ostrom 1965; E. Ostrom 1998a,b) has also been used in different contexts. Ultimately, however, they settled on the phrase "institutional analysis" as the most accurate label for their approach, but its lack of specificity makes that also a potentially confusing term. For this reason, and others, we will use the term Bloomington School as a shorthand label for the approach to research pioneered by Vincent and Elinor Ostrom.

2 That is to say it was doing more than merely developing a simple market model, derived from neoclassical economic theory, and applying it to a non-market setting in the public choice tradition. Its goals are much bolder: "We thought an indication that quasi-market mechanisms were operable in a public service economy would imply important new dimensions for a theory of public administration" (V. Ostrom 1972). In other words, they were restructuring scholars' basic conceptualization of the public sector (Ostrom *et al.* 1961).

3 In a monocentric political system the prerogatives for determining and enforcing the rules are "vested in a single decision structure that has an ultimate monopoly over the legitimate exercise of coercive capabilities." In a polycentric system "many officials and decision structures are assigned limited and relatively autonomous prerogatives to determine, enforce and alter legal relationships" (V. Ostrom [1972] in McGinnis 1999b: 55–60). In a polycentric system no one has an ultimate monopoly over the legitimate use of force. The "rulers" are constrained and limited under a "rule of law." Ultimately, polycentric systems are rule of law systems. Incentives alignment in the enforcement of general rules of conduct provides the legal framework for a polycentric order: "If individuals or units operating in a polycentric order have incentives to take actions to enforce general rules of conduct, then polycentricity will become an increasingly viable form of organization" (V. Ostrom 1972). Another condition is freedom of entry and exit in a particular system. The establishment of new decision centers under the existing rules should not be blocked. The freedom of entry ensures the evolution and adaptation of the system. Finally, another key condition is that spontaneity should be manifested in the reformulation and revision of the basic rules that define the framework of a specific polycentric order. The idea is that individuals should be free not only to play the game or have the incentives to self-enforce the rules of the game but also to change those rules in an orderly way. Understanding and learning from experience are in fact the vectors of an ongoing process of knowledge integration in the institutional system and the prerequisites of subsequent adaptations to the changing environment. (V. Ostrom [1972] in McGinnis 1999b).

4 The specific form of this framework has varied considerably over time; important stages in its development can be seen at Kiser and Ostrom (1982), E. Ostrom (1990), Ostrom *et al.* (1994), McGinnis (2000), E. Ostrom (1998a, 2005, 2007b, 2010b) and Poteete *et al.* (2010). The IAD framework is also related to earlier work on public service industries and local public economies (Ostrom *et al.* 1961; Ostrom and Ostrom 1977; E. Ostrom 1983; Ostrom *et al.* 1993; McGinnis 1999b; Oakerson 1999) as well as more recent work on social-ecological systems (E. Ostrom 2007a, 2009). For a recent overview of all of these related frameworks, see McGinnis (2011a).

5 "Policy analysis," writes Vincent Ostrom, is based on the presumption that "appropriate forms of collective choice and collective action will contribute to a more effective resolution of common problems and an advancement in the aggregate well-being experienced by members of collectivities" (V. Ostrom in McGinnis 1999a: 394).

6 Due to the very specific and contextual nature of knowledge required for the assessment of a case, "in finite time and place exigencies," the need to get the local knowledge, and perceptions and ideas of the actors involved is even more stringent. One has to derive criteria for choosing one alternative over the other and to assess their consequences. In other words, the applied dimension presses the problem of norms not only at an analytical level but also at the decision-making one.

7 Much of contemporary policy analysis appears to be largely institution-free except for abstract allusions to the government, or the state (meaning nation-states).

> Policy formulations presume a clean slate as though the failure to proclaim a General National Policy implied the absence of an Energy Policy, an Urban Policy, a Housing Policy, an Educational Policy, or any other specifiable policy. It is as though all political systems were unicentric, hierarchical in order, and run from the top down. The same modes of analysis and policy prescriptions can presumably be used anywhere in the world.
>
> (Ostrom, V. *The Meaning of American Federalism: Constituting a Self-governing Society*. ICS Press, 1991: 2)

## Bibliography

Aligica, P. and P. Boettke. 2009. *Rethinking Institutional Analysis and Development: The Bloomington School.* London: Routledge.

Bish, R. 1971. *The Public Economy of Metropolitan Areas.* Chicago: Markham Press.

Kiser, L.L. and S. Percy. 1980. 'The concept of coproduction and its prospects for public service delivery,' Working Paper No. W80-6, Workshop in Political Theory and Policy Analysis, Bloomington, IN: Indiana University.

McGinnis, M.D. 1999a. *Polycentric Governance and Development: Readings from the Workshop in Political Theory and Policy Analysis.* Ann Arbor, MI: University of Michigan Press.

—— 1999b. *Polycentricity and Local Public Economies: Readings from the Workshop in Political Theory and Policy Analysis.* Ann Arbor, MI: University of Michigan Press.

—— 2000. *Polycentric Games and Institutions: Readings from the Workshop in Political Theory and Policy Analysis.* Ann Arbor, MI: University of Michigan Press.

—— (2011a). 'An Introduction to IAD and the Language of the Ostrom Workshop: A Simple Guide to a Complex Framework', *Policy Studies Journal* 39 (1) (March 2011), 163–77.

—— 2011b. 'Networks of adjacent action situations in polycentric governance', *Policy Studies Journal* 39(1): 45–72.

Kiser, L. and E. Ostrom. 'The three worlds of action,' in *Strategies of Political Inquiry*, ed. E. Ostrom, Beverly Hills, CA: Sage, 179–222.

Mitchell, W.C. 1988. 'Virginia, Rochester, and Bloomington: Twenty-five years of public choice and political science', *Public Choice* 56(2): 101–19.

Oakerson, R.J. 1999. *Governing Local Public Economies: Creating the Civic Metropolis.* San Francisco: ICS Press.

——and R.B. Parks. 1988. 'Citizen voice and public entrepreneurship: The organizational dynamic of a complex metropolitan county', *Publius: The Journal of Federalism* 18(4): 91–112.

Ostrom, E. 1972. 'Metropolitan reform: Propositions derived from two traditions', *Social Science* Quarterly 53: 474–93.

—— 1983. 'A public choice approach to metropolitan institutions: Structure, incentives, and performance', *Social Science Journal* 20(3): 79–96.

—— 1986. 'An agenda for the study of institutions', *Public Choice* 48: 3–25

—— 1990. *Governing the Commons: The Evolution of Institutions for Collective Action.* New York: Cambridge University Press.

—— 1996, 'Crossing the great divide: Coproduction, synergy, and development', *World Development* 24 (6): 1073–87.

—— 1998a. 'A behavioral approach to the rational choice theory of collective action', *American Political Science Review* 92(1): 1–22.

—— 1998b. 'The comparative study of public economies', presented upon acceptance of the Frank E. Seidman Distinguished Award in Political Economy, Memphis, TN, P.K. Seidman Foundation.

—— 2005. *Understanding Institutional Diversity.* Princeton, NJ: Princeton University Pres

—— 2007a. 'A diagnostic approach for going beyond panaceas', *Proceedings of the National Academy of Sciences* 104(39): 15181–7.

—— 2007b. 'Institutional rational choice: an assessment of the institutional analysis and development framework' in P.A. Sabatier (ed.) *Theories of the Policy Process,* 2nd edn. Boulder, CO: Westview Press, 21–64.

—— 2009. 'A general framework for analyzing sustainability of social-ecological systems', *Science*, vol. 325, no. 5939: 419–22.

—— 2010a. 'Analyzing collective action', *Agricultural Economics* 41(S1): 155–66.

—— 2010b. 'Beyond markets and states: polycentric governance of Complex economic systems', *American Economic Review* 100(3): 641–72.

—— 2011. 'Background on the institutional analysis and development framework', *Policy Studies Journal* 39 (1): 7–27.

——, Larry Schroeder and Susan Wynne. 1993. *Institutional Incentives and Sustainable Development: Infrastructure Policies in Perspective.* Boulder, CO: Westview Press.

——, R. Gardner and J. Walker. 1994. *Rules, Games, and Common-Pool Resources.* Ann Arbor, MI: University of Michigan Press.

Ostrom, V. 1964. 'Editorial comment: Developments in the "no-name" fields of public administration', *Public Administration Review* 24(1): 62–3.

—— 1971. *The Political Theory of a Compound Republic: Designing the American Experiment*, 2nd edn. Lincoln, NE: University of Nebraska Press.
—— 1972. 'Polycentricity', Workshop Archives, Workshop in Political Theory and Policy Analysis, Bloomington, IN: Indiana University. Presented at Annual Meeting of the American Political Science Association, September 5–9, Washington, DC. Reprinted in McGinnis 1999b. *Polycentry and Public Economies*, Ann Arbor, MI: University of Michigan Press.
—— 1973. *The Intellectual Crisis in American Public Administration*, 2nd edn. Tuscaloosa, AL: University of Alabama Press.
—— 1991. 'Some ontological and epistemological puzzles in policy analysis', Working Paper No. W82-16, Workshop in Political Theory and Policy Analysis, Bloomington, IN: Indiana University.
—— 1997. *The Meaning of Democracy and the Vulnerability of Democracies: A Response to Tocqueville's Challenge*. Ann Arbor, MI: University of Michigan Press.
——, C.M. Tiebout and R. Warren. 1961. 'The organization of government in metropolitan areas: A theoretical inquiry', *American Political Science Review* 55: 831–42.
—— 1990. 'American constitutionalism and self-governance', in M. Rozbicki (ed.) *European and American Constitutionalism in the Eighteenth Century*. Vienna: US Regional Program Office.
——, R. Bish and E. Ostrom. 1988. *Local Government in the United States*. San Francisco: ICS Press.
Ostrom, V. and E. Ostrom. 1965. 'A behavioral approach to the study of intergovernmental relations', *The Annals of the American Academy of Political and Social Science* 359: 137–46.
—— 1971. 'Public choice: A different approach to the study of public administration', *Public Administration Review* (31): 203–16.
—— 1977. 'Public goods and public choices', in McGinnis 1999b. *Polycentry and Public Economies*, Ann Arbor, MI: University of Michigan Press.
Parks, R.B. 1993. 'Comparative metropolitan organization: Service production and governance structures in St. Louis (MO) and Allegheny County (PA)', *Publius* 23(1): 19–39.
——and R.J. Oakerson. 1989. 'Metropolitan organization and governance: A local public economy approach', *Urban Affairs Quarterly* 25(1): 18–29.
Poteete, Amy, Marco Janssen and Elinor Ostrom. 2010. *Working Together: Collective Action, the Commons, and Multiple Methods in Practice*. Princeton, NJ: Princeton University Press.
Simon, H.A. 1955. 'A behavioral model of rational choice', *Quarterly Journal of Economics* 69(1): 99–118.
Tiebout, C.M. 1956. 'A pure theory of local expenditures', *Journal of Political Economy* 64: 416–35.
Toonen, Theo A.J. 1998. 'Networks, management and institutions: Public administration as "normal science"', *Public Administration* 76: 229–52.
Whitaker, G. 1980. 'Coproduction: Citizen participation in service delivery', *Public Administration Review* 40(3): 240–6.

# 8 Postpositivism and the policy process

*Raul Perez Lejano*

Our understanding of what policy-making is, and what policy analysts do, evolved beyond a clear conception of policy-making as a linear, rational exercise to a more unsettled but pragmatic view of it as a complex, plurivocal, indeterminate, and often controversial act. This marked transition has been referred to as the argumentative (or discursive, linguistic, communicative) turn in policy (Fischer and Forester 1993). As will be discussed, this opening up to a broader landscape has both enlivened and fractured the policy discipline (to the extent that the word discipline is itself problematic). It has moved scholars and practitioners of policy to wonder, "what is our science?" or perhaps, more appropriately, "what is our folly?"

## Turning points in the practice of policy

The notion of policy-making and analysis as a rational process is traced to the rise of systems and decision analysis, beginning with the Second World War. This era saw the use of mathematics and the increasingly powerful growth in computer processing toward the systematic allocation of resources, first for military purposes but soon thereafter to large-scale social projects. The first policy think tanks, of which the RAND Corporation is perhaps emblematic, arose as seats of a grand planning endeavor, in which numerical optimization could be translated into optimal outcomes in the battlefield, in the emerging mega-cities and suburbs, in schools, hospitals, and other sites of social activity. This heritage draws, first and foremost, from the pioneering work of von Neumann and Morgenstern (1944) in conceptualizing a theory of games and decisions. This powerful analytical lens begins and ends with the notion of individual rationality as self-utility maximization, and of society as a collection of rational individuals. Translation of this system of rational thought to actual application would not be long, e.g. Schelling's treatment of war and conflict as multi-player games among rational actors (1980) or to Buchanan and Tullock's use of the same model to analyze political instituitons (1962). A central figure in the translation of the rational model to the public realm of allocation of goods and services is Karl Mannheim (1940), who provided an early vision of democratic social planning. In this modernist vision, exemplified by Le Corbusier's utopian cities, society can be designed.

Where, then, did the turn away from the rational model occur? In part, we can trace some of it to a turn to reflection occasioned by a seeping disillusionment in these grand experiments in rational policy-making. Several key examples will suffice. But first, we ask the reader to excuse an inescapable "US-centricity" to this account. Much of the self-reflection one finds in the literature occurs in US academia and media. At the same time, we occasionally bring in examples from other regions to guard against monocentricity and, at times, as a counterpoint to some of these observations.

Disillusionment with the state's grand social experiments began early. From the experience of Lyndon Johnson's war on poverty, ending with ever-increasing disparities between rich and poor, to the military rational planning of the Cold War, ending in national defeat to the North Vietnamese, United States ventures have failed in grand manner. In city planning, the rational design of large-scale Corbusian housing complexes ends with the demolition of the grandiose Pruitt-Igoe tenements in Chicago.

But this was not just the American experience. Indeed, one cannot look back on the great leaps in agricultural productivity of post-feudal China without recalling, at the same time, the social ills of the Cultural Revolution. Across the world, grand state-led social engineering, led by institutions like the World Bank, resulted in large state agencies in developing nations that failed to deliver goods and services effectively and failed to eliminate entrenched poverty (Rapley 1996).

In fact, much of this was foretold many decades earlier, in Weber's description of the sweeping rationalization of society (Weber 1904). In this account, rationalization involved the increasingly narrow reduction of social processes and institutions into means-end technocracies in which easily calculable or accountable outputs would be optimized in rationally designed institutions. In this type of *Zweckrationalität*, bureaus would maximize bureaucratic imperatives to the exclusion of deeper, perhaps more elusive social goals, e.g. energy departments would maximize energy output to the exclusion of environmental quality; transportation agencies would maximize road capacity to the detriment of walkable neighborhoods, etc. In his incisive critique of the Tennessee Valley Authority, Selznick described how the state agency itself became captured by the very entities it regulated (the power companies) because their interests coincided (1949). Skepticism over institutions grew ever deeper during the Watergate era, to be repeated from administration to administration, from the Iran-Contra affair to Iraq. A good summary account of the failures of the rational, modernist state is found in Scott's description of high modernism (Scott, J. 1998).

In contrast to the rationalist goal of clearly defined objectives and alternatives, Rittel and Webber describe pressing social issues as wicked problems—namely those for which no right or wrong exists, with ends for which there is no consensus in society, with alternatives and consequences that cannot be determined by technical analysis, and no good way to even ascertain if the problem has been solved or not (Rittel and Webber 1973). In such a milieu, the maximizing impulse gives way to the question, "what is it exactly that we want to optimize?" and the consequentialist framework gives way to the question, "how do we act when we just don't know what will result?"

Wicked problems are all around us. As this chapter is being written, society in the US in 2012 is caught in an ideological divide. As fiscal conservatives forced the country into a near default in pursuit of an ideological commitment to small government, low taxes, and defeating an incumbent President, it became apparent how intractable the gulf was. The question quickly became that of choosing between maximizing individual wealth or social equity, and society itself was divided over the choice just as the liberals and conservatives in congress were. As to predicting consequences of one action versus another, one side clearly believed that budget-cutting would create growth, while the other believed that stimulus and near-term spending would pump-prime the economy. What is right when one side's notion of rationality is a polar opposite of the other? At this time, there is evolving yet another turn in policy thought being precipitated by the Depression of 2008, and it is unclear how the policy disciplines will change from this time forward—that book is still being written.

## Turning points in policy thought

At the same time as the grand experiment at social intervention was beginning to waver, a revolution in the theoretical underpinnings of policy was evolving.

Part of the intellectual movement owes its trajectory to the "linguistic" turn in the social sciences and humanities. The reference to language owes to the advancement in the field of linguistics, beginning with Saussure's structural theory of meaning (1916). Saussure posited that the meaning of words is not inherent in the words themselves but something that arises in the place of the word in the constellation of other words forming the language system. Thus, the word "poor" means what it means only in juxtaposition to words like "destitute," "rich," "wealthy," "penniless," and all the other words that, by virtue of its position relative to each other, determine their respective meanings. Meaning is purely positional, which is why Saussure's is said to be a structural theory of meaning. Post-structuralism comes on the heels of Saussure's theory by positing further that not only is meaning relative and positional, it is not even fixed this way. Meaning is never determined and, instead, is always subject to the free play or polysemy of language (Derrida 1978).

Parallel developments include Wittgenstein's philosophical treatise on logic, in which, contrary to logicians who maintain that fundamental truths can be arrived at by beginning with foundational facts and building logically outward, all truth claims are contingent. There is no logical truth, only language games wherein truth is established only within a particular language system, but never established categorically (Wittgenstein [1922]61). Truth is socially constructed, subject to conventions established in social discourse, but always contextual, never categorical. In the sociology of knowledge, much of the unraveling of the notion of absolute knowledge is traced to Lyotard, who began by contrasting technical-scientific knowledge with narrative or folk knowledge, then argued that both were language games, no one more privileged than the other to any claim to truth (Lyotard 1979). Lyotard's declamation against universality of knowledge (what he called grand narratives) is thought to be the first emphatic statement of a new, postmodern age where there are no definitive truth claims, social norms, or teleological principles, but only individual and particular voices in a discursive babble (or paralogy, in Lyotard's words).

This turning away from modernity, with its pursuit of universal truths and its espousal of the enlightenment of rationality and scientific inquiry, and a turning toward a never-ending questioning of purpose and meaning, had a profound effect on policy thought (and, as will be argued, a later and less dramatic effect on practice). Berger and Luckmann wrote about institutions as social constructs, subject to artifice and ever-changing convention (1966). This easily lends to a questioning of the institutional foundations of policy—the meaning of the state, the legislature, or the legal process. Others questioned even the primacy of science as a truth—establishing endeavor, showing that the scientific process itself is very much a cultural practice as other cultural practices such as taboo or courtship (Latour 1987; and see Douglas 1966 for an earlier statement of modernity and culture).

The effect of these intellectual revolutions on thinking about policy, and the institutions in which policy happens, has been deeply felt. Consider the linguistic turn and its turning away from logocentricity, which is the notion that words point to objective truths which language accurately represents. And consider the turn toward the idea that words themselves are not fixed in meaning but subject to play and debate. This extends immediately to the most physical object of policy, which are statements of policy, policy documents, and law. In this poststructural age, even a statement like "We hold these truths to be self-evident, that all men are created equal, that they are endowed by their Creator with certain unalienable Rights, that among these are Life, Liberty and the pursuit of Happiness" itself ceases to be self-evident. The words are enshrined for all of history, but their meaning changes. Equality and liberty mean different things today than when first written in Jefferson's time. And what they mean today is itself subject to debate. Does equality mean extending the same bundle of rights and privileges to undocumented immigrants? If not, then these persons are consituted as less than citizens, which is what the Declaration of Independence meant by persons (which, in Jefferson's time, referred to white, male landowners).

The telos of policy is also uncertain. What is the maximand of rational policy-making if we cannot even come to agreement over what liberty, rights, and public good mean? There is no transcending ethic that all can come to agreement over. In the context of the ideological debates in the US Congress, some have tried to appeal to an overweening ethical principle "Nation before Party!" but even this is questioned, as the nation's good has been conflated on all sides with the party's. As Sarah Palin said:

> Politics isn't just a game of competing interests and clashing parties. The people of America expect us to seek public office and to serve for the right reasons. And the right reason is to challenge the status quo and to serve the common good.
>
> *(http://www.npr.org/templates/story/story.php?storyId=94118910 (downloaded December 10, 2011))*

Everyone, even the political maverick, lays claim to the public good.

The deconstruction of institutions has also had a profound effect, beginning with the decentering of the state (which parallels the decentering of the author as the font of meaning of the logos) away from the presumption that the state represents the people and acts for the greatest good of the greatest number (Mill 1863). Devolution away from the state has been most marked in the "government to governance" literature in which focus turns to networks of policy actors acting in often innovative ways (Koppenjan and Klijn 2004; Edelenbos *et al.* 2010; Schout *et al.* 2010).

It is perhaps no accident that a central figure in linguistics, Noam Chomsky, would emerge as one of the foremost critics of the new order, characterizing the state as a conglomerate of military, industrial, government, and big business interests (Chomsky and Herman 1988). But perhaps the most trenchant critique would come from the French sociologist, Michel Foucault, who posited all modern institutions to be modeled after the same basic mold of the penal institution, designed to disipline the public and channel all human activity toward the furthering of the interests of the powerful (1977). And as the policy-making institutions go, so does the very integrity of the policy that emerges from them. Thus, in a skeptical age, an action such as the TARP (Troubled Asset Relief Program), the US Federal Reserve's lending instrument that kept large financial institutions from bankruptcy in 2008, could be so casually described by political commentators in terms such as:

> The bailout money is just going to line the pockets of the wealthy, instead of helping to stabilize the economy or even the companies receiving the bailouts: Bailout money is being used to subsidize companies run by horrible business men, allowing the bankers to receive fat bonuses, to redecorate their offices, and to buy gold toilets and prostitutes.
>
> *(www.worldcrisisnewswatch.com/2011/05/tarp-bailout-scam-explained-government.html)*

Thus, the postpositivist turn has come to mean not just a turning away from the notion that the public good was measurable and subject to systematic analysis and optimization. In fact it questioned the foundational meaning of policy itself, not only uncertainty over the correlation between policy actions and the public's welfare, but that the very intent of policy could not be presumed to be aligned with such collective good.

## Policymaking in an interpretive world

To sum up the state of affairs thus far, if:

- policy goals cannot be set definitively, in a manner achieving broad consensus over them;
- policy situations cannot be described or analyzed in a positivist manner (i.e. their truth determined by some definitive measures);
- policy instruments and policy texts cannot be unambiguously determined with regard to their meaning;
- policy-making and implementing institutions cannot be assumed to have the capacity to realize policy targets, nor assumed to be aligned with them in purpose

then what policy should be and how policy should be enacted cannot be determined in objective manner and, instead, a matter of interpretation. This is not a trivial proposition, inasmuch as the essence of community and political life, as Aristotle said in the *Politics*, is their "establishment with a view to some good." If we cannot agree on what "good" means for the community, then how do we set policy and go about attaining its ends?

In an interpretive world, where meaning and good ends are subject to deliberation and debate, policy-making is less about measuring and projecting the optimal trajectory for policy but the crafting of a compelling and consensus-building story that captures the public's moral imagination and moves people and groups to action. In this account, we refer to a number of key works in the postpositivist policy literature—at this point, a handful of useful summary treatments can be found in Stone, Roe, Fischer and Forester, Fischer, Hajer, Kaplan, Schneider and Ingram, Yanow, Schon and Rein, and Dryzek.

Making sense of the world, and policy situations encountered in it, requires seeking satisfactory interpretations of these situations. For Ricoeur, people make sense of the world by crafting coherent narratives about it (1981; also Bruner 1991). In Ricoeur's words, "By means of the [narrative's] plot, goals, causes, and chance are brought together within the temporal unity of a whole and complete action" (1984: ix). So it is, then, that by reconstructing a person's underlying narrative account, we can best reproduce their experience of a situation. To do this, Ricoeur espouses a hermeneutic approach to narrative interpretation (1976, 1981).

Goffman said something similar when he evoked the idea of frames, which were interpretive constructs used to create coherent meaning in an otherwise complex and incomprehensible situation (1974). Frames, as Goffman introduced them, are interpretive schemes that selectively highlight aspects of the issue and introduce a specific perspective that then allows one to capture reality in a simpler manner (1974; also Schön and Rein 1994). But seldom found in this research is the explicit recognition that, very often or perhaps generally, these mental models, cultural models, and frames take on the appearance and essence of story. Bruner is one of the few to make this explicit connection (1987). As others have expressed it: "Given the amount of uncertainty about the world, people create cause-and-effect stories to fill in the blanks. Frames—also known as mental models, schemas—are essentially such stories" (Wesselink and Warner 2010). Stone talks about how "causal stories" are used to craft and process policy ideas through the process (1997)—though, we might add, the causal story is just one of the genres one finds in the policy field (i.e. others include moral fables, epic myths, tales of chivalry, surrealist fiction, etc.). And so, for example, along with the proposal for TARP was the narrative of how financial institutions like Goldman Sachs were "too big to fail." In this interpretive model, it is on the strength of the policy story that policies win or lose.

As a result, over several decades now, scholars have called for the systematic use of narrative analysis in public administration and policy research (Roe 1989, 1994; Yanow 1992, 2007; Balfour and Mesaros 1994; Sköldberg 1994; Schram and Neisser 1997; Hajer and Wagenaar 2003; Ospina and Dodge 2005; Hampton 2009; Lejano and Leong 2012). This is joined by an already considerable literature on narrative approaches to studying organizational process and design (e.g. see Martin 1982; Boje 1991; Weick 1995; Boyce 1995; Czarniawska 1998; Patriotta 2003).

The move towards narrative approaches began with the interpretive turn in the social sciences (Berger and Luckmann 1966; Rabinow and Sullivan 1979, 1987). In the 1970s and 1980s, scholars like Fischer and Forester (1993) argued for an interpretive approach to public policy studies. The then prevalent positivist-instrumentalist bent of the social sciences had failed in carrying out its promise of giving a good account of what goes on in government and society at large (Dryzek 1982). The deductive approach of technical knowledge, with its search for objective measures and universal principles, failed to account for the fact that social phenomena mean different things to different people, and that such social constructions are highly contextual (ibid.: 310; also Fischer and Forester 1993). The primacy of technical knowledge was questioned and, increasingly, narrative knowledge began to be seen as equally valid (Lyotard 1979; Jameson 1984).

Among the first to use narrative analysis to study public controversies was Emery Roe (1989, 1994). His point was that narratives are one of the richest vehicles for the multiple and complex meanings that different stakeholders bring to a public issue. Martha Nussbaum says something similar when she describes how complex normative positions are best expressed in narrative form (1990). Deborah Stone speaks to the power of "causal stories" which public managers and politicians craft, to construct reality in a way that best captures their interests and policy goals (1997). Given this irreducible element of social construction, she argues, understanding deliberation in the public realm requires an interpretive approach (Stone 1997). In our work, we look for stories that are told by different publics, including citizens' groups and media.

In this discussion, we understand a narrative to simply mean a story, composed of a coherent sequence of events, involving a set of characters, which are actors with definite traits (e.g. see Ryan 2007; Bal 2009). When we reconstruct a narrative underlying an issue, we are simply composing a story, with events and characters, as if a narrator were recounting it to us directly. It is possible that no one source (whether a respondent or a text) ever gives us a complete narrative *in toto*, or that it gives us only one particular account of a larger narrative, and it is the analyst's role to construct a story that reflects the different aspects of the issue in a coherent way. The resulting, reconstructed narrative is akin to the *fabula* (or storyline) of a literary piece—namely it presents the plot even when it cannot be found in any single narrator's particular account (Bal 2009). Stories, then, are used to capture the imagination and support of decision-makers and public to rally around a policy initiative and form a coalition in support of it. Sometimes, in fact, the stories themselves organize these coalitions and networks of policy actors—literally, policy movements and networks are emplotments of characters and events into one coherent narrative (Lejano *et al.* 2013). Most recently, Lejano and Leong (2012) develop a hermeneutic approach for analyzing the multiple dimensions of public debate.

But this should not be thought of as mere political "spin doctoring", as the stories one finds in the policy realm can be taken at face value or critiqued, and can engender belief or incredulity. So the question is: ow can we tell a good, from a bad, narrative interpretation of a public issue? There are different ways, and Kaplan (1986) discusses some. In Kaplan's terms, good narratives should be empirically verifiable, rich, and coherent. First, a narrative can be tested against known empirical information, events, etc. Secondly, given two narratives that both meet empirical tests, the one that is able to account for more facets of experience, empirical reality, and people's personal accounts, should be regarded as the better, richer one. Lastly, the test of coherence suggests that we assess the strength by which different accounts, different facets of the story, the sequence of events, etc. are connected by some logical (or other) scheme. For example, the passage "I saw a bird flying. I started weeping." is not as coherent as this one: "I saw a bird flying above me. The majesty and utter simplicity of this reality made me feel so alive, I could not but begin to weep." There are other prescriptions for how one distinguishes a better story from an inferior one, but in practice, this poses no problem for us in everyday life. To cite a trivial example, everyone knows Rocky I was a far better story than Rocky V, without even needing to explicitly describe the complex mode by which we come to such judgements.

The pragmatism test lies in the ability of the reconstructed narrative to explain the different contingencies and particularities surrounding the issue. Does it help us better to understand the motivations of the different actors and their actions? In the case study to be taken up herein, does it help us to understand why opposition to the project was so strong and effective, and why attempts by the agency at knowledge transfer did not suffice to quell this opposition?

Why is there a need to find meanings beyond the surface of what people say or write? First of all, there may be processes or conditions, like ocean currents beneath a surface calm, that influence the proceedings even though these processes may be well removed from the matter at hand. Tradition, power, culture, and other forces of structuration act like this. Second, there may be issues that stakeholders, consciously or subconsciously, relegate to the background. Yanow notes that in public decision-making, some issues are verboten—namely "publicly unspeakable because there is no explicit public consensus underlying them" (1992: 400). This is also tied up with political necessities such as maintaining "public silences about contradictions" (1992: 418).

## Policy institutions and the postmodern condition

In the previous section, we took up the task of analyzing policy ends and determining policy directions when truth and good could not be unambiguously stated. We then, now, ask the closely related question of what is the policy enacting institution (an agency, a community, or an individual) to do under such uncertainty? How do policy actors proceed to act in the public realm?

If, taking a cue from Lyotard, all policy discussions were simply nothing other than language games, then policy-making must then be simply a competition over the best discourse. This can devolve into the classic pluralist model of competition over policy agendas. In this game, the better, more influential, better resourced interest group wins the policy battle. But this process can take different forms, in part determined by how policy institutions view the policy question.

Karl Popper's epistemological framework viewed the establishment of truth and good as unachievable by any objective, scientific model but rather the contingent and defeasible setting of truth claims. By defeasible, we mean a process whereby claims are constantly subject to testing and confirmation or revision in the world of practical implementation (Popper 1994). This incrementalist view of knowledge leads to a pluralist model such as that of Lindblom's mutual partisan adjustment, wherein, through a tug of war of competing interests, society finds some reasonably optimal trajectory that is cognizant of the differing interests and their strength of preference (1965). In this model, process determines the right.

But process can determine what is right in other ways. Habermas believed in the possibility of a kind of rationality that had a transcendent moment that allowed the diverse and conflictual set of policy actors to come to agreement over what is right (1984). In this model, what is true and good is not available a priori but reached through a process of agonistic debate. It is still a tug of war, carried out through dialogue, but with a difference: in this model, policy actors can come to a mutually agreed resolution of what is right and good, through the force of better argument. The key, in this communicative model of rationality, is the practice of the ideal speech situation, where all have an ability to speak and be heard and communication is nondistorted. This epistemological framework finds its application in different practical models for public deliberation and consensus-building (Bobrow and Dryzek 1987; Healey 1996; Innes and Booher 2009; Susskind *et al.* 1999). In these situations, consensus can be reached through compromise across fixed but divergent interests (Fisher *et al.* 1991), or through the construction of new understandings of a situation that move policy actors to reconsider their positions or to realize a higher goal that exceeds the provincial limits of individual preference (Schön and Rein 1994).

The social construction of policy pertains not just to the identification of solutions to pressing social problems, but the active construction of the problems themselves. As Schneider and Ingram depicted it, what the issue is, what the stakes are, who the stakeholders are, and what their roles in the policy issue as constructed might be—that is, as targets, beneficiaries, victims, or agents of policy (1997). In this framework, the key step is reached well before problem-solving begins but in the earlier phase of issue identification and stakeholder analysis. This view of policy lends a constructionist interpretation to the issue-salience and policy windows model of the policy process (see Kingdon 1984). Issues do not exist a priori to be solved—rather, they are constructed in response to the priorities of agenda-setters. In some cases, policy solutions preexist issues and can take the form of policy responses waiting for appropriate problems to be identified in order for them to be employed (March and Simon 1958). From this point of view, military action (to take one example) is seen not as a response to an emergent conflict, but the other way around, namely conflicts are identified (or designed) as a response to an unmet demand for military action.

In this type of policy milieu, ideas (which are what social constructions are, after all) and the rhetorical skill by which they are deployed become the focus of policy attention (Throgmorton 1991; Howlett and Rayner 2008).

Models of the policy process taken up in the first section of this book still pertain. We are well advised to not jettison the idea of a policy process template. In the context of the linguistic turn, however, each of the stages in the policy cycle are now seen as forums for public deliberation, namely as part of an extended communicative process. As Laswell first suggested, an initial step still remains that of issue identification, but since meaning of policy can no longer be fixed, interpretations of issues (and their salience in the public mind) continues all throughout the policy process. Moreover, in the postmodern era, these processes need not necessarily lead to outcomes, at least not idealized ones, nor to a transition from one stage to another. Habermas' speech situation need not lead to decisions, as the focus is on the communicative process. In Lyotard's model of paralogy, consensus is never envisioned—it is enough to simply have debate and an airing of disparate views. In the postpositivist age, talk is action.

But this is just a short step away from a complete rethinking of the policy process.

## Deconstructing the policy process

Classic models of the policy process, involving stages or cycles of issue identification, analysis, and finally, implementation are actually translations of the rational model into institutional form. The classic rational model of analysis involves just these stages, from identification of overall goals or values, enumeration of policy alternatives, evaluation, decision, and enaction. The idealized policy process is a hypostatization of the model of rationality.

But just as, not merely postructural theory, but the practice and follies of real-world policy has forced us to reconsider the rational model, so is it possible to deconstruct the entire policy process.

In part, this deconstructionist turn is guided by the new institutionalism that emerged from the fields of public administration and organization theory. In this postmodern view, institutions are themselves social constructions (e.g. March and Olsen 1989) that themselves are crafted after well-constructed narratives (Weick 1995). When institutions take on a repeatable form, it is not because of some objective property of these institutions, but rather, because their social constructions become norms or standards that diffuse from polity to polity (DiMaggio and Powell 1991).

While the turn away from logocentricity involved an undoing of the idea that meaning is fixed in the words of policy, it also undoes the primacy of the author as the center of meaning. From this point onward, policy will be, as Barthes put it, a "writerly" text (1975), where the implementors and targets of policy are just as much authors as the writers of policy. This turns the policy process inside out. For example, where and at what stage is policy designed? In a deconstructed process, policy is not simply designed in a central location and diffused outward; rather, it undergoes transformation and redesign as new policy actors take on the institutional norm and make use of it (Howlett and Rayner 2008). Consider a policy on conditional cash transfers for the poor, wherein payments are made to recipients so long as the latter pledge to or prove that they use the money for medical or educational purposes. Then consider a situation wherein field agents who implement the policy by making the actual transfers to recipients and collect information, decide to allow a women's cooperative to pool their outlays and obtain credit from a local bank. Are the field agents not also participating in design of the policy, not as formally laid out but as actualized in the field?

As Pressman and Wildavsky showed, neat boundaries between the policy design and implementation become blurred in practice (1979). In practice, all such conceptualizations of the policy process do blur in many different ways. For this reason, one can take a phenomenological approach to analyzing policy processes. Instead of beginning, in positivist fashion, from the universal concept and applying it to actual processes deductively, one can instead begin and end with the actual process in place, in actual context, as Husserl, the pioneer of phenomenological thought, put it: to the thing itself (1900). That is, do not analyze the process according to a pre-constructed template, whether it be one of stages or cycles of policy-making; rather, describe it as it is, as experienced and observed in place. For example, Argyris and Schön wrote about how actual programs might be characterized by theories-in-practice rather than theories underlying their design (1974).

An example of phenomenological description is seen in Lejano (2008), wherein habitat conservation policy is described not according to its formal design, but in the informal, dynamically evolving practices that made up the policy as experienced. In such a mode of description, formal descriptors of policy processes (e.g. designers, implementors, organizational roles and rules, bureaucratic structure) all blur into sometimes new categories requiring new modes of description. For example, in the aforementioned study, instead of describing the program as a set of rules, the author modeled it as a web of relationships, all cohering with each other in dynamic fashion.

Another mode of studying a deconstructed policy process is to study it in the same way as one might study the social construction of a narrative that is shared with others. The formation of such a narrative is congruent with the formation of the network of actors that share it. Latour, Callon, Law, and others have sought to describe the process by which such actor-networks are formed (Latour 2005; Callon 1986; Law 1992). Callon describes it as the translation of the policy story into forms that can be assimilated by (or, perhaps more accurately, can emplot) other actors. In this translation process, he posits four stages (1986):

- *Problematisation*: defining a problem that requires joint action, and set of actors who are potentially enmeshed in it.

- *Interessement*: the negotiation of actors' involvement and roles in the initiative.
- *Enrollment*: actors' acceptance and acting out of these roles.
- *Mobilization*: the expansion of the network to include communities of support.

It is not an accident that the above sequence also resembles the exposition of a story's plot—namely identification of the conflict, description of the setting and cast of characters, and mobilization of action on the characters' part. The description of the network process is not far from the act of emplotment—in fact, they are essentially one and the same.

The turn away from the positivist notion of determinate problem solutions and a functionalist notion of the policy process leads to a turning toward, instead of the linear process of locating solutions, the discursive process of issue construction and deliberation. The focus is not on the location of the optimal solution, but on the gathering together of a critical coalition (or network) that supports and champions a policy idea to completion. Callon and Latour took this same road by focusing on the network formation process. Howlett and Ramesh (1998) discussed how to delineate the characterized policy subsystems (which are almost the same as the networks described above) in terms of their openness to new policy ideas and disposition to policy change. In this literature, the postpositivist focus is not so much on the narrative and its narration, but on the formation of coalitions and shifts in memberships and allegiances (Sabatier and Jenkins-Smith 1993), which one reasons, leads to shifts in their shared narratives. By retaining the classic notion of interest-based coalitions, these theories are able to combine frame, interests, and knowledge base in one process theory.

There are other ways to modify the otherwise linear, rational process model. As Goffman had shone light onto social and organizational processes that occurred "backstage" (e.g. on the street, at home, in the coffee shop, smokey room, etc.) rather than the foreground of policy-making (e.g. senate floor, parliament, executive boardroom, etc.), researchers began paying attention to informal processes (e.g. Innes and Booher 2010), decentralized decision-making in the field (e.g. Lipsky 1980), or policy-making within complex networks (e.g. Kickert *et al.* 1997). The transition away from formal institutional processes finds its most ambitious form in a growing literature on practice (e.g. Bourdieu 1977; Giddens 1984). The modernist impulse would seek to find universal rules in the structures that govern individuals in society (as in dialectical materialism or classic political institutional theory) or within the individual (as in rational choice or behavioralist theories). In contrast, theorists of practice aim to represent meaning and action as traversing the structure-agency divide. For example, Bourdieu discusses how individual decision-making is an improvisation guided by sometimes rigid controls, often not transparent to the individual and often immanent in the body's own habitual movements (1990). In this framework, enacting of reproductive health policy, as an example, is as much or more determined by the everyday routines women and men follow subconsciously than formal rules and programs—the functioning of political institutions if steered by similar habitual patterns, such as talk and dress and relationships between members of an organization. Such focus on practice, while by now well established in the organizational literature, is just beginning to have an effect on policy studies.

Furthermore, if policy-making proceeds through the construction of a policy narrative, then perhaps it is also through narrative means by which the process is best described. This involves soliciting stories from policy actors caught up in the process (as in Pentland 1999; also Lejano *et al.* 2012). Description of the process is captured by narrative. These stories can vary from place to place—perhaps aligned with easily recognized templates (e.g. policy stages) in some respect, but finely and richly different in the way it unfolds. Through a postpositivist lens, these fine differences are as important as the general commonalities. Whereas the positivist lens emphasizes deductive reasoning from universal principles (e.g. policy stages), postpositivism focuses on the particulars of the phenomenon.

To sum up: why are processes not so easily circumscribed in a postpositivist frame of analysis? Because policy no longer can be seen as an object that can be objectively determined, and neither can we place exactly where policy is crafted and how. Policy meanings cannot be pinned down and, so, where there used to be analysis, we have deliberation all throughout the policy process, and where there used to be pure implementation, we now have redesign and reinterpretation of policy. Authorship of policy is not fixed and determinate, and where a policy is authored is similarly deconstructed to include a new constellation of policy actors.

## The problem of social construction

Contrary to a radical constructionist interpretation of policy, most of the scholars cited above do not espouse simple constructionism (Fischer 2003). Policy stories are not simply fictions crafted out of sheer artifice. We discussed, earlier, certain tests of validity and pragmatic value that allow us to discern whether one narrative is more credible than another. Just because we weaken the notion of objective standards for truth does not mean an inability to tell better from worse policy narratives. Social constructs have to be coherent, and the parts of their story have to be internally logically consistent.

Just as importantly, policy stories have to, ultimately, be grounded in the real experiences of policy actors. The last ten years have been a sobering experience for us all, but especially policy scholars. Notwithstanding the concerted effort to build momentum for the war in Iraq, at some point, policy-makers had to reconcile their policy narrative with the nagging fact that there were no weapons of mass destruction (WMDs) in Iraq. Despite the degree to which the homeownership narrative captured the public psyche, at some point in the last few years, the socially constructed value of property had to reconcile with the limitations of earning power of the would-be property owners, and bubbles began to burst. There is not an infinite array of narratives that can capture the public agenda, but only those that cohere with how people and policy-makers understand themselves and the world around them. Such understandings are borne by learning over lifetimes of experience.

Whether bubbles or WMDs, what confronts the public today is the turning back of the pendulum away from a hapless constructionism to a sober realization that policy narratives are not fictions but rather attempts to represent reality. The failure of cherished institutions (market, state, and community) have created a void in the way we idealize policy process.[1] What are needed now are approaches that reconcile the desire for objective foundations for policy-making with the inescapable intedeterminate nature of policy. Perhaps what we are beginning to see is a turn toward a *post-constructionist* understanding of policy and its processes (Lejano 2006). Doubtless, we perceive this in the recent focus on evidence-based policy-making (Pawson 2006; Bochel and Duncan 2007; Khagram and Thomas 2010). But another part of it may be a reversion to pure ideology. It seems that polities, the world over, are now caught in a divide between requiring more and better-informed judgments from decision-makers or giving up on rational process altogether and relying on exhortations from political extremists (and the latter occur in many forms—pastors, mullahs, talk show hosts, governors and former governors). In this ironic age, the new freedoms of digital communication and social networks seem to go hand in hand with the increasing demise of free and democratic public discourse.[2] The challenge for political life is to discover a new middle ground where polities are free to imagine and craft new futures while grounding deliberation on the realities of everyday life.

Policy studies have to find such middle (or higher) ground, as well (Lejano 2006). As De Leon writes concerning positivism and postpositivism: "it would seem foolish to set the two concepts at odds, in a zero-sum game, as opposed to use them to inform and support one another" (1998, p.157). Perhaps as a necessity, policy scholars who take the route of postpositivism have espoused a deep critique, and often wholesale rejection, of the positivist model. But this has created a bifurcated literature, with neither side wary of the achievements of the other. Doctoral students in the fields of policy and public administration are asked, early in their academic careers, to choose one or other of these alternatives. To postpositivists, quantitative models seem to merely scratch the surface of institutions, and to positivists, discursive approaches appear to be pure artifice. If the first decade of this new century is any indication, measurement and discourse need a new reconciliation.

As one recalls the turn that policy studies took after the crises of the 1960s and 1970s, one wonders what corner we are turning now.

## Notes

1 As an example, the ongoing financial crisis gripping the European Union threatens institutional models that envision new regional modes of collaborative policy-making. Asian models of state-sponsored interventions in the market begin to reveal wicked trade-offs between productivity and quality of life and liberty. And as for the American model, we all know too well about its crises and ideological standoffs.

2 As this chapter is being written, the author's own university in Irvine, California, is undergoing a crisis over free speech—e.g. students arrested for writing with chalk on pavement in protest against runaway tuition fee increases.

## Bibliography


Argyris, Chris and Donald Schön. 1974. *Theory in Practice: Increasing Professional Effectiveness*. San Francisco: Jossey-Bass.

Bal, Mieke. 2009. *Narratology: Introduction to the Theory of Narrative*, 3rd edn. Toronto: University of Toronto Press.

Balfour, Danny L. and William Mesaros. 1994. 'Connecting the local narratives: Public administration as a hermeneutic science', *Public Administration Review* 54: 559–64.

Barthes, Roland. 1975. *S/Z: An Essay*. New York: Hill and Wang.

Berger, Peter and Thomas Luckmann. 1966. *The Social Construction of Reality*. New York: Doubleday.

Bobrow, Davis and John Dryzek. 1987. *Policy Analysis by Design*. Pittsburgh, PA: University of Pittsburgh Press.

Bochel, H.M. and S. Duncan. 2007. *Making Policy in Theory and Practice*. Bristol: Policy Press.

Boje, David M. 1991. 'The storytelling organization: A study of story performance in an office-supply firm', *Administrative Science Quarterly* 36(1): 106–26.

Bourdieu, Pierre. 1977. *Outline of a Theory of Practice*. Cambridge: Cambridge University Press.

—— 1990. 'Structure, habitus, practice', in Pierre Boudieu (ed.) *The Logic of Practice*, Richard Nice (trans.). Palo Alto, CA: Stanford University Press.

Boyce, Mary E. 1995. 'Collective centring and collective sense-making in the stories and storytelling of one organization', *Organization Studies* 16(1): 107–37.

Bruner, Jerome. 1987. 'Life as narrative', *Social Research: An International Quarterly* 71(3): 691–710.

—— 1991. 'The narrative construction of reality', *Critical Inquiry* 18(1): 1–21.

Buchanan, James and Gordon Tullock. 1962. *The Calculus of Consent*. Ann Arbor, MI: University of Michigan Press.

Callon, Michel. 1986. 'Some elements of a sociology of translation: Domestication of the scallops and the fishermen of St Brieuc Bay', in John Law (ed.) *Power, Action and Belief: A New Sociology of Knowledge*. London: Routledge and Kegan Paul.

Chomsky, N. and E. Herman 1988. *Manufacturing Consent: The Political Economy of the Mass Media*. New York: Pantheon Books.

Czarniawska, B. 1998. *A Narrative Approach to Organization Studies*. Thousand Oaks, CA: Sage.

Derrida, Jacques. 1978. *Writing and Difference (L'Écriture et la Différence)*, A. Bass (trans.). Chicago: University of Chicago Press.

de Leon, P. 1998. 'Models of policy discourse: Insights versus prediction', *Policy Studies Journal* 26(I): 147–161.

de Saussure, Ferdinand. 1916. *Cours de Linguistique Générale*, C. Bally and A. Sechehaye (eds) with the collaboration of A. Riedlinger. Lausanne and Paris: Payot; *Course in General Linguistics*, W. Baskin (trans.), 1977. Glasgow: Fontana/Collins.

DiMaggio, Paul and Walter Powell. 1991. 'The iron cage revisited: Institutional Institutional isomorphism and collective rationality in organization fields', in P. DiMaggio and W. Powell (eds) *The New Institutionalism in Organizational Analysis*. Chicago: University of Chicago Press.

Douglas, M. 1966. *Purity and Danger: An Analysis of Concepts of Pollution and Taboo*, Routledge and Keegan Paul, London.

Dryzek, J. 1982. 'Policy analysis as hermeneutic activity', *Policy Science* 14(4): 309–29.

Edelenbos, J., N. van Schie and L. Gerrits. 2010. 'Organizing interfaces between government institutions and interactive governance', *Policy Sciences* 43(1): 73–94.

Fischer, Frank. 2003. *Reframing Public Policy: Discursive Politics and Deliberative Practices*. Oxford: Oxford University Press.

——and John Forester (eds). 1993. *The Argumentative Turn in Policy Analysis and Planning*. Durham, NC: Duke University Press.

Fisher, R., W. Ury, and B. Patton. 1991. *Getting to Yes: Negotiating Agreement Without Giving In*. New York: Penguin.

Forester, John. 1999. *The Deliberative Practitioner*. Cambridge, MA: MIT Press.

Foucault, Michel. 1977. *Discipline and Punish: The Birth of the Prison*, Alan Sheridan (trans.). New York: Pantheon.

Giddens, Anthony. 1984. *The Constitution of Society: Outline of the Theory of Structuration*. Berkley, CA: University of California.

Goffman, E. 1974. *Frame Analysis: An Essay on the Organization of Experience*. Cambridge, MA: Harvard University Press.

Habermas, Jürgen. 1984. *Reason and the Rationalization of Society*, vol. 1 of *The Theory of Communicative Action*, Thomas McCarthy (trans.). Boston: Beacon Press.

Hajer, Maarten A. and Hendrik Wagenaar (eds). 2003. *Deliberative Policy Analysis*. Cambridge: Cambridge University Press.

Hampton, Greg. 2009. 'Narrative policy analysis and the integration of public involvement in decision making', *Policy Sciences* 42: 227–42.

Healey, Patsy. 1996. 'The communicative turn in planning theory and its implications for spatial strategy-making', *Environment and Planning B: Planning and Design* 23(2): 217–34.

Howlett, Michael and M. Ramesh 1998. 'Policy subsystem configurations and policy change: Operationalizing the postpositivist analysis of the politics of the policy process', *Policy Studies Journal* 26(3): 466–81.

——and Jeremy Rayner. 2008. 'Third generation policy diffusion studies and the analysis of policy mixes: Two steps forward and one step back?', *Journal of Comparative Policy Analysis: Research and Practice* 10(4): 385–402.

Hysing, E. 2009. 'From government to governance? A comparison of environmental governing in Swedish forestry and transport', *Governance* 22 (4), 647–72.

Husserl, Edmund. 1900. *Logical Investigations* (*Logische Untersuchungen*) vol. 1, J.N. Findlay (trans.). New York: Routledge.

Innes, Judith E. and David E. Booher. 2010. *Planning with Complexity: An Introduction to Collaborative Rationality for Public Policy*, New York, NY: Routledge.

Jameson, Frederic. 1994. 'Postmodernism, or the cultural logic of late capitalism', *New Left Review* 1: 146.

Khagram, S. and C.W. Thomas. 2010. 'Toward a platinum standard for evidence-based assessment by 2020', *Public Administration Review* 70(s1): S100–S106.

Kaplan, Thomas. 1986. 'The narrative structure of policy analysis', *Journal of Policy Analysis and Management* 5(4): 761–78.

Kickert, Walter J.M., Erik-Hans Klihn and Jopp F.M. Koppenjan. 1997. *Managing Complex Networks: Strategies for the Public Sector*. London and Thousand Oaks: Sage.

Kingdon, John. 1984. *Agendas, Alternatives, and Public Policies*. Boston: Little, Brown.

Koppenjan, J. and Klijn, E.H. 2004. *Managing Uncertainties in Networks: A Network Approach to Problem Solving and Decision Making*. London: Routledge.

Latour, Bruno. 1987. *Science in Action*. Cambridge, MA: Harvard University Press.

——2005. *Reassembling the Social: An Introduction to Actor-Network-Theory*. Oxford: Oxford University Press.

Law, John. 1992. 'Notes on the theory of the actor network: Ordering, strategy, and heterogeneity', Available at: www.lancs.ac.uk/fass/sociology/papers/law-notes-on-ant.pdf

Lejano, Raul. 2008. 'The phenomenon of collective action: Modeling institutions as structures of care', *Public Administration Review* May/June: 491–504.

——and Ching Leong. 2012. 'A hermeneutic approach to explaining and understanding public controversies', *JPART Journal of Public Administration Research and Theory* (http://jpart.oxfordjournals.org/content/early/2012/04/04/jopart.mus001.abstract).

——, Helen Ingram and Mrill Ingram. 2013. *The Power of Narrative in Networks: Relating Alternative Ecologies.* Cambridge, MA: MIT Press.

Lipsky, Michael. 1980. *Street-level Bureaucracy: Dilemmas of the Individual in Public Services.* New York: Russell Sage Foundation.

Lindblom, Charles. 1965. *The Intelligence of Democracy: Decision Making Through Mutual Adjustment.* New York: Free Press.

Lyotard, Jean-François 1979. *The Postmodern Condition: A Report on Knowledge.* Minneapolis, MN: University of Minnesota Press.

Mannheim, Karl. 1940. *Man and Society in an Age of Reconstruction.* London: Routledge.

March, James and Herbert Simon. 1958. *Organizations.* New York: Wiley.

——and Johan Olsen. 1989. *Rediscovering Institutions: The Organizational Basis of Politics.* New York: Free Press.

Martin, J. 1982. 'Stories and scripts in organizational settings', in A.H. Hastorf and A.M. Isen (eds) *Cognitive and Social Psychology.* Amsterdam: Elsevier, 255–305.

Mill, John Stuart. 1863. *Utilitarianism.* London: Parker, Son, & Bourn.

Nussbaum, Martha C. 1990. *Love's Knowledge: Essays on Philosophy and Literature.* New York: Oxford University Press.

Ospina, Sonia M. and Jennifer Dodge. 2005. 'It's about time: Catching method up to meaning—the usefulness of narrative inquiry in public administration research', *Public Administration Review* 65(2): 143–57.

Patriotta, Gerardo. 2003. 'Sensemaking on the shop floor: Narratives of knowledge in organizations', *Journal of Management Studies* 40(2): 349–76.

Pawson, R. 2006. *Evidence-based Policy: A Realist Perspective.* London: Sage.

Pentland, Brian. 1999. 'Building process theory with narrative: From description to explanation', *Academy of Management Review* 24(4): 711–24.

Popper, Karl. 1994. *All Life is Problem Solving.* New York: Routledge.

Powell, Walter and Paul DiMaggio. 1991. *The New Institutionalism in Organizational Analysis.* Chicago: University of Chicago Press.

Pressman, J. and A. Wildavsky. 1979. *Implementation: How Great Expectations in Washington are Dashed in Oakland: Or, Why It's Amazing that Federal Programs Work at All, This Being a Saga of the Economic Development Administration as Told by Two Sympathetic Observers Who Seek to Build Morals on a Foundation of Ruined Hopes.* Berkeley, CA: University of California Press.

Rabinow, P. and W. Sullivan (eds). 1979 and 1987. *Interpretive Social Science: A Reader.* Berkeley: University of California Press.

Rapley, John. 1996. *Understanding Development: Theory and Practice in the Third World.* Boulder, CO: Lynne Rienner.

Ricoeur, Paul. 1976. *Interpretation Theory: Discourse and the Surplus of Meaning.* Texas: Christian University Press.

—— 1981. *Hermeneutics and the Human Sciences: Essays on Language, Action and Interpretation,* John B. Thompson (ed. and trans.). Cambridge: Cambridge University Press.

——. 1984. *Time and Narrative,* vol. 1, K. McLaughlin and D. Pellaver (trans.). Chicago: Chicago University Press.

—— 1992. *Oneself as Another,* Kathleen Blamey (trans.). Chicago: University of Chicago Press.

Rittel, Horst and Melvin Webber. 1973. 'Dilemmas in a general theory of planning' *Policy Sciences,* vol. 4. Amsterdam: Elsevier Scientific, 155–69. (Reprinted in N. Cross (ed.) 1984. *Developments in Design Methodology,* Chichester: John Wiley & Sons 135–44.

Roe, Emery M. 1989. 'Narrative analysis for the policy analyst: A case study of the 1980–1982 medfly controversy in California,' *Journal of Policy Analysis and Management* 8: 251–73. doi:10.2307/3323382.

—— 1994. *Narrative Policy Analysis: Theory and Practice.* Durham, NC: Duke University Press.

Ryan, Marie-Laure. 2007. 'Toward a definition of narrative', in David Herman (ed.) *The Cambridge Companion to Narrative.* Cambridge: Cambridge University Press, 22–35.

Sabatier, P.A. and H.C. Jenkins-Smith. 1993. *Policy Change and Learning: An Advocacy Coalition Approach.* Boulder, CO: Westview Press.

Schelling, Thomas C. 1980. *The Strategy of Conflict*, reprinted, illustrated and revised. edn. Cambridge, MA: Harvard University Press.

Schneider, Anne and Helen Ingram. 1997. *Policy Design for Democracy*. Lawrence, KS: University of Kansas.

Schön, Donald and Martin Rein. 1994. *Frame Reflection: Toward the Resolution of Intractable Policy Controversies*. New York: Basic Books.

Schout, Adriaan, Andrew Jordan, and Michelle Twena. 2010. 'From "old" to "new" governance in the EU: Explaining a diagnostic deficit', *West European Politics* 33(1): 154–70.

Schram, Sanford and Philip T. Neisser. 1997. *Tales of the State: Narrative in Contemporary U.S. Politics and Public Policy*. Langham, MD: Rowman & Littlefield.

Scott, James C. 1998. *Seeing like a State: How Certain Schemes to Improve the Human Condition Have Failed*. New Haven, CT: Yale University Press.

Scott, W. Richard. 1998. *Organizations: Rational, Natural, and Open Systems*. Englewood Cliffs, NJ: Prentice Hall.

—— 2001. *Institutions and Organizations*. 2nd edn. Thousand Oaks, CA: Sage.

Selznick, Philip. 1949. *TVA and the Grass Roots: A Study in the Sociology of Formal Organization*. Berkeley: University of California Press.

Sköldberg, Kaj. 1994. 'Tales of change: Public administration reform and narrative mode', *Organization Science* 5: 219–38.

Stone, Deborah. 1997. *Policy Paradox: The Art of Political Decision-Making*. New York: Norton.

Susskind, Lawrence, Jennifer Thomas-Larmer and Sarah McKearnen. 1999. *The Consensus Building Handbook: A Comprehensive Guide to Reaching Agreement*. Thousand Oaks, CA: Sage.

Throgmorton. J.A. 1991. 'The rhetorics of policy analysis', *Policy Sciences* 24: 153–79.

van Neumann, John and Oskar Morgenstern. 1944. *Theory of Games and Economic Behavior*. Princeton, NJ: Princeton University Press.

Weber, Max. 1958. *The Protestant Ethic and the Spirit of Capitalism*. New York: Charles Scribner [1904].

Weick, K.E. 1995. *Sensemaking in Organizations*. Thousand Oaks, CA: Sage.

Wesselink, Anna and Jeroen Warner. 2010. *Reframing Floods: Proposals and Politics, Nature and Culture* 5(1): 1–14.

Wittgenstein, Ludwig. [*c.* 1922] 1961. *Tractatus Logico-Philosophicus: Suivi De Investigations Philosophiques*. Paris: Librairie Gallimard.

Yanow, Dvora. 1992. 'Silences in public policy disclosure: Organizational and policy myths', *Journal of Public Administration Research and Theory* 2: 399–423.

—— 2001. *Conducting Interpretive Policy Analysis*. Thousand Oaks, CA: Sage.

—— 2007. 'Interpretation in policy analysis: On methods and practice', *Critical Policy Studies* 1: 110–22.

# Part III

# Modelling the policy process

## Frameworks for analysis

# 9

# The institutional analysis and development framework

*Ruth Schuyler House and Eduardo Araral Jr.*

As a relatively young discipline and an intrinsically complex science, public policy has yet to congeal into a clear-cut school of thought. Rather, its borders are diffuse, both overlapping with and comprising multiple "pure" disciplines of the social and natural sciences. Indeed, the complexities of the open systems subject to study necessitate a multidisciplinary approach that pragmatically draws from the fields most germane to the particular issues at hand. Further, by drawing from different approaches, scholars can develop constructively competitive views of a context in order to come to a more enlightened understanding about the potential effects of public action.

Institutional scholars' engagement with classical economics, political science, law, sociology, psychology, natural science, and a host of other fields in the pursuit of understanding the policy process has generated an incredibly rich and variant body of scholarship united by a common focus on institutions and their roles (among other important factors) in shaping, constraining, and enabling human behavior. By focusing on rule sets and the major physical and social constructs characterizing a particular situation, institutional scholars seek to grapple with *both* macro-level social structures and individual agency and also move beyond the market versus hierarchy division to identify a more elemental set of components comprising any and all situations of human interaction.

We believe that institutional analysis makes an important contribution to the study of public policy for a number of reasons, in particular its established record of drawing from multiple fields as discussed already. For one, institutional research over the past 25 years has advanced Douglass North's early challenge to progress economics from a static to dynamic theory of human exchange (North 1990, p.107). Indeed, institutions have come to be commonly recognized as a critical factor shaping political and economic behavior, but we have yet to fully understand what types of institutions (if any) are requisite for the development and the maintenance of functioning democracies, let alone how to manage and control processes of "institution building" and institutional change. Moreover, institutional analysis—and more specifically, the institutional analysis and development (IAD) framework developed largely by Elinor Ostrom and her colleagues at the Workshop in Political Theory and Policy Analysis at Indiana University—comes as close as any approach to offering a framework that is generally applicable to comparatively studying a wide variety of social situations. Finally, as entirely new and sometimes blended structures of organization emerge in an increasingly complex, globalized political economy, we need to utilize theoretical frameworks that are capable of encompassing multitudinous patterns of human interaction.

## Frameworks, theories, and models

Before delving into the IAD framework, we must clarify what a "framework" is, and how it relates the many theories and models—each with their own constructs and vocabularies—used to understand public policy. Ostrom herself offers a clear explanation distinguishing between theories, frameworks, and models (2007, p.25). Most broadly, a *framework* identifies a set of general variables and relationships that should be studied in order to understand a particular phenomenon, but assigns no values to the variables and does not specify the direction of relationships between them. In essence, the framework is an organizing tool that allows the comparison of different theories, many of which may be compatible with a particular framework. According to Ostrom, frameworks "attempt to identify the *universal* elements that any theory relevant to the same kind of phenomena would need to include" (2005, p.826).

A *theory* specifies a more coherent set of assumptions about elements within the framework, including their relationships with each other, their importance to answering particular kinds of questions, and expectations about interactions and outcomes. For example, game theory, classical economic theory, transaction cost theory, and a host of other theories have been extensively used alongside the IAD framework.

Finally, a *model* is used to represent a specific situation and makes explicit assumptions about the values of variables and the expected outcomes of a situation given a particular set of parameters (Ostrom 2007, p.26). Since there exist numerous ways in which a particular system of human organization or governance might be studied and understood, the IAD framework becomes useful to engage in comparative study across disciplines and draw nearer toward generalized understandings about the creation, implementation, interaction, and outcomes of rules arrangement in different contexts.

## Institutions

Before jumping into the application of the IAD framework, we must first come to a common understanding of its primary focus: *institutions*. What, then, are institutions, and why do they constitute an important unit of analysis? Perhaps the most commonly cited definition of institutions is Douglas North's: institutions are "the rules of the game of a society, or, more formally, the humanly devised constraints that structure human interaction" (1990), including formal laws and regulations and informal constraints, such as conventions and social norms. Emphasizing their functionality, Menard and Shirley define institutions as the "rules, norms, and constraints that humans devise to reduce uncertainty and control their environment" (2005). While scholars of different strands of institutionalism differ in opinion about the human intentionality of institutional forms, the rational choice or "actor-centered" institutionalists who most commonly utilize the IAD framework see institutions as constructs intentionally devised by political or economic actors to serve particular purposes. Ostrom describes rules as "shared prescriptions (must, must not, or may) that are mutually understood and enforced in particular situations in a predictable way by agents responsible for monitoring conduct and for imposing sanctions" and norms as "shared prescriptions known and accepted by most of the participants themselves involving intrinsic costs and benefits rather than material sanctions or inducements" (2005, p.824).

The varied use of multiple definitions of the term "institution" (for example, when used to refer to physical buildings like hospitals or organizations like the UN as opposed to rule sets) is one among many challenges of institutional research. Furthermore, institutions are invisible and are thus very difficult to describe, define, and measure. And quite often, the most influential rules governing a system of interaction are the *informal* norms and conventions—the "rules-in-use"—rather than the "rules-in-form" on formal record (Ostrom 2007, p.23). The effects of particular rules are also difficult to study in isolation, as rules and norms consistently interact with the constellation of other rules and exogenous factors that define a particular situation.

Finally, rules exist at multiple levels, and rules at any one level are embedded in the next higher tier. The nestedness of lower levels in higher tiers is important to understanding how rule changes (and thereby institutional change) at one level are influenced by rules and contextual factors at other levels. Thus, institutional analysis becomes akin to untangling the relationships between rules within and across levels. As Kiser and Ostrom point out, rules exist at the *operational level* that govern the "every day" activities and decisions of agents in an interactive situation. Moving higher, there exists a set of *collective choice level* rules that constrain those at the operational level and determine how operational rules are set. And at the *constitutional choice level,* rules that govern the process of rule-setting, including who may be involved and how, frame the collective-choice and operational situations (Kiser and Ostrom 1982).

Oliver Williamson, the prominent transaction cost scholar, proposes a similar delineation of institutional tiers, where human exchanges lie at the most immediate level. These transactions are constrained by governance structures, which are in turn shaped by the "institutional environment" set by property rights rules, the bureaucracy, legislative processes, etc. Finally, all of these rule structures are couched within rules at the level of embedded norms and traditions, which change most slowly and are often studied via application of social theory (Williamson 1998). Despite minor variations, the point is that most theorizing related to institutions incorporates the recurring themes of nestedness, configurative relationships, and interrelatedness—characteristics that make institutional analysis complex and prescriptions for institutional reform often quite tentative.

## The IAD framework

Given the complexity of studying institutions, along with the observed differences in approaches to understanding institutions, the Institutional Analysis and Development (IAD) framework unifies the multidisciplinary study of rules and norms in a common analytical framework comprising a number of key variables that define a particular *action situation*. The framework is applicable to both "snapshot" analyses as well as process-oriented studies of institutional change, where feedback becomes an important part of the analysis. Furthermore, the framework allows the researcher to focus on particular components of an action situation, for example the external physical variables, the actors' characteristics, or the rules-in-use. Ultimately, the IAD framework is intended to allow researchers to model the strategies players adopt within particular rule configurations and to better understand how the mixture of participants, rules, strategies, community attributes, and external variables, results in certain outcomes, and thereafter, how these outcomes and participants' responses to them pressure changes to the prevailing rule sets.

Like any good framework, the IAD framework maps out the broad variables applicable to any institutional form (including markets, hierarchies, and collective action systems) that may be studied by different theories and models. These broad variables, which Ostrom terms *action arenas,* are nested subassemblies of a broader, interrelated social structure.

Action arenas are comprised of two lower-level subassemblies: the *actors* and the *action situation* (Ostrom 2007, p.28). The actors and action situation interact and are simultaneously affected by exogenous variables including physical conditions (e.g. the nature of a resource in a common pool situation); community attributes (the social and cultural context); and the rules in use, or institutional arrangements (ibid.; Ostrom *et al.* 1994).

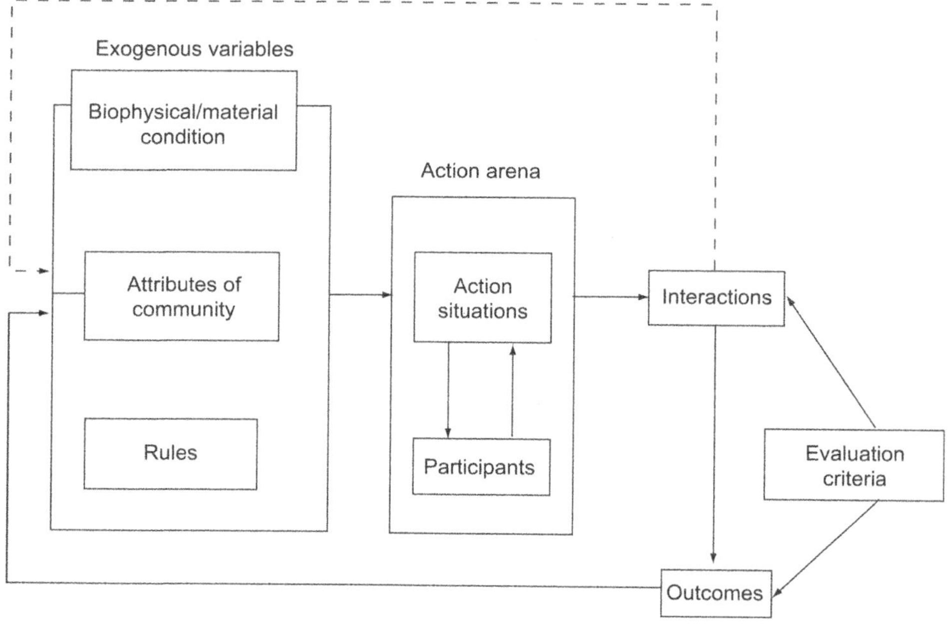


*Figure 9.1* A framework for institutional analysis
Source: Ostrom (1999: 42)

## The action arena

The action arena under study is "the social space where individuals interact" and is comprised of the participants and their action situation (Ostrom 2005, p.829). Ostrom describes *action situations* as collections of seven variables: first, the participants; second, their positions; third, the set of potential outcomes; fourth, information available; fifth, the costs and benefits associated with the set of outcomes; sixth, the degree of control participants have over choices and strategies, and seventh, relationships between actions and outcomes (Ostrom 2005, p.828). Also germane to describing the situation is the frequency and duration of interactions and whether the situation is recurrent or singular.

The *actors,* be they conceptualized as individuals, loose groups, or formal organizations, exhibit different attributes affecting their behaviors. The researcher must investigate and make assumptions about participants' preferences, goals, values, beliefs, and decision-making strategies (Ostrom 2007, p. 30). The actors may be characterized according to values of four variables: the resources they control; the values they assign to various actions and outcomes; the way they use information; and the processes they use for selecting strategies (Ostrom 2007, p. 28). It is also important to note that, in the tradition of institutional economics, neoclassical economics, assumptions of pure rationality and full information are discarded and replaced by a conceptualization of individual actors as boundedly rational (Simon 1957) and typically lacking full information about the situation at hand.

## External variables

A set of three important external contextual variables structure the arena: the rules-in-use, the physical conditions of the good under study and the surrounding context, and the characteristics of the community of participants (Kiser and Ostrom 2000).

### Rules-in-use

Returning to the notion of rules-in-use, a critical component of institutional analysis is discovering how the nested, interlinked rules-in-use that affect potential payoffs and losses, demarcate the set of allowable or feasible strategies, and influence actors' behaviors. These rules are subject to the limits of human cognition, understanding, and language, and can only be discovered through rigorous research of the *understood* "do's and don'ts"—rules that may, indeed, be quite different from or supersede the rules that exist on formal record (Ostrom 2005, p.832).

Which rules, then, are important to analyzing a particular action arena? Ostrom and Crawford developed a typology of rules that should be specified in order to determine first, their impact on the action situation and actors, and second, the impact of one rule change upon another. In cataloging the rules governing a particular situation and making note of their configurations, scholars can thereafter better explain and predict the results of rule changes on the situation and the likelihood of change itself. The set of important rules governing any situation includes *boundary rules* that set who can participate and how easy is it for them to join or exit the arena; *position rules* which assign positions of leadership, subservience, rank, etc.; *authority rules* which define what actions participants in different positions may or may not take; *scope rules* which restrict the set of possible outcomes; *aggregation rules* which define the degree of control an actor has at a decision point; *information rules* which affect the availability of information for different participants; and *payoff rules* which assign the costs and benefits linked to different actions. All of the many possible configurations of these rule sets define different *institutions* (Ostrom and Crawford 2005).

Beyond understanding the rules-in-use governing a situation, it is also important to understand where the rules themselves originated, the history of their evolution, and the stability of their configuration. The stability of a rule set's configuration depends on multiple factors, including enforcement capacity (Gibson *et al.* 2005; Ostrom 2005, p.833), the frequency of interactions, and the degree to which rules are similarly understood and valued by participants (Ostrom 2005, p.833).

### Attributes of the material context

Another critical factor that influences the action arena is the "state of the world" in the arena at hand—the physical context, material conditions, and the type of good under study in the situation. These conditions delimit what kinds of strategies and outcomes are at all possible and how particular strategies relate to different outcomes (Ostrom 2005, p.837). Furthermore, regarding the good under study, it becomes important for the researcher to ask critical questions about the nature of the good, including the ability to exclude beneficiaries and the "subtractability of the flow" (ibid.)—or the degree of rivalry, in neoclassical economic terms. These two attributes are used to distinguish between public and private goods, common pool resources, and club goods, each of which is associated with a set of assumptions and expectations related to their production and provision and the incentives of participants that utilize, control, trade, allocate, acquire, or produce them. Additionally, it may be important to consider the size of the good, whether it can be stored and transported, and how consistently it can be made available (Ostrom 2005, p.840).

### Attributes of the community

The final set of external variables that affect the action arena is the attributes of the larger community, sometimes referred to as the *culture* (Ostrom 2005, p.841). According to Ostrom, the attributes that are important to shaping behaviors in the action arena include "the norms of behavior generally accepted in the community, the level of common understanding potential participants share about the structure of particular types of action arenas, the extent of homogeneity in the preferences of those living in a community, and the distribution of resources among those affected" (Ostrom 2005, p.841). By specifically accounting for the role of culture and shared conventions, the IAD framework incorporates lines of enquiry more typical of sociological and anthropological research into understanding policy situations—a shift responsive to long-standing critique of the strict positivist tradition in policy science.

## Linking arenas and studying institutional change

In addition to studying the effects of the aforementioned factors on a particular action situation, it is also often important to uncover the linkages and relationships between factors in different action arenas. More specifically, the relationships between institutions at different levels—the operational, collective choice, and constitutional—are critical to processes of institutional change. For the researcher, it is necessary to acknowledge that rules changes in one arena are constrained by rules at a deeper level, and that changes in successively deeper levels are typically more costly and difficult to make (Ostrom 2005, p.842). Because there are multiple sources of institutional change with networked effects, sustained change in one component is difficult without concurrent change in others (Saleth and Dinar 2004). Further, change is difficult to coordinate and depends not only on changing organization but also changing human behavior, the institutional environment, and the institutions of governance at higher levels (Williamson 1998).

As for applying the framework to understand institutional change, exogenous variables are assumed to be fixed at the beginning of analysis, and resultant outcomes are thereafter judged by participants according to criteria such as perceived efficiency, equity, adaptability, accountability, and conformance to morality and general social norms. If outcomes are unproductive, deemed unfair, or are otherwise displeasing to the actors in the arena, those actors will strategize to change the rule structure. In this way, the IAD framework may be applied to research the iterative, ongoing nature of policy-making.

## Applications of the IAD framework

A key test of a framework's utility is the extent to which it has been applied to a variety of settings and research programs. The IAD framework meets this test as it is now extensively used in teaching, research, and policy advice worldwide and is arguably one of the most utilized frameworks in the US and Western Europe (Sabatier 2007) as well as in East, Southeast and South Asia.

For instance, in teaching, dozens of graduate programs in public policy, political science, economics, sociology, and ecology around the world use the IAD framework or elements of it used in their curriculum. Examples include universities in Asia (Tsinghua University in China, the National University of Singapore, Hong Kong University, Seoul National University, China University of Political Science and Law, Asian Institute of Technology), Europe (Humboldt University, Stockholm School of Economics, Delft University Technology (Netherlands), Erasmus University), North America (Indiana University, Arizona State University, University of Colorado, Rice University, University of California, Carleton University, UNAM (Mexico), Duke University, University of Michigan, University of Nevada,) among others.

In terms of empirical and experimental research, the IAD framework has been extensively used in a wide range of research programs. These include the commons research agenda such as fisheries (Basurto 2008; de Castro 2000), irrigation (Bruns 2009; Araral 2006); ground water (Steed 2010; Wang 2006), forestry (Andersson 2003; Hayes 2007; Pacheco 2007; Persha 2008;

Jagger 2009; Marquez 2011); watersheds and river basins (Myint 2005; Heikilla *et al.* 2011); and land use (Donnelly 2009).

The IAD framework has also been used not just for common pool natural resources but also research on knowledge as commons (Hess and Ostrom 2006); infrastructure in developing countries (Schroeder *et al.* 1993); property rights (Kauneckis 2005; Mwangi 2003); foreign aid and bureaucratic incentives (Araral 2008); federalism and constitutional order (V. Ostrom 1991; Jillson and Wilson 1994; Wang 2006; Oyerinde 2006); local public economies (Oakerson and Parks 2011); public housing (Choe 1992); nongovernmental organizations (NGOs) and non-profits (Bushouse 1999; Elliott-Teague 2007; Sabet 2005); global commons (McGinnis and Ostrom 1996; Dolsak 2000; Allen 2005) as well as collective action problems and social dilemmas (Dudley 1993; Ahn 2001; Coleman 2009; Araral 2009; van Laerhoven 2008).

Finally, in terms of policy advice, the IAD framework has been used in diverse policy settings such as peace and nation-building in Liberia (Sawyer 2005), foreign aid (India, Kenya) (Gibson *et al.* 2005); health care (United States), forestry policy in Bolivia (Andersson 2003), irrigation in the Philippines (Araral 2006), among others.

## Conclusion

The rich body of research used to develop the IAD framework alludes to the complexity of institutional analysis and the problems associated with prescribing institutional reform without a full study of the interrelations of the rules at work, particular social contexts, goods in question, and underlying social norms. Nevertheless, the diverse community of institutional scholars contributing to this line of enquiry has contributed to the growing sophistication of institutional analysis. With luck, continued advancements in understanding the multiple rules at play and the relationships between institutional arrangements and economic growth will allow for more appropriate reform prescriptions, greater appreciation of the limitations of outside intervention, and realistic expectations about changing institutional arrangements and growth patterns.

While it is increasingly accepted that there exist no "right" institutions for any and all contexts, Ostrom's and her colleagues' studies of successful and failed institutions via application of the IAD framework have allowed her to identify some general design principles including first, a clear definition of group boundaries; second, rules that are matched to local conditions; third, active participation of individuals affected by rules; fourth, respect of community rule-making rights by external authorities; fifth, monitoring systems managed by community members; sixth, established sanction systems; seventh, low-cost conflict resolution mechanisms; and eighth nested systems of governance in larger systems (Ostrom 1991). Further, increasing emphasis on the importance of informal institutions should afford policy-makers a healthy dose of modesty when designing and implementing "institution-building" programs, for as North warns, policy tools are "blunt instruments." We are often only able to significantly change formal rules, while we can exert very limited control over informal institutions (North 2008).

Finally, Robert Putnam reminds us of the ultimate goal of institutions—that of achieving purpose, not just agreement. Institutions shape politics by way of the rules and standard operating procedures employed to reach political outcomes. And these institutions are influenced by their particular historical and social contexts (Putnam *et al.* 1993). So then, understanding the collective goals that motivate institutional formation, how those institutions shape social action and value systems, and again how those social goals lead to further institutional change allow for a process-oriented, evolutionary understanding of economic growth and social organization.

## Bibliography

Ahn, T.K. 2001. 'Foundations for cooperation in social dilemmas' PhD dissertation, Bloomington, IN: Indiana University.

Allen, Linda. 2005. 'The politics of structural choice of the commission for environmental cooperation: The theoretical foundations of the design of international environmental institutions', PhD dissertation, Bloomington, IN: Indiana University.

Andersson, Krister P. 2002. 'Can decentralization save Bolivia's forests? An institutional analysis of municipal forest governance', unpublished dissertation, Bloomington, IN: Indiana University.

—— 2003. 'What motivates municipal governments? Uncovering the institutional incentives for municipal governance of forest resources in Bolivia', *Journal of Environment and Development* 12(1): 5–27.

Araral, Eduardo K. 2006. 'Decentralization puzzles: A political economy analysis of irrigation reform in the Philippines', PhD dissertation, Bloomington, IN: Indiana University.

—— 2008. 'The strategic games that donors and bureaucrats play: An institutional rational choice analysis', *JPART* 19: 853–871.

—— 2009. 'What explains collective action in the commons? Theory and evidence from the Phillipines', *World Development* vol. 37, no. 3, 687–697.

Basurto, Xavier. 2008. 'Biological and ecological mechanisms supporting marine self-governance: The Seri Callo de Hacha fishery in Mexico', *Ecology and Society* 13(2): 20.

Bruns, Bryan Rudolph. 2009. 'Solving Samaritan's dilemmas in irrigation investment'. Available at: www.indiana.edu/~workshop/colloquia/materials/papers/Bruns-Solving%20Samaritan's%20Dilemmas%20in%20Irrigation%20DRAFT090925.pdf

Bushouse, Brenda K. 1999. 'The mixed economy of child care: An institutional analysis of nonprofit, for profit, and public enterprises', PhD dissertation, Bloomington, IN: Indiana University.

Choe, Jaesong. 1992. 'The organization of urban common-property institutions: The case of apartment communities in Seoul,' PhD dissertation, Bloomington, IN: Indiana University.

Colfer, C.J.P. and R.G. Dudley. 1993. *Shifting Cultivators of Indonesia: Marauders or Managers of the Forest. Rice Production and Forest use among the Uma' Jalan of East Kalimantan*. Rome: Food and Agriculture Organization of the United Nations.

Coleman, Eric. 2009. 'Essays on the effects of institutions and trust on collective action', PhD dissertation, Bloomington, IN: Indiana University.

Croissant, Cynthia. 2005. 'Uses and landscape patterns: A study of relationships between human activities and spatial patterns of land use and land cover on private parcels in Monroe County, Indiana', PhD dissertation, Bloomington, IN: Indiana University.

De Castro, Fabio. 2000. 'Fishing accords: the political ecology of fishing intensification in the Amazon', PhD dissertation, Bloomington, IN: Indiana University.

Dolsak, Nives. 2000. 'Marketable permits: Managing local, regional, and global commons', PhD dissertation, Bloomington, IN: Indiana University.

Donnelly, Shanon. 2009. 'Linking land use, land cover, and land ownership at the parcel scale in the midwest United States', PhD dissertation, Bloomington, IN: Indiana University.

Elliott-Teague, Ginger. 2007. 'NGOs in policymaking in Tanzania: The relationships of group characteristics, political participation and policy outcomes', PhD dissertation, Bloomington, IN: Indiana University.

Gibson, C.C., J.T. Williams and E. Ostrom. 2005. 'Local enforcement and better forests', *World Development* 33(2): 273–84.

——, Krister Andersson, Elinor Ostrom and Sujai Shivakumar. 2005. *The Samaritan's Dilemma: The Political Economy of Development Aid*. Oxford: Oxford University Press.

Hayes, Tanya. 2007. 'Forest governance in a frontier: An analysis of the dynamic interplay between property rights, land-use norms, and agricultural expansion in the Mosquitia forest corridor of Honduras and Nicaragua', PhD dissertation, Bloomington, IN: Indiana University.

Heikkila, Tanya, Edella Schlager and Mark W. Davis. 2011. 'The role of cross-scale institutional linkages in common pool resource management: Assessing interstate river compact', *Policy Studies Journal* 39(1): 121–45.

Hess, C. and E. Ostrom. 2006. *Understanding Knowledge as a Commons*. Cambridge, MA: MIT Press.

Jagger, Pamela. 2009. 'Can forest sector devolution improve rural livelihoods? An analysis of forest income and institutions in Western Uganda', PhD dissertation, Bloomington, IN: Indiana University.

Jillson, Calvin C. and Rick K. Wilson. 1994. *Congressional Dynamics: Structure, Coordination, and Choice in the First American Congress, 1774–1789*. Stanford, CA: Stanford University Press.

Kauneckis, Derek. 2005. 'The co-production of property rights: Theory and evidence from a mixed-right system in southern Mexico', PhD dissertation, Bloomington, IN: Indiana University.

Kiser, L. and E. Ostrom. 1982. 'The three worlds of action: A metatheoretical synthesis of institutional approaches', in E. Ostrom (ed.) *Strategies of Political Inquiry*. Thousand Oaks, CA: Sage, 179–222.

——and E. Ostrom. 2000. 'The three worlds of action: A metatheoretical synthesis of institutional approaches', in Robert D. Putnam and Robert Leonardi (eds) *Making Democracy Work*. New York: Greenwood Publishing Grou.

McGinnis, Michael and Elinor Ostrom. 1996. 'Design principles for local and global commons', in Oran R. Young (ed.) *The International Political Economy and International Institutions*, Vol.2. Cheltenham: Edward Elgar.

Marquez, Lilian. 2011. 'The effect of institutions on Guatemalan forests: Conceptual, methodological and practical implications', PhD dissertation, Bloomington, IN: Indiana University.

Menard, C. and M.M. Shirley. 2005. *Handbook of New Institutional Economics*. Dordrecht: Kluwer.

Mwangi, Esther. 2003. 'Institutional change and politics: The transformation of property rights in Kenya's Maasailand', PhD dissertation, Bloomington, IN: Indiana University.

Myint, Tun. 2005. 'Strength of "weak" forces in multilayer environmental governance: Cases from the Mekong and Rhine River basins', PhD dissertation, Bloomington, IN: Indiana University.

North, D.C. 1990. *Institutions, Institutional Change, and Economic Performance*. Cambridge: Cambridge University Press.

—— 1996. 'Institutions, organizations and market competition', *Economic History* 9612005, EconWPA.

—— 2005. 'Institutions and the performance of economies over time', in C. Ménard and M. Shirley, (eds) *Handbook of New Institutional Economics*. Dordrecht: Springer, 21–30.

Oakerson, R. and Parks, R. 2011. 'The study of local public economies: Multi-organizational, multi-level institutional analysis and development', *Policy Studies Journal*, vol. 39, 1(february): 147–167.

Ostrom, E. 1991. *Governing the Commons: The Evolution of Institutions for Collective Action* Cambridge: Cambridge University Press.

—— 2005. 'Doing institutional analysis digging deeper than markets and hierarchies', *Handbook of New Institutional Economics*, Dordrecht: Springer, pp. 819–48.

—— 2007. 'Institutional rational choice: An assessment of the institutional analysis and development framework', in *Theories of the Policy Process*, 2nd edition, edited by P.A. Sabatier, Boulder, CO: Westview Press, 21–34.

——, Larry Schroeder and Susan Wynne. 1993. *Institutional Incentives and Sustainable Development: Infrastructure Policies in Perspective*. Boulder, CO: Westview Press.

——, R. Gardner and J. Walker. 1994. *Rules, Games, and Common-pool Resources*. Ann Arbor, MI: University of Michigan Press.

——and S. Crawford. 2005. *Classifying Rules. Understanding Institutional Diversity*. Princeton, NJ: Princeton University Press, 187–215.

Ostrom, V. 1991. *The Meaning of American Federalism: Constituting a Self-Governing Society*, San Francisco, CA: Institute for Contemporary Studies Press.

Oyerinde, Oyebade Kunle. 2006. 'The constitution of order among the Yoruba of Nigeria' PhD dissertation, Bloomington, IN: Indiana University.

Pacheco, Diego. 2007. 'An institutional analysis of decentralization and indigenous timber management in common-property forests of Bolivia's lowlands', PhD dissertation, Bloomington, IN: Indiana University.

Persha, Lauren. 2008. 'Decentralized forest management, anthropogenic disturbance patterns and forest change in the Usambara Mountains, Tanzania', PhD dissertation, Bloomington, IN: Indiana University.

Putnam, Robert D. and Robert Leonardi. 2002. *Making Democracy Work*. New York: Greenwood Publishing Group.

Reiners, Derek. 2006. 'Institutional effects on decision-making and performance in public land agencies: The case of wildfire in the interior west of the United States', PhD dissertation, Bloomington, IN: Indiana University.

Sabatier, Paul A. (ed.). 2007. *Theories of the Policy Process*. Boulder, CO: Westview Press.

Sabet, Daniel M. 2005. 'Thickening civil society: nonprofit organizations and problems of water and sanitation along Mexico's northern Border', PhD dissertation, Bloomington, IN: Indiana University.

Saleth, R.M. and A. Dinar. 2004. *The Institutional Economics of Water: A Cross-country Analysis of Institutions and Performance*. Cheltenham: Edward Elgar.

Sawyer, A. 2005. *Beyond Plunder: Toward Democratic Governance in Liberia*.

Schoon, Michael. 2008. 'Building robustness to disturbance: Governance in Southern African Peace Parks', submitted to the faculty of the University Graduate School in partial fulfillment of the requirements for the joint degree Doctor of Philosophy in the School of Public and Environmental Affairs and the Department of Political Science, Bloomington, IN: Indiana University.

Simon, H.A. 1957. *Models of Man, Social and Rational: Mathematical Essays on Rational Human Behavior in a Social Setting*. New York: John Wiley.

Smith, Ronald S. 2006. 'Discerning differences in social capital: the significance of interpersonal network and neighborhood association structure on citizen participation', PhD dissertation, Bloomington, IN: Indiana University.

Steed B. 2010. 'Natural forces, human choices: an over time analysis of responses to ecological and human induced disturbances in southern California water basin governance'. PhD dissertation, Bloomington, IN: Indiana University.

van Laerhoven, Frank. 2008. 'Local governance and the challenge of solving collective action dilemmas', PhD dissertation, Bloomington, IN: Indiana University.

Wang, Jianxun. 2006. 'Political economy of village governance in contemporary China', PhD dissertation, Bloomington, IN: Indiana University.

Williamson, O.E. 1998. 'Transaction cost economics: How it works: where it is headed', *The Economist* 146(1): 23–58.

# 10

# The advocacy coalition framework

## Coalitions, learning and policy change

*Christopher M. Weible and Daniel Nohrstedt*

## Introduction

Policy process research is the study of public policy over time and the surrounding actors, contexts, and events. The formal academic study of policy processes began in the 1950s and 1960s, led by the likes of Lerner and Lasswell (1951), Freeman (1955), Simon (1957), Lindblom (1959), Dawson and Robinson (1963), Easton (1965), Ranney (1968), and Walker (1969). Policy process research sprung, in part, from dissatisfaction with political scientists' focus on governing institutions (courts, legislatures, and executives), a theoretical desire to understand broader political systems, optimism following successes of the social sciences during World War II, and a practical desire to benefit society.

Since the 1960s, a number of complementary research programs have emerged for describing and explaining various aspects of policy processes (e.g. Sabatier 1999, 2007). Among these research programs is the advocacy coalition framework (ACF) created by Paul Sabatier and Hank Jenkins-Smith in the 1980s (Sabatier 1987, 1988; Jenkins-Smith 1990; Sabatier and Jenkins-Smith 1993, 1999).[1] Sabatier and Jenkins-Smith established the ACF in response to several perceived shortcomings in policy process research: a dissatisfaction with the policy cycle or stages heuristic as a causal theory; a need to take more seriously the role of scientific and technical information in policy processes; dissatisfaction with the top-down and bottom-up perspectives of the implementation literature; a need to take a long-term time perspective to understand policy processes; and a need to develop theories that assume more realistic human agents other than the rational actor models found in microeconomics.

The ACF resulted as an amalgam inspired partly from previous studies of issue networks (Heclo 1978), implementation (Pressman and Wildavsky 1973; Mazmanian and Sabatier 1981; Hjern and Porter 1981), learning (Heclo 1974; Weiss 1977), policy subsystems (Griffith 1939; Freeman 1955), belief systems (Ajzen and Fishbein 1980; Putnam 1976; Peffley and Hurwitz 1985; Hurwitz and Peffley 1987), scientific and technical information in policy debates (Mazur 1981; Jenkins-Smith 1990), and a model of the individual based on bounded rationality and cognitive filters (Simon 1957). The ACF serves as an analytical guide for answering questions principally about advocacy coalitions, policy-oriented learning, and policy change.

## The framework

Following Laudan (1977: 70–120) and Ostrom (2005: 27–9), frameworks serve as a platform for groups of scholars to work together toward common understandings and explanations of phenomena. Frameworks provide assumptions, specify the scope of inquiry, and establish conceptual categories with basic definitions and general relations. Frameworks support the development and testing of theory that, in turn, narrow the scope of inquiry, offer testable hypotheses, and postulate causal relationships among concepts. This section introduces the ACF as an actual "framework" by describing its assumptions, scope, and the basic concepts and the general relations among them. The next sections describe the major theoretical emphases supported by the ACF.

### *Assumptions*

Sabatier and Jenkins-Smith based the ACF on several foundational assumptions (1993: 17–20):

*The policy subsystem is the primary unit of analysis for understanding policy processes.* Policy subsystems are defined by a substantive topic and territorial domain along with a set of people actively involved in shaping subsystem affairs. Subsystems are simultaneously semi-autonomous while also nested and interdependent (Sabatier 1998; Nohrstedt and Weible 2010). For example, a water policy subsystem at local level will likely be nested in a regional policy subsystem which is nested within a national policy subsystem. This same water policy subsystem at a local level overlaps to various extents with other subsystems (e.g. a local-level transportation policy subsystem). To attract the attention and involvement of actors, policy subsystems usually entail some degree of authority or potential for authority to alter behavior and shape subsystem outcomes.

*The set of relevant subsystem actors include any person attempting to influence subsystem affairs.* As policy process research developed in the 1950s and 1960s, the emphasis was on symbiotic relations between legislative committees, interest groups, and the government agencies (what has been referred to as the "iron triangle"). The ACF broadens the set of subsystem actors essentially to include any person attempting to influence subsystem affairs, including government officials, members of the private sector and nonprofits, scientists and consultants, and members of the media.

*Individuals are boundedly rational with limited ability to process stimuli, motivated by belief systems, and prone to experience the "devil shift."* The actors involved in policy subsystems are boundedly rational, meaning they are goal-oriented but hampered by their cognitive abilities to process stimuli (Simon 1985). To overcome these limitations, actors simplify the world through hierarchical belief systems consisting of normative deep core beliefs, subsystem specific policy core beliefs, and narrow secondary beliefs (Putnam 1976; Peffley and Hurwitz 1985; see Sabatier and Jenkins-Smith 1999: 133). These belief systems are used as heuristics to filter and interpret stimuli (Lord *et al.* 1979; Munro *et al.* 1997; Munro *et al.* 2002). Furthermore, the ACF borrows from prospect theory to assume that actors remember losses more than gains (Quattrone and Tversky 1988). The result is what the ACF calls the "devil shift," which is the tendency for individuals to exaggerate both the power and maliciousness of their opponents (Sabatier *et al.* 1987).

*Subsystems are simplified by aggregating actors into one or more coalitions.* Given the large number and diversity of actors involved in subsystem affairs, there is a need to simplify while not overly distorting reality. The ACF directs researchers toward aggregating actors into one or more coalitions. These coalitions are defined by their shared policy core beliefs and coordination patterns.

*Policies and programs incorporate implicit theories and assumptions reflecting the translated beliefs of one or more coalitions.* Subsystems consist of boundedly rational actors working together in coalitions toward shaping policy outputs and outcomes. Given the importance of beliefs systems, the ACF assumes that policy outputs are merely the translations of beliefs of the winning coalition or coalitions (Pressman and Wildavsky 1973).

*Scientific and technical information is important for understanding subsystem affairs.* Most subsystems involve issues that are usually difficult to describe and explain in terms of problem seriousness, causes, and potential impacts of proposals. Scientific and technical information, thus, becomes an important resource for coalition members for a variety of uses from argumentation with opponents to the mobilization of supporters.

*Researchers should adopt a longterm time perspective (e.g, of 10 years or more) to understand policy processes and change.* Policy process research is largely the study of public policy over time. The ACF recommends that researchers examine their phenomenon as a point in the ongoing development of the policy subsystem. Part of the rationale for taking a long-term perspective is to allow for ample time to evaluate the outcomes of any policy decision, to assess political reactions, and to study learning within and between coalitions.

### *Scope*

A framework should provide a scope of inquiry for guiding scholars toward a shared research agenda. The traditional foci of the ACF are descriptions and explanations of advocacy coalitions, learning within and among coalition allies and opponents, and policy change. These emphases should be viewed as general categories for both research inquiry and theory development. Certainly other areas of research are permitted and have been conducted (e.g. Montpetit 2011; Shanahan *et al.* 2011).

## General conceptual categories and relations

A framework provides a common vocabulary including the major conceptual categories and general relations among them. Figure 10.1 shows the ACF flow diagram (adapted from Sabatier and Weible 2007) featuring a policy subsystem with coalitions, their resources and beliefs, and the policy outputs and outcomes. Policy subsystems are embedded in a broader political system with relatively stable parameters and external events, where the latter is more prone to change than the former.

For researchers wanting to apply the ACF, it is important to consider the following basic concepts: (1) public policy topic that defines the subsystem; (2) actors who are involved in subsystem affairs; (3) institutions (e.g. rules) that structure overall subsystem interactions and the behaviors within particular venues; (4) relative stable parameters and external events; (5) interdependencies with other subsystems; and, finally, (6) time to permit observations of coalition behavior, learning, and policy change.

The next step is to articulate the theoretical emphases within the ACF. Theories serve different functions than frameworks in a research program. Theories narrow the scope of inquiry, link concepts usually in the form of expectations, propositions, or observable implications, and establish rationales (causal mechanisms) that explain how concepts interrelate. There are three major theoretical emphases of the ACF.

## First theoretical emphasis: advocacy coalitions

The first area of theoretical emphasis focuses on advocacy coalitions. Advocacy coalitions are defined as groups of actors sharing policy core beliefs and coordinating their behavior in a non-trivial manner. Advocacy coalitions emerge and persist because actors vary in their belief systems

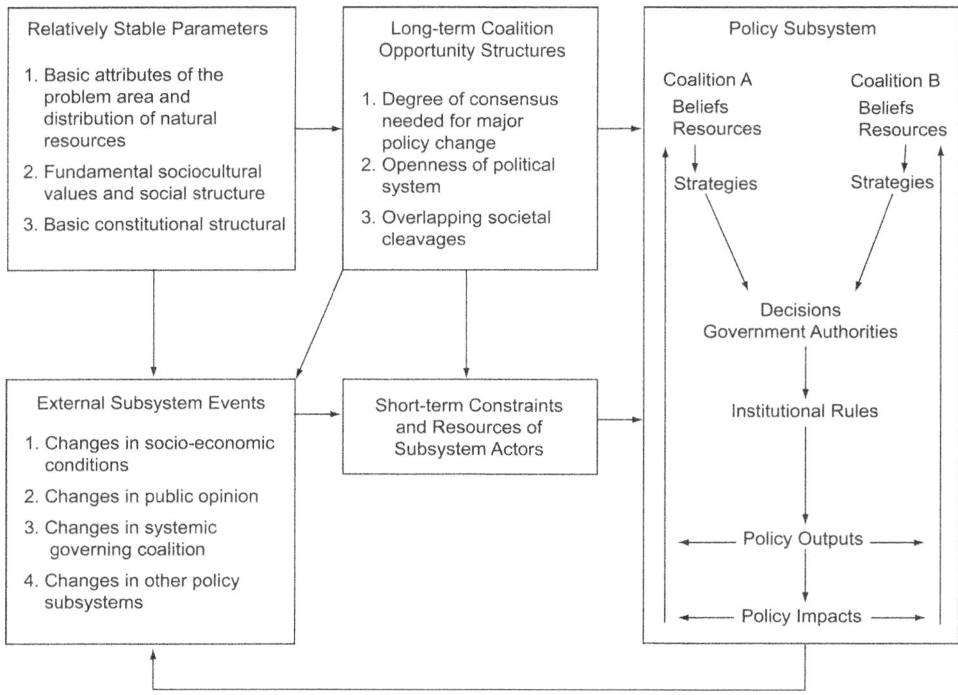


*Figure 10.1* Flow diagram of the advocacy coalition framework
Source: Adapted from Sabatier and Weible (2007)

(e.g. normative values regarding a particular policy topic) and seek to form alliances to translate their beliefs into actual policies before actors with different belief systems can do the same.

The ACF offers three reasons that permit subsystem actors to overcome threats to collective action in mobilizing coalition activity (Zafonte and Sabatier 1998; Sabatier and Weible 2007: 197). First, similar beliefs among coalition allies reduce transaction costs of coordination. Second, the level of coordination varies with some actors engaging in weak coordination (modifying their behavior to achieve shared goals or information exchange) and others in strong coordination (jointly developing and executing action plans) (Fenger and Klok 2001). Third, in high conflict situations, the "devil shift" occurs when actors exacerbate the power and maliciousness of opponents. When under the devil shift, coalition members will overestimate the threats from shared opponents and the imposed costs of inaction.

Empirical research across subsystems and political systems have confirmed that policy subsystems are regularly composed of one to five advocacy coalitions fighting over resources, access to venues, and influence on the formation of public policy (Weible *et al.* 2009). Occasionally, these coalitions interact competitively showing intervals, sometimes spanning decades, of one-upmanship. In other situations a single, "dominant" coalition will largely control a subsystem for extended periods of time over a largely nonexistent, inactive, or disorganized opposition. Key descriptive questions regarding coalition formation and development include:

- What is the structure of the networks and belief systems of advocacy coalition members?
- How stable is coalition membership over time?
- What is the role of different organizations within coalitions?

- How much consensus is there among coalition members?
- What are the patterns of coordination among subsystem actors?
- What strategies and resources do coalitions use to achieve their policy goals?

Within the scope of the emphasis on coalitions are also a set of explanatory questions addressing the formation of coalitions and the interaction and behavior of coalition members:

- Why do coalitions form?
- How do coalition members overcome threats to collective action?
- Why do coalition allies negotiate with opponents?

These questions are usually pursued in the form of testing and developing hypotheses. The most important hypotheses aiming at the composition and development of advocacy coalition include:

| | |
|---|---|
| Hyphothesis 1 | On major controversies within a policy subsystem when policy core beliefs are in dispute, the lineup of allies and opponents tends to be rather stable over periods of a decade or so. |
| Hypothesis 2 | Actors within an advocacy coalition will show substantial consensus on issues pertaining to the policy core beliefs, although less so on secondary aspects. |
| Hypothesis 3 | An actor (or coalition) will give up secondary aspects of his or her (its) belief system before acknowledging weaknesses in the policy core beliefs. |
| Hypothesis 4 | Within a coalition, administrative agencies will usually advocate more moderate positions than their interest group allies. |
| Hypothesis 5 | Elites of purposive groups are more constrained in their expression of beliefs and policy positions than elites from material groups. |

*(Sabatier and Weible 2007: 220)*

Hypotheses 1–5 specify some of the fundamental components of the ACF, including the hierarchy and stability of belief systems and the distinction between different types of organizations. Important contributions in the study of coordination networks and belief stability and change within coalitions can be found in Jenkins-Smith *et al.* (1991), Zafonte and Sabatier (1998), Weible and Sabatier (2005), Weible (2005), Ingold (2011), Henry *et al.* (2010), Henry (2011), Matti and Sandström (2011), and Pierce (2011). Previous empirical research provides mixed results regarding these hypotheses by showing patterns of both stability and defection of coalition members over time (Jenkins-Smith and St. Clair 1993; Jenkins-Smith *et al.* 1991; Sabatier and Brasher 1993; Zafonte and Sabatier 2004; Andersson 1999; Munro 1993).

While coalition resources have been a regular feature within the ACF since its inception (Sabatier and Jenkins-Smith, 1993: 29), Sabatier and Weible (2007: 201-4) and Weible (2007) placed more emphasis on the area by offering a typology of coalition resources: (1) formal legal authority to make policy decisions; (2) public opinion; (3) information; (4) mobilizable troops; (5) financial resources; and (6) skillful leadership. The access and use of these resources is theoretically argued to be important for forming and maintaining coalitions and for policy change. However, the empirical investigation of coalition resources has only recently been examined by scholars (Nohrstedt 2011; Ingold 2011; Albright, 2011).

The formation and stability of advocacy coalitions over time and their political behavior is conditioned by subsystem institutions and events outside the control of subsystem actors. The most important institutional factors that constrain subsystem actors are first, the openness of the political system and second, norms of consensus, which affect the level of inclusiveness of coalitions, exchange of information across coalition boundaries, and access to policy venues (Sabatier and Weible 2007). Institutions shape the level of coordination within a coalition, primarily by setting legal impediments that constrain formation of formal alliances paving the way for weaker forms of coordination as a viable political strategy (Zafonte and Sabatier 1998; Fenger and Klok 2001; Nohrstedt 2010). Events are likely to affect coalition behavior, particularly by providing opportunities for exploitation of new resources (including mobilization of new coalition members) and strategy in terms of venue exploitation.

## Second theoretical emphasis: policy-oriented learning

Learning has been a central focus of the ACF since its inception (Sabatier 1988). Policy-oriented learning is defined as "enduring alterations of thought or behavioral intentions that result from experience and which are concerned with the attainment or revision of the precepts of the belief system of individuals or of collectives" (Sabatier and Jenkins-Smith 1993: 42–56). To study policy-oriented learning is to study changes in belief system components of coalition members over time. Policy-oriented learning may entail better understanding of political goals, the causal relationship among key factors in the subsystem, and effective strategic behaviors, especially as used in analytic debates.

Important descriptive questions that guide inquiry into learning are the following:

- What belief system components are changing through learning?
- To what extent is one coalition learning more than another coalition?

Explanatory questions deal with issues of when, why, and how actors learn within and between coalitions and include:

- What contexts and events foster learning by coalition members?
- How does learning diffuse among allies within a coalition?
- What contexts and events foster learning by brokers?
- To what extent, if at all, does a broker facilitate learning between coalitions?
- Why does learning occur, if at all, between some members of opposing coalitions and not others?

On the whole, the intent of the ACF's focus on policy-oriented learning is to understand and explain what constitutes learning and why learning occurs within coalitions and between coalitions. Four general factors are important for explaining policy-oriented learning. The first involves the attributes of professional forums (see Jenkins-Smith 1990). Professional forums are venues of discussion involving subsystem actors. Forums are structured by different sets of institutional arrangements. Some forums are structured by open participation rules (open forum) and others by closed participation rules (closed forum). Professional forums are based on common analytical training and norms and are postulated to increase the likelihood for learning between coalitions (ibid.).

The second variable conditioning learning is the level of conflict between coalitions (Jenkins-Smith 1990; Weible 2008). The expectation is that there is an inverted quadratic relationship between conflict and cross-coalition learning. On one extreme at low levels of conflict, there is little cross-coalition learning as the opposing coalitions place their attention on other, more pressing issues. On the other extreme at high levels of conflict, there is also little cross-coalition learning as opposing coalitions are motivated to defend their positions and refute claims by their opponents. The conditions most conducive for cross-coalition learning would then be intermediate levels of conflict where there is enough of a threat to attract the attention of rivals but not too much of a threat to entrench opponents in rigid policy positions.

The third variable is attributes of the stimuli or data prompting learning. The stimuli can come from many different sources including scientific and technical information, actors, and events. One important attribute of stimuli relates to the level of analytical tractability of the phenomenon (Jenkins-Smith 1990: 97–9). Subsystems with highly intractable issues are marked by uncertainty and high levels of disagreement about the scientific and technical aspects of the issue (e.g. about the quality of the data or theories used). In general, highly intractable issues are expected to be associated with lower levels of cross-coalition learning.

The fourth variable that conditions learning involves attributes of individuals, including belief systems, resources, and network contacts. Are actors with extreme beliefs less likely to learn from their opponents than actors with moderate beliefs? Are some actors more or less supported by their analytical training in learning than others? Are actors with network contacts—either within their coalitions or with opposing coalitions—more likely to learn?

Central to the arguments about cross-coalition learning is a certain type of individual: the policy brokers. Sabatier and Jenkins-Smith (1993: 27) define brokers as "a category of actors … whose dominant concerns are keeping with the level of political conflict within acceptable limits and reaching some 'reasonable' solution to the problem." Sabatier and Jenkins-Smith argue that identifying brokers is an empirical question and is not dependent upon organizational affiliation. These broker may learn, possibly prior to the coalitions, and then facilitate cross-coalition learning later in the process (Sabatier and Jenkins-Smith 1993: 218–19).

Given the research questions and categories above, the theoretical emphasis on policy-oriented learning within the ACF is built into five hypotheses:

| | |
|---|---|
| Hypothesis 1 | Policy-oriented learning across belief systems is most likely when there is an intermediate level of informed conflict between the two coalitions. This requires that: (a) each have the technical resources to engage in such a debate; and that (b) the conflict be between secondary aspects of one belief system and core elements of the other or, alternatively, between important secondary aspects of the two belief systems. |
| Hypothesis 2 | Policy-oriented learning across belief systems is most likely when there exists a forum which is: (a) prestigious enough to force professionals from different coalitions to participate; and (b) dominated by professional norms. |
| Hypothesis 3 | Problems for which accepted quantitative data and theory exist are more conducive to policy-oriented learning across belief systems than those in which data and theory are generally qualitative, quite subjective, or altogether lacking. |
| Hypothesis 4 | Problems involving natural systems are more conducive to policy-oriented learning across belief systems than those involving purely social or political systems because in the former many of the critical variables are not themselves active strategists and because controlled experimentation is more feasible. |
| Hypothesis 5 | Even when the accumulation of technical information does not change the views of the opposing coalition, it can have important impacts on policy – at least in the short run – by altering the views of policy brokers. |

A review of ACF applications in Weible *et al.* (2009) indicates that, of the five learning hypotheses, the first two have been tested the most and the last two the least. From this review, they found evidence suggesting that learning within coalitions reinforces beliefs and mixed results about the likelihood of cross-coalition learning. For example, Larsen *et al.* (2006) find that cross-coalition learning occurs at the secondary level of belief systems (as expected) but also at the policy-core level (not expected). Similar mixed results can be found with the measurement and findings involving professional forums. If there is any area within the ACF needing more attention at both the theoretical and operational levels, it is policy-oriented learning.

## Third theoretical emphasis: policy change

The third theoretical emphasis in the ACF involves policy change. The ACF assumes that policies are translations of beliefs and can be conceptualized and measured hierarchically like belief systems. Policy components that span, and are salient to, a policy subsystem represent the policy core aspects of the subsystem. Policy components that deal with only a part of a subsystem or technical components of a policy represent secondary aspects of the subsystem. A change in policy core aspects indicates a major change in the direction of the subsystem and is defined as "major policy change." A change in secondary aspects indicates a minor change in the subsystem and is defined as "minor policy change" (Sabatier and Jenkins-Smith 1999: 147–8).

The descriptive questions in the study of policy change include:

- To what extent does major and minor policy change occur within the subsystem over time?
- What is the content of minor and/or major policy change?

Explanatory questions on the topic of policy change are several:

- Why do some events and contexts lead to minor and major policy change?
- What are the mechanisms linking internal and external events to minor and major policy change?
- How do negotiated agreements lead to policy change?
- When does policy-oriented learning lead to policy change?

As reflected in these questions, the ACF specifies four pathways to policy change (Sabatier and Weible 2007). The first two paths involve events either external or internal to the policy subsystem. External events occur outside the territorial boundaries of the subsystem and/or the topical policy boundaries of the subsystem and are, hence, largely outside the control of subsystem actors. Internal events occur inside the territorial and/or the topical area of the policy subsystem and are more likely affected by subsystem actors. The two types of events differ in their effect on coalition behavior and policy change. Most importantly, attribution of blame or success is higher after internal subsystem events are compared to after external subsystem events (see Nohrstedt and Weible 2010).

Policy-oriented learning is the third path and is said to lead to policy change through altering the beliefs of coalition members. Policies may change after a dominant coalition learns or after learning occurs between adversarial coalitions.

The fourth path is said to occur through negotiated agreements. Sabatier and Weible (2007: 205–6) describe nine prescriptions fostering negotiation between coalitions and then policy change. These nine prescriptions include: a hurting stalemate, broad representation, leadership, consensus, funding, commitment by actors, importance of empirical issues, trust, and lack of alternative venues. From this list, the most important for instigating negotiations between coalitions is a hurting stalemate. A hurting stalemate occurs when both coalitions view the status quo as unacceptable and do not have access to alternative venues for achieving their objectives.

The original version of the ACF offered two hypotheses involving major policy change:

Hypothesis 1 Significant perturbations external to the subsystem are a *necessary, but not sufficient,* cause of change in the *policy core* attributes of a governmental program.

Hypothesis 2 The policy core attributes of a governmental program in a specific jurisdiction will not be significantly revised as long as the subsystem advocacy coalition that instituted the program remains in power within that jurisdiction—except when the change is imposed by a hierarchically superior jurisdiction.

These two hypotheses for policy change have existed since the original version (Sabatier 1987, 1988). After the introduction of the other paths to policy change in 2007, new hypotheses were not added to encompass this expansion in logic. To better reflect the theoretical arguments c. 2007, a revised Hypothesis 1 would read as follows:

Hypothesis 1 Significant perturbations external to the subsystem, a significant perturbation internal to the subsystem, policy-oriented learning, negotiated agreement, or some combination thereof are *necessary, but not sufficient,* cause of change in the policy core attributes of a governmental program.

The underlying logic of the ACF suggests that none of the four paths are necessary and sufficient to produce policy change. Thus, one underdeveloped area within the ACF is the explanation that traces any path or combination of paths from its occurrence to policy change or stasis. This research should center on one or more exploitive coalitions that seek to capitalize on the opportunity afforded by one of the paths. But how a coalition will exploit an opportunity is largely unknown from a theoretical perspective, with notable explorations into the topic taken by Smith (2000), Ameringer (2002), Albright (2011), Ingold (2011), and Nohrstedt (2005, 2008, 2010, 2011). Developing knowledge in understanding the links from one or more of the four paths to policy change will most likely involve the analysis of how resources are redistributed between coalitions within the subsystem. It is likely, for example, that external events or internal events or even learning might alter the distribution of resources or how those resources are used leading to a more empowered coalition. Another theoretical area open for inquiry is the interdependencies of the four paths or multiple occurrences within the same path. For example, when do multiple external or internal events lead to learning and possibly negotiated agreements among adversarial coalitions? Similarly, when do a number of events occurring over time accumulate into sufficient momentum for a coalition to capitalize to produce major policy change (Smith 2000)? Finally, the role and behavior of dominant coalition actors in processes leading to policy change must be clarified (Nohrstedt 2010: 23). Under what conditions do dominant coalition members promote stability and defend the status quo and when do they seek change? What approaches to policy change (reformist or conservative) do dominant coalitions take following external and internal events and why? By definition, dominant coalition members control key political resources—primarily formal legal authority—and thereby policy programs (Nohrstedt 2011). Therefore, understanding the motivations of dominant coalition actors is an important avenue for future research.

## Conclusions

The ACF has continued for a quarter of a century and has made progress in understanding and explaining policy processes across the globe. The theoretical emphasis in the ACF reflects the specialization among people applying the framework as well as natural partitions of the hypotheses. Clearly, the hypotheses are overlapping. Whereas a theoretical emphasis on the structure and stability of networks and beliefs might be the dependent variable for one study about coalitions, changes in coalition structure and stability might be the independent variable for another study about policy change (Weible *et al.* 2011). Researchers should not view the theoretical emphases as sharply distinct but rather as signifying helpful partitions that permit specialized inquiry into questions about coalitions, learning, and policy change.

Among the next steps in applying the ACF is to continue to develop the theoretical descriptions and explanations within each of these areas of emphases as well as to develop other unexplored areas within the framework. It is quite possible, for example, that there is another theoretical emphasis centered on the role of scientific and technical information and scientists in policy subsystems (Jenkins-Smith 1990; Weible 2008; Montpetit 2011). Policy narratives are another area that offers opportunities for theoretical growth based in part on the ACF (Shanahan *et al.* 2011). Scholars can also develop better theoretical understanding about how specific concepts or categories of concepts interrelate within the framework; for example, the role of political opportunity structures (Sabatier 1998; Kübler 2001). Most importantly, the ACF is increasingly serving as a framework for guiding researchers from around the world in conducting comparative public policy analysis. As such, what is needed is a clearer articulation of how subsystems operate in different political systems and political cultures. One likely approach for international comparisons is, first, to focus on political system differences (e.g. the continuum from corporatism to pluralism) and, second, to compare and contrast subsystem institutions (e.g. subsystem specific rules and norms) and their effects on coalition formation, policy learning and change.

Given the continued and growing momentum of the ACF research program, this effort must ask the question: to what end? The immediate objective of the ACF is a better understanding and explanation of policy processes. Such knowledge serves academia in research and teaching. Another tradition in public policy is the service to society outside the networks of academics. In this context, extant approaches for this aspiration can be found in various forms of engaged scholarship (Van de Ven 2008), advocacy, and direct service. For scholars applying the ACF and seeking practical benefits, one question should be how the framework can be used for theoretically-guided research toward academic ends and as a tool in providing advice to subsystem actors toward better societal outcomes.

## Note

1 See Sabatier and Jenkins-Smith (1993) for a thorough description of the framework's underpinnings. Additionally, readers interested in gaining a deeper understanding of the ACF are encouraged to read Sabatier (1987, 1988, 1998), Jenkins-Smith (1990), Sabatier and Jenkins-Smith (1999), Sabatier and Weible (2007), Weible *et al.* (2009), and Weible *et al.* (2011).

## Bibliography


Ajzen, Icek and Martin Fishbein. 1980. *Understanding Attitudes and Predicting Social Behavior*. Englewood Cliffs, NJ: Prentice Hall.

Albright, Elizabeth A. 2011. 'Policy change and learning in response to extreme flood events in Hungary: An advocacy coalition approach', *Policy Studies Journal* 39(3): 484–511.

Ameringer, Carl F. 2002. 'Federal antitrust policy and physician discontent: Defining moments in the struggle for congressional relief', *Journal of Health Politics, Policy and Law* 27(4): 543–74.

Andersson, Magnus. 1999. *Change and Continuity in Poland's Environmental Policy*. Dordrecht: Kluwer.

Dawson, Richard and James Robinson. 1963. 'Interplay competition, economic variables, and welfare policies in the American states', *Journal of Politics* 25 (May): 265–89.

Easton, David. 1965. *A Framework for Political Analysis*. Chicago: University of Chicago Press.
Fenger, Menno and Pieter-Jan Klok. 2001. 'Interdependency, beliefs, and coalition behavior: A contribution to the advocacy coalition framework', *Policy Sciences* 34: 157–70.
Freeman, J. Leiper. 1955. *The Political Process*. New York: Random House.
Griffith, Ernest. 1939. *The Impasse of Democracy*. New York: Harrison Hilton Books.
Heclo, Hugh. 1974. *Social Policy in Britain and Sweden*. New Haven, CT: Yale University Press.
—— 1978. 'Issue networks and the executive establishment', in Anthony King (ed.) *The New American Political System*. Washington, DC: AEI.
Henry, Adam. 2011. 'Power, ideology, and policy network cohesion in regional planning', *Policy Studies Journal* 39(3): 361–83.
——, Mark Lubell and Michael McCoy. 2010. 'Belief systems and social capital as drivers of policy network structure: The case of California regional planning', *Journal of Public Administration Research and Theory* 21(3); 419–44.
Herron, Kerry G. and Hank C. Jenkins-Smith. 2006. *Critical Masses and Critical Choices: Evolving Public Opinion on Nuclear Weapons, Terrorism, and Security*. Pittsburgh, PA: University of Pittsburgh Press.
Hirschi, Christian and Thomas Widmer. 2010. 'Policy change and policy stasis: Comparing Swiss foreign policy toward South Africa (1968–94) and Iraq (1990–91)', *Policy Studies Journal* 38(3): 537–63.
Hjern, Benny and David Porter. 1981. 'Implementation structures: A new unit of administrative analysis', *Organizational Studies* 2: 211–27.
Hurwitz, Jon and Mark Peffley. 1987. 'How are foreign policy attitudes structured? A hierarchical model', *American Political Science Review* 81: 1099–120.
Ingold, Karin. 2011. 'Network structures within policy processes: Coalitions, power and brokerage in Swiss climate policy', *Policy Studies Journal* 39(3): 434–59.
Jenkins-Smith, Hank. 1990. *Democratic Politics and Policy Analysis*. Pacific Grove, CA: Brooks/Cole.
——and Gilbert St. Clair. 1993. 'The politics of offshore energy: Empirically testing the advocacy coalition framework', in Paul Sabatier and Hank Jenkins-Smith (eds) *Policy Change and Learning*. Boulder, CO: Westview Press, 149–75.
——, Gilbert St. Clair and Brian Woods. 1991. 'Explaining change in policy subsystems: Analysis of coalition stability and defection over time', *American Journal of Political Science* 35 (November): 851–72.
Kübler, Daniel. 2001. 'Understanding policy change with the advocacy coalition framework: An application to Swiss drug policy', *Journal of European Public Policy* 8(4): 623–41.
Larsen, Jakob Bjerg, Karsten Vrangbaek and Janine M. Traulsen. 2006. 'Advocacy coalitions and pharmacy policy in Denmark', *Social Science and Medicine* 63(1): 212–24.
Laudan, Larry. 1977. *Progress and Its Problems: Towards a Theory of Scientific Growth*. Berkeley, CA: University of California Press.
Lerner, Daniel and Harold D. Lasswell (eds). 1951. *The Policy Sciences*. Stanford, CA: Stanford University Press.
Lindblom, Charles E. 1959. 'The science of muddling through', *Public Administrative Review* 59: 78–88.
Lord, Charles, Lee Ross and Mark Lepper. 1979. 'Biased assimilation and attitude polarization: The effects of prior theories on subsequently considered evidence', *Journal of Personality and Social Psychology* 37: 2098–109.
Matti, Simon and Annica Sandström. 2011. 'The rationale determining advocacy coalitions: Examining coordination networks and corresponding beliefs', *Policy Studies Journal* 39(3): 385–410.
Mazmanian, Daniel and Paul Sabatier. 1981. *Implementation and Public Policy*. Lanham, MD: University Press of America.
Mazur, Allan. 1981. *The Dynamics of Technical Controversy*. Washington DC: Communications Press.
Montpetit, Eric. 2011. 'Scientific credibility, disagreement, and error costs in 17 biotechnology policy subsystems', *Policy Studies Journal* 39(3): 513–33.
Munro, John. 1993. 'California water politics: Explaining change in a cognitively polarized subsystem', in Paul Sabatier and Hank Jenkins-Smith (eds) *Policy Change and Learning*. Boulder, CO: Westview Press, 105–28.
Munro, Geoffrey D. and Peter H. Ditto. 1997. 'Biased assimilation, attitude polarization, and affect in reactions to stereotype-relevant scientific information', *Personality and Social Psychology Bulletin* 23(6): 636–53.
——, Peter H. Ditto, Lisa K. Lockhart, Angela Fagerlin, Mitchell Gready and Elizabeth Peterson. 2002. 'Biased assimilation of sociopolitical arguments: Evaluating the 1996 US Presidential debate', *Basic and Applied Social Psychology* 24(1): 15–26.

Nohrstedt, Daniel. 2005. 'External shocks and policy change: Three Mile Island and Swedish nuclear energy policy', *Journal of European Public Policy* 12(6): 1041–59.

—— 2008. 'The politics of crisis policymaking: Chernobyl and Swedish nuclear energy policy', *Policy Studies Journal* 36(2): 257–78.

—— 2010. 'Do advocacy coalitions matter? Crisis and change in Swedish nuclear energy policy', *Journal of Public Administration Research and Theory* 20: 309–33.

—— 2011. 'Shifting resources and venues producing policy change in contested subsystems: A case study of Swedish signals intelligence policy', *Policy Studies Journal* 39(3): 461–84.

——and Christopher M. Weible. 2010. 'The logic of policy change after crisis: Proximity and subsystem interaction', *Risks, Hazards, and Crisis in Public Policy* 1(2): 1–32.

Ostrom, Elinor. 2005. *Understanding Institutional Diversity*. Princeton, NJ: Princeton University Press.

Peffley, Mark and Jon Hurwitz. 1985. 'A hierarchical model of attitude constraint', *American Journal of Political Science* 29: 871–90.

Pierce, Jonathan J. 2011. 'Coalition stability and belief change: Advocacy coalitions in US foreign policy and the creation of Israel, 1922–44', *Policy Studies Journal* 411–34.

Pressman, Jeffrey and Aaron Wildavsky. 1973. *Implementation*. Berkeley, CA: University of California Press.

Putnam, Robert. 1976. *The Comparative Study of Political Elites*. Englewood Cliffs, NJ: Prentice Hall.

Quattrone, George A. and Amos Tversky. 1988. 'Contrasting rational and psychological analysis of political choice', *American Political Science Review* 82: 719–36.

Ranney, Austin. 1968. *Political Science and Public Policy*. New York: Markham.

Sabatier, Paul, A. 1987. 'Knowledge, policy-oriented learning, and policy change: An advocacy coalition framework', *Knowledge: Creation, Diffusion, Utilization* 8(4): 649–92.

—— 1988. 'An advocacy coalition model of policy change and the role of policy-oriented learning therein', *Policy Sciences* 21 (autumn): 129–68.

—— 1991. 'Toward better theories of the policy process', *PS: Political Science and Politics* 24(2): 147–56.

—— 1998. 'The advocacy coalition framework: revisions and relevance for Europe', *Journal of European Public Policy* 5 (March): 98–130.

—— 1999. 'The need for better theories', in *Theories of the Policy Process*. Boulder, CO: Westview Press, 3–17.

—— 2007. *Theories of the Policy Process*. Boulder, CO: Westview Press.

——and Anne M. Brasher. 1993. 'From vague consensus to clearly differentiated coalitions: environmental policy at Lake Tahoe, 1964–1985', in Paul Sabatier and Hank Jenkins-Smith (eds) *Policy Change and Learning*. Boulder, CO: Westview Press, 177–208.

——and Hank C. Jenkins-Smith. 1993. *Policy Change and Learning: An Advocacy Coalition Approach*. Boulder, CO: Westview Press.

——and Hank Jenkins-Smith. 1999. 'The advocacy coalition framework: An assessment', in Paul Sabatier (ed.) *Theories of the Policy Process*. Boulder, CO: Westview Press, 117–68.

——and Christopher M. Weible. 2007. 'The advocacy coalition framework: Innovations and clarifications', in Paul Sabatier (ed.)*Theories of the Policy Process*, 2nd edn. Boulder, CO: Westview Press, 189–222.

——and Matthew Zafonte. 2001. 'Policy knowledge, advocacy organizations', in Neil J. Smelser and Paul B. Baltes (eds) *International Encyclopedia of the Social and Behavioral Sciences* 17. Oxford: Pergamon Press, 11563–68.

——, Susan Hunter and Susan McLaughlin. 1987. 'The devil shift: Perceptions and misperceptions of opponents', *Western Political Quarterly* 40: 51–73.

Schlager, Edella. 1995. 'Policy making and collective action: Defining coalitions within the advocacy coalition framework', *Policy Sciences* 28: 243–70.

Shanahan, Elizabeth, Michael D. Jones and Mark K. McBeth. 2011. 'Policy narratives and policy processes', *Policy Studies Journal* 39(3): 535–61.

Simon, Herbert A. 1957. *Models of Man: Social and Rational*. New York: John Wiley.

—— 1985. 'Human nature in politics: The dialogue of psychology with political science', *American Political Science Review* 79 (June): 293–304.

Smith, Adrian. 2000. 'Policy networks and advocacy coalitions: Explaining policy change and stability in UK industrial pollution policy?' *Environment and Planning C: Government and Policy* 18: 95–114.

Van de Ven, Andrew H. 2008. *Engaged Scholarship: A Guide for Organizational and Social Research*. Oxford: Oxford University Press.

Walker, Jack, L. 1969. 'The diffusion and innovation among the American states', *The American Political Science Review* 63(3): 880–99.

Weible, C.M. 2005. 'Beliefs and perceived influence in a natural resource conflict: an advocacy coalition approach to policy networks', *Political Research Quarterly* 58(3): 461–75.

—— 2007. 'An advocacy coalition framework approach to stakeholder analysis: understanding the political context of California marine protected area policy', *Journal of Public Administration Research and Theory* 17: 95–117.

—— 2008. 'Expert-based information and policy subsystems: A Review and synthesis', *Policy Studies Journal* 36(4): 615–35.

——and Paul A. Sabatier. 2005. 'Comparing policy networks: Marine protected areas in California', *Policy Studies Journal* 33(2): 181–204.

——, Paul A. Sabatier and Kelly McQueen. 2009. 'Themes and variations: Taking stock of the advocacy coalition framework', *Policy Studies Journal* 37(1): 121–40.

——, Paul A. Sabatier, Hank C. Jenkins-Smith, Daniel Nohrstedt and Adam Douglas Henry. 2011. 'A quarter century of the advocacy coalition framework: An introduction to the special issue', *Policy Studies Journal* 39(3): 349–60.

Weiss, Carol. 1977. 'Research for policy's sake: The enlightenment function of social research', *Policy Analysis* 3 (autumn): 531–45.

Zafonte, Matthew and Paul A. Sabatier. 1998. 'Shared beliefs and imposed interdependencies as determinants of ally networks in overlapping subsystems', *Journal of Theoretical Politics* 10 (4): 473–505.

——and Paul A. Sabatier. 2004. 'Short-term versus long-term coalitions in the policy process: Automotive pollution control, 1963–89', *The Policy Studies Journal* 32(1): 75–107.

# 11

# The punctuated equilibrium theory of agenda-setting and policy change

*Graeme Boushey*

## Introduction

On March 23, 2010, President Barack Obama signed into law the Patient Protection and Affordable Care Act (PPACA), marking a major shift in the organization and structure of health care in the United States. The statute outlined a series of dramatic reforms to the provision, funding and regulation of public and private health insurance, controversially requiring that all Americans carry qualifying health coverage, directing state governments to regulate new health insurance exchanges, expanding the coverage of poor and uninsured children, and designating a comparative effectiveness research institute to track the effectiveness of preventative and clinical public health (Kaiser Family Foundation 2010).[1] Although there is currently considerable uncertainty regarding the future implementation of the health care reforms, the passage of the act is nonetheless remarkable in the size and scope of policy change. The PPACA has triggered significant policy-making attention across the legal, executive, and legislative branches of both the state and federal governments. If the statute survives the current legal challenges, the PPACA will radically alter the US health care system.

The sweeping policy reform highlights a familiar puzzle to students of the punctuated equilibrium theory (PET) in public policy-making. Public policy change is typically characterized by tremendous stability, as broad policy change usually faces considerable political and institutional barriers. Yet policy change can occur through sweeping positive feedback cycles as radical new innovations are adopted in a relatively short time frame.[2] Most changes in US health policy have occurred through incremental adjustment, as Congress approved modest reforms to national and state programs. However, at key moments national policy-making attention has focused squarely on the problem of underinsurance, leading to sweeping policy reforms such as the Medicare and Medicaid programs, the expansion of the Medicare prescription drug benefit, and most recently the passage of the PPACA. Viewed over time, public policy-making is characterized by punctuated dynamics.

As a policy process model, punctuated equilibrium theory documents how shifts in macro political attention result in both negative and positive feedback cycles in policy-making. *Negative feedback cycles* emerge as a result of the delegation of routine policy-making to policy subgovernments, as a core group of institutional actors make marginal adjustments to policy in response to a dominant policy image. *Positive feedback cycles* result when mass political attention focuses system-wide attention on a new dimension of a policy problem. When this occurs, policy change occurs rapidly as new political actors and new jurisdictions become involved in policy-making.

These distinct patterns of *incremental* and *non-incremental* policy change result from the disproportionate allocation of issue attention in public policy-making (Baumgartner and Jones 2009; Jones and Baumgartner 2005). Governments have limited agenda space but face thousands of competing policy problems annually (Baumgartner and Jones 2009; Jones and Baumgartner 2005). Because mass political attention is rarely focused on a single issue, policy-making is generally delegated to policy subgovernments, where actors within political institutions work to manage an overwhelming supply of information demanding political action. When system-wide political attention is focused on a single issue, the pressures reinforcing equilibrium in a policy subsystem are ruptured, leading to broad political change.

To understand forces leading to both policy stability and rapid change in a single political system, punctuated equilibrium theory approaches the study of public policy longitudinally by exploring how focusing events, institutional venues, policy ideas and policy entrepreneurs interact to produce policy change. The allocation of government attention is unpredictable, yet PET identifies systematic processes that lead to the dynamic processes of policy change over time through the study of comparative issue dynamics across institutional and historical contexts.

This chapter provides an overview of the theory and methods of the punctuated equilibrium theory of public policy. The chapter begins with a review of the decision-making model underlying punctuated equilibrium theory, explaining how pressures facing individual and institutional decision-making precipitate punctuated dynamics in agenda setting. The chapter then focuses on PET as a policy process model, reviewing how focusing events, policy ideas, institutional venues and interest groups interact to produce both stability and sudden policy change over time. The chapter concludes with a review of recent methodological advances in comparative policy dynamics, highlighting major empirical and methodological findings as PET has evolved as a general model of policy-making across historical and institutional contexts. With these factors working together, the review points to a number of new opportunities for evaluating the causes of punctuated dynamics in public policy-making.

## Negative feedback cycles and policy incrementalism[3]

Models of political decision-making begin with an important observation about the demands of information processing in public policy-making. Political actors are constrained by a scarcity of time, resources and political attention. Because political decision-makers must address a multitude of different issues on a daily basis—negotiating budget appropriations, designing regulatory policy, sitting in hearings and attending to casework—decision-makers cannot dedicate the time and resources needed to engage in a comprehensive solution search for each and every policy problem (Lindblom 1959; Hayes 1992).

The challenges presented by the sheer volume of issues demanding political attention are compounded by the complexity of emerging public policy problems (Workman *et al.* 2009). Policy problems are multidimensional, and policy-makers are challenged by considerable uncertainty regarding the appropriate solutions and potential outcomes of new policy interventions. For example, policy-makers faced with growing concern over about air pollution must consider difficult trade-offs between protecting population health, protecting the environment, and providing for the continued competitiveness of industry. The development of appropriate regulations are further complicated when the costs and expected outcomes of regulatory intervention are unknown. Policy-makers face considerable challenges when problems are complex, solutions are costly, and outcomes are uncertain.

To compensate, policy-makers engage in incremental decision-making, limiting solution searchers to a small set of local alternatives and making small adjustments to existing policy regimes (Lindblom 1959; Wildavsky 1964). This implies a conservative approach to policy-making, as risk-averse policy-makers make gradual changes to existing policies through "successive limited comparison" rather than risking large-scale policy failure (Lindblom 1959; Robinson 2006). For example, when faced with the considerable uncertainty of the consequences of new air quality regulations, policymakers may prefer to make minor adjustments to the existing policy—such as adopting slightly more stringent energy efficiency standards for cars or manufacturers—rather than advocating for a large-scale change such as a cap and trade system for greenhouse gas emissions. This approach has the advantage of reducing the uncertainty regarding the cost and efficacy of policy change. In this regard, incremental decision-making can resemble path dependency theory, as policy and solutions become locked in over time (Robinson and Meier 2006).

## Institutions and negative feedback cycles

The tendency toward incremental decision-making is reinforced by policy-making institutions, which help decision-makers organize information, set agenda priorities, develop solutions, and choose among alternatives. In political institutions, policy-making is generally delegated to *policy subsystems,* specialized policy-making jurisdictions charged with the development of public policy within a specific issue area.

The delegation of policy-making to subgovernments helps to overcome the challenges presented by oversupply of information by facilitating *parallel processing* where different subgovernments "address multiple, diverse issues simultaneously" (Workman *et al.* 2009: 79). In the United States, policy-making in Congress is channeled through the committee system, a series of specialized subgovernments charged with policy development across specific issue areas. The committee system reduces the problem of information oversupply by committees acting as gatekeepers, selectively filtering information for the larger legislative body.

The organization of policy-making institutions reinforces the bias toward incremental policy-making by imposing strict decision costs on policy-making that pressure against sudden policy change (Workman *et al.* 2009). Deliberative bodies may have supermajority requirements to enact certain forms of legislation, or require multiple legislative bodies to approve policy prior to enactment. Broad policy change is therefore generally difficult to achieve, as it requires the coordination and cooperation of multiple veto players with distinct preferences across policy-making institutions (Tsebelis 2002). Actors face considerably less opposition at the subgovernment level, where policy-making occurs through marginal, consensual adjustment to prior policy regimes.

Negative feedback in public policy-making is maintained by the stability of participants engaged in policy subsystems. When policy subsystems are dominated by a specific interest in the policy process, policy-making is dictated by a *policy monopoly*, a narrow coalition of elected officials, bureaucrats and interest group representatives controlling the legislative agenda at the subgovernment level (Baumgartner and Jones 2009; True *et al.* 2007).[4] As beneficiaries from the status quo, these policy monopolies have little incentive to undertake radical reforms in policy-making. Instead, policy monopolies offset outside calls for reform and policy change by making minor or superficial adjustments to policy, allowing the subsystem to appear responsive without radically adjusting public policy.

For example, faced with the challenge of conserving natural resources and energy in the United States, the Senate Committee on Energy and Natural Resources has historically recommended increasing the fuel efficiency of automobiles and heavy trucks, and consistently working to reduce the nation's energy dependence by regulating the fuel consumption of passenger vehicles. By making minor adjustments to vehicle fuel efficiency, policy-makers incrementally move toward the overall goal of energy conservation while simultaneously reducing the uncertainty of new policy for industry, consumers and government. Such incremental adjustments prevail at a subsystem level where constraints on attention and information demand that policy-makers routinely focus on limited alternatives in developing new solutions.

Finally, negative feedback cycles dominate in policy subsystems because of the relative stability of the *policy image*—the collective understanding and ideas regarding the problems and issues at stake (Baumgartner and Jones 2009; Walgrave and Varone 2008). Although policy problems are complex and multidimensional, decision-makers operating within a policy monopoly tend to focus only on specific dimensions of a public policy problem. Within a policy monopoly there is little disagreement over the nature of the policy problem. Without change in the monopoly dynamic, policy solutions become routine over time, and policy though subsystem-level responses to well-defined policy problems become repetitive. For much of recent history, energy and natural resources have largely been understood as a problem of conservation and efficiency. Government has focused largely on regulating the individual consumption of oil through speed limits, fuel efficiency standards, and highway and infrastructure investment. These solutions all respond to a common and widely shared understanding of the challenges of energy conservation.

The tremendous policy stability that typically explains policy-making results from the constraints that individuals working within complex political institutions face as they address complex policy problems. Policy-makers rarely have the time, resources or incentive to engage in crafting radical new solutions to each and every policy problem. Even if an actor pushes for a radical new program, they usually face institutional barriers that reroute toward gradual and consensual policy adjustment.

## Disproportionate information processing and positive feedback cycles

Policy change generally occurs gradually, but at other times issues explode onto the policy agenda, leading to sweeping changes in public policy that cannot be explained neatly by conservative incremental policy-making theory. These periods of policy disequilibrium result when a focusing event directs system-wide attention onto a new salient dimension of a public policy issue, elevating it to the forefront of the institutional and mass political agendas (Baumgartner and Jones 2009; Jones and Baumgartner 2005; Kingdon 1984; Shattschneider 1975). When elevated issue attention expands the scope of conflict to new jurisdictions, the policy monopolies that sustained the prior equilibrium are destroyed as new participants introduce legislation responding to the shift in governments' understanding of the policy problem (Baumgartner and Jones 2009). Sudden periods of agenda instability and policy disequilibrium are the result of positive feedback cycles in public policy-making, as new pressures for policy change destabilize long-standing policy regimes (Jones and Baumgartner 2005).

In recent years, punctuated equilibrium theory has extended the theory of bounded rationality to model how individual and organizational choice can explain both incremental adjustment and sudden shifts in policy regimes. Punctuated policy dynamics are the result of disproportionate information processing in public policy processes (Jones 2001; Jones and Baumgartner 2004, 2005; Workman *et al.* 2009). Decision-making is limited less by the supply of available information and more by the scarcity of attention (Jones 1994: 87). The key insight is that patterns of policy change result from the selective allocation of attention in decision-making. Individuals pressed with the demands of making decisions across a multitude of issues reduce information costs through incremental decision-making; however, when a subset of issues receives substantial political attention, it leads to more extensive problem representation and solution search than is typical (Jones 2001). These attention shifts occur as individuals filter new information, focusing attention squarely on decisions that elevate a sense of urgency, fear or anxiety. While individuals may intend to make proportional, rational decisions that are appropriate for the problems they face, emotional cues often lead them to under-respond to some pressures, and over-respond to others. Neither individuals nor institutions respond to information and policy relevant signals equally (ibid.).

The bias toward incremental responses to routine problems contributes to disproportionate information processing in decision-making. Because most problems are addressed through incremental adjustment, people routinely fail to incorporate new policy-relevant information when making daily decisions. When attention is squarely focused on an emerging policy problem, individuals then over-respond to new information as a wide range of new policy relevant information is suddenly incorporated into choice (Jones and Baumgartner 2004). In this regard, the status quo bias of incrementalism begets large shifts in attention exactly because it reinforces a disjointed pattern of neglect and sudden response to information (Jones and Baumgartner 2005).

Individual preferences also shift suddenly in response to changes in the context of new policy-relevant information. Although policy problems are multidimensional, decision-makers tend to focus narrowly on a limited set of dimensions highlighted in the most immediate problem at hand. As research in framing effects has demonstrated, preferences for policy can shift radically depending on the specific contextual cues (Iyengar 1996; Jones 2001). Preferences may therefore shift dramatically when policy-makers react to information that highlights a new and previously overlooked component of a policy problem.

In focusing on the disproportionate allocation of individual attention, punctuated equilibrium theory demonstrates that incrementalism is not the only mechanism of preference formation and choice implied by bounded rationality. Shifts in individual attention can lead to disproportionate responses to new information. Rather than following a single path of incremental choice, individuals instead often shift attention and preferences suddenly.

## Positive feedback cycles and institutional choice

As with the pressures leading to negative feedback cycles, the processes leading to positive feedback result from the interaction of individuals and institutions in public policy-making. Although the organization of policy-making in the United States generally imposes a conservative pressure against rapid policy change, policy entrepreneurs and interest group activists across national and sub-national jurisdictions constantly pressure for new policy reform or innovation. When a new idea or initiative takes hold and becomes legitimized across political venues, sudden shifts in policy follow.

Punctuated equilibrium theory contends that the formalized process of agenda-setting and political decision-making in political institutions amplifies disproportionate information processing (Jones and Baumgartner 2004, 2005). Most policy issues are handled as routine developments and are delegated to policy subgovernments (Baumgartner and Jones 2009; True *et al.* 2006; Baumgartner and Jones 2002). However, at any given moment a small subset of issues receives system-wide political attention. When this occurs, widespread participation of actors across venues and the incorporation of new information can trigger rapid and extensive policy change (Baumgartner and Jones 2009; True *et al.* 2007; Jones and Baumgartner 2005).

Studies of punctuated dynamics begin by identifying the factors leading to the shift in macro-political attention preceding radical policy reforms. Elevated issue attention caused by a focusing event that galvanizes mass public and political attention can open a "window of opportunity," creating conditions for rapid and non-incremental policy change (Baumgartner and Jones 2009; Birkland 1997; Kingdon 1984). Exogenous shocks work to suddenly galvanize mass political attention on an issue area, revealing a critical policy problem that demands political intervention. The tsunami leading to the Fukushima nuclear reactor meltdown in 2011 focused international political attention of the safety of nuclear power, leading governments to suspend new projects or adopt more restrictive regulatory regimes for monitoring safety.

Exogenous shocks are not the only mechanism that can lead to shifts in public policy images over time. Baumgartner and Jones (2009) observe that changes in policy indicators, as well as changes in the tone of media coverage, can both redirect public and political perceptions of policy problems. Furthermore, policy entrepreneurs play a key role in influencing perceptions of a policy problem. Strategic issue definition and redefinition (Baumgartner *et al.* 2008; Baumgartner and Jones 1993; Jones and Baumgartner 2005) and policy targeting (Boushey 2010; Donovan 2001; Schneider and Ingram 1993) can draw public attention to new dimensions of a problem, leading to swings in public opinion and support for new policy ideas. It is not simply that focusing events elevate government attention, but perhaps more importantly that these events redirect mass political understandings of the underlying policy problem.

These pressures have a common impact on political decision-making, especially when a new policy idea expands the scope of conflict and brings new voices into a policy arena (Shattschneider 1975). As this occurs, the policy monopoly that had sustained policy equilibrium at the subgovernment level is destroyed. In its place, government generates new legislation, regulations, and institutions to respond to the emerging policy problem, as new stakeholders across political jurisdictions and venues are mobilized to engage in previously neglected policy arenas. Policy punctuations represent the output of these periods of instability, as government reorganizes to effectively respond to the new policy image.

Finally, although the allocation of political attention universally follows the rules of disproportionate information processing, different institutions impose decision costs that lead to *stick slip* dynamics in public policy-making, as pressures for policy change contend with institutional rules that impose friction or gridlock on the policy process (Baumgartner *et al.* 2009). Here, institutional decision rules shape long-term patterns of policy equilibrium. As pressure for change accumulates, more responsive institutions will see smaller but more frequent reversals in policy-making, updating policy more rapidly in response to shifting preferences. Institutions with higher decision costs will be generally resistant to large-scale policy change. In these intuitions, positive feedback cycles of sudden policy change will occur more rarely, but be larger in size and scope. This dynamic is illustrated in Jones and Baumgartner's (2005) comparison of the historical distributions of policy change across US policy-making institutions. Where institutional decision-costs are lower (for example executive orders), punctuated dynamics are less pronounced. Where institutional costs are highest (for example in budgeting) the distribution of policy change suggested rare but more extreme policy change.

These observations underpin what Jones and Baumgartner (2005) refer to as the *general punctuation hypothesis*, as cognitive and individual constraints interact to produce punctuated dynamics in political decision-making. Because cognitive limitations leading to punctuated dynamics are universal, punctuated dynamics will emerge across policy-making contexts, and policy-makers will respond disproportionately to information. However, punctuated dynamics are also contingent on the degrees of friction imposed by institutional rules, leading to "a greater likelihood of punctuations in some institutions of government than others" (ibid.: 20).

The dynamics of punctuated equilibrium have been documented across issue areas and institutional contexts. For example, researchers have documented punctuated dynamics across

US policy-making institutions (Baumgartner and Jones 2005; Jones *et al.* 2003) as well as state (Breunig and Koski 2009) and local government budgeting (Jordan 2003). The patterns of policy stasis and change have been documented in policy areas as distinct as gun control (True and Utter 2002), crime control (Schneider 2006), environmental regulation (Repetto 2006), tobacco control (Wood 2006), education finance (Robinson 2006) and international infectious disease policy (Shiffman *et al.* 2002). Perhaps more impressively, research in recent years has expanded beyond the study of American politics to evaluate the general punctuation hypotheses in other institutional contexts. Scholars have documented punctuated dynamics across Western democracies (Baumgartner *et al.* 2009; Jones *et al.* 2009; Baumgartner *et al.* 2008). This growing body of work suggests that that punctuated dynamics emerge from pressures of political decision-making that are generalizeable across eras and institutional contexts (Baumgartner and Jones 2009).[5]

## Policy entrepreneurs, venue shopping, issue framing and policy change

Punctuated equilibrium theory suggests that interest groups and policy entrepreneurs play a prominent role in developing and introducing new ideas in the political system. Punctuated dynamics are shaped by the mobilization of competing interest groups and activists in public policy-making. Organized interests that assume privileged positions in policy monopolies help to reinforce the status quo, providing expert testimony and support for maintaining a stable policy regime at the subsystem level. Conversely, the strategic choices of marginalized interest groups are pivotal for understanding how new ideas enter the political system.

The effect of the participation of interest groups is therefore critical for understanding how policy images evolve over time. While policy monopolies maintain policy stability, marginalized or outsider interest groups do not simply acquiesce to the bias of policy monopolies across subgovernments. Instead, these organizations work to shape policy change at all levels of government. This section briefly discusses how the strategies adopted by outsider or marginalized interests lead to periods of policy change. In so doing, it highlights one major mechanism leading to policy change across political systems. Most organized efforts fail to disrupt the status quo, but when an interest group succeeds, its activities can lead to sweeping changes across institutions.

The first major implication of punctuated equilibrium theory is that interest groups are not complacent when they are excluded from policy-making at the subgovernment level. Interest groups shut out of one policy venue often strategically look for agenda access elsewhere. Organized interest groups engage in *venue shopping*, strategically moving across jurisdictions to secure legislative change (Boushey 2010; Baumgartner and Jones 2009; Cashore and Howlett 2006; Pralle 2003). In federal systems, interest groups may pressure for reforms across municipal and state governments, adopt litigation strategies to secure change through the courts, or employ state and local ballot initiative campaigns to introduce legislation directly before the voters as part of the initiative system. The logic is that institutions and policy-making jurisdictions are not equally receptive to new appeals for policy reform. For example, Cashore and Howlett (2006) discovered differences in jurisdictional susceptibility to widespread policy reform in federal and state forestry policy, indicating that various institutions respond differently to nearly identical pressures for policy change.

More broadly, research in state-level policy innovation and diffusion has documented considerable variation in the responsiveness of state governments to calls for policy change. Researchers have developed a robust understanding of how differences in the ideology, resources and professionalism of state and provincial governments shape their responsiveness to new reform initiatives over time (Boushey 2010; Karch 2007; Berry and Berry 1999). Boushey (2010) observes that venue shopping in federalism can lead to punctuated patterns of policy diffusion across subnational governments in federalism. The ability of interest groups to secure policy change at select venues can result in gradual policy adoptions across jurisdictions as they succeed in pushing reforms through at state and municipal governments over time. However, in rare instances venue-shopping strategies can trigger positive feedback cycles as an issue becomes the focus of broader system-wide policy-making attention (ibid.).

Organized interests not only experiment with the selection of venues but also actively engage in the framing and reframing of legislative ideas in the hope of expanding public support for policy change (Baumgartner *et al.* 2008; Smith 2007). Activists seeking to shape public responsiveness to their policy programs experiment with framing legislation in response to changes in the political environment, looking to attribute new meaning or justification for their preferred policy proposals (Baumgartner and Jones 1993).

Interest groups adopt one of two strategies when attempting to frame a policy problem. One is simply to attach a new justification for an existing policy proposal. For example, interest groups justify policy reforms in the context of the major salient "issues of the day," such as pushing for tax reform legislation as a solution to a major financial crisis or advocating for a ban on factory farming in the wake of food safety concerns. Such framing and coupling strategies are employed to redirect public attention to a different dimension of a policy problem that is more favorable to the policy agenda of a given interest group.

The second form of strategic interest group framing happens with policy targeting. In this case, interest groups narrow or expand the conflict surrounding a proposal by narrowing or expanding the scope and application of the policy proposal. (Schattschneider 1975). Marijuana reform activists have pushed for the legalization of medical marijuana, rather than the immediate end of marijuana prohibition (Boushey 2010). Targeting policies in this manner does not simply offer new justification for the policy proposal; it alters the scope of the policy itself.

Of course, efforts to redefine or reframe a policy debate generally fail to generate broad support for a new policy reform. Even when a new way of describing a policy problem succeeds, opposing interest groups often succeed in diminishing the impact of an emerging frame with a counterargument. However, when issue framing or venue-shopping strategies successfully unite broad and distinct social interests around a cause, rapid policy change may follow. This points to an important feature of the broader policy-making processes leading to punctuated dynamics in public policy-making: although the formal organization of policy-making institutions works to slow pressures for sudden policy change, the multiple access points and proliferation of interest groups also encourages the proliferation of policy ideas.

The role that interest groups play in shifting national political attention through issue framing and venue-shopping strategies have been well-documented in case studies of interest group mobilization. For example, the passage of the Eighteenth Amendment prohibiting alcohol in the United States emerged from a century of political pressure, as prohibitionists pushed for local, state, and national alcohol reform, constantly shifting the justification for prohibition (Boushey 2010; Aaron and Musto 1981). The Tobacco Master Settlement agreement was secured through judicial venue shopping, as 46 states joined in a giant lawsuit against the tobacco industry to recover state Medicaid expenditures incurred covering smoking-related illness (Baumgartner and Jones 2009; Wood 2006). Finally, the longer-term decline in public support for the death penalty in practice occurred as the death penalty abolitionists succeeded in shifting the focus of the debate towards the very real possibility that governments were executing the innocent. The movement to stay the death penalty also followed a venue-shopping strategy, as activists have pressured for moratoriums on capital punishment in receptive states, legitimizing the policy reform gradually (Baumgartner *et al.* 2008).

Although these cases highlight strategies of groups operating within federalism, there is no reason to believe that this strategic choice is limited to this institutional context. Venue shopping can occur within single institutions, as actors petition distinct subgovernments to place an issue on the agenda. For example, activists concerned with the dangers of genetically modified foods may bypass the Department of Agriculture and instead petition the Food and Drug Administration to regulate new crops. The essential insight is that organized interests and policy entrepreneurs play a key role in developing and introducing ideas into the system. Policy entrepreneurs selectively direct issue attention toward new dimensions of a problem in the hopes of securing a change of policy over time. Furthermore, they labor to introduce these policies into the political system, probing for receptive venues and petitioning for widespread policy adoption. In these two ways, interest groups play a pivotal role in precipitating punctuated dynamics in public policy.

## Empirical approaches in punctuated equilibrium

The complex processes contributing to negative and positive feedback processes over time make it difficult to evaluate punctuated equilibrium theory. Positive feedback cycles result from stochastic processes, and it is nearly impossible to anticipate when or how exogenous shocks will galvanize macropolitical attention over time (Jones and Baumgartner 2005). Sudden shifts in systemic issue attention can be triggered by factors as distinct as an unexpected environmental crisis, a coordinated social movement, changes in media coverage regarding a new problem, or a long-term shift in policy indicators leading to heightened political concern about a new problem. These unpredictable punctuations are the result of complex interactions between available policy solutions, participants, and receptive venues at a critical moment. Studies of agenda-setting assert that shifts in policy-making occur when factors converge to open a window of opportunity for policy change, but these approaches have offered no universal method for understanding when such shifts in policy attention will occur.

Preliminary research in punctuated equilibrium theory focused on explaining how complex interactions precipitate negative and positive feedback cycles in public policy-making, drawing heavily on longitudinal case studies to illustrate how exogenous shocks, changes in the policy image, the receptivity of institutional venues, and the participation of interest groups interact over time to produce policy change within a specific case (Baumgartner and Jones 2009). These studies of comparative issue dynamics confirmed the patterns of attention allocation leading to widespread policy change (with the exception of Givel 2006).[6] These studies provided a robust understanding of the process leading to negative and positive feedback cycles across institutions and issue areas, and have further permitted researchers to isolate how shifts in the policy image (Baumgartner and Jones 2009; Baumgartner *et al.* 2009), the participation of interest groups and policy entrepreneurs (Boushey 2010), venue shopping (Pralle 2003) and the decision rules of distinct institutional venues (Baumgartner *et al.* 2009) contributed to punctuated dynamics in public policy-making.

To test the broader implications of punctuated equilibrium theory, researchers have shifted their focus to aggregate patterns of policy outputs across issues and institutions over time, exploring longitudinal changes in budgetary outlays, law-making, executive orders, public opinion, media attention and other agenda-setting processes. Over the last decade, researchers working to understand the evolution of issue attention in government have gathered impressive collections of data that captures government attention over time. In the United States, Bryan Jones, Frank Baumgartner, and John Wilkerson have organized the Policy Agendas Project, an invaluable resource regarding trends in the federal budget, congressional hearings, important problem public opinion data, media coverage, executive orders and other indicators of national policy-making attention from 1946 onward.[7] The success of this initial project inspired the Comparative Agendas

Project, a collaborative endeavor documenting parallel indicators of longitudinal policy attention across 14 Western democracies.[8] These resources have classified policy attention by major and subtopic codes, allowing researchers to evaluate both aggregate patterns of policy change while also tracking the rise and fall of specific issues and policy problems across governments over time.

Punctuated equilibrium theorists have relied on these resources to evaluate how cognitive constraints and institutional rules shape policy outputs over time. This research focused initially on the general punctuation hypothesis, exploring whether policy change over time could be best explained through incrementalism or disproportionate information processing. More recently, this research has branched out to model how institutions shape information processing.

Because of the overwhelming complexity and unpredictability of policy change in political systems, punctuated equilibrium theory has employed stochastic process models to evaluate punctuated dynamics in public policy-making (Breunig and Jones 2011; Breunig and Koski 2009; Baumgartner *et al.* 2009; Robinson and Caver 2006; Jones and Baumgartner 2005; Jordan 2003; True *et al.* 1999; Padgett 1980). To evaluate the general punctuated hypothesis, punctuated equilibrium has examined the underlying probability density distributions of policy inputs and outputs data, beginning with research on public budgeting (True *et al.* 1999) and expanding out to shifts in policy-making in other institutional contexts such as elections, bill introductions and question periods, legislative hearings, shifts, and media coverage of events over time (Baumgartner *et al.* 2009; Jones and Baumgartner 2005; Jones *et al.* 2003). This research has followed Padgett's (1980) seminal application of stochastic process models in public budgeting, which demonstrated that aggregate distributions of policy change over time could be used to distinguish between incremental and non-incremental patterns of change.

This approach is justified by the theoretical distributions associated with incremental decision-making and disproportionate information processing. Incrementalism implies a normal distribution, as policy change occurs through a gradual adjustment with larger shifts in policy occurring equally around the mean (Breunig and Jones 2011; Baumgartner and Jones 2005; True *et al.* 1999; Padgett 1980). Punctuated equilibrium theory implies leptokurtic distributions, described by "fat tails (indicative of internal reprioritizations and external policy punctuations), and sharp central peaks (indicative of internal inattentiveness and external temporal stability)" (Breunig and Jones 2011; Jones and Baumgartner 2005).

Figure 11.1 illustrates policy change distributions associated with incremental and disproportionate information processing. The *incremental* histogram on the left follows a normal distribution of budgetary change over time. Here, annual changes in budgets are clustered around the mean, and larger changes are evenly distributed, with extremely large punctuation representing extremely rare events. In the *punctuations* histogram budgetary change is typically very small, as evidenced by the central cluster of data around the mean. Moderate policy adjustment occurs less frequently and major policy change more frequently than anticipated by incremental model. This is consistent with a process of volatile policy change that occurs through long periods of neglect and sudden moments of extreme change.

Researchers have supplemented these ocular checks of punctuated dynamics with several statistical measures of the distribution of policy change data.[9] Most commonly, researchers have estimated the L-Kurtosis (LK) or "peakedness" of a given distribution. A normal distribution can be described as mesokurtic, and is smooth and symmetrical around the mean. Leptokurtic distributions are indicated by sharp central peaks and fat tails. LK provides a simple method for distinguishing between mesokurtic and leptokurtic distributions, returning values in intervals between 0 and 1, with higher values indicating non-normality.[10] The incremental histogram in Figure 11.1 produces an LK score of 0.12, indicative of a normal distribution. The punctuated curve on the right produces a value of 0.17, indicative of an exponential or power law distribution.

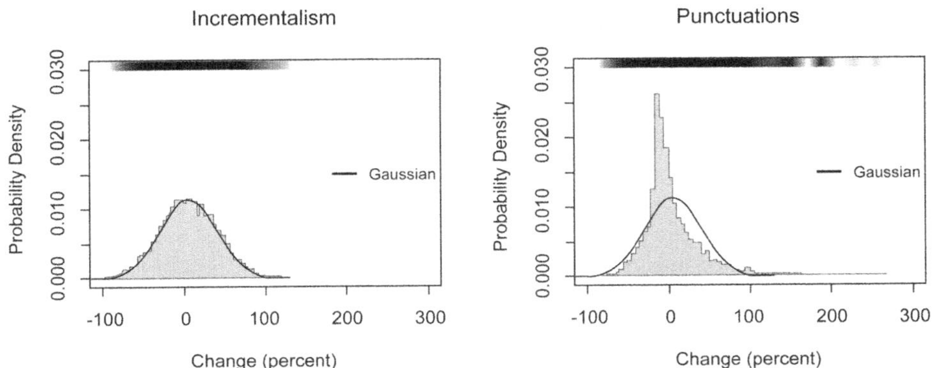


*Figure 11.1* Incremental and punctuated policy change distributions
Source: Breunig, Christian and Chris Koski. 2009. 'Punctuated Budgets and Governor's Institutional Powers', *American Politics Research* 37(6): 1116–38.

Applied to the study of policy change over time, stochastic process models therefore provide a relatively simple method for distinguishing between policy-making driven by strict incrementalism and policy-making driven by punctuated equilibrium. Policy change distributions that are normally distributed indicate a process of incremental decision-making. Policy change distributions producing sharp central peaks and fat shoulders imply decision-making processes consistent with punctuated dynamics in policy-making (Jones and Baumgartner 2005).

Punctuated equilibrium theory has made use of stochastic process models to assess patterns of decision-making across institutional and historical contexts. These studies have provided robust support for the general punctuation hypothesis, as virtually all patterns of policy change over time produce punctuated dynamics consistent with disproportionate information processing. Distributions of policy change data consistent with punctuated equilibrium theory have been identified in studies of public budging in federal budgeting (Jones and Baumgartner 2005), state budgeting (Breunig and Koski 2006), and local government budgeting (Jordan 2003). A comparison of national budgeting across the United States, France, Germany, Great Britain, Denmark and Canada confirmed that budget change across nations produces punctuated dynamics (Jones *et al.* 2009). This growing body of research suggests that incrementalism is one process of decision-making embedded in a larger model of disproportionate information processing.

More recently studies of punctuated equilibrium have employed stochastic process models to understand how different institutions shape punctuated dynamics in policy-making. Here, researchers have compared the shape and kurtosis of change data to understand how the institutional context shapes punctuated dynamics in policy-making. Some institutions impose considerable friction against policy change while others are more responsive. This research has qualified PET's earlier understanding of disproportionate information processing, illustrating that variation in the decision rules and transaction costs imposed across institutions shapes the frequency and magnitude of policy punctuations. Baumgartner and his coauthors (2009) compare the kurtosis values associated with policy change distributions across multiple policy-making institutions in the United States, Denmark and Belgium, finding that institutions that impose larger barriers to policy change are also more susceptible to large policy punctuations. Although all policy-making departs from normal incremental decision-making process, there is considerable variation in the slip stick dynamics imposed by different forms of institutions. Government activities such as elections produce smaller L-kurtosis values than more rigid policy output processes, such as lawmaking and budgeting (Baumgartner *et al.* 2009). Breunig and Koski (2009) confirm these dynamics in their study in US state-level gubernatorial powers. The executive's ability to shape state budgets and veto undesirable legislation contributed to larger punctuations than states with weaker executive offices.

## Conclusion

The renewed focus on stochastic process models points to one of the most promising areas for future research in punctuated equilibrium. The initial research testing the general punctuation hypothesis has demonstrated that policy-making cannot uniformly be explained as resulting from an incremental decision-making process. However, research has only recently started to identify distributions commonly associated with disproportionate information processing in policy-making (Breunig and Jones 2011). Future research will allow us to differentiate between incremental decision-making, sudden punctuations in response to exogenous shocks, and policy change triggered by changes in factors endogenous to a given political system. PET researchers have already begun to test how closely policy change distributions associated with different policy processes match specific outcome distributions such as the power law or exponential distributions that result from distinct decision-making processes (Jones *et al.* 2009). Identifying the distributions attached to specific mechanisms of policy change beyond incrementalism will help us understand the processes leading to policy change over time. Boushey (2010) integrated research from agenda-setting and epidemiology to distinguish between incremental and punctuated patterns of policy diffusion in the United States. This research suggested that innovations that encourage positive feedback cycles in policy-making could produce steep S-shaped distributions representative of internal contagion, leading to rapid diffusion across states, or stark R-shaped exponential distributions in response to exogenous factors.

The data resources prepared in the Policy and Comparative Agendas projects will also lead to new discovery in the field. These resources provide leverage not only for testing how different institutions shape punctuated dynamics in policy-making, but also for testing how the interaction of policy-makers and policy ideas across systems shapes patterns of policy change over time. The time series measures of attention across countries will eventually provide researchers with a powerful resource for understanding how the serial allocation of political attention across countries shapes patterns of agenda-setting and policy adoption over space and time. For example, research focusing on the policy responses of domestic and international political systems to exogenous shocks will help us to understand how different institutions respond to common exogenous shocks. Current research shows how aggregate patterns of policy change generally unfold across different institutional contexts. Future research will identify how different institutions interact with common exogenous signals in policy-making.

Over the last two decades, researchers have expanded on the initial model of punctuated equilibrium theory presented in *Agendas and Instability in American Politics*. On the one hand, PET has added a much richer account of the decision-making model leading to incremental adjustment and sudden positive feedback cycles. This has grounded punctuated equilibrium theory, illustrating how disproportionate information processing leads to shifts in attention and policy preferences in individuals and the institutions they populate. At the same time, PET theory has expanded on the macropolitical implications of punctuated equilibrium theory, moving from a study of policy change in the United States to a more general model of agenda-setting and policy-making within organizations. The assumptions of PET theory have been evaluated in case studies across issue areas and at the aggregate level across institutions. The broad interest in the theory has generated a strong consensus regarding how policy change occurs over time, and points to a promising research agenda as new scholars identify how the allocation of policy attention in organizations and institutions leads to profound shifts in public policy.

## Notes

1 This section highlights only the subset of the major health reforms in the PPACA. An interested reader may wish to refer to the Kaiser Family Foundation's (2010) "Summary of the new health reform law" for a succinct 13-page summary of the key provisions of the PPACA.

2 To conceptualize the pressures leading to incremental and sudden policy change within a single political system over time, Baumgartner and Jones (1993) borrowed from evolutionary biology and paleontology, drawing on Eldredge and Gould's punctuated equilibrium theory of speciation (1972). For a comparison of the PET framework in biology and public policy, see Robinson (2006). For a critique of the metaphor, see Givel (2010).

3 Punctuated equilibrium theory borrows heavily from prior research in bounded rationality in policy-making to explain pressures leading to policy stability and change. For more extensive reviews of bounded rationality or incrementalism in policy-making, refer to Jones and Hayes' chapters in this volume.

4 The stability of participants at the subgovernment level has been well-documented in the study of American politics. Researchers have alternately labeled this organization of elected officials, interest group activists and bureaucrats as iron triangles, policy subsystems, or issue networks.

5 For far more expansive lists of the many contributions of punctuated equilibrium theory, refer to the publications page at the Comparative Agendas Project web page (www.comparativeagendas.org/publications) or the Policy Agendas publication web page (www.policyagendas.org/biblio).

6 Givel (2006) contends that punctuated equilibrium theory fails to explain the stability of tobacco policy in the face of widespread pressure for policy reform. Baumgartner and Jones (2009) revisit the case of tobacco reform in the second edition of *Agendas and Instability in American Politics*. They argue that the pro-industry tobacco policy monopoly has been thoroughly destroyed at the federal level, and that radical reforms to tobacco control and regulation have occurred at the state and local levels of government.

7 These data are available at the policy agendas website at: www.policyagendas.org.

8 More detailed information on the Comparative Agendas Project can be accessed at: www.CAP.org.

9 Researchers have employed other simple tests evaluate the normality of a given probability density function. Tests such as the Shapiro-Wilk, Anderson Darling or the Kolmogorov–Smirnov test indicate whether a given distribution is consistent with a normal (incremental) decision-making process.

10 Prior research in punctuated equilibrium employed standard measures of kurtosis (K) to estimate the shape of the distribution. For K, normal distributions have kurtosis values of 3, with larger values indicating leptokurtic distributions. Breunig and Jones (2011) suggest L-Kurtosis as an alternative, as this measure results in more stable estimates of the overall shape of the distribution.

## Bibliography

Aaron, Paul and David Musto. 1981. 'Temperance and prohibition in America: A historical overview', in Mark Moore and Dean Gerstein (eds) *Alcohol and Public Policy: Beyond the Shadow of Prohibition*. Washington, DC: National Academy Press, 125–81.

Baumgartner, Frank and Bryan D. Jones. 1993. *Agendas and Instability in American Politics*. Chicago: University of Chicago Press.

——and Bryan D. Jones. 2002. 'Positive and negative feedback in politics', in *Policy Dynamics*. Chicago: University of Chicago Press

——and Bryan Jones. 2009. *Agendas and Instability in American Politics*, 2nd edn. Chicago: University of Chicago Press.

——, Suzanna De Boef and Amber Boydstun. 2008. *The Decline of the Death Penalty and the Discovery of Innocence*. New York: Cambridge University Press.

——, Christoffer Green-Pedersen and Bryan D. Jones (eds). 2008. *Comparative Studies of Policy Agendas*. New York: Routledge.

——, Christian Breunig, Christoffer Green-Pedersen, Bryan D. Jones, Peter B. Mortensen, Michiel Nuytemans and Stefaan Walgrave. 2009. 'Punctuated equilibrium in comparative perspective', *American Journal of Political Science* 53(3): 603–20.

Berry, Frances S. and William D. Berry. 1999. 'Innovation and diffusion models in policy research', in Paul A. Sabatier (ed.) *Theories of the Policy Process*. Boulder, CO: Westview Press, 169–200.

Birkland, Thomas A. 1997. *After Disaster: Agenda Setting, Public Policy, and Focusing Events*. Washington, DC: Georgetown University Press.

Boushey, Graeme. 2010. *Policy Diffusion Dynamics in America*. Cambridge: Cambridge University Press.

Breunig, Christian and Chris Koski. 2006. 'Punctuated equilibria and budgets in the American states', *Policy Studies Journal* 34(3): 363–79.

——and Chris Koski. 2009. 'Punctuated budgets and governors' institutional powers', *American Politics Research* 37(6): 1116–38.

——and Bryan Jones. 2011. 'Stochastic process methods with an application to budegetary data', *Political Analysis* 19(1): 103–17.

Cashore, Benjamin and Michael Howlett. 2006. 'Behavioral thresholds and institutional rigidities as explanations of punctuated equilibrium processes in Pacific Northwest Forest Policy Dynamics', in Robert Repetto (ed.) *Punctuated Equilibrium in US Environmental Policy*. New Haven, CT: Yale University Press, pp. 137–61.

Donovan, Mark. 2001. *Taking Aim: Target Populations and the Wars on Aids and Drugs*. Washington, DC: Georgetown University Press.

Eldredge, Niles and Stephen Gould. 1972. 'Punctuated equilibria: An alternative to phyletic gradualism', in T. Schopf (ed.) *Paleiobiology*, San Francisco: Freeman, Cooper, 82–115.

Givel, Michael. 2006. 'Punctuated equilibrium in limbo: The tobacco lobby and US state policy making from 1990 to 2003', *Policy Studies Journal* 43(3): 405–18.

—— 2010. 'The evolution of the theoretical foundations of punctuated equilibrium theory in public policy', *Review of Policy Research* 27(2): 187–98.

Hayes, Michael. 1992. *Incrementalism and Public Policy*. New York: Longman.

Holyoke, Thomas. 2003. 'Choosing battlegrounds: Interest group lobbying across multiple venues', *Political Research Quarterly* 56: 325–36.

Iyengar, Shanto. 1996. 'Framing responsibility for political issues', *Annals of the American Academy of Political and Social Science* 546(1): 59–70.

Jones, Bryan D. 1994. *Reconceiving Decision-Making in Democratic Politics: Attention, Choice, and Public Policy*. Chicago: University of Chicago Press.

—— 2001. *Politics and the Architecture of Choice: Bounded Rationality and Governance*. Chicago: University of Chicago Press.

——and Frank Baumgartner. 2004. 'Representation and agenda setting', *Policy Studies Journal* 32: 1–25.

——and Frank Baumgartner. 2005. *The Politics of Attention: How Government Prioritizes Problems*. Chicago: University of Chicago Press.

——, Tracy Sulkin and Heather Larsen. 2003. 'Punctuations in American political institutions', *American Political Science Review* 97(1): 151–69.

——, Frank R. Baumgartner, Christian Breunig, Christopher Wlezien, Stuart Soroka, Martial Foucault, Abel François, Christoffer Green-Pedersen, Peter John, Chris Koski, Peter B. Mortensen, Frédéric Varone and Stefaan Walgrave. 2009. 'A general empirical law of public budgets: A comparative analysis', *American Journal of Political Science* 53(4): 855–73.

Jordan, Meagan. 2003. 'Punctuations and agendas: A new look at local government budget expenditures', *Journal of Policy Analysis and Management* 22: 345–60.

Kaiser Family Foundation. 2010. 'Summary of new health reform law', *Focus on Health Reform*. Available at: www.kff.org/healthreform/upload/8061.pdf (accessed 23 November 2011).

Karch, Andrew 2007. 'Emerging issues and future directions in state policy diffusion research', *State Politics and Policy Quarterly* 7(1): 54–80.

Kingdon, John. 1984. *Agendas, Alternatives, and Public Policies*. Boston: Little, Brown.

Lindblom, Charles. 1959. 'The science of muddling through', *Public Administration Review* 19: 79–88.

Padgett, John F. 1980. 'Bounded rationality in budgetary research', *American Political Science Review* 74: 354–72.

Pralle, Sarah. 2003. 'Venue shopping, political strategy, and policy change: A case study of Canadian forest advocacy', *Journal of Public Policy* 23: 233–60.

Repetto, Robert (ed.). 2006. *Punctuated Equilibrium and the Dynamics of US Environmental Policy*. New Haven, CT: Yale University Press.

Robinson, Scott. E. 2006. 'Punctuated equilibrium models in organizational decision making', in Goktug Morcol (ed.) *Handbook on Human Decision Making*. Boca Raton, FL: CRC Press, 133–49.

—— and Floun'say R. Caver. 2006. 'Punctuated equilibrium and Congressional policymaking', *Political Research Quarterly* 59(1): 161–6.

—— and Kenneth J. Meier. 2006. 'Path dependence and organizational behavior: Bureaucracy and internal standards', *American Review of Public Administration*, 36(3): 241–60.

Schattschneider, Elmer E. 1975. *The Semi-sovereign People*. Hinsdale, IL: Dryden Press.

Schneider, Anne Larason. 2006. 'Patterns of change in the use of imprisonment in the American states: An integration of path dependence, punctuated equilibrium and policy design approaches', *Political Research Quarterly* 59(3): 457–70.

—— and Helen Ingram. 1993. 'The social construction of target populations: Implications for politics and policy', *American Political Science Review* 87(2): 334–47.

Shiffman, Jeremy, Tanya Beer and Yonghong Wu. 2002. 'The emergence of global disease control priorities', *Health Policy and Planning* 17(3): 225–34.

Smith, Mark A. 2007. *The Right Talk: How Conservatives Transformed the Great Society into the Economic Society*. Princeton, NJ: Princeton University Press.

True, James and Glenn Utter. 2002. 'Saying "yes", "no", and "load me up" to guns in America', *The American Review of Public Administration* 32(2): 216–41.

——, Bryan Jones and Frank Baumgartner. 1999. 'Punctuated-equilibrium theory: Explaining stability and change in American policymaking', in Paul Sabatier (ed.) *Theories of the Policy Process*. Boulder, CO: Westview Press, 155–88.

——, Bryan Jones and Frank Baumgartner. 2007. 'Punctuated equilibrium theory: explaining stability and change in American policymaking', in Paul Sabatier (ed.) *Theories of the Policy Process*, 2nd edn. Boulder, CO: Westview Press, 155–88.

Tsebelis, George. 2002. *Veto Players: How Political Institutions Work*. Princeton, NJ: Princeton University Press.

Walgrave, Stefaan and Frédéric Varone. 2008. 'Punctuated equilibrium, and agenda setting: Bringing parties back in. Policy change after the Dutroux crisis in Belgium', *Governance: An International Journal of Policy and Administration* 21(3): 365–95.

Wildavsky, A. 1964. *The Politics of the Budgetary Process*. Toronto: Little, Brown.

Wood, Robert. 2006. 'Tobacco's tipping point: the master settlement agreement as a focusing event', *Policy Studies Journal* 34(3): 419–36.

Workman, Samuel, Bryan D. Jones and Ashley E. Jochim. 2009. 'Information processing and policy dynamics', *Policy Studies Journal* 37(1): 75–92.

# 12

# Policy network models

*Chen-Yu Wu and David Knoke*

## Defining policy networks

The overarching goal of policy network analysis is to understand how relationships between actors involved in policy-making determine the outcomes of collective policy decisions (Compston 2009; Knoke 2011). To this end, policy network analysis consists of two distinct components. First, one has to identify the important actors involved in the policy-making process. Although policies are proposed, debated, and passed by legislators and other governmental entities, extra-governmental actors such as non-governmental organizations (NGOs), interest groups, or even influential individuals can be involved in influencing policies. Second, one has to describe the type of social interactions that occur between actors during the policy-making process. Both components are vital to enabling the researcher to explain or predict policy outcomes.

In short, policy network analysis provides scholars with an analytical framework to *describe* the social network dimensions of policy-making. However, policy network analysis can also be used to answer the fundamental research questions of social network analysis, namely: how these networks form, how and why they persist over time, and also how they change.

## Social network theory

Social network analysis consists of theories and methods for examining structural relations among social actors and for explaining the consequences of those connections. Network theories can apply to structures and processes occurring either in small, closed social systems (such as artificially constructed experimental groups, or natural settings such as classrooms and work teams) or in larger, open systems (such as communities, markets, and international relations). Network theories and data analyses may apply to the egocentric, interpersonal, subgroup, or complete network levels of analysis, as well as to cross-level and time-dependent effects. At the micro-level, network analysts examine how people form, change, or drop ties such as friendship, giving assistance and advice, exchanging information, and quarreling. Interpersonal interactions aggregate into meso-level social structures that affect collective actions and performance outcomes of small groups such as gangs, teams, and crews. Macro-level systems of cities, economies, nations, and transnational relations may be studied using conceptual and methodological techniques developed through decades of social network theory and research. The interdisciplinary field originated in anthropology, small group, social psychology, and sociology in the mid-twentieth century, and really took off around 1970 as theoretical interest in structural analysis converged with increasingly sophisticated computer software for analyzing network data based on matrix algebra methods. The exponential growth of social research and proliferation of academic specialties introduced social network analysis to increasing numbers of basic, substantive, and applied disciplines, including political sociology, political science, and public administration.

As a minimum a social network consists of a set of actors (people, groups, organizations, nations) and one or more relations that connect some of them (e.g., communication, trust, purchase, attack). A boundary- or scope-condition specifies which actors are included within a particular network; for example, by formal membership as in a social club; by residence as in a neighborhood; or by informal criteria such as attendance at flea markets. Network theories typically make three core assumptions about the mutual influences among actors: (1) the social structure of any complex system consists of the stable patterns of repeated interactions connecting actors to one another; (2) these social relations are the primary explanatory units of analysis, rather than the attributes and characteristics of the individual actors; and (3) the perceptions, attitudes, and actions of actors are shaped by the multiple structural networks within which they are embedded, and in turn their behaviors can change these networks' structures (Knoke 2001: 63–4). Political networks are a subset of social networks in which the primary relations among actors involve inequalities in power. Asymmetrical power rarely depends on overt coercive force and more often relies on taken-for-grant beliefs about the possession of authority to issue commands and to expect compliance with orders (Max Weber's legitimate power). Political power is inherently relational: one or more actors seek resources and other advantages despite resistance by others. Hence, social network theory is well-suited to investigate the diverse structures and consequences of power, from the bedroom to the boardroom to the battlefield. Political networks can be observed at micro-levels, where friends and kin try to persuade one another to vote and participate in electoral campaigns. At the most macro-level, political networks in the international system are evident in shifting patterns of military alliances and interstate aggression (e.g. Maoz 2010). This chapter concentrates on meso-level political networks comprised mainly of formal organizations engaged in collective efforts to influence public policy decisions within nation-states.

To explain public policymaking at various governmental levels, network theorists draw attention to the *policy network* as an appropriate unit of analysis. In local governments, important political actors are typically powerful individuals (e.g. mayor, council members). But, at national levels, influential actors are more often formal organizations such as political parties, legislative committees, executive agencies, ministries, and interest organizations including labor unions, business associations, and public interest groups. Kenis and Schneider (1991: 41) argued, "Policy networks should be conceived as specific structural arrangements in policymaking." They defined a policy network as set of public and private corporate actors linked by communication ties for exchanging information, expertise, trust, and other political resources:

> A policy network is described by its actors, their linkages and its boundary. It includes a relatively stable set of mainly public and private corporate actors. The linkages between the actors serve as channels for communication and for the exchange of information, expertise, trust and other policy resources. The boundary of a given policy network is not in the first place determined by formal institutions but results from a process of mutual recognition dependent on functional relevance and structural embeddedness.
>
> *(ibid.)*

A closely related concept, the *policy domain*, is socially constructed by political actors who mutually recognize that their preferences on policy events must be taken into consideration by other domain participants (Laumann and Knoke 1987: 10). A policy domain is defined as any political subsystem

> identified by specifying a substantively defined criterion of mutual relevance or common orientation among a set of consequential actors concerned with formulating, advocating, and selecting courses of action (i.e., policy options) that are intended to resolve the delimited substantive problems in question.
>
> *(Knoke and Laumann 1982: 256)*

Some policy domain examples are education, agriculture, national defense, welfare (Laumann and Knoke 1987: 10), health, energy, and transportation (Burstein 1991: 328). The policy network and the policy domain concepts are interrelated, with a policy domain delineating a bounded system within which its organizational participants are interconnected by one or more policy networks.

Five basic types of interorganizational relations exhibiting distinctive policy network structures, include: resource exchange; information transmission; power relations; boundary penetration; and sentimental attachments (Knoke 2001: 65). Resource exchanges in policy networks, such as money or personnel, are usually voluntary transfers, although occasional government mandates impose interorganizational connections. Information exchanges range from technical and scientific data to policy advice and advocacy. Power relations include both formal and informal inequalities in authority and dominance, with public sector entities usually controlling more power than private sector organizations to impose their interests on a domain. Boundary penetration refers to two or more actors coordinating their actions for a common goal, such as lobbying as discussed below. Sentimental attachments are subjective and emotional affiliation expressing solidarity and political support as exemplified by labor unions and social movement organizations. The five basic types of interorganizational relations can be operationalized by a multitude of empirical indicators and jointly analyzed to reveal network structures connecting policy domain organizations in complex patterns.

An interorganizational perspective on policy domains and policy networks comprised the theoretical and methodological basis for the organizational state model of policymaking that Edward Laumann, David Knoke, and Franz Pappi constructed for investigating the US national energy and health domains (Laumann and Knoke 1987), and comparative network analysis of the US, German, and Japanese labor domains (Knoke *et al.* 1996). See Knoke (1998) for a detailed overview of these and related projects. The organizational state model views national policy-making processes as dynamic influence actions among formal organizations, with elite persons acting as agents of these organizational principals. Within every policy domain, the set of core organizational players are drawn from both the public and private sectors. Some key organizations may have intense interests in numerous policy issues and participate in efforts to affect the policy outcomes of dozens of legislative, executive, and judicial decisions. Other organizations focus more narrowly on a single issue and mobilize only rarely to pursue their interests. Given the diversity of organizational interests, limited resources, and complexity of influence dynamics, no organization or small subset has the capacity to control, let alone dominate, a policy domain's policy-making processes. Instead, most policy fights consist of multiorganizational coalitions brought temporarily together to work collectively on shaping policy proposals and advocating a specific preferred policy solution to those authorities capable of rendering a binding decision on a particular policy event (e.g. a regulatory ruling, legislative act, court decision).

A policy domain's communication and resource exchange networks enable interested organizations to identify collaborators and opponents that can be mobilized on competing sides of a policy event. Frequently, some members of an *action set*—organizations that all hold the same outcome preference on the event, are connected in a communication network, and coordinate their policy to influence actions—pool their political resources and launch coordinated campaigns to pressure governmental decision-makers into choosing the policy outcome favored by the coalition members.

Some organizations work solo but chances of a favorable outcome are usually greater when coalitions create an efficient division of labor that maximizes their strengths and expertise. Broad-based membership organizations such as labor unions mobilize mass constituencies to man phone banks and email legislators. Organizations with well-funded staff assemble research evidence to present during testimony at public legislative and regulatory hearings. Political consultants produce persuasive head-counts at closed-door meetings with elected officials. And deep-pocketed political action committees always have an open door to make their cases to cash-starved politicians. Lobbying proceeds neither by political bribery nor by striking overt quid pro quo deals, but by making a more persuasive case in an appropriate decision-making arena (Brown 1998). Lobbyists succeed by providing policy-makers with useful information and data, substantive arguments, proposed policy language, and astute political arguments for supporting one side of a policy fight over the alternatives.

After a binding policy decision is made, the coalitions disband as new policy events attract different combinations of organized interest groups. Viewed over time, the policy network structures of policy domain appear continually in flux. Yet, despite much instability at the micro-level, relatively durable macro-level cleavages may emerge and persist. Examples of such enduring cleavages are the business-vs.-labor, rural-vs.-urban, and religious-vs.-secular divisions occurring in many nations. Many national policy domains contain fairly stable policy networks whose boundaries and components persist over substantial time (Burstein 1991). However, as "social constructions, created through interactions among organizations and given meaning by culture" (1991: 345), policy domains are susceptible to reconceptualization and evolutionary transformations. Scant theory seeks to explain the historical origins of new policy domains or the transformation of existing domains. An exception is Knoke's (2004) schematic model of six elements (focusing events, technological innovations, political entrepreneurs, issue framing, policy networks, and institutionalization), which he offered as "a provisional framework to initiate empirical research on the sociopolitical construction of national policy domains" (2004: 94). So far, no takers.

## History and development of policy network analyses

According to Knoke (2011), the term "policy network" was first used by Katzenstein (1976) in his article comparing the foreign economic policies of France and the United States. Although Katzenstein did not explicitly define policy networks, he emphasized that policy networks form a crucial link between state and society. Additionally, he proposed a simple continuum for describing types of policy networks. One ideal type (to use the Weberian term) is the state-centered policy network, which is defined by political power and dominance; the other ideal type is the society-centered policy network, which in contrast is defined by economic power. In practice, Katzenstein stated that all policy networks in "advanced industrial states" would fall somewhere between the two extremes.

Since the publication of Katzenstein's article, the volume of work on policy networks has grown immensely. These works encompass policy-making on all levels, from the local level (e.g. Laumann and Pappi 1976) to comparative (e.g. Marsh 1998), regional (e.g. Adshead 2002), and transnational analyses (e.g. McGann and Sabatini 2011; Witte *et al.* 2000). As the field of policy network analysis expanded, three distinct schools of thought emerged. In the following subsections, we will briefly discuss the US, British, and German perspectives on policy network analysis.

*United States*. The American approach to policy network analysis is rooted in Laumann and Pappi's 1973 study, *New Directions in the Study of Community Elites*. In the study, as well as subsequent replications (e.g. Galaskiewicz 1979; Laumann *et al.* 1978), researchers employed the network analysis of power structures and found that actors in central network positions were more engaged in local civic life, and as a result, enjoyed a better chance of influencing public policy debates in their favor.

Laumann and Knoke extended this framework to national policy domains and the formal organizations within them in *The Organizational State* (1987), and found that the networks among these organizations enabled organizations with opposing interests to pool their resources and mobilize them in pursuit of commonly-desired policy outcomes. Furthermore, the authors found that, at the national level, it is often the case that different organizations simultaneously have common and opposing policy interests.

In another study, Knoke *et al.* (1996) found that, like policy-making at the local level, actors in centrally located network positions could more easily influence policy decisions. In their comparative study of US, German, and Japanese policy domains, they make the distinction between communication networks (characterized by exchanges of information) and support networks (characterized by resource exchanges), and found that occupying a central position in communication networks provided organizations with more political influence in the US and Germany, while the opposite was true for Japan (1996: 120). These findings suggest that the processes involved in policy-making are not necessarily universal, but rather culturally determined.

*Germany*. The German approach to policy network analysis, like the American approach, is rooted both in the previously discussed study by Laumann and Pappi (1973), and also in Lehmbruch's (1984, 1989) studies of corporatist politics the Federal Republic of Germany (FRG). Compared to other more centralized states, such as the United Kingdom, the FRG's relative noncentralized policy networks necessitated exchanges of resources among many organizations involved in policy-making (Lehmbruch termed this corporatist concertation). In this policy environment, Lehmbruch (1984) found that these interorganizational policy networks serve as an important structural and institutional constraint moderating the outcomes of collective policy decisions. Equally importantly, Lehmbruch (1989) concluded that the formal organizations involved in the policy-making process can influence the structure and dynamics of policy networks.

*Great Britain*. Unlike the American and German approaches, which analyze policy networks using theories of power structures, British scholars' analytical framework involves highlighting the contrasts between different networks' pluralist and corporatist characteristics (e.g. Rhodes 1985, 1990). Additionally, unlike American and German scholars, British policy network analysis places more emphasis on more fluid and unpredictable policy communities rather than entrenched governmental and subgovernmental units (Richardson 2000; Rhodes 1990). As such, British scholars produced a wide range of literature on self-organizing groups involved in the policy-making processes for policy domains such as agriculture, employment, and informational technology.

Within the British school of thought, one of its more influential works is Marsh and Rhodes' (1992) book, *Policy Networks in British Government*, which provided an analytical approach emphasizing the importance of structural relations between governmental entities, interest groups, and informal actors, as opposed to interpersonal relations among individual actors. Equally importantly, their approach established a unidirectional direct link between policy networks and policy outcomes. Critics of this approach, notably Dowding (1995, 2001), have argued that it has two glaring weaknesses: first, it lacks a theoretical basis; and second, it does not provide any basis for explaining network transformation (which is, as previously mentioned, an important objective for policy network scholars). In response, various authors (e.g. Marsh and Smith 2000; Kisby 2007) have offered explanations and models addressing these criticisms.

## Key ideas in modern policy network analysis

One of the features that all of these views of policy network analysis share, to some extent, is the idea of resource dependency (Benson 1982; Rhodes 1985). In other words, in the realm of policy-making, every actor desires resources that other actors control. As a result, every actor is prepared to exchange or give up some resources in order to obtain resources which they do not have (Compston 2009: 7). These exchanges are not unregulated or arbitrary; rather, actors employ specific strategies which conform to mutually accepted "rules of the game" (Rhodes 1985: 4–5). These rules can either be formally codified (e.g. laws regulating campaign contributions from interest groups) or informal (e.g. hiring former government officials to serve as consultants and advisers to interest groups).

A common example in modern-day democracies is the exchange of resources between law-makers and interest groups. As previously mentioned, legislators and other government officials are the only people who can legally introduce, debate, and ultimately pass policy in the halls of government. Such political authority is a key resource that all other actors lack, and therefore seek access to. These actors, however, control other resources coveted by these legislators. Namely, interest groups—and the members they represent—hold both the votes that legislators need to win elections and the funds legislators require to wage successful campaigns. Hence, actors like interest groups can influence or pressure legislators to push for legislation advocating for their preferred policy outcomes.

This example highlights two key characteristics in every policy network. First is the assumption that policy actors are rational, and that actors agree to participate in these resource exchanges if they stand to benefit from them. To illustrate, an official with a largely conservative electorate is unlikely to heed the demands of a liberal/progressive interest group, nor accept its donations, since the official does not "need" the votes of the minority to secure re-election, nor does the official wish to alienate his or her base constituency. This characteristic can also explain why legislators are much less likely to compromise with colleagues with opposing views when their political parties hold a majority in government.

The second characteristic is that all policy exchanges stem from power imbalances—political, economic, or ideological—and that all policy exchanges result in power imbalances, although not necessarily the same ones as before the exchange. In theory, if the playing field was level for all actors, there would be no need to exchange resources. Another way to approach this characteristic is to understand that all resource exchanges result in losers as well as winners (Compston 2009). In democracies, it is rarely the case that an individual legislator is subjected to the lobbying efforts of a single nongovernmental actor; it is more likely that individual legislators are simultaneously considering the requests of multiple competing actors. Hence, after every exchange, there will be some actors which are more well-off as a result, and others who are less so.

## Policy network theory and empirical research

Like every analytical framework, policy network theory has strengths and weaknesses. For instance, early critics of policy network theory charged that policy network research largely failed to develop testable theories of both policy development and outcomes (Knoke 2011). Additionally, as mentioned previously, other critics—notably Dowding (1995)—claim that the discourse of policy network theory is not only merely descriptive, but more importantly that the precise definitions of many concepts in policy network research have not been agreed upon universally by the scholars conducting this research. More recent work (e.g. Mikkelson 2006) has highlighted some confusion among scholars about whether policy networks should be treated as dependent or independent variables. In other words, is policy network theory a better framework for understanding why and how these networks form, or is it a better tool for predicting the outcomes and consequences of this type of collective action?

Despite these criticisms, policy network theory continues to be an extremely valuable analytical tool for understanding both social network theory in general, but also the policy-making process. A large volume of recent work was produced by European scholars, probably due to both the creation of new nation-states following the fall of the Soviet Union in 1991, and also the increased prominence of the European Union in European political and civic life (Knoke 2011). The increased volume of policy network research has also seen scholars expand their foci, including: from government to strategies of governance; from centrally focused policy-making to multilayered policy-making (McGann and Sabatini 2011; von Winter 2001); from top-down hierarchies to grassroots influences (von Winter 2004); and from policy formation and outcomes to policy implementation (e.g. Greenaway *et al.* 2007).

Although policy network research in the United States has not kept pace with Europe, American scholars have made some significant contributions. For instance, some scholars uncovered new insights into policy theory and social network theory in general through the re-examination of older studies, while others chose to focus on and expand research on policy domains (Knoke 2011). These new studies remain very much rooted in the American perspective of power structures. For instance, Carpenter *et al.* (2003) found that as actors' needs for policy-related information increases, they are much more likely to invest their efforts and resources in building stronger communication links to their allies, rather than reaching out to their opponents. The downside of this approach, however, is that by engaging in such cliquish behavior, network actors expose themselves to an increased risk of network failure due to their inability to obtain complete information (2003: 433).

American scholars continue to be active in research into the social construction (and reconstruction) of policy domains. Policy domain research—particularly research into changes in policy domains—is a significant component of policy network theory, as it provides researchers with a link between culture and policy-making (Knoke 2004). In other words, changes in policy domains "potentially transforms shared cultural meanings, taken-for-granted assumptions, normative understandings, classificatory schemas, and tacit knowledge" (2004: 3). Its implications for policy network theory are fairly clear: new domains necessitate new policy-making strategies to comply with new legal regulations and bureaucratic practices, as well as other unanticipated changes.

Analyses of policy networks in non-Western states remain rare (Knoke 2011). This dearth is most likely due to various factors, such as the lack of cultural or political traditions of civic participation or, more basically, the inability to participate in civic life under certain forms of government. Additionally, the few studies that have been conducted tended to be descriptive, rather than theoretically grounded empirical research. As a result, there is a huge potential for growth for policy network literature on non-Western countries, as well as cross-national and comparative studies.

Another impetus for the growth of policy network analysis is the increased scholarly interest in globalization. According to McGann and Sabatini (2011), since globalization is commonly characterized by the global movement of capital and services, policy networks are ideal for the study of globalization due to the ability to identify and incorporate actors across social, political, governmental, and geographical boundaries. Additionally, two factors which occurred almost hand-in-hand with globalization also encouraged the proliferation of policy network research: namely, increased political and economic liberalization across the globe, and technological advances particularly in information exchange (e.g. the Internet). These developments allow civic-minded individuals and organizations more easily to establish transnational relationships and maintain their channels of communication (ibid.: 67–8).

While almost all research on globalization and policy networks is relatively recent, the work has the potential of encouraging even more growth for this analytical framework. The reason is that global polities of governance differ significantly from national governments, or even regional alliances. United Nations global policy-making bodies differ from national and regional alliances in that they tend to be decentralized, and that they tend to lack means of enforcing policies (for instance, nations can choose not to ratify or implement UN resolutions usually without any fear of retribution). Consequently, network strategies employed by actors on the global stage will inevitably differ from the strategies examined in current literature, reflecting the different challenges required to gain actors' acquiescence and avoid disagreements.

## Future directions for policy network research

We reiterate the central research questions which motivate policy network research, namely, how these networks form, how and why they persist over time, and also how they change. Presently, most literature focuses on the second question: scholars have amassed a trove of information about how routine activities occur within the context of already-established policy domains and policy networks. Large gaps still exist in the literature on the origins of policy networks, as well as how they change.

Some scholars have taken steps to address these shortcomings. For instance, Knoke (2004) proposed an analytical framework which would enable researchers to study how policy domains—and consequently policy networks—change. He argued that changes which are disruptive to routine activities—which he terms "focusing events"—are central to these changes. A prominent example of a focusing event, which permanently altered actors' perceptions of the world around them, is the September 11 terrorist attacks. Other focusing events include the exponential growth of the Internet (Rethemeyer 2007), which enabled and empowered organizational and individual actors alike to accomplish much more (particularly in terms of communications and networking) than was ever possible before.

Other analytical frameworks include Marsh *et al.*'s (2009) attempt to merge Grant's (1978) distinction between "insider" and "outsider" groups with Marsh and Rhodes' (1992) policy network classification system, reasoning that each approach makes up for each others' shortcomings. They applied this analytical framework to a case study, and concluded that the amalgamation of the two approaches could allow scholars to develop a better classification system of the types of interest groups and policy networks. Another recent framework proposed by Sandström and Carlsson (2008) argued that while network orientation has long been a vital part of policy science, most existing research does not focus on how a network's structure affects its performance. Their framework proposes that an effective policy network—that is, one that is both efficient and innovative—consists of a heterogeneous set of actors working very closely together. Voets *et al.* (2008) noted that existing research on policy networks focuses specifically on efficiency and effectiveness as measures of network performance, and argued that network activity entails additional costs, such as democratic quality and capacity building. Thus, the authors employed the discourse of New Public Management to provide new assessment criteria to measure these "other" costs of policy network activity.

Another frequently voiced criticism of the policy network approach is its lack of a theoretical grounding. Consequently, researchers have ample opportunities for developing new ideas and theoretical frameworks to address this gap. For instance, some researchers (e.g. Knoke 2009; Siegel 2008) have proposed analyzing policy networks using the concept of political capital, which is the political network equivalent of social capital (Knoke 2011).

Another possible theoretical framework for policy network research is the incorporation of the advocacy coalition framework (ACF) to policy network analysis (Weible and Sabatier 2007). Like policy network analysis, ACF assumes that actors cooperate with allies who share similar policy preferences and outcomes. Additionally, ACF—unlike policy network analysis—provides researchers with mechanisms that can explain policy changes.

Other researchers have tried incorporating new research methodology into the study of policy networks. For example, Bevir and Richards (2009) and Pal and Ireland (2009) echo previous criticism that policy network theory cannot be used to provide causal generalizations, and consequently, legitimate advice to policy-makers. To address this shortcoming, Bevir and Richards proposed a "decentered" approach towards the study of policy networks, arguing that research methods such as textual analysis and ethnography would allow researchers to understand meanings behind traditions of networks—in other words, understanding how network participants view themselves and their world. In pursuit of a similar goal, Pal and Ireland noted the importance of creating a comprehensive map of global policy networks so that researchers can understand broader issues affecting their networks of interests, not just narrow issues and specific organizations and individuals.

Another critique of policy network theory is that existing theory does a poor job explaining the genesis and evolution of policy networks. Scholars have tried to address this shortcoming by incorporating other theoretical lines of thought; for example deLeon and Varda (2009) proposed a theory based on collective action theory to develop "structural signatures of exchanges" among network participants. Others offered completely new theories. For example, Provan and Kenis (2008) proposed three models of governance with distinctive structural properties and tried to understand why network actors choose to adopt one form over another. Ultimately, they sought to understand the impact that each form of governance has on network outcomes, including the evolution of both the network and of governance strategies.

Ideally, policy network research will continue to develop until it achieves characteristics we take for granted in other more established fields of social research: a distinct and grounded theoretical framework that explains not only how established policy networks operate, but also how these networks form and change over time. Additionally, this theoretical framework should enable interested scholars to generate testable hypotheses and identify distinct variables which would enable these hypotheses to be tested empirically.

## Bibliography

Adshead, M. 2002. *Developing European Regions? Comparative Governance, Policy Networks and European Integration*. Burlington, VT: Ashgate.

Benson, J.K. 1982. 'A framework for policy analysis', in D.L. Rogers and D. Whetten (eds) *Interorganizational Coordination: Theory, Research and Implementation*. Ames, IA: Iowa State University Press.

Bevir, M. and D. Richards. 2009. 'Decentering policy networks: A theoretical agenda', *Public Administration* 87: 3–14.

Browne, W.P. 1998. *Groups, Interests, and US Public Policy*. Washington, DC: Georgetown University Press.

Burstein, P. 1991. 'Policy domains: Organization, culture, and policy outcomes', *Annual Review of Sociology* 17: 327–50.

Carpenter, D., K. Esterling and D. Lazer. 2003. 'The strength of strong ties: A model of contact-making in policy networks with evidence from US health politics', *Rationality and Society* 15: 411–40.

Compston, H. 2009. *Policy Networks and Policy Change*. New York: Palgrave Macmillan.

deLeon, P. and D.M. Varda. 2009. 'Toward a theory of collaborative policy networks: Identifying structural tendencies', *Policy Studies Journal* 37: 59–74.

Dowding, K. 1995. 'Model or metaphor? A critical review of the network approach', *Political Studies* 43: 136–58.

—— 2001. 'There must be an end to confusion: Policy networks, intellectual fatigue, and the need for political science methods courses in British Universities', *Political Studies* 49: 89–105.

Galaskiewicz, J. 1979. *Exchange Networks and Community Politics*. Beverly Hills, CA: Sage.

Grant, W. 1978. 'Insider groups, outsider groups and interest group strategies in Britain', Warwick: University of Warwick Department of Politics Working Party no. 19.

Greenaway, J., B. Salter and S. Hart. 2007. 'How policy networks can damage democratic health: A case study in the government of governance', *Public Administration* 85: 717–38.

Katzenstein, P. 1976. 'International relations and domestic structures: Foreign economic policies of advanced industrial states', *International Organization* 30: 1–45.

Kenis, P. and V. Schneider. 1991. 'Policy networks and policy analysis: Scrutinizing a new analytical toolbox', in B. Marin and R. Mayntz (eds) *Policy Networks: Empirical Evidence and Theoretical Considerations*. Boulder, CO, Frankfurt: Campus Verlag and Westview Press.

Kisby, B. 2007. 'Analyzing policy networks: Towards an ideational approach', *Policy Studies* 28: 71–90.

Knoke, D. 1998. 'The organizational state: Origins and prospects', *Research in Political Sociology*, 8: 147–63.

—— 2001. *Changing Organizations: Business Networks in the New Political Economy*. Boulder, CO: Westview Press.

—— 2004. 'The sociopolitical construction of national policy domains', in C.H.C.A. Henning and C. Melbeck (eds) *Interdisziplinäre Sozialforschung: Theorie und empirische Adwendungen*. Frankfurt: Campus Verlag.

—— 2009. 'Playing well together: Creating corporate social capital in strategic alliance networks', *American Behaviorial Scientist* 52: 1690–708.

—— 2011. 'Policy networks', in J.P. Scott and P. Carrington (eds) *The Sage Handbook of Social Network Analysis*, Thousand Oaks, CA: Sage.

——and E.O. Laumann. 1982. 'The social structure of national policy domains: an exploration of some structural hypotheses', in P.V. Marsden and N. Lin (eds) *Social Structure and Network Analysis*. Beverly Hills, CA: Sage Publications.

——, F.U. Pappi, J. Broadbent and Y. Tsujinaka. 1996. *Comparing Policy Networks: Labor Politics in the US, Germany and Japan*. New York: Cambridge University Press.

Laumann, E.O. and F.U. Pappi. 1976. *Networks of Collective Action: A Perspective on Community Influence Systems*. New York: Academic Press.

——, J. Galaskiewicz, and P.V. Marsden. 1978. 'Community structure as interorganizational linkages', *Annual Review of Sociology* 4: 455–84.

——and D. Knoke. 1987. *The Organizational State: A Perspective on the Social Organization of National Energy and Health Policy Domains*. Madison, WI: University of Wisconsin Press.

——and F.U. Pappi. 1973. 'New directions in the study of community elites', *American Sociological Review* 38: 212–230.

Lehmbruch, G. 1984. 'Concertation and the structure of corporatist networks: Order and conflict in contemporary capitalism', in J.H. Goldthorpe (ed.) *Order and Conflict in Contemporary Capitalism*. Oxford: Oxford University Press.

—— 1989 'Institutional linkages and policy networks in the federal system of West Germany', *Publius* 19: 221–35.

McGann, J.G. and R. Sabatini. 2011. *Global Think Tanks: Policy Networks and Governance*. New York: Routledge.

Maoz, Z. 2010. *Networks of Nations: The Evolution, Structure, and Impact of International Networks, 1816–2001*. New York: Cambridge University Press.

Marsh, D. (ed.). 1998. *Comparing Policy Networks*. Buckingham: Open University Press.

——and R.A.W. Rhodes (eds). 1992. *Policy Networks in British Government*. Oxford: Clarendon Press.

——and M. Smith. 2000. 'Understanding policy networks: Towards a dialectical approach', *Political Studies* 48: 4–21.

——, D. Toke, C. Belfrage, D. Tepe. and S. McGough. 2009. 'Policy networks and the distinction between insider and outsider groups: The case of the Countryside Alliance', *Public Administration* 87: 621–38.

Mikkelson, M. 2006. 'Policy network analysis as a strategic tool for the voluntary sector', *Policy Studies* 27: 17–26.

Pal, L.A. and D. Ireland. 2009. 'The public sector reform movement: Mapping the global policy network', *International Journal of Public Administration* 32: 621–57.

Provan, K.G. and P. Kenis. 2008. 'Modes of network governance: Structure, management, and effectiveness', *Journal of Public Administration Research and Theory* 18(2): 229–52.

Rethemeyer, R.K. 2007. 'Policymaking in the age of internet: Is the internet tending to make policy networks more or less inclusive?' *Journal of Public Administration Research and Theory* 17: 259–84.

Rhodes, R.A.W. 1985. 'Power dependence, policy communities and inter-governmental networks', *Public Administration Bulletin* 49: 4–29.

—— 1990. 'Policy networks: A British perspective', *Journal of Theoretical Politics* 2: 293–317.

Richardson, J. 2000 'Government, interest groups and policy change', *Political Studies* 48(5): 1006–25.

Sandström, A. and L. Carlsson. 2008. 'The performance of policy networks: The relation between network structure and network performance', *Policy Studies Journal* 36: 497–524.

Siegel, J. 2008. 'Contingent political capital and international alliances: Evidence from South Korea', *Administrative Science Quarterly* 52: 621–66.

Voets, J., W. Van Dooren and F. de Rynck. 2008. 'A framework for assessing the performance of policy networks', *Public Management Review* 10: 77–90.

—— 2004. 'From corporatism to lobbyism: A change of paradigm in the theory and analysis of advocacy', *Zeitschrift für Parlamentsfragen*, 35: 761–76.

von Winter, T. 2001. 'From corporatism to etatism: Changes in the structure of the German poverty policy network', *Zeitschrift für Politikwissenschaft* 11: 1573–608.

Weible, C.M. and P.A. Sabatier. 2007. 'A guide to the advocacy coalition framework: Tips for researchers', in F. Fischer, G.J. Miller and M.S. Sidney (eds) *Handbook of Public Policy Analysis: Theory, Methods, and Politics*. London: CRC Press.

Witte, J. M., W.H. Reinicke and T. Benner. 2000. 'Beyond multilaterialism: Global public policy networks', *Internationale Politik und Gesellschaft* 2: 176–88.

# Part IV

# Understanding the agenda-setting process

# 13

# Policy agenda-setting studies

## Attention, politics and the public

*Christoffer Green-Pedersen and Peter B. Mortensen*

## Introduction

The agenda-setting approach has a long tradition in public policy studies. Seminal work by Schattschneider (1960) and Bachrach and Baratz (1962) pointed to the crucial role of attention to policy problems. The allocation of attention was the "second face of power" (Bachrach and Baratz 1962), and the "conflict of conflicts" is crucial in politics (Schattschneider 1960). From these seminal studies grew the literature known as policy agenda-setting studies (Baumgartner *et al.* 2006). The crux of this tradition is precisely the focus on attention. Policy-making cannot be understood without understanding the agenda-setting process, which draws attention to policy problems that need to be addressed through policy decisions. The first studies in policy agenda-setting were classics like Cobb and Elder (1983) and Kingdon (1995). They mostly applied a case study perspective and focused on how agenda-setting leads to policy decisions. Kingdon (1995: Chapter 23) became influential in the study of policy decisions from an agenda-setting perspective.

A new tradition in the policy agenda-setting tradition took off with the publication of Baumgartner and Jones' (1993) seminal book *Agendas and Instability in American Politics*, which pushed policy agenda-setting studies in a different direction in several related ways. Most notably, while previous studies focused on the role of agenda-setting dynamics in relation to specific policy decisions (see e.g. Zahariadis 1995), Baumgartner and Jones (1993) focused on more general patterns of agenda-setting in political systems. Instead of focusing on individual policy decisions, they focused on how attention to broader policy issues changed over time and how these changes paved the way for often dramatic changes in public policy. Another effect of the change in focus was the establishment of extensive datasets to measure attention dynamics over time and across a large number of policy issues, for instance through coding of attention to different issues in congressional hearings.

In recent years, the policy agenda-setting tradition has taken a new turn through a surge in comparative work following the path laid out by Baumgartner and Jones. Part of this work has been related to a comparative evaluation of the punctuated equilibrium model (see Chapter 12). However, the recent interest in comparative policy agenda-setting studies goes far beyond testing the punctuated equilibrium model to an interest in understanding attention dynamics and how they are shaped by factors like party competition and political institutions. These questions lead to new insights into how public opinion and elections affect public policy. This chapter reviews this recent trend and focuses on how the new insights into agenda-setting dynamics inform our understanding of public policy and policy change.

## Comparative studies of policy agendas

Over the past five years, a network of scholars (www.comparativeagendas.org) studying agenda-setting across a wide range of Western countries has emerged. The network emphasizes attention dynamics rather than policy change. A central element is the establishment of comparative large-scale datasets on attention to policy issues in, for instance, executive speeches (e.g. speeches at the opening of parliament), party manifestos, mass media and parliamentary activities (bills, interpellations, parliamentary questions, etc.). Many of these attention dynamics studies have clear implications for our understanding of policy dynamics and will therefore be introduced below.

One of the network's research areas is attention dynamics in executive speeches. While they do not directly represent policy decisions, they often contain a government's policy intentions or plans for the coming year and therefore their dynamics are of obvious interest in relation to policy dynamics. Some of the studies test the punctuated equilibrium model (see Chapter 12) (e.g. John and Jennings 2010); one study of the UK focuses on the responsiveness to public opinion (Jennings and John 2009); another examines the effect of factors like coalition composition and government life-cycle in the Dutch context (Breeman *et al.* 2009).

A central issue for comparative investigation of executive speeches has been the role of elections and government change (Mortensen *et al.* 2011). This discussion is closely linked to the "politics matters" approach in policy studies. From this perspective, elections are an important driver of policy change. They often lead to a change in the color of the government and a government of a different color will pursue different policy goals (cf. Schmidt 1996; Imbeau *et al.* 2001). Based on this theory, one would expect that elections—when they lead to a change in government color—lead to a change in issue priorities in executive speeches. A government of a different color would focus on different policy issues. However, the studies of executive speeches over the past 50 years in three West European countries (the UK, the Netherlands and Denmark) found that elections and changes in government color had very little effect. Only in the UK, the political system where one should expect the strongest effect, are there signs of a small effect from a change in government color (Mortensen *et al.* 2011). In other words, the color of the government has surprisingly little effect on the policy agenda of modern governments. The issues and thus policy problems, which they attend to, seem to be driven by other factors than the color of the government.

Nevertheless, the limited effect of elections and change in government color should not be interpreted as a sign of no change in the policy priorities of government. In the long run, they change substantially. Core issues like economy and defense have lost their dominance of executive agendas (Jennings *et al.* 2011) and issues like health care, the environment and crime have gained importance across countries. This does not imply that party competition is irrelevant for understanding what issues governments prioritize, but rather that we learn little about the timing of such processes if we focus on elections. To attract attention to issues, political parties need policy problems defined in a favorable way. And since policy problem developments are independent of elections, little is gained from focusing on elections when we want to understand the timing of major changes in government agendas. This comparative study indicates that it is more important whether or not parties find themselves in government or opposition because policy responsibility is key to shaping governments' prioritization of issue attention.

This idea is further explored in Green-Pedersen and Mortensen (2010). Once a government holds power, it is also expected to provide solutions to whatever societal problems emerge. So when the banking system collapses, major pollution events happen or the media report on waiting lists for hospital treatment, it is the government's problem, no matter whether the present government's policies have caused these problems in any way. Health care is a good example. All governments in the Western world face a difficult dilemma between a huge surge in the possibilities of detecting and treating diseases and the need to keep health care costs under control (Green-Pedersen and Wilkerson 2006). Thus, health care is a policy issue that governments in the Western world, regardless of party color, have been more or less forced to pay increasing attention to (Mortensen *et al.* 2011). Consistent with this idea of the "burden" of policy responsibility of being in government, Green-Pedersen and Mortensen (2010) have developed a model of issue competition that points to the agenda-setting power of opposition parties. A central implication of the model is that opposition parties are freer to focus continually on issues that are advantageous to them, whereas government parties are forced to respond more often to issues brought up on the so-called party system agenda. Using data on issue competition in Denmark covering 25 years and 23 issue categories, the empirical evaluation of this model clearly shows how opposition parties are capable of raising issues that the government needs to address later in executive speeches, for instance.

Paying attention is of course not the same as making policy. However, from an agenda-setting perspective increasing attention is very likely to lead to policy measures. There are limits to how much a government can talk about health care, for instance, without doing something in terms of policy. A recent study of law and order in Denmark (Seeberg 2011) shows that it can lead to significant policy changes when opposition parties raise an issue like law and order. The government's first response is most likely to address the issue in speeches, and so on, but if the issue does not die out in terms of attention, the government will also respond by changing policies, in this case by introducing longer and stricter sentences. Where the above study of attention to different issues in executive speeches focuses on similarities in attention to issues across countries, other studies focus on explaining cross-national differences in attention to policy issues and investigating the policy consequences. These cross-national studies often focus on cross-national differences in how much attention political parties pay to different policy issues. The underlying idea is that certain issues are politicized, which implies that all political parties will pay attention to them, whether or not they want to.

Green-Pedersen and Krogstrup (2009), for instance, study the politicization of immigration in Denmark and Sweden. The issue has been politicized in Denmark but not in Sweden and the explanation for this lies in the composition of the right-wing bloc of parties and the incentives this offers for mainstream right-wing parties. In Denmark the Liberals and the Conservatives dominate the right-wing bloc in terms of parliamentary seats. After 1993, when they found themselves in opposition, their strategy was to gain a majority with the extreme right. This involved a successful attempt to politicize immigration, even though it meant a conflict with the center-right party, the Social Liberals, which had supported the right-wing government before 1993. Sweden only has one mainstream right-wing party: the Conservatives. In terms of gaining a parliamentary majority, the mainstream right in Sweden is thus very dependent on the three center-right parties, and collaboration with the extreme right, including an attempt to politicize immigration, has thus not been an attractive option. The policy consequences of these differences in politicization are significant despite considerable skepticism toward immigration in both countries. In Denmark the consequence has been a significant tightening of the rules on immigration and for acquiring citizenship. This has not happened in Sweden.

The same basic explanatory model, where differences in party incentives to politicize issues lead to cross-national differences in issue politicization, which again generate cross-national differences in public policies, has been used to explain cross-national differences in policies with regard to morality issues like abortion and euthanasia. Green-Pedersen (2007) has investigated why euthanasia is legal in the Netherlands, but not in Denmark and found that the explanation was a conflict between religious and secular parties in the Dutch party system. In times of increasing secularization, morality issues have been used by the secular parties to put pressure on religious parties, such as the Christian Democrats. These parties have based their continuing electoral survival on issues like the welfare state and on avoiding issues such as abortion where their distinctive religious profile has become an increasing liability. The secular parties tried to politicize morality issues by demanding more permissive regulation of abortion and euthanasia, for instance. In Denmark, there is no conflict between religious and secular parties. Political parties are generally uninterested in morality issues. They are considered "non-political," ethical issues, which are not relevant for party competition. The policy consequences of this definition of the issues are mixed. On the subject of euthanasia, there has been no drive for permissive regulation in Denmark, whereas a permissive abortion regulation was adopted in the early 1970s. However, there has been no general move toward the more permissive regulation that is found in the Netherlands (cf. also Engeli *et al.* 2012). The two countries thus differ in their policy profile on morality issues despite similarities in public opinion. In both countries, there is support for legalizing euthanasia, but it plays no role in Denmark because of the non-political character of the issue (Green-Pedersen 2007).

These recent studies all show how important it is to study party incentives and party competition in terms of understanding primarily cross-national differences in attention to policy issues, but also cross-national differences in public policy. The difference in regulation of euthanasia in Denmark and the Netherlands cannot be explained without understanding the cross-national differences in party incentives to politicization and the same goes for the difference in immigration policies between Denmark and Sweden.

## Linking attention, public opinion and policy change

While the comparative studies have focused on explaining cross-national variation in attention to policy issues and then looked at the policy consequences of these changes, other studies have focused on how agenda-setting actually affects national policy-making. Do changes in the political agenda foreshadow changes in public policies? And does the effect of changes in the political agenda depend on the policy preferences expressed by the mass public?

By integrating the study of political agendas with classic assumptions about re-election oriented representation it has been hypothesized that the political agenda—defined as the collective attention of elected national policy-makers—matters to public policies, but the direction of the effect is crucially dependent on the policy opinions expressed by the mass public, because the potential electoral costs of unpopular policies increase with the issues' importance on the political agenda (see Mortensen 2010).

Macro-political institutions like Congress or national parliaments handle hundreds of issues every year, most of which are not very important from a re-election perspective because they, for various reasons, are subject to relatively low or decreasing political attention. Mass media coverage tends to fluctuate with the tides of the political agenda and if an issue does not attract much attention in macro-political venues like national parliaments or Congress it probably does not receive much attention among a broader public audience either (see e.g. Bennett 1990; Bennett *et al.* 2007). Hence, on many issues national policy-makers have some leeway to legislate as they see fit without much concern about being punished at the next election by retrospective voting. On the other hand, debates and activities in macro-political arenas both reflect and reinforce outside attention to the issue. Hence, re-election concerns about a given issue are assumed to rise with increased macro-political attention to that issue (see also Sulkin 2005). When that happens, the argument goes, the majority of the re-election-oriented national policy-makers seek to change policies toward the position expressed by the mass public on those issues. In other words, the policy effects of changes in the political agenda depend upon the policy preferences expressed by a majority of the mass public. For instance, in terms of public spending the implication is that popular spending issues where most of the public prefers increased spending do benefit in terms of monetary appropriations from increasing attention in the macro-political arena. Unpopular spending domains where most of the public prefers decreased public spending, on the other hand, are expected to suffer from increasing macro-political attention. Conversely, in times of decreasing macro-political attention where public opinion (and hence re-election motives) presumably will be less important to national spending decisions, unpopular spending domains may benefit relatively.

Using public spending as a measure of public policy, this agenda-policy hypothesis has been evaluated empirically in statistical time series regressions utilizing a Danish dataset of public spending attitudes, public spending, and the political agenda covering six issues from 1980 to 2003 (see Mortensen 2010). Across the issues, the results show that public opinion clearly affects policy changes after taking account of other potentially relevant agenda and spending determinants. For instance, in popular spending domains (in Denmark issues like law and order, pollution control, health and primary education where a majority over time and in every poll has expressed a preference for increased spending), there is a positive relationship between changes in macro-political attention and changes in public spending on these issues. In unpopular spending domains (in Denmark these may be issues like defense, development aid and culture) there is a negative relationship between changes in macro-political attention and changes in public spending.

A theoretically more elaborate version of this basic agenda-policy hypothesis has been presented and evaluated in a US study of the relationship between changes in congressional attention and federal budget appropriations across 12 spending domains and 33 years (1970–2003) (see Mortensen 2009). The modified claim is that the policy (spending) effects of attention shifts are strongest when the trade-off between re-election incentives and intensive group interests is low, which is the case when attention to popular issues peaks and attention to unpopular issues declines. Put differently, when popular issues are subject to increased macro-political attention congressional policy-makers can satisfy both public spending attitudes and specialized spending advocates by increasing spending on such issues. On the other hand, when popular issues attract decreasing attention policy-makers may become more hesitant to follow a narrow re-election incentive and withdraw monetary resources because of (anticipated) fierce opposition from vested spending interests. Thus, in popular spending domains the association between attention and spending changes is expected to be driven mainly by increased attention followed by relatively large spending increases, not by decreased attention followed by relatively large budget cuts.

Conversely, in spending domains in which a majority of the US public prefers less spending, the relationship between congressional attention and public spending may be driven by decreased congressional attention followed by increased spending investments advocated by special interest in times of less outside visibility, not by congressional attention peaks paving the way for large publicly supported spending cuts. Subsystem loyalties or fierce opposition from groups or agencies with intensive interests in a given unpopular spending program may not suffice to fully avoid cutbacks during macro-political attention peaks. However, as opposed to popular spending programs, unpopular programs are certainly not expected to benefit from increased macro-political attention, but to be built up in quieter times of decreasing macro-political attention (see Mortensen 2009).

Utilizing data from the US policy agendas project (see www.policyagendas.org) the empirical analyses support this conditional model of the agenda-policy relationship. In popular spending domains such as crime, environment, and health where most of the US public in every poll since 1970 has expressed a preference for increased spending, increases in congressional attention to these domains are followed by spending increases. In comparison, decreases in attention to popular spending domains are not to a similar extent followed by spending cuts. The reverse happens in unpopular spending domains where a majority of the US public in all polls since 1970 has expressed a preference for reduced spending (i.e. space exploration, foreign aid and welfare). Here, decreases in congressional attention are followed by spending increases, whereas attention increases do not show a spending effect. In other words, well-organized spending coalitions working within domains that are not very popular with the general public can better pursue their spending interests in times of decreasing outside attention and may be able to block large spending cuts when attention increases.

While these results are consistent with Redford's (1969) classic conception of macro and subsystem politics (see also Baumgartner and Jones 1993), the two studies offer the first large N empirical illustration of these ideas and advocate a more explicit confluence of the policy agenda-setting perspective developed by Baumgartner and Jones and more mainstream perspectives on representation and congressional policy-making. Furthermore, they demonstrate that policy changes also happen when issues are not politicized, but these changes can hardly be explained by factors like party competition and public opinion.

More important in times of low attention is subsystem politics dominated by organized interest groups, experts, advocacy coalitions, and bureaucrats with vested interests in the given subject. A good example of policy change without a major surge in macro-political attention is tobacco regulation, which in many West European countries has undergone substantial change over the past few years without being subject to party competition or strong support in public opinion. Western Europe has seen a surge in restrictions on smoking that is hard to explain by a surge in macro-political attention (cf. Albæk *et al.* 2007). Thus, a change in macro-political attention is an important, but not a necessary condition for policy change, and it is not a satisfactory stand-alone explanation if we want to understand directions of policy change.

One should note how these agenda-setting-inspired models of the attention-policy link differ from opinion-policy studies focusing on the broader concept of public saliency (see e.g. Page and Shapiro 1983; Soroka 2003; Baumgartner and Jones 2004). While the latter tend to focus on an issue's saliency to the public, the former focus on the policy-making process and the preferences of the relevant policy-makers. For instance, an issue might be salient to the general public without being subject to macro-political intervention because party competition does not form around that issue, just as macro-political intervention may anticipate, reduce, or perhaps even prevent increased public saliency of an issue. Furthermore, some problems do not have simple cures and will turn into major problems despite political action, but from a governmental re-election point of view, it may be too late to respond at that time. In a similar vein, as also implied by Redford's (1969) distinction between subsystem and macro-political actors, all policy-makers are most likely neither equally nor constantly concerned about potential voter reactions. This explicit focus on the policy-makers and the policy-making process also suggests that one considers not only the majority attitudes of the general public but also the demands and interests of specialized policy advocates with more intensive interests in the given policy programs. In other words, the findings reported in this section seem to call for a more general model of public policy-making that transcends the classic division between models of electoral competition and responsiveness to the mass public, on the one hand, and models that stress the power of special interests and subsystem actors, on the other. In this way, Schattschneider's (1960) strong legacy is still very significant in current developments in the literature on agenda-setting and public policy.

## Conclusion

While early agenda-setting studies were somewhat narrowly concerned with describing different agendas and studying agenda-setting per se, the recent wave of agenda-setting studies is much more inspired by and in dialogue with other major approaches to the study of public policy. Examples include literature on party competition, for instance the "politics matters" approach, literature on government coalitions, institutionalism, representation and the role of public opinion, mediatization of politics, as well as more classical literature on public spending and budgeting.

This, of course, implies that there is no narrow theoretical focus uniting the new scholars of agenda-setting and public policy, for instance the mandate theory underlying the major research program on party manifestoes (see e.g. Klingemann *et al.* 1994). What characterizes the group of agenda-setting scholars is a common interest in the concept of attention as well as rather strictly standardized approaches to how agenda-setting data are collected and coded across time and countries.

Still, it is possible to draw some general insights about what we have recently learned from an agenda-setting approach to public policy. First, shifts of party governments and elections are not strongly related to shifts in government agendas and policy. As the review of studies shows, this does not imply that political parties and their competition for electoral support are unimportant for political agendas and thus public policies, but only that elections, even when they lead to a change in government color, are not very central for understanding the dynamic of political agenda and public policy. Instead, the competition ongoing in-between elections between government and opposition parties has, for instance, been shown to be important for policy change.

Second, changes in attention have important policy consequences but this does not imply that policy change only happens as a result of changes in attention, nor does it imply a linear relationship where changes in attention push public policies in certain directions. Rather, changes in attention are important for public policy because they change the policy process. When an issue suddenly reaches the macro-political agenda, factors like party competition and public opinion become important to explain public policies. When issues receive limited macro-political attention, public policies are better explained by the nature of the political subsystems related to the issue.

Third, attention to political issues and thus the public policy agenda shows less cross-national variation than one would expect from an institutional approach. As the health care example showed, the issues and related problems matter and they might be universal at least across rather closely integrated (e.g. West European, countries). This does not mean that variation does not exist as the examples about immigration in Denmark and Sweden and morality issues in Denmark and the Netherlands showed. However, different dynamics of party competition seem to be a more important cause of variation than institutional differences.

## Bibliography

Albæk, Erik, Christoffer Green-Pedersen, Lars Beer Nielsen. 2007. 'Making tobacco consumption a political issue in the United States and Denmark: The dynamics of issue expansion in comparative perspective', *Journal of Comparative Policy Analysis: Research and Practice* 9(1): 1–20.

Bachrach, Peter and Morton S. Baratz. 1962. 'Two faces of power', *American Political Science Review* 56: 947–52.

Baumgartner, Frank R. and Bryan D. Jones. 1993. *Agendas and Instability in American Politics*. Chicago: University of Chicago Press.

—— and Bryan D. Jones. 2004. 'Representation and agenda-setting', *Policy Studies Journal* 32(1): 1–24.

——, Christoffer Green-Pedersen and Bryan D. Jones. 2006. 'Comparative studies of policy agendas', *Journal of European Public Policy* 13(7): 955–70.

Bennett, W. Lance. 1990. 'Toward a theory of press-state relations in the United States', *Journal of Communication* 40(2): 103–25.

——, Regina C. Lawrence and Steven Livingston. 2007. *When the Press Fails. Political Power and the News Media From Iraq to Katrina*. Chicago: University of Chicago Press.

Breeman, G., D. Lowery, C. Poppelaars, S. L. Resodihardjo, A. Timmermans and J. de Vries. 2009. 'Political attention in a coalition system: Analyzing queen's speeches in the Netherlands 1945–2007', *Acta Politica* 44(1): 1–27.

Cobb, Roger W. and Charles D. Elder. 1983. *Participation in American politics. The Dynamics of Agenda-building*. Baltimore, MD: Johns Hopkins University Press.

Engeli, Isabella, Christoffer Green-Pedersen and Lars T. Larsen (eds). 2012. *Morality Politics in Western Europe: Parties, Agendas, and Policy Choices*. London: Palgrave Macmillan.

Green-Pedersen, Christoffer. 2007. 'The conflict of conflicts in comparative perspective: Euthanasia as a political issue in Denmark, Belgium, and the Netherlands', *Comparative Politics* 39(3): 273–91.

——and John Wilkerson. 2006. 'How agenda-setting attributes shape politics: Problem attention, agenda dynamics and comparative health policy developments in the US and Denmark', *Journal of European Public Policy* 13(7): 1039–52.

——and Jesper Krogstrup. 2009. 'Immigration as a political issue in Denmark and Sweden', *European Journal of Political Research* 47(5): 610–34.

——and P.B. Mortensen. 2010. 'Who sets the agenda and who responds to it in the Danish parliament? A new model of issue competition and agenda-setting', *European Journal of Political Research* 49(2): 257–81

Imbeau, Louis M., François Petry and Moktar Lamari. 2001. 'Left-right party ideology and government policies: A meta-analysis', *European Journal of Political Research* 40(1): 1–29.

Jennings, W. and P. John. 2009. 'The dynamics of political attention: public opinion and the queen's speech in the United Kingdom', *American Journal of Political Science* 53(4): 838–54.

——, Shaun Bevan, Arco Timmermans, Laura Chaques, Gerard Breeman, Sylvain Brouard, Christoffer Green-Pedersen, Peter John, Peter B. Mortensen and Anna Palau. 2011. 'Effects of the core functions of government on the diversity of executive agendas.' *Comparative Political Studies* 59(1): 74–98.

John, P. and W. Jennings. (2010. 'Punctuations and turning points in British politics: The policy agenda of the Queen's speech, 1940-2005', *British Journal of Political Science* 40(3): 561–86.

Kingdon, John W. 1995. *Agendas, Alternatives, and Public Policies*. New York: HarperCollins College Publishers.

Klingemann, Hans-Dieter, Richard Hofferbert and Ian Budge. 1994. *Parties, Policies, and Democracy*. Boulder, CO: Westview Press.

Mortensen, Peter B. 2009. 'Political attention and public spending in the United States', *Policy Studies Journal* 37(3): 435–55.

—— 2010. 'Political attention and public policy: a study of how agenda-setting matters', *Scandinavian Political Studies* 33(4): 356–80.

——, Cristoffer Green-Pedersen, Gerard Breeman, Laura Chaqués Bonafont, Will Jennings, Peter John, Anna M. Palau Rogué, Arco Timmermans. 2011. 'Comparing government agendas: Executive speeches in the Netherlands, United Kingdom, and Denmark', *Comparative Political Studies* 44(8): 973–1000.

Page, Benjamin I. and Robert Y. Shapiro. 1983. 'Effects of public opinion on policy', *American Political Science Review* 77(1): 175–90.

Redford, Emmette S. 1969. *Democracy in the Administrative State*. New York: Oxford University Press.

Schattschneider, Elmer E. 1960. *The Semisovereign People*. New York: Holt, Rinehart and Winston.

Schmidt, Manfred G. 1996. 'When parties matter: A review of the possibilities and limits of partisan influence on public policy', *European Journal of Political Research* 30(2): 155–83.

Seeberg, Henrik. 2011. 'Parties and politics: how policy changes when the opposition party sets the agenda', Aarhus University Department of Political Science.

Soroka, Stuart N. 2003. 'Media, public opinion and foreign policy', *Harvard International Journal of Press and Politics* 8(1): 27–48.

Sulkin, Tracy. 2005. *Issue Politics in Congress*. Cambridge; Cambridge University Press.

Zahariadis, Nikolaos. 1995. *Markets, States and Public Policy: Privatization in Britain and France*. Ann Arbor, MI: University of Michigan Press.

# 14

# Focusing events and policy windows

*Thomas A. Birkland and Sarah E. DeYoung*

## Introduction: focusing events in the agenda-setting process

Policy scholars have long argued that the "stages" model of the policy process is not a useful model for generating testable hypotheses about policy-making (Nakamura 1987; Sabatier 1988; Sabatier 1991a, 1991b). But scholars still find the stages as useful "sites" for the study of important elements of the policy process, from problem recognition through implementation (deLeon 1999). Among the most intensively studied stages is agenda-setting, which is the process by which some issues gain and others lose attention among policy-makers and the public. Agenda-setting is important to all theories of the policy process because "the definition of the alternatives is the supreme instrument of power" (Schattschneider 1975: 66). Groups—or, more specifically, advocacy coalitions, in Sabatier's Advocacy Coalition Framework—engage in rhetorical battles, in many different venues, to gain access to the agenda while attempting to deny agenda access to other actors (Cobb and Ross 1997). Group competition, a major driving force in agenda-setting, can be fierce because of the limited capacity of any system or institution to accommodate all issues and ideas (Walker 1977; Baumgartner and Jones 1993; Cobb and Elder 1983). This competition is over both which problems are most important, and over what causes and solutions surround any one problem (Hilgartner and Bosk 1988; Lawrence and Birkland 2000, 2004; Birkland and Lawrence 2009). The agenda-setting process is therefore a system of sifting issues, problems and ideas, and implicitly assigning priorities to these issues.

## Focusing events as an aspect of agenda-setting

John Kingdon argues that agenda change is driven by two broad phenomena: changes in indicators of underlying problems, which lead to debates over whether and to what extent a problem exists and is worthy of action; and *focusing events*, or sudden shocks to policy systems that lead to attention and potential policy change.

John Kingdon used the term "focusing event" within a general discussion of "Focusing Events, Crises, and Symbols" (Kingdon 2003, 94–100). Kingdon calls focusing events a "little push" "like a crisis or disaster that comes along to call attention to the problem, a powerful symbol that catches on, or the personal experience of a policymaker." Kingdon found that some policy domains are less prone to sudden events than are low-visibility policy domains that are prone to sudden shocks (Birkland 1997) which trigger a great deal of rapid attention, followed by a steep drop-off in attention after the acute phase of a disaster or crisis (Downs 1972). Kingdon further notes that focusing events gain their agenda-setting power by aggregating their harms in one place and time. A plane crash that kills 200 people gets more attention than 200 single fatal car wrecks; aviation is therefore a domain that is more prone to focusing events than is automobile safety, where problems tend to be discovered through the accumulation of information. A starker example in the United States would be the example of the 9/11 attacks, which were socially, politically, and economically devastating, even though the death toll of about 3,000 people is less than 10 percent of annual road fatalities in the United States. Other problems—cancer, heart disease, other forms of accidents—kill far more people than terrorist attacks, but focusing events are much more sudden, and their harms more easily spoken of in terms of a place ("Oklahoma City") or a time ("9/11").

Before Kingdon's book was published, there was a broad acknowledgment that disasters and crises were important in the policy process, but little systematic research on their agenda-setting power. Cobb and Elder examine events they call "circumstantial reactors," such as the 1969 Santa Barbara oil spill, "that led to a reconsideration of the whole question of offshore drilling regulations" (1983: 83). Broader ecological change, such as population growth, economic shifts, and black migration, are also circumstantial reactors, but these changes are much more subtle than natural disasters or technological accidents, and are therefore less likely to serve as a time—and space—definite rallying point for group attention and mobilization. As Kingdon argues, subtle changes are less likely to be viewed as "events" than are sudden, dramatic, and visible problems. These elements of the policy process have a greater influence on the problem stream and on the accumulation of ideas and evidence to justify policy change.

Traditionally, sudden events were thought to "simply bowl over everything standing in the way of prominence on the agenda" (Kingdon 2003: 96). Kingdon portrays focusing events as being more varied and subtle, and includes as focusing events personal experiences of policy-makers with matters of personal interest, such as disease that affect them or their families. Kingdon also argues that "the emergence and diffusion of a powerful symbol" is a focusing event that "acts … as reinforcement for something already taking place" (2003: 97). When symbols of events propagate—the elderly woman in New Orleans sheltering herself from the rain with an American flag, the raising of the flag at Ground Zero in a manner reminiscent of the raising of the flag at Iwo Jima, or the images of oil-soaked wildlife after oil spills—these symbols would not have their power if it were not for *the event itself*. The propagation of the symbol amplifies the focusing power of the event, particularly if the symbol is particularly evocative (Birkland and Lawrence 2002). But Kingdon seems to argue that the sudden uptake of a symbol or idea—what scholars in the new media call a *meme*—is itself a focusing event.

Kingdon's notion of a focusing event is important, but the term has often been uncritically adopted in the literature, often as a term of art that is never precisely defined. This may be because Kingdon defined and described focusing events in a way that is too broad to guide focused empirical research. He conflates sudden crises and shocks with individual experience and symbol propagation that are often reflective of what Peter May (1992) calls political learning about more effective policy arguments, which is less about the idea of *focusing* attention through an *event*, the latter term suggesting a phenomenon that is easily placed in time.

Second, Kingdon compares sudden events with political events, such as protest activity, that are purposefully caused, such as the 1963 March on Washington for Jobs and Freedom, a key event in the history of the civil rights movement. Including these events in the definition of focusing events confuses the role of political mobilization in the "politics" stream with the revelation and depiction of problems in the "problem" stream. "Shocking" and sudden focusing events are not purposefully caused, and can be viewed as exogenous to a policy community or domain, even if the policies and practices adopted by key members of that community make such events more likely.

Third, Kingdon's definition of a focusing event is retrodictive, which is unsurprising given the nature of his research method. While this definition is suggestive of a way of empirically studying the agenda-setting effects of events, it was insufficient to develop a testable model of focusing event politics. Birkland (1997, 1998) focused his model of *potential* focusing events on policy domains prone to crises more on the crisis and disaster aspect of this definition, a direction that has been broadly adopted, as we show here. Birkland defines a *potential focusing event* as an event that is sudden, relatively rare, can be reasonably defined as harmful or revealing the possibility of potentially greater future harms, inflicts harms or suggests potential harms that are or could be concentrated on a definable geographical area or community of interest, and that is known to policy-makers and the public virtually simultaneously (1997: 22).

The term *potential* highlights that an event may influence the agenda, but one cannot say with certainty precisely what, if any, that effect will be, and that one can only study that event's effects compared with a similar class of events. While we may "know" intuitively that an event—the Deepwater Horizon Oil Spill, 9/11, or Hurricane Katrina—will gain a lot of attention, it is difficult to know in advance how *focal* that event will be. Will the event make a more significant and discernible difference on the agenda than competing events and issues? Will that event have any discernible influence on policy changes? But we cannot collect a set of events from one particular class of event and a priori decide that these events are equally and significantly influential. Only careful analysis can do so.

## Foundations of focusing event theory

Focusing event theory is part of the broader scholarship on the agenda-setting process; it relies heavily on the idea that agenda space is limited, and that groups and interests compete for attention. One strand of this research focuses on the nature of the problems themselves including their expansion to a larger more attentive audience (Cobb *et al.* 1976; Cobb and Elder 1983; Cobb and Ross 1997) and how long that attention may last (Downs 1972). The nature of the actors and the nature of the problems interact with each other to promote or impede issue expansion. These theories are important because they help us to understand how groups seek to find or express the "meaning" of an event (Schattschneider 1975; Molotch and Lester 1974, as cited in Best 2010; Nohrstedt 2010).

A focusing event, by definition, increases attention to a public issue or problem. Baumgartner and Jones (1993) note that this attention is usually *negative* attention, and negative attention often yields further attention, thereby moving issues closer to potential policy changes. However, political elites do not always resist change, even if policy monopolies are reorganized. Focusing events, particularly in policy domains characterized as "policies without publics," (May 1990) yield "internal mobilization" efforts to promote the change that policy elites prefer (Cobb and Elder 1983). Indeed, Best (2010) cites Molotch and Lester's (1975) claim that "actor-promoted events" (APEs, in her term) are more likely to generate attention when the actors are elites with which news media already have steady contacts, and whose actions are considered important by definition. The messages these actors seek to convey are generally pro-status quo, or at least pro-elite, to the extent that elites sometimes desire policy change, particularly in "policies without publics" (May 1990). Later we consider Best's challenge to this proposition in her groundbreaking work on purposive events and agenda-setting in the news media.

A second strand is the use of language, stories, metaphors, and symbols, to advance or retard issues on the agenda. Contained in this strand is the process of social construction, by which societies collectively define and explain the nature and cause of problems. Students of the media explain how issues gain the attention of journalists, how journalists and their sources use symbols and stories to explain complex issues, and how news consumers respond to these issues and symbols (Edelman 1967, 1988; Stone 1989, 2002; Majone 1989; Schneider and Ingram 1991). Related to this is the literature on problem framing in government and the mass media (Entman 1993; Burnier 1994; Lawrence 2000), which has been profitably applied to studies of focusing events (Glascock 2004; Gunter 2005; Liu *et al.* 2011). Framing theory argues that that participants in policy debate frame stories about problems to fulfill news-gathering routines designed to make the story both efficient and compelling (Bennett 2003), and to motivate action by its supporters, inaction by its opponents, or both. These symbols are promoted by a policy entrepreneur, who is an individualactive in the policy community because of their technical expertise in their field, political expertise, and ability to broker deals that lead to new programs and policies (Kingdon 2003; Mintrom 1997; Mintrom and Vergari 1998). Recent studies referencing focusing events have further restated the roles of policy entrepreneurs (Gunter 2005; Wood 2006). Focusing events often gain their power from the propagation of symbols, involvement of policy entrepreneurs, as well as through group mobilization—all of which can overlap with one another in order to cause momentum for agenda change and potential policy change.

## The special role of group coalescence and mobilization

A third theoretical strand that is important for understanding focusing events within the agenda-setting tradition is group coalescence and mobilization, "because of the impact of the nature of the policy community on the policy process" (Baumgartner and Jones 1993: 43). Groups coalesce to form advocacy coalitions based on mutual interests and values. Sabatier predicts that two to four advocacy coalitions will form in most policy domains. However, some domains prone to sudden disasters may be characterized as "policies without publics" (May 1990), in which policy-making is often the domain of technical experts, with little public mobilization around particular policy changes after a major crisis or disaster, (Birkland 1998) beyond the usual diffuse claims that policies should work "better" in some way. These domains are characterized by one advocacy coalition, which may be quite weak. In many policy domains characterized by focusing events, the events drive an "internal mobilization" effort among existing group members to resolve a problem about which the public is broadly concerned, but is generally unable or unmotivated to organize around. In other words, focusing events are not always triggers for mass mobilization or sustained public attention.

However, policy domains that are part of the broader political and policy debate can see very intense group activity. Birkland's 1997 study found that the earthquake and hurricane policy domains were very much characterized by an internal mobilization model of agenda-setting and policy change, while in the oil spill and nuclear power policy domains, there were discernible advocacy coalitions that were engaged in direct competition. Even here, though, there are important differences. Birkland argued that oil spills have a much greater likelihood of mobilizing groups to oppose oil shipping and exploration because of the very visible and deeply felt damage done by these spills, as evidence by images of oily otters after *Exxon Valdez*, or idled fishing boats after the Deepwater Horizon spill. In this case, oil companies sought to "contain the scope of conflict," in Schattschneider's terms, while the highly polarized nuclear power policy domain was less influenced by the dominant event, the Three Mile Island nuclear accident. The degree of polarization therefore influences post-event politics (Walgrave and Verhulst 2009).

Focusing events may trigger greater attention to problems and solutions because they increase the likelihood of more influential and powerful actors entering the conflict on the side of policy change (Schattschneider 1975; Baumgartner and Jones 1993), by way of greater claims of policy failure and a more active search for solutions, leading to a greater likelihood of policy change (Birkland 2006).

But one must not make too much of event-triggered group mobilization. Sometimes we attribute greater power to events than they deserve. Kingdon notes that we cannot trace the discovery or the propagation of a policy idea to its first instance, lest we engage in "infinite regress." In a similar manner, in some events we have to ask: Which came first, the problem, or the event? Among the public there is widespread belief that the Three Mile Island (TMI) nuclear power plant accident in 1979 was the event that stalled the movement toward more nuclear power plants for generating electricity. As Baumgartner and Jones note in their chapter on nuclear power, the "policy image" of nuclear power had eroded before TMI—the major milestones in that erosion were the creation of the Nuclear Regulatory Commission (NRC) and the abolition of the Atomic Energy Commission and its congressional champion, the Joint Committee on Atomic Energy (JCAE). Birkland (1997: Chapter 5) found that, at the time of TMI, the nuclear power policy domain was highly polarized and the policy community was already fiercely debating both the meaning of TMI (which was not, is still not, self-evident) and the nature of nuclear power generally. The lack of one clear interpretation of the nature and meaning of the TMI accident meant that all the participants in the debate could use the accident for their own rhetorical ends: as evidence either for the "defense in depth" notion of nuclear safety, or for the idea that nuclear power contained unknown risks, that other incidents were equally or more serious than TMI, and that heretofore poorly understood systems accidents could yield catastrophic disasters (Perrow 1999). In the end, TMI was an important event, and it was focal in its agenda-setting meaning, but its role in group mobilization and actual policy-making is less clear.

Apart from group efforts to expand issues, major events often reach the agenda without group promotion through media propagation of news and symbols of the event. This coverage of a sudden and shocking event, such as a particularly horrific airline crash, or school shooting, makes the public aware of these events without efforts on the part of group leaders to induce attention. This media propagation of symbols gives less powerful groups another advantage in policy debates. Pro-change groups are relieved of the obligation to create and interpret powerful images and symbols of the problem. Rather, groups only need to repeat the already existing symbols that the media have seized upon as the most important in the current crisis. These obvious symbols are likely to carry more emotional weight than industry or governmental assurances that policy usually works well. Carpenter and Sin (2007) found that the images of fragile children who had been poisoned by Sulfanilamide were influential in triggering a strong outcry that led to more stringent regulation and licensing for medications in the Food and Drug Act of 1938. Thus, media-generated symbols of health, environmental, or other crises or catastrophes are often used by groups as an important recruiting tool – thereby expanding the issue—and as a form of evidence of the need for policy change.

To conclude, all these theoretical strands assume that agenda-setting is not a neutral, objective, or rational process. Rather, it is the result of a society, acting through its political and social institutions, building a consensus on the meanings of problems and the range of acceptable solutions. There are many possible constructions that compete with each other to tell the story of why a problem is a problem, who benefits or is harmed by the problem, whose fault it is, and how it can be solved (Gusfield 1981; Schneider and Ingram 1991; Schneider 2008; Stone 1989, 2002).

## Some empirical applications of focusing event theory

In this section we show how the application of the focusing event concept can reveal important features of agenda-setting, group activity, and potential convergence or divergence in what a policy community deems to be the "real" problem revealed by a focusing event.

*Ab initio,* the influence of a particular event on the formal agenda of the news media and political institutions should be detectable because focusing events are more sharply defined in time than are social, demographic, or ideological changes. Take, for example, both news media and congressional attention to terrorism before and after the September 11 terrorist attacks (Figure 14.1). In this figure, data on the number of *New York Times* articles and the number of witnesses appearing before congressional hearings on these issues are normalized to the same scale, for ease of comparison. The key focusing event in this data is obvious, but the increase in attention is much more acute in the news media than in Congress. The news media tend to focus to a much greater extent on the seeming novelty of a particular event itself, while Congress tends to be seized by the broader problem—in this case, terrorism—for a longer time than the media, whose interest in the broader problem drops off rather rapidly.

The pattern shown in Figure 14.1 is not particularly surprising. But attention is not the same as the substance of the agenda. Birkland found that the dominant topic of discussion in congressional hearings can change considerably when testimony is offered about a particular event, compared with testimony about the general problem itself, as shown in Table 14.1.

## Differences in the substance of discussion after focusing events

We know that focusing events gain increased attention, and we can plot that attention in terms of media coverage and congressional activity. However, does the substance or content of the discussion change in the presence of a recent event from the "typical" discussion?

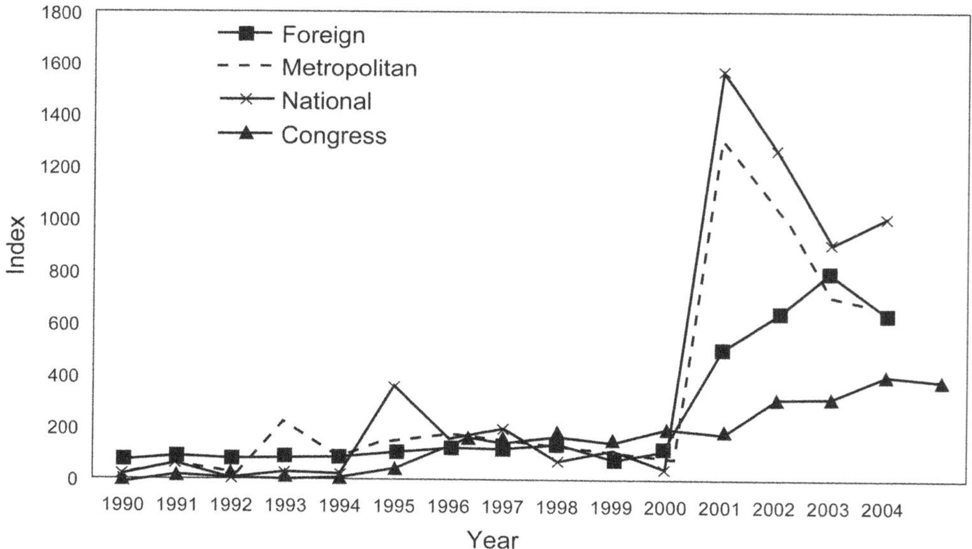


*Figure 14.1* Comparative attention to terrorism
Source: LexisNexis search for term terrorism in headline, lead, or key terms, by desk; testimony in LexisNexis congressional testimony database, by term terrorism. Birkland 2006, Figure 2.1

*Table 14.1* The substance of the agenda when events are or are not mentioned in testimony

| | *Testimony on specific event* | *All other testimony* | *All testimony* |
|---|---|---|---|
| *Earthquake* | Disaster relief | NEHRP | Disaster relief |
| *Hurricane* | Disaster relief | Disaster relief | Disaster relief |
| *Oil spill* | Spill cleanup and costs | Liability, compensation and costs | Liability, compensation and costs |
| *Nuclear Power* | Cleanup | Licensing | Licensing |

Source: Birkland (1998), Table 1

In most policy domains that are prone to sudden, dramatic events, there are two discernible dominant topics: those that dominate inter-event periods, when focusing events are often dim memories, and periods in which an issue dominates the agenda as a direct consequence of a recent event. Table 14.1 reflects this proposition. These categories were designed so that parallels could be drawn among the four domains: the term "disaster relief," for example, is roughly analogous to the term "cleanup" in the industrial domains because they both involve the immediate response to a disaster or accident. In all but the hurricane domains, the dominant issue on the agenda changes when an event is specifically mentioned. In the other domains, the existence of an event on the agenda influences the actual substance of discussion in the domain. The oil spill and nuclear power policy domains have at two broad advocacy coalitions, generally a pro-industry and pro-environment coalition. There appears to be one advocacy coalition in earthquake policy, a professional community that works to educate Congress and to advocate for policy change intra-disaster. Such a community is not present, or not called upon, by Congress, and most testimony in the hurricane domain is therefore about the rapid and generous delivery of disaster relief.

This research led Birkland to suggest that focusing events led to a convergence of opinion about the *nature* of problems on the agenda, and to assume that an event led to something like convergence toward a policy solution. Indeed, in the oil spill domain, this supposition was strongly confirmed by the passage of the Oil Pollution Act of 1990 soon after the *Exxon Valdez* oil spill; the oil spill broke a 14-year legislative logjam. This convergence proposition was also built on the normative conviction that there *should* be some convergence on one or very few problem definitions, which should yield a narrow range of policy options from which to choose.

Contrary to this supposition, Hilgartner and Bosk (1988) and Lawrence (2000) argued that the elevation of an issue on the agenda can yield a competition over how to frame or describe the problem, thereby creating a proliferation of "causal stories" (Stone 1989) about why some events happened, and what should be done. Lawrence and Birkland found that in the case of a particular focusing event—the Littleton school shootings—considerable attention was paid to the "school violence" problem, broadly conceived, but the causal stories vary considerably, as shown in Figure 14.2.

Here, we see considerable divergence in the dominant frames or causal stories, where the news media assigned more importance to guns, rank and file members of Congress to guns, pop culture, and a potpourri of other causes, while the creation of additional school programs—or the increased funding or enforcement effort devoted to them—was the modal frame in legislation. The explanation is simple: Congress, not being directly responsible for the management of schools, politically constrained on the gun issue, and constitutionally constrained to regulate speech and expression, settled on where it can have the most visible influence. In this case, Congress, in seeking a policy solution, largely turned to distributive spending to encourage greater efforts by schools to engage in a wide range of social service programs to prevent school violence (Birkland and Lawrence 2009).

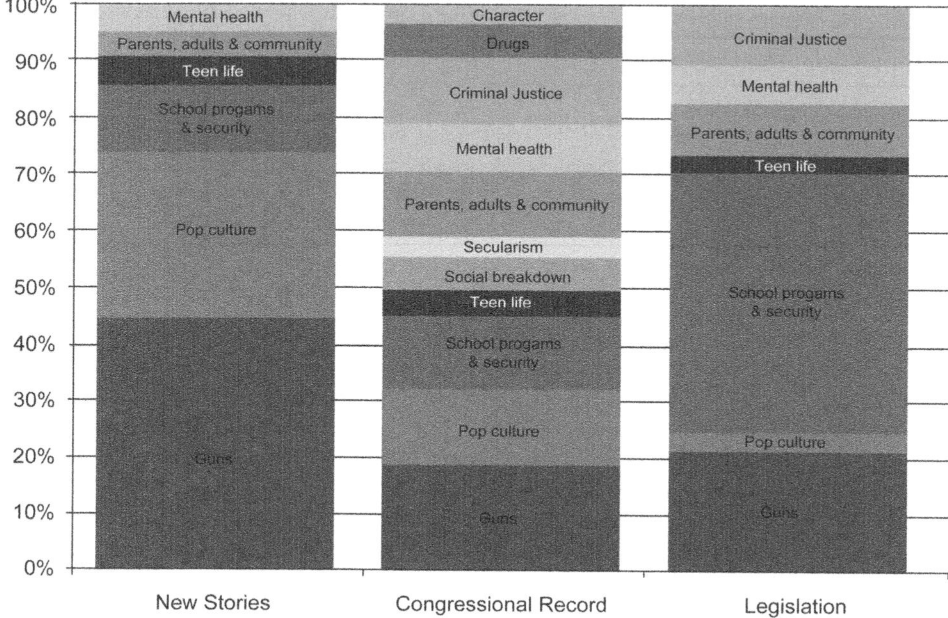


*Figure 14.2* Dominant problem frames in school violence, by venue
Source: Based on Table 1 in Lawrence and Birkland (2004)

Finally, it is possible to study the ideas contained in legislation in a disaster-prone domain and consider whether legislative ideas converge to a focused few ideas, or expand to cover much wider ground. The results of this analysis are provided in Table 14.2, which shows the main ideas contained in legislation that followed major aviation security incidents (including the aftermath of the 1996 ValuJet and TWA crashes, the latter of which was widely believed to have been the result of a terrorist bombing, even though it was not).

This empirical work shows that thinking on focusing events has evolved, from the simple idea that focusing events "bowl over" other issues, to the more sophisticated idea that focusing events have variable influences on policy communities, on the nature of policy debate, and the content of policy ideas in different policy domains.

## Broader applications of the focusing event idea

Since Birkland's (1997) refinement of Kingdon's (2003) definition of focusing events, other scholars have applied or mentioned focusing event theory as an important aspect of the policy process. This work generally falls into three broad categories: research that cites Kingdon or Birkland uncritically, accepting the definitions without any critical analysis, often simply to acknowledge that events matter; work that cites Kingdon or Birkland and use the focusing event theory to build, reinforce, or expand the definitions of focusing events and their causal mechanisms; and work that seems to us to misapply the focusing event concept to other phenomena that better explain the processes being described.

A great deal of work relies on Kingdon's or Birkland's discussion of focusing events by simply acknowledging the importance of focusing events, without careful dissection of agenda-setting theory. Works that cite Kingdon only (e.g. Oakley 2009; Prince 2010; Vaughan and Arsneault

*Table 14.2* Key issues addressed in aviation security legislation

| *Topic* | *Aviation Security Improvement Act of 1990* | *Federal Aviation Authorization Act of 1996* | *Federal Aviation Administration Authorization Bill* | *Airport Security Improvement Act of 2000* | *Aviation and Transportation Security Act* | *Homeland Security Act of 2002* |
|---|---|---|---|---|---|---|
| Airport access control | • | | | | • | |
| Baggage matching | • | • | | | • | |
| Background checks of employees | • | • | | • | • | |
| Cargo and mail security | • | • | | | • | |
| Cockpit security | | | | | • | |
| Employee ID systems | | | | | • | |
| Explosives and explosives detection | • | • | • | | • | • |
| Create or restore air marshals | | | | | • | |
| Modify existing organizations | • | | | | | • |
| Create new organizations | | | | | • | • |
| Passenger profiling | | • | | | • | |
| Allow pilots to carry fatal weapons | | | | | • | • |
| Allow pilots to carry nonfatal weapons | | | | | • | |
| Certification of screening companies | | • | | | | |
| Require screening personnel be US citizens | | | | | | • |
| Require all airport personnel be screened (including flight crews) | | | | | • | |
| Screeners—general issues | • | | | | • | |
| Make screeners federal employees | | • | | | • | |
| Provide security training to the aircrew | | | | | • | |
| Provide security training to pilots | | | | | • | |
| *Total* | 7 | 8 | 1 | 1 | 17 | 5 |

Source: Birkland (2004).

2008) are works that contain overviews of major agenda-setting theory, with a focus on the streams model, but that fall short of carefully differentiating focusing events from other drivers of agenda change. Similarly, works that cite Birkland but not Kingdon (e.g. Ackleson 2005; Chenoweth and Clarke 2010; Davis 2006; Einsiedel 2000; Melis and Pulwarty 2001; Verhulst and Walgrave 2009) often simply recapitulate Birkland's definition of a focusing event testing the definition or the underlying theory. The second body expands on theory by applying a case and then building an argument for whether the case or event can be considered as a focusing event, usually by using quantitative and qualitative data to reinforce or analyze how the case adheres to the focusing event concept. These studies may also reconsider the definition of focusing events in light of the new data and interpretation. For example, Busenberg (2000) makes an interesting case for the second-order effects of policy changes that can be engendered by focusing events. He showed how the enactment of the Oil Pollution Act (OPA) of 1990 soon after the *Exxon Valdez* oil spill created an atmosphere in which coalitions and oil companies were more willing to collaborate to prevent and mitigate future spills, and that the OPA induced companies more open to innovative strategies than they had been before the spill and the OPA.

A particularly promising study is Best's (2010) analysis of how local newspapers in Denver treated news events related to homelessness. Best coded story frames to consider, among other things, whether stories were episodic or thematic, and whether the events being covered were "actor promoted events" (APEs) or "non-actor promoted events" (NAPEs). Best draws on a wide range of literature on problem framing to develop sophisticated models to find that NAPEs were highly likely to trigger thematic stories about the problem of homelessness, which appears to support the idea, implicit in Birkland's work and explicit in work by Lawrence (2000) and Molotch and Lester (1975) that NAPEs will trigger greater thematic coverage. But, as we described earlier, the idea that an event triggers a broader discussion does not mean that the potential explanations in the media focus on broader systemic problems.

Best found that, in news coverage of high-profile murders of homeless men in Denver, newspapers were more prone to "problematize" (in Lawrence's term) individual choices to remain homeless than they were to cast light on systemic causes of homelessness. Contrary to her expectations, APEs were found to be more likely to challenge the status quo, which Best claims is contrary to Molotch and Lester's theory that APEs promote the status quo. But focusing event theory and agenda-setting theory could explain the pro-change orientation of elites as a form of internal mobilization among a set of elite who perceive homelessness to be a problem deserving attention and policy change. Best also notes that the articles that contained content that promoted change and homelessness amelioration were most often written or promoted by organizations that were dedicated to social change (2010: 87).

The third category of literature is characterized by a form of overreaching in which other phenomena are characterized as focusing events. For example, Collins and Kapuçu (2008) discuss the importance of warning systems for tornadoes, using "tornadoes as a focusing event." But their use of the term is synonymous with a presumably attention-grabbing event (the tornado itself). Indeed, many uses of the term do not delve beyond this meaning.

Another common misuse of the concept comes when the surprising result of an election is cited as a focusing event, as when Béland (2005) and Blankenau (2001) state or imply that the 1991 election of Harris Wofford to the US Senate was a focusing event that propelled health care reform onto the agenda. In Kingdon's streams metaphor, these surprising results are best understood as a change in the political stream that can be harnessed, as was done by health care reformers, to claim that the political atmosphere has changed such that a window of opportunity for policy change is more likely. An election is not a focusing event because it is expected, planned, and part of normal governmental routine. And it is very difficult to discern whether

Wofford's election was more a reflection of growing attention to health care reform than a trigger of it. In any case, the election is better accommodated in other aspects of Kingdon's model, and need not be force-fitted into the focusing event framework.

Similarly, some researchers imply that indicators are synonymous with focusing events, and they confuse an indicator change with a focusing event, as in the following inference: "Indicators are inherently interconnected with focusing events and feedback in the sense that they reflect an objective measure of the former and are prone to subjective constructs regarding the latter" (Galland and McDaniels 2008: 519). This claim is problematic because indicators are as much symbols as they are facts. But while the essential idea that indicators and focusing events interact is a good insight, what distinguishes the agenda-setting power of a focusing event is its symbolic power in a particular place and time, not in indicators of a problem. This is not to deny the idea that a focusing event can trigger a search for more and better indicators of the problem revealed by the event.

Finally, we also found examples in which focusing events are mentioned without reference to the literature at all, as when Green-Pederson (2007: 624) argues that "Focusing events ... are hard to predict or even include in variable-oriented explanations." The latter claim may be true, but without any theoretical warrant or appeal to the literature as the basis for this claim.

Most of the studies we found were not comparative studies of similar types of events within a broader class of events, such as "disasters" or "natural disasters" or "industrial accidents." Birkland's 1997 study revealed considerable differences in the outcomes of event-driven debates. By contrast, the studies we reviewed here made few such comparisons of policy community comparisons for "matching" focusing events with corresponding communities. Most research focuses on policy changes over time in connection with one event in one community. (e.g. Carpenter and Sin 2007) or comparing the policy differences across countries (Lowry 2006), rather than across events within similar domains, such as Birkland's (1997) comparison of hurricane and earthquake coalition organization.

Fishman (1999) makes a valuable distinction between Type One (common) and Type Two (novel) focusing events. This distinction is crucial in understanding the way in which the event may cause a "window of opportunity" (Kingdon 2003) because the event type will have varying contextual factors that will influence possible policy solutions, as well as on framing and symbol propagation.

## Conclusion and future directions: focusing events and policy change

A common feature of the focusing event literature is that it often enthusiastically applies the focusing event concept to all manner of events. Many of these events are not rare, or sudden, or harmful, in the sense that Birkland's definition suggests. For those policy domains in which focusing events are important one can at least make a prima facie case that events can often be precursors—or, if we might be so bold, to be triggers—of policy change. Birkland shows this phenomenon in studying how the *Exxon Valdez* oil spill broke a 14-year-long legislative deadlock over comprehensive oil spill liability legislation. The September 11 terrorist attacks are widely understood to have triggered major policy change in the United States (in the form of homeland security initiatives and the restructuring of the Federal Emergency Management Agency (FEMA) into the Department of Homeland Security (DHS)), although the shape and nature of that change is very broad and cannot be said to have resulted from some sort of sudden consensus about *the* problem revealed by the event. Instead, the event influenced many policy communities and policy regimes (May *et al.* 2006). But the mechanism by which agenda change is turned into policy change is not yet well defined; we can tell stories about these changes, but the theory remains thin.

Birkland (2006) outlined a theory of event-driven policy change and learning which is beyond the scope of this chapter. To summarize, he argues that focusing events reveal policy failures—which are the fodder for interest group debate, because these failures reveal the problems that policy entrepreneurs join to "solutions" in the post-event window of opportunity. But, as we have discussed, any event is a *potential* focusing event that has the *potential* to open a window, and, even if the window opens, has the potential to yield policy change. Birkland's model allows, therefore, for an accumulation of knowledge driven by events, until, at some point, an event brings together all other event-driven knowledge at a point where it is possible for the policy system to show evidence of "learning" from the accumulation of events. This formulation is attractive, because it ties to the literature on ideas and learning from the policy process and from organizational theory. However, these bodies of literature are not fully reconciled in a way that would support policy change. But recent research shows that the theoretical construction is promising and can be accommodated in broader theoretical frameworks, such as the ACF (Albright 2011).

Among the works we reviewed for this chapter, there seems to be a sense—not explicitly stated, however—that Birkland's definition of *focusing event* may be so restrictive that there would be few events to study, thereby defining too small a set of phenomena as focusing events. The variability of the implicit or explicit definitions of the term focusing event suggest that it may be useful to attempt to create some categories or typologies of events, much as Birkland (1997: Chapter 6) did. Neither Birkland nor other scholars have followed up on these tentative categories with more careful research, but Fishman's (1999) notion of Type One and Type two events is promising. To the extent that future research is undertaken on focusing events, our goal should be to improve the explanatory and predictive power of any theory of these events. Such a theory should lend itself to replication and testing across multiple policy domains over many years. A good foundation has been laid in the social sciences, and with continued sudden, dramatic, and unsettling events gaining attention, there is no paucity of cases or of policy domains subject to these events, all of which provide fruitful material for research.

## Bibliography


Ackleson, Jason. 2005. 'Border security technologies: Local and regional implications', *Review of Policy Research* 22(2): 137–55.

Albright, Elizabeth A. 2011. 'Policy change and learning in response to extreme flood events in Hungary: An advocacy coalition approach', *Policy Studies Journal* 39(3): 485–511.

Baumgartner, Frank R. and Bryan D. Jones. 1993. *Agendas and Instability in American Politics.* Chicago: University of Chicago Press.

Béland, D. 2005. 'Ideas and social policy: An institutionalist perspective', *Social Policy and Administration* 39(1): 1–18.

Bennett, W. Lance. 2003. *News, The Politics of Illusion.* New York: Longman.

Best, R. 2010. 'Situation or social problem: The influence of events on media coverage of homelessness', *Social Problems* 57(1): 74–91.

Birkland, Thomas A. 1997. *After Disaster: Agenda Setting, Public Policy and Focusing Events.* Washington, DC: Georgetown University Press.

—— 1998. 'Focusing events, mobilization and agenda setting', *Journal of Public Policy* 18(3): 53–74.

—— 2004. 'Learning and policy improvement after disaster: The case of aviation security', *American Behavioral Scientist* 48(3): 341–64.

—— 2006. *Lessons of Disaster.* Washington, DC: Georgetown University Press.

—— and Regina G. Lawrence. 2002. 'The social and political meaning of the Exxon Valdez oil spill', *Spill Science and Technology Bulletin* 7(1–2) (June): 17–22.

——and Regina G. Lawrence. 2009. 'Media framing and policy change after Columbine', *American Behavioral Scientist* 52(10): 1405–25.

Blankenau, Joe. 2001. 'The fate of national health insurance in Canada and the United States: A multiple streams explanation', *Policy Studies Journal* 29(1): 38–55.

Burnier, DeLysa. 1994. 'Constructing political reality: Language, symbols and meaning in politics: A review essay', *Political Research Quarterly* 47(1): 239–53.

Busenberg, George J. 2000. 'Innovation, learning and policy evolution in hazardous systems', *American Behavioral Scientist* 44(4): 679–91.

Carpenter, Daniel and Gisela Sin. 2007. 'Policy tragedy and the emergence of regulation: The Food, Drug and Cosmetic Act of 1938: 1', *Studies in American Political Development* 21(2): 149.

Chenoweth, E. and S.E. Clarke. 2010. 'All terrorism is local: Resources, nested institutions and governance for urban homeland security in the American federal system', *Political Research Quarterly* 63(3): 495–507.

Cobb, Roger W. and Charles D. Elder. 1983. *Participation in American Politics: The Dynamics of Agenda-Building*. Baltimore, MD: Johns Hopkins University Press.

——and Marc Howard Ross. 1997. *Cultural Strategies of Agenda Denial: Avoidance, Attack, and Redefinition*. Lawrence, KS: University Press of Kansas.

——, Jeannie-Keith Ross and Marc Howard Ross. 1976. 'Agenda building as a comparative political process', *American Political Science Review* 70(1): 126–38.

Collins, Matthew, L. and Naim Kapuçu. 2008. 'Early warning systems and disaster preparedness and response in local government', *Disaster Prevention and Management* 17(5): 587–600.

Davis, Charles. 2006. 'Western wildfires: A policy change perspective', *Review of Policy Research* 23(1): 115–27.

deLeon, Peter. 1999. 'The stages approach to the policy process: What has it done? Where is it going', in *Theories of the Policy Process*. Boulder, CO: Westview Press.

Downs, Anthony. 1972. 'Up and down with ecology: The issue attention cycle', *The Public Interest* 28 (Summer): 38–50.

Edelman, Murray J. 1967. *The Symbolic Uses of Politics*. Urbana, IL: University of Illinois Press.

—— 1988. *Constructing the Political Spectacle*. Chicago: University of Chicago Press.

Einsiedel, Edna F. 2000. 'Cloning and its discontents; A Canadian perspective', *Nature Biotechnology* 18(9): 943–44.

Entman, Robert M. 1993. 'Framing: Toward classification of a fractured paradigm', *Journal of Communication* 42(4): 51–9.

Fishman, Donald, A. 1999. 'ValuJet Flight 592: Crisis communication theory blended and extended', *Communication Quarterly* 47(4): 345.

Galland, Daniel and Timothy McDaniels. 2008. 'Are new industry policies precautionary? The case of salmon aquaculture siting policy in British Columbia', *Environmental Science and Policy* 11(6) (October): 517–32, doi:10.1016/j.envsci.2008.05.002.

Glascock, Jack. 2004. 'The Jasper dragging death: Crisis communication and the community newspaper', *Communication Studies* 55(1): 29.

Green-Pedersen, Christoffer. 2007. 'The growing importance of issue competition: The changing nature of party competition in Western Europe', *Political Studies* 55(3): 607–28.

Gunter, Valerie J. 2005. 'News media and technological risks', *Sociological Quarterly* 46(4): 671–98.

Gusfield, Joseph. 1981. *The Culture of Public Problems: Drinking Driving and the Symbolic Order*. Chicago: University of Chicago Press.

Hilgartner, James and Charles Bosk. 1988. 'The rise and fall of social problems: A public arenas model', *American Journal of Sociology* 94(1): 53–78.

Kingdon, John W. 2003. *Agendas, Alternatives, and Public Policies*, 2nd edn, Longman Classics in Political Science. New York: Longman.

Lawrence, Regina G. 2000. *The Politics of Force: Media and the Construction of Police Brutality*. Berkeley, CA: University of California Press.

——and Thomas A. Birkland. 2000. 'The politics of event driven problem definition: School violence, media frames, and policy responses', paper presented at the annual meeting of the American Political Science Association. Washington, DC.

——and Thomas A. Birkland. 2004. 'Guns, Hollywood, and criminal justice: Defining the school shootings problem across public arenas', *Social Science Quarterly* 85(5): 1193–207.

Liu, X.S., E. Lindquist and A. Vedlitz. 2011. 'Explaining media and congressional attention to global climate change, 1969–2005: An empirical test of agenda-setting theory', *Political Research Quarterly* 64(2): 405–19.

Lowry, William. 2006. 'Potential focusing projects and policy change', *Policy Studies Journal* 34(3): 313–35.

Majone, Giandomenico. 1989. *Evidence, Argument and Persuasion in the Policy Process*. New Haven, CT: Yale University Press.

May, Peter J. 1990. 'Reconsidering policy design: Policies and publics', *Journal of Public Policy* 11(2): 187–206.

—— 1992. 'Policy learning and failure', *Journal of Public Policy* 12(4): 331–54.

——, Joshua Sapotichne and Samuel Workman. 2006. 'Policy coherence and policy domains', *Policy Studies Journal* 34(3): 381–403.

Melis, T.S and Pulwarty, R.S. 2001. 'Climate extremes and adaptive management on the Colorado River: Lessons from the 1997–1998 ENSO event', *Journal of Environmental Management* 63(3): 307.

Mintrom, Michael. 1997. 'Policy entrepreneurs and the diffusion of innovation', *American Journal of Political Science* 41(3) (July): 738–70.

——and Sandra Vergari. 1998. 'Policy networks and innovation diffusion: The case of state education reforms', *The Journal of Politics* 60(1): 126–48.

Molotch, Harvey and Marilyn Lester. 1974. 'News as purposive behavior', *American Sociological Review* 39(February): 101–13.

——and Marilyn Lester. 1975. 'Accidental news: The great oil spill as local occurrence and national event', *American Journal of Sociology* 81(2): 235–61.

Nakamura, Robert T. 1987. 'The textbook policy process and implementation research', *Policy Studies Journal* 7(1): 142–54.

Nohrstedt, D. 2010. 'Do advocacy coalitions matter? Crisis and change in Swedish nuclear energy policy', *Journal of Public Administration Research and Theory* 20(2): 309–33.

Oakley, M.R. 2009. 'Agenda setting and state policy diffusion: The effects of media attention, state court decisions and policy learning on fetal killing policy', *Social Science Quarterly* 90(1): 164–78.

Perrow, Charles. 1999. *Normal Accidents Replacement: Living With High-Risk Technologies*. Princeton NJ: Princeton University Press.

Prince, M.J. 2010. 'Avoiding blame, doing good, and claiming credit: Reforming Canadian income security', *Canadian Public Administration—Administration Publique du Canada* 53(3): 293–322.

Sabatier, Paul A. 1988. 'An advocacy coalition framework of policy change and the role of policy-oriented learning therein', *Policy Sciences* 21: 129–68.

—— 1991a. 'Political science and public policy and toward better theories of the policy PR', *PS: Political Science and Politics* 24 (June):144–56.

—— 1991b. 'Toward better theories of the policy process', *PS: Political Science and Politics* 24(2): 144–56.

Schattschneider, E.E. 1975. *The Semisovereign People*. Hinsdale, IL: The Dryden Press.

Schneider, Anne and Helen Ingram. 1991. 'The social construction of target populations: Implications for politics and policy', *American Political Science Review* 87(2): 334–48.

Schneider, Saundra. 2008. 'Who's to blame? (Mis) perceptions of the intergovernmental response to disasters', *Publius: The Journal of Federalism* 38(4) (September 1): 715–38. doi:10.1093/publius/pjn019.

Stone, Deborah A. 1989. 'Causal stories and the formation of policy agendas', *Political Science Quarterly* 104 (2): 281–300.

—— 2002. *Policy Paradox: The Art of Political Decision Making*. New York: Norton.

Vaughan, Shannon K. and Shelly Arsneault. 2008. 'Not-for-profit advocacy: Challenging policy images and pursuing policy change', *Review of Policy Research* 25(5): 411–28.

Verhulst, J. and S. Walgrave. 2009. 'The first time is the hardest? A cross-national and cross-issue comparison of first-time protest participants', *Political Behavior* 31(3): 455–84.

Walgrave, S. and J. Verhulst. 2009. 'Government stance and internal diversity of protest: A comparative study of protest against the war in Iraq in eight countries', *Social Forces* 87(3): 1355–87.

Walker, Jack L. 1977. 'Setting the agenda in the US senate: A theory of problem selection', *British Journal of Political Science* 7: 423–45.

Wood, Robert S. 2006. 'Tobacco's tipping point: The master settlement agreement as a focusing event', *Policy Studies Journal* 34(3): 419–36.

# 15

# Agenda-setting and political discourse

## Major analytical frameworks and their application

*David A. Rochefort and Kevin P. Donnelly*

Three questions are central to the agenda-setting perspective in public policy analysis:

1 Among all competing concerns of individuals and groups, what determines which ones will succeed in gaining the active attention of political decision-makers?
2 How do problems and solutions come to be matched together in public policy formulation?
3 Who are the key actors in agenda-setting, and by what means do they pursue their objectives?

At times, circumstances are such that it is neither puzzling nor questionable why officials would be preoccupied with a given predicament. That is, the perception of threat is so reflexive, the dimension of calamity so tangible and evident, no intermediation is necessary between social awareness of a problem, on the one hand, and government engagement, on the other. Yet issues of this type, which do not merely *occupy* space on the radar screen of government but *command* it, are exceptional. The broader class of misfortunes and ills in society do not receive automatic attention from public policy-makers. Rather, they must vie for standing within an appropriate institutional arena—legislative, administrative, or judicial—already busy with matters current and pending.

Powerful interests outside and inside government can be influential in gaining consideration for an issue. However, the more visible an issue, the more widespread its significance, and the more controversial its claims, the less likely will it be that some narrow group of actors, however well positioned and resourceful, might control its fate. In the politics of public policy-making, most issues are malleable entities subject to interpretation and prioritization in a contest over the construction of meaning. Although factual information helps to document a problem's existence, rarely is there consensus about which facts are most relevant, how they should be assembled to create a picture of the whole, or what the implications are concerning those things government should, or should not, do in remedying a situation. Sorting out these possibilities may be likened to an exercise in collective political cognition, one rooted in opinion, values, and beliefs as much as objective analysis.

The "argumentative turn" in policy studies is a phrase that has come into usage as a way of referring to the critical role of discourse within this disorderly process (Fischer and Forester 1993). Majone has written:

> Argumentation is the key process through which citizens and policymakers arrive at moral judgments and policy choices. Public discussion mobilizes the knowledge, experience, and interest of many people, while focusing their attention on a limited range of issues. Each participant is encouraged to adjust his view of reality, and even to change his values, as a result of the process of reciprocal persuasion.
>
> *(1989: 2)*

Language is more than just a serviceable instrument of conflict and compromise in public debate, however. Language can also be a vehicle for expressing identity, affirming or challenging the hierarchical status quo, and embedding discussion of issue specifics within larger categories of social understanding (see, e.g., Edelman 1988). All are pertinent to a polity's response to demands for change through effective policy choice.

The purpose of this chapter is to review three major veins of research on the role of political discourse in public policy development with special focus on the identification and typing of issues within the agenda-setting phase. The three areas of scholarship are *problem definition*, *framing*, and *political narrative*. Each possesses elements distinctive from the concerns and approaches of the other two, although important points of overlap exist. All perspectives arise from multiple disciplinary sources. Perhaps owing to this intellectual admixture, scholars situated within particular literatures often have not adequately acknowledged the relevance of similar work in other fields. Our aim, therefore, is to promote a synthesis toward greater interrelationship and accumulation of knowledge going forward. Following an overview of main concepts within these parallel bodies of work, we will demonstrate their applicability via a pair of case studies of recent public policy controversies in Great Britain and the United States.

## Problem definition

In a slim volume called *The Semisovereign People* published in 1960, E. E. Schattschneider outlined an understanding of the linkage among social conflict, issue creation, and government response that continues to inspire research and writing in the public policy field several decades later. Schattschneider's main interest was the "mobilization of bias" determining which concerns get organized into and out of the "political game." One critical asset in the competition for political attention is large-scale public support, which can either be enhanced or reduced by the way an issue is defined. Indeed, for Schattschneider, "the definition of the alternatives is the supreme instrument of power" (1960: 69).

Building on this work, Cobb and Elder (1972) elaborated a model of agenda-setting that identifies issue characteristics as a key factor in conflict expansion. In general, issues successfully cast in terms of certain qualities—ambiguity and abstraction, social significance, long-term relevance, lack of technical complexity, and familiarity—possess greater potential for visibility and salience. Thus, the description of issues, or problems, by "policy entrepreneurs" can be an important strategy for gaining advantage in the process of political gate keeping that limits the policy agenda (Kingdon 1995).

As noted by Cobb *et al.* (1976: 126), "Agenda building is a process ideally suited to comparative analysis" (see also Baumgartner *et al.* 2006). This is so because all political communities face the same basic challenge of deciding which issues should be given priority in official decision-making. These scholars suggest a framework for cross-cultural investigation centering on the major characteristics of issue careers, including the way public issues are initiated, the degree to which issue demands are specific or general in form, the process of issue expansion, and an issue's method of entrance onto the formal agenda. Use of language is pervasive across these dimensions of the policy process and can help to explain both issue-specific and regime-specific tendencies.

Rochefort and Cobb (1993, 1994) examined more closely the categories of claims within the discourse of problem definition. Providing an "anatomy of problem description," they focused on five areas of discussion that repeatedly arise in political debate over social issues: problem causation; nature of the problem (severity, incidence, novelty, proximity, crisis status); characteristics of the problem population; end-means orientation of problem definer; and nature of the solution. In effect, this listing of categories provides a template for analyzing problem definition as "a distinctive form of rhetoric made up of a habitual vocabulary" (1994: 15).

Each of these dimensions of description can be addressed in a way calculated to maximize a problem's perceived importance and handling as a "public issue" rather than as a "private trouble" (Mills 1959). Problems attributed to social causes beyond individual control, that are widespread in scope, have severe impacts, threaten the "average citizen," have reached a dangerous crisis point, involve sympathetic problem populations, and point to solutions viewed as effective and affordable represent predictable items of attention inside the political arena. At the same time, the polarity of these same dimensions can be reversed by problem definers seeking to "contain" public support for an issue and deem it unworthy of decision-makers' precious time and resources. Hirschman (1991) identified a counter-rhetorical strategy evident across various periods of history to undermine reform proposals by portraying them as "perverse" (likely to backfire), "futile" (beyond the effective capability of government), and "jeopardizing" (prone to damage an existing policy or system). Hirschman presents these arguments as the archetypal conservative response to progressive proposals, although they are equally apt in patterning the discourse of objection by liberals to policy innovations from the political right.

As Stone (2002) notes, the "language of counting" is prominent in problem definition. Numbers serve to document both the occurrence of a problem and its impacts. Numbers may lend the appearance of precision to policy arguments, but, in fact, they are subject to manipulation, open to differing interpretations, and can acquire symbolic meanings just as happens with words and images. It is not merely that most social problems are associated with "high" and "low" estimates. Measurements can differ widely as a result of time frame selected, categorization of people and events, the reference points and comparisons used in establishing context, and other choices supportive of, or detrimental to, the interests of a problem definer.

In the effort to persuade, practitioners of problem definition resort to language that is factual and language that is figurative, sometimes combining the two for maximum impact. Figurative language refers to words, phrases, and comparisons that convey meanings beyond their literal content. Analogies are statements that compare problems, or issues, by asserting a logical equivalence, often leaving to inference the nature and extent of similarities between the two. Analogies can be used to underscore the severity of a situation, suggest causal relationships, and make predictions about the likely outcome of policy action or neglect. Metaphors are a closely related form of comparison that link items through implied argument. British scholar Adrian Beard (2000) observes: "Metaphor is deeply embedded in the way we construct the world around us and the way that world is constructed for us by others" (p.21). Especially prominent in the world of politics, Beard notes, are metaphors of sport and war.

One area of problem definition scholarship that draws directly from the discipline of sociology, particularly the "social construction of reality" perspective, is the consideration of problem ownership (see, e.g., Gusfield 1981). Sometimes what is at stake in definitional disputes is the determination of which group in society will gain recognition as established experts for explaining and resolving a given social problem. Status, influence, and resources all potentially hinge on which professional, disciplinary, or moral point of view wins out.

Although problem definition is integral in issue creation, it also relates to the function of policy design. Causation is a basic feature of description that can steer attention to a certain method, level, or object of government intervention because it is in keeping with a problem's attributed origins. Sometimes problems achieve agenda standing when they are defined as well suited for the application of a policy approach already well established and widely supported. In this sense, it is said, solutions give rise to problems, as well as the other way around. Characterization of problem populations—the individuals and groups who are seen as affected by, or the source of, a social problem—conditions the types of instruments viewed by policy-makers as appropriate forms of treatment due to judgments about blame, deservingness, deviancy, and potential for change. Not just the substance of programmatic action, namely benefits and burdens, is shaped by these components of problem definition, but also the techniques of program implementation and the rhetoric that imbues the chosen policy (Schneider and Ingram 1997; Rochefort 1986).

## Framing

That reality is complex, multidimensional, inherently confusing, and overwhelming in its entirety constitutes the fundamental premise of the "framing" perspective. A natural cognitive process is to narrow the field of perception to make reality more manageable for interpretation and for use as a guide to action. As Noakes and Johnston (2005: 2) write: "In the simplest of terms, framing functions in much the same way as a frame around a picture: attention gets focused on what is relevant and important and away from extraneous items in the field of view."

Framing enables individuals and groups to make sense of the world, but because it is selective with regard to information considered, many different coherent meanings are possible. Rein and Schön (1993: 147) discuss the creation of multiple social realities, which leads people facing a common situation to "see different things, make different interpretations of the way things are, and support different courses of action concerning what is to be done, by whom, and how to do it." The framing approach echoes the problem definition perspective in underscoring the "malleability" of social problems and, in particular, the divergent impressions that result when a causal picture having multiple, simultaneous, and sequential influences is cast in partial terms. However, the framing paradigm weaves this insight into a model broad enough to encompass thematic, ideological, cultural, group identity, and motivational elements (Noakes and Johnston 2005).

The intellectual sources of framing analysis are multidisciplinary to an exceptional degree. Anthropologist Gregory Bateson was one of the earliest scholars to make use of the concept of a frame (Noakes and Johnston 2005). Subsequently, various applications of framing have appeared in linguistics, social psychology, media studies, and artificial intelligence, in addition to political science and policy analysis. The framing perspective has also emerged as one of the most influential paradigms for theoretical and empirical research on social movements, an inherently cross-disciplinary area with bearing on public policy initiation.

In tracing the impact of framing within political science, Druckman (2010) focuses on two main types of application. First is the question of how an individual forms preferences, that is "a rank ordering of a set of objects or alternative actions" (2010: 280). By representing the item under consideration in different ways or contexts, framing has been shown to produce different valuative outcomes. Second is the role of framing in political communication and a speaker's ability, at times, to evoke varying audience reactions depending on which facet or dimension of a topic has been emphasized. Iyengar (1996) pursued a similar line of inquiry with respect to public affairs information in the media, finding, for example, that "episodic" treatment of social problems focusing on isolated instances versus more contextual "thematic" reports tends to result in viewers favoring individualistic explanations for those problems. As Entman (1993) has noted, to the extent that public opinion proves susceptible to manipulation, framing research confirms the possibility of elite control, thereby raising far-reaching implications for democratic theory.

Rein and Schön's (1993) work on "frame analysis" represents a methodical, conceptually sophisticated extension of these ideas into the policy realm (see also Schön and Rein 1994). These authors examine policy controversies in terms of rival frames that are distinguished by alternative factual interpretations, social meanings, and normative recommendations. The policy process is a battle to set the agenda by means of one of these divergent models of reality. How this battle turns out will serve the symbolic and material interests that shape, and are advanced by, a certain complex of beliefs, values, and perspectives. None of this means frames are easy to identify, however. On the contrary, frames exist in the world of (often unspoken) mental constructs. Further, similar policy actions may align with different frames, or the same frame can give rise to multiple policy solutions. And yet, when a frame has been successfully decoded, it not only has great explanatory power, it can also be the first step in an emotional and cognitive transaction by which starkly contending interests begin to find common ground.

A frame sets the larger tableau within which political language is used. Statements of causality, metaphorical comparisons, claims of professional ownership, and larger story narratives all may animate a policy debate, although the proposition of scholars in this field is that relevance and impact will be determined by compatibility with the dominant understanding of what is at stake in an issue conflict. In their study of the US death penalty, Baumgartner *et al.* (2008) found that media coverage shifted in line with the rise of the innocence frame, with elements critical of capital punishment becoming much more common in news stories.

Often, language performs the crucial function of naming a policy terrain so as to accentuate the overarching frame of interpretation (Rein and Schön 1993): female liberation, health care rights, environmental justice, workforce competitiveness, and so on. Since frames consist of *tone* as well as *substance*, there is also a relationship between framing and the expressive aspects of policy discourse, as would be seen, for example, in harsh condemnation of "shiftless welfare cheats," sympathetic support for "victims of cancer," and compassionate identification with neighbors "at the mercy of rising prices at the gas pump." In a study of Druze Arabs in Israel, Krebs and Jackson showed the importance of political rhetoric in framing a campaign for expanded citizenship rights as the collective reward for military sacrifice:

> In short, the Druze trapped Jewish leaders in a rhetorical cul-de-sac in which … they maneuvered their Jewish opponents onto a rhetorical playing field on which the Druze could not lose, for no rebuttal would have been acceptable to key audiences, both domestic and international.
>
> *(2007: 52).*

In so far as framing contributes to an issue's or a problem's perceived degree of importance, it has obvious repercussions for determination of agenda priorities. Framing is also relevant when analyzing the content of disputes in the politics of agenda-setting, although researchers differ on the pattern. Baumgartner and Jones (1993) have stressed "noncontradictory argumentation" in which rival frames are advanced without direct challenging of the alternatives, while other scholars have focused on the clash between opposing frames and the discursive and other tactics used by advocates to gain the upper hand within such competitions (see, e.g., Cobb and Ross 1997).

## Narrative

Many of the same observations made about problem definition and framing apply to the narrative perspective on public policy-making. Scholars view narratives as devices that bring order and meaning to a situation. Patterson and Monroe (1998: 315) state that narrative "refers to the ways in which we construct disparate facts in our own worlds and weave them together cognitively in order to make sense of our reality." Further, Jones and McBeth (2010: 330) write that "narrative cognition may be fundamental to a meaningful human existence." Narratives make use of metaphors, symbols, analogies, synecdoche, and other forms of figurative language in heightening a message's impact (Stone 2002). Narrative analysis also has its roots in disparate fields, most notably anthropology, literary theory, history, marketing, neuroscience, psychology, and psychoanalysis.

What is distinctive about the study of narratives and public policy is the focus on stories as a means for representing reality. A story is an account with a guiding arc structured around a beginning, middle, and end. Most simply, there is a problem, an explanation for occurrence of the problem, and a tension-resolving solution (Fischer 2003). In fulfilling the form of a story, policy narratives contain predictable elements (Patterson and Monroe 1998). There are *characters or actors*, with special prominence given to the roles of victims, villains, and heroes. There is a *point of view*, which is the speaker's perspective of what is important, true, worthy of comment, and goes without saying. There is a *sequential ordering of events* to give coherence to a problem's origins and development. And there is the *setting*, which is the socio-cultural context in which a speaker embeds the account.

The purpose of constructing such a story is neither neutral nor desultory. Rather, it is to make a point, to register an objection, and to recommend a remedy or, as some put it, to propound a moral. In other words, policy narratives have a normative element centrally concerned with human intention. As Fischer (2003: 163) states, "the narrative is especially geared to the goals of the actors and the way changing goals and intentions causally contribute to social change. It seeks to comprehend and convey the direction and purpose of human affairs." A full-bodied, well-articulated story can go far in dispelling the confusing facts and conflicting voices surrounding a public policy issue, superimposing an interpretation of events that is "both lovely and useful" (Kaplan 1993: 176).

Stepping back from the particulars, it is possible to recognize the repetition of several common story lines within public policy discourse. Stone (2002) identifies two main types, "stories of decline" and "stories of control." The former describes circumstances in which conditions are deteriorating, disaster looms, and therefore swift action is needed to avert catastrophe. Stone calls attention to subtypes of stories of decline: the "stymied progress story" (positive change in an area is being undone), and the "change is only an illusion story" (contrary to appearances, reality is worse or better than appreciated). Stories of control focus on problems that had been understood as beyond effective social intervention, but in fact can now be meliorated by public policy action. Different versions of this story form develop themes of "conspiracy" (powerful groups or entities have actually been controlling things behind the scenes for their own advantage), or "blaming the victim" (people affected by problems have brought these difficulties on themselves). With respect to the latter, Douglas Torgerson (1996), a Canadian policy specialist, emphasizes the need for deconstructing stigmatized identities in social policy to uncover the discursive opposition of a "privileged center" versus a "neglected margin." Whatever the genre, all policy narratives are likely to intermingle statistics, journalistic reporting, anecdotal portrayals, and other factual and emotive supports for the sake of an explicit or implicit argument.

Ross examines competing narratives with regard to sense making of the attacks of September 11, 2011, from different national perspectives. He bases his discussion on the succinct premise that:

> Narratives are explanations for events (large and small) in the form of short, common-sense accounts (stories) that often seem simple. However, the powerful images they contain and the judgments they make about the motivations and actions of their own group, and others, are emotionally significant for groups and individuals.
>
> *(2011: 1)*

A dominant narrative for Americans, which depicts the attack as evil behavior motivated by religious and political extremism, construes 9/11 as an act of war. Here, the response that seems appropriate is massive military intervention abroad to defend the United States proactively by tracking down and eliminating the terrorists and their supporters. A different narrative that is heard in many parts of the Islamic world may or may not deem the attack as evil incarnate, but relates it to objectionable activities by the United States in the Middle East over a period of years. The American military response is predicted to extend these past injustices by harming innocent Muslim populations while ignoring the precipitating factors and conditions that gave rise to 9/11. Analyzing the contradictions between such narratives, Ross underscores the significance of divergent group beliefs and experiences, facts that are selectively remembered and interpreted, and preexisting narratives within a culture that guide collective responses to stress.

Jones and McBeth (2010) have introduced a Narrative Policy Framework (NPF) for assessing the impact of policy narratives by means of empirical quantitative methodology. Their goal, in short, is to subject a postpositivist concept to positivist standards of evaluation. As outlined, NPF takes into account the principal elements of narrative form (plot, setting, characters, and moral) while categorizing generalized story content with respect to ideology (or another belief system). The methodology then uses these inputs to generate hypotheses concerning the potential impact, or utility, of narrative for individuals and groups within a policy dispute. Elaborating on this approach, Shanahan *et al.* (2011) drew upon the NPF to formulate an additional set of hypotheses incorporating independent and dependent variables of interest concerning policy outcomes, policy learning, policy change, public opinion, and strategy from Sabatier and Jenkins-Smith's (1993) well known Advocacy Coalition Framework.

## Two cases

During the summer of 2011 London experienced days of rioting marked by violence, social unrest, and destruction on a massive scale. The turbulence generated a sweeping national examination of conscience in British society on topics ranging from income inequality to the decline of moral virtue. The fall of 2011 witnessed an outpouring of citizen protests on Wall Street and in dozens of cities around the United States. Few anticipated this "Occupy" movement and the strong chord its message struck with large segments of the American people. A brief review of each of these cases will serve to illustrate the potent role of language in political situations surrounding the emergence (and reemergence) of divisive social issues.

### *Riots in the United Kingdom*

Late in the evening of Saturday, August 6, 2011, riots broke out in the north London neighborhood of Tottenham. Rioters set buildings on fire, clashed with police, and smashed the windows of local shops. In subsequent days, the violence and destruction spread to neighboring cities and towns. According to the *Guardian* newspaper, by the third night "Buildings were torched, shops ransacked, and officers attacked with makeshift missiles and petrol bombs as gangs of hooded and masked youths laid waste to streets right across the city" (Dodd and Davies 2011).

Calm did not return until the fourth night following Prime Minister David Cameron's decision to deploy an additional 10,000 police officers across the streets of London.

Both during and immediately following the riots, political commentary focused on a central question of problem definition and narrative composition: Who or what was to blame for this historic display of social unrest? The immediate precipitant was obvious. Days earlier, police had shot and killed Mark Duggan when attempting to arrest him in an investigation of gun violence. A peaceful protest in Tottenham denouncing the police role in Duggan's death, which some suggested was racially motivated, ultimately got out of hand (Faiola 2011). Yet, according to the *New York Times*, "the circumstances of Mr. Duggan's death appeared to be remote from the forces driving the riots, at least in the assessment of many of those who are most familiar with the neighborhoods affected." Instead, this incident was simply the "original trigger for the violence" (Burns 2011). While most seem to accept the truth of this observation, this is where agreement ended in regard to underlying cause of the riots.

Drastic cuts to services, or "austerity measures," surfaced as one prominent culprit noted in the media. Consider the following account offered by Nina Power of the *Guardian*, who suggested a "context to London's riots that can't be ignored."

> Since the coalition came to power just over a year ago, the country has seen multiple student protests, occupations of dozens of universities, several strikes, a half-a-million-strong trade union marches and now unrest on the streets of the capital ... Each of these events was sparked by a different cause, yet all take place against a backdrop of brutal cuts and enforced austerity measures. The government knows very well that it is taking a gamble, and that its policies run the risk of sparking mass unrest on a scale we haven't seen since the early 1980s. With people taking to the streets of Tottenham, Edmonton, Brixton and elsewhere over the past few nights, we could be about to see the government enter a sustained and serious losing streak.
>
> *(8 August 2011)*

Power also proposed basic income inequality as a critical driver of the riots. After first establishing the link between inequality and social issues, Power stated that "[d]ecades of individualism, competition and state-encouraged selfishness—combined with a systematic crushing of unions and the ever-increasing criminalisation of dissent—have made Britain one of the most unequal countries in the developed world." Ravi Somaiya of the *New York Times* echoed this view in stating that "Economic malaise and cuts in spending and services instituted by the Conservative-led government have been recurring flashpoints for months" (Somaiya 2011). Political commentators were not the only ones delivering this message. In the aftermath of the riots, Labour Party leader Ed Miliband called the cause of the riots "complex," but frequently pointed to Britain's "unequal society" as a key contributor (Dunt 2011). The long-term pattern of deterioration within this constructed narrative is consistent with Stone's (2002) "stories of decline." By assigning blame to the Government as a guilty party in igniting the riots, this interpretation also pointed to a logical solution—roll back the cuts and create a more equal society. Little in the way of specific policy proposals has yet accompanied the linking of inequality to the rioting. However, in a major speech delivered against the backdrop of his old secondary school, Miliband set the stage for possible future action by urging the governing party to establish a formal "commission of inquiry" to investigate the cause of the riots, and he tasked it, in particular, with examining "issues of inequality" (Miliband 2011).

Other commentary, however, tagged the rioters as reckless law-breakers skilled at exploiting New Age social media outlets. Quickly dispensing with the notion that the riots were in some way a valid political expression, *The Daily Telegraph* offered the following:

> What we have experienced in London and elsewhere since Saturday night is a wholly new phenomenon: violent disorder whose sole intent is criminal. These are not protesters, as the BBC stupidly insisted on calling them: they are looters and vandals and thieves. The unstructured nature of their violence has made it exceedingly difficult for the police to gather any worthwhile intelligence on them. Yet their sophisticated use of social media allows them to muster at will. They have had the whip hand for four days and the police have constantly had to play catch-up.
>
> (Telegraph View *2011)*

Government officials in London expressed parallel sentiments. During a press conference just days following the initial night of rioting, deputy assistant commissioner to the Metropolitan police, Steve Kavanagh, blamed the rioting on "really inflammatory, inaccurate" messages on Twitter, adding that "[s]ocial media and other methods have been used to organise these levels of greed and criminality" (Halliday 2011). Going further, Mike Butcher, a digital aide to London's mayor, told the BBC that "[m]obile phones have become weaponised in their capability of spreading information about where to target next." Butcher remarked it was "unbelievable" that BlackBerry Messenger had not been shut down during the riots (Minicucci 2011). Ultimately, government authorities chose not to interrupt service. However, this criminal, rather than political, framing of the riots impacted solution development. London police authorities launched an official investigation into the use of BlackBerrys as an organizing tool by the rioters.

A broader theme in discourse about the riots was the issue of moral decay. Prime Minister Cameron pointed to the UK's "slow-motion moral collapse" as overriding cause of the riots:

> These riots were not about race: the perpetrators and the victims were white, black and Asian. These riots were not about government cuts: they were directed at high street stores, not Parliament. And these riots were not about poverty: that insults the millions of people who, whatever the hardship, would never dream of making others suffer like this.
>
> No, this was about behaviour. People showing indifference to right and wrong. People with a twisted moral code. People with a complete absence of self-restraint.
>
> *(15 August 2011)*

Cameron announced that his plan to fix a "broken" Britain would be back on the "top of [his] political agenda." This policy vision, which centered on the goal of reversing general social decay, originated during the previous 2010 election, but it was dusted off as the ideal response to the current violence.

In a *Wall Street Journal* op-ed, Britain's chief rabbi, Jonathan Sacks, wrote that no one should have been surprised by the London riots. In his view, "Britain is the latest country to pay the price for what happened half a century ago in one of the most radical transformations in the history of the West. In virtually every Western society in the 1960s there was a moral revolution, an abandonment of its entire traditional ethic of self-restraint" (Sacks 2011). Not to be outdone, another religious leader, the Archbishop of Canterbury, Rowan Williams, sermonized on moral failings by criticizing an "educational philosophy at every level [that] has been more and more dominated by an instrumentalist model; less and less concerned with a building of virtue, character and citizenship." The solution, according to Dr. Williams, could be found in "rebuilding the skills of parenting in some of our communities, [and] in rebuilding education itself" (Walton 2011). These, of course, are not new ideas in socially conservative circles. In effect, the riots provided a context, not to mention a *pretext*, for attaching existing solutions to a new problem, which is a well-known sequence in problem definition (Kingdon 1995). The dynamic of religious figures asserting the relevance of their special brand of expertise also represents a striking illustration of the struggle for "problem ownership" that frequently occurs in public policy debate.

## *Occupy Wall Street*

On September 17, 2011, a protest movement emerged on the streets of Lower Manhattan, the likes of which had not been seen in the US for decades. On that day, a small group of protesters gathered to "occupy" parts of Wall Street and camp out in nearby Zuccotti Park in a dramatic attempt to draw attention to growing inequalities in American wealth and income. Although this initial action turned out to be fairly modest in scope, within weeks similar demonstrations cropped up in dozens of cities across the nation and the world. Increasingly larger groups of protesters claiming solidarity with the Occupy movement set up encampments in city parks and other public spaces from Boston to Oakland, Nashville to Reno. Proudly "leaderless" and vague in its goals, the Occupy movement nonetheless captured the attention of law-makers and dramatically shifted the focus of American political discourse.

In the early days of the Occupy protests, political commentary focused on explaining the movement itself. An array of competing narratives resulted. Tying the movement to the "story of our economic woes," Paul Krugman (2011), a liberal columnist for the *New York Times*, outlined the following "three acts":

> In the first act, bankers took advantage of deregulation to run wild (and pay themselves princely sums), inflating huge bubbles through reckless lending. In the second act, the bubbles burst—but bankers were bailed out by taxpayers, with remarkably few strings attached, even as ordinary workers continued to suffer the consequences of the bankers' sins. And, in the third act, bankers showed their gratitude by turning on the people who had saved them, throwing their support—and the wealth they still possessed thanks to the bailouts—behind politicians who promised to keep their taxes low and dismantle the mild regulations erected in the aftermath of the crisis. Given this history, how can you not applaud the protesters for finally taking a stand?

Starkly different was the take of conservative columnist for the *Washington Post*, Charles Krauthammer, who linked the Occupy movement to President Obama's recent calls for the rich to "pay their fair share":

> To the villainy-of-the-rich theme emanating from Washington, a child is born: Occupy Wall Street. Starbucks-sipping, Levi's-clad, iPhone-clutching protesters denounce corporate America even as they weep for Steve Jobs, corporate titan, billionaire eight times over. These indignant indolents saddled with their $50,000 student loans and English degrees have decided that their lack of gainful employment is rooted in the malice of the millionaires on whose homes they are now marching—to the applause of Democrats suffering acute Tea Party envy and now salivating at the energy these big-government anarchists will presumably give their cause.
>
> *(13 October 2011)*

Aside from reflecting the ideological predispositions of these two pundits, such accounts spoke to a broader effort on the part of media figures to contextualize the ongoing social unrest.

Certain political commentators drew analogies to other grassroots movements. Nicholas Kristof, an international news reporter for the *New York Times*, drew a parallel between the Occupy movement and the pro-democracy protesters in Cairo's Tahrir Square:

> [T]here is the same cohort of alienated young people, and the same savvy use of Twitter and other social media to recruit more participants. Most of all, there's a similar tide of youthful frustration with a political and economic system that protesters regard as broken, corrupt, unresponsive and unaccountable.
>
> *(Kristof 2011)*

Use of this particular analogy sent a powerful message by framing the Occupy movement as part of a global phenomenon in which a virtuous younger generation had stood up to an ineffective and illegitimate power structure. Other observers, including President Obama, compared the Occupy and Tea Party movements, the latter coalescing two years earlier around the goals of shrinking government and an originalist interpretation of the Constitution. During an interview Obama suggested:

> In some ways, they're not that different from some of the protests that we saw coming from the Tea Party. Both on the left and the right, I think people feel separated from their government. They feel that their institutions aren't looking out for them.
>
> *(Dwyer 2011).*

This comparison both anointed (prematurely) the Occupy movement as a potent political force and presented the idea that a counterweight to the Tea Party movement was now emerging. The formulation of comparisons to movements as diverse as the Arab Spring and the Tea Party is testament to the amorphous nature of the Occupy protests. However, it also illustrates the extent to which analogies portray political events in dramatically different lights in the creative application of political discourse.

Despite its ambiguity, the Occupy movement articulated an agenda clear and motivating enough to draw thousands of Americans into the streets. This may be due, in part, to the fact that protesters proposed a new framework for debating US economic policy. Unlike during the previous two years, in which the national debt, government spending, and draconian cost-cutting measures dominated the discourse, the Occupy movement spotlighted *economic inequality* as a transcendent issue. A *New York Times* editorial chastised the "chattering classes [who] keep complaining that the marchers lack a clear message and specific policy prescriptions," and offered the following defense:

> At this point, protest is the message: income inequality is grinding down that middle class, increasing the ranks of the poor, and threatening to create a permanent underclass of able, willing but jobless people. On one level, the protesters, most of them young, are giving voice to a generation of lost opportunity.
>
> (New York Times *Editorial 2011)*

Along with their physical presence, the protesters supported their inequality frame with powerful sloganizing. Put simply, "We are the 99%." This phrase effectively hit home the movement's essential complaint—that wealth is highly concentrated in the top 1 percent of the population while the status quo serves the financial elite at the expense of the many. Similarly, by featuring a "raised fist"—the universal symbol of solidarity and resistance—on the Occupy

Wall Street website and at rallies across the nation, the group reinforced the scope of their solution: "A revolution of the mind as well as the body politic" (OccupyWallSt.org).

Critics of the Occupy movement portrayed its participants in a negative light to discredit their message. In her appearance on the Fox News "Hannity" program, conservative author and commentator Ann Coulter assured the viewing audience that "none of these kids at 'Occupy Wall Street' are coming from places like Yale, they are coming from the most bush league schools which is why none of them can even say why they are there." Further, Coulter expressed confidence that "Americans are reacting the way they should, which is with hilarity and revulsion" (Coulter 2011). Even more contemptuously, talk radio show host Rush Limbaugh told his audience:

> [W]hen I was ten years old … I was more self-sufficient than this parade of human debris calling itself Occupy Wall Street … If you look at the minutes and read their website, these people are announcing that they're parasites, that they are not self-sufficient and that they are totally dependent on the very things and people they're protesting.
>
> *(Limbaugh 2011)*

Here was a classic tactic of conflict containment via rhetoric: defuse the issue and block its expansion by means of a direct verbal attack on a protest group and its leaders (Cobb and Elder 1972).

Other more mainstream critics elected to challenge the inequality frame head on. Representative Paul Ryan, in a prominent speech before the Heritage Foundation, asked the audience to consider "[w]hether we are a nation that still believes in equality of opportunity, or whether we are moving away from that, and toward an insistence on equality of outcome." The latter, Ryan suggested, constitutes "the moral basis of class warfare—a false morality that confuses fairness with redistribution, and promotes class envy instead of social mobility" (Ryan 2011). Mitt Romney, front-runner for the 2012 Republican presidential nomination, responded to a question about the Occupy protests by saying: "I think it's dangerous, this [is] class warfare" (Boxer 2011). The contest of economic frames was classic: inequality versus competition, fairness versus winner-take-all.

The fact that prominent Republicans saw the need to *defend*, not merely promote, their preferred economic frame illustrates the surprising strength of the Occupy movement. What remains unclear at the time of this writing, however, is the long-term impact of such rhetorical point-counterpoint on US politics and public policy.

## Discussion and conclusion

The two cases we have discussed may be notable for their timeliness and for the significance of issues being raised, but they are not unique from a discursive standpoint. The patterns of argumentation, descriptive construction, and storytelling are commonplace, making it easy to demonstrate the applicability of the problem definition, framing, and narrative perspectives across the political landscape. This should not be surprising if it is true, as has sometimes been claimed, that "all language is political" and "all politics is language." Yet the very pervasiveness of political discourse inclines the subject to certain ambiguities that should be noted at the close of this review.

First, although much work in the field of discourse analysis has been devoted to typing the rhetorical strategies that recur in politics, the raw material in any given case study is always unique, with its own combination of themes, accents, and emotions. This situation makes it likely that no two analysts will interpret a case precisely the same way, either in identifying critical elements of language or in explicating their role in the outcome of a conflict. The focus on politics as a "text" has, in short, opened the door to all the creativity and all the inconsistency that one finds in other fields of textual analysis, such as literary studies. Thus, even though it is possible to recognize a close connection among the problem definition, framing, and narrative approaches, these frameworks have oddly served as alternative lenses at times, that is, as intellectual spheres with their own reference points, observational criteria, and conceptual intentions. Whether this pluralism has proved boon or bane to the broad community of scholars and students interested in the impact of political language is questionable.

Second, it is understandable that the fluidity of political discourse analysis has now given rise to attempts to pin down crucial variables through quantitative measurement. The Narrative Policy Framework of Jones and McBeth (2010) has already been cited as an illustration of this quantifying impulse, one that aims to gain a place for language variables within the policy studies literature with respect to such basic processes as policy change and policy learning. Similarly, the specification, tabulation, and interrelating of basic numerical indicators has been highly useful in documenting the rise and fall of rival policy frames for those working within this perspective (see, e.g., Baumgartner *et al.* 2008; Baumgartner and Jones 1993). Various media and survey studies have also confirmed hypothesized relationships between language constructions and political attitudes of different kinds. So far, however, the ambitiousness of this quantitative vein of work, worthwhile though it may be, continues to outstrip its accomplishments, nor has it done much to integrate the divergent traditions of scholarship within this area.

Third, a persistent barrier to positivist analysis in searching for regularities in the expressions of political language, on the one hand, and their impact on agenda setting, on the other, is the shifting meaning of similar language and narratives depending on context. Within the American national healthcare debate, it has been intriguing to note the contradictory uses of what might be called the "rhetoric of foreign standards." In the hands of different polemicists, the same examples of national health systems elsewhere have been used either to shame the United States for being a "laggard" in providing universal coverage and cost control, or to praise the US health care system as the "best in the world." Even aside from such blatant paradoxes, important nuances of discursive meaning are likely whenever attention shifts from one policy domain to another. Thus, Rochefort *et al.* (1998) found substantial differences in rhetorical uses of the concept of "community" within policy debates concerning mental health, criminal justice, and social service programs in the US and Canadian province of Quebec. Underlying similar sounding language were both divergent value assumptions and alternative pathways for policy design.

A concern with the potent use of language in politics is not new. It dates back at least as far as Plato's academy in ancient Greece and the first formal analyses of rhetoric written by Aristotle, former student and faculty member there. Today, however, researchers from many different disciplines who share an interest in the politics of public policymaking are injecting new energy and concepts into this field of study. This academic focus is being matched and doubtless heightened by a dramatic expansion in the techniques and forms of media available to the practitioners of political language, inside and outside government. The purpose of this chapter has been to signal promising trends in the major scholarly approaches surrounding this development while encouraging greater awareness of their intellectual common ground.

## Bibliography

Bardach, Eugene. 2009. *A Practical Guide for Policy Analysis*. Washington, DC: CQ Press.

Baumgartner, Frank R. and Bryan D. Jones. 1993. *Agendas and Instability in American Politics*. Chicago: University of Chicago Press.

——, Green-Pedersen, and Bryan D. Jones. 2006. 'Comparative studies of policy agendas', *Journal of European Public Policy* 13(7): 959–74.

——, Suzanna L. De Boef and Amber E. Boydstun. 2008. *The Decline of the Death Penalty and the Discovery of Innocence*. Cambridge: Cambridge University Press.

Beard, Adrian. 2000. *The Language of Politics*. London: Routledge.

Boxer, Sarah B. 2011. 'Romney: Wall Street protests "Class Warfare', *National Journal*, 5 October. Available at: http://nationaljournal.com/2012-presidential-campaign/romney-wall-street-protests-class-warfare–20111004.

Burns, John F. 2011. 'Cameron deploys 10,000 more officers to riots', *New York Times*, 10 August, p. A4.

Cameron, David. 2011. Speech on the fight-back after the riots, Witney, Great Britain, 15 August. Available at: http://www.newstatesman.com/politics/2011/08/society-fight-work-rights.

Cobb, Roger W. and Charles D. Elder. 1972. *Participation in American Politics: The Dynamics of Agenda-Building*. Boston: Allyn & Bacon.

——and Marc H. Ross (eds). 1997. *Cultural Strategies of Agenda Denial: Avoidance, Attack, and Redefinition*. Lawrence, KS: University Press of Kansas.

——, Jennie Keith-Ross and Marc Howard Ross. 1976. 'Agenda building as a comparative political process', *American Political Science Review* 70(1): 126–38.

Coulter, Ann. 2011. 'Remarks on Fox News' "Hannity",' 14 October. Available at: http://www.foxnews.com/on-air/hannity/2011/10/17/ann-coulter-sounds-brainless-wall-street-protesters.

Dodd, Vikram and Caroline Davies. 2011. 'London riots escalate as police battle for control', *The Guardian*, 8 August. Available at: http://www.guardian.co.uk/uk/2011/aug/08/london-riots-escalate-police-battle.

Druckman, James N. 2010. 'What's it all about? Framing in political science', in Gideon Keren (ed.) *Perspectives on Framing*. New York: Psychology Press, 279–302

Dunt, Ian. 2011. 'Miliband: if Cameron doesn't hold an inquiry I will', Politics.co.uk, 12 August. Available at: http://www.politics.co.uk/news/2011/08/12/miliband-pushes-for-national-inquiry-into-eng.

Dwyer, Devin. 2011. 'Obama: Occupy Wall Street "not that different" from Tea Party protests', ABC News, 18 October. Available at: http://abcnews.go.com/blogs/politics/2011/10/obama-occupy-wall-street-not-that-different-from-tea-party-protests/.

Edelman, Murray. 1988. *Constructing the Political Spectacle*. Chicago: University of Chicago Press.

Entman, Robert M. 1993. 'Framing: Toward clarification of a fractured paradigm', *Journal of Communication* 43(4): 51–8.

Faiola, Anthony. 2011. 'Riots breakout in London neighborhood', *Washington Post*, 7 August. Available at: http://www.washingtonpost.com/world/riots-break-out-in-london-neighborhood/2011/08/07/gIQAn0sA0I_story.html.

Fischer, Frank. 2003. *Reframing Public Policy: Discursive Politics and Deliberative Practices*. Oxford: Oxford University Press.

——and John Forester (eds). 1993. *The Argumentative Turn in Policy Analysis and Planning*. Durham, NC: Duke University Press.

Gusfield, Joseph R. 1981. *The Culture of Public Problems*. Chicago: University of Chicago Press.

Halliday, Josh. 2011. 'London riots: BlackBerry to help police probe Messenger looting "role"', *Guardian*, 8 August. Available at: http://www.guardian.co.uk/uk/2011/aug/08/london-riots-blackberry-messenger-looting.

Hirschman, Albert. 1991. *The Rhetoric of Reaction: Perversity, Futility, Jeopardy*. Cambridge, MA: Belknap Press.

Iyengar, Shanto. 1996. 'Framing responsibility for political issues', *Annals of the American Academy of Political and Social Science* 546(1): 59–70.

Jones, Michael D. and Mark K. McBeth. 2010. 'A narrative policy framework: Clear enough to be wrong?' *Policy Studies Journal* 38(2): 329–53.

Kaplan, Thomas J. 1993. 'Reading policy narratives: beginnings, middles, and ends', 167–85, in Frank Fischer and John Forester (eds) *The Argumentative Turn in Policy Analysis and Planning*. Durham, NC: Duke University Press.

Kingdon, John. 1995. *Agendas, Alternatives, and Public Policies*. Boston: Little, Brown.

Krauthammer, Charles. 2011. 'The scapegoat strategy', *Washington Post*, 13 October. Available at: http://www.washingtonpost.com/opinions/the-scapegoat-strategy/2011/10/13/gIQArNWViL_story.html.

Krebs, Ronald R. and Patrick Thaddeus Jackson. 2007. 'Twisting tongues and twisting arms: The power of political rhetoric', *European Journal of International Relations* 13(1): 35–66.

Kristof, Nicholas. 2011. 'The bankers and the revolutionaries', *New York Times*, 1 October, SR11.

Krugman, Paul. 2011. 'Confronting the malefactors', *New York Times*, 6 October, A27.

Limbaugh, Rush. 2011. 'Remarks on the "Rush Limbaugh Show"', 5 October. Available at: http://www.rushlimbaugh.com/daily/2011/10/05/anti_capitalist_protestors_face_dilemma_should_they_buy_stuff.

Majone, Giandomenico. 1989. *Evidence, Argument, and Persuasion in the Policy Process*. New Haven, CT: Yale University Press.

Miliband, Ed. 2011. Speech on the London riots, Haverstock School in Chalk Farm, Great Britain, 15 August. Available at: http://www.newstatesman.com/politics/2011/08/society-young-heard-riots.

Mills, C. Wright. 1959. *The Sociological Imagination*. Oxford: Oxford University Press.

Minicucci, Daniela. 2011. 'The role of digital and social media in the London riots', *Global News*, 9 August. Available at: http://www.globalnews.ca/feature/6442461111/story.html.

*New York Times* editorial. 2011. 'Protesters against Wall Street: It's obvious what they want', *New York Times*, 9 October, p. SR10

Noakes, John A. and Hank Johnston. 2005. 'Frames of protest: A roadmap to a perspective', 1–29, in Hank Johnston and John A. Noakes (eds) *Frames of Protest: Social Movements and the Framing Perspective*. Oxford: Rowman and Littlefield.

OccupyWallSt.org. 2011. 'A modest call to action on this September 17th', 17 September. Available at: http://occupywallst.org/article/September_Revolution/.

Patterson, Molly and Kristen Renwick Monroe. 1998. 'Narrative in political science', *Annual Review of Political Science* 1: 315–31.

Power, Nina. 2011. 'There is a context to London's riots that can't be ignored', *Guardian*, 8 August. Available at: http://www.guardian.co.uk/commentisfree/2011/aug/08/context-london-riots.

Rein, Martin and Donald Schön. 1993. 'Reframing policy discourse', 145–66, in Frank Fischer and John Forester (eds) *The Argumentative Turn in Policy Analysis and Planning*. Durham, NC: Duke University Press.

Rochefort, David A. 1986. *American Social Welfare Policy: Dynamics of Formulation and Change*. Boulder, CO: Westview Press.

——and Roger W. Cobb. 1993. 'Problem definition, agenda access, and policy choice', *Policy Studies Journal* 21(1): 56–71.

——and Roger W. Cobb. 1994. 'Problem definition: An emerging perspective' in David A. Rochefort and Roger W. Cobb (eds) *The Politics of Problem Definition: Shaping the Policy Agenda*. Lawrence, KS: University Press of Kansas, 1–31.

——, Michael Rosenberg and Deena White. 1998. 'Community as a policy instrument: A comparative analysis', *Policy Studies Journal* 26(3): 548–68.

Ross, Marc H. 2011. 'The political psychology of competing narratives: September 11 and beyond', Social Science Research Council. Available at: http://essays.ssrc.org/sept11/essays/ross.htm.

Ryan, Paul. 2011. Remarks before the Heritage Foundation, Washington, DC, 26 October. Available at: http://blog.heritage.org/2011/10/26/video-rep-paul-ryan-on-saving-the-american-idea/.

Sabatier, Paul A. and Hank Jenkins-Smith. 1993. *Policy Change and Learning: An Advocacy Coalition Approach*. Boulder, CO: Westview Press.

Sacks, Jonathan. 2011. 'Reversing the decay of London undone', *Wall Street Journal*, 20 August. Available at: http://online.wsj.com/article/SB10001424053111903639404576516252066723110.html.

Schattschneider, E.E. 1960. *The Semisovereign People: A Realist's View of Democracy in America*. Hinsdale, IL: Dryden Press.

Schneider, Anne and Helen Ingram. 1997. *Policy Design for Democracy*. Lawrence, KS: University of Kansas Press.

Schön, Donald A. and Martin Rein. 1994. *Frame Reflection: Toward the Resolution of Intractable Policy Controversies*. New York: Basic Books.

Shanahan, Elizabeth A., Michael D. Jones and Mark K. McBeth. 2011. 'Policy narratives and policy processes', *Policy Studies Journal* 39(3): 535–61.

Somaiya, Ravi. 2011. 'London sees twin perils converging to fuel riot', *New York Times*, 8 August, A4.

Stone, Deborah. 2002. *Policy Paradox: The Art of Political Decision Making*. New York: Norton.

*Telegraph View* editorial. 2011. 'The criminals who shame our nation', *The Telegraph*, 9 August. Available at: http://www.telegraph.co.uk/comment/telegraph-view/8691352/The-criminals-who-shame-our-nation.html.

Torgerson, Douglas. 1996. 'Power and insight in policy discourse: Post-positivism and problem definition', in Laurent Dobuzinskis, Michael Howlett, and David Laycock (eds) *Policy Studies in Canada: The State of the Art*. Toronto: University of Toronto Press, 266–98.

Walton, Jeff. 2011. 'Church of England bishops: Lack of virtue at fault for London riots', The Institute on Religion and Democracy, 22 August. Available at: http://www.theird.org/page.aspx?pid=2012.

# 16

# Mass media and policy-making

*Stuart Soroka, Stephen Farnsworth, Andrea Lawlor and Lori Young*

Mass media can, and often do, play a critical role in policy-making. The typical view of media is that they matter in the early stages of the policy process—that media can help to set an agenda, which is then adopted and dealt with by politicians, policy-makers, and other actors. The impact of media is rarely so constrained, however. Our argument here, in short, is that media matter, not just at the beginning but throughout the policy process.

Many of the standard accounts of policy-making have a much too narrow view of the timing of media effects. That said, the ways in which mass media can matter are relatively well understood. Existing work tells us that media can draw and sustain public attention to particular issues. They can change the discourse around a policy debate by framing or defining an issue using dialogue or rhetoric to persuade or dissuade the public. Media can establish the nature, sources, and consequences of policy issues in ways that fundamentally change not just the attention paid to those issues, but the different types of policy solutions sought. Media can draw attention to the players involved in the policy process and can aid, abet or hinder their cause by highlighting their role in policy-making. Media can also act as a critical conduit between governments and publics, informing publics about government actions and policies, and helping to convey public attitudes to government officials.

Allowing for the possibility that any and all of these effects can be evident not just in the early stages but throughout the policy process makes clear the potentially powerful impact we believe that media can have on policy. Indeed, mass media are in the unique position of having a regular, marked impact on policy, but from outside the formal political sphere, often without even being recognized as a policy player.

This chapter reviews the state of the literature on media and policy-making. It reviews two of the most prominent theories in the study of media and policy-making: agenda-setting and issue framing. It then considers some of the normative implications of the regular impact of media on policy-making. Is the fact that media matter to policy-making a good thing? There are benefits, to be sure, but also costs, and we consider below the costs associated with the well-known event-driven, sensationalist tendencies in media content. We then finish with a brief example from Canadian environmental news coverage; an example which illustrates some of the problematic tendencies in media content, and highlights some of the issues with media as a policy actor.

## Agenda-setting and issue attentiveness

The policy agenda-setting literature has its roots in early work in political behavior focused on how media coverage of political events impacts electoral outcomes. Berelson *et al.'s* (1954) seminal study on voting, for instance, notes that the media persuades individuals by prioritizing particular stories over others, or by airing a greater volume of stories related to some policy domains, but not others. McCombs and Shaw's (1972) Chapel Hill study, which spawned a vast literature on public agenda-setting, examines the media's role in focusing public attention on particular issues, concluding that the media can effectively "set" the public agenda by consistently and prominently featuring issues in their news coverage. Cobb and Elder's (1972) early work is the policy-oriented equivalent, and these authors were followed by a growing body of literature focused on the sources of the policy agenda, that is, the "general set of issues that are communicated in a hierarchy of importance at a point in time" (Cobb and Elder [1972]1983: 14).

Though by no means the only source of the policy agenda, existing work suggests that media can be an important one. Consider work by Flickinger (1983) and Mayer (1991), for instance, on the role of media in the rise of consumer protection as a policy issue, or Pritchard's (1986) work on the impact of media coverage on the decision to prosecute murderers (also see Pritchard's (1992) review of the role of the news media in public policy). All of this work points toward an impact of media on policy-makers that is very similar to what Cohen famously observed about the public, namely, that the mass media "may not be successful much of the time in telling people what to think, but it is stunningly successful in telling its readers what to think about" (Cohen 1963: 13). The policy equivalent—mass media may not define the nature or direction of policy change, but can certainly steer attention towards certain policy domains over others—is of no small consequence. Recent work by both Kingdon (1995) and Baumgartner and Jones (1993) has made this especially clear. For each, issue attentiveness is a critical precursor of policy change.

The same was true in Anthony Downs' (1972) work on the "issue attention cycle," the canonical model of public issue attentiveness. Downs suggested that (policy) issues move cyclically in and out of the public consciousness. The life cycle of an issue moves incrementally from periods of low to high salience, ultimately retreating to the background after the public has moved onto to other issues. The notion itself is not earth-shattering, but Downs' description of the process is valuable. It also points to the role of media in affecting change in issue salience.

Note too that while most of the preceding work focuses on the role of media in affecting some kind of aggregate policy agenda, the role of media in setting the policy agenda can also be seen at the individual level, that is, impacting individual political and policy actors directly. Politicians are affected by media in the same way as ordinary citizens (Eilders 2001; Dearing and Rogers 1996). They rely on media cues to prioritize information and to disseminate public opinion (Walgrave and Van Aelst 2006: 100; Cook *et al.* 1983). Politicians can be even more susceptible to media content depending on whether they are subject to electoral punishment on a set of issues (Kingdon 1984). However, legislators, like voters, cannot pay attention to all issues at a given time; their attention is finite, and therefore they tend to focus on key issues that are beneficial to their constituents, country and indeed, their own career. Unsurprisingly, there are often high levels of congruence among these issues and the issues that are of concern to the public (Baumgartner *et al.* 1997: 350).

Of all this said, media quite clearly do not matter to all policy issues all the all the time, and there is a growing body of work exploring the ways in which media influence varies systematically across issues. Some work has compared the impact of media across issues directly. Soroka (2002), for instance, argues for three different issue types, where "sensational" issues—characterized by low complexity and the possibility for dramatic events—are those for which media are most likely to play a leading role. (Also see Walgrave *et al.* 2007.) Indeed, there are a number of studies suggesting that the complexity of issues seriously constrains the potential for media effects, on both the public and policy-makers (e.g. Zucker 1978; Yagade and Dozier 1990), and a series of studies that focus on the role of often sudden and unexpected "focusing events" in attracting media, and then policy, attention to issues (e.g. Birkland 1998; Kingdon 1994). The impact of media on policy also appears to be contingent on the source of the news: reliable and respected news outlets have more impact than marginal and questionable news sources (Bartels 1996). Additionally, the possibility that media have a marked impact on the political agenda increases when there is heightened coverage of the same issue, at the same time, by different media outlets (Eilders 2000, 2001).

Even with these caveats, the accumulated literature suggests an important (and often independent) role for media in determining which issues are important, and when—for the public, and for policy-makers as well. Setting the agenda is just one way in which media may matter to policy, however. We explore a second below.

## Issue framing

As with agenda-setting, the framing literature spans analyses of both policy-making and public opinion. Druckman offers a cogent definition:

> a framing effect is said to occur when, in the of describing an issue or event, a speaker's emphasis on a subset of potentially relevant considerations causes individuals to focus on these considerations when constructing their opinions.
>
> *(2001: 1042; drawing on work by Rabin 1998, among others)*

The extent to which this kind of framing is seen as separate from agenda-setting varies somewhat—some authors choose to see framing mainly as shifts in attentiveness to sub-issues (see, e.g. McCombs *et al.* 1997; McCombs 2004). Others argue that while agenda-setting looks at story selection as determinants of public perceptions of issue importance, framing looks at the way those issues are presented (see, e.g. Price and Tewksbury 1997: 184). We take the view here, in line with a vast body of work on policy-making, that it is worth considering framing as distinct from agenda-setting.

Framing theory is based on the belief that how an issue is characterized to an audience will influence how it is understood (see, e.g. Scheufele and Tewksbury 2007). Put differently, issue framing refers to the selective exposure of information to an audience with the intent of shaping their understanding of an issue; it is the "selection of—and emphasis upon—particular attributes for the news media agenda when talking about an object" (McCombs 2004: 87). Media can apply frames to issues in order to organize a storyline around a series of events (e.g. Gamson and Modigliani 1987), or to instruct or persuade the audience in how to evaluate the information being given to them in a predictable way (e.g. McQuail 1994). Framing issues presuppose that the information presented to the public will change the way that they view an issue. In other words, framing an issue involves "select[ing] some aspects of a perceived reality … in such a way as to promote a particular problem definition, causal interpretation, moral evaluation, and/or treatment recommendation" (Entman 1993: 52). To frame a story is to often withhold some information or prioritize some facts over others. In fact, most frames are, according to Entman (1993), as defined by what they omit or obscure as what they include. (And note that motives for inclusion or exclusion of information may be conscious or unconscious, see Gamson 1989.)

Frames often influence the direction of policy by pulling values or emotion into the discussion. Stone argues that problem identification often focuses on framing a story in a way that attributes cause and assigns blame (1989: 282). According to Iyengar (1991), thematic frames (those that give information about general trends such as poverty or social welfare) tend to promote a sense of social or institutional responsibility, while episodic frames (those that reference individuals or personal experiences or and stories) place responsibility on the individual. Frame types prime social values differently, and simultaneously establish the salience of the subject and promote a particular policy direction (Sniderman *et al.* 1991).

Framing is not an activity for media alone, of course. Policymakers are not simply affected by issue framing in media, but they actively engage in policy framing. Indeed, the policy literature on framing is much more focused on the ways in which policy re-framing by politicians and/or bureaucrats can shift attentiveness to or attitudes towards an issue. Consider Edelman's (1997) work on the role of language and symbols in politics, for instance, connected to a broader body of constructionist accounts of the policy process (e.g. Lasswell 1949; Spector and Kitsuse 1977; Rosenau 1993). Consider also Fischer's (2003) discussion of politicians' use of rhetorical devices to frame an issue and sway public opinion. Using the example of hiring policy, Gamson and Modigliani (1987) show that formal terms in thematic, policy-oriented frames (i.e. "affirmative action") may lend the frame more credibility than vernacular or emotionally charged language (i.e. "preferential treatment"), thereby impacting how audiences receive the frame and accept policy direction from elites (see also Gamson 1992).

## Media as a policy actor: challenges

Clearly, media matter to policy, throughout the policy process, and in many different ways. Is this a good thing? It is an inevitable thing, surely—it is nearly impossible to imagine modern politics and policy-making without some kind of media involvement, after all. Even so, we should consider some of the issues related to media's role in the policy process. Here, we review the considerable body of work that criticizes the nature and tone of media content on policy issues. As we shall see, this work raises serious questions about the potential for and difficulties with the role of mass media in policy-making.

Note first that work in political communication routinely offers largely critical assessments of the ability of news content to contribute to informed public debate, particularly with respect to television news. Biases in reporter coverage and the use of active conflict frames—key journalistic tools in other areas of media coverage—are highlighted as important constraints. Studies fault reporters for focusing on the trivial, for being too closely tied to official sources, for not providing their viewers with enough context to understand contentious policy options, for their bias and for a lack of technical proficiency in the matters about which they write (Entman 2004; Farnsworth and Lichter 2006, 2011; Herman and Chomsky 1988; Iyengar 1991; Iyengar and Kinder 1987; Larson 2001; McChesney 1999; Patterson 1994).

Research also questions the possibility that journalistic norms serve to create misleading news stories. Coverage of environmental issues stands as one example of this phenomenon. Even with major issues that have been repeatedly featured in the media, such as the global warming debate, scholars note that attempting to provide roughly equal treatment of both sides of a story can "distort" the reality of widespread scientific agreement regarding climate change (Boykoff 2005). Rather than focus on the preponderance of scientific evidence that supports the global warming hypothesis, scholars argue that US news reports have tended to give roughly equal weight to skeptics with little peer-reviewed evidence (Boykoff 2005; Mooney 2004).

Other journalistic norms may also reduce the likelihood of effective/informative policy discussion in the mass media. Reporters often prefer conflict frames to increase news consumer interest, but the news reports that emerge often lack sufficient context (Iyengar 1991; Iyengar and Kinder

1987). Emphasizing the conflict frame of environmental debates decreases public awareness of the scientific consensus regarding the existence of human-triggered climate change, for instance (Corbett and Durfee 2008; Nisbet and Myers 2007). Content analyses of climate change news in the *New York Times*, the *Washington Post*, the *Los Angeles Times* and the *Wall Street Journal* from 1998 through 2002 suggest that the journalistic attempts to be even-handed sowed far greater public doubts about global warming than exist within the scientific community (Boykoff and Boykoff 2007). Studies of television news have found that these attempts to provide balance in stories made scientific findings on climate change appear to the public as far more tentative than they actually were (Boykoff 2007a).

Additional problems with media coverage of complicated policy domains have emerged in other studies. First, scientific uncertainty and other technical matters tend to be papered over by reporters who do not mention that correlation is not causation, or that preliminary findings are tentative (Murray *et al.* 2001). Complexities, in other words, that too often are ignored in favor of a more compelling and definitive, if less accurate, narrative. In cases where policy specialists offer an interpretation that is too nuanced or too technical (others might say "accurate"), reporters are tempted to rely on environmental activists who are quicker with a pithy quote, even though they may not possess the credentials of the less-quotable scientific experts (Lichter and Rothman 1999). Part of the problem may be the relatively limited policy expertise possessed by many reporters. Work suggests, for instance, that a lack of expertise has been important in journalists' susceptibility to marginal claims of potential health hazards, such as the relative dangers posed by pesticides on apples or Bisphenol A (BPA) in water bottles when compared, for example, to cigarette smoking or obesity (Murray *et al.* 2001; Lichter 2009).

Second, when elected officials weigh in on policy, political issues tend to become increasingly prominent in the public discussion. That is, the interaction of politics and policy in the media tends to reduce attention to substantive policy matters and refocus concern on estimations of politically viable policy options (Miller *et al.* 1990; Wilkins and Patterson 1991).

Third, and perhaps most relevant, one problem in policy coverage by the media is that the very long-term nature of some policy domains works against the traditional newsroom norms of timeliness and novelty (McCright and Dunlap 2003; Trumbo 1995). While news coverage can focus intensely on scientific issues when a hurricane makes landfall or when a severe drought decimates crop yields, media attention can evaporate as quickly as it emerges (Mazur 2009; Mazur and Lee 1993). For instance, content analysis of climate change reports in the *New York Times* and *Washington Post* from 1980 to 1995 shows an attention cycle of media interest in global warming, where coverage increases in the early stages of discussion but erodes over time (McComas and Shanahan 1999). Early coverage was anchored by dire projections from scientists, while a middle phase of coverage focused on disagreements among scientists to maintain interest, and a later phase of reduced coverage concentrated on the economic costs and political debates over potential remedies. The rapid turnover of issues in mainstream news works against gradual long-term stories like climate change, particularly if the dire early predictions do not appear to come to pass shortly after they are made (Stevens 1993).

## An expository analysis: environmental coverage in Canada[1]

The preceding section has drawn on work focused on environmental policy in particular for good reason: there is a growing body of work dealing with the problems with media coverage of environmental issues. A recurring theme is the tendency for a strong connection between environmental coverage and major events—or, more precisely, a lack of environmental coverage in the absence of major weather or climate events. For instance, a comparison of global warming news in top circulation newspapers in the US and the UK found a much greater volume of coverage in the UK, though the number of news reports in both nations increased notably (and temporarily) around key environmental events, such as new expert reports on greenhouse gas emissions caused by air travel (a key issue of the G8 summit in June 2005), and the release of Al Gore's film, *An Inconvenient Truth*, a year later (Boykoff 2007a).

The biggest challenge in media coverage of environmental politics may be, then, that despite the long-term nature of many environmental issues, environmental news is really not all that different from other types of news: as with coverage of a wide range of policy issues, events with immediate impacts are both easier and more attractive to cover than continuous monitoring of a known issue. And in the absence of such events, regardless of the actual state of the environment, environmental issues will disappear from the media agenda (and quite possibly the policy agenda as well).

This event-driven tendency in media is relatively easily illustrated. We focus here on a body of content-analytic data of all news stories from the nightly newscast for CTV in Canada (the nightly newscast with the largest audience shares in each country) from 1999 to 2009. Data were gathered using full-text indices in Nexis, and relying on the Nexis topic field to identify stories for which a "major theme" (based on the Nexis subject-coding scheme) was the environment. In total, the database includes 1,789 news stories.

We begin by subject-coding stories based on an iterative automated process. We first look at frequencies for all words and phrases in the stories (analyzed together), using WordStat. We then take the most common words and phrases—those relating to the environment—and build a dictionary of commonly used terms. We add these terms, gradually, to the topic dictionary—the product of a combination of data processing and common sense. A story is then coded as a given topic if at least two keywords for that category were present in the text. The resulting codes thus are indicators of the prevalence of specific language relating to various environmental issues.

Our focus here is on two topics in particular: pollution/climate change, and weather and natural disasters.[2] Figure 16.1 shows trends in coverage for both topics over time. What is most important to draw from the figure is (a) the tendency for weather and natural disasters to produce more news than pollution and climate change and (b) the lack of any upward trend in coverage of environmental issues in spite of increasing environmental difficulties worldwide. Media coverage of pollution and climate change does not, at least in terms of the volume of coverage, appear to reflect trends in environmental indicators.

The more striking finding from these data is shown in Table 16.1, however. The table presents results from a relatively simple Granger causality test—a statistical test of the temporal relationship between the number of articles relating to disasters/weather and the number of articles dealing with pollution/climate change.

Analyses rely on weekly data, and Granger tests proceed as follows. Total current coverage of disasters/weather is regressed on the last week's coverage of disasters/weather, as well as the last week's coverage of pollution/climate change. Results show, controlling for past coverage of disasters/weather, whether pollution/climate change coverage systematically leads to disasters/weather coverage. The same model is also estimated in the opposite direction: pollution/climate change coverage is regressed on last week's coverage of pollution/climate change, and last week's coverage of disasters/weather. Drawing on both models, we have a good sense of the extent to which disasters/weather leads pollution/climate change, and vice versa.

Both models are estimated simultaneously using OLS vector autoregression; estimated coefficients are shown in Table 16.1. In the first column, we see that current coverage of disasters/weather is related to the previous week's coverage of disasters/weather. (The coefficient is .32, and is statistically significant.) The same is not true for the previous week's coverage of

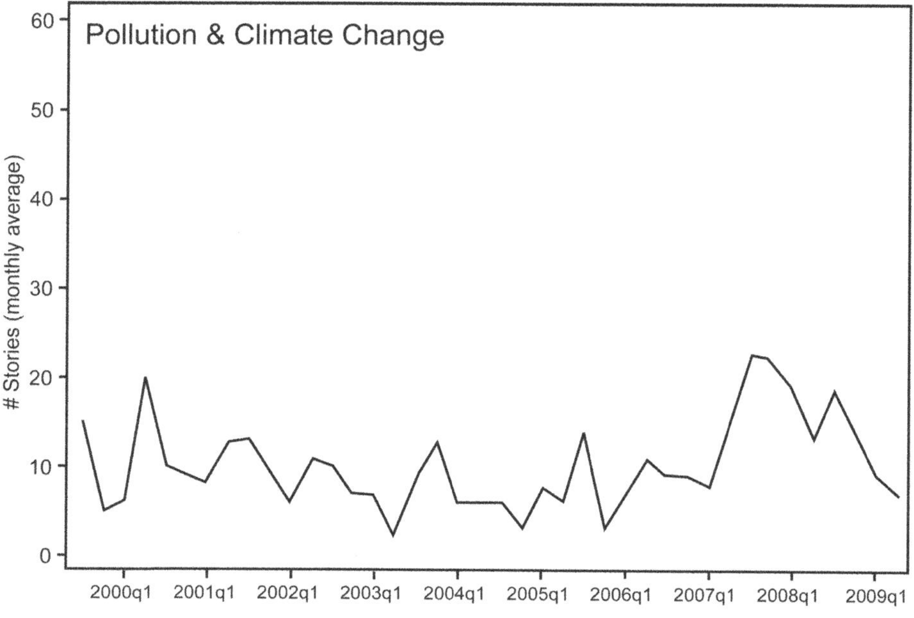


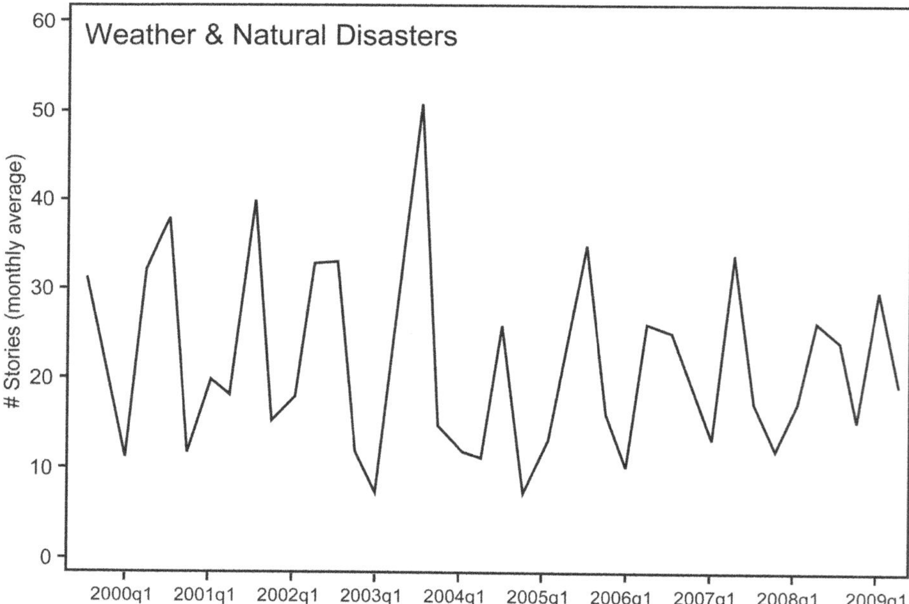


*Figure 16.1* Coverage of natural disasters/weather and pollution/climate change by year
Source: Stuart Soroka, Stephen Farnsworth, Lori Young and Andrea Lawlor (2009) 'Environment and energy policy: Comparing reports from US and Canadian television news'. Paper presented at the Annual Meeting of the American Political Science Association, Toronto.

*Table 16.1* Coverage of natural disasters/weather and pollution/climate change

| | *DV: disasters/ weather* $_t$ | *DV: pollution/climate Change* $_t$ |
|---|---|---|
| Disasters/weather $_{t-1}$ | .315* | .061[a] |
| | (.109) | (.035) |
| Pollution/climate Change $_{t-1}$ | .019 | .259* |
| | (.051) | (.043) |
| Constant | 1.114* | .776* |
| | (.109) | (.090) |
| R-sq | .101 | .079 |

Notes: N=520. * $p < .05$; a $p < .10$. Estimates rely on weekly data. Cells contain coefficients from an OLS vector regression, with standard errors in parentheses.
Source: Author

pollution/climate change. That is, there is no relationship between current coverage of weather or disasters, and the preceding week's reports on pollution or climate change.

The second column includes the model for current coverage of pollution or climate change. Here, we see that current coverage of pollution and climate change is related to last week's coverage of climate change (a coefficient of .26), but also to last week's coverage of disasters and events (a coefficient of .06). There is, then, evidence here of a unidirectional causal effect: coverage of pollution and climate change is systematically (and positively) led by coverage of weather and disasters. (Put differently, coverage of disasters and events "Granger-causes" coverage of pollution and climate change.)

In sum, these data suggest that substantive coverage of environmental themes such as air pollution, global warming and climate change increases after major weather-related disasters and events. Indeed, one interpretation—drawing on the literature discussed above—is that coverage of pollution and climate change is dependent on weather-related disasters and events. As we might expect, reporters apparently find it hard to write about climate change without reference to high temperatures and weather-related disasters. A sustained conversation on the environment is unlikely, our findings suggest, to exclude a steady stream of floods, hurricanes, ice storms, power blackouts, and other climate mayhem.

## Conclusions

There is little doubt that mass media play an important role in policy-making. A growing body of literature highlights this role, both in terms of issue attentiveness and policy framing. We have argued here, however, that it is important to note, first, that media matter not just at the beginning but throughout the policy process, and second, that media's involvement in the policy process poses some real difficulties. In short, the complexities of policy-making are likely not to be well served by well-known tendencies in media coverage. That media matter to policy-making seems beyond doubt. Whether their contribution tends to be positive on balance is, however, up for discussion.

## Notes

1 This section draws on analyses in Soroka *et al.* 2009.
2 The first is captured using the following keywords: acid rain, air, carbon, climate change, emission*, global warming, greenhouse gas*, pollution, pollute*, toxic, toxin*, ozone; the second is based on: flood*, forest fire*, wildfire*, wild fire*, hurricane*, storm*, drought*, rain*, wind*, ice, weather, tornado*.

## Bibliography

Bartels, L.M. 1996, September. 'Politicians and the press: Who leads, who follows? in *APSA*. San Francisco, CA.

Baumgartner, Frank R. and Bryan D. Jones. 1993. *Agendas and Instability in American Politics*. Chicago: University of Chicago Press.

——, Bryan D. Jones and Beth L. Leech. 1997. 'Media attention and Congressional agendas', in Shanto Iyengar and Richard Reeves (eds) *Do the Media Govern? Politicians, Voters, and Reporters in America* Thousand Oaks, CA: Sage.

Berelson, Bernard R., Paul F. Lazarsfeld and William N. McPhee. 1954. *Voting: A Study of Opinion Formation in a Presidential Campaign*. Chicago: University of Chicago Press.

Berger, B. 2001. 'Private issues and public policy: Locating the corporate agenda in agenda-setting theory', *Journal of Public Relations Research* 13(2): 91–126.

Birkland, Thomas A. 1998. 'Focusing events, mobilization, and agenda setting', *Journal of Public Policy* 18(1): 53–74.

—— 2007. 'Agenda setting in public policy', in Frank Fischer, Gerald J. Miller and Mara S. Sidney (eds) *Handbook of Public Policy Analysis*. London: Taylor & Francis.

Boykoff, Maxwell. 2005. 'The disconnect of news reporting from scientific evidence', *Nieman Reports, Harvard University*, winter: 86.

—— 2007a. 'From convergence to contention: United States mass media representations of anthropogenic climate change science', *Transactions of the Institute of British Geographers* 32: 477–89.

—— 2007b. 'Flogging a dead norm? Newspaper coverage of anthropogenic climate change in the United States and the United Kingdom from 2003–2006', *Area* 39: 470–81.

——and Jules M. Boykoff. 2007. 'Climate change and journalistic norms: A case study of US mass media coverage', *Geoforum* 38: 1190–204.

Cobb, R.W. and C.D. Elder. [1972]1983. *Participation in American Politics: The Dynamics of Agenda-Building*. Boston: Allyn & Bacon.

Cohen, Bernard C. 1963. *The Press and Foreign Policy*. Princeton, NJ: Princeton University Press.

Cook, Fay Lomax, Tom R. Tyler, Edward G. Goetz, Margaret T. Gordon, David Protess, Donna R. Leff, and Harvey L. Molotch. 1983. 'Media and agenda setting: Effects on the public, interest group leaders, policy makers, and policy', *The Public Opinion Quarterly* 47(1): 16–35.

Corbett, Julia B. and Jessica Durfee. 2008. 'Testing public (un)certainty of science: Media representations of global warming', *Science Communication* 26: 129–51.

Dearing, James W. and Everett M. Rogers. 1996. *Agenda-Setting*. Thousand Oaks, CA: Sage.

Downs, Anthony. 1972. 'Up and down with ecology: The "issue attention cycle"', *The Public Interest* 28: 35–50.

Druckman, James N. 2001. 'On the limits of framing effects: Who can frame?' *The Journal of Politics* 63: 1041–1066.

——and Michael Parkin. 2005. 'The impact of media bias: How editorial slant affects voters', *The Journal of Politics* 67(4): 1030–49.

Edelman, M. 1964. *The Symbolic Uses of Politics*. Chicago: University of Illinois Press.

—— 1977. *Political Language*. New York: Academic Press.

Eilders, C. 2000. 'Media as political actors? Issue focusing and selective emphasis in the German quality press', *German Politics* 9(3): 181–206.

—— 2001. *Conflict and Consonance in Media Opinion: Political Positions of Five German Quality Papers*. Berlin: WZB Discussion Papers.

Entman, Robert. 1993. 'Framing: Toward clarification of a fractured paradigm', *Journal of Communication* 43(4): 51–8.

—— 2004. *Projections of Power: Framing News, Public Opinion and Foreign Policy*. Chicago: University of Chicago Press.

Farnsworth, Stephen J. and S. Robert Lichter. 2006. *The Mediated Presidency: Television News and Presidential Governance*. Lanham, MD: Rowman & Littlefield.

—— and S. Robert Lichter. 2011. *The Nightly News Nightmare: Media Coverage of US Presidential Elections, 1988–2008*. Lanham, MD: Rowman and Littlefield. Third Edition.

Fischer, Frank. 2003. *Reframing Public Policy: Discursive Politics and Deliberative Practices*. Oxford: Oxford University Press.

Flickinger, Richard. 1983. 'The comparative politics of agenda-setting: The emergence of consumer protection as a public policy issue in Britain and the United States', *Policy Studies Review* 2(3): 429–44.

Gamson, W.A. 1989. 'News as framing: Comments on Graber', *American Behavioral Scientist* 33: 157–66.
—— 1992. *Talking Politics*, New York, NY: Cambridge University Press.
——and A. Modigliani. 1987. 'The changing culture of affirmative action', in R.G. Braungart and M.M. Braungart (eds) *Research in Political Sociology*. Greenwich, CT: JAI Press.
Gandy, O.H., Jr. 1982. *Beyond Agenda Setting: Information Subsidies and Public Policy*. Norwood, NJ: Ablex.
Herman, Edward S. and Noam Chomsky. 1988. *Manufacturing Consent: The Political Economy of the Mass Media*. New York: Panetheon.
Hilgartner, Stephen and Charles L. Bosk. 1988. 'The rise and fall of social problems: A public arenas model', *American Journal of Sociology* 94(1): 53–78.
Iyengar, Shanto. 1991. *Is Anyone Responsible? How Television Frames Political Issues*. Chicago: University of Chicago Press.
—— 1993. 'Agenda-setting and beyond: Television news and the strength of political issues', in William Riker (ed.) *Agenda Formation*. Ann Arbor, MI: University of Michigan Press.
——and Donald R. Kinder. 1987. *News That Matters*. Chicago: University of Chicago Press.
Jensen, Carsten. 2009. 'Policy punctuations in mature welfare states', *Journal of Public Policy* 29(3): 287–303.
Kingdon, John. 1984. *Agenda-Setting, Alternatives and Public Policies*. New York: Harper Collins.
—— 1995. *Agendas, Alternatives, and Public Policies*. New York: HarperCollins College Publishers.
Lang, Kurt and Gladys Engel Lang. 1966. 'The mass media and voting', in Bernard Berelson and Morris Janowitz (eds) *Reader in Public Opinion and Communication*. New York: Free Press.
Larson, Stephanie. 2001. 'Poll coverage of the 2000 presidential campaign on network news', paper delivered at the 2001 Annual Meeting of the American Political Science Association, San Francisco.
Lasswell, Harold D. 1949. 'Style in the language of politics', in Harold Lasswell and N. Leites (eds) *The Language of Politics: Studies in Quantitative Semantics*. New York: George Stewart, 20–39.
Lichter, S. Robert. 2009. 'Are chemicals killing us? Experts speak out', STATS (21 May report). Available at: http://stats.org/stories/2009/are_chemicals_killing_us.html (accessed 2 August, 2009).
Lichter, S. Robert, and Stanley Rothman. 1999. *Environmental Cancer: A Political Disease?* New Haven, CT: Yale University Press.
McChesney, Robert. 1999. *Rich Media, Poor Democracy: Communications Politics in Dubious Times*. New York: Times Press.
McComas, Katherine and James Shanahan. 1999. 'Telling stories about global climate change: Measuring the impact of narratives on issue cycles', *Communication Research* 26: 30–57.
McCombs, M. 2004. *Setting the Agenda: The Mass Media and Public Opinion*. Malden, MA: Blackwell Publishing Inc.
——and Donald L. Shaw. 1972. 'The agenda-setting function of mass media', *Public Opinion Quarterly* 36(2): 176–87.
——and J.H. Zhu. 1995. 'Capacity, diversity, and volatility of the public agenda: Trends from 1954 to 1994', *Public Opinion Quarterly* 59: 495–525.
——, D.L. Shaw, and D. Weaver. 1997. *Communication and Democracy: Exploring the Intellectual Frontiers in Agenda-Setting Theory*. Mahwah: NJ: Lawrence Erlbaum.
McCright, Aaron M. and Riley E. Dunlap. 2003. 'Defeating Kyoto: The conservative movement's impact on US climate change policy', *Social Problems* 50: 348–73.
McQuail, D. 1994. *Mass Communication Theory: An Introduction*, 3rd edn. Thousand Oaks, CA: Sage.
Mayer, Robert N. 1991. 'Gone yesterday, here today: Consumer issues in the agenda-setting process', *Journal of Social Issues* 47(1): 21–39.
Mazur, Allan. 2009. 'American generation of environmental warnings: Avian influenza and global warming', *Human Ecology Review* 16: 17–26.
——and Linling Lee. 2003. 'Sounding the global alarm: Environmental issues in the US national news', *Social Studies of Science* 23: 681–720.
Miller, S. M., A. Evers and H. Winterberger. 1990. 'The evolving welfare state mixes', in *Shifts in the Welfare Mix: Their Impact on Work, Social Services and Welfare Policies*. Frankfurt: Campus Verlag, 371–88.
Mooney, Chris. 2004. 'Blinded by science: How 'balanced' coverage lets the scientific fringe hijack reality', *Columbia Journalism Review*, November/December.
Murray, David, Joel Schwartz and S. Robert Lichter. 2001. *It Ain't Necessarily So: How Media Make and Unmake the Scientific Picture of Reality*. Lanham, MD: Rowman & Littlefield.
Nelson, Barbara. 1984. *Making an Issue of Child Abuse: Political Agenda-Setting for Social Problems*. Chicago: University of Chicago Press.

Nisbet, Matthew C. and Teresa Myers. 2007. 'Twenty years of public opinion about global warming', *Public Opinion Quarterly* 71: 444–70.

Patterson, Thomas E. 1994. *Out of Order.* New York: Vintage.

Peters, B. Guy and Brian W. Hogwood. 1985. *The Pathology of Public Policy.* New York: Oxford University Press.

Price, V. and D. Tewksbury. 1997. 'News values and public opinion: A theoretical account of media priming and framing', in G.A. Barett and F.J. Boster (eds) *Progress in Communication Sciences: Advances in Persuasion.* Greenwich, CT: Ablex.

Pritchard, David. 1986. 'Homicide and bargained justice: The agenda-setting effect of crime news on prosecutors', *Public Opinion Quarterly* 50(2): 143–59.

—— 1992. 'The news media and public policy agendas', in. D. Kennamer (ed.) *Public Opinion, the Press and Public Policy.* Westport, CT: Praeger.

Rabin, Matthew. 1998. 'Psychology and Economics', *Journal of Economic Literature* 36: 11–46.

Rosenau, Pauline V. 1993. 'Anticipating a post-modern policy current?' *Policy Currents* 3: 1–4.

Schattschneider, E.E. 1960. *The Semisovereign People.* New York: Rineheart and Wilson.

Scheufele, Dietram A. and David Tewksbury. 2007. 'Framing, agenda setting, and priming: The evolution of three media effects models', *Journal of Communication* 57(1): 9–20.

Sniderman, P.M., R.A. Brody and P.E. Tetlock. 1991. *Reasoning and Choice: Explorations in Political Psychology.* Cambridge: Cambridge University Press.

Soroka, Stuart. 2002. *Agenda-Setting Dynamics in Canada.* Vancouver: University of British Columbia Press.

——, Stephen Farnsworth, Lori Young and Andrea Lawlor. 2009. 'Environment and energy policy: Comparing reports from US and Canadian television news', paper presented at the Annual Meeting of the American Political Science Association, Toronto.

Spector, Malcolm and John I. Kitsuse. 1977. *Constructing Social Problems.* Menlo Park, CA: Cummings.

Stevens, W.K. 1993. 'Scientists confront renewed backlash on global warming', *New York Times*, 14 September.

Stone, Deborah. 1989. 'Causal stories and the formation of policy agendas', *Political Science Quarterly* 104(2): 281–300.

Trumbo, Craig. 1995. 'Longitudinal modeling of public issues: An application of the agenda-setting process to the issue of global warming', *Journalism and Mass Communication Monographs* 152(August): 1–57.

—— 1996. 'Constructing climate change: Claims and frames in US news coverage of an environmental issue', *Public Understanding of Science* 5: 269–83.

Tuchman, G. 1978. *Making News: A Study in the Construction of Reality.* New York: Free Press.

Walgrave, Stefaan and Peter Van Aelst. 2006. 'The contingency of the mass media's political agenda setting power: toward a preliminary theory', *Journal of Communication* 56(1): 88–109.

——, Stuart Soroka and Michiel Nuytemans. 2007. 'The mass media's political agenda-setting power: A longitudinal analysis of media, parliament, and government in Belgium (1993 to 2000)', *Comparative Political Studies* 41(6): 814–36.

Wilkins, Lee and Philip Patterson. 1991. 'Science as symbol: The media chills the greenhouse effect', in Lee Wilkins and Philip Patterson (eds) *Risky Business: Communication Issues of Science, Risk and Public Policy.* Westport, CT: Greenwood, 159–76.

Yagade, A. and Dozier D.M. 1990. 'The media agenda-setting effect of concrete versus abstract issues', *Journalism Quarterly* 67: 3–10.

Zhu, J.H. 1992. 'Issue competition and attention distraction: A zero-sum theory of agenda setting', *Journalism Quarterly* 69: 825–36.

Zucker, H.G. 1978. 'The variable nature of news media influence', in B.D. Ruben (ed.) *Communication Yearbook,* vol 2. New Brunswick, NJ: Transaction Books.

# Part V

# Understanding the formulation process

# 17

# Policy design and transfer

*Anne Schneider*

Policy design, whether conceptualized as a verb referring to the process of formulating public policy, or as a noun describing the content of public policy remains largely uncharted territory. This chapter reviews what we know about policy designs and develops ideas about how the study of policy design can contribute to an understanding of policy transfer and diffusion. Policy scholars have long been interested in understanding how policies are copied, stolen, or diffuse across jurisdictions, but much of the attention has been on the politics and geographic proximity of the "innovating" states—that is, the ones that were early adopters (Walker 1969). The focus in this chapter is on what types of policy designs are most likely to transfer and which ones may be subject to truncated transfer or to not move at all (Schneider and Ingram 1988). Theories of policy invention and expert decision-making suggest that individuals search through large amounts of relevant information stored in memory, reason by analogies, make comparisons, and either copy or simulate patterns of information to produce desired consequences. These consequences may focus on "good" public policy that resolves important collective problems, or on gaining political capital, or a broad array of more narrow-gauged goals. On the other hand, social psychologists have documented that even experts are subject to a wide range of cognitive biases, and these biases find their way into public policy designs (Kahneman *et al.* 1982). Rather than simply a benign process of efficient decision-making, cognitive biases may operate at the expense of policy that would serve democratic ends. In the remaining parts of this chapter, I will first explore policy designing as it commonly occurs with an emphasis on the role of decision heuristics and cognitive biases, and then develop a framework for analyzing policy design—that is, policy content. From the analysis of the elements of design found in almost all public policies, it is possible to identify a number of commonly copied designs and their implications for democracy.

## Background

Two very different approaches to the study of policy design have emerged in the literature (Schneider and Ingram 1988, 1993, 1997, 2005; Howlett and Lejano 2011; Linder and Peters 1985; Bobrow and Dryzek (1987). What these approaches have in common is a desire to improve the consequences of public policy—the outputs or outcomes of policy. They differ considerably, however, in the focus of attention, define the term differently, and also come at the problem of producing what might be considered "good" public policy from very different perspectives.

The rationalist approach defines policy design as a rational and systematic effort to achieve effective and efficient policy. Howlett and Lejano (2013), for example, define policy design as

> the effort to more or less systematically develop efficient and effective policies through the application of knowledge about policy means gained from experience, and reason, the development and adoption of courses of action that are likely to succeed in attaining their desired goals or aim.
>
> *(forthcoming: 3)*

Design, in this approach, is mainly used as a verb and is a particular type of process emphasizing rational, scientific, and logical thinking toward identifying the most effective and efficient means to a given end.

The second tradition, best developed by Schneider and Ingram (1997), but tracing its roots also to Dahl and Lindblom (1953), Forester (1989), Schőn (1994); Stone (1988) begins with policy design as policy content—broadly understood—and not just those aspects of the policy text and practices that are rationalistic, grounded in science or logic, or even systematically put into place. Policy design, according to Schneider and Ingram (1997: 2)

> refers to the content or substance of public policy—the blueprints, architecture, discourses, and aesthetics of policy in both its instrumental and symbolic form.

Policy *designing* is the process through which this policy content is produced, and (again) not just the systematic and rational in terms of clearly stated public policy goals, but also the cognitive biases embedded in the policy as well as attributes damaging to the linkage between public policy and democratic principles, such as the intentionally manipulative, deceptive, illogical, mean-spirited, and unscientific factors that influenced the choice of design elements.

This chapter begins with the presumption that policy design is more a process of copying and adaptation than of invention, at least at the policy-maker level. Model legislation and guidelines commonly are drafted by policy entrepreneurs who attempt to spread a particular policy idea throughout the nation. And, policy-makers pay close attention to the policy designs being used elsewhere, as has been well-documented in the studies of policy diffusion (Karch 2007). Second, the process of designing is not necessarily intended to produce the policy goals that are touted as the probable result, but are filled with compromises, attempts to build sufficient support for passage, rationales that may have little to do with the actual motivations, and outright deception. Policy-makers have both political and policy goals, as well as personal goals that influence their choice of design elements. Designs contain embedded social constructions, images, and symbols that send messages to target populations and the broader public about who is deserving of what, and why (Schneider and Ingram 1993, 1997, 2005). Designs embed, as well, the cognitive biases and decision heuristics of those who crafted the content of the policy. For these reasons, it is essential that analysts develop a framework for systematically analyzing and comparing policy designs (content). It is no longer sufficient just to say that it is "education policy," or "three strikes and you're out," or an "anti-immigration" bill. More information is needed about the actual array of elements in the design. The study of policy transfer, innovation, and diffusion typically has not paid much attention to actually what was transferred or copied across jurisdictional lines, other than the very broad popularized title for the policy—such as an immigration law "as tough at Arizona's." Thus, a more careful and comprehensive approach to the study of policy design can contribute to a number of areas of policy and political research.

To limit the study of policy design entirely to those aspects that are rational and systematic is not necessary and makes a serious mistake in understanding the reasons certain designs are chosen and the consequences of those designs for democracy. Policy designs can fruitfully be understood with an analogy to the design of a city. A city probably has some elements that were designed intentionally to be efficient and effective—such as the system of streets and roads, the placement of light rail and traffic lights, the water and power delivery systems. But some aspects—many in fact—of a design were not put in place by any overall intentional or systematic or scientific process. The used car parked on the sidewalk is an aspect of the design of a city at a particular moment, as is the green grass or desert landscaping at a new housing development. At any given moment, every element in the city is a part of its design. And, the design of a city is constantly changing as new houses are built, new roads put in place, changes in traffic patterns, landscaping, and so on. Yet, it is possible to stop the scene at any moment and capture the exact design of that city, at that moment.

This chapter builds on an understanding of how policy designs are crafted and chosen. First, ample research points out that designs often are copied, borrowed, or stolen from similar policies elsewhere (Schneider and Ingram 1988). With the exception of some very early studies of policy diffusion (Gray 1973), most of the research has largely ignored the characteristics of the policies themselves, and focused on which kinds of cities, states, or nations are most "innovative"—defined as "early adopters." Thus, a huge uncharted area of research is why some kinds of policy designs are copied and spread whereas others are truncated and others never even begin to move across jurisdictional lines (see Karch 2007). Second, the reasoning process through which people arrive at decisions relies heavily on decision heuristics—deviations from rational decision-making—that introduce biases into policy design. And equally important, knowledge about how people reason has become a fundamental tool of political leaders who manipulate media and citizens by using policy arguments and designs as a technique to gain public support for policy that actually will not produce the consequences touted for it and may work to the actual disadvantage of those that the rhetoric implies will gain from it. Third, this chapter draws on Schneider and Ingram's theory of degenerative policy-making and policy design to identify characteristics of policy that often are copied and appropriated from other jurisdictions (Schneider and Ingram 1993, 1997).

## Policy design as a verb: cognitive biases and decision heuristics

This discussion begins with the insight from sociology and social psychology that people have a tendency to identify with an "in" group and embellish its virtues as well as find "the other" from which they not only distance themselves, but socially construct as dangerous, undeserving, lazy, stupid, or other undesirable epitaphs. This apparently fundamental trait of modern human beings plays a central role in the ways that decision heuristics and cognitive biases affect politics and public policy.

The "in group" preference along with the theory of decision heuristics and cognitive biases form the micro-level theory of this approach to policy design. Kahneman *et al.* (1982) and others have identified a number of common heuristics (rules of thumb) that people—even experts—rely on to make decisions. One of the most common in the process of policy design is *availability*. Availability refers to the ease by which a particular instance or occurrence or causal event is brought to mind. Those that are most easily brought to mind include those that are more recent, more dynamic or colorful, more consistent with biases and prejudices. Why, for example, have the American states altered their policies since the early 1970s to produce the highest incarceration rate in the world? One could contend that it is simply to gain political capital. But that brings up the next question—why does it work to produce political capital? And a promising explanation is that most people find it easy to imagine that if you threaten enough, and punish severely enough, and catch people when they commit a crime; they will stop committing crimes. Why has "tough on immigration" legislation spread like wildfire across the United States in the past several years, but the "Utah Compact" that advocates a much more benign approach even though thoroughly grounded in the principles of conservatives has gained almost no traction? Saying that "tough on immigration" produces political capital, again, is not enough: why does it "work" to produce such presumably large political payoffs? Decision theory suggests it is easy for people to buy into the notion that people who are in this country illegally are deceptive, criminal, lazy, dangerous and other negative social constructions. Decision theory suggests that this image is considerably easier to imagine than one in which "illegal aliens" as they are commonly called, are good, honest, hard-working people who value their families. Why did policy-makers leading up to the 2012 elections tie every conceivable policy proposal to "job creation"? Decision theory suggests that it is easier for people to imagine that if businesses both large and small had more money (through tax cuts), they would create more jobs than to believe that if the government spent more money, it would create more jobs. The highly negative social construction of "government," compared with the far more positive construction of "business" in the first decade of the twenty-first century is a prime reason. As Stimson (1991) has shown, "national "moods" exist and exert a powerful influence over what it is that people find "easy to believe." Social psychologists have also documented an "availability cascade" in which an assertion is repeated often enough that the simple repetition adds to the perception of its accuracy.

The combination of policy-makers themselves relying on cognitive biases when they propose policy and the ease of convincing the public of their contentions has produced an alarming lack of rationality in the designing process. As David Brooks (2011) said, the American public is suffering from intellectual laziness of massive proportions. He speaks specifically of the problems introduced by contribution bias. Research has shown consistently that people sort through all of the purported facts and evidence that comes to their attention, but they primarily focus only on the facts, studies, and anecdotal incidents that confirm what they already know and they easily dismiss even the most prestigious studies if those contradict their current knowledge. Challenges to the methodology of global warming studies, for example, come almost exclusively from those who already believe that either global warming is not occurring or that humans have no hand in it. In spite of massive scientific consensus, leading candidates for president such as Rick Perry of Texas in 2012 repeatedly paid attention only to the "facts" that already supported his beliefs. Others play into this same tendency toward intellectual laziness when they use specific incidents, such as Hurricane Katrina, as "proof" that global warming is occurring.

Closely related to "availability," illusory correlations are another example of cognitive bias that influences policies designs. Illusory correlations are those that are easy to imagine but have no scientific basis. For example, it is easy to believe that if a business has more money, it will expand and create more jobs. If America sends its military forces into a small, weak country like Vietnam, Iraq, or Afghanistan, the war will be won quickly and easily. And if not, it is easy to justify the mistaken correlation on the grounds, for example, that enough troops were not sent.

Anchoring is another heuristic important in understanding policy designing. The idea here is that people start from a particular point and then make small adjustments in various directions but commonly do not make adequate adjustments. Change the anchor point, and a different policy design will emerge. Another heuristic is overconfidence in the prediction of effects—even experts become over time more confident that a highly unlikely event will actually occur. For example, scientists involved in nuclear energy research consistently overestimate the likelihood of nuclear accidents (Kahneman *et al.* 1982).

Decision-makers have become considerably more savvy about the persuasive techniques that may be used to gain public support (or opposition) and the arguments surrounding policy choices have become particularly disingenuous. The findings of the social psychologists are used not to correct for cognitive biases, but to rely on them as ways to shift public opinion and opinion leaders toward a particular point of view. The social construction of "government" has become so negative that everyone wants to run as an outsider. The social construction of the word "socialist" is viewed as so antithetical to American values that simply labeling a policy proposal as "socialist" is commonly used as a way to kill the idea even though the United States has dozens, even hundreds, of programs that by almost any definition are "socialist" ranging from public schools to the ownership of the Green Bay Packers!

An example of how public officials use the insights from cognitive and decision research to reinforce certain biases is found in Senator John McCain's response when he was asked what he thought about the cause of Arizona's most destructive forest fire in history—the Wallow fire of 2011. He had just been briefed about the Wallow fire, and it had been compared to the second most destructive fire in Arizona history, the Rodeo-Chedeski fire, both of which occurred in the northeast part of Arizona. McCain was asked:

> How do you explain two massive record wildfires, all being said, human caused, but how do you explain such huge fires and how do you fix this from happening?
>
> *(Arizona Republic, B1)*

His response:

> Well first of all we are concerned about particular areas down on the border where there is substantial evidence that some of these fires are caused by people who have crossed our border illegally. They have set fires because they want to signal others, they have set fires to keep warm, and they have set fires in order to divert law enforcement agents and agencies from them. So the answer to that part of the problem is, get a secure border.

Liberals quickly jumped all over this comment as there was no evidence that immigrants had started the fire and both of these fires were more than 300 miles away from the Mexican border. McCain retaliated, pointing out that he did not say the Wallow fire was caused by an illegal immigrant—and it was factually correct that he had not made that statement. (Two white male campers had been arrested for letting their campfire get out of control and starting this fire that destroyed more than 500,000 acres). His office retaliated with this statement:

> The facts are clear. For years, federal, state and local officials have stated that smugglers and illegal immigrants have caused fires on our southern border.

This statement went on to say that McCain's office had asked for a study and that it would be out in about a month. And on July 8, 2011, Jim Pena, a US Forest Service associate deputy chief, testified before the House Subcommittee on National Parks, Forests and Public Lands that between 2002 and 2011, 457 fires were determined to be human-caused in the southwest border area of the Coronado National Forest. Pena added, "Forest Service investigators have been able to identify the individuals responsible in 31 of those fires. Of those 31 fires, it was determined that undocumented aliens were responsible for starting five."

The *Arizona Republic*'s "fact check" upheld McCain's position that he had not specifically said that illegal immigrants had caused the fire. Yet, there was a clear association being made between illegals and fire—an illusory correlation that played directly from the "availability heuristic" to make it "easier to believe" that illegal immigrants are dangerous and the border must be secured to protect Arizonans from wildfires and other dangers that illegal immigrants bring into the state. Furthermore, although it is true that the statement from McCain's office only said that "facts are clear" and that "illegal immigrants have caused fires on the southern border," the statement deceives the reader by not going on to say that five of 431 fires were known to have been started by illegal immigrants.

Framing effects are well known in the public policy literature and policy-makers have taken advantage of these to draw together a number of different cognitive biases as a way to make a persuasive argument. Policy analysts (and media "fact checkers") may contribute significantly to improved policy design by paying careful attention not only to "fact checking" but also to the types of cognitive biases built into the rationales and the ways that political leaders are using the "intellectual laziness" of the public to gain support for legislation. It is not enough to just look for the rational, instrumental logic of policy but to unmask the persuasive devices being used to thwart rational, logical thinking and reliance on well-established facts.

## Policy design as a noun (policy content)

Public policy has a common-sense understanding of being everything that government, or government agencies or street-level case workers do. This understanding means that public policy includes documents such as constitutions, statutes, and court cases as well as agency guidelines, state and local laws, and actual practices such as the ways that street-level case workers apply the policy to a particular person or organization. Each of these contains a policy design, but at different levels of analysis. At whatever level the focus might be, an adequate empirical description of policy design is essential. Development of particular types of designs—with elements that tend to cluster together—is essential for linking politics to policy design and policy design to policy consequences. Particular types and styles of political dynamics do not produce policy outcomes directly, as is sometimes implied. Policy design is not a black box that has no bearing on consequences. Rather, political dynamics produce policy designs and these, in turn, "feed forward" to produce not only policy results but also to influence the subsequent "politics" of the society. In fact, it will be argued below that certain kinds of political dynamics are associated with certain types of policy designs and that these designs, in turn, have consequences for achievement (or lack thereof) of the purported policy goals, and also systematic consequences for social identity, political participation, justice, political gain or loss, and democracy in the broad sense of the word. Policy designs embed aspects of the politics that created them, and the designs tend to reproduce the same kinds of politics from which they emerged (Schneider and Ingram 1993, 2005).

This approach to policy design places its study within the empirical and normative tradition of Lasswell's "who gets what, why, and how" (Lasswell 1936). Thus, the study of policy design—as policy content—is a broad, coherent, and essential part of political science. This approach has led to a new very important area of study called "policy centric" orientation; and it has led to new ways of thinking about the empirical and normative aspects of the policy-making process itself (see Mettler and Soss 2004).

From a normative perspective, public policy in a democracy is charged with the task of creating democratic institutions; encouraging and promoting an active, engaged, and informed citizenry; promoting justice as fairness for all people; and solving collective problems in ways that are efficient and effective.

From an empirical perspective, all public policies contain a set of central elements that can be described, studied and compared. The argument made below is that these tend to cluster in identifiable patterns that can be identified and classified as certain types of policy designs. The question is then, what kinds of policies, under what kinds of conditions, are most likely to be copied, stolen, or borrowed by what kinds of political entities?

The fundamental elements of designs include goals or problems to be solved, target populations, benefits or burdens to distribute, and linkage mechanisms of tools, rationales, underlying assumptions, an implementation structure, and social constructions (of targets, goals, and other elements) (Schneider and Ingram 1997). These elements are found in all levels of policy—from constitutions, to statutes, to agency guidelines, to state and local laws, and even to the discretion that street-level agents of government use when they actually put a policy to work.

*Goals* of a policy at times may seem obvious, since written policy often contains a statement of the problem to be solved or goals to be achieved. Goals or problems to be solved refer (on the one hand) to the intentional aspects of designs and indicate what the purported consequences are desired to be. On the other hand, actual goals may be masked and the policy itself strategically attached to some widely acknowledged public problem that the policy has no realistic chance of impacting with its true goals being largely hidden from sight (Stone 1988; Kingdon 1984). For example, in the run-up to the 2012 election, "job creation" was the purported number one priority of almost all candidates from every party; yet policy proposals directly conflicting with one another attached themselves to this goal with utter disregard of the logic in the connection. Perhaps the most memorable example of policies conveniently attaching themselves to a problem came in the summer and fall before the 2000 presidential election when candidate George Bush was arguing that tax cuts were needed because the government had a substantial surplus. As the economy deteriorated in late summer and early fall, he switched his argument saying that tax cuts were needed to stimulate the economy and ward off a recession.

Arizona's Senate Bill 1070, widely characterized as the strictest law again undocumented people in the United States, carries the beneficent title, "Support Our Law Enforcement and Safe Neighborhood Acts." The stated intent of the law is to make "attrition through enforcement the public policy of all of Arizona." The purpose, in other words, is to rid the state of undocumented immigrants. The governor's rationale for signing the bill, however, focused on crime, violence, Mexican drug cartels, and the failure of the federal government in keeping undocumented people out of the country. Opponents argued that Arizona's economy would be severely damaged by the legislation both because of a likely boycott and because ridding the state of workers and consumers is not the way to "grow the economy." The political consequences of the Hispanic vote were largely disregarded also even though almost one-third of the Arizona adult population are of Hispanic origin. No evidence was presented or needed that undocumented people damage the quality of life in Arizona—illusory correlations, "availability" and the apparent desire to identify and punish the "other" were sufficient. An early poll showed that 70 percent of the population agreed with the legislation, although that number dropped substantially over several months.

*Target populations* are the people, groups, and organizations that are impacted by the policy. Target populations are critical to policy effectiveness, since the target groups must coproduce or behave in ways intended by the policy if the policy is to achieve its purported goals. In the example above regarding Arizona's Senate Bill 1070, one of the reported purposes is to rid the state of undocumented people. These people must either "get the message" and leave, or the provisions of the law that enable local law enforcement to identify the undocumented and refer them to federal authorities for deportation must be operative. Further, the federal officials are the only ones that can actually deport someone. Target populations, however, may not be chosen on the basis of goal achievement, at all. If the goal is to reduce crime, then shifting law enforcement responsibilities from crime prevention and detection to finding undocumented people who have not committed any crime, may not be an effective or efficient method of crime prevention. Target groups may be selected on the basis of their direct linkage to goal achievement, but they also are selected on the basis of political power, wealth, images (particularly whether they are "deserving" or "undeserving," or other principles that send messages about the values of the society. Furthermore, people's experiences with government as targets shapes their view of government and their understanding of their role in government. As Schneider and Ingram argued:

> the way targets are treated by policy is central to justice, citizenship, support for democratic institutions, and democratic problem solving. Policy can either reinforce or undermine government legitimacy and sense of civic duty.
>
> *(1997: 85)*

Policy-makers have a choice among different target groups that can be involved or excluded from policy. To create jobs, for example, policy can develop public works programs that actually create job programs that hire people and put them to work on road construction, bridges, libraries, tutoring for school children, and aides for child protective services. Alternatively, policy can cut corporate taxes with the contention that cutting corporate taxes will enable corporations to expand thereby hiring people. Or policy can create jobs by providing tax credits for new hires, and so on.

Policies allocate values—*benefits and burdens*—to target groups and this, too, offers policy-makers a wide range of choices for solving any given problem. An entire chain of target groups may be involved as intermediate linkages between policy design and goal achievement. Some may be in line for benefits, others for burdens. Target groups are sent messages by policy design of what they deserve or do not deserve. Persons without jobs during the virtual collapse of the US economy were told, on the one hand, that they deserved jobless benefits and that the amount of time they would be eligible would be extended, and on the other hand, that paying jobless benefits encouraged people to not look for jobs and in fact became a factor that prolonged unemployment.

*Rules* refer to who is to do what, when, with what resources and limitations. Rules include the eligibility criteria for receiving benefits, as well as the behaviors that would lead to arrest and punishment. *Tools* are the incentive and disincentives built into the design intended to insure that agencies and target groups and any other players in the system take the policy-preferred actions. Tools have been categorized in terms of the underlying behavioral assumptions: authority (just doing what one is told to do); positive incentives, negative incentives or punishment, actual force, symbolic and hortatory tools (persuasive devices), learning tools, and capacity-building tools are examples. Tools are quite interchangeable and policy designers have a wide range of choices regarding how to get target groups to follow the rules.

*Implementation structures* are often built into the policy design. These may be top-down command and control types of implementation or follow the ideas of adaptive management and leave considerable discretion to the local implementers.

*Rationales* are the reasons, justifications, or legitimations for the design itself. These may be straightforward or deceptive, logically consistent or inconsistent, and based on a wide range of different values ranging from justice-oriented rationales to economic, scientific or religious. Rationales may reflect the actual reasons, or the real reasons may be carefully masked as policy-makers attempt to tie the policy to a popular problem for the purpose of gaining political capital and support. *Underlying assumptions* typically are not laid out in the policy design itself but are brought to the analysis by the policy analyst. There are three types of assumptions: technical assumptions that are scientific and can be tested with scientific research (including social sciences); normative assumptions that the policy design is fair, just, compassionate, treats people as they ought to be treated, consistent with prevailing values; and behavioral assumptions about what people need to be motivated to act in policy-preferred ways.

Policy designs contain—in addition to these empirical elements—other more judgmental characteristics such as the type of message (positive, negative) being sent to target populations; the extent of deception in the design and the rationales used to justify it; and the strength of the logic holding the elements together. These, too, are important aspects of design for the policy analyst to unmask.

## Commonly copied policy designs

One of the least developed aspects of the study of policy design is in the development of design patterns – clusters of elements that commonly go together. The approach that will be presented here builds from my work and that of my colleague Helen Ingram to classify design types in terms of the power and the social construction of the target populations and whether benefits or burdens are being distributed. We hypothesized that certain design elements tend to be used, depending on this classification. Furthermore, subsequent work has contended that some types of policy design will be more subject to path dependency than other types, and in the remaining part of this chapter, the point will be made that some types are more likely to transfer than others.

Schneider and Ingram have argued that a great deal can be understood about the elements of policy design by taking into account the political power of target populations, their social construction (such as "deserving" or "undeserving") and whether benefits or burdens are being distributed. Using this two-dimensional framework, target populations can be clustered generally into one of four types: *advantaged groups* (politically powerful and positively constructed as deserving, intelligent, hard-working, and other positive values of the society); *contenders* who are politically powerful but carry a negative image as "greedy," "dishonest," "undeserving of what they have"; *dependents* (politically weak but constructed as "good but weak or helpless" people); and *deviants* (politically weak and carrying the image of dangerous, violent, mean, selfish). Most of the research using this framework has focused on the allocation of benefits and burdens consistent with the theory and on the consequences of policy design for political attitudes and participation.

Far less has been done with the ideas that some types of designs are more apt to transfer or diffuse across jurisdictions than others, or are more (or less) likely to converge over time. Schneider (2006) has shown that a particular type of design—policies that inflict harsh punishment on those who break the law have been far more path-dependent, over time, than policies that utilize rehabilitation, probation, house arrest, fines, or other less draconian policies. This study based on state-level incarceration data from 1927 through 2003 showed far longer periods of continuous increases in incarceration rates across almost all states than periods of decreases. The research also found that state-level incarceration rates tend to change in the same direction, at the same time, as if some kind of national "mood" were influencing all of them at once, or that policy designs were diffusing rapidly throughout the nation even though decisions about incarceration are made at the state and local level and in response to the state and local laws.

The most likely designs to transfer are those that fit the dominant patterns identified by Schneider and Ingram. The first of these is providing benefits to advantaged groups. The design elements are expected generally to be quite similar across jurisdictions: strong statutes; tight implementation structures but very little oversight or assessment of results; "popular" rationales that fit into prevailing values, capacity building and learning tools for target groups; and universalistic rules of eligibility. These designs are politically popular regardless of whether one is liberal or conservative since the target populations are considered deserving of what they receive and the rationales are structured carefully to fit prevailing values. Also, it is difficult to generate opposition except on rational/instrumental or scientific grounds that the means will not produce the desired ends—but since most do not pay much attention to such logic, opposition is difficult to generate. Strong statutes provide sufficient detail to ensure that the benefits are actually delivered and not sidetracked in some ways. Once a program area, however, becomes "oversubscribed"—whereby so many benefits are being provided that it becomes politically risky and difficult to sustain the rationales or create new ones—implementing agencies can be expected to be given discretion to determine eligibility. Implementation structures are tight in that there are clear lines of authority and responsibility for carrying out the statutory intent. If policy is not clear on the linkages between funding and desired outcomes, however, learning and capacity-building tools may be used to help to guarantee that the programs work. Oversight, however, is weak or nonexistent or largely illusory except to prevent fraud that would endanger the program. Rationales will depend on the prevailing "ideas in good currency." If jobs are needed and valued, the benefits will be touted as contributing to job creation. If national security is involved, the rationale will be based on national security. If fairness or justice is involved and if that is a value currently in vogue, then it would be used. Policy tools will be largely benign—learning tools providing adequate discretion even to target populations, capacity building, and direct handouts. Rules will tend toward the universalistic without means testing and without other tight restrictions. Benefits will tend to be provided now, not well into the future, and significant sums of money or tax breaks can be expected. Far less likely to transfer are designs that inflict burdens on advantaged populations, but when regulations are transferred, design elements will tend to have weak statutes (providing multiple loopholes for advantaged groups to escape), highly particularistic (only some of the advantaged are subject to the rules), and regulatory activities can expect to be underfunded.

A second commonly copied type of design is expected to be providing punishment and discipline to deviant groups. These designs are expected also to involve universalistic rules (everyone who breaks a particular law is supposed to be treated the same way as others); the rationales focus on negative social constructions of the target groups as "dangerous," "untrustworthy," "already had their chance," "violent," and so on. The logic connecting design elements to desired results is largely unimportant provided that the target groups can continue to be constructed as undeserving. Even though there is considerable political gain and ideological commitment to punishing the undeserving, the political leaders do not want to spend much money on this task if it can be avoided. Evaluation to discern program effectiveness is seldom used when punishment is provided to "undeserving" people.

A third commonly copied design involves the provision of services or the discipline of various kinds of dependent populations (children, women, mothers, disabled, etc.). These designs can generally be expected to involve very particularistic rather than universalistic rules, typically means-tested, far more "talk" than "funding," especially from the federal level; tools to induce desired behavior can be expected to rely on authority, persuasion, and expectations that the clients will establish their own eligibility—no one will help them to do that. Rules contained in these policies especially when benefits are being distributed are expected to be strict, with complex eligibility requirements. In contrast to the types of design discussed above where benefits are provided to advantaged groups or punishment to deviant groups, provision of benefits to dependents typically will require evaluation studies to "prove" the worthiness of the policy. Rationales will focus on justice, fairness, and when discipline or punishment is involved—it is "for their own good."

A fourth type of commonly copied designs pertains to attempts to provide benefits to contenders (such as Wall Street, corporations, "big labor", "big banks") at the same time that the public stance is to discipline and restrict these groups. Whether the design elements that are likely to transfer will be the same across jurisdictions simply is not known but the theory strongly suggests that beneficial policy for contenders will transfer and will be the most deceptive of all the types of designs.

## Conclusions

Given the fact that public policies have increasingly been used for political and ideological purposes rather than to find the best solution to a collective problem, policy analysts are well advised to study carefully the design elements and analyze them not simply in terms of their rationality, but also in terms of who gets what, who wins and who loses, whose image is emboldened and who is denigrated, and what are the messages being sent to the target populations and the broader public. What are the impacts on political participation and attitudes? Is it the case that policy designs embed the social constructions and assumptions and then reproduce that same pattern of politics? Is policy itself partly responsible for the politics that ensue, as Lowi so famously argued many years ago? It is not sufficient to simply analyze policy designs in terms of their technical logic and whether they achieve their purported goals? The full array of elements along with the images, hidden messages, underlying assumptions, deception, and illogic need to be probed by the policy analyst.

## Bibliography


Arizona Republic, 'Sen. John McCain ties fires to illegal border crossings', June 20, 2011, B1.

—— 'The issue: McCain's comments on migrants, Wallow Fire', by Ginger Rough, August 27, 2011.

Bobrow, Davis B. and John Dryzek. 1987. *Policy Analysis by Design*. Pittsburgh, PA: University of Pittsburgh Press.

Brooks, David. 2011. *The Social Animal: The Hidden Sources of Love, Character, and Achievement*. New York: Random House Digital, Inc.

Dahl, Robert and Charles Lindblom. 1953. *Politics, Economics, and Welfare*. New York: Harper.

Forester, John. 1989. *Planning in the Face of Power*. Cambridge, MA: MIT Press.

Gray, Virginia. 1973. 'Innovation in the states: A diffusion study', *American Political Science Review* 67(4): 1174–85.

Howlett, Michael and Raul Lejano. 2013. 'Tales from the crypt: The rise and fall (and rebirth?) of policy design', *Administration and Society* (forthcoming)

Ingram, Helen and Anne L. Schneider. 1990. 'Improving implementation through framing smarter statutes', *Journal of Public Policy* 10(1): 66–87.

——and Anne L. Schneider. 1991. 'The choice of target populations', *Administration and Society* 23(3): 333–56.

James, Oliver and Martin Lodge. 2003. 'The limitations of "policy transfer" and "lesson drawing" for public policy research', *Political Studies Review* 1: 179–93.

Kahneman, Daniel, Paul Slovic and Amos Tversky. 1982. *Judgment under Uncertainty: Herusitics and Biases*. Cambridge: Cambridge University Press.

Karch, Andrew. 2007. *Democratic Laboratories: Policy Diffusion among the American States*. Lansing, MI: University of Michigan Press.

Kingdon, John. 1984. *Agendas, Alternatives, and Public Policies*. New York: Longman.

Lasswell, Harold. 1936. *Who Gets What, When, and How?* New York: McGraw Hill.

Lieberman, Robert, Helen Ingram and Anne Schneider. 1995. 'Social constructions', *American Political Science Review* 89(2): 437–44.

Linder, Stephen H. and Guy Peters. 1985. 'From social theory to policy design', *Journal of Public Policy* 4(3): 237–59.

Mettler, Suzanne and Joe Soss. 2004. 'The consequences of public policy for democratic citizenship: bridging policy studies and mass politics', *Perspectives on Politics* 2(1): 55–73.

Schneider, Anne Larason. 2006. 'Patterns of change in the use of imprisonment in the American states: An integration of path dependence, punctuated equilibrium and policy design approaches', *Political Research Quarterly* 59(3): 457–70.

——and Helen Ingram. 1988. 'Systematically pinching ideas: A comparative approach to policy design', *Journal of Public Policy* 8(1): 61–80.

——and Helen Ingram. 1990. 'Behavioral assumptions of policy tools', *Journal of Politics* 52(2): 510–29.

——and Helen Ingram. 1993. 'The social construction of target populations', *The American Political Science Review* 87(2): 334–46.

——and Helen Ingram. 1997. *Policy Design for Democracy*. Lawrence, KS: University of Kansas Press.

——and Helen Ingram (eds). 2005. *Deserving and Entitled: Social Construction and Public Policy*. Albany, NY: SUNY Press.

——and Mara Sidney. 2009. 'What's next for policy design/social construction theory?', *Policy Studies Journal* 37(1): 103–19.

Schön, Donald and Martin Rein. 1994. *Frame Reflection: Toward the Resolution of Intractable Controversies*. New York: Basic Books.

Stone, D.A. 1988. *Policy Paradox and Political Reason*. Glenview, IL: Scott, Foresman.

Stimson, James. 1991. *Public Opinion in America*. Boulder, CO: Westview Press.

Utah Compact. 2011. http://www.deseretnews.com/article/700080758/Official-text-of-Utah-Compact-declaration-on-immigration-reform.html (Accessed 10 September 2011).

Walker, Jack. 1969. 'The diffusion of innovations among the American states', *American Political Science Review* 63(3): 880–99.

# 18
# Epistemic communities

*Claire A. Dunlop*

## Introduction

Peter M. Haas formulated the epistemic communities framework as a means of exploring the influence of knowledge-based experts in international policy-making. Specifically, the approach was designed to address decision-making instances characterized by technical complexity and uncertainty. Control over the production of knowledge enables epistemic communities to articulate cause-and-effect relationships and so frame issues for collective debate and export their policy projects globally. Despite the framework being two decades old, there are still relatively few studies which explicitly test or develop the concept theoretically, thus making it difficult to assess what we have collectively and cumulatively learned about this topic. This chapter attempts to systematize key developments in the literature. The first section outlines the concept locating it in the politics of ideas literature. The second explores the state of the art in the empirical studies deploying the epistemic communities framework. The third section considers the theoretical challenges that researchers face when attempting to study epistemic communities. Discussion here proposes five possible causal pathways through which we can explain how epistemic communities help decision-makers learn. The chapter closes with a brief sketch of potential future research frontiers for scholars interested in the power of knowledge and epistemic communities in public policy.

## Epistemic communities and the politics of ideas

Epistemic communities are groups of professionals, often from a variety of different disciplines, which produce policy-relevant knowledge about complex technical issues (Haas 1992a: 16). Such communities embody a belief system around an issue which contains four knowledge elements:

> (1) a shared set of normative and principled beliefs, which provide a value-based rationale for the social action of community members; (2) shared causal beliefs, which are derived from their analysis of practices leading or contributing to a central set of problems in their domain and which then serve as the basis for elucidating the multiple linkages between possible policy actions and desired outcomes; (3) shared notions of validity – that is, intersubjective, internally defined criteria for weighing and validating knowledge in the domain of their

> expertise; and (4) a common policy enterprise – that is, a set of common practices associated with a set of problems to which their professional competence is directed, presumably out of the conviction that human welfare will be enhanced as a consequence.
>
> *(1992a: 3)*

The concept was the subject of an *International Organization* (*IO*) special edition in 1992 edited by Haas. In this, the full framework was articulated (1992a) and empirically explored in environmental, security, trade and international political economy cases studies. This volume still represents the keystone of the epistemic communities literature. Emphasizing experts' influence over decision-maker learning as a potentially central mechanism effecting policy development and change, the epistemic communities framework aims to make sense of policy-making in conditions of uncertainty and technical complexity. In these settings, decision-makers' preferences will be less clear to them transforming policy-making into an exercise in learning rather than bargaining.

As the main vehicles for authoritative consensual knowledge, epistemic communities have the ability to help formulate policy in three main ways: elucidating cause-and-effect relationships and providing advice on the likely results of various courses of action; shedding light on the complex interlinkages between issues, and helping to define the self-interest of states (Haas 1992a). The 'value added' of the approach is that it highlights the importance of actors that are able to define complex problems, particularly in the early policy design stages of the policy cycle where the uncertainty of novel policy problems is at its peak. The framework is intended to complement existing theories of policy-making that focus upon interests and the calculation of costs and benefits (rational choice), identities and socialization (constructivism), policy legacies (historical institutionalism) and the use of words and discourse (poststructuralism) (1992a: 6). The core analytical point here is that in the absence of epistemic communities to frame complex issues and proffer new ideas, policy-making would follow more conventional, unreflective paths (Haas 2011).

The advent of the epistemic communities framework should be seen as part of the wider 'renaissance of knowledge' (Radaelli 1995). In political science in the 1990s, scholars were reminded that, along with the traditional interests and institutions, there was a third 'i'. Ideas also matter in explaining political decision-making. Although material power, identities and policy legacies have not disappeared from analysis, this ideational turn emphasizes decision-makers as 'sentient' agents (Schmidt 2010). As such, they are sensitive to new ideas or new representations of existing ones. The politics of ideas agenda has been followed enthusiastically and resulted in empirical analysis that sheds light on how public policy emerges from new ways of thinking, beliefs, rhetoric and discourse. The contribution of the epistemic communities framework is to remind us that 'ideas would be sterile without carriers' (Haas 1992a: 27). This is an anthropomorphic conceptualization of knowledge (Radaelli 1997: 169) where those experts who create the knowledge on which decision-makers depend are central to political analysis. Thus, to identify an epistemic community is to identify a set of actors with the professional and social stature to make authoritative claims on politically pertinent and socially relevant issues of the day. Their success is dependent, not simply on their epistemic resources but also on their political acumen. Epistemic communities must persuade decision-makers, and successfully navigate the machinery of government by insinuating themselves into bureaucratic positions, if their consensual knowledge is to inform policy choices.

## The empirical analysis of epistemic communities

The first step in mapping the field of epistemic communities' scholarship involves exploring the empirical analysis deploying the term. Bibliographic analysis provides the broad canvas on which we can sketch out some of the significant details. Using a citation search, we identified some 638 articles, book chapters and books citing Haas's 1992 introductory article to the *IO* special edition.[1] Results confirm that the idea of epistemic communities is firmly embedded in the social sciences lexicon; in the past two decades, the concept has travelled across a wide range of disciplines – 54 in fact (see Figure 18.1[2]). Such wide appeal fits with the framework's aim to explain the role of experts in the technically complex policy problems which dominate the policy process in contemporary society. As we would expect Government and Law, Public Administration and International Relations (IR) lead the way in citations, though interestingly IR lags a little way behind the first two political science sub-fields (see Figure 18.2).

Despite epistemic communities' obvious resonance across social scientific disciplines, a review of the literature reveals superficial engagement. Specifically, the actual identification of epistemic communities using the fourfold belief system that defines them remains rare. Rather, the term is more frequently used metaphorically to describe any group of experts giving policy advice. A succinct explanation for this state of affairs is offered by Wright: '[A]ctually identifying these communities … can be a difficult process' (1997: 11). Practical obstacles, such as identifying, locating and gaining access to those believed to be members of an epistemic community, may frustrate attempts to engage with the approach as an analytical tool.

Identification of an epistemic community's belief system presents a further empirical challenge. In most cases, authors delineate beliefs using the qualitative 'soaking and poking' (Fenno 1986)

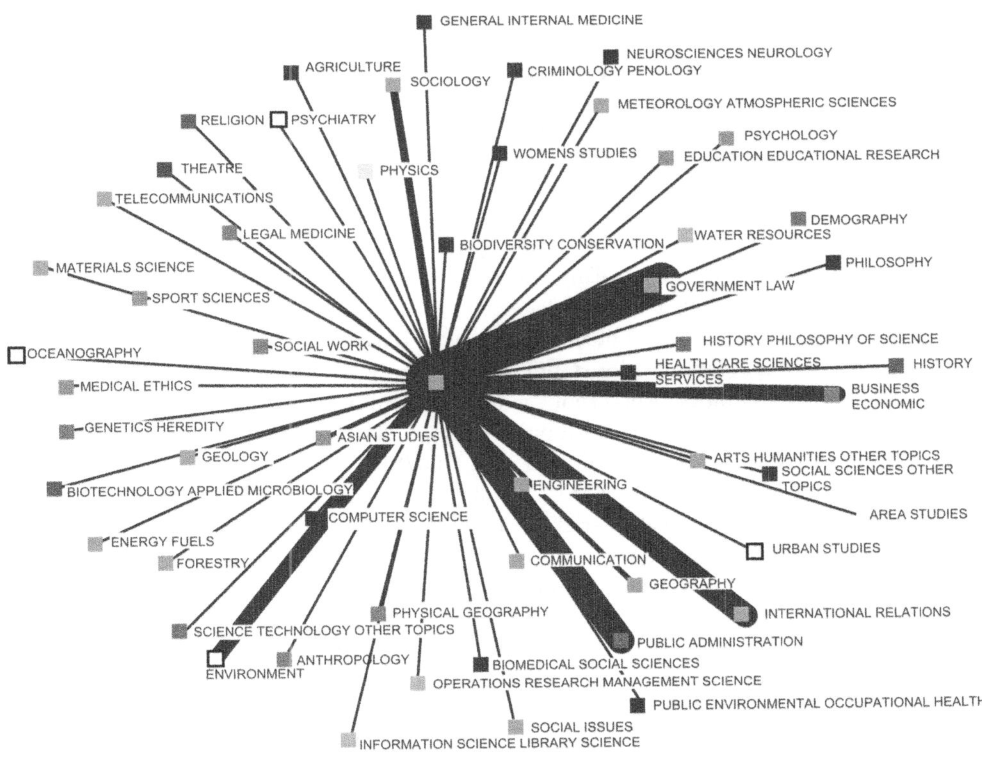


*Figure 18.1* Bibliographic analysis of 638 articles, book chapters and books citing Haas's 1992 introductory article to the *IO* special edition
Source: Author

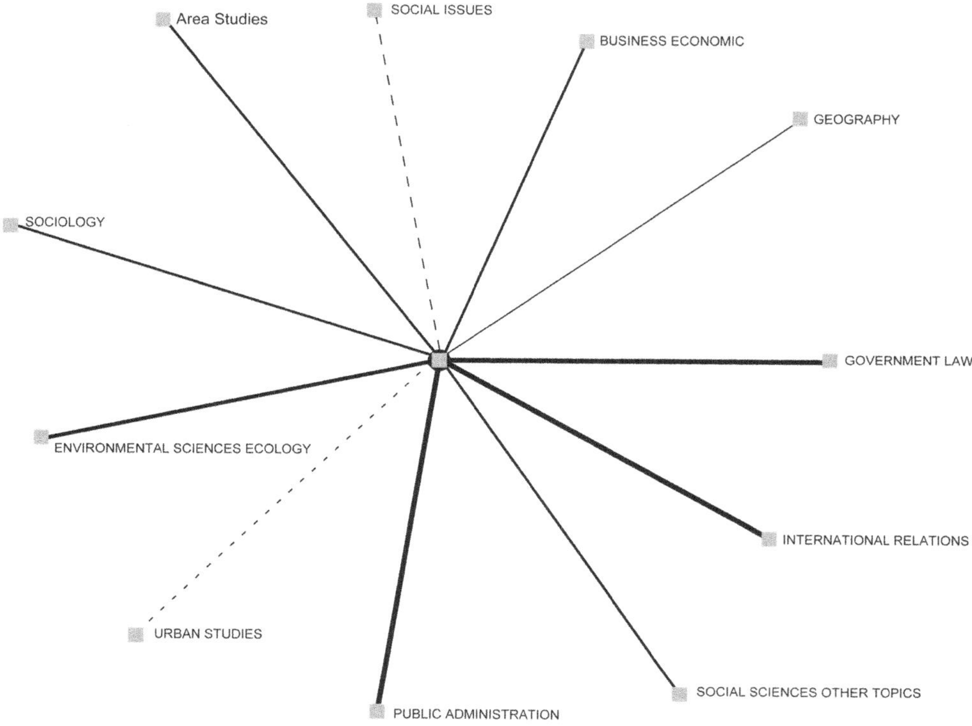


*Figure 18.2* Bibliographic analysis of 638 articles, book chapters and books citing Haas's 1992 introductory article to the *IO* special edition (subject areas receiving 11 citations or more)
Source: Author

strategies advocated by Haas. This is especially appropriate when attempting to uncover what can be sensitive information – particularly experts' normative and policy beliefs about an issue. However, in addition to analysing scientific documents and conference proceedings, and conducting interviews, some scholars have used quantitative surveys (Radaelli and O'Connor 2009; Wright 1997) to gather this kind of information. Criticisms have, however, been voiced about the neglect of how epistemic communities' beliefs about an issue are mediated by experts' own deeper socio-political beliefs and psychological motivations (Finlayson 2004; Zelikow, 1994). This question of social conditioning is explored by Mitchell *et al.* (2007) in relation to nuclear scientists in the United States (US) and European Union (EU) member states. Using survey data, they conclude that values (expressed on the traditional left-right spectrum) and national context matter for epistemic communities' policy preferences.

The challenges of using epistemic communities as an analytical framework are not only practical. Getting to grips with the structure and power dynamics that may exist within an epistemic community is important if we are to understand belief system formation and message framing. For example, in their study of an epistemic community of legal scholars, van Waarden and Drahos (2002) uncover a hierarchical structure where some actors are more equal than others: 'it matters not only what some member says, but who says it' (2002: 930). In a related vein, Drake and Nicolaïdis's (1992) and Dunlop's (2009) case studies illustrate the impact that a division of labour between disciplines within these groups can have on belief system formation and communication. Yet, in the politics literature, these examples are the exception rather than the rule. In most cases, where scholars do map out the beliefs which epistemic communities embody, the community itself is rarely the centre of analytical attention – usually losing out to interest groups and institutions. Disciplinary preferences provide a plausible explanation for this. Political scientists' attention is naturally drawn toward political institutions rather than the world of professionals and experts. Here, the increasing attention being paid by sociologists, well-schooled in the power of professions (Abbott 1988), will be valuable to the epistemic communities approach.[3] For example, Roth's (2008a, 2008b) analysis of epistemic communities of embryologists and zebrafish experts, respectively, forms the basis for a discussion on the internal structure and politics of these communities. Lorenz-Meyer's (2010) recent work on the membership configurations within communities, and experience of actually being a member, is similarly promising. By exploring the internal workings of epistemic communities, analysts can uncover how experts expand their political power and ability to influence.

The epistemic communities framework was originally developed to explain the role of transnational experts in fostering international policy coordination – something reflected in the pronounced number of studies focussing on the EU (for example, Kaelberer 2003; van Waarden and Drahos 2002; Zito 2001).[4] The bibliographic review also reveals, however, that these communities are not restricted to inter-, trans- or supranational levels. Epistemic communities can be located at any level of government. Indeed, they are commonly national entities, and policy transfer concepts (see Chapter 17 of this volume) have usefully been deployed to explore what happens to ideas as they move from an epistemic community in one jurisdiction to another (Albert and Laberge 2007; Prince 2010; Melo 2004). Studies have also highlighted the more antagonistic relationship that can develop between epistemic communities in different places. In her studies of hormone growth promoters and the biotech milk yield enhancer bovine somatotrophin (rbST), Dunlop illustrates how epistemic communities in the EU and US, offering contrasting interpretations of the same scientific evidence, were used to justify international policy divergence (2007, 2009, 2010). Harrison's cross-national study of dioxins in pulp mill effluents and paper products reports a similar role for experts in cross-national policy divergence (2002). This underlines the fact that the concept's analytical leverage is founded on the potentially powerful role experts and knowledge can play in overcoming collective action dilemmas in uncertain contexts *regardless* of jurisdiction and government level. Empirical studies have also successfully applied epistemic communities to more local settings – for example exploring interagency cooperation in California (Thomas 1997); forest policy change in British Columbia (Kamieniecki 2000); medical ethics in the Czech Republic (Simek *et al.* 2010) and transport policy in Belgium (Albrechts, 2001).

The empirical literature also highlights research design issues associated with locating epistemic communities in dynamic policy environments. Two main challenges are evident: how to explore epistemic communities' interactions with other actors in policy arenas, and designing research that is able to capture the temporal dimension of epistemic communities' influence.

To understand how epistemic communities interact with other policy actors, we first need some background on what distinguishes epistemic communities from others in the policy process. Their blend of beliefs and highly specialized expertise distinguish epistemic communities from interest groups and policy networks (Haas 1992a: 22). This enables them to make legitimate claims to being *the* main producers of knowledge in an issue area (Dunlop 2009). This specification of difference does not imply that Haas attempts to advance epistemic communities as morally superior to other actors in the policy process (see the debate between Toke 1999 and Dunlop 2000). Rather, the aim is to record the view that expert groups' main interactions are expected to be with decision-makers and that they are *not* a brand of specialized interest groups with non-material aims (Haas 1992a: 19). For Haas, the crucial claim to distinctiveness rests on elements (2) and (3) of their belief system which result in consensual knowledge. Haas consistently implies the non-negotiable nature of these two elements – without them, the epistemic community ceases to function as an authoritative voice of advice. Accordingly, in the event of a serious challenge to the causal 'world view' of the community (2) which could not be settled internally (3), the community would withhold policy advice: 'Unlike an interest group, if confronted with anomalous data, they would retract their advice or suspend judgement' (Haas 1990: 55).

But what of the real world of politics – where constellations of political actors interact, argue and bargain? Being 'apolitical' (yet 'politically empowered') seems unfeasible. The emphasis on consensual knowledge may overstate the influence these expert enclaves *alone* can have. Interest groups and rival scientific groups interact with epistemic communities learning from and arguing with them. The need to explore epistemic communities' propensity to build alliances was a theme taken up by James Sebenius in the 1992 *IO* special edition. Using insights from negotiation analysis, Sebenius argues that an epistemic community's influence may emanate from *bargaining* with other actors in an attempt to convert their 'natural coalition' of believers into a 'winning coalition', pushing forward a shared policy enterprise (characteristic (4) of an epistemic community) (Sebenius 1992: 325). Therefore, epistemic communities have to be politically proactive players to convey their message, interacting with a multiplicity of other actors where it is to be expected that influence is variable and contingent as wider strategic games are played out. In such a scenario, the full potential of consensual knowledge may only be realized through the involvement of other, more politically astute, groups.

In the literature, this interaction is often captured by subsuming epistemic communities within interest-based approaches. Most commonly, empirical studies which explore alliances between epistemic communities and interest groups use the advocacy coalition framework (for example, Dudley and Richardson 1996; Elliott and Schlaepfer 2001; Meijerink 2005). However, with the interest-based approaches doing the analytical work, epistemic communities' conceptual development is stunted. Alliances with interest groups raise key issues that are still to be addressed. What happens to the epistemic community itself as alliances stabilize? What aspect(s) of an epistemic community's belief system are most vulnerable to change, if any? Unlike Sabatier's advocacy coalition framework approach, the epistemic communities framework does not explicitly explore the weight of the beliefs relative to one another. Exploring the susceptibility of a belief system to change would tell analysts a good deal about a community's propensity towards coalition building in a given policy area. Exploring the extent to which one element could dominate another, and how this is influenced by the membership of a community, could also help build bridges with the emerging research on interest groups. For example, by delineating the relative importance of normative and policy-oriented beliefs, synergies may be possible between epistemic communities and advocacy networks (Keck and Sikkink 1998) and epistemic communities and Communities of Practice (Wenger 1999).

While we have empirical studies of cooperation, there is little evidence that epistemic communities are willing to engage in conflict with interest groups. Rather, conflict appears reserved for other expert groups. For example, the epistemic battles between rival groups of experts, anticipated by Haas (1990: 57, 1992b: 44), has been explored empirically by Youde (2007). In his study of health policy in South Africa, Youde identifies the emergence of both an epistemic community and a 'counter-epistemic community' offering fundamentally different understandings of AIDS and radically different policy prescriptions.

This intervention is extremely valuable. In the two decades since the epistemic communities concept was first introduced, communication technology has changed beyond all recognition with the advent of the Internet. Simultaneously, the technical policy dilemmas that decision-makers encounter have increased in quantity and complexity – most notably climate change. The democratization of information (if not knowledge) and increased urgency of complex policy-making has resulted in a huge expansion in the number and types of groups that classify themselves as experts. These trends are reflected in the increased willingness of scholars to talk in terms of multiple epistemic communities (Stephens *et al.* 2011) that engage in 'contests of credibility' (Epstein 1996: 3). The prescience of the approach is also reflected by the empirical cases studies. The framework has been used to explore policy problems as diverse as agricultural policy (for example, Coleman and Skogstad 1995); financial policy (Rethel 2010); economics and banking (for example, Ikenberry 1992); forestry (Shankland and Hasenclever 2011); defence and security (Howorth 2004); health policy (for example, Ogden *et al.* 2003), and transport (for example, Schot and Schipper 2011). Reflecting the approach's empirical roots, environmental case studies are by far the most common – something which is set to continue (for example, Haas 1990, 1992b; Peterson 1992). Nine of the 118 articles citing Haas's 1992a introduction in 2010 and 2011 were directly related to climate change and sustainable development (for example, Lovell and MacKenzie 2011).

While epistemic communities are discrete actors, they are located in dynamic policy environments. This dynamism requires not only that research is designed in ways which illuminate how epistemic communities relate to other policy actors; we must also attend to the temporal dimension of policy-making. A focus on the 'here and now' of policy-making means that analysis may miss epistemic communities' influence. There are three reasons for taking the long view; the first concerns the internal operation of an epistemic community. While we might expect experts' influence to be biased towards the early stages of the policy process, the back story of how a group of experts came together, and the process of knowledge creation, still matters. Scientific consensus takes time to construct; knowledge is often incomplete and judgements of cause and effect partial. If we focus only on what has occurred when the consensus has been reached and the community has entered the political arena, we may miss earlier episodes of political behaviour where the expert enclave has, for example, refined its position in order to gain access to decision-makers (Dunlop 2007).

In the same vein, empirical studies are required to illuminate what happens to epistemic communities over time, as they interact with decision-makers and other actors in the policy process. This issue of time is again something which Haas acknowledges in pointing out that the knowledge consensus represents a '*temporally* bounded notion of truth' (1992a: 23, emphasis added). Over time, this particular 'truth' will evolve, be challenged and altered, or debunked and replaced, as new discoveries dictate. We need to empirically explore what happens to these communities *during* this evolutionary process. Of specific interest is the impact that political exposure has on an epistemic community's belief system. Adler and Haas state that: '[A]s epistemic communities consolidate and expand their political and bureaucratic influence internationally, additional ideas may be incorporated into the core community beliefs' (1992a: 374). Successful examination of the stability and strength of the different elements of an epistemic community's belief system requires that the four elements' characteristics are problematized clearly in empirical studies and their importance relative to each other elucidated (Dunlop 2000).

A second reason for analysing epistemic communities over time concerns when epistemic communities are located in the policy cycle. It is well established that experts are active in the early agenda-setting and issue framing stages of policy-making and less visible as decisions are being set and policy implemented. However, if we only front-load our attention to these early stages, analysis may miss a reappearance or reincarnation of an epistemic community in the policy evaluation and feedback stages.

Finally, the causal mechanism associated with the approach also requires that we take the long view. Learning processes have their own temporal dimension – with 'policy-oriented learning' and 'enlightenment' happening over protracted periods of time (Sabatier 1988; Weiss

1979). And so, we must look at the 'moving picture' rather than the 'snapshot' (Pierson 1996). Long after an epistemic community has left the political arena, its ideas may be influencing policy-making.

## Theoretical challenges

While the epistemic communities framework is empirically well travelled, the analytical horizons of the approach have not been broadened to the same extent. Despite being *the* conceptual name to drop in studies of technical issues in political science and beyond, very little work has been done to interrogate and develop the concept theoretically. The tendency in the discipline to commit substantial time and resources to refining and reforming such conceptual frameworks – for example the last three decades' refinement of policy networks (for example Thatcher 1998; see Chapter 12 of this volume) and the advocacy coalition framework (most recently Weible *et al.* 2011; see Chapter 10 of this volume) – has not been repeated in the case of epistemic communities. Given the empirical, practical and disciplinary barriers outlined already, such underdevelopment is perhaps unsurprising. This is not to say that the analytical challenges associated with the approach are unknown, however. On the contrary, many of the articles citing Haas's work offer conceptual criticisms. But these are made in passing and have not been related back to the framework itself. This section outlines some of the analytical gauntlets that have been thrown down and proposes ways that these might be picked up by future scholars focused on explanatory analysis of epistemic communities.

To understand how epistemic communities influence decision-makers' learning we must first clarify our dependent variable. Asking what is actually being explained in epistemic community analysis is perhaps not as self-evident a question as it may seem. In his case studies, Haas uncovers epistemic communities as the catalysts for international policy coordination (1990, 1992a). This policy outcome should not however be the standard against which an epistemic community's influence is judged. These cases show the maximum influence experts can have; they are extreme examples. If we look only for international policy coordination, the results are liable to disappoint. Epistemic communities are rarely 'live' actors at the decision-making or implementation stages of the policy cycle. So, we must lower our expectations and give epistemic communities their proper analytical place. What we are interested in is how epistemic communities help decision-makers learn. Policy outputs should not be the primary focus as epistemic communities' influence over those will usually be indirect.

So, what do decision-makers learn from epistemic communities? In his exposition of the epistemic communities' framework, Haas provides a clear definition of learning. Learning is a process of informing decision-makers' beliefs about the four key components of complex technical issues embodied by epistemic communities with particular attention drawn to epistemic communities' influence on the 'substantive nature of … policy arrangements' and their more overtly political role as the 'nonsystemic origins of state interests' (1992a: 4). Experts' potential to stimulate learning is assured by the control they enjoy over the production of knowledge relating to an issue (ibid.: 2) and the influence they exert is a function of decision-makers' uncertainty.

Despite this clarity and specificity, we still know relatively little about the possible forms of learning that may arise between epistemic communities and decision-makers. The framework emphasizes a form of learning that depicts control over knowledge as something which epistemic communities have and decision-makers, whose bounded rationality initiates their call for advice, do not have (1992a: 14–16). This definition of uncertainty is problematic, however. Epistemic communities' entry into the policy arena is a function of decision-makers' technical uncertainty, however by conflating this uncertainty with comprehensively bounded rationality we are left with a single learning category where decision-makers experience extreme epistemic deficiencies which need to be filled. And so, despite disaggregating belief systems into individual components in the definition of what an epistemic community actually is, the epistemic resources experts pass on to decision-makers are portrayed as a unified good.

This 'deficit model' of learning (Dunlop 2009), where epistemic communities are required to fill gaps in decision-makers' knowledge, reflects the empirical case which informed the original development of the epistemic communities approach. Haas's major study *Saving the Mediterranean* (1990) illustrates the extreme level of influence that epistemic communities can have. In this case, the epistemic community had the power to make decision-makers cooperate and develop policies in ways they would not otherwise have. Such ideal typical cases yield important examples of what is possible, however they also highlight extreme phenomena. If it is to explain the role of epistemic communities in 'who learns what, when, to whose benefit and why' (Adler and Haas 1992: 370), the analytical framework must be able to account for the *variety* of these actors' learning interactions. While epistemic communities' central role in information production gives them the authoritative status to occupy this role, we cannot assume that they will be able to exert control over *every* aspect of what is known about an issue or that the control they do enjoy will be uniform across time and space. To understand the different roles epistemic communities occupy in the policy process, we must have a clear, coherent and systematic way of describing variation in this explanandum.

One promising way of characterizing the learning that epistemic communities can effect is to focus upon the ways in which decision-makers' preferences *mediate* the learning processes in which they engage. This is something that Haas himself acknowledges, describing a scenario where decision-makers rely on epistemic communities for only *certain aspects* of policy knowledge (1992a: 15). Where decision-makers' preferences are unclear or controversial, uncertainty is generated and gaps appear into which epistemic communities can insinuate themselves. Learning may also be differentiated across time and space as well as knowledge components; epistemic communities can be 'called in' to provide one type of input and find that the scope and intensity of their influence may increase, decrease or change in emphasis (ibid.: 16).

In recent research, a typology has been developed to capture the variety of ways in which decision-makers actually learn from epistemic communities (Dunlop 2009). Using a flexible definition of uncertainty for example, Dunlop (ibid.) suggests that variety is best captured by differentiating between the control enjoyed by decision-makers and epistemic communities over the production of substantive knowledge – or *means* – that informs policy on the one hand and the policy objectives – or *ends* – to which that knowledge is directed on the other. The four components identified by Haas can be reclassified quite simply into the foci of means and ends with shared normative beliefs (component 1) cause and effect postulates (component 2) and intersubjective understandings of validity (component 3) making up the substantive means produced around an issue and the most overtly political component of epistemic communities the common policy enterprise (component 4) equating to the end objectives. The implications of this distinction for the types of epistemic community-decision-maker learning exchanges that may prevail are elaborated using a typology of adult learning from the education literature which delineates the *four* possible learning situations (see Dunlop 2009 for an exposition of the typology).

Dunlop's empirical exploration of the typology provides grounds for optimism suggesting that each of the types are readily distinguishable from one another and provide a parsimonious account of learning exchanges and basis for ordering empirical findings across cases and comparison within them. Of course, further empirical assurances are required that the typology does not contain self-contradictory ideas. Suffice it to say that research needs to unpack the nature of uncertainty and what it is in epistemic terms that decision-makers are open to learning from epistemic communities.

With regard to the independent variable, we can break down the explanatory challenges posed by epistemic communities. Following Coleman (1986), explanation of epistemic communities' influence in the policy process consists of unpacking three elements in turn: (a) the microfoundations of the macro-level independent variable (i.e. epistemic communities and the learning they effect); (b) the micro-micro causal logics that characterize the learning interactions between epistemic communities and decision-makers (and other policy actors), and (c) the mechanisms that turn learning at the micro level into macro outputs of the dependent variable (i.e. learning in government and, ultimately, policy outputs). Against Coleman's 'bathtub' ideal of rigorous research, the epistemic communities' literature reveals the various conceptual challenges to be met.

a. *Microfoundations of epistemic communities and learning:* To uncover the microfoundations of epistemic communities' influence in the policy process, we must focus on the conditions of their emergence. Empirical studies reveal at least two distinct epistemic community types – each distinguished by the extent to which decision-makers exert control over their existence (Dunlop, 2010). Epistemic communities were originally conceived as 'evolutionary' entities; self-regulating enclaves of experts that existed 'out there' in the academic and research world that entered the political arena by responding to decision-makers' call for advice (Haas 1989, 1992a). In such 'ideal typical' scenarios, decision-makers' uncertainty is such that epistemic communities are able to offer *both* substantive policy advice (means) and policy proposals (ends). However, another type of expert enclave is apparent in the literature. Some epistemic communities are what can be described as 'governmental' – where members have been deliberately selected by decision-makers to justify a predetermined policy decision (Dunlop 2010) or depoliticize an emotive issue (Peterson 2001). For example, in Ikenberry's study of Anglo-American post-war economic settlement (1992), an epistemic community was *assembled* by decision-makers to provide technical and normative guidance to facilitate a move away from policies based on unregulated free trade. A similar instance of decision-makers delimiting the policy ends is provided by Verdun in her study of the Delors' Committee that was appointed to provide the substantive epistemic means to supranational elites aiming to deliver the policy end of Economic and Monetary Union (EMU) in the EU (1999). It is only by identifying epistemic communities' microfoundations, that the scope of decision-makers' epistemic needs, and the likely range of epistemic communities' influence, can be discerned.
b. *Explaining learning interactions between epistemic communities and policy elites:* On the micro-micro interactions between epistemic communities and decision-makers, the causal mechanism associated with the framework is obviously learning. However, learning as an explanation takes many forms. Indeed, a closer look at the epistemic communities literature suggests that learning is a 'master mechanism' (see Hedström and Swedberg 1998 for a deeper discussion of causal mechanisms) which can be unpacked into a variety of specific causal logics. The five causal pathways with most analytical potential are suggested and discussed in turn.
   *i* *Learning as instrumental:* Haas's epistemic communities framework, as it stands, implies two causal rationales. The first of these treats decision-maker learning as underpinned by the Lasswellian desire to make 'better public policy'. Here, interactions between epistemic communities and decision-makers are guided by a functional logic where beliefs are updated in a Bayesian manner (Radaelli 2009). Epistemic communities' supply the policy-relevant information required by decision-makers to update their beliefs. Public policy, in this view, is a matter of trial-and-error and experts' role is more overtly technical than political.
   *ii* *Learning as persuasion and socialization:* Haas also emphasizes that the framework is underpinned by 'limited constructivism' (1992a: 23) stressing the importance of persuasion and reflection in the redefinition of decision-makers' interests and identities (Checkel

2001; Jacobson 2000: 160–1). In Haas's Mediterranean study (1990) for example, the epistemic community which grew from the United Nations Environment Programme (UNEP) persuaded decision-makers across nations to internalize a new set of environmental standards and common understanding of the problem. The international diffusion of new environmental norms resulted in effective policy coordination.

iii *Learning as calculation:* Moving beyond the causal logics originally envisaged for epistemic communities, more overtly political learning styles may exist where interaction is underpinned by a 'logic of consequence' and behaviour a function of calculation. In such interest-driven accounts, epistemic communities and decision-makers act in ways that maximize their utility where their engagement in a learning relationship is a product of the sanctions and rewards they perceive such behaviour will bring. The benefit of this logic is that it enables a move away from simply treating learning as something which is value driven, or based on technical rationale. Rather, decision-makers can control a policy domain or gain political advantage by using and, perhaps sourcing, specialist knowledge in a strategic manner (Chwieroth 2007; Dunlop and James 2007; Kohler-Koch 2000; Niemann 1998). For example, principal-agent modelling has been used to explore the role of epistemic communities is delivering pre-determined policy choices in an efficient and credible manner (Dunlop 2010). We should be clear, it is not simply decision-makers that can be treated as rational actors. Epistemic communities' belief systems suggest that while they do not have direct pecuniary incentives, they are still interested parties. Because of their socio-political beliefs these are experts who *want* rather than need to be in the policy arena. They are self-selecting policy actors driven by normative and policy beliefs. Moreover, as creators of knowledge, they are essentially 'residual claimants' (Alchian and Demsetz 1972); long-term shareholders in a product who may compete with other 'claim makers' to control an epistemic field.

iv *Learning as legitimacy:* The sociologies of science, knowledge and professions have obvious, but rarely used, insights for epistemic communities. Specifically, the logic of practice thesis (Bourdieu 1990) can be used to illuminate the interaction between experts and decision-makers as a game where action is informed by the cultural dispositions of the two sets of actors involved. In relation to advisory games, epistemic communities as symbols of authority and legitimacy has been criticized in the Science and Technology Studies (STS) literature (Jasanoff 1996; Lidskog and Sundqvist 2002; Walker 2001) and this field offers important analytical resources for the framework. Epistemic communities' practices as authority claiming actors can be explored using Gieryn's (1983) notions of boundary work. In contrast to the logic of appropriateness, epistemic communities in this view draw a firm line, a boundary, between themselves and the decision-makers they advise. By emphasizing the differences in their professional identities, epistemic communities monopolize epistemic resources and aim to impose their view of the world by dint of their epistemic authority. Decision-maker learning in this scenario is not about uncovering 'what works', but rather is symbolic and legitimacy seeking.

v *Learning as unreflective:* The idea of learning as unreflective is more than a little contradictory. But, we can imagine scenarios where learning from an epistemic community is an automatic response from decision-makers. Following Hopf's thesis on the 'logic of habit' in international relations (2010), habitual behaviour flourishes in environments where uncertainty is absent. Where an epistemic community has become institutionalized, and has successfully attenuated uncertainty and advisors' trustworthiness is assured (ibid.: 16), decision-makers may be content to unquestioningly adopt its ideas thereafter. The proposition that epistemic communities' interpretations could be adopted wholesale through routinized behaviour of decision-makers is perhaps not as controversial as it may at first appear. Epistemic communities that have been institutionalized in bureaucracies may command considerable resources – institutional as well as epistemic (Finnemore 1993). This is especially plausible in technically complex policy domains where the political stakes are relatively low or remain hidden.

Of course, if considered in isolation, each of these conceptual lenses may obscure as much as they reveal. Certainly, mono-causal explanation will not take analysts very far in the complex world of policy learning. Rather, these logics are better used in combination. For example, in her study on hormone growth promoters, Dunlop (2010) found that explanations emphasizing a calculative logic were important at the start of the relationship between European Commission officials and their epistemic community but gave way to learning underpinned by socialization further down the line.

*vi* *Relating the micro world of learning to the macro world of policy outputs:* Finally, research must relate the micro world of epistemic community-decision-makers' interactions to the macro-level world of government learning and policy outputs. The challenges posed by such aggregation are considerable. Analysts must capture how decision-maker learning becomes transformed into learning at a systemic level. They must also pinpoint the source of those lessons as being the epistemic community. Methodological choices may hold the key here. The painstaking qualitative process-tracing originally advocated by Haas (1992a) remains the most suitable method to uncover whether socially accepted ideas can actually be traced back to a group of experts. Counterfactual analysis, also suggested by Haas, is a valuable yet underused tool which can help to construct a rigorous account of learning that would not have occurred in the absence of an expert enclave creating new policy relevant ideas.

## Conclusions and future research agenda

The epistemic communities approach speaks directly to the complex challenges faced by decision-makers in uncertain policy environments. Accordingly, the approach has proved valuable in explaining the role of experts in a variety of political settings and has remarkable disciplinary reach beyond its roots in IR. Yet arguably, we are still some way off the 'reflective research program' envisaged two decades ago (Adler and Haas 1992).

Empirical research on epistemic communities has ensured that the term is now part of the social science lexicon. To deepen our understanding, research is required that explores how epistemic communities emerge in the first place and what happens to them as they interact with decision-makers and other policy actors over time. Moving from exploratory to explanatory mode, future research interrogating the causal mechanism of learning would be welcome. In particular, following major analytical themes which have emerged in political science in the past few years, the role of professional practice and habit in how decision-makers learn from epistemic communities would represent important additions to the research agenda. Finally, with regard to methodology, again epistemic communities should take inspiration from where analytical energies are being deployed in the social sciences. Specifically, it would be useful for scholars to invest research time in two areas: the role of temporal variables in epistemic communities' influence and the transformation of learning at the micro level to learning at the systemic level.

## Acknowledgements

Claire A. Dunlop gratefully acknowledges the support of the Economic and Social Research Council (grant R00429034387) and European Research Council, grant on Analysis of Learning in Regulatory Governance, ALREG, available at: http://centres.exeter.ac.uk/ceg/research/ALREG/index.php.

## Notes

1 The citation search involved two steps. The first was to perform a citation search using the ISI social sciences database – this yielded 583 articles. The second was a manual search for works not cited in the ISI—a further 55 articles, books and book chapters citing Haas (1992a) were uncovered at this stage.
2 The ego-network analysis of the citation data presented in Figures 18.1 and 18.2 were conducted using UCINET network analysis software (Borgatti *et al.* 1999).
3 There have been 45 research articles citing Haas's 1992 *IO* introduction in journals classified under Sociology by the Web of Science. Just over half of these have been published since 2006 (Web of Science citation search 22 July 2011). Perhaps surprisingly, only 17 of these are published in journals which identify as including Science and Technology Studies (STS).
4 It is instructive to note that the leading journal publishing work citing epistemic communities is the *Journal of European Public Policy* (which recorded 40 of the 583 articles listed in the ISI).

## Bibliography


Abbott, A. 1998. *The System of Professions*. Chicago: University of Chicago Press.

Adler, E. and P.M. Haas. 1992. 'Conclusion: Epistemic communities, world order and the creation of a reflective research program', *International Organisation* 46(1): 367–90.

Albert, M. and S. Laberge. 2007. 'The legitimation and dissemination processes of the innovation system approach: The case of the Canadian and Quebec science and technology policy', *Science Technology and Human Values* 32(2): 221–49.

Albrechts, L. 2001. 'How to proceed from image and discourse to action: As applied to the Flemish diamond', *Urban Studies* 38(4): 733–45.

Alchian, A.A. and H. Demsetz. 1972. 'Production, information costs and economic organization', *American Economic Review* 62, 777–95.

Borgatti, S.P., M.G. Everett and L.C. Freeman. 1999. *UCINET 6.0 Version 1.00*. Natick, MA: Analytic Technologies.

Bourdieu, P. 1990. *Logic of Practice*. Stanford, CA: Stanford University Press.

Checkel, J. 2001. 'Why comply? Social learning and European identity change', *International Organization* 55(3): 553–88.

Chwieroth, J. 2007. 'Neoliberal economists and capital account liberalization in emerging markets', *International Organization* 61(2): 443–63.

Coleman, J.S. 1986. 'Social theory, social research, and a theory of action', *American Journal of Sociology* 91: 1309–35.

——and G. Skogstad. 1995. 'Neo-liberalism, policy networks, and policy change: Agricultural policy reform in Australia and Canada', *Australian Journal of Political Science* 30(2): 242–63.

Drake, W.J. and K. Nicolaïdis. 1992. 'Ideas, interests and institutionalisation: "Trade in services" and the Uruguay Round', *International Organization* 46: 1, 37–100.

Dudley, G. and J.J. Richardson. 1996. 'Why does policy change over time? Adversarial policy communities, alternative policy arenas and British trunk roads policy, 1945–1995', *Journal of European Public Policy* 3(1): 63–83.

Dunlop, C.A. 2000. 'Epistemic communities: A reply to toke', *Politics* 20(3): 137–44.

—— 2007. 'Up and down the pecking order, what matters and when in issue definition: the case of rbST in the EU', *Journal of European Public Policy* 14(1): 39–58.

—— 2009. 'Policy transfer as learning: Capturing variation in what decision-makers learn from epistemic communities', *Policy Studies* 30(3): 291–313.

——. 2010. 'Epistemic communities and two goals of delegation', *Science and Public Policy* 37(3): 205–17.

——and O. James. 2007. 'Principal-agent modelling and learning: The European commission, experts and agricultural hormone growth promoters', *Public Policy and Administration* 22(4): 403–22.

Elliott, C. and R. Schlaepfer. 2001. 'Understanding forest certification using the advocacy coalition framework', *Forest Policy and Economics* 2(3–4): 257–66.

Epstein, S. 1996. *Impure Science: AIDS, Activism, and the Politics of Knowledge*. Berkeley, CA: University of California Press.

Fenno, R.F. 1986. 'Observation, context, and sequence in the study of politics', *American Political Science Review* 80(1): 3–15.

Finlayson, A. 2004. 'Political science, political ideas and rhetoric', *Economy and Society* 33(4): 528–49.

Finnemore, M. 1993. 'International organizations as teachers of norms: The United-Nations Educational Scientific and Cultural Organization and Science Policy', *International Organization* 47(4): 565–97.
Gieryn, T.F. 1983. 'Boundary-work and the demarcation of science from non-science: Strains and interests in professional ideologies of scientists', *American Sociological Review* 48(6): 781–95.
Haas, P.M. 1989. 'Do regimes matter? Epistemic communities and Mediterranean pollution control', *International Organization* 43(3): 377–403.
—— 1990. *Saving the Mediterranean – The Politics of International Environmental Co-operation*. New York: Columbia University Press.
—— 1992a. 'Introduction: Epistemic communities and international policy co-ordination', *International Organization* 46(1): 1–36.
—— 1992b. 'Obtaining international environmental protection through epistemic consensus', in I.H. Rowlands and M. Greene (eds) *Global Environmental Change and International Relations*. Basingstoke: Palgrave Macmillan.
—— 2011. 'Epistemic communities', in *IPSA Encyclopedia of Political Science*, New York: Sage.
Harrison, K.A. 2002. 'Ideas and environmental standard-setting: A comparative study of regulation of the pulp and paper industry', *Governance* 15(1): 65–96.
Hedström, P. and R. Swedberg (eds). 1998. *Social Mechanisms*. Cambridge: Cambridge University Press.
Hopf, T. 2010. 'The logic of habit in international relations', *European Journal of International Relations* 16(4): 539–61.
Howorth, J. 2004. 'Discourse, ideas, and epistemic communities in European security and defence policy', *West European Politics* 27(2): 211–34.
Ikenberry, G.J. 1992. 'A world economy restored: Expert consensus and the Anglo-American postwar settlement' in *International Organization* 46: 1, 289–322.
Jacobson, H.K. 2000. 'International institutions and system transformation', *Annual Review of Political Science* 3: 149–66.
Jasanoff, S. 1996. 'Science and norms in global environmental regimes', in F. Hampson Osler and J. Reppy (eds). *Earthly Goods: Environmental Change and Social Justice*. Ithaca, NY: Cornell University Press.
Kaelberer, M. 2003. 'Knowledge, power and monetary bargaining: Central bankers and the creation of monetary union in Europe', *Journal of European Public Policy* 10(3): 365–79.
Kamieniecki, S. 2000. 'Testing alternative theories of agenda setting: Forest policy change in British Columbia, Canada', *Policy Studies Journal* 28(1): 176–89.
Keck, M. and K. Sikkink. 1998. *Activists Beyond Borders: Advocacy Networks in International Politics*. Ithaca, NY: Cornell University Press.
Kohler-Koch, B. 2000. 'Framing; the bottleneck of constructing legitimate institutions', *Journal of European Public Policy* 7(4): 513–31.
Lidskog, R. and G. Sundqvist. 2002. 'The role of science in environmental regimes: The case of LRTAP', *European Journal of International Relations* 8(1): 77–101.
Litfin, K.T. 1994. *Ozone Discourses: Science and Politics in Global Environmental Cooperation*. New York: Columbia University Press.
Lorenz, D. 2010. 'Possibilities of enacting and researching epistemic communities', *Sociological Research Online* 15(2).
Lorenz-Meyer, Dagmar. 2010. 'Possibilities of enacting and researching epistemic communities', *Sociological Research Online* 15(2). Available at: http://www.socresonline.org.uk/15/2/13.html.
Lovell, H. and D. MacKenzie. 2011. 'Accounting for carbon: The role of accounting professional organisations in governing climate change', *Antipode* 43(3): 704–30.
Meijerink, S. 2005. 'Understanding policy stability and change. The interplay of advocacy coalitions and epistemic communities, windows of opportunity, and Dutch coastal flooding policy 1945–2003', *Journal of European Public Policy* 2(6): 1060–77.
Melo, M.A. 2004. 'Institutional choice and the diffusion of policy paradigms: Brazil and the second wave of pension reform', *International Political Science Review* 25(3): 320–41.
Mitchell, N.J., H. Jenkins-Smith, K. Herron and G. Whitten. 2007. 'Elite beliefs, epistemic communities and the Atlantic divide: Scientists' nuclear policy preferences in the United States and European Union', *British Journal of Political Science* 37: 753–64.
Niemann, A. 1998. 'The PHARE programme and the concept of spillover: Neofunctionalism in the making', *Journal of European Public Policy* 5(3): 428–46.
Ogden, J., G. Walt and L. Lush. 2003. 'The politics of "branding" in policy transfer: The case of DOTS for tuberculosis control', *Social Science and Medicine* 57(1): 179–88.

Peterson, J. 2001. 'The choice for EU theorists: Establishing a common framework for analysis', *European Journal of Political Theory* 39(3): 289–318.
Peterson, M.J. 1992. 'Whalers, cetologists, environmentalists and the international management of whaling', *International Organization* 46(1): 147–86.
Pierson, P. 1996. 'The path to European integration: A historical institutionalist analysis', *Comparative Political Studies* 29(2): 123–63.
Prince, R. 2010. 'Globalizing the creative industries concept: Travelling policy and transnational policy communities', *Journal of Arts Management Law and Society* 40(2): 119–39.
Radaelli, C.M. 1995. 'The role of knowledge in the policy process', *Journal of European Public Policy* 2(2): 159–83.
—— 1997. *The Politics of Corporate Taxation in the EU: Knowledge and International Policy Agendas*. London: Routledge.
—— 2009. 'Measuring policy learning: Regulatory impact assessment in Europe', *Journal of European Public Policy* 16(8): 1145–64.
—— and K. O'Connor. 2009. 'How bureaucratic elites imagine Europe: Towards convergence of governance beliefs?', *Journal of European Public Policy* 16(7): 971–89.
Rethel, L. 2010. 'The new financial development paradigm and Asian bond markets', *New Political Economy* 15(4): 493–517.
Roth, C. 2008a. 'Epistemic networks: Formalizing distributed cognition', *Sociologie Du Travail* 50(3): 353–71.
—— 2008b. 'Co-evolution of authors and concepts in epistemic networks the "zebrafish" community', *Revue Francaise de Sociologie* 49(3).
Sabatier, P.A. 1988. 'An advocacy coalition framework of policy change and the role of policy oriented learning therein', *Policy Sciences* 21: 129–68.
Schmidt, V.A. 2010. 'Taking ideas and discourse seriously: Explaining change through discourse institutionalism as the fourth "new institutionalism"', *European Political Science Review* 2(1): 1–25.
Schot, J. and F. Schipper. 2011. 'Experts and European transport integration, 1945–1958', *Journal of European Public Policy* 18(2): 274–93.
Sebenius, J.K. 1992. 'Challenging conventional explanations of international co-operation: Negotiation analysis and the case of epistemic communities' in *International Organisation* 46(1): 323–65.
Shankland, A. and L. Hasenclever. 2011. 'Indigenous peoples and the regulation of REDD plus in Brazil: Beyond the war of the worlds?', *International Development Bulletin* 42(3): 80–8.
Simek, J., L. Zamykalova and M. Mesanyova. 2010. 'Ethics committee or community? Examining the identity of Czech ethics committees in the period of transition', *Journal of Medical Ethics* 36(9): 548–52.
Stephens, J.C., A. Hansson, Y. Liu, H. de Coninck and S. Vajjhala. 2011. 'Characterizing the international carbon capture and storage community', *Global Environmental Change-Human and Policy Dimensions* 21(2): 379–90.
Thatcher, M. 1998. 'The development of policy network analyses', *Journal of Theoretical Politics* 10(4): 389–416.
Thomas, C.W. 1997. 'Public management as interagency co-operation: Testing the epistemic community theory at the domestic level', *Journal of Public Administration Research and Theory* 7(2): 221–46.
Toke, D. 1999. 'Epistemic communities and environmental group', in *Politics* 19(2): 97–102.
van Waarden, F. and M. Drahos. 2002. 'Courts and (epistemic) communities in the convergence of competition policies', *Journal of European Public Policy* 9(6): 913–34.
Verdun, A. 1999. 'The role of the Delors Committee and EMU', *Journal of European Public Policy* 6(2): 308–29.
Walker, K.J. 2001. 'Uncertainty, epistemic communities and public policy', in J. Handmer, T. Norton and S. Dovers. (eds) *Ecology, Uncertainty and Policy*. Englewood Cliffs, NJ: Prentice Hall.
Weible, C.M., P.A. Sabatier, H.C. Jenkins-Smith, D. Nohrstedt, A.D. Henry and P. deLeon. 2011. 'A quarter century of the advocacy coalition framework', *Policy Studies Journal* 39(3): 349–60.
Weiss, C. 1979. 'The many meanings of research utilization', *Public Administration* 39: 426–31.
Wenger, E. 1999. *Communities of Practice*. New York: Cambridge University Press.
Wright, K. 1997. 'Knowledge and expertise in European conventional arms control negotiations: an epistemic community?', *The European Policy Process Occasional Papers*, No. 41 Department of Government, University of Essex.
Youde, J. 2007. *AIDS, South Africa and the Politics of Knowledge*. Aldershot: Ashgate.
Zelikow, P. 1994. 'Foreign policy engineering: From theory to practice and back again', *International Security* 18(4): 143–71.
Zito, A.R. 2001. 'Epistemic communities, European Union governance and the public voice', *Science and Public Policy* 28(6): 465–76.

# 19
# Policy appraisal

*John Turnpenny, Camilla Adelle and Andrew Jordan*

## Introduction

For anyone interested in the role of knowledge in policy-making, these are fascinating times. Terms like policy analysis, policy formulation, impact assessment and policy appraisal are frequently used, and not just by academics: the media, government, non-governmental organisations, interest groups and research funders are all visibly concerned with how evidence is collected, marshalled, communicated, digested and used. One might be forgiven for using such terms interchangeably, or at least rather loosely, but they are quite distinct, and distinctive. This chapter is specifically about the role of *policy appraisal* in knowledge collection, review and utilisation processes.

There are several important reasons why policy appraisal should interest public policy scholars. First, it belongs to a family of other, perhaps, more familiar concepts. We argue policy appraisal is a very specific type of *policy analysis*, a term which covers the use of analytical methods – formal or informal – in any part of policy-making from agenda-setting to implementation. So-called *ex ante* policy appraisal – the focus of this chapter – specifically relates to *policy formulation:* 'how policy options are formulated within government' (Howlett 2011: 18). While part of the process of formulation involves a choice among instruments for implementing policy objectives, like regulation, taxes and voluntary agreements (Bardach 2005; Howlett and Ramesh 2003), the process of formulation *itself* involves activities such as appraising knowledge or evidence, engaging in dialogue about the nature of policy problems and solutions, and identifying and assessing the impacts of different policy options (Howlett 2011).

Second, policy appraisal is a symptom of broader changes in policy-making which began in the latter part of the twentieth century. Many jurisdictions have since embarked on reform programmes intended to better structure and manage their regulatory processes (Allio 2007). This interest in 'Better Regulation' was ignited in part by the need to cope with the increased competition created by more globalised markets, as well as the international diffusion of the Organisation for Economic Co-operation and Development's (OECD) core principles of regulatory reform (ibid.). Radaelli (2007: 191) describes Better Regulation as a type of meta-governance because of 'its emphasis on standards and rules which, instead of governing specific sectors or economic actors, steer the process of rule formulation, adoption, enforcement, and evaluation'.

As we will see below, policy appraisal has become an important enabler of Better Regulation among other things, spreading rapidly throughout the OECD and beyond.

Third, having now secured this role, appraisal processes have themselves become important new sites of political behaviour (Turnpenny *et al.* 2009). Thus, investigating how policy appraisal systems are structured and operate in practice provides another way to study governance via its policy instruments (see Hood 2007 and Lascoumes and Le Galès 2007 among others). While the idea of policy appraisal owes a theoretical debt to the founding fathers of policy analysis (e.g. Lasswell 1947; Simon 1976), paradoxically, contemporary policy analysts have been slow to explore appraisal's policy and political consequences. Appraisals are contested sources of legitimacy, accountability and normative justification for public action. Accordingly, they inform us of the theoretical presuppositions and legitimacy standards embedded in public policy (Lascoumes and Le Galès 2007). Investigating the use of appraisal can also improve our understanding of the *administrative capacity and effectiveness* of public policy (Chaker *et al.* 2006; Hahn and Tetlock 2008). There is great potential to inform political science discussion on capacity and implementation. Finally, as a highly visible form of evidence use, appraisal offers a fresh angle on some rather old debates in public policy such as decision-making (Russel and Jordan 2009), policy coordination (Schout and Jordan 2007), and the development and (non)-utilisation of evidence in politics (Dowie 1996; Pawson 2002; Sanderson 2006). In fact, in this chapter we argue that policy appraisal is a recent and more institutionalised manifestation of policy formulation activities which have always been carried out in various forms.

This chapter provides an introduction to the principles and dynamic practices of policy appraisal. We first examine differing ideas about what appraisal is, or could be, starting from the most basic definitions and how these have evolved over time as ever more ambitious expectations have emerged as to what it can deliver in practice. We then discuss how policy appraisal has been working in practice in different contexts – particularly how it has become institutionalised in many jurisdictions since the mid-1990s. These observations illustrate well the politicised nature of knowledge use in policy-making and the obstacles to its institutionalisation. We then show how several distinct types of research on these subjects have developed, sometimes in parallel with practices, sometimes apart from them. The literatures on appraisal are advancing rapidly, but we show that they often take us back to many fundamental debates in policy analysis, namely between proponents of fairly linear models of knowledge transfer between experts and policy-makers, and those adopting more 'post-positivist' positions. In the final section, we assess the relationship between research and practice across different types of policy appraisal research, and question some of the basic assumptions made about appraisal in the light of theory, research and practice. Finally, we speculate on the possible future direction of policy appraisal research and practice.

## What is policy appraisal?

Definitions of policy appraisal abound. One of the most widely cited is: '[that] family of *ex ante* techniques and procedures. … that seek to inform decision makers by predicting and evaluating the consequences of various activities according to certain conventions' (Owens *et al.* 2004: 1944). Another, less well-known definition, is 'a test or judgment of some policy, with the aim to inform the decision makers on the suitability, desirability, effectiveness or efficiency of it" (de Ridder 2006: 21). Regardless of the definition, we are arguably living in "an age of assessment" (Rayner 2003: 163). The assessment or 'appraisal' of *projects* (e.g. through Environmental Impact Assessment—EIA) has been routinely undertaken in many countries since the 1970s (Jay *et al.* 2007). This was followed by attempts to institute appraisal at the more strategic level of *plans and programmes* (e.g. Strategic Environmental Assessment—SEA) (Bina 2007).

Put simply, policy appraisal is appraisal conducted at the policy level. It attempts to formalise the decision-making process in a series of steps to be undertaken when developing a policy. The end product is a report which describes the results of each step. The steps vary depending on the jurisdiction applying the system (see the section 'How is policy appraisal practised?'), but at a general level they usually include: identifying the problem to be addressed by the proposed policy; defining the objectives of the proposed policy; identifying the different policy options to pursue these objectives; analysing the potential impacts of each option; comparing the options by weighing up the negative and positive impacts for each; and setting out plans for monitoring and evaluating the policy once it is implemented.

These are very similar to the standard steps in EIA and SEA (e.g. Barrow 1997). However, the motives for appraising have varied enormously across jurisdictions and policy fields, from environmental protection through to reducing regulatory burdens and promoting a neo-liberal economic agenda (Kirkpatrick and Parker 2007; Jacob *et al.* 2007; Hertin *et al.* 2009b; OECD 2008). Different subtypes have emerged such as Regulatory Impact Assessment (RIA) (e.g. Radaelli 2004b) and Sustainability Impact Assessment (SIA) (e.g. Kirkpatrick and Lee 2001), each with a slightly different conception of the basic steps outlined above. Appraisal systems in turn harness a wide range of policy appraisal tools such as cost-benefit analysis, scenario analysis and computer modelling (Carley 1980; de Ridder *et al.* 2007; Nilsson *et al.* 2008). Until now, we have mostly been concerned with textbook definitions and understanding of appraisal. In the next section we turn to look at the very varied ways that policy appraisal has actually been practised over the past 20 years or so.

## How is policy appraisal practised?

Precursory forms of policy appraisal, which focused mainly on the assessment of economic and administrative impacts of regulation, were introduced as early as 1966 (Denmark) and 1971 (USA) (OECD 2009). However, the practice spread only slowly at first, with Finland and Canada following in the 1970s and Australia, the UK, the Netherlands and Germany adopting some form of policy appraisal in the mid-1980s. There was, however, a rapid rise in adoption in the second half of the 1990s, following OECD recommendations on regulatory reform (OECD 1995), and again in the mid-2000s following the launch of the European Commission's Impact Assessment system in 2003 (European Commission 2002). 'Better Regulation' has ranked high on the European Union's (EU) agenda for well over a decade now (Allio 2007), and the EU, and especially the European Commission, was a highly visible adopter of policy appraisal, as part of a number of measures designed to improve and streamline its decision-making processes in order 'to improve the quality and coherence of the policy development process' (European Commission 2002: 2).

Many of the early policy appraisal systems were subsequently revised to include a wider range of impacts. For example, the UK system introduced in 1986 as a Compliance Cost Assessment was replaced in 1996 by a broader system of regulatory appraisal, but it did not appear in anything near its current form of RIA until 1998. All 31 OCED countries had by 2008 either adopted, or were in the process of adopting, policy appraisal (OECD 2009). A recent survey of 17 European countries found that all of them had adopted some form of policy appraisal, although some countries were still in the early stages of implementation (Adelle *et al.* 2010). The most recent countries to adopt policy appraisal have tended to be EU member states in Central and Eastern Europe (CEE) such as Estonia and Lithuania (ibid.; De Francesco 2010), although there are some geographical exceptions such as Ireland which only introduced its system in 2005 (Adelle *et al.* 2010). There are also early CEE adopters like Hungary (1994) (see Staronova 2010). Recent adoption appears to be one of the predictors of weak implementation of policy appraisal, with many of the more sophisticated and robust systems being found in the older EU member states (Adelle *et al.* 2010). In addition, policy appraisal is beginning to spread beyond the OECD and EU (De Francesco 2010) and become a 'global norm' (Jacobs 2006). Interest in policy appraisal in middle- and lower-income countries is increasing, albeit from a relatively low base (Kirkpatrick and Parker 2004; Kirkpatrick *et al.* 2004).

This widespread diffusion of policy appraisal systems has not, however, led to a standard appraisal approach. Radaelli (2005: 924) argues that it is an idea which has 'travelled lightly' around the world producing 'diffusion without convergence'. He claims that this has led to the introduction of a policy appraisal 'bottle' which contains many different 'wines'. Essentially most policy appraisal systems (the 'bottle') draw on certain common elements: they are often – but not always – supported by a legislative act making their application mandatory; they consist of similar procedural steps set out in official 'guidance' documents (see above); they are undertaken by the official responsible for policy development; and they result in a written document, which may or may not be made public via a government website.

However, these common features disguise the many different ways policy appraisal is implemented in practice (the 'wine'). For example, in some cases, policy appraisal only exists on paper as a 'tick-box' exercise (Radaelli 2005). Radaelli attempted to account for this variety by examining how institutional and political context matters in the process of diffusion. A number of comparative surveys of policy appraisal practices around Europe have indeed revealed vast diversity in the practice of policy appraisal. They have uncovered different institutional frameworks, objectives, uses of policy appraisal tools, quality of reports, as well as the effects of cultures and the place of appraisal within policy processes (e.g. Jacob *et al.* 2008; Adelle *et al.* 2010; Hertin *et al.* 2009a). These and other insights into the everyday practices of policy appraisal have emerged from a rapidly developing academic literature, which we summarise in the next section.

## Policy appraisal research

Policy appraisal research falls into different broad types. Some is strongly (although often implicitly) premised on the *positivist* belief that more 'rational' policy-making can be achieved by applying analytical tools. The idea that appraisal exists to bring in evidence to counter interest-based policy-making, to integrate cross-cutting issues, and to increase cooperation between different departments is widespread, not least in the guideline documents prepared for government officials. It is based on a 'rational model' of linear knowledge transfer between experts and policy-makers.

Other research draws on a *post-positivist* epistemology, and emphasises the importance of revealing, understanding and working with normative values in studying the relationship between evidence and policy-making. Such an approach fundamentally challenges the underlying assumption that policy appraisal is purely about informing (and thus 'improving') policy, and hence challenges the straightforward definition of what policy appraisal is – is it a tool, a method, an instrument of public policy (e.g. Radaelli 2008: 6) or an administrative coordination mechanism (Jordan and Schout 2006) for example? Policy appraisal can also, with varying degrees of explicitness, be used to delay or dilute unwanted regulation, or to exert political control on government departments and agencies.

### *Positivist approaches*

Turnpenny *et al.* (2009) tried to make sense of these advances by subdividing the literature into four main types. The first two may be thought of as broadly positivist, while the third and fourth are more post-positivist in their orienation. The first type concerns the *design of appraisal systems* themselves. This often highly technical literature is rooted in the environmental management, economics and policy analysis communities. It addresses the design of specific tools and methods for policy appraisal such as Cost Benefit Analysis, the so-called Standard Cost Model, and more general tools such as computer models and scenarios (e.g. Quade 1989; Dunn 2004). It also includes attempts to inform the design of appraisal systems (e.g. Lee 2006; OECD 2008), and often takes the form of 'how to' textbooks (e.g. Barrow 1997) and handbooks (e.g. European Commission 2009), for which there is a steady demand amongst the practitioners who perform appraisals. For useful overall reviews of this type of literature, see Eales *et al.* 2005; Ness *et al.* 2007; de Ridder *et al.* 2007 and Tamborra 2002.

The second type of research concerns the *assessment of the operation of policy appraisal* designs 'in practice', in individual jurisdictions and internationally (e.g. Lee and Kirkpatrick 2004; Renda 2006; Jacob *et al.* 2007; Hertin *et al.* 2009b; EEAC 2006). Initial attempts (e.g. Harrington *et al.* 2000) measured quality by comparing the *contents* of appraisal reports with official guidance. Subsequent research extended this approach somewhat to emphasise aspects of the *process* of appraisal using a more in-depth case study approach, often including interviews with those involved (e.g. TEP 2007). This research has generated a fairly consistent picture of the empirical 'reality' of appraisal, namely that: there is a gap between the aims of appraisal and its implementation; the economic aspects of policy all too easily crowd out other (e.g. social and environmental) aspects; appraisals tend to be performed at a relatively late stage in the policy process and consequently have little or no influence over the final decisions made; consultation is often limited to the 'usual suspects' who have participated before or who have large resources; and formal appraisal tools such as computer modelling are patchily used despite the strong political invocation to use them. Most studies identify recommendations to policy-makers on how to improve the quality of their appraisal systems. Many such recommendations focus on micro-level constraints, such as calls for more training and guidance (EEAC 2006; DBR 2004; Jacobs 2006; NAO 2007; TEP 2007; Wilkinson *et al.* 2004). Another common recommendation is to start the policy appraisal earlier in the policy process, when more options are likely to be open (Renda 2006; TEP 2007; Wilkinson *et al.* 2004). Researchers such as Turnpenny *et al.* (2008) also emphasised the need to address higher-level constraints through, for example: stronger political leadership (Jacob *et al.* 2008; Russel and Jordan 2007); the creation of oversight and quality assurance mechanisms (DBR 2004; TEP 2007; Torriti 2007; Wilkinson *et al.* 2004); and a greater understanding, acceptance and use of appraisal tools (Jacob *et al.* 2008; Nilsson *et al.* 2008; de Ridder *et al.* 2007; Turnpenny *et al.* 2008).

## Post-positivist approaches

Research of the third and fourth types adopts a more post-positivist view. In the third type, analysts have tried to go beyond calling for micro-level changes such as better training and political support, and explored the wider political and institutional context in which appraisal systems operate. Policy appraisal is, as all evidence use in policy-making is, a political activity (see, for example, Hall (1989) on evidence generally, Richardson (2005) on EIA, and Turnpenny *et al.* (2008) on policy appraisal). Such research searches for evidence that appraisal has led to policy change via processes of learning, and attempts to understand what is affecting such processes, such as the constraining effect of the institutional context in which appraisal takes place (Jacob *et al.* 2008; Russel and Jordan 2009; Thiel 2008; Turnpenny *et al.* 2008). For example, Thiel (2008) revealed how appraisal in the European Commission is shaped by departmental cultures and prior experiences of appraisal. There are a relatively small number of studies employing this type of research (e.g. Cashmore *et al.* 2008; Hertin *et al.* 2009a; Hertin *et al.* 2009b; Jacob *et al.* 2008; Nilsson 2006; Thiel and König 2008; Torriti 2007; Turnpenny *et al.* 2008). A distinction is often made between *single-loop* (or instrumental) learning where 'knowledge directly informs concrete decisions by providing specific information on the design of policies' (Hertin *et al.* 2009a: 1187), and *double-loop* (or conceptual) learning where 'knowledge "enlightens" policy-makers by slowly feeding new information, ideas and perspectives into the policy system' (ibid.). Clearly the former is more consistent with a positivist epistemology, whereas the latter is more consistent with a post-positivist one. Much of this literature explicitly endorses more deliberative approaches (e.g. Bond and Morrison-Saunders 2011; Cashmore *et al.* 2008; Owens *et al.* 2004). However, a positivist epistemology continues to provide the foundation for most methodological development (Bond and Morrison-Saunders 2011; Hertin *et al.* 2009a, 2009b). As a consequence, while policy appraisal could potentially provide a new venue for conceptual learning, it appears that this rarely occurs in practice (Hertin *et al.* 2009a: 1196).

The fourth type of research investigates the underlying motivations for appraising in the first place, such as to facilitate political control of bureaucracy (e.g. Radaelli and Meuwese 2010; Radaelli 2008), following perceived 'best practice' in other states (e.g. Radaelli 2005), and attempts to 'modernise' the state (Hood and Peters 2004; Radaelli and Meuwese 2010). Studies of the diffusion of policy appraisal practices across and within jurisdictions have emphasised how different actors shape appraisal structures and practices to suit their preferences (Radaelli 2004a, 2004b, 2005). Research has also focused on the intended and unintended consequences of policy appraisal. It treats appraisal as 'a good lens on the changing nature of the regulatory state in the EU and its member states' (Radaelli and Meuwese 2009: 651). In such accounts, the claim is that politically contested questions (such as who is in charge of the law-making process?) are transferred into more technocratic venues such as policy appraisal processes, where they can be more easily resolved (Radaelli and Meuwese 2010: 143). Appraisal thus becomes a way to unite otherwise incompatible political visions; in many respects, a form of politics by more technocratic means.

## Policy appraisal research-practice relationships

There have been developments in both the research on, and practice of, policy appraisal, but to what extent have research and practice actually informed each other? Susan Owens and her colleagues (2004) expected the practices of, and the research on, appraisal to co-evolve in a steadily more reflexive, or mutually informing, direction. But while there are signs that policy appraisal *research* is moving away from its positivist roots, both research and practice remain heavily informed by it.

According to Adelle *et al.* (2012), research on the *design of appraisal systems* continues apace. Consequently, there are now myriad policy appraisal designs and tools that can be consulted. However, the practices of policy appraisal appear to be informing such research only in a rather general sense, namely through demands from policy-makers for policy appraisal tools, methods and process designs. Consequently, there remains a gap between 'sophisticated tool knowledge and pragmatic policy-making' (de Ridder *et al.* 2007: 436). Thus, while both research and practice still appear to be heavily informed by the positivist model, it is questionable if innovation in both is proceeding in a mutually informative manner.

Regarding research on the *assessment of the operation of policy appraisal*, while at first there was little evidence that such research was producing changes in policy appraisal practices (e.g. Cecot *et al.* 2007; Renda 2006), the picture is now changing (e.g. European Court of Auditors 2010). There is some evidence that as a direct consequence of research, policy appraisal systems in some jurisdictions have been revised to improve the impact of appraisals on political decision-making, for example by setting up dedicated bodies to review the quality of appraisal and/or moving responsibility for appraisal from specialised departments to the heart of government (Jacob *et al.* 2008: 11). However, such changes have not (yet) amounted to a serious reconsideration of the theoretical underpinnings of appraisal practices or research. In mainly pursuing change at the micro and occasionally meso levels, they essentially remain rooted in a positivist epistemology. At present practitioners seem content to commission yet more research on the quality of the policy appraisal systems in their jurisdictions (e.g. European Court of Auditors 2010; NAO 2009), without really investigating some of the underlying contextual issues.

There is still relatively little *post-positivist* work. Perhaps this is not surprising considering the difficulties associated with studying learning processes over long time periods (Owens *et al.* 2004; Radaelli 2009). Nonetheless, if research and practices were proceeding in parallel we would expect to find more evidence of policy appraisal practices being informed by post-positivistic recommendations, such as more deliberative approaches. There is currently little evidence of such 'innovative' approaches within policy appraisal practice or research.

## The role of appraisal in policy analysis

Another way to understand the current place of policy appraisal is to view it against the backdrop of policy analysis more generally. Doing this reveals that appraisal raises some very old questions. Modern policy analysis is usually held to date from the late 1940s, particularly forged by the work of Lasswell, Simon and Lindblom. But each of these had very different ideas about the nature and goals of policy, and hence disagreed about the form and function of policy analysis. It is possible to divide the history of policy analysis into three broad 'waves'. The first wave, from roughly the late 1940s to the late 1970s, corresponded to widespread use, and implicit faith in, rationally based appraisal tools like cost-benefit analysis, operations research and assessment (Rossi *et al.* 2004; Wollmann 2007). But the limits to such tools soon became evident, and the promise of analytically based answers to every policy question soon faded.

The 'second wave' (Wollmann 2007) began as limits on the ability to predict every eventuality became clearer, and the politics surrounding use of analysis became more intense (Weiss 1979; Palumbo 1987). During the early 1980s, an 'anti-analytical' mood of government coupled with budgetary retrenchment pressure, particularly in the USA and the UK, resulted in a scaling back of the policy units who once espoused analytical methods. But since the mid-1990s, there has been a revival in the use of policy analytical tools in practical policy-making, including policy appraisal. This shift corresponded with a drive to more 'evidence-based' approach to policy-making in an era of New Public Management (e.g. Radaelli 1995; Dowie 1996; Pawson 2002; Sanderson 2006; Nutley *et al.* 2007). Critically – and somewhat in tension with this 'third wave' of use – there has been a blossoming of more sophisticated research on the discursive, argumentative and political aspects of policy analysis (e.g. Majone 1989; Fischer 1995; John 1998). The tone of this research has changed from 'discover and predict' to a recognition of the 'power of language, persuasion and argument' (John 1988: 154) – the importance of revealing, understanding and working with normative values expressed in a 'post-positivist epistemology' (Fischer 1995). However, as we have seen, this 'post-positivist turn' has made little impact so far on policy appraisal research or practice. Policy appraisal is thus both a symptom of these long-term trends in policy analysis, and a site of everyday politics around the use of knowledge in the policy process.

## Conclusion

In this chapter we have shown that policy appraisal is an important aspect of policy analysis which has spread rapidly and secured a high profile. It now appears in many different guises, each with different aims. It is variously: a method or procedure for analysis; a policy instrument; a site of political behaviour; and a technique for policy harmonisation across states. As it enjoys its current and relatively rapid phase of proliferation, research on policy appraisal is moving towards the mainstream of public policy research, on several different fronts. The broadly 'positivist' and broadly 'post-positivist' approaches to understanding policy appraisal reflect wider debates within policy analysis and evidence use. But while policy appraisal has emerged as a significant part of the policy-making process in the last ten years or so, research and practice are only weakly informed by post-positivist research developments elsewhere (Adelle *et al.* 2012). This is partly because of the lack of a ready audience for such work. Many policy appraisal practitioners have made a significant political and/or resource commitment to forms of policy appraisal informed by the 'rational' model which they are reluctant to surrender. In part it is also due to the nature of the post-positivist research, which questions the very purpose of doing appraisal.

What might this mean for the future of policy appraisal? In the second decade of the twenty-first century, perhaps another policy analysis 'wave' is breaking. The tension between the broadly positivist 'evidence-based policy' underpinning of policy appraisal in practice, and the post-positivist challenges to it, echo the transition from the first to the second wave in the mid-late 1970s. Challenges to the evidence-based policy-making discourses of the early 2000s in the light of economic crises and ideological retrenchment may have significant implications for the future direction of policy appraisal. Its continued rise, coupled with more political pressure, offers many opportunities for research which examines underlying motivations for appraisal, and methods for deducing this. Research could lead to a fuller understanding of when, why and how appraisal practices depart from the positivist model, depending on the specific context(s) in which appraisal is deployed. Work which seeks to mediate between the positivist and the post-positivist approaches will also play a more significant role. Policy appraisal researchers are well placed to shape new developments. These are indeed fascinating times.

## Bibliography


Adelle, C., A. Jordan, J. Turnpenny, S. Bartke, T. Bournaris, K. Jacob, H. Kuittinen, K. Mäkinen, C. Moulogianni, T. Nõmmann, L.E. Larsen, K. Peterson, M. Perez Soba, L. Roupioz, B. Sánchez, D. Wascher, and S. Weiland. 2010. 'A summary of user needs and expectations with regards to impact assessment'. Unpublished LIAISE project report prepared under contract from the European Commission. Contract No. 243826.

——, A. Jordan and J.R. Turnpenny. 2012. 'Proceeding in parallel or drifting apart? A systematic review of policy appraisal research and practices', *Environment and Planning C* 30(3): 400–414.

Allio, L. 2007. 'Better regulation and impact assessment in the European Commission', in C. Kirkpatrick and D. Parker (eds) *Regulatory Impact Assessment: Towards Better Regulation?* Cheltenham: Edward Elgar.

Bardach, E. 2005. *A Practical Guide for Policy Analysis: The Eightfold Path to More Effective Problem-Solving*. Washington, DC: CQ Press.

Barrow, C.J. 1997. *Environmental and Social Impact Assessment*. London: Arnold.

Bina, O. 2007. 'A critical review of the dominant lines of argumentation on the need for strategic environmental assessment', *EIA Review* 27: 585–606.

Bond, A. and A. Morrison-Saunders. 2011. 'Re-evaluating sustainability assessment: Aligning the vision and the practice', *EIA Review* 31(1): 1–7.

Carley, M. 1980. *Rational Techniques in Policy Analysis*. London: Heinemann.

Cashmore, M. 2004. 'The role of science in Environmental Impact Assessment: Process and procedure versus purpose in the development of theory', *EIA Review* 24: 403–26.

——, A. Bond and D. Cobb. 2008. 'The role and functioning of environmental assessment: Theoretical reflections upon an empirical investigation of causation', *Journal of Environmental Management* 88: 1233–48.

Cecot, C., R.W. Hahn and A. Renda. 2007. 'A statistical analysis of the quality of impact assessment in the European Union', AEI- Brookings Joint Center for Regulatory Studies. Working Paper 07-09.

Chaker, A., K. El-Fadl, L. Chamas and B. Hatjian. 2006. 'A review of strategic environmental assessment in 12 selected countries', *EIA Review* 26(1): 15–56.

DBR (EU Directors of Better Regulation Group). 2004. 'A comparative analysis of regulatory impact assessment in ten EU countries', report prepared for the EU DBR Group, Dublin, May 2004 (accessed 15 August 2011). Available at: http://www.betterregulation.ie/eng/Publications/A_COMPARATIVE_ANALYSIS_OF_REGULATORY_IMPACT_ASSESSMENT_IN_TEN_EU_COUNTRIES.html (accessed 15 August 2011).

De Francesco, F. 2010. 'The diffusion process of regulatory impact analysis in EU and OECD member states'. PhD thesis, University of Exeter.

de Ridder, W. 2006. *Tool Use in Integrated Assessment: Integration and Synthesis Report.* Bilthoven: Netherlands Environmental Assessment Agency.

——, J. Turnpenny, M. Nilsson and A. von Raggamby. 2007. 'A framework for tool selection and use in integrated assessment for sustainable development', *Journal of Environmental Assessment Policy and Management* 9(4): 423–41.

Dowie, J. 1996. '"Evidence-based", "cost-effective" and "preference-driven" medicine: decision analysis based medical decision making is the pre-requisite', *Journal of Health Services Research and Policy* 1(2): 104–13.

Dunn, W.N. 2004. *Public Policy Analysis – An Introduction*, 3rd edn. Mahwah, NJ: Pearson Prentice Hall.

Eales, R., S. Smith, C. Twigger-Ross, W. Sheate, E. Özdemiroglu, C. Fry, P. Tomlinson and C. Foan. 2005. 'Emerging approaches to integrated appraisal in the UK', *Impact Assessment and Project Appraisal* 23(2): 113–23.

EEAC (European Environment and Sustainable Development Advisory Councils). 2006. 'Impact assessment of European Commission policies: Achievements and prospects', statement of the EEAC Working Group on Governance, April.

European Commission. 2002. 'Impact assessment' (COM (2002) 276), Commission of the European Communities, Brussels.

—— 2009. 'Impact assessment guidance' (SEC(2009)92), Commission of the European Communities, Brussels.

European Court of Auditors. 2010. 'Impact assessments in the EU institutions: Do they support decision-making?' Special Report No. 3, European Court of Auditors, Luxembourg.

Fischer, F. 1995 *Evaluating Public Policy.* Boulder, CO: Wadsworth.

Hahn, R.W. and P.C. Tetlock. 2008. 'Has economic analysis improved regulatory decisions?', *Journal of Economic Perspectives* 22(1): 67–84.

Hall, P.A. (ed.). 1989. *The Political Power of Economic Ideas.* Princeton, NJ: Princeton University Press.

Harrington, W., R.D. Morgenstern and P. Nelson. 2000. 'On the accuracy of regulatory cost estimates', *Journal of Policy Analysis and Management* 19: 297–322.

Hertin, J., J. Turnpenny, A. Jordan, M. Nilsson, D. Russel and B. Nykvist. 2009a. 'Rationalising the policy mess? Ex ante assessment and the utilisation of knowledge in the policy process', *Environment and Planning A* 41: 1185–1200

——, K. Jacob, U. Pesch and C. Pacchi. 2009b. 'The production and use of knowledge in regulatory impact assessment: An empirical analysis', *Forest Policy and Economics* 11(5–6): 413–21.

Hood, C. 2007. 'Intellectual obsolescence and intellectual makeovers: Reflections on the tools of government after two decades', *Governance* 20(1): 127–44.

——and B.G. Peters. 2004. 'The middle aging of New Public Management: Into the age of paradox?', *Journal of Public Administration Research and Theory* 14: 267–82

Howlett, M. 2011. *Designing Public Policies: Principles and Instruments.* London: Routledge.

——and M. Ramesh. 2003. *Studying Public Policy: Policy Cycles and Policy Subsystems.* Oxford: Oxford University Press.

Jacob, K., J. Hertin and A. Volkery. 2007. 'Considering environmental aspects in integrated Impact Assessment: Lessons learned and challenges ahead', in C. George and C. Kirkpatrick (eds) *Impact Assessment for a New Europe and Beyond.* Cheltenham: Edward Elgar.

——, J. Hertin, P. Hjerp, C. Radaelli, A. Meuwese, O. Wolf, C. Pacchi, and K. Rennings. 2008. 'Improving the practice of impact assessment', EVIA (Evaluating Integrated Impact Assessments) project report. Project No. 028889, European Commission Sixth Framework Programme.

Jacobs, S.H. 2006. 'Regulatory impact analysis in regulatory process, method, and co-operation: Lessons for Canada from international trends'. Policy Horizons Canada Working paper 026. Government of Canada, Ottawa.

Jay, S., C. Jones, P. Slinn and C. Wood. 2007. 'Environmental impact assessment: Retrospect and prospect', *EIA Review* 27: 287–300.

John, P. 1998. *Analysing Public Policy*. London: Continuum.

Jordan, A. and A. Schout. 2006. *The Coordination of the European Union*. Oxford: Oxford University Press.

Kirkpatrick, C. and N. Lee. 2001. 'Methodologies for sustainability impact assessments of proposals for new trade agreements', *Journal of Environmental Assessment, Policy and Management* 3(3): 395–412.

——and D. Parker (eds). 2007. *Regulatory Impact Assessment: Towards Better Regulation?* Cheltenham: Edward Elgar Publishing.

——and D. Parker. 2004. 'Regulatory impact assessment and regulatory governance in developing countries', *Public Administration and Development* 24(4): 333–44.

——D. Parker and Y.-F. Zhang. 2004. 'Regulatory impact assessment in developing and transition economies: A survey of current practice', *Public Money and Management* 24(5): 291–6.

Lascoumes, P. and P. Le Galès. 2007. 'Introduction: Understanding public policy through its instruments: From the nature of instruments to the sociology of public policy instrumentation', *Governance* 20(1): 1–21.

Lasswell, H.D. 1947. *The Analysis of Political Behavior: An Empirical Approach*. London: Routledge.

Lee, N. 2006. 'Bridging the gap between theory and practice in integrated assessment', *EIA Review* 26: 57–78.

——and C. Kirkpatrick. 2004. 'A pilot study on the quality of European Commission extended impact assessment'. Draft For Consultation. Impact Assessment Research Centre, Institute for Development Policy and Management, University of Manchester, 21 June.

Majone, G. 1989. *Evidence, Argument and Persuasion in the Policy Process*. New Haven, CT: Yale University Press.

NAO (National Audit Office). 2007. *Evaluation of Regulatory Impact Assessments 2006–07*. London: The Stationery Office.

—— 2009. *Delivering High Quality Impact Assessments*. London: The Stationery Office.

Ness, B., E. Urbel-Piirsalu, S. Anderberg and L. Olsson. 2007. 'Categorising tools for sustainability assessment', *Ecological Economics* 60: 498–508.

Nilsson, M. 2006. 'The role of assessments and institutions for policy learning: A study on Swedish climate and nuclear policy formation', *Policy Sciences* 38: 225–49.

——, A. Jordan, J. Turnpenny, J. Hertin, B. Nykvist and D. Russel. 2008. 'The use and non-use of policy appraisal in public policymaking: An analysis of three European countries and the European Union', *Policy Sciences* 41(4): 335–55.

Nutley, S.M., I. Walter and H.T.O. Davies. 2007. *Using Evidence: How Research Can Inform Public Services*. Bristol: The Policy Press.

OECD (Organisation for Economic Co-operation and Development). 1995. *Recommendation of the Council of the OECD on Improving the Quality of Government Regulation*. Paris: OECD.

—— 2008. *Building an Institutional Framework for Regulatory Impact Assessment: Guidance for Policy-makers*. Paris: OECD Publications.

—— 2009. *Indicators of Regulatory Management Systems*. Paris: OECD Publications.

Owens, S., T. Rayner and O. Bina. 2004. 'New agendas for appraisal: Reflections on theory, practice and research', *Environment and Planning A* 36: 1943–59.

Palumbo, D.J. 1987. 'Politics and evaluation', in D.J. Palumbo (ed.) *The Politics of Program Evaluation*. Newbury Park, CA: Sage, 12–46.

Pawson, R. 2002. 'Evidence-based policy: In search of a method', *Evaluation* 8(2): 157–81.

Quade, E.S. 1989. *Analysis for Public Decisions*, 3rd edn. Mahwah, NJ: Prentice Hall.

Radaelli, C. 1995. 'The role of knowledge in the policy process', *Journal of European Public Policy* 2: 159–83

—— 2004a. 'Getting to grips with quality in the diffusion of regulatory impact assessment in Europe', *Public Money and Management* 5: 271–6.

—— 2004b. 'The diffusion of regulatory impact analysis: Best practice or lesson-drawing', *European Journal of Political Research* 43: 723–47.

—— 2005. 'Diffusion without convergence: How political context shapes the adoption of regulatory impact assessment', *Journal of European Public Policy* 12: 924–43.

—— 2007. 'Whither better regulation for the Lisbon agenda?', *Journal of European Public Policy* 14(2): 190–207.

—— 2008. 'Evidence-based policy and political control: What does Regulatory Impact Assessment tell us?', paper for the European Consortium for Political Research Joint Sessions, workshop on 'The politics of evidence-based policy-making', Rennes, 11–16 April.

—— 2009. 'Measuring policy learning: Regulatory impact assessment in Europe', *Journal of European Public Policy* 16: 1145–64.

——and A.C.M. Meuwese. 2009. 'Better regulation in Europe: Between public management and regulatory reform', *Public Administration* 87: 639–54.

——and A.C.M. Meuwese. 2010. 'Hard questions, hard solutions: Proceduralisation through impact assessment in the EU', *West European Politics* 33: 136–53.

Rayner, S. 2003. 'Democracy in the age of assessment: Reflections on the roles of expertise and democracy in the public sector decision making', *Science and Public Policy* 3: 163–70.

Renda, A. 2006. *Impact Assessment in the EU: The State of the Art and the Art of the State*. Brussels: Centre for Policy Studies.

Richardson, T. 2005. 'Environmental assessment and planning theory: Four short stories about power, multiple rationality and ethics', *EIA Review* 25: 341–65.

Rossi, P.H., M.W, Lipsey and H.E. Freeman. 2004. *Evaluation: A Systematic Approach*, 7th edn. Thousand Oaks, CA: Sage.

Russel, D. and A. Jordan. 2007. 'Gearing-up governance for sustainable development: Patterns of policy appraisal in UK central government', *Journal of Environmental Planning and Management* 50: 1–21.

——and A.J. Jordan. 2009. 'Joining up or pulling apart? The use of appraisal to coordinate policy-making for sustainable development', *Environment and Planning A* 41(5): 1201–16.

Sanderson, I. 2006. 'Complexity, "practical rationality" and evidence-based policy making', *Policy and Politics* 34(1): 115–32.

Schout, A. and A. Jordan. 2007. 'What do "new" modes of governance demand of public administrations?', paper presented at the Connex Workshop on Governing the European Union: Policy instruments in a multi-level polity, Paris, 21 and 22 June. Sciences Po—Centre d'études européennes.

Simon, H.A. 1976. *Administrative Behavior: A Study of Decision-making Processes in Administrative Organization*, 3rd edn. London: Collier Macmillan.

Staronova, K. 2010. 'Regulatory impact assessment: Formal institutionalization and practice', *Journal of Public Policy* 30(1): 117–36.

Tamborra, M. 2002. *Tools for Sustainability Impact Assessment of EU Policies: The Contribution of the EU Socio-economic Research*. Brussels: European Commission.

TEP (The Evaluation Partnership). 2007. 'Evaluation of the Commission's Impact Assessment system'. Final Report Submitted to Secretariat-General of the European Commission (Contract Number SG-02/2006).

Thiel, A. 2008. 'Changing administrative culture and political debate? A review of impact assessment practices in the European Commission', *Zeitschrift für Umweltpolitik and Umweltrecht* 31: 5–27.

——and B. König. 2008. 'An institutional analysis of the use of modelling tools within the European Commission', in K. Helming and and H. Wiggering (eds) *Sustainability Impact Assessment of Land Use Policies*. Heidelberg: Springer.

Torriti, J. 2007. 'Impact assessment in the EU: A tool for better regulation, less regulation, or less bad regulation?' *Journal of Risk Research* 10(2): 239–76.

Turnpenny, J., M. Nilsson, D. Russel, A. Jordan, J. Hertin and B. Nykvist. 2008. 'Why is integrating policy assessment so hard? A comparative analysis of the institutional capacities and constraints', *Journal of Environmental Planning and Management* 51(6): 759–75.

——, C. Radaelli, A. Jordan and K. Jacob. 2009. 'The policy and politics of policy appraisal: Emerging trends and new directions', *Journal of European Public Policy* 16: 640–53.

Weiss, C. 1979. 'The many meanings of research utilization', *Public Administration Review* 39(5): 426–31.

Wilkinson, D., M. Fergusson, C. Bowyer, J. Brown, A. Ladefoged, C. Monkhouse and A. Zdanowicz. 2004. *Sustainable Development in the European Commission's Integrated Impact Assessments for 2003: Final Report*. London: Institute for European Environmental Policy.

Wollmann, H. 2007. 'Policy evaluation and evaluation research', in F. Fischer, G.J. Miller and M.S Sidney (eds) *Handbook of Public Policy Analysis: Theory, Politics and Methods*. London: CRC Press, 393–402.

# 20

# Policy analytical styles

*Igor S. Mayer, C. Els van Daalen and Pieter W.G. Bots*

## Introduction: perspectives on policy analysis: a framework for understanding and design[1]

Policy analysis is a multifaceted field in which a variety of different activities and ambitions have found a place. Some policy analysts conduct quantitative or qualitative research while others reconstruct and analyse political discourse or set up citizen forums. Some policy analysts are independent researchers, some are process facilitators, while others act as political advisers (Dror 1967; Jenkins-Smith 1982; Durning and Osuna 1994). The debate on the discipline – for example, on its foundations, underlying values and methods – is conducted in a fragmented way (Dunn [1981] 1994; Brewer and DeLeon 1983; Hogwood and Gunn 1984; Bobrow and Dryzek 1987; Wildavsky 1987; DeLeon 1988; MacRae and Whittington 1997; Hawkesworth 1988; House and Shull 1991; Weimer and Vining 1992; Fischer and Forester 1993; White 1994; Radin 1997; Mayer 1997; Hoppe 1998; Shulock 1999; Lynn 1999).

This is a pity, because it tends to sideline a reflection on the relationship between applied research, the use and development of methods in relation to policy advice and policy processes.

The variety and multifaceted nature of policy analysis makes it clear that there is no single, let alone 'best', way of conducting policy analyses. The discipline consists of many different schools, approaches, roles and methods. The observed diversity of policy analysis does give rise to numerous questions. If we are unable to construct cohesion and unity behind this great diversity, we cannot speak of a discipline. What relationship exists between the different schools and activities of policy analysis? Do they exclude each other or are there – in practice – numerous hybrids and combinations? What conceptual framework do we have at our disposal if we need to demarcate the discipline, design new methods and approaches, or evaluate projects? Can we enrich the methodological toolbox by adding new methods? What is the relationship between policy analysis methods and new insights from the policy sciences, such as interactive policy development and process management (Edelenbos 1999; de Bruijn *et al.* 2002)? These are important questions that we obviously cannot answer in full and all at once, but for which we modestly hope to provide a framework.

## Untangling and explaining

The great diversity of views, schools and methods easily causes confusion and gives rise to the need for insight into the discipline for insiders and outsiders alike (Radin 1997; Lynn 1999).

Various attempts have been made to untangle and explain policy analysis as a methodical discipline. Some well-known examples of models in which activities and methods are systematically related can be found in Dunn (1994), Brewer and DeLeon (1983), Hogwood and Gunn (1984), Bobrow and Dryzek (1987), Miser and Quade (1985), Patton and Sawicki (1986), Weimer and Vining (1992) and Mayer (1997).

It is precisely because of the varied developments in policy analysis and the diffuse image that they create of the field, that this chapter seeks to make the field transparent and to structure it with the help of a framework or conceptual model. Structuring will not take place by choosing a specific author, perspective or school, but rather by displaying the variety of views of policy analysis. It is not our intention to adopt a normative standpoint on what the most preferable form or style of policy analysis should be. This chapter provides a framework for positioning the different perspectives and for highlighting the implications of choosing a perspective when designing or evaluating a policy analysis project.

The presented conceptual model therefore has three functions. First, structuring the field into activities and styles provides a greater insight into and overview of the diversity of policy analysis. The model is a means to demarcate and understand the field as a whole. Second, when designing a particular policy analysis project, the analysts will select methods and tools they consider to be appropriate. The model can support choosing existing methods and designing new methods. Third, we believe that the quality of a policy analysis project can be judged from different perspectives. The model helps to formulate the values pertaining to a perspective, values from which criteria for the evaluation of a policy analysis project can be derived.

## Research approach

In our attempt to (re)structure the different styles and construct a conceptual model, we reviewed the authoritative literature on the development of policy analysis and policy analysis styles. This review led to an important observation. All characterisations of policy analysis are inclusive of a limited number of preferred styles but are also exclusive of other styles, either because these are not considered at all or because they are criticised as not being (effective) policy analysis (e.g. Lawlor 1996). From the present literature, a preliminary classification of policy analysis activities, roles and values was constructed.

## A set of interacting activities

Our strategy in developing the model has been to first address the question: 'What general activities do policy analysts perform when it comes to supporting policy and policy processes?' We identified six major clusters of activities. They are:

1 Research and analyse: this cluster of activities matches with a perspective on policy analysis as knowledge generation. Knowledge institutions, such as statistical agencies, semi-scientific research institutions, and research agencies, gather and analyse, on request and on their own initiative, knowledge and information for policy purposes. It is possible that the political agenda influences their research priorities, but the results of their autonomous research activities may also influence the political agenda. Translation of the results of their research into a policy design or recommendation is not a primary part of their task or mission. It is up to the political system to identify consequences and draw conclusions from the best available knowledge.
2 Design and recommend: when sufficient data and information have been gathered in earlier research, a policy analysis will focus on translating the available knowledge into new

policy, either by making recommendations or by making a complete policy design. Recommendations will typically be the result of comparing the effects of different policy alternatives and weighing the options based on various criteria. Policy analysts in this way are supportive to the policy process by translating available knowledge into new policy either by advising or by making (partial) policy designs in terms of 'actions-means-ends'. A complete policy design typically involves generating a set of alternative strategies that each consists of several tactics aimed at achieving particular objectives or sub-goals (see Walker 1988).

3 Clarify arguments and values: there will always be implicit normative and ethical questions and opinions behind public policy. Prolonged conflicts and social issues that turn into stalemates often come about through fundamental normative and argumentative differences (van Eeten, 2001; Fischer and Forester 1993). Abortion, euthanasia and drilling for natural gas in protected areas are examples of such issues. Policy analysis may not only make instrumental recommendations for policy-making; it may also analyse the values and argumentation systems that underpin social and political debate. Moreover, policy analysis seeks to improve the quality of debate by identifying the one-sided or limited nature of arguments or showing where blind spots exist in the debate (Hoppe 1998).
4 Provide strategic advice: policy analysis will often be a strategic, client-oriented activity. The substantive or procedural advice will be made dependent on the analysis of the field of forces that exist, namely the environment in which the client and his problem are located. The policy analyst will advise the client on the most effective strategy for achieving certain goals given a certain political constellation, namely the nature of the environment in which the client operates, the likely countersteps of opponents, and so on.
5 Democratise: in the 'democratise' cluster of activities, policy analysis does not have a value-free orientation, but a normative and ethical objective: it should further equal access to, and influence on, the policy process for all stakeholders (DeLeon 1988, 1994; Lerner and Lasswell 1951). Experts and elites are more likely to be involved and carry greater weight than ordinary citizens and laymen (Fischer 1990). Policy analysis can try to correct this inequality by calling attention to views and opinions typically overlooked in policy-making and decision-making (Fischer 2000).
6 Mediate: policy analysts can play a role in enhancing the knowledge actors have about their own position, about the actors' room for manoeuvring, and in looking for possible compromises and win-win options. In addition, they can be involved in designing the rules and procedures for negotiating in a policy-making or decision-making process and managing the interaction and progress of that process. The mediation cluster comprises different types of activities, with a focus on analysing contextual factors (e.g. dependency analysis, transaction analysis), and designing, and possibly also facilitating, meetings in which different stakeholders and decision-makers consult and negotiate. The policy analyst can be involved during the design of the negotiation process as well as its execution.

In real-life cases and projects, a policy analyst will combine one or more activities, albeit not all at the same time. When more activities are combined, a policy analysis project will become richer and more comprehensive, but also more complex.

The hexagon in Figure 20.1 is a diagrammatic representation of these six activities. The theoretical foundation will be discussed later in this chapter, when we show the policy analysis styles and values on which the clustering of activities has been based. In this section, we focus on the six activities and illustrate these with the help of examples based on policy analyses.

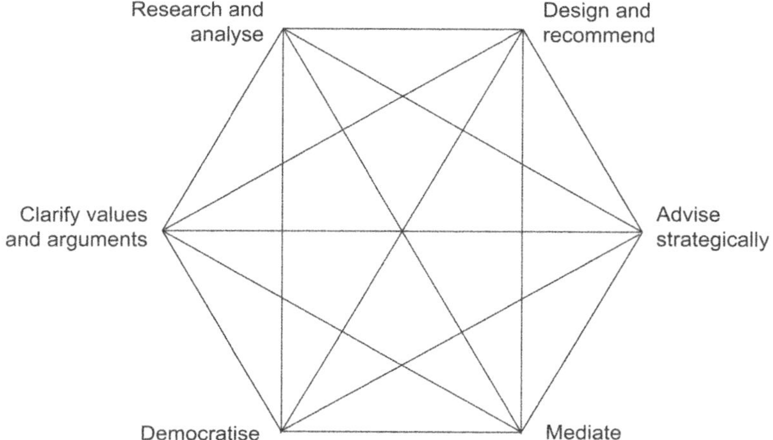


*Figure 20.1* Policy analysis tasks
Source: Mayer *et al.*. 2004. 'Perspectives on policy analysis: A framework for understanding and design', *International Journal of Technology, Policy and Management* 4(1): 169–91

At the end of this section, we will look at the relations between the various activities in more detail.

## Policy analysis styles

It is the objective of our model to clarify and understand the discipline of policy analysis. Numerous schools of thought, paradigms and models can be found in the policy analysis literature (Bobrow and Dryzek 1987; DeLeon 1988; Hawkesworth 1988; House and Shull 1991; Mayer 1997). In this chapter, we will refer to styles of policy analysis rather than to a paradigm, model or school. Based on the schools discussed in the literature and the framework of our model, we have identified six policy analysis styles. They are:

1 a rational style;
2 an argumentative style;
3 a client advice style;
4 a participatory style;
5 a process style;
6 an interactive style.

Figure 20.2 shows how these styles relate to the activities discussed above. Below, we will briefly discuss the styles in an archetypical manner. We will focus on the arguments that are used by proponents of these styles.

### *The rational style*

The rational style is shaped to a large degree by assumptions about knowledge and reality, and by a relatively large distance between the object and subject of study: it is assumed that the world is to a large extent empirically knowable and often measurable. Knowledge used for policy must be capable of withstanding scientific scrutiny. The role of knowledge in policy is a positive

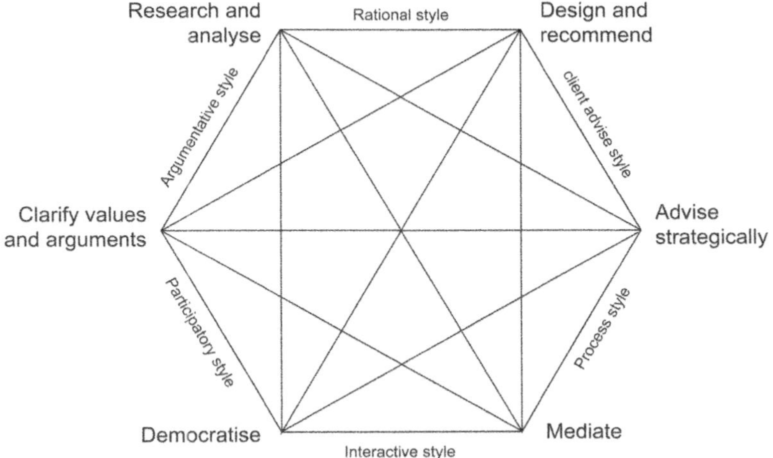


*Figure 20.2* Policy analysis styles
Source: Mayer *et al.* (2004) 'Perspectives on policy analysis: A framework for understanding and design', *International Journal of Technology, Policy and Management* 4(1): 169–91

one, namely a greater insight into causes, effects, nature and scale produces better policy (Weiss and Bucuvalas 1980). Policy should come about – preferably – in neat phases, from preparation to execution, with support through research in each phase. An example of this policy analysis approach is the systems analysis method developed by the RAND Corporation (Quade 1989; Miser and Quade 1985). The advice on policy regarding the Eastern Scheldt storm surge barrier in the Netherlands was obtained using this method (Goeller *et al.* 1977). This style is discussed in many general textbooks on methods of policy analysis (Patton and Sawicki 1986; MacRae and Whittington 1997; House and Shull 1991).

## Argumentative style

This style assumes that policy is made, defended and criticised through the medium of language. The basic assumption of the argumentative style is therefore that when analysing policy, it is important to devote attention to aspects related to the language game that takes place around a policy problem or issue. Attention will shift to the debate and the place in the debate of arguments, rhetoric, symbolism and stories (Fischer and Forester 1993; Fischer 1995; van Eeten 2001). Arguments aim to have an effect on the public. The positions of parties and the argumentations in a policy discourse are not always clear and unambiguous, however. Therefore, policy analysis will make policy easier to understand by illustrating the argumentations and the quality thereof schematically and making a judgement based on criteria such as justification, logic and richness (Dunn 1982, 1994). But the ambition of argumentative policy analysis is to use such an analysis to produce recommendations and improvements in situations where parties have been talking at cross-purposes for many years: a dialogue between the deaf (van Eeten 2001). The argumentative style assumes that it can make the structure and progress of the discourse transparent by means of interpretive and qualitative methods and techniques, and can also bring about improvements by identifying caveats in the debate or searching for arguments and standpoints that can bridge the gap between opponents. This style of policy analysis centres on discourse and argumentation analyses so as to frame the different standpoints of clusters of parties and, if possible, change and influence them.

## Client advice style

In a number of respects, the client advice style is based on assumptions that policy-making occurs in a complex and rather chaotic arena. There are numerous players, with different interests and strategies (de Bruijn and ten Heuvelhof 2000; de Bruijn *et al.* 2002). Therefore, it is wise to gain insight into the various objectives, means and interests of the actors involved. For that reason, the analysis of this complex environment is important and can be undertaken analytically and systematically by such means as stakeholder analyses, although intuition and soft information definitely play a role. Besides knowledge and insights gained through research, policy analysis is largely a question of politico-strategic insight and skills including client-analyst communication. In addition to being a skill, methodical and explicit, policy analysis is also an art in which tacit knowledge plays an important role (Wildavsky 1987). Depending on orientation, the client advice style involves a more design-oriented approach or a strategic, process-driven approach.

## Participatory style

Participatory policy analysis views the relationship between research and advice on the one hand and policy and politics on the other by looking at society critically (Fischer 1990, 2000). Here it is assumed that not all sections of the population have ready access to policy systems. Researchers, economic elites, institutionalised non-governmental organisations and politicians dominate policy discussions and decisions about major social issues (Jasanoff 1990). Researchers, stakeholders and policy-makers will even change roles and positions within one and the same system. Certain subjects and also certain groups of actors are often excluded from the social debate. This is referred to as the technocratic criticism of policy analysis (Fischer 1990). Participatory policy analysis assumes that citizens can have a voice and be or become interested enough to deliberate on substantive and politically difficult questions (Dryzek 1990; Fishkin 1991; Durning 1993; DeLeon 1994; Mayer 1997; Fischer 2000). The policy analyst can take on a facilitating role in such a debate by promoting equality and openness in the design and by giving ordinary citizens and laymen a role alongside others (Mayer 1997).

## Process style

Just as in a game of chess, the parties that participate in a policy-making process will exhibit strategic behaviour in the pursuit of their own objectives and achievement of the best possible positions, even if such action runs counter to the public interest formulated in policy (de Bruijn *et al.* 2002). It is perfectly understandable that, in controversial and complex issues, opponents will underpin their case with conflicting research reports. Impartial experts do not exist and a solution by way of new reports and studies can aggravate the problem in a certain sense. In fact, knowledge is (not much more than) negotiated knowledge. It is better to negotiate and reach agreements about the use of the results of a study or jointly contracting research (de Bruijn *et al.* 2002). The process style of policy analysis is based on the assumption that substantive aspects of a policy problem are, in fact, coordinate or perhaps even subordinate to the procedural aspects of a policy problem. The analyst or process manager creates 'loose coupling' of procedural aspects and substantive aspects of a problem. Procedural aspects are understood to be the organisation of decision-making or the way in which parties jointly arrive at solutions to a problem. To that end, agreements can be reached through 'mediation and negotiation'. If the procedural sides of a policy-making or decision-making process have been thought through properly, it will greatly increase the likelihood of substantive problems being resolved. Substantive problems can be made part of a process design, for example, by placing the different substantive aspects on the agenda.

## Interactive style

The interactive style of policy analysis assumes that individuals – experts, analysts, clients, stakeholders and target groups – have or may have differing views of the 'same' policy problem. An insight relevant to policy can be obtained by bringing about a confrontation and interaction of different views. The interactive style has a strong socio-constructive foundation. Different views of reality can be valid simultaneously. Through continuous interaction and interpretation – the 'hermeneutic circle' – it is possible to gain an 'insight' (Guba and Lincoln 1989).

In an interactive style of policy analysis, target groups and stakeholders are usually invited to structure problems or devise solutions in structured working meetings at which policy analysis techniques may be used (Mason and Mitroff 1981). This brings about a multiple interaction whereby the views and insights of the analyst, the client and also the participants are enriched (Edelenbos 1999). In other words, participants learn about their own views in relation to those of others, and have an opportunity to refine those views. The selection of views is obviously crucial. Political considerations – the power to obstruct – and enrichment arguments – what citizens really think – may be interwoven. What matters is the quality of the obtained insights in combination with the heterogeneity of opinions and interests. If policy analysis concerns the redevelopment of a city square, for example, stakeholders such as local residents and business people can be consulted by means of workshops about the problems they experience with the present arrangement of the square and their wishes with regard to the new plans. The interactive style assumes that a process like this is informative for decision-makers and planners, is more likely to lead to acceptance and fulfilment of the plans, and can bring about all kinds of positive effects among the participants (learning about each other and about policy processes) (ibid.).

## Definition of archetypal styles

Figure 20.3 shows the policy analysis styles placed in an 'archetypal' way between the different activities. This rightly suggests that a style balances on two important activities. This balance does not necessarily need to be in equilibrium. Participatory policy analysis balances between democratisation and clarification of values and arguments. The emphasis may be more on one activity than on the other: citizens can be directly involved in discussions about genetic technology, or the analyst may be mainly interested in the value systems, arguments and opinions of citizens about the technology and may want to systematise them for the purpose of policy advice.

The argumentative style balances between research and analysis and clarification of values and arguments. Some argumentative policy analysts attempt to improve the quality of policy by testing the policy design as thoroughly as possible, or by building on consistency, validity and so on, of the underlying arguments (Dunn 1994). This is based on the principle that 'claims' must be substantiated up by facts ('backings'). The 'formal logic' is dominant in this setting. Others reconstruct arguments, not in relation to scientific quality, but according to their variety and richness. This allows greater scope for normative systems, religion and intuitive arguments (Fischer 1995).

In a similar way, the rational style balances between researched analysis and advisory design; the interactive style between democratisation ambitions and mediation activities; the client advice

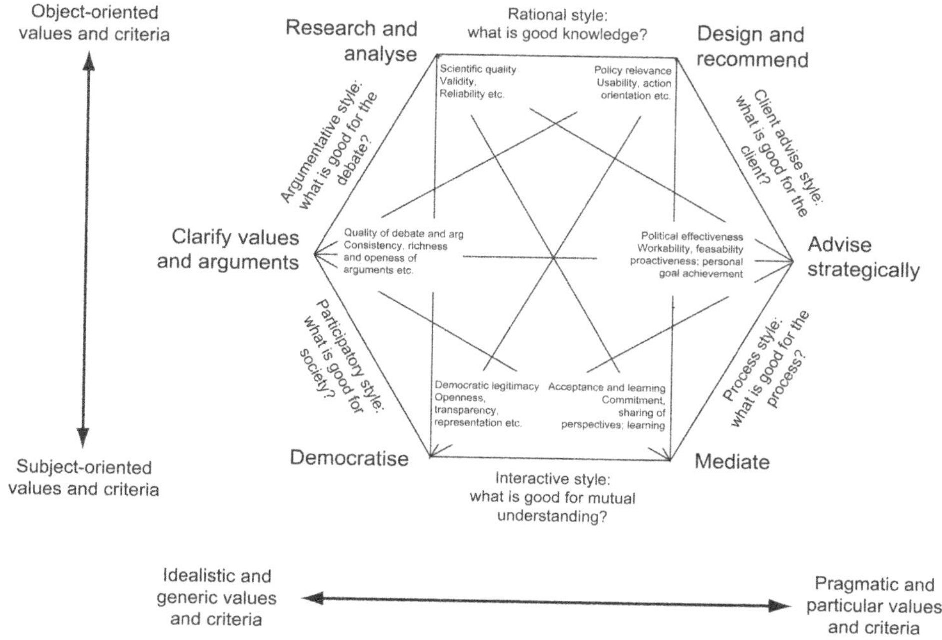


*Figure 20.3* The underlying values and criteria of policy analysis
Source: Mayer *et al.* (2004) 'Perspectives on policy analysis: A framework for understanding and design', *International Journal of Technology, Policy and Management* 4(1): 169–91

style between substantive design and strategic advice; and the process style between strategic advice and mediation. The styles of policy analysis may thus have different manifestations and emphases. A focus on a certain activity may result in a style leaning more towards one activity than to another.

## Combining activities

In the preceding sections of this chapter, we have differentiated between the policy analysis styles by showing that they balance between two activities. It is also possible to let go of the balance and to make combinations of activities that are not adjacent to one another. In other words, a policy analytic arrangement will be made whereby two or more activities that are opposite, rather than adjacent, to each other in the hexagon of Figure 20.1 can be combined. This kind of combination or arrangement, symbolised by the dashed diagonals in the hexagon, is achievable in two ways:

1 The activities can be carried out sequentially or separately, either in various parts of one policy analysis project or in different complementary or competing projects; i.e. a form of methodological triangulation of activities. As part of a policy analysis project focusing on climate change, for example, first research can be conducted by experts using climate models (activity: research) and subsequently the perceptions and arguments of ordinary citizens and laymen regarding climate change can be mapped out (activity: clarify arguments).
2 The various activities can be integrated into one design or method. As part of a project focusing on climate change, for example, climate models can be used to get various groups

of stakeholders, experts, politicians and so on to jointly generate and test policy proposals, while obtaining feedback from representative citizen panels. Such a design would integrate various activities: research, design, democratise and mediate.

## Underlying values

### *Evaluation criteria*

In addition to demarcating and understanding the field of policy analysis and designing a policy analysis project, our model has a third function: evaluation of policy analysis projects and methods (Twaalfhoven 1999). The various activities and styles are based on underlying values and orientations. The values determine in what way a policy analyst or others will view the quality of the policy analysis study and the criteria that will be applied to examine it. These criteria can be made explicit by addressing the following questions:

- Rational style: what is good knowledge?
- Argumentative style: what is good for the debate?
- Client advice style: what is good for the client/problem owner?
- Participatory style: what is good for democratic society?
- Process style: what is good for the process?
- Interactive style: what is good for mutual understanding?

Figure 20.3 shows that the activities in the top half of the hexagon are primarily object-oriented activities: a system, a policy design, an argumentative analysis. The activities at the bottom are subject-oriented activities. They focus primarily on the interaction between citizens, stakeholders, the analyst and the client. Whereas the top-half activities are usually captured in a product – e.g. a report, a design, a computer model – the effects of the bottom-half activities are usually captured in the quality of the process itself: increased support base, mutual understanding, citizenship, learning. The distinction 'object–subject' translates into the types of evaluation criteria to be applied. Object-oriented policy analysts will judge the quality of a policy analysis by its scientific rigor or the substantive insights it has yielded. Subject-oriented policy analysts will base their judgement on the contribution of the orchestrated interaction between stakeholders to the decision-making process. The turning point between object and subject-oriented activities lies with 'clarification of values and arguments' and 'provision of strategic advice'. These can be either object-oriented and/or subject-oriented.

Figure 20.3 also shows that the activities on the left-hand side are judged by idealistic and generic criteria for good policy analysis, such as validity, reliability, consistency, fairness, equality or openness. The activities on the right-hand side of the hexagon are judged by pragmatic and particular criteria, such as workability, usability, opportunity, feasibility or acceptance.

These criteria for evaluating the quality of a policy analysis project or method are summarised in Box 20.1 and appear in the corners of the hexagon in Figure 20.3.

### *The role of the policy analyst*

As the presented model is based on activities, styles and their associated values, it also generates and organises the positive and negative images, the metaphors, of the policy analyst (Dror 1967; Jenkins-Smith 1982; Durning and Osuna 1994). Some policy analysts allow themselves to be guided mainly by their wish to conduct objective scientific research; these are the objective

## *Box 20.1* Translation of values into quality criteria

### *Research and analyse*

Policy analysis will be judged by substantive (scientific) quality criteria, such as validity and reliability, the use and integration of state-of-the-art knowledge, the quality of data gathering and the formal argumentation and validation of conclusions.

### *Design and recommend*

Policy analysis will be judged by instrumental criteria of policy relevance, such as usability and accessibility for policy-makers, action orientation and utilisation, presentation and communication of advice, weighing up of alternatives, clear choices and so on.

### *Clarify values and arguments*

Policy analysis will be judged by quality of argumentation and debate criteria such as formal logic (consistency), informal logic (rhetoric and sophism), and quality of the debate in terms such as richness, layering and openness of arguments.

### *Advise strategically*

Policy analysis will be judged by pragmatic and political effectiveness criteria, such as the 'workability' of advice, political cleverness and proactive thinking, greater insight (for the client) in the complex environments (political and strategic dynamics, forces and powers), targeting and achievement of goals.

### *Democratise*

Policy analysis will be judged by democratic legitimacy criteria, such as openness and transparency of the policy-making process, representation and equality of participants and interests, absence of manipulation and so on.

### *Mediate*

Policy analysis will be judged by external acceptance and learning criteria, such as the agreement that mutually independent actors reach on the process and/or content, support for and commitment to the negotiating process and solutions, learning about other problem perceptions and solutions.

technicians. In contrast, others seek interaction with their client; these are the client advisers or counsellors. Some advocate a clear standpoint such as a more stringent environmental policy; these are the issue activists. How the role of a policy analyst is perceived depends on one's own values and position in a policy process. A skilful strategic advisor, for example, may be highly appreciated by his/her client, but portrayed as a hired gun by his/her client's opponents. In Table 20.1, positive and negative images of the role of the policy analysts are depicted for each activity.

*Table 20.1* Positive and negative images of the policy analyst

| *Activity* | *Positive role image* | *Negative role image* |
|---|---|---|
| Research and analyse | Independent scientist; objective researcher. | A-moral researcher; technocrat. |
| Design and recommend | Independent expert; engineer; impartial adviser. | Desk expert; 'back seat driver'. |
| Clarify values and arguments | Logician or ethicist; narrator. | Linguistic purist; 'journalist'. |
| Advise strategically | Involved client adviser; client counsellor; policy entrepreneur | 'Hired gun' |
| Democratise | Democratic (issue) advocate. | Missionary; utopian. |
| Mediate | Facilitator; mediator; process manager. | Manipulator; 'relativist'. |

Source: Mayer *et al.* (2004). 'Perspectives on policy analysis: A framework for understanding and design', *International Journal of Technology, Policy and Management* 4(1): 169–91

## Perspectives on the field of policy analysis

Figure 20.4 presents the complete conceptual model in which policy analysis activities are related to underlying styles and values and the policy analyst's roles. The figure enables us to demarcate all manifestations and varieties of policy analysis and also to develop new approaches and methods. Methods developed mainly within one style of policy analysis can be combined with insights from another style and adapted to new activities. Below, we will briefly recapitulate the functions of the model, namely demarcate, design and evaluate.

### *Reflection on policy analysis*

Policy analysis is characterised by ambitions but also by ambivalences. Various approaches criticise each other and it is very difficult to define and describe what policy analysis is. The added value of our model is that it shows why policy analysis is ambivalent and elusive, namely because the proponents and opponents reason from different points of departure, about what they are doing, why they are doing it, and the limitations or conversely the richness of the discipline. It is not our intention in this chapter to adopt a position on our preferred form of policy analysis, even if we were to have one. Depending on one's own position, one may accept the wide picture of policy analysis as depicted in our model, but it is likely that many will argue that certain styles or activities are not (proper) policy analysis (e.g. Lawlor 1996): for those critics, the hexagon may turn into a straight line, a triangle or a square. The problem, of course, is that there will be no disciplinary consensus on what activities and styles to cut from the hexagon and on what grounds. For every policy analytic style there are both proponents and critics. Given the actual and desirable development of the various definitions of policy analysis, we are of the opinion that it is better to define the discipline too widely than too narrowly. The integrated conceptual model offers full scope without losing the unity of the policy analysis and causing the disintegration of the field. The model offers the possibility to examine policy analyses already performed and to relate these to each other. The model seeks to provide a foothold, or a framework, for demarcating the wide field of work.

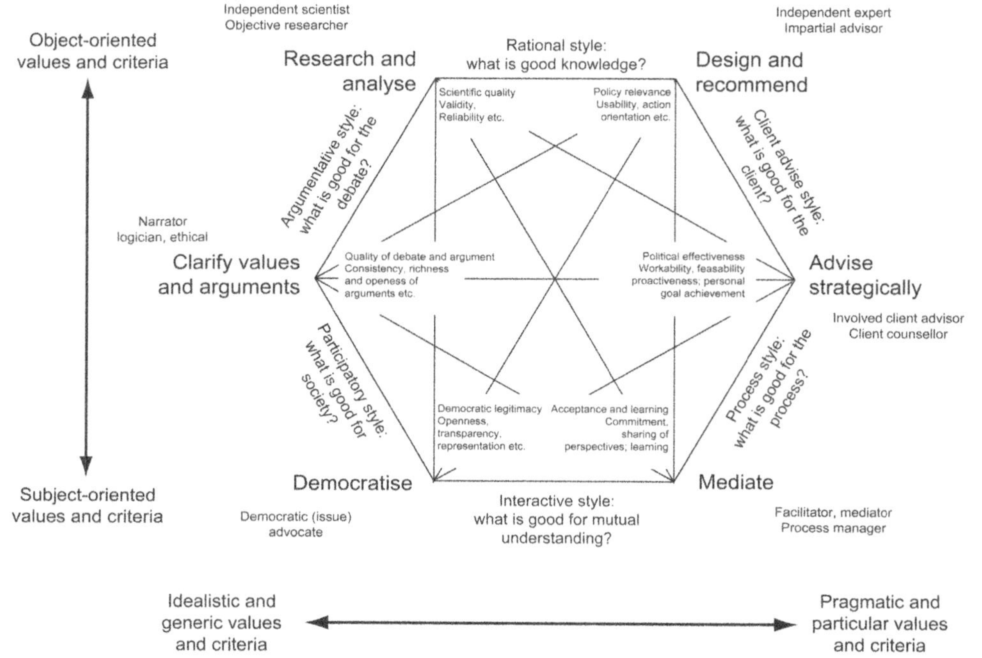


*Figure 20.4* Overview of the complete hexagon model of policy analysis
Source: Mayer *et al.* (2004). 'Perspectives on policy analysis: A framework for understanding and design', *International Journal of Technology, Policy and Management* 4(1): 169–91

## *Design of a policy analysis*

The model provides an overview of the wealth of possibilities of policy analysis studies and the interrelationships between them, and can be of help in reflecting consciously and creatively on the design of a policy analysis. As a rule, policy analysis projects require a customised design. It is possible, however, to fall back on standard methods of policy analysis, although the choice and combination of methods will depend on the problem under examination. The model definitely does not seek to prescribe instrumentally how a policy analysis should be designed. The opposite is the case, because we advocate creativity and innovation in designing approaches, actions and methods. Innovative combinations of researching, designing, recommending, mediating, argumentation and democratisation can be made. If desired, a rational style of policy analysis may be combined, for example, with a process style. This would 'interweave' analytical or scientific study in mediation processes between parties (de Bruijn *et al.* 2002).

We consider the design of policy analysis to include the development of new methods of policy analysis so as to allow a good integration of sub-activities. In point of fact, the history of policy analysis is characterised by the repeated application of creative and intelligent combinations of methods; methods that originated in one domain are translated into applications for other domains. The, by now, classical Delphi and scenario methods came about as methods for studying the future, but are currently used for strategic advice, mediation and even democratisation in policy Delphis, interactive scenario methods and scenario workshops (Mayer 1997). Cross-impact techniques and stakeholder analysis techniques, which came about as methods for advising clients, now have principally interactive applications and are used for mediation. Consensus conferences that came about as a method for study and mediation between leading experts in medical scientific controversies have been transformed into methods for democratising and for public participation (Mayer 1997; Fischer 2000).

### *Evaluation of a policy analysis*

Each policy analysis activity is based (implicitly) on values concerning the quality and purposes of the policy analysis. Therefore, policy analysis projects can be examined from different perspectives. This may lead to different opinions about success or failure, quality or shortcomings. A substantively thorough and valid study can be unusable for a client. A brilliant and workable compromise that breaks a stalemate may be based on negotiated nonsense (van de Riet 2003) or may violate or manipulate the interests of legitimate participants. Conflicts like these are almost inherent in every evaluation of sizeable policy analysis projects. In the design and evaluation, the policy analyst attempts to cope as well as possible with these tensions and dilemmas, either by making choices or by finding new routes.

## Conclusion

In this chapter we have presented a model for policy analysis based on six archetypal policy analysis activities. This subdivision makes it possible to relate various policy analysis styles found in the literature to each other and to analyse the characteristics of and differences between the styles. Additionally, the activities provide pointers for evaluating policy analyses. By explicitly identifying which activities are being pursued with the policy analysis, it is possible to use that information as a basis for identifying success criteria for the policy analysis. The developed framework seeks to map out transparently the enormous variety of different types of policy analyses and to allow them to be viewed in relation to each other. The model can also be used to design policy analysis studies. By making explicit which activities are relevant in a particular policy analysis, a conscious choice can be made for a certain policy analysis style and the policy analysis methods can be selected in a well-founded way for the contribution made by the method or technique to the activities that must be carried out.

While the developed framework provides pointers for reflection, design and evaluation, it is not intended to be a rigid, prescriptive model. Rather, the intention is for the policy analyst to be consciously working on the goal of the analysis in relation to the policy-making process and to produce his own policy analysis design and evaluation.

## Note

1 This chapter is a condensed and slightly adapted version of a journal article previously published as: I.S. Mayer; P.W.G. Bots and C.E. van Daalen. (2004). 'Perspectives on policy analysis: A framework for understanding and design', *International Journal of Technology, Policy and Management* 4(2): 169–91. The material has been reused with permission of the copyright owner.

## Bibliography

Bobrow, D. and J. Dryzek. 1987. *Policy Analysis by Design*. Pittsburgh, PA: University of Pittsburgh Press.
Brewer, G. and P. DeLeon. 1983. *The Foundations of Policy Analysis*. Homewood, IL: Dorsey.
de Bruijn, J. and E. ten Heuvelhof. 2000. *Networks and Decision-Making*. Utrecht: Lemma.
——, E. ten Heuvelhof and R. in 't Veld. 2002. *Process Management, Why Project Management Fails in Complex Decision-Making Processes*. Dordrecht: Kluwer.

DeLeon, P. 1988. *Advice and Consent: The Development of the Policy Sciences*. New York: Russell Sage Foundation.

—— 1994. 'Democracy and the policy sciences: Aspirations and operations', *Policy Studies Journal* 22: 200–12.

Dror, Y. 1967. 'Policy analysts: A new professional role in government service', *Public Administration Review* 27(3): 198.

Dryzek, J. 1990. *Discursive Democracy; Politics, Policy and Political Science*. Cambridge: Cambridge University Press.

Dunn, W. [1981]1994. *Public Policy Analysis: An Introduction*, 1st and 2nd edns. Englewood Cliffs, NJ: Prentice Hall.

—— 1982. 'Reforms as arguments', *Knowledge, Creation, Diffusion, Utilization* 3(3): 293–326.

Durning, D. 1993. 'Participatory policy analysis in a social service agency: A case study', *Journal of Policy Analysis and Management* 12(2): 297–322.

——and W. Osuna. 1994. 'Policy analysts, roles and value orientations: An empirical investigation using Q methodology', *Journal of Policy Analysis and Management* 13(44): 629–57.

Edelenbos, J. 1999. 'Design and management of participatory public policy making', *Public Management* 1(4): 569–78.

—— 2000. *Process in Shape*. PhD thesis. Lemma: Utrecht.

Fischer, F. 1990. *Technocracy and the Politics of Expertise*. Newbury Park, CA: Sage.

—— 1995. *Evaluating Public Policy*. Chicago: Nelson-Hall.

—— 2000. *Citizens, Experts and the Environment. The Politics of Local Knowledge*. Durham, NC: Duke University Press.

——and J. Forester (eds). 1993. *The Argumentative Turn in Policy Analysis and Planning*. Durham, NC: Duke University Press.

Fishkin, J. 1991. *Democracy and Deliberation: New Directions for Democratic Reform*. New Haven, CT: Yale University Press.

Goeller, B., A. Abrahamse, B.H. Bigelow, J.G. Bolten, D.M. De Ferranti, J.C. DeHaven, T.F. Kirkwood, R. Petruschell. 1977. *Protecting an Estuary from Floods: A Policy Analysis of the Oosterscheld*, vol. 1. Santa Monica, CA: Summary Report, prepared for the Netherlands Rijkswaterstaat.

Guba, E. and Y. Lincoln. 1989. *Fourth Generation Evaluation*. Newbury Park, CA: Sage.

Hawkesworth, M. 1988. *Theoretical Issues in Policy Analysis*. Albany, NY: State University of New York Press.

Hogwood, B. and L. Gunn. 1984. *Policy Analysis for the Real World*. Oxford: Oxford University Press.

Hoppe, R. 1998. 'Policy analysis, science, and politics: From "speaking truth to power" to "making sense together"', *Science and Public Policy* 26(3): 201–10.

House, P. and R. Shull. 1991. *The Practice of Policy Analysis; Forty Years of Art and Technology*. Washington, DC: Compass.

Jasanoff, S. 1990. *The Fifth Branch. Science Advisors as Policymakers*. Cambridge, MA: Harvard University Press.

Jenkins-Smith, H. 1982. 'Professional roles of policy analysts', *Journal of Policy Analysis and Management* 2(1): 88–100.

Lawlor, E. 1996. Book review of *The Argumentative Turn in Policy Analysis and Planning*, F. Fischer and J. Forester. (eds) *Journal of Policy Analysis and Management* 15(1): 110–46.

Lerner, D. and Lasswell, H. (eds). 1951. *The Policy Sciences, Recent Developments in Scope and Methods*. Stanford, CA: Stanford University Press.

Lynn, L. 1999. 'A place at the table: Policy analysis, its postpositive critics, and the future of practice', *Journal of Policy Analysis and Management* 18(3): 411–24.

MacRae, D. and D. Whittington. 1997. *Expert Advice for Policy Choice: Analysis and Discourse*. Washington, DC: Georgetown University Press.

Mason, R. and I. Mitroff. 1981. *Challenging Strategic Planning Assumptions. Theory, Cases and Techniques*. New York: John Wiley and Sons.

Mayer, I. 1997. *Debating Technologies: A Methodological Contribution to the Design and Evaluation of Participatory Policy Analysis*. Tilburg: Tilburg University Press.

——, C. Els van Daalen and Pieter W.G. Bots. 2004. 'Perspectives on policy analysis: A framework for understanding and design', *International Journal of Technology, Policy and Management* 4(1): 169–91.

Miser, Hugh J. and E.S Quade. 1985. *Handbook of Systems Analysis*. New York: North-Holland.

——and E. Quade. 1988. *Handbook of Systems Analysis: Craft Issues and Procedural Choices*. Chichester: John Wiley & Sons.

Patton, C. and D. Sawicki. 1986. *Basic Methods of Policy Analysis and Planning*. Englewood Cliffs, NJ: Prentice Hall.
Quade, E. 1975. *Analysis for Public Decisions*. New York: Elsevier.
Radin, B. 1997. 'Presidential address: The evolution of the policy analysis field: \from conversation to conversations', *Journal of Policy Analysis and Management* 16(2): 204–18.
Shulock, N. 1999. 'The paradox of policy analysis: If it is not used, why do we produce so much of it?', *Journal of Policy Analysis and Management* 18(2): 226–44.
Twaalfhoven, P. 1999. *The Success of Policy Analysis Studies: An Actor Perspective*. Delft: Eburon.
van De Riet, O. 2003. *Policy analysis in Multi-Actor Settings: Navigating between Negotiated Nonsense and Superfluous Knowledge*. Delft: Eburon.
van Eeten, M. 2001. 'Recasting intractable policy issues: The wider implications of the Netherlands civil aviation controversy', *Journal of Policy Analysis and Management* 20(3): 391–414.
Walker, W. 1988. 'Generating and screening alternatives', in H. Miser and E. Quade (eds) *Handbook of Systems Analysis: Craft Issues and Procedural Choices*. Chichester: John Wiley & Sons.
Weimer, D. and A. Vining, A. 1992. *Policy Analysis: Concepts and Practice*. Englewood Cliffs, NJ: Prentice Hall.
Weiss, C. and M. Bucuvalas. 1980. *Social Science Research and Decision-Making*. New York: Columbia University Press.
White, L. 1994. 'Policy analysis as discourse', *Journal of Policy Analysis and Management* 13(3): 506–25.
Wildavsky, A. 1987. *Speaking Truth to Power: The Art and Craft of Policy Analysis*. New Brunswick, NJ: Transaction Books.

# Part VI

# Understanding the decision-making process

# 21

# Bounded rationality and public policy decision-making

*Bryan D. Jones and H.F. Thomas III*

Underlying most approaches to the study of policy processes is a model of human choice.[1] This model rests upon critical aspects of the cognitive and emotional architectures of decision-makers. The particular aspects of human psychology that informs the major approaches in policy studies differ, but all share the common focus of requiring some assumptions about human nature. The Advocacy Coalition Framework is based on an analysis of the attitudes, beliefs and values of coalition participants. Punctuated Equilibrium Theory is based on shifts in the focus of collective attention, which requires an individual choice model based on attention and short-term memory. The Institutional Analysis and Development Framework centers on rational action by strategic actors, but with an understanding of the limits of full rationality and a focus on the abilities of citizens in smaller associations to focus on collective rather than individual benefits. In each case, some elements of cognitive processing beyond the maximization of goals assumed in the model of instrumental rationality, which is used in economics and in public choice and neo-institutional analyses in political science, are present.

It is not much of a stretch to argue that the model underlying virtually all studies of policy processes is bounded rationality. In this model, humans pursue goals, but they often fall prey to mistakes in doing so. These mistakes are not simple, but complex results of human cognitive architectures, and because the environments human decision-makers face is complex. Because they are fundamentally related to human psychology, they are liable to be repeated. This approach has the benefit of keeping the traditional role of strategic action in the picture, but allows for major deviations from optimum strategies.

In this chapter we review the genesis and development of bounded rationality and show how it has influenced the study of policy processes. Further, this chapter reviews the general research on bounded rationality relevant to the policy-making process, focusing specifically on bounded rationality as a microfoundational underpinning for the study of public policy. We show how bounded rationality is a superior microfoundation for most aspects of public policy, most particularly the prioritization of policy problems, and show how the theory of preferences can be reconciled with bounded rationality.

## Genesis and development of bounded rationality

Most scholars studying politics and government care little about the fine details of the specifics of human cognition; we are quite content to leave that to biologists, psychologists, and cognitive scientists. What we cannot escape, however, is the need for some firm foundation capable of linking human behavior to policy processes. That foundation must fulfill three criteria: first, it must do no harm (it should not mislead); second, it must allow us to move between individual-level processes and organizational processes in a more or less seamless manner; and third, it should be efficient, in that it does not drag in specifics of human behavior that are not needed to understand the policymaking process.

As we show below, the model of bounded rationality, as initially articulated by Herbert A. Simon and expanded by Simon, organizational theorists such as James A. March, and cognitive scientists, especially Allen Newell, does that, and that foundation has been available since 1958.

Simon made the first bold step toward the development of a model of decision-making capable of aiding the understanding of collective choice in organizations with the publication of *Administrative Behavior* (Simon 1945). Simon admits that the model articulated there consisted largely of "residual categories, and the positive characterization of the process of choice is very incomplete" (Simon 1977: xxix). By 1958, however, all the elements for producing an organizational and policy science based on a positive model of choice were in place. The basic elements of that model have been confirmed and reconfirmed by cognitive scientists in the laboratory and by students of organizations and policy processes in the field. Yet the approach, rather than serving as the undisputed decisional foundation for modern social science, has engendered much confusion and controversy. In political science, much time was spent fighting Simon's approach as "too scientific" for the humanistic study of politics; later the public choice approach simply ignored the model. Economists "went on counting angels on the heads of neoclassical pins" (Simon 1999: 113).

It is no accident that the behavioral model of choice came more or less directly from the behavioral discipline of political science. Simon gives great credit to his participation as a student in Charles Merriam's behavioral revolution at the University of Chicago's Department of Political Science in the 1930s (Simon 1996a: Chapter 4). The scientific tenets of political behavioralism were strong on observation and quantification and not so strong on theory; the movement had a clearly inductive flavor. It demanded real-world observation—Merriam wanted to make a difference in the conduct of public policy as well as in the conduct of scientific inquiry.

## The tenets of bounded rationality

Simon developed bounded rationality as a critique of fully rational decision-making; what Simon later termed the "behavioral theory of choice" was an attempt to state the positive aspects of a theory of human choice based on scientific principles of observation and experiment rather than the postulation and deduction characteristic of theoretical economics. We first review the principles of bounded rationality, and then turn to the modern conceptions of the behavioral theory of choice. The tenets of bounded rationality can be summarized in four straightforward principles. While research in many fields of social science has advanced our understanding over the years, the basic formulation occurred in *Administrative Behavior* (Simon 1945).

*Principle of intended rationality*. Simon's model is enshrined in the crucial principle of intended rationality. That is, it starts with the notion that people are goal-oriented, but often fail to accomplish this intention because of the interaction between aspects of their cognitive architectures and the fundamental complexity of the environment they face (Simon 1977: xxvii; March 1994). Intellectually, this notion did not begin with Simon; it probably began with Vilfredo Pareto. In *Mind and Society* he distinguished logical, illogical, and non-logical behavior (Pareto 1935).[2] Logical behavior is rational choice; it is ends-means reasoning where means are appropriate to goals. Illogical behavior is behavior not rooted in ends-means thinking; Pareto thought little human behavior (at least of interest to a social scientist) was illogical. Non-logical thought involved "sentiments and residues" that could interfere with logical thinking. In a way, then, we might term the principle of intended rationality the "Pareto-Simon Principle".

The principle of intended rationality implies that we look at the goal-directed behavior of people, and investigate the manner in which their cognitive and emotional constitutions concomitantly promote and interfere with goal-directed behavior. It implies, of course, that "Rationality does not determine behavior... Instead, behavior is determined by the irrational and nonrational elements that bound the area of rationality" (Simon 1945: 241).

Bounded rationality is not simply a lack of calculational ability (see Lupia *et al.* 2000: 9). Simon, March, and Newell all stressed that calculations were a minimal part of the difficulty, easily solved via notepads, calculating machines, or a bureau of accountants. Simon does write extensively, however, about attention, emotion, habit, and memory, exploring the functionality and dysfunctionality of these aspects of the architecture of human cognition. And it is true that a prime component of the behavioral model of choice is difficulty in planning and executing long behavior sequences in complex environments (Jones 2001: 61). But this aspect of the model should not be confused with calculational difficulties.

*Principle of adaptation.* The principle of adaptation stems most directly from the studies of Allen Newell and Herbert Simon in human problem-solving, and is best stated in Simon's *The Sciences of the Artificial* (1996b). The claim is that most human behavior is explained by the nature of the "task environment." Given enough time, human thought takes on the shape of the tasks facing it—that is, human thought is adaptive and basically rational. Simon put it this way: "There are only a few 'intrinsic' characteristics of the inner environment of thinking beings that limit the adaptation of thought to the shape of the problem environment. All else in thinking and problem-solving behavior ... is learned and is subject to improvement" (Simon 1996b: 54). From this principle comes the inference that, in general, the more time one spends on a problem, the more likely the decision-maker's understanding of the problem will approximate the actual task environment, and the limitations of human cognitive architecture fades (Newell 1990).

Psychologists stress the distinction between central and peripheral mental processing (Fiske and Taylor 1991: 475–80). Kuklinski and Quirk put it this way:

> In central processing, used when attention and motivation are high, people employ more mental resources, think more systematically, and allow data to shape inferences. In peripheral processing, used when attention and motivation are low, they employ fewer resources, rely on simple heuristics, and use top-down, stereotypic inferences.
>
> *(2000: 163)*

*Principle of uncertainty:* One of the major contributions of decision theory has been to understand uncertainty in light of the calculus of probabilities. We speak of "expected utility" and think of outcomes as following a probability distribution. Unfortunately this does not tell the full story of uncertainty in human decision-making. Students of human choice in real-world or in laboratory situations again and again find that people have great difficulties in working with probabilities, assessing risk, and making inferences where uncertainty is involved. Indeed, a whole field of endeavor has emerged that studies the factors responsible for perceptions of risk; clearly these perceptions are not just rooted in "nature" but also involve human psychology.

An underlying tenet of bounded rationality from its early years centered on how human cognitive architecture interacted with an uncertain world; bounded rationalists saw uncertainty as far more fundamental to choice than the probability calculus implied (March 1994). If one's understanding of the causal factors involved in a problem is hazy or ambiguous, then the uncertainty is not contained, but reverberates through the entire thought process. If one is uncertain about how to specify outcomes, then one must also be uncertain about how to specify one's utility function. Simon termed this difficulty "the design problem" to denote that the fundamental nature of specifying a problem-space within which to solve problems.

*Principle of trade-offs.* People have a very difficult time with trading off one goal against another in a choice (Slovak 1990; Tetlock 2000). The classical economic model depicts trade-offs as smooth indifference curves, and modern rational choice theory offers little new in the theoretical study of trade-offs. The first behavioral tool for understanding trade-offs was Simon's notion of "satisficing." His idea that "administrative man"—an individual in an organization—chooses alternatives that are "good enough" has led critics to claim that the notion is just a poverty-stricken version of maximization (Lupia *et al.* 2000: 9). However, if one adds information and decision-making cost constraints to choice, this will not cause bounded rationality to dissolve into maximizing behavior. Satisficing describes the cognitive difficulties people have with trade-offs. Because of the operation of limited attention spans, people work on goals sequentially. As a consequence, trade-offs among goals is very difficult. The response, argues Simon, is for people to set "aspiration levels" on the goals they wish to achieve. If a choice is "good enough" (that is, if it exceeds aspiration levels) on all goals, then it is chosen.

Other models of choice among multiple goals have been developed, including the *lexicographic strategy* (choose the strategy that maximizes gain on the most salient goal and ignore the rest) and elimination by aspects (use a lexicographic strategy unless there is a tie among alternatives; then and only then use a second goal to break the tie). In an important particular, people have considerable difficulty in trading off benefits against losses, something that standard utility maximization theory treats as straightforward (Kahneman and Tversky 1979).

## The behavioral theory of choice

While great strides have been made in recent years by psychologists and behavioral economists studying choices in the controlled arrangements of the laboratory, only serious field study can indicate how real choices are made in the "structured yet dynamic" environments of real choice situations. Bounded rationality and the behavioral theory of choice came from organization theory; indeed, March (1994) once noted that breakthroughs in the study of human cognition were likely to come from a study of organizations. Laboratory findings of systematic violations of principles of behavior based on expected utility calculation are dramatic and widespread (Camerer 1998; Camerer and Thaler 1995; Thaler 1991, 1992), yet this says little about choice in the field where behavior can be adaptive and responsive to multiple feedback streams (Laitin 1999). As a consequence of the single-minded focus on experimental design and rejecting various tenets of expected utility, behavioral economists have termed their own literature "the anomalies literature" (Thaler 1988, 1992). Several political scientists have criticized experimental psychology and the behavioral economics literature for its seeming ad hoc nature, building findings experimental effect by experimental effect. David Laitin (1999) notes that in everyday actions people are adaptive, avoiding many of the traps set for them in experiments.

Much recent debate has centered on the viability of expected utility theory given the laboratory findings. This debate is to a large extent misplaced, because since the late 1950s a full model of choice, the behavioral model of choice, has been available. It avoids the "anomalies" problem, is parsimonious, and yields more accurate predictions on aggregate choices such as we observe in studying policy processes than does comprehensive rationality.

Bounded rationality points to the limits of rational adaptation; behavioral choice theory provides a body of literature that shows how human choice works. As we noted above, bounded rationality and the associated behavioral theory of choice are open-ended; we do not know everything about human choice and we learn more every year. But we know a lot, and we know enough to specify the outlines of what aspects of human cognition must be incorporated to formulate a general theory of human choice. We would cite the following:

1 *Long-term memory:* humans learn by encoding experience (direct or secondary) into rules that specify action to be taken in response to categories of stimuli.
2 *Short-term memory:* human cognitive capacities include a "front end" that extracts features from the world around them, categorizes them as relevant or irrelevant (in the former case, they become "stimuli") and prioritizes them.
3 *Emotions set priorities:* in an initial encounter with a choice situation, the major mechanism for weighting the relevance of stimuli is emotion.
4 *Central versus peripheral processing:* when attention and emotion are aroused, information processing shifts toward problem analysis and search. When they are not, the decision-maker relies on prepackaged solutions.
5 *The preparation-search trade-off:* if the front-end system indicates a need for action, humans can take two paths: draw upon previously prepared and stored rules specifying how to respond to the category that the stimulus has been placed in, or search for new responses.
6 *Identification:* People identify emotionally with the previously prepared solutions that they have encoded in memory. They tend to become emotionally attached to their current repertoire of encoded solutions, even as the problems they face evolve. As a consequence, reliance on prepared solutions dominates search.

## Heuristics

Heuristic decision-making plays a key role in most of the basic theories of policy processes. The notion was a critical component of the problem-solving studies of Newell and Simon (1972). Heuristics, or shortcuts, are strategies that people employ to cope with the bounds of their cognitive architectures. Jon Bendor (2010: 1) notes that political science harbors two orientations toward heuristics. On the one hand some political scientists report that "decision-makers often manage to do 'reasonably well'—even in complex tasks—despite their cognitive limitations." He puts Lindblom's theory of "muddling through" (1959) and Wildavsky's (1964) budgetary studies in this category. On the other hand, in the work of other political scientists, "the emphasis is on how people make mistakes even in simple tasks," an orientation common in much of psychology (where the terms "heuristics and biases" often go together), and in studies of voting behavior in political science. Newell and Simon saw that both facets were operative at once. For example, in their experiments, when people found that a problem-solving strategy would not work, they found another through trial and error search. In contrast, when presented with a problem logically similar to the one they just addressed, many went back to the failed first-choice strategy of the earlier problem.

A critical component of the problem-solving approach of Newell and Simon is the separation of problem from solution spaces (Newell 1990). Most decision-making occurs without much analysis of the problem-space. Decision-makers assume that they know the dimensions of a problem and apply a known solution from memory. Basically, decision-makers can either search memory for a prepackaged solution, or they can engage in search for new solutions. Because it is less costly to use a prepackaged solution from memory, this is the route most typically taken.

The separation of problem-space and solution-space is a fundamental component of the policy process field. The garbage can theory of organizational decision-making rests on this distinction (Cohen *et al.* 1972), as does the work of Kingdon (1984) on agenda-setting and public policy. In these studies, solutions and problems are not linked causally, but are unified by collective attention. When a problem emerges, solutions are likely to be attached without prior analysis of the problem-space.

Fernandes and Simon (1999) applied the process-tracing methodology initially developed by Newell and Simon (1972) in their problem-solving experiments to the complex and ill-structured problems characteristic of policy issues. Fernandes and Simon wondered if the professional identifications among doctors led to different problem-solving strategies. They found a heavy reliance on what they termed a *Know* → *Recommend* strategy among many participants that hindered their use of information in problem-solving.

Ill-structured problems lend themselves to the application of prepackaged solution sets that participants bring to the problem-solving enterprise. These prepackaged "solution sets" (Jones and Bachelor 1993) can derive from ideology, or professional identification, or current organizational practices. Whatever its source, it suggests a major limitation in one of the fundamental principles of bounded rationality: what we termed the principle of adaptation above. But it operates *away from* comprehensive rationality, and it cannot be construed as some sort of "heuristic" shortcut for limiting search costs. It may be in moderation, but current studies suggest that it is overused to the point of interfering with adaptation. This is an important finding capable of being linked to collective decision-making (see Brown 2001).

The *Know* → *Recommend* strategy has powerful implications for public policy. In many cases in which attention and emotion are aroused, people may insist on rigidly reaching for old solutions to problems, regardless of their applicability to the current issue. Hinich and Munger (1994) note that ideologies organize the political (and policy) world, so it is not surprising that solutions more amenable to a particular ideological world view are viewed as appropriate, even when evidence shows them to have failed in the past. Jones and Williams (2008), who studied tax policies, and Schrad (2010), who studied alcohol control, show in two very different policy-making situations the role of bad policy ideas in leading to policy failures. Bad policy ideas are defined as those resulting in a policy that "isn't working, hasn't ever worked, and runs the risk of causing great damage" (Schrad 2010: 208). Yet, the committed activists in both cases rushed to claim effects for policies that had already been discredited.

This commitment to prior solutions, based on cognitive and emotional identification, provide an important limit to the principle of adaptation. In such cases, much central processing effort is expended, but most of it goes to justifying previously employed solutions—a condition known as *motivated reasoning* (Kunda 1990; Lodge and Taber 2000).

## Organizations

The six aspects of human cognition, and their influences on heuristic decision-making, obviously do not deal with every aspect of human behavior that could influence the policy process, but they cover much ground, and lay the basis for a general behavioral theory of choice in organizations and institutions. Most importantly, they form a basis for "scaling up" the behavior of humans to organizations and policy processes. One of the continuing challenges for those scholars working in the bounded rationality tradition is the movement from models of human decision-making to those characterizing organizations and interactions of organizations in policy-making systems.

While organizations clearly free humans by extending their capacities to achieve goals, being human inventions they also fall prey to aspects of human cognitive architecture in predictable ways. Major aspects of the behavioral theory of organization parallel major facets of the behavioral theory of human choice:

1 *Organizational memory:* organizations encode experience into rules, routines, and standard operating procedures that specify action to be taken in response to categories of stimuli.
2 *Agenda-setting:* organizational capacities include a "front end" that extracts features from the world, categorizes them as relevant or irrelevant (in the former case, they become "stimuli") and prioritizes them. Agenda-setting in organizations parallels the short-term and attention "bottleneck" (Simon's term) afflicting human cognition.
3 *Parallel processing:* a major way that organizations expand human capacities is the ability to process information in parallel. By decentralizing and delegating, organizations can process multiple streams of input simultaneously (Simon 1983; Jones 1994). This organizational strategy presupposes considerable "peripheral processing" relying on preprogrammed solutions.
4 *Serial processing:* the search for new solutions is activated only when previously prepared solutions encoded in organizational routines are judged to be inadequate. Then organizations move from peripheral to central processing (or from parallel processing to serial processing).
5 *Emotional contagion:* in policy-making, emotional commitment and contagion are crucial elements in mobilizing for major initiatives. Moving from parallel to serial processing is invariably accompanied by emotional arousal by participants (Jones 1994).
6 *Identification:* people identify emotionally as well as cognitively with the organizations they participate in, or even parts of an organization, which Simon termed "sub-goal identification." Organizational identification is a great resource for leaders. Patriotism or religious zeal or even pride in performing their jobs can push people to actions that would be unthinkable in a calm cost-benefit analysis. But it also can make it difficult for leaders to shift strategies when they find it necessary to do so.

The relationships between organizational decision-making and individual decision-making are not metaphorical; they are *causal* (Jones 2001). One cannot really understand how organizations operate without a strong sense of how individuals process information and make decisions. As a consequence, a firm scientific foundation for policy studies must be rooted in a behavioral approach to organizations (see Green and Thompson 2001).

## Information-processing

A political science relying on behavioral choice theory will invariably be drawn toward the study of information-processing and problem-solving. It will be less focused on questions of preferences and equilibria. The nature of the behavioral assumptions influences the choice of topics for study. It is not that preferences and equilibria are not interesting subjects, well worthy of study. It is that they have been attended to far out of proportion to their explanatory power.

The focus on equilibrium processes has as its underpinning a narrow conception of choice, based on the notion of fixed preferences that lead actors to choose strategies that maximize those preferences. It is often found in modern studies of legislatures and public agencies. Early students of public administration were concerned with how organizations and democracy were intermeshed, whether a pluralism of interests generated by Roosevelt's "alphabet soup" of regulatory agencies could fit with a single "overhead control" model of democracy. However, much recent scholarship has relied heavily on the principal agent approach, in which the issue for a principal, such as collectively acting legislature, involves controlling the actions of a delegate, such as a bureaucratic agency, which receives delegated authority. This has resulted in a public administration that has overly focused on the single issue of control—and control solely through formal incentives (primarily punishment). The rich insights of behavioral choice have devolved into a discredited Skinnerian psychology—the incentive controls the behavior. It is ironic that

Skinner's study of pigeons and mice and the comprehensive rationality of economics both lead to the same impoverished model of human choice: only formal incentives matter.

The adoption of an overly limited model of human behavior has led to inadequate development of other aspects of bureaucratic behavior. Models based on principal agency have problems in confirmation (see, for example, Brehm and Gates 1997; Balla 1998; Carpenter 1996; Balla and Wright 2001). Brehm and Gates (1997: 578) comment that "the primary contribution is ... our finding of the overwhelming importance of attributes of the organizational culture in determining subordinates' levels of compliance." Miller (1992) has shown the critical importance of organizational culture as well.

In addition, public bureaucracies are important in the process of providing and interpreting information for the legislative branch. Because the environment of policy-making is both uncertain and ambiguous, delegating information processing to public agencies is common and necessary in legislatures. One cannot control what one does not understand (Workman *et al.* 2009).

## Attention-driven choice in public policy

The basis for the behavioral model of choice is the processing of information. Information is not predefined or packaged; rather it is often vague, ambiguous, and most importantly, is generated from multiple sources. The receiver of the information is as important as the sender (Jones 2001: Chapter 4). In modern complex environments, neither individuals nor organizations respond simply to stimuli. They must attend, prioritize, and select an appropriate response. As a consequence, there is no clear, one-to-one mapping between potential stimuli or events and actions.

A major key to understanding information-processing in people and in organizations is the allocation of attention. In his study of municipal budgeting, John Crecine (1969) noted that city agencies developed *attention rules* that indicated what aspects of the environment ought to be monitored for indicators of change that could need addressing. These rules did not tell the agency what to do; only what to attend to. Similarly Jones (1980) found in a study of Chicago building code enforcement that informal norms generally supplanted the complexities of the code, but that supervisors occasionally sent out signals to field inspectors that all violations were to be recorded in potentially "hot" cases. Differential code enforcement resulted as a consequence of these attention rules. Research by Armstrong *et al.* (2003) indicates that media attention to disease is not simply related to mortality and morbidity of disease, and this attention seems to mediate output indicators, such as investment in cures and related science.

Attention is different from any other resource type variable because one cannot allocate it proportionally to one's priorities at any one instance. Attention is selective; select one aspect of an environment for study and inattention must be paid to the rest of the environment. Attention is partially under the control of a decision-maker, but cognitively we possess no comprehensive system for monitoring when enough attention has been devoted to a topic. As a consequence, shifts in attentiveness are in large part hostage to emotional arousal. Because attention shifts are governed by emotion, they are unavoidably disjointed. Since, in many cases, the devotion of other resources follows attention, past decisions are a residue of past allocations of attention. They may or may not be consistent—great inconsistencies in choices are a result of attention.

The allocation of attention strongly affects the manner in which individuals or organizations prioritize problems for action. Because attention is disjointed and episodic, so is problem-prioritization. Because problems are prioritized in policy-making systems through attention, and attention is disjointed, policy-making is disjointed and episodic, not necessarily related to the severity of indicators. Similarly attention to solutions given that a problem has been prioritized is governed by attention—oftentimes directed at solutions that have been used before, even when they have been unsuccessful in the past (Jones and Williams 2008; Schrad 2010).

## Disproportionate information-processing and institutional friction

So far, we have addressed the scaling up of the model of bounded rationality to the level of the single organization. Now we will need to address full policy-making systems—those composed of interacting organizations. The key to this scaling up is the notion of *disproportionate information-processing* (Jones 2001). A policy-making system may be considered fully adaptive to the extent that it responds appropriately to the information coming in from its environment. Yet systems comprised of boundedly rational decision-makers are not capable of responding proportionately—a direct implication of attention-driven choice and other mechanisms rooted in bounded rationality (Jones and Baumgartner 2005). The result is episodic policy-making as policy-makers shift from addressing one set of problems to a different set.

Research focusing on explaining the episodic nature of policy change over time cites two mechanisms: institutional friction and positive feedback. Disproportionate information-processing in policy-making systems stems from a continual interaction between the conservative forces of policy stasis governed by negative feedback processes and the cascades of policy action governed by a collective sense of urgency among policy-makers. Jones and Baumgartner (2005) examine how government attends to, interprets, and prioritizes diverse incoming information streams within a boundedly rational framework. In their approach, human cognitive processing interacts with policy-making institutions to determine responses to incoming information.

In the model, institutional friction results from the interaction of two kinds of costs: *decision costs*, which are those imposed by the operation of institutional rules (such as those required by the constitutional system of divided powers in American federal government) and *cognitive costs* associated with boundedly rational decision-makers operating in a complex and changing environment (Jones *et al.* 2003; Jones and Baumgartner 2005). Baumgartner *et al.* further define the mechanism:

> Institutional friction in the form of sunk costs, long-term budgetary commitments, identification with means rather than ends, and bureaucratic inertia makes it hard for governments to reduce attention to issues that are improving just as it inhibits them from paying attention to problems that are just emerging.
>
> *(2009: 608)*

Empirical results in the US and elsewhere show that increased friction from these sources lead to more pronounced patterns of overreaction and underattention in policy-making. If friction is understood as strong resistance to change over time (and not as the static concept of 'gridlock'), major shifts in policy can occur when it is overcome (Jones and Baumgartner 2005). This generally occurs when "errors accumulate"—that is, when the system is "far enough" out of balance with its environment that it lurches forward.

## Disproportionate information-processing and positive feedback

The friction approach to incorporating disproportionate information processing into a model of policy change is essentially passive—pressures build up and cause attention to shift from one problem to another, which is then addressed. This resistance is in part a function of cognitive limitations and heuristic decision-making, so it incorporates elements of bounded rationality. A second aspect of disproportionality, based on positive feedback, is active. Positive feedback operates to amplify a process rather than to damp it down (as is the case for negative feedback processes). Positive feedback mechanisms can lead to contagion effects and the breakdowns of control mechanisms, and are well known in both natural and social sciences.

Well-ordered and equilibrium processes always involve negative feedback systems. The "wisdom of crowds" argument (Surowiecki 2004) claims that decisions or judgments made through the aggregation of individual choices often leads to accurate and rational conclusions. So it seems that rational decisions in systems stem from averaging out the individual errors. The theory is based on independent decision-making, each actor making his or her own judgment. Unfortunately, communication and interaction among individuals can easily lead to the rapid breakdown of the theory, as mimicking can bias outcomes. Experimental evidence in sociology confirms this argument, suggesting that the breakdown of the "wisdom of crowds" effect can be undermined through social influence among actors (Lorenz *et al.* 2010).

A weight-guessing game, perhaps involving a carnival crowd offering suggestions on a particular hog's size, offers an illustrative example. Here, the independence of individuals and a lack of communication would likely yield a close prediction of the hog's actual size at the average (Galton 1907). Yet if carnival attendees are allowed to communicate and discuss their potential guesses while they examine the hog and place their bets, a bounded rationality microfoundation would predict considerable deviation from the actual weight of the hog as cue-taking and information cascades ensue. A propensity to mimic neighbors and authority figures, take cues to reduce decisions costs, and the cascade of information (say from one side of the hog to the other) would generate a set of guesses subject to fluctuation, bias, and inaccuracy.

This amplification mechanism is found in political bandwagons, in fads of fashion, and in financial markets, bubbles and crashes (Mackay 1841). Shiller (2005) discusses the psychology of herding, or irrational exuberance, among investors whereby price increases beget further price increases in a consecutive loop of speculative confidence. Sornette (2004) and Youssefmir *et al.* (1998) focus on how unchecked feedback can generate asset-pricing bubbles and cause their subsequent collapse. Beyond finance, examples of positive feedback and cascades abound, and include: city growth (Gabaix 1999), the superstardom of pop musicians (Chung and Cox 1994), fashion trends and cultural change (Bikhchandani *et al.* 1992), website links (Barbási 2002), restaurant popularity (Becker 1991), standing ovations (Miller and Page 2004), and credit for scientific findings (Merton 1968), among others.[3]

Political scientists address feedback mechanisms in research spanning the discipline (see Baumgartner and Jones 2002 for a review). For example, scholars of the news media (Boydstun 2008), interest group behavior (Baumgartner and Leech 2001; Leech *et al.* 2005; Halpin 2011), agenda-setting (Baumgartner and Jones 1993), state-level diffusion of innovations (Boushey 2011), decision-making in Congress (Kingdon 1977; Matthews and Stimson 1975), presidential primaries (Bartels 1988), collective action (Lohmann 1994) and social movements (Chong 1991) all discuss the amplifying role of positive feedback in terms of cue-taking, bandwagons, cascades, contagion, and momentum related to various political phenomena.[4]

Linking these two mechanisms of positive feedback and institutional friction, Jones and Baumgartner (2005) argue that cascades may be critically important to our understanding of policy outcomes. They describe a gap between a distribution of real-world budget outlays and another predicted by their friction model, and conclude that friction alone does not fully explain budget distributions. They see positive feedback as a likely candidate for the difference, and suggest that "it may turn out that cascades are the key to understanding how friction is overcome in policy systems" (ibid. 139).

## Bounded rationality and stochastic processes

In rational models of action, people act proportionately to the information they receive. They attend to everything simultaneously and make trade-offs effortlessly. They avoid punctuated outputs except where inputs are disjointed and episodic, or where rules do not allow for the easy adjustment of outputs to inputs. Organizations composed of rational participants respond directly and efficiently to information discounted by costs. Organizations composed of boundedly rational participants cannot avoid punctuated outputs, because they cannot adjust their behaviors to incoming information of any degree of complexity.

Bounded rationality and behavioral choice lead to predictions about policy outcomes that imply that organizational outputs will be disjointed and episodic regardless of first, the input stream and second, the cost structure of the organization. It is clear that decision costs in the policy-making process can cause disjoint outputs. For example, in the American system of separated powers, considerable changes in the preferences of policy-makers can occur without producing policy change because of the need to assemble majorities in all responsible branches (Hammond and Miller 1987). If we were able to discount these "decision costs" bounded rationality implies that disjointed and episodic behavior would still occur. Examination of a number of different distributions of outcomes from political institutions and the policy-making process in the US, finds that, regardless of the institutional cost structure, outputs are punctuated (Jones *et al.* 2003; Jones and Baumgartner 2005).

Because of the disproportionate information processing described above, the traditional approaches to analysis based on point prediction and regression analysis can be misleading. It is too difficult (and perhaps meaningless) to try to tie a particular event of flow of information to a particular outcome. Students of organizational processes have begun to make use of stochastic process approaches, in which efforts are made to understand the processes underlying an entire distribution of outputs rather than a particular response to a policy innovation or other change (Padgett 1980, 1981; Jones *et al.* 2003). Disproportionate information processing implies leptokurtic ("fat-tailed") distributions of output changes (such as annual changes in a government's budget) regardless of the input distribution. Because of the phenomenon of disproportionate information-processing, decision-makers are forever underreacting to stimuli that require action, and overreacting with cascading behavior when the problem is fully recognized (Jones 2001; Jones *et al.* 2003). The underreacting results in the slender peak of the leptokurtic distribution, while the fat tails indicate the rapid changes that occur in the overreacting stage.

## Concluding comments

Psychologists, neuroscientists, behavioral economists, and students of political behavior have accumulated a great amount of information since the studies of Newell and Simon 40 years ago. Not only have these studies shown where failures in human rationality exist, they have also found adaptive capacities in human action, even in complex modern environments (Gigerenzer and Goldstein 1996; Gigerenzer 2001). In general, while the tenets of cognitive rationality have been repeatedly undermined by these studies, those of bounded rationality have fared much better.

Policymaking systems are comprised of multiple organizations, each of which incorporates numerous human actors. In order to serve as a microfoundation for understanding policy process, we need to avoid getting overly consumed by the details of human cognition (see Bendor 2010: 44–7 for a discussion). What are the important elements of a microfoundation for the study of policy processes, one rooted in the scientific and empirical findings on human cognation and information-processing?

In this chapter we have discussed those elements of human cognition that we see as critical for policy process scholars to understand, and shown how those elements may be scaled up to the levels of the organization and the policy-making system. While models of strategic interaction among rational actors are (relatively) easy to scale up, the same cannot be said for a more realistic empirically based cognitive foundation. As a consequence, less effort has been expended in achieving this scaling up than we think desirable.

## Notes

1 This chapter draws heavily on Jones (2003).
2 Our thanks to Fred Thompson for drawing this link.
3 See Schelling 1978 for an early overview as well as Miller and Page 2007 for a recent review of positive feedback in complex adaptive systems.
4 See also Pierson (2000) for a discussion of 'increasing returns' in political processes.

## Bibliography


Alt, James E., Margaret Levi and Elinor Ostrom. 1999. *Competition and Cooperation: Conversations With Nobelists About Economics and Political Science*. New York, Russell Sage Foundation.

Armstrong, Elizabeth M., Dan Carpenter and Marie E. Hojnacki. 2003. 'Whose deaths matter? Attention to disease in the public arena', paper presented at the Conference on the Politics of Biomedical Research, Woodrow Wilson School of Public and International Affairs. Princeton, NJ: Princeton University, March.

Balla, Steven J. 1998. 'Administrative procedures and political control of the bureaucracy', *American Political Science Review* 92: 663–73.

——and John R. Wright. 2001. 'Interest groups, advisory committees, and congressional oversight', *American Journal of Political Science* 45: 799–81.

Barabási, Albert-László. 2002. *Linked*. New York: Penguin.

Baumgartner, Frank R. and Bryan D. Jones. 1993. *Agendas and Instability in American Politics*. Chicago: University of Chicago Press.

——and Bryan D. Jones, eds. 2002. *Policy Dynamics*. Chicago: University Press of Chicago.

——and Beth L. Leech. 2001. 'Issue niches and policy bandwagons: Patterns of interest group involvement in national politics', *Journal of Politics* 63: 1191–213.

——, Christian Breunig, Christoffer Green-Pedersen, Bryan D. Jones, Peter B. Mortensen, Michiel Nuytemans and Stefaan Walgrave. 2009. 'Punctuated equilibrium in comparative perspective', *American Journal of Political Science* 53(3): 603–20.

Becker, Gary S. 1991. 'A note on restaurant pricing and other examples of social influence on price', *Journal of Political Economy* 99: 1109–16.

Bendor, Jonathan. 2010. *Bounded Rationality and Politics*. Berkeley, CA: University of California Press.

Bikhchandani, Sushil, David Hirshleifer and Ivo Welch. 1992. 'A theory of fads, fashion, custom, and cultural change as informational cascades', *Journal of Political Economy* 100: 992–1026.

Boushey, Graeme. 2011. *Policy Diffusion Dynamics*. Cambridge: Cambridge University Press.

Boydstun, Amber E. 2008. 'How policy issues become front-page news', PhD dissertation, Penn State University.

Brehm, John and Scott Gates. 1993. 'Donut shops and speed traps: Evaluating models of supervision on police behavior', *American Journal of Political Science* 37: 555–81.

—— 1997. *Working, Shirking, and Sabotage*. Ann Arbor, MI: University of Michigan Press.

Brown, Steven R. 2001. 'Structural and functional information: A cautionary note to Fernandes and Simon', paper presented at the annual meeting of the Society for the Policy Sciences New Haven, Connecticut.

Camerer, Colin F. 1998. 'Behavioral economics and nonrational organizational decision making' in Jennifer J. Halpern and Robert N. Stern (eds) *Debating Rationality*. Ithaca, NY: Cornell University Press.

——and Richard F. Thaler. 1995. 'Ultimatums, dictators and manners', *Journal of Economic Perspectives* 9: 209–19.

Carpenter, Daniel. 1996. 'Adaptive signal processing, hierarchy, and budgetary control in federal regulation', *American Political Science Review* 90: 283–302.

Chong, Dennis. 1991. *Collective Action and the Civil Rights Movement*. Chicago: University of Chicago Press.

Chung, Kee H. and Raymond A.K. Cox. 1994. 'A stochastic model of superstardom: An application of the Yule distribution', *Review of Economics and Statistics* 76(4): 771–5.

Cohen, Michael D., James G. March and Johann P. Olsen. 1972. 'A garbage can model of organizational choice', *Administrative Science Quarterly* 17: 1–25.

Crecine, John. 1969. *Government Problem-Solving*. Chicago: Rand-McNally.

Fernandes, Ronald and Herbert A. Simon. 1999. 'A study of how individuals solve complex and ill-structured problems', *Policy Sciences* 32: 225–45.

Fiske, Susan and Shelly Taylor. 1991. *Social Cognition*. New York: McGraw-Hill.

Galton, Francis. 1907. 'Vox populi', *Nature* 75: 450–1.

Gabaix, X. 1999. 'Zipf's Law and the growth of cities', *American Economic Review* 89(2): 129–32.

Gigerenzer, Gerd. 2001. *The Adaptive Toolbox*. Cambridge, MA: MIT Press.

——and Daniel G. Goldstein. 1996. 'Reasoning the fast and frugal way: Models of bounded rationality', *Psychological Review* 103: 650–69.

Granovetter, M.S. 1973. 'The strength of weak ties', *American Journal of Sociology* 78(6): 1360–80.

—— 1978. 'Threshold models of collective behavior', *American Journal of Sociology* 83(6): 1420.

Green, Mart T. and Fred Thompson. 2001. 'Organizational process models of budgeting', in John Bartle (ed.) *Research in Public Administration: Evolving Theories of Budgeting*. San Francisco: JAI Press.

Halpin. D. 2011. 'Organized interests and cascades of attention: Unpacking policy bandwagon dynamics', *Governance*, 24(2); 205–30.

Hammond, Thomas and Gary J. Miller. 1987. 'The core of the constitution', *American Political Science Review* 81: 1155–74.

Hinich, Melvin and Michael Munger. 1994. *Ideology and the Theory of Political Choice*. Ann Arbor, MI: University of Michigan Press.

Jones, Bryan D. 1980. *Service Delivery in the City: Citizen Demand and Bureaucratic Response*. New York: Longman.

—— 1994. *Reconceiving Decision-Making in Democratic Politics*. Chicago: University of Chicago Press.

—— 2001. *Politics and the Architecture of Choice*. Chicago: University of Chicago.

—— 2003. 'Bounded rationality and political science: Lessons from public administration and public policy', *Journal of Public Administration and Theory* 13(4): 395–412.

——and Lynn W. Bachelor. 1993. *The Sustaining Hand: Community Leadership and Corporate Power*. Lawrence, KS: University Press of Kansas.

——and Frank R. Baumgartner. 2005. *The Politics of Attention: How Government Prioritizes Problems*. Chicago: University of Chicago Press.

——and Walter Williams. 2008. *The Politics of Bad Ideas*. New York: Pearson Longman.

——, Tracy Sulkin and Heather Larsen. 2003. 'Punctuations in political institutions', *American Political Science Review* 97: 151–69.

——, Heather Larsen-Price and John Wilkerson. 2009. 'Representation and American governing institutions', *Journal of Politics* 71: 277–90.

Kahneman, Daniel and Amos Tversky. 1979. 'Prospect theory: An analysis of decision-making under risk', *Econometrica* 47: 263–91.

Kingdon, John W. 1977. 'Models of legislative voting', *The Journal of Politics*, 39(3): 563–95.

—— 1984. *Agendas, Alternatives, and Public Policies*. Boston: Little, Brown.

Kuklinski, James and Paul Quirk. 2000. 'Reconsidering the rational public: Cognition, heuristics and mass opinion', in Arthur Lupia, Mathew D. McCubbins and Samuel L. Popkin (eds) *Elements of Reason*. Cambridge: Cambridge University Press.

Kunda, Ziva. 1990. 'The case for motivated reasoning', *Psychological Bulletin* 108: 480–98.

Laitin, David. 1999. 'Identity choice under conditions of uncertainty: reflections on Selten's dualist methodology', in James Alt, Margaret Levi and Elinor Ostrom (eds) *Competition and Cooperation: Conversations with Nobelists about Economics and Political Science*. New York: Russell Sage.

Leech, Beth L., Frank R. Baumgartner, Timothy La Pira and Nicolas A. Semanko. 2005. 'Drawing lobbyists to Washington: Government activity and interest-group mobilization', *Political Research Quarterly* 58(1) (March): 19–30.

Lindblom, Charles E. 1959. 'The science of "muddling through"', *Public Administration Review* 19(2): 79–88.

Lodge, Milton and Charles Taber. 2000. 'Three steps toward a theory of motivated political reasoning', in Arthur Lupia, Mathew D. McCubbins and Samuel L. Popkin (eds) *Elements of Reason*. Cambridge: Cambridge University Press, 183–213.

Lohmann, Susanne. 1994. 'The dynamics of informational cascades: The Monday demonstrations in Leipzig, East Germany, 1989–1991', *World Politics* 47: 42–101

Lorenz, Jan, Hekio Rauhut, Frank Schweitzer, and Dirk Helbing. 2010. 'How social movements can undermine the wisdom of crowd effect', *PNAS* 108(22): 9020–9025.

Lupia, Arthur, Mathew D. McCubbins and Samuel L. Popkin. 2000. 'Beyond rationality: Reason and the study of politics', in Arthur Lupia, Mathew D. McCubbins and Samuel L. Popkin (eds) *Elements of Reason*. Cambridge: Cambridge University Press.

Mackay, Charles. 1841. *Extraordinary Popular Delusions and the Madness of Crowds*. New York: Broadway.

March, James 1994. *A Primer on Decision-Making*. New York: The Free Press.

——and Herbert A. Simon. 1958. *Organizations*. New York: John Wiley & Sons.

Matthews, D.R. and James A. Stimson. 1975. 'Yeas and nays: Normal decision-making in the US House of Representatives', New York: John Wiley & Sons.

Merton, Robert K. 1968. 'The Matthew effect in science', *Science* 159: 56–63.

Miller, G.J. 1992. *Managerian Dilemmas: The Political Economy of Hierarchy*. New York: Cambridge University Press, 216–333.

Miller, John H. and Scott E. Page. 2004. 'The standing ovation problem', *Complexity* 9: 8–16.

——and Scott E. Page. 2007. *Complex Adaptive Systems*. Princeton, NJ: Princeton University Press.

Mladenka, Kenneth. 1978. 'Rules, service equity and distributional decisions', *Social Science Quarterly* 59: 192–202.

Newell, Allen.1990. *Unified Theories of Cognition*. Cambridge, MA: Harvard University Press.

——and Herbert A. Simon. 1972. *Human Problem Solving*. Englewood Cliffs, NJ: Prentice Hall.

Padgett, John F. 1980. 'Bounded rationality in budgetary research', *American Political Science Review* 74: 354–72.

—— 1981. 'Hierarchy and ecological control in federal budgetary decision making', *American Journal of Sociology* 87: 75–128.

Pareto, Vilfredo. 1935. *Mind and Society*. New York: Kessinger Publishing.

Pierson, Paul. 2000. 'Increasing returns, path dependence, and the study of politics', *The American Political Science Review* 94(2): 251–67.

Robinson, Scott. 2003. 'Punctuated equilibrium, bureaucratization, and budgetary changes in schools', paper presented at the Midwest Political Science Association, Chicago, April 4–6.

Schelling, Thomas. C. 1978. *Micromotives and Macrobehaviour*, New York: Norton.

Schrad, Mark Lawrence. 2010. *The Political Power of Bad Ideas*. Oxford: Oxford University Press.

Shiller, R.J. 2005. *Irrational Exuberance*. Princeton, NJ: Princeton University Press.

Simon, Herbert A. 1945. *Administrative Behavior*. New York: Macmillan.

—— 1977. 'The logic of heuristic decision-making', in R.S. Cohen and M.W. Wartofsky (eds) *Models of Discovery*. Boston: D. Reidel.

—— 1983. *Reason in Human Affairs*. Stanford, CA: Stanford University Press.

—— 1996a. *Models of My Life*, MIT edn. Cambridge, MA: MIT Press.

—— 1996b. *The Sciences of the Artificial*, 3rd edn. Cambridge, MA: MIT Press.

—— 1999. 'The potlatch between political science and economics', in James Alt, Margaret Levi and Elinor Ostrom (eds) *Conflict and Cooperation: Conversations with Nobelists about Economics and Political Science*. New York: Russel Sage.

Slovak, Paul. 1990. 'Choice', in Daniel N. Osherson and Edward E. Smith (eds) *Thinking: An Invitation to Cognitive Science*, vol. 3. Cambridge, MA: MIT Press.

Sornette, D. 2004. *Why Stock Markets Crash*. Princeton, NJ: Princeton University Press.

Surowiecki, James. 2004. *The Wisdom of Crowds*. New York: Doubleday.

Thaler, Richard H. 1991. *Quasi Rational Economics*. New York: Russell Sage.

—— 1988. 'Anomalies: the ultimatum game', *Journal of Economic Perspectives* 2: 195–206.

—— 1992. *The Winner's Curse: Paradoxes and Anomalies of Economic Life*. Princeton, NJ: Princeton University Press.

Tetlock, Philip. 2000. 'Coping with trade-offs: Psychological constraints and political implications', in Arthur Lupia, Mathew D. McCubbins and Samuel L. Popkin (eds) *Elements of Reason*. Cambridge: Cambridge University Press.

True, James L. 2000. 'Avalanches and incrementalism: Making policy and budgets in the United States', *American Review of Public Administration* 30: 3–18.

——, Bryan D. Jones and Frank R. Baumgartner. 1999. 'Punctuated equilibrium theory', in Paul Sabatier (ed.) *Theories of the Policy Process*. Boulder, CO: Westview Press.

Tversky, Amos. 1972. 'Elimination by aspects: A theory of choice', *Psychological Review* 79: 281–99.

Wildavsky, Aaron. 1964. *The Politics of the Budgetary Process*. Boston: Little, Brown.

Workman, Samuel, Bryan D. Jones and Ashley E. Jochim. 2009. 'Information processing and policy dynamics', *Policy Studies Journal* 37(1): 75–92.

Youssefmir, Michael, Bernadro A. Huberman, and Tad Hogg. 1998. 'Bubbles and market crashes', *Computational Economics* 12(2): 97–114.

# 22
# Incrementalism

*Michael Hayes*

Incrementalism is a pluralistic process of policy-making involving mutual adjustment among multiple actors who typically disagree on objectives and start off from very different conceptions of the problem at hand. Incomplete knowledge and time constraints limit attention to alternatives differing only marginally (incrementally) from previous policies. The necessity for bargaining and compromise virtually assures incremental outcomes. Major policy change will occur gradually, if at all, as experience with policies generates demands for modification or expansion in subsequent policy cycles.

Charles Lindblom advanced incrementalism as both an explanatory and a prescriptive model of the policy process (Dahl and Lindblom 1953; Lindblom 1959, 1965, 1979; Braybrooke and Lindblom 1963). In his view, incrementalism provides the best explanation of the policy process because it is the best way to make policy, allowing policy-makers to proceed when the rational-comprehensive ideal has broken down.

The first section of this chapter will review how rational decision-making breaks down in most cases and how incrementalism departs from the rational method on all points. The second section will identify some circumstances under which nonincremental policy change may occur. The third section will explore whether incrementalism really is the best way to make public policies, as Lindblom asserts.

## Incrementalism as an alternative to the rational ideal

Ideally, policies would result from a rational analysis culminating in a value-maximizing choice after a thorough examination of all relevant alternatives. Unfortunately, this almost never happens, for a variety of reasons.

*The breakdown of rationality:* For decisions to be made rationally, public problems must be perceived and defined accurately. In reality, there is no guarantee that problems will be perceived at all and almost no likelihood that they will be defined the same way by all participants. Items will reach the agenda because they have attracted political support from organized interests or the mass public, not because they have been rationally or scientifically identified.

Moreover, policy-makers must agree on objectives. This means more than just sharing the same broad goals. All involved must also share the same priorities, ranking goals in the same way and agreeing on exactly how to allocate finite resources. This condition is almost never satisfied.

Third, policy-makers must estimate accurately the consequences of all alternatives. Policy-makers are almost never able to do this. On the contrary, the question of what consequences will follow from various alternatives is almost always vigorously contested.

Clearly, rational decision-making is unattainable most of the time. Where there is no agreement on objectives, it is impossible to say which values should be maximized. Where the knowledge base is inadequate, there is no way to say which alternatives have the best consequences.

Incrementalism rejects the very idea of policies as the product of decisions. According to Lindblom, policies are not the products of rational choice but rather the political resultants of *partisan mutual adjustment* among various actors possessing different information, adhering to different values, and driven by different individual or group interests (Lindblom 1965).

*The advantages of incrementalism:* by contrast, incrementalism requires neither comprehensive information nor agreement among policy-makers on objectives. It permits action where the rational ideal offers no guidance to policy-makers.

For example, policy-makers almost never face a "given" problem (Lindblom 1980: 24). Rather, problems are brought to government through a process Lindblom terms the *social fragmentation of analysis* (Braybrooke and Lindblom 1963: 104–6). No single actor possesses comprehensive information on the problem. Rather, each brings to the table some portion of the knowledge that is required to analyze the problem. The dispersal of essential knowledge throughout the system makes some form of social fragmentation of analysis inevitable. No policy-maker could accurately specify the varying value preferences of different individuals or assess the impact of policy proposals on different groups without some input from these groups. Because disagreements can be accommodated through bargaining, problems may be, and often are, acted on without ever being fully defined.

Incrementalism avoids the need to secure agreement on objectives by focusing on concrete problems to be alleviated (for example, unemployment) rather than on abstract ideals to be attained (a self-actualized citizenry). The process moves away from problems rather than toward ideals, which can never be specified with sufficient precision to permit rational analysis. Lindblom terms this element of the model *remediality* (Braybrooke and Lindblom 1963, 102–4).

Ends and means are typically considered simultaneously because different alternatives embody different trade-offs among values. When policy-makers choose one of several alternatives, they are also choosing which trade-offs should be made among values. In practice, ends and means cannot be separated as called for by the rational model, with a decision on values preceding any decision on alternatives. Any decision among alternatives is inherently and necessarily a decision about values. Lindblom terms this element of the model *the adjustment of objectives to policies* (Braybrooke and Lindblom 1963: 93–8).

Time constraints preclude a comprehensive examination of all alternative solutions. Policy-makers must somehow limit their attention to a manageable number of options. In practice, they accomplish this by *limiting their focus to incremental alternatives* (Braybrooke and Lindblom 1963: 88–90). Major policy departures are unlikely to be enacted. Established policies acquire powerful supporters opposed to any significant changes in policy. Thus prolonged consideration of nonincremental policy proposals is likely to be a waste of time. Moreover, policy-makers build up a reservoir of knowledge through experience with existing policies that they will be reluctant to throw away by moving in an entirely different direction. It makes more sense to build on past policy than to begin again from the ground up.

Policy-makers further reduce the costs of analysis by focusing on the increments by which various proposals differ from one another and from past policies. Lindblom terms this process *margin-dependent choice* (Braybrooke and Lindblom 1963: 83–8). In the budgetary process, for example, legislators normally make no attempt to evaluate federal policies comprehensively.

Rather, they focus on the increments by which spending will go up or down for various programs under different proposals. Focusing on the margins permits an intelligent comparison of proposals where a comprehensive analysis of the various competing policies would be infeasible (Wildavsky 1992: 82–3).

Finally, the policy process is *serial*, or repetitive (Braybrooke and Lindblom 1963: 99–102). Because policies can be modified in subsequent policy cycles, unanticipated consequences do not pose a serious problem for incrementalism. They merely generate new problems to be dealt with at a later date. Problems are considered unsolved as long as some publics continue to express dissatisfaction with existing policies. By the same token, a policy may be regarded as "solved" when it finally disappears from the agenda, crowded off by other problems now considered more pressing (Wildavsky 1974: 60).

## Preconditions for nonincremental change

While Lindblom is correct that policy-making will be incremental most of the time, research suggests that nonincremental policy change may occur in response to crises, an aroused mass public opinion, or the attainment of the conditions for rational decision-making. These three favorable circumstances will be covered in turn below.

*Crises as a source of nonincremental change:* Lindblom identified conditions for nonincremental change in a volume he coauthored with David Braybrooke (Braybrooke and Lindblom 1963: 66–79). He characterized problems as falling within four quadrants defined by two continuous dimensions. The first dimension measured the policy-makers' understanding of the problem at hand; the second measured the degree of change a proposal would make from previous policy. The four quadrants are shown below (see Table 22.1):

Within this scheme, rational decision-making is confined to a relatively small number of cases, primarily technical decisions made by professionals in the middle levels of the bureaucracy—e.g. high understanding of problems is limited to policy alternatives that are incremental in scope. There will be, in Lindblom's view, no cases in which nonincremental policy proposals are well understood. Most policy-making will occur within the realm of normal incrementalism, where understanding is low and policy-makers confine themselves to incremental proposals.

Nonincremental policy change is possible in the remaining quadrant, which Braybrooke and Lindblom term the realm of wars, revolutions, and grand opportunities. On a less sweeping level, policy-makers may opt for nonincremental change any time a particular policy is judged to be broken beyond repair. Under such circumstances a "calculated risk" is warranted, and

*Table 22.1* Four quadrants of policy change

| | *Incremental* | *Nonincremental* |
|---|---|---|
| *High understanding* | Rational decision-making is possible for small, technical problems | This quadrant is empty; no cases occur here |
| *Low understanding* | The realm of normal incrementalism; most cases fit here | Nonincremental change possible here; realm of "wars, crises, and grand opportunities" |

Source: Hayes (1992) *Incrementalism and Public Policy*, New York: Longman

policy-makers may opt for major policy change even though all involved recognize the limits of their inability to predict the consequences of their actions (Dahl and Lindblom 1953: 85).

*Aroused mass public opinion as a catalyst for nonincremental change:* Charles O. Jones's case study of the Clean Air Amendments of 1970 showed that nonincremental policy outcomes can result where mass public opinion is aroused on an issue, forcing policy-makers to satisfy a "pre-formed majority." Although incrementalism provided a good description of policy-making on the air pollution issue from 1941–1967, the increased salience of the issue in 1970 produced a very different kind of policy process, necessitating the development of an alternative model to describe events (Jones 1974, 1975).

Under normal "majority-building incrementalism," as understood by Jones, mass public opinion is typically inattentive and ill-informed. Policy development takes place within policy communities, consisting of congressional committees or subcommittees with jurisdiction over the issue, executive agencies with responsibility for administering laws within the issue area, and clientele groups with a stake in the policies developed by these policy communities. As bills work their way through multiple veto points, the need for bargaining and compromise virtually guarantees that proposals will emerge weaker than they were initially. Jones terms this process "tapering demands from the optimal down to the acceptable."

Majority-building incrementalism could not explain air pollution policy-making in 1970, however. Public opinion polls pointed to a dramatic rise in public concern over the pollution issue, and the sharp rise in issue salience triggered the formation of many new interest groups representing environmental interests. This public pressure for dramatic federal action constituted a kind of "pre-formed majority," obviating the normal need for tapering down. Policy-makers who had shown little interest in the issue before (including the president) now saw it as having electoral potential. This expanded circle of policy-makers scrambled to satisfy the highly aroused, pre-formed majority, and air pollution legislation grew steadily stronger as it moved through the House and Senate through a process Jones termed "policy escalation."

The end result, according to Jones, was a nonincremental policy change: Congress gave the federal government sweeping new authority and set technology-forcing, health-based air quality standards. However, the strong new law was not the product of any expansion in the scientific knowledge base available to policy-makers but rather was driven primarily by the need to appease an aroused mass public. For this reason, Jones characterized the 1970 policy outcome as "legislating beyond capability."

*Attainment of the conditions for rational decision-making:* throughout all his works on incrementalism, Lindblom identified two preconditions for rational decision-making: agreement among participants on objectives and the possession of a knowledge base sufficient to permit accurate estimation of the consequences associated with various alternatives. In Lindblom's view, incrementalism describes how policy is made under normal circumstances because these two conditions are almost never met.

While Lindblom is doubtless correct in asserting that these two conditions are not satisfied for most policy problems, the failure to meet these two conditions should not be taken for granted. For example, participants may agree on values without engaging in a comprehensive review of alternative value mixes. The attainment of consensus on objectives changes the policy process significantly even where it results from the failure of policy-makers to examine any other goals or the inability of interests with contrary values to mobilize. In the same way, policy-makers may understand some problems better than others, or at least think that they do. While a complete understanding of cause-and-effect relationships is almost never attained, there are nevertheless issues for which participants have achieved a consensus on basic facts. Robert Rothstein has termed this condition "consensual knowledge":

> a body of belief about cause-effect and ends-means relationships among variables (activities, aspirations, values, demands) that is widely accepted by the relevant actors, irrespective of the absolute or final "truth" of these beliefs.
>
> *(1984: 736)*

As with consensual objectives, the policy process is fundamentally altered whenever policy-makers agree on how the world works for a given issue whether this shared understanding of cause-and-effect relationships is ultimately vindicated or disconfirmed.

Combining these two dimensions produces a typology of four quadrants that differs significantly from the one advanced earlier by Braybrooke and Lindblom. It should be noted that where issues fit within the typology is properly determined by their placement on the underlying dimensions and not by the names attached to the categories. Thus initial placement of a particular issue within one of the four cells in no way precludes its movement over time into one of the other cells. Issues will move from one category to another whenever the degree of agreement on values or the adequacy of the knowledge base is affected by events.

Where conflict over objectives is combined with an inadequate knowledge base that leads to disagreement over policy consequences (conflictual knowledge), as in cell A, incrementalism is virtually inevitable. The policy process will exhibit all the characteristics of normal incrementalism and policy outcomes will necessarily be incremental. Lindblom is almost surely right in assuming that this will be the normal case.

By contrast, cell B consists of what might be termed pure problems of value conflict. Here the knowledge base is not the problem and policy-makers exhibit what Rothstein called consensual knowledge. While policy *outcomes* are likely to be incremental at best in this cell, the process by which these outcomes are determined will be much more conflictual than Lindblom envisioned for normal incrementalism. Within normal incrementalism, problems are complex and the self-interest of various participants will be poorly understood, thus tempering conflict to at least some extent. By contrast, where problems are well understood, the clarity of the stakes for all involved will intensify conflict. For example, social security is a difficult issue for policy-makers precisely because all reforms have immediate and readily understood redistributive consequences. The fight is over who will bear the costs of repairing the system.

The policy process will be different again for pure problems of knowledge base (cell C). Here, a consensus on objectives exists and rational policy-making is precluded only by an inadequate understanding of the problem. Policy-making here will monitor information from the environment and adapt to changing circumstances through feedback. Macroeconomic policy-making provides a good example here,

Finally, where consensual knowledge is combined with consensual objectives, as in cell D, rational decision-making is attainable. While many of the issues for which these two conditions

*Table 22.2* A typology of decision environments

| | *Conflictual objectives* | *Consensual objectives* |
|---|---|---|
| *Conflictual or contested knowledge* | (A) Realm of normal incrementalism | (C) Pure problems of knowledge base |
| *Consensual knowledge* | (B) Pure problems of value conflict | (D) Realm of rational decision-making |

Source: Hayes (2001) *The Limits of Policy Change: Incrementalism, Worldview and the Rule of Law*. Washington, DC: Georgetown University Press

are satisfied may involve relatively small technical or administrative problems, as Lindblom has suggested (Braybrooke and Lindblom 1963: 61–79), nonincremental policy departures are also possible here. Where policy-makers agree on objectives and share a consensual knowledge base, there is nothing to preclude large change if large change seems warranted.

*The life cycle of policies:* when are the conditions for rational decision-making most likely to be met? All policies go through a predictable life cycle, and the preconditions for rational decision-making are most likely to be attained late in the life cycle of policies.

Lindblom saw policy-makers as typically building on past policies. This presumes the existence of past policies to build on. Most policy problems have in fact been around for many years, taxing the capacities of policy-makers and resisting any final solution. However, all policies began as brand new policies at some point in time. Building on the earlier research of Lawrence D. Brown (1983), we may call legislative enactments establishing a new federal responsibility *federal role breakthrough policies.* This is the first stage in the life cycle of policies.

Over time, policy communities develop around these new programs. Congressional committees are assigned responsibility for legislative oversight, executive agencies are given statutory authority to administer the new law, and affected interest groups establish close ties with these legislators and administrators. Because new policies are unlikely to be well-understood or to generate consensual goals, policy-making will typically exhibit characteristics of normal incrementalism for many years. Brown termed policies aimed at reforming or improving government programs already in existence "rationalizing policies." Because such rationalizing policies tend to exhibit the characteristics of normal incrementalism for many years, we may call this second stage of the life cycle the stage of *incremental rationalizing policies.*

For many policies, this will be the final stage in the life cycle. For at least some policies, however, workable solutions to problems may emerge after many years. As policy-makers come to understand problems better over time through accumulated experience with policy implementation, a consensus on both objectives and knowledge base may develop. Where this occurs, the conditions for rationality are met, permitting the development of what we may term *rationalizing breakthroughs.* Such initiatives are rationalizing policies because they seek to reform existing government programs, but they also constitute breakthrough policies of a very special sort inasmuch as they represent a dramatic shift in thinking and policy design that permits effective action in addressing enduring problems.

Thus the conditions for rational policy-making are more likely to emerge at the end of the life cycle than the beginning. While nonincremental policy change may result from crisis conditions or in response to an aroused mass public opinion, it will be most effective and lasting where it constitutes a rationalizing breakthrough in the final stage in the life cycle of an issue. Policies do not reach this final stage without going through the two prior stages, however. There are no shortcuts to rational decision-making.

## Can incrementalism be trusted to yield good policies?

Is incrementalism the best way to make policies, as Lindblom asserts? There will never be complete agreement on this point because attitudes toward incrementalism depend on underlying assumptions about human nature and what it is possible to achieve through analysis. In this regard, Hayek (1948), Sowell (1987), and Spicer (1995) identified two distinct worldviews, which may be termed rationalist and anti-rationalist (see also Hayes 2001: 7–50).

Rationalists reject Lindblom's thesis that rational-comprehensive analysis is unattainable. They are optimistic about human nature and believe that all social problems can be solved through the exercise of reason. By contrast, anti-rationalists are pessimistic about human nature and see distinct limits on what can be achieved through human reason (Hayes 2001: 8–11). Where rationalists see solutions as emerging from analysis, anti-rationalists see good public policies as emerging from a policy process that is pluralistic and typically conflictual. In Sowell's terms (1987), rationalists believe in articulated rationality while anti-rationalists believe in systemic rationality. Wildavsky (1979) makes this same distinction, characterizing the alternatives as intellectual cogitation vs. social interaction.

Rationalists reject incrementalism for a variety of reasons. They dislike the muddled compromises that emerge from pluralistic political processes, eschew piecemeal and gradual social reforms in favor of sweeping policy proposals, and decisively reject any strategy for building on a status quo they view as inherently flawed. By contrast, anti-rationalists embrace incrementalism, accepting incrementalism's core tenet that good policies are more likely to result from pluralistic processes and endorsing incrementalism's stress on learning through seriality.

Critics have advanced a variety of indictments against incrementalism (see the various authors reviewed in Weiss and Woodhouse 1992: 252–68). While some of these indictments are essentially rationalist in orientation, others are anti-rationalist, accepting the need for policy-making through social interaction but pointing to inherent flaws in the policy process. By and large, the rationalist critiques can be easily dismissed; the anti-rationalist critiques are more compelling.

*Rationalist indictments:* here there are four main criticisms: (1) that incrementalism is insufficiently goal-oriented; (2) that it is hostile to analysis; (3) that it is inherently reactive rather than proactive; and (4) that it cannot anticipate "sleeper effects."

1. Critics of incrementalism want policy-making to be purposive, or goal-oriented. This criticism assumes it is actually possible to identify agreed upon ends. For example, Dryzek (1987: 424) defines the concept of instrumental rationality as "the capacity to devise, select, and effect good means to *clarified ends*" (emphasis added). By contrast, Lindblom sees multiple and conflicting objectives as the normal case. While participants may agree on the desirability of all the ends, agreement on objectives implies agreement on priorities—a much higher standard to satisfy.

   In this vein, rationalists and anti-rationalists tend to differ in their handling of trade-offs (Sowell 1995: 135–42). Anti-rationalists recognize that desired goals are often in conflict and cannot be satisfied simultaneously. On the contrary, to gain more of one value, you must give up some of the other. Understood in this way, agreement on objectives implies a consensus among participants on exactly how to make these trade-offs, a consensus that is typically unattainable. By contrast, rationalists tend to focus on one goal at a time, ignoring or denying the existence of trade-off relationships with other goals. Any attempt at rational analysis that achieves agreement on objectives by focusing on a single goal may facilitate coherent, purposeful decision-making but only at the expense of neglecting alternative values that do not go away just because they are ignored.
2. A related criticism charges that incrementalism is hostile to analysis. This charge misrepresents how incrementalism works. Anti-rationalists, including Lindblom, expect participants to employ analysis both in pursuing their self-interest and in attempting to identify workable solutions to public problems. Anti-rationalists see distinct limits on the ability of any one actor to formulate comprehensive, workable solutions to public problems. Those limits flow out of inherent limitations on man's cognitive capacities and the dispersion of pertinent information throughout the population. Accordingly, good policies are more likely to emerge from the interplay of multiple actors, each of whom can be expected to marshal the best arguments they can in defense of their positions. Policy-making by social interaction (systemic rationality) is not just a balance of power among participants; it is also a competition among ideas.

3 The third criticism holds that incrementalism is inherently reactive rather than proactive. According to Lindblom, policy-making is reactive by necessity. Where values are multiple and in conflict with one another, as is usually the case, proactive policy-making is virtually impossible. Fortunately, policy-makers do not need to secure agreement on goals. To the contrary, they can consider ends and means together through the adjustment of objectives to policies. Because different options embody different value trade-offs, to choose one alternative over others is to choose a value trade-off, and conflict over which option to choose represents a conflict over value trade-offs. Policy-making is meliorative as a consequence, moving away from concrete problems rather than toward abstract ideals.
4 The final rationalist critique stresses the the inability of incrementalism to deal with what are called sleeper effects. These are negative policy consequences that remain invisible through many policy cycles only to show up suddenly at a point when it has become difficult, if not impossible, to change course. A contemporary example would be global warming; here reliance on fossil fuels as an energy source has created a greenhouse effect. The consequences of this greenhouse effect for climate change only began to be understood by scientists when an irreversible threshold was about to be crossed.

Although sleeper effects clearly pose a serious problem for incrementalism, it is not clear how late-blooming negative consequences could be identified earlier through efforts at rational-comprehensive analysis (Weiss and Woodhouse 1992: 265). Indeed, it is hard to see how any decision-making method could anticipate policy consequences which are beyond the available knowledge base by definition. In theory, at least, sleeper effects should pose less of a threat to a process in which policy changes occur gradually, in small steps. If sleeper effects can be likened to lemmings running off a cliff (Dryzek 1983), it would seem better to approach the cliff at reduced speed. In the case of global warming, the science has taken decades to develop, and understanding is still incomplete. How would nonincremental policy-making magically solve the problem of an inadequate knowledge base?

The rationalist critiques just reviewed all treat incrementalism as a strategy for policy-making that can be chosen or discarded at will. However, policy-making is not pluralistic and conflictual because participants have chosen incrementalism over rationality as a strategy for policy-making. Rather, it is pluralistic and conflictual because one or more of the conditions for rational decision-making have broken down, as is the case in three of the four quadrants identified earlier.

*Anti-rationalist criticisms:* anti-rationalist critiques acknowledge the superiority of policy-making by social interaction but point to inherent flaws in the policy process. Here the main criticism is that incrementalism is inherently conservative, first because it encourages policy-makers to focus exclusively on small increments, and second because the interplay of multiple interests will necessarily favor organized elites (especially corporations) with disproportionate political power.

First, critics indict incrementalism for rejecting fundamental changes in the status quo and focusing instead on gradual policy change through incremental steps (Weiss and Woodhouse 1992: 260–2). This argument ignores the potential for continual improvement in policies through modification in subsequent policy cycles. Seriality allows policy-makers to converge on a solution through trial and error. While any given outcome may be incremental, significant policy change is possible through an accumulation of small changes over time. In fact, significant change may occur sooner through a rapid succession of small steps than through an occasional nonincremental policy change (Lindblom 1979: 520–1).

If significant change is clearly possible through seriality, can incrementalism be legitimately charged with a conservative bias? Admittedly, it makes a degree of sense to view rationalists as liberals because of their optimistic view of what it is possible to achieve through politics. Similarly, anti-rationalists might be characterized as conservative to the extent that they are more skeptical regarding what it is possible to achieve through politics. Sowell (1995) characterizes the two worldviews in precisely this way.

This simple, dichotomous distinction is misleading, however, as incrementalism may be employed to pursue liberal policies. As Karl Popper observed:

> This method [incrementalism, or "piecemeal social engineering" in Popper's terms] can be used … in order to search for, and fight against, the greatest and most urgent evils of society, rather than to seek, and to fight for, some ultimate good … But a systematic fight against definite wrongs, against concrete forms of injustice or exploitation, and avoidable suffering such as poverty or unemployment, is a very different thing from the attempt to realize a distant ideal blueprint of society.
>
> *(1994: 91–2)*

Clearly, the fact that incrementalism is meliorative rather than utopian, and that it pursues policy change through seriality rather than once-and-for-all solutions, does not make the strategy inherently conservative. In this regard, Hayes (2001) distinguishes between rationalist liberals (which he terms utopian visionaries) and anti-rationalist (or meliorative) liberals, as well as between nostalgic (rationalist) and adaptive (anti-rationalist) conservatives. Within this scheme, both Lindblom and Popper would qualify as meliorative liberals (ibid.: 28–41).

Second, incrementalism has also been characterized as conservative because the interplay of multiple interests will tend to favor organized elites with disproportionate power (Weiss and Woodhouse 1992: 260–2). Two conditions in particular must be met for incrementalism to yield good public policies. First, all affected interests must succeed in mobilizing. Lindblom was overly optimistic on this point in his early writings, assuming that every important social interest would have its watchdog (Lindblom 1959: 85). The free rider problem prevents many groups from organizing at all, however (Olson 1970), creating a systemic bias in favor of small groups over large diffuse groups like consumers or taxpayers. Inasmuch as membership groups face a free rider problem that never goes away, they will be at a disadvantage vis-à-vis institutions, which are already organized for other purposes and thus face no free rider problem. Finally, groups mobilizing affluent constituencies will have an advantage over groups attempting to mobilize the poor inasmuch as the affluent can more easily afford membership dues (on these points, see the sources cited in Hayes 2001: Chapter 4).

The second condition that must be met for incrementalism to operate efficiently is a rough equality in power across groups. Just as economic markets work badly whenever some firms have market power, incrementalism works badly whenever some actors possess disproportionate political power. Lindblom (1977, 1982) argued that corporations will occupy a privileged position within capitalist societies. Because corporations can deliver or withhold prosperity, they have unparalleled legitimacy to the extent that policy-makers equate the class interest of business with the public interest (Miliband 1969). This legitimacy gives corporations both a veto power over policies that threaten them and a form of indirect influence ("control without trying"), as corporations receive favorable tax or regulatory benefits from policy-makers that they have not actively sought.

Lindblom is not advancing a power elite thesis here; rather, he sees the policy process as pluralistic but skewed toward the interests of corporations. His primary concern is that business power hampers the proper operation of incrementalism, keeping some items off the agenda entirely and channeling disproportionate benefits to business groups. Although this concern is valid, disproportionate business power would plague any policy-making method: "[I]t is the socio-political power structure that favors organized elites, not incrementalism or any other decision strategy" (Weiss and Woodhouse 1992: 262).

While corporations may occupy a privileged position in capitalist societies, Lindblom's analysis is overstated. Business groups do not win all the time, and their ability to block policies they oppose is overrated (Hayes 2006: 63–79). While business groups do win more than any other group in contemporary American politics, they also suffer defeats, and there are many issues on which they take no position at all. The larger question is whether the American system features dispersed or cumulative inequalities (Dahl 2005). In a system of dispersed inequalities, the money or manpower of some groups might be offset by the legitimacy or expertise of other groups. In a system of cumulative inequalities, by contrast, some groups will rank high on all or most dimensions of influence while others will rank low across the board. Right now, corporations possess vast wealth and unparalleled legitimacy. They also have an advantage in expertise on technical regulatory issues, and, with their ability to deliver or withhold prosperity, they occupy a strategic position within the economy.

While this business advantage in resources may seem insurmountable, it is worth recalling that Dahl (2005) found a surprising evolution in New Haven over time from a system of cumulative inequalities to one of dispersed inequalities. This occurred through the natural development of new sources of power that none of the original power-holders could have anticipated and which they were powerless to block. Policy-makers bent on dispersing inequalities could take action both to facilitate mobilization of previously unorganized interests and to ameliorate inequality in tangible resources across groups through a system of public financing for congressional campaigns (Hayes 2001: 162–6). Although such reforms would mitigate the problem of cumulative inequalities, they would not eliminate completely the privileged position corporations will always occupy within any capitalist society—a problem that would plague any decision-making method, as noted above.

*Special problems plaguing incrementalism in the American context:* two additional anti-rationalist critiques may be offered that would apply with special force in the United States. The first stems from our system of checks-and-balances. The second flows out of the potential for divided government in an era of polarized political parties.

First, in Lindblom's view (and mine), there is no viable alternative to incrementalism under most circumstances. The question is not whether policy-making should be incremental, but rather whether incrementalism is functioning efficiently. Lindblom is right that more can be achieved through a rapid succession of small steps than through an occasional major policy change. However, aspects of the political system may preclude revisiting policies on a regular basis, thus preventing the kind of rapid succession of small steps Lindblom envisions. Under such circumstances, incrementalism can be properly accused of a conservative bias. Lindblom (1979) believes our system of checks-and-balances impedes the proper operation of incrementalism in precisely this way by making it extremely difficult to pass any kind of legislation. Too often, incrementalism in the United States features small policy changes a generation or more apart. This problem has become especially acute in recent years with the development of the party filibuster and the 60-vote Senate (more on this below).

Second, for any system of policy-making through social interaction to function properly, all affected interests must be effectively represented. We have already seen how unrealistic this is. The development in recent years of a system of polarized parties makes the representation of a broad range of interests even more problematic. While our contemporary parties help voters hold politicians accountable by functioning as responsible parties, they also hamper the effective operation of incrementalism. To the extent that each party represents a narrow range of interests, unified government could produce a policy equilibrium that is necessarily incomplete, representing only the range of views held by members of the majority party.

Seen in this light, divided government might seem to force consideration of a more complete range of viewpoints by giving effective leverage to both parties. Where the two parties are as polarized as ours are today, however, they are more likely to be completely opposed on most major issues, making gridlock more likely than cooperation. This tendency toward gridlock may be reinforced by electoral incentives, as neither party wants to cooperate on issues that might otherwise be used against the other party in the next election. In a world of polarized parties, then, unified government may be a necessary condition for passing controversial legislation. As we have seen in recent years, the 60-vote Senate gives the minority party some leverage even under conditions of unified government.

Under such circumstances, incremental policy changes a generation apart may be all we can hope for. While meliorative liberals like Lindblom would view this as the worst of all policy-making worlds, it is not inconsistent with the vision of the framers. While the checks-and-balances built into the constitution may foster incrementalism, they were never intended to foster efficient policy-making via a rapid succession of small steps.

In conclusion, incrementalism is clearly not a utopian method of policy-making. While the rationalist critiques are rooted in a misunderstanding of how the policy process operates, the anti-rationalist critiques point to real problems with the method. It must be noted, however, that Lindblom never characterizes incrementalism as functioning to yield optimal policies in every instance. Rather, he argues that incrementalism will outperform misguided efforts to employ rational-comprehensive analysis. Indeed, as noted in an earlier section of this chapter, once rationality breaks down, there is no longer any criterion for determining whether policy outcomes are good or bad. One can only hope that good policy processes will yield good policy outcomes, at least most of the time. Ultimately, Lindblom's case for incrementalism as a policy-making method is meliorative rather than utopian. While corporate power and the failure of some interests to mobilize make for a "rigged competition" (Weiss and Woodhouse 1992: 262), incrementalism—however imperfect—is still the only viable way to make policy when the conditions for rationality break down.

## Bibliography


Braybrooke, David, and Charles E. Lindblom. 1963. *A Strategy of Decision: Policy Evaluation as a Social Process*. New York: Free Press of Glencoe.

Brown, Lawrence D. 1983. *New Policies, New Politics: Government's Response to Government's Growth*. Washington, DC: Brookings Institution.

Dahl, Robert A. 2005. *Who Governs? Democracy and Power in an American City*, 2nd edn. New Haven, CT: Yale University Press.

——and Charles E. Lindblom. 1953. *Politics, Economics, and Welfare: Planning and Politico-Economic Systems Resolved into Basic Social Processes*. New York: Harper & Row, Harper Torchbooks.

Dryzek, John S. 1983. 'Present choices, future consequences: A case for thinking strategically, *World Futures* 19: 1–19.

—— 1987. 'Complexity and rationality in public life', *Political Studies* 35: 424–42.

Hayek, Friedrich. 1948. *Individualism and Economic Order*. Chicago: University of Chicago Press.

Hayes, Michael T. 1992. *Incrementalism and Public Policy*. New York: Longman.

—— 2001. *The Limits of Policy Change: Incrementalism, Worldview, and the Rule of Law*. Washington, DC: Georgetown University Press.

—— 2006. *Incrementalism and Public Policy*. Lanham, MD: University Press of America.

Jones, Charles O. 1974. 'Speculative augmentation in federal air pollution policy-making', *Journal of Politics* 36(May): 438–64.

—— 1975. *Clean Air: The Policies and Politics of Pollution Control*. Pittsburgh, PA: University of Pittsburgh Press.

Lindblom, Charles E. 1959. 'The science of "muddling through', *Public Administration Review* 19 (Spring): 79–88.
—— 1965. *The Intelligence of Democracy: Decision-Making Through Mutual Adjustment*. New York: Free Press.
—— 1977 *Politics and Markets: The World's Political Economic Systems*. New York: Basic Books.
—— 1979. 'Still muddling, not yet through', *Public Administration Review* 39(6): 517–26.
—— 1980. *The Policy-Making Process*, 2nd edn. Englewood Cliffs, NJ: Prentice Hall.
—— 1982. 'The market as prison', *Journal of Politics* 44: 324–36.
Miliband, Ralph. 1969. *The State in Capitalist Society*. New York: Basic Books/Harper Colophon Books.
Olson, Mancur, Jr. 1970. *The Logic of Collective Action: Public Goods and the Theory of Groups*. New York: Schocken Books.
Popper, Karl. 1994. *The Poverty of Historicism*. London and New York: Routledge and Kegan Paul.
Rothstein, Robert L. 1984. 'Consensual knowledge and international collaboration: Some lessons from the commodity negotiations', *International Organization* 38: 733–62.
Sowell, Thomas. 1987. *A Conflict of Visions: Ideological Origins of Political Struggles*. New York: William Morrow, Quill Books.
—— 1995. *The Vision of the Anointed: Self-Congratulation as a Basis for Social Policy*. New York: Basic Books.
Spicer, Michael. 1995. *The Founders, the Constitution, and Public Administration*. Washington, DC: Georgetown University Press.
Weiss, Andrew and Woodhouse, Edward. 1992. 'Reframing incrementalism: A constructive response to the critics, *Policy Sciences* 25: 255–73.
Wildavsky, Aaron. 1974. *The Politics of the Budgetary Process*. Boston: Little, Brown.
—— 1979. *Speaking Truth to Power: The Art and Craft of Policy Analysis*. Boston: Little, Brown.
—— 1992. *The New Politics of the Budgetary Process*, 2nd edn. New York: HarperCollins.

# 23

# Models for research into decision-making processes

## On phases, streams, rounds and tracks of decision-making[1]

*Geert R. Teisman and Arwin van Buuren*

### Models for the reconstruction of decision-making

Public administration scholars agree that decision-making has become more complex. Several reasons can be identified for this increased complexity. Two important ones are increased uncertainty about the dynamics and interdependencies in global networks and the power-sharing characteristics or that 'network society'. In networks, local circumstances can change quickly due to networks dynamics. At the same time, decisions are taken in a society where nobody is in charge (Bryson and Crosby 1992; Kickert *et al.* 1997). These two system changes do make public decision-making complex. Situations can change quickly and any decision taken interacts with decisions taken by others.

This chapter is based on the assumption of increased complexity. As such, it fits in with many others. Often the focus is on the consequences of and challenges for governments or governance systems. Complexity is clearly taken into account in the wider discussion on governance in networks. This was already the case before 2000 (for example: in Germany Marin and Mayntz 1991 and Scharpf 1997; in France Crozier and Friedberg 1980; in Great Britain Rhodes 1996b; and in the United States E. Ostrom 1990; Smith 1998). After 2000, many other publications have elaborated the complexity-government/governance relation (Strand 2002; Teisman and Klijn 2002; Duit and Galaz 2006; Wagenaar 2007; Gerrits 2008, Teisman *et al.* 2009).

Complexity, however, also raises questions for researchers of complexity. What kinds of models can researchers in decision-making apply to describe, analyse and evaluate decision-making and how do these models deal with complexity? Attention was paid to this topic by Mintzberg (1973), Kingdon (1984), Butler (1991) and Teisman ([1992, 1995] 1998). They generated images of decision-making as phases, as streams and as rounds. After 2000, van Buuren and Gerrits (2008) and Haynes (2008) contributed to the thinking about this topic by introducing concepts as tracks and traces as well as timelines and rates of change to indicate dynamics in processes. These authors pay special attention to the compounded, erratic and unpredictable characteristics of decision-making processes. By looking at processes they focus far less on the decision and more on the emergence of outcomes from a variety of more or less coupled decisions of a variety of actors. To indicate this configuration of ecology of decisions as an important object of study Teisman, van Buuren and Gerrits (2009: 231–49) introduce the concept of process systems. This concept underlines the embeddedness of individuals and their decisions in groups of individuals and their decisions into an organizational and institutional context where many more (in terms of content unrelated) decisions are taken that can emerge into important ones for the progress in decision-making on the level of individuals and groups.

This chapter focuses on the question of how to depict decision-making which evolves in complex network structures. We will concentrate on the characterization of successive decision-making activities and of concurrent decision-making activities. We will also discuss the assumed relations between the activities, in sequential as well as parallel combinations. The following research questions can be formulated:

1 Which assumptions are made with respect to chains of activities in decision-making processes? We will analyse different criteria used to distinguish between strands of activities, typologies of decision-making as a whole and elements of this process, and signs of progress in decision-making.
2 What sorts of assumptions are made with respect to simultaneous activities in decision-making processes? Specifically, we will distinguish here between (more or less relevant) actors, the relationship between problems and solutions, and the content of decision-making in terms of ambitions, frames and facts.

To analyse decision-making, the researcher needs to make a reconstruction of the study object. Such a reconstruction will be selective in nature. Observation is not simply an effort to learn what is going on. Rather it is a process where observations are made to conform to sets of assumptions (Edelman 1971). The gathering and classification of empirical observations into meaningful information is based on the a priori images of decision-making used. We cannot depict decision-making without making assumptions about its appearance. Various terms are used to describe such a set of assumptions: model, image, metaphor, referential framework or methodology. In this chapter the term 'model' will be used. Models help us to understand decision-making in distinctive yet partial ways (Morgan 1997: 4).

Four models will be discussed in this chapter. Two of these are generally accepted and respected, namely the so-called *phase model* and the *stream model*. The phase model is the most common approach, both in science (e.g. Anderson 1979; Bryson and Crosby 1992) and in policy practice (procedures are often based on the concept of phasing). Decision-making is represented in terms of a number of distinct stages (Mintzberg 1976). Phase models distinguish between (at least) policy formation, policy adoption and policy implementation. Each phase has its specific characteristics and participants. Ministries, for instance, are often divided into departments that are responsible for policy formation and others responsible for implementation.

The stream model depicts decision-making as a combination of three separate concurrent streams (Kingdon 1984). One stream consists of problems, another of policies/solutions, and a third one of politics/participants. Like the phases, streams have their own characteristics, but they exist side by side. A decision results out of the coincidence of streams.

The third model, the round model, has become more and more accepted as a conceptual approach to analyse decision-making in the context of complex networks (van Bueren *et al.* 2003; Howlett 2010). In this so-called *rounds model* decision-making is assumed to consist of different decision-making rounds. In all sets of rounds, the interaction between different actors results in one or more definitions of problems and solutions. In addition to Teisman (2000) we will present a fourth approach of complex decision-making, elaborated by van Buuren (2006) based upon the assumption that we can interpret decision-making as three co-evolving tracks: of fact-finding, framing and will-forming (cf. van Buuren and Gerrits 2008; van Herk *et al.* 2011).

In the round model the interaction between varieties of actors is the primary focus of the researchers. All participants can score points in each round, in terms of a leading definition of the problem and the (preferred) solution. By doing so, they define the beginning of a next round. But at the same time each new round can change the direction of the match: new players can appear, and in some cases the rules of the game can even be changed. The rounds model was developed during years of research in the field of urban and infrastructural planning. The first author was fascinated by the long duration of decision-making processes and by the changes in course these processes often take. Another remarkable result of his research was that the actors involved in decision-making often did not agree on the classification of a certain stage in the process, in terms of formation, adoption and implementation. Although he was able to identify several official decisions taken by ministers, Parliament, Parliamentary committees, etc., none of these decisions could be clearly depicted as the moment of adoption. Some of the official decisions were followed by actions which could not possibly be seen as the implementation of these decisions. This brought the first author to a fascinating conclusion: in complex decision-making results are achieved without the existence of the decision that marks the switch from the preparation phase into the implementation phase. Furthermore, the distinction between what the problem is and what the solutions are proved to be more complicated than assumed in the stream model. What was a solution for one actor could easily be a problem for another. Participants bring along closely intertwined problems and solutions.

In order to understand these dynamics and variety in perceptions, Teisman gradually altered his conceptual definition of decision-making. Due to the fact that the central decision could not be found, he began to collect all the decisions that were taken in a certain case. Second, he no longer assumed that the decisions were arranged on the basis of an a priori order and hierarchy. On the contrary, it was the task of research to clarify the empirical relation between decisions. In order to do so, decision-making was redefined as an intertwined 'clew' of a series of decisions taken by various parties, leading to a new analytical model. Progress is described in terms of successive rounds.

The second author (2006) took this insight as point of departure to answer the question: but how can we understand the evolution of the content of decision-making processes when it comes to the issues at stake? What are the various elements which constitute the content of decision-making? And how do they influence each other? To answer this question there are numerous points of departure to be chosen. Many authors (implicitly or explicitly) depart from a distinction between elements of ambition, interest and stake, versus elements of knowledge, analysis and information. This distinction can be traced back to Lindblom and Woodhouse (1992) who distinguish between activities to gather information and activities to exert influence, and to Heclo (1974) who uses the concepts of powering and puzzling to depict the same phenomena.

More recently, much literature has appeared which deals with a third element, the role of interpretation and thus of frames or belief systems in decision-making processes (Feldman 1989; Schön and Rein 1993; Fischer 2003; Sabatier 1999). Frames are the normative and subjective perceptions of actors within decision-making processes. Frames are important in decision-making because they determine which knowledge questions are taken into account, but also which ambitions are seen as fitting in a specific problem context.

Each actor brings in his own facts, frames and ambitions within a decision-making process and negotiates with other actors to agree about them. These elements evolve in a dynamic and erratic way and influence each other. Decisions can be seen as temporal selections of facts, frames and ambitions. This temporal 'equilibrium' can be easily challenged when the content of its constituting tracks changes.

The tracks model (elaborated in Figure 23.1) is based upon the assumption that it is helpful to describe the evolution in these three tracks separately, to be able to explain (the consequences of) their mutual interaction and their influence on the decisions realized.

After having examined all four models, they will be compared with each other. A four-fold analysis of decision-making about the Betuwe freight railway line will be carried out, and finally we shall draw some conclusions regarding the added value of the tracks and rounds models compared to the phase and streams model.

## Concepts within and principles of the phase model

In policy process analyses 'policy can be understood and examined as a combination of several processes, which are interrelated but can still be conceived as distinct components that are determinants of government actions' (Sato 1999). The phase model assumes that decision-making is 'the succession of different situations in the formulation, adoption, implementation and evaluation of a policy' (Bryson and Crosby 1992: 57–66)[2]. Often formation is divided into a phase of problem definition and a phase wherein solutions are presented. The first stage of the traditional policy process, problem definition, involves the emergence and recognition of some problem or crisis. In the second stage a policy to address specific problems is formulated by various governmental and non-governmental actors such as legislators, executive branch officials, the courts, citizens and special interest groups. Special policy proposals are adopted in the third stage. The fourth stage is policy implementation, wherein the adopted alternatives are executed by administrative units. Finally, in the policy evaluation stage, policy-makers determine whether the policy has achieved its goals (Altman and Petkus 1994).

Policy formulation is described as 'the collecting and analysing of information and the formulating of advice regarding the policy to be followed'. Parts of this phase include recognition, diagnosis, search for information, design and evaluation of the different alternatives that are designed. Policy adoption involves the 'taking of decisions about the contents of a policy'. During implementation the chosen means are applied: 'Decision-making is a sequence of steps which, if followed, should lead to the best solution; that is, to action which optimises the decision maker's utility' (Butler 1991: 43–4).

Analysts using the phase model are aware of the fact that reality does not reflect the assumption of the model: 'Planning in shared-power situations hardly ever follows a rigidly structured sequence from developing problem definitions and solutions to adopting and implementing proposals.

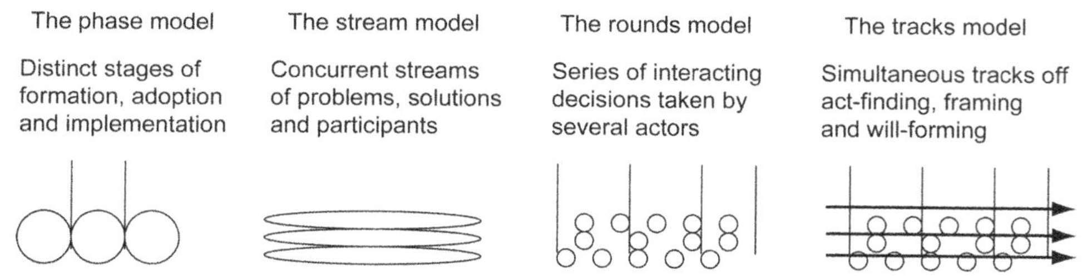


*Figure 23.1* A depiction of four models for the analysis of decision-making processes
Source: Teisman (2000) 'Models for research into decision-making processes: On phases, streams and decision-making rounds', *Public Administration* 78(4): 937–56

Serious difficulties arise when people try to impose this rigidly sequential approach on situations in which no one is in charge' (Bryson and Crosby 1992: xiv). 'Nonetheless, to be steadily effective, it is essential to have an organised approach of some sort' (ibid.: xiv). Several scientists reach the same conclusion (Hoogerwerf 1982; Mintzberg *et al.* 1976). They are aware that empiricism deviates from this, but feel it is worthwhile to reconstruct policy-making as though it was taking place in phases. The phase metaphor allows scientists to develop different theories regarding the various stages. To reconstruct the policy formation phase, concepts such as 'problem definition', 'generating alternative solutions' and 'policy design' are used. To analyse the adoption of policies, analysts look for the central decision which demarcates the transition from formation to implementation. During this phase, the policy proposal needs to be determined that is optimally suited to achieve the set objectives. Many parties are involved in this phase, but in the end only one or two actors determine which means are used to achieve the objectives. During the implementation phase, the researcher focuses on how chosen means were used and how any opposition was handled.

### *Problems preceding the search for and choice of solutions*

Scientists using the phase model assume that decision-making is problem-oriented (Scharpf 1997). There is, or at least there should be, one actor whose decision supersedes those of others and who therefore determines the problem and the policy. 'We therefore define public policy as substantive decisions, commitments, and actions made by those who hold or affect government positions of authority, as they are interpreted by various stakeholders' (Bryson and Crosby 1992: 63). Even though Bryson and Crosby (ibid.: 159) agree with Rittel and Webber (1973) that public problems are 'wicked' in the sense that they have no definite formulation, cannot be solved immediately and are unique, they still assume that problems do exist and should be known before a search for solutions can begin. Developing a 'problem definition to guide action' is seen as the first and most important phase in decision-making, which should be carried out before the adoption of a policy by the policy-maker can take place. Bryson and Crosby also assume that a solution can be formulated at a single point and place (see Figure 23.2). It is on these points that the stream and rounds models use different assumptions.

## Concepts within and principles of the stream model

Some researchers assume that the horizontal division of activities is a more crucial distinction to analyse processes than the vertical division used in the phase model. In their view, the analysis of the various phases does not result in specific theories on policy formation, policy adoption and implementation. Based on this point of view, the so-called stream model was developed in 1972 by Cohen *et al.* In 1984 Kingdon elaborated this model further. His model was based on the idea that policy-making consists of three streams: problems, solutions/policies and politics. As opposed to the phase model, here decision-making is dissociated from a specific participant. The idea is that decision-making consists mainly of a stream in which problems are discussed, a stream in which solutions are discussed and a stream consisting of things such as the attitude of the public, campaigns by pressure groups, and ideological contributions (Kingdon 1984: 152). Politicians can determine the problems and solutions they wished to concentrate on. For this reason, they are likely to rush from one combination of problem and solution to another. As a result of this, the level of participation in decision-making is likely to vary strongly. This is partly because these processes develop unpredictably (March and Olsen 1976: 10–23). Thus, the temporal sequence of the phase model is replaced by the postulate of simultaneousness (Koppenjan 1993: 26).

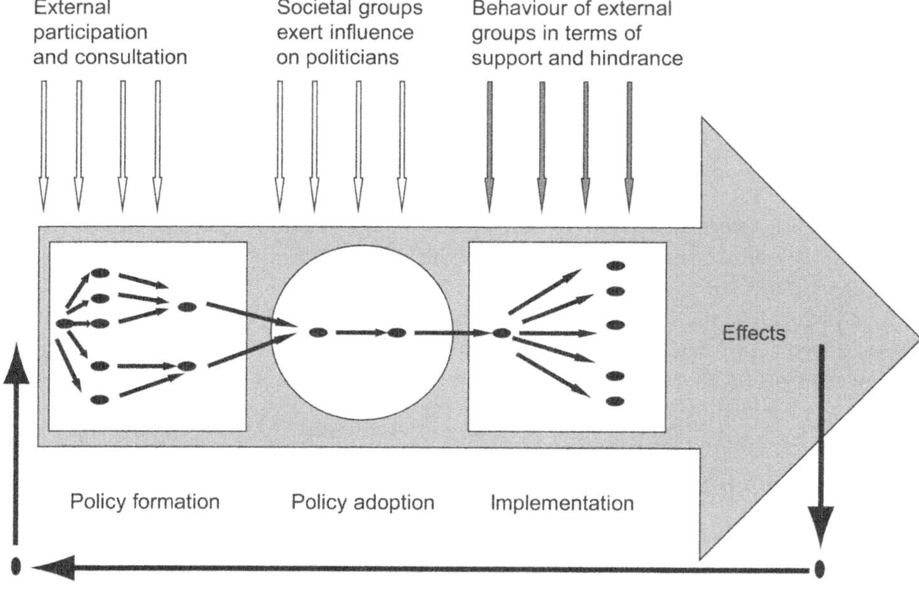


*Figure 23.2* The concept of decision-making used in the phase model
Source: Teisman (2000) 'Models for research into decision-making processes: On phases, streams and decision-making rounds', *Public Administration* 78(4): 937–56

The three streams exist simultaneously. 'They are largely independent of one another, and each develops according to its own dynamics and rules' (Kingdon 1984: 20). There are three separate worlds where specific products are developed and transformed into their own dynamics and therefore are not linked in any temporal sequence. 'While there are indeed different processes, they do not necessarily follow one another through time in any regular pattern' (Kingdon 1984: 83). Actors with solutions in the policy stream are looking for problems and political commitment, while politicians are looking for both solutions and problems with which they can 'score'. According to this conceptual model, major policy changes are likely to occur only if the three streams become linked. Such linkages can occur especially if there is a favourable momentum, a so-called 'policy window' (Kingdon 1984: 174; Anglund 1999). The researcher can make decision-making transparent by investigating to what extent links are forged and why they are forged. Thus decision-making is not primarily separated into vertical strands, in the sense of consecutive steps over time, but rather in horizontal strands, in the sense of streams existing simultaneously side by side (see Figure 23.3).

## The rounds model of decision-making: interacting decisions

In the rounds model, actors are once again the focal point of analysis. The assumption here is that solutions/policy and problems are relevant to a policy process, insofar as they are presented by an actor during this process (Scharpf *et al.* 1978; Teisman 1998) In contrast to the phase model, here the researcher assumes that problems and solutions are not linked to a single actor (policy-maker) and are therefore not fixed at the single moment at which the policy is adopted. Many actors are involved in decision-making, and they will introduce their own perceptions of

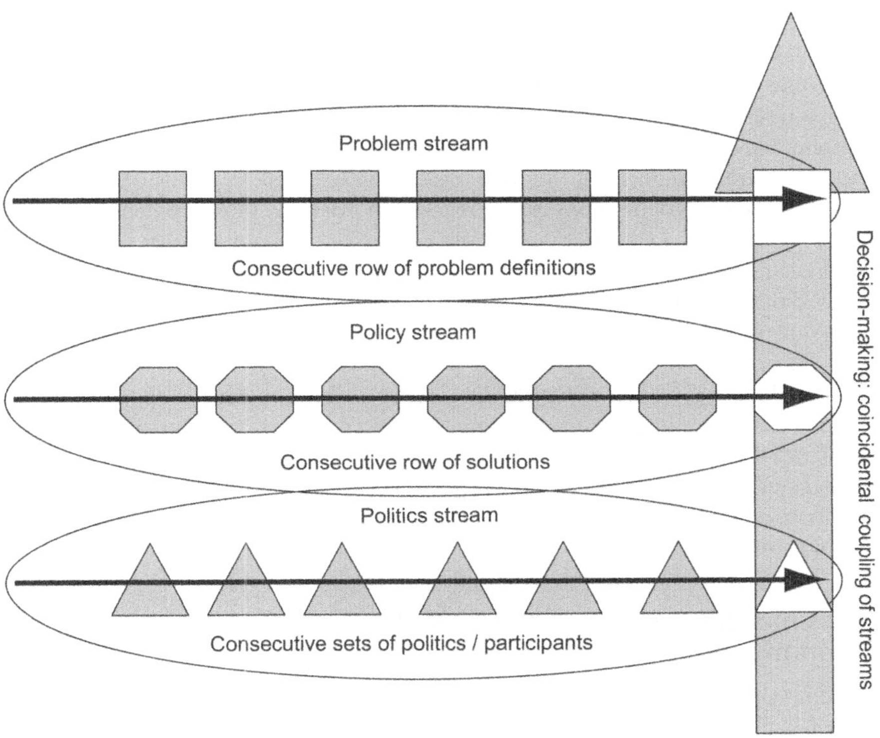


*Figure 23.3* The concept of decision-making used in the stream model
Source: Teisman (2000) 'Models for research into decision-making processes: On phases, streams and decision-making rounds', *Public Administration* 78(4): 937–56

relevant problems, possible solutions and political judgement. In order to understand decision-making, the researcher focuses on the variety of actors, objectives and solutions, their dynamics as well as the interaction between these elements. Complex decision-making involves many policy-makers who take decisions.

The rounds model can be seen as an interactive approach (Scharpf 1997). Policies, in terms of the actual interventions that take place in society, do not stem from an intended course of action formulated by one actor, but result from of a series of decisions taken by different actors (see Figure 23.3, from Teisman 2000).

> Political scientists ... should be interested in the fact that many or most of the well-designed policy proposals will never get a chance to become effective. The reason is that public policy is not usually produced by a unitary actor with adequate control over all required action resources and a single-minded concern for the public interest. Rather it is likely to result from the strategic interaction among several or many policy actors, each with its own understanding of the nature of the problem and the feasibility of particular solutions, each with its own individual and institutional self-interest and its own normative preferences, and each with its own capabilities or action resources that may be employed to affect the outcome.
>
> *(Scharpf 1997: 11)*

The focus, therefore, should be on the interaction among purposeful actors. To gain insight into policy-making, the researcher depicts which actors are participating at what time. Actors are units capable of developing a recognisable course of action (individuals, groups or collective/corporate entities).

To separate strands of decision-making, the train of thought of the phase model is combined with that of the stream model. On the one hand, a *vertical* classification of decision-making is made, by looking at series of decisions that were taken in that time. On the other hand a *horizontal* classification is applied by looking at interactions concerning the same subject, even if actors are unaware of each other's decisions at the moment they take these decisions. The division into time periods differs from that of the phase model in a number of respects. It is not the feature of the time period as such (i.e. this is preparation and this is implementation) that is being determined, but rather the starting and concluding points of a certain period. Such a period is called a 'decision-making round'. The researcher demarcates decision-making rounds by determining the most crucial decisions of decision-making in retrospect. This concerns particularly the choice of decisions that in a later period of decision-making serve as an important point of reference for the behaviour of the actors that are present at the time (Teisman 1998).

The application of the rounds model yields a picture of decision-making, particularly focusing on the ability of parties to handle their dependency on other parties in interaction (see Figure 23.4).

## The tracks model of decision-making: looking at the ingredients of interaction processes

The rounds model gives us an impression of how we can understand the intermittent development of decision-making processes and the way in which consecutive decisions emerge. It explains

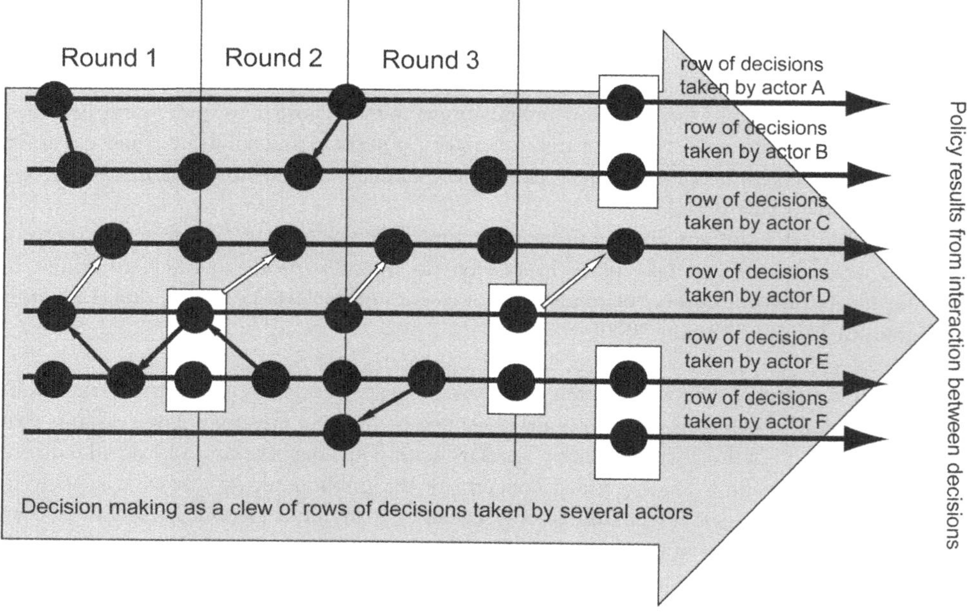


*Figure 23.4* The concept of decision-making used in the rounds model
Source: Teisman (2000) 'Models for research into decision-making processes: On phases, streams and decision-making rounds', *Public Administration* 78(4): 937–56

how strategies of individual actors result in collective outcomes. At the same time, it has less relevance for the content of a decision-making process, an element which is quite central to Kingdon's streams model and is also important in the phase model when it comes to the rational approach of policy-making and the central role of policy analysis (Quade 1972).

The tracks model emerged out of the recognition that decision-making has to do with three ingredients brought in by participants (cf. van Buuren and Gerrits 2008). First of all, they bring in their ambitions, based upon their material interests or normative goals. They participate because they have something to win or lose. But second, these actors also have the opportunity to mobilize factual evidence in favour of their ambitions (Sabatier 1988). They criticize evidence when this is not in accordance with their point of view. Due to the fragmentation within the knowledge domain, they do have many opportunities to mobilize counter-evidence to attack the evidence used by formal policy initiators. But third, implicitly or explicitly, all participants in decision-making processes do have their own problem perceptions, mental frame or belief system. They use a specific interpretation of the problem at stake and also a specific interpretation of the future they are convinced to be desirable (Feldman 1989). We can find a comparable idea in Vickers (1965) who distinguishes between action judgements, reality judgements and value judgements.

Facts, frames and ambitions are the ingredients of interaction processes. During these interaction processes these ingredients evolve, merge and disappear, due to endogenous and exogenous developments. The evolution of these elements is influenced by internal dynamics but also by their mutual interaction: facts can influence frames as can ambitions and vice versa. Actors negotiate about which facts are authoritative, which meta-frames are constructed and which ambitions can be combined or traded. New facts are mobilized in order to break through a situation of frame fixation and frame reflection can be initiated when negotiations stagnate. The tracks model thus analyses the evolution of these tracks separately as well as by their mutual interaction.

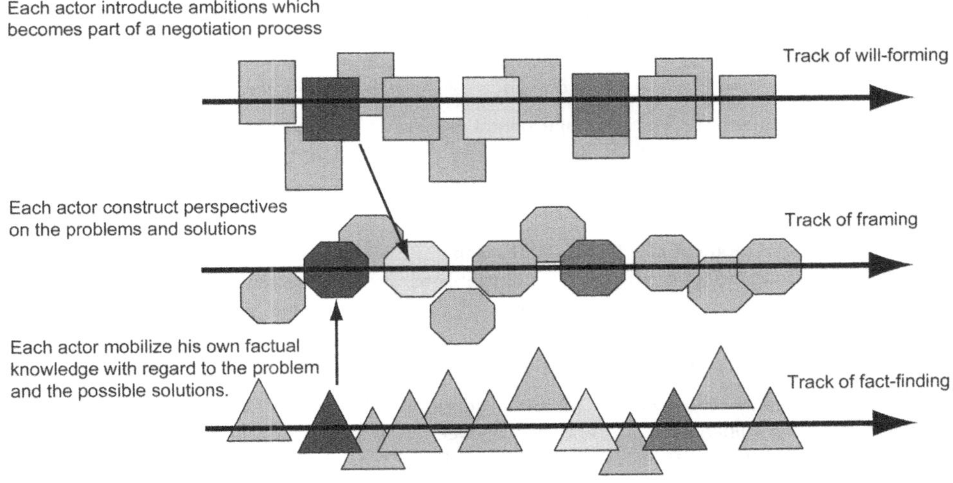


*Figure 23.5* The concept of decision-making used in the tracks model
Source: Author

From this perspective decisions are seen as (temporal and dynamic) selections of facts, frames and ambitions. These selections are only temporary: developments within one of the tracks (for example new facts or changing ambitions) can distort such an equilibrium and can trigger new decisions (van Buuren and Gerrits 2008; van Buuren *et al.* 2009). In more consensus-oriented decision-making processes, the extent to which there is consensus within these three tracks is an important selection criterion, while in more adversarial processes this selection depends upon the outcome of a power struggle between actors. Actors easily can mobilize new facts, construct new frames or air other ambitions to challenge this equilibrium.

## A comparative analysis to highlight the relative value of the four models

In the previous sections we have examined four models. The phase model provides an insight into the subsequent stages a focal actor goes through. The stream model focuses on links between problems, solutions and politics. The rounds model provides an insight into the interaction between actors. Mutual adjustment (by way of co-operation, conflict or avoidance) leads to policy results (see Table 23.1). And finally, the tracks model explains the way in which the content of decisions evolves.

In order to argue what the added value of the rounds model can be, three themes will be dealt with. The first looks at the issue of actors, problems and solutions, the second with policy adoption as a yardstick, event or result and the third with criteria for the evaluation of decision-making. Finally, the rounds model will be considered as a useful tool for developing the governance theories further.

*Table 23.1* Comparative perspectives on the phase model, the stream model and the rounds model

| | *Phase model* | *Stream model* | *Rounds model* | *Tracks model* |
|---|---|---|---|---|
| Criteria for the separation of strands of activities | Stages a focal organization goes through | Different concurrent streams of problems, solutions and politics | Rows of decisions taken by actors, creating rounds through interaction | Tracks of different types of content, brought in by various actors |
| Characterization of decision-making | Sequence of formation, adoption and implementation | Coincidental or organized links between streams | Interaction between decisions taken by various actors | Co-evolving tracks of fact-finding, framing and will-forming |
| Assumptions about the nature of the process | One moment of policy adoption holds way over other decisions and guides the process | A simultaneous stream of problems, solutions and politics, linked more or less at random | Decisions that conclude a round and initiate a new round, without fixing its progress | Decisions as temporary constellations of facts, frames and ambitions |
| Assumptions about the content of the process | A focal actor adopts a dominant definition of the problem solution, creating governmental policy | Dynamics within and links between streams determine major policy changes | Interdependent actors take decisions separately or jointly, leading to governance policies | Content evolves dynamically due to the evolution within and between the three tracks |

Source: Authors

### *Actors, problems, solutions and interaction*

It is generally accepted that various actors are involved in decision-making. The phase model, however, places certain actors in a more central position than others on an a priori basis. The rounds model refrains from doing this. When dealing with complexity, it is not sensible to exclude actors in advance or to assume that certain actors can be characterized on a priori grounds as policy designers, adopters or implementers. Rather, it is advisable to start out with all the (potential) participants who perform in decision-making. In the rounds model, decision-making is not about a single issue, nor about separated streams of problems, solutions and participants, but about dynamic combinations of sets of problems and solutions represented by different actors. Complications in decision-making often appear when a solution adopted by one or more actors constitutes a problem for others. Progress is often made when a solution is provided which deals with sets of problems and the ambitions of several of the actors involved. For this reason the rounds model focuses on the *interaction* between actors, during which they can negotiate acceptable combinations of problems and solutions. To understand this interaction in more detail, the tracks model focuses on the evolution of the ingredients of decisions during this interaction process.

## Policy adoption, yardstick, event or result

The phase model assumes that policies are set at a certain moment. The stream model assumes that policy streams from an event in which the streams coincide. The rounds model, in contrast, assumes that this moment does not exist. Policies result from a series of decisions taken by various actors. The dynamics of combining problems and solutions and the relation between the two account for the course of decision-making. A round of decision-making begins and ends with the adoption of a certain combination of a problem definition and a (virtual) solution by one or more actors.

The assumption is that the actors assess to what extent other actors share their definition of reality and proceed to interact on this basis. In contrast to the phase model, none of the definitions are seen as final or permanent. Research based on the rounds model will focus on perceived problems and solutions and will subsequently analyse whether and how actors have managed to combine perceptions to such an extent that they are willing to support a joint solution (Termeer 1993: 44, 48–51). Adoption then becomes the consolidation of a problem-solution combination (in terms of a specific constellation of facts, frames and ambitions) over a longer period of several decision rounds.

### *Policy evaluation and evaluation criteria, shifting from a government to a governance approach*

In the phase model, the public interest as defined by the focal organization is often used as guideline for evaluation. Evaluation focuses on the 'fit' between policy result and policy formulated in advance by the focal organization. The rounds model questions this criterion. Policy intentions at the beginning of a process are not necessarily the best indicator of public interest. It could be argued that a posteriori opinions and judgments are at least as good an indicator. Second, it is assumed that network society as a whole, and the government in particular, are fragmented. As a result, the representation of the public interest is distributed over various parts of government and organizations outside the government. Policy evaluation becomes more meaningful if all these intentions are taken into account in the analysis. A fitting overall concept is joint interest (Teisman 1992: 91–2). Evaluation then no longer focuses on the question whether the policy result agrees with a single policy intention, but whether it is based upon agreed facts between participants, a shared problem frame and an attractive combination of the various ambitions, and to what extent it responds to the objectives of all the parties involved at the moment policy effects can be distinguished.

### *The shift in orientation from government to governance*

By doing so, the rounds model can contribute to the discussion about the shift from government to governance within several scientific communities involved in public administration.

In response to empirical studies by Mackintosh (1977) and Jones (1975), which undermined some of the assertions of the Westminster model, Rhodes (in Rhodes and Dunleavy 1995) suggested a new framework of analysis. This framework should focus on the complex web of institutions, networks and practices surrounding the prime minister, Cabinet, Cabinet committees and their official counterparts, namely the less formal ministerial 'clubs' or meetings, bilateral negotiations, interdepartmental committees, and so on (Rhodes 1995: 12). From this insight it was a logical next step to focus on complexity of interactions between actors (see Smith 1998: 47). Government is depicted as an institutional framework, not as an actor. Governance is about steering without presuming the presence of hierarchy (Rosenau 1992: 14). It refers to relational contracting, organized markets in group enterprises, clans, networks, trade associations and strategic alliances (Jessop 1995). Departments have to be seen as one of many competing centres of authority (Rhodes 1996a, 1996b).

It is within this perspective that the rounds and tracks model must be placed. Consideration should be given to the idea of using the rounds model in empirical research focusing on governance. The model offers a way to reconstruct a basically unlimited complexity of events that can be combined into a decision-making process. This will provide us with additional, more detailed insights into these processes, thereby creating a basis for more management theories about networks (Kickert *et al.* 1997).

## A fourfold analysis of the Betuwe railway line

In this section we will present an in-depth case study of decision-making processes regarding the construction of a new freight railway line between Europe's largest port, Rotterdam, and Germany. The so-called Betuwe line is one of the most disputed projects of the last decade in the Netherlands. The parties involved have even called it a 'battle'.[3] Despite all the problems and opposition, construction of the railway line is still continuing. Therefore, we may consider this to be a successful decision-making process, in which the ministry, the cabinet and the parliament were able to undertake a strategic project that fitted in with their policies.

At the same time, however, many questions can be raised. The expected growth of freight transport by rail did not take place. It is far from clear whether or not the German section of the line can support the number of trains needed to make the Betuwe railway line viable. There are no private parties that want to invest in the line or exploit it, even though this was assumed to be the case by the cabinet when the policy was being adopted.

Studies have questioned the positive environmental impact of transport by rail compared with that by road and waterways. The costs of the line have risen from 2.5 billion initially to 9.35 billion in 1998. Recently the transport minister decided to forgo the construction of the Northern branch of the Betuwe line in order to avoid any further increase in expenditure. A fourfold analysis of this case is presented below.

## Application of the phase model: a central actor, a defined problem and a good solution

In the Netherlands, the central government, specifically the Ministry of Traffic and Waterways, is responsible for the planning of new infrastructure. To properly organie decision-making, the ministry uses a formal procedure known as the Planning Central Decision Procedure (in Dutch: PKB). At the end of the 1980s, the ministry was faced with congestion on existing freight connections from Rotterdam to the hinterland, combined with an expected growth in freight transport. In previous policy memoranda, the Government had appointed the distribution sector as a core activity for the Dutch economy. The two main Dutch ports, Schiphol Airport and the port of Rotterdam, should be enabled to function optimally and the main transport lines should be provided with sufficient capacity. The capacity of the hinterland connection could be increased by three different means: road, waterways or a new railway line. Because road traffic was seen as having a negative impact on the environment and transport by water was not seen as a viable option, the ministry decided in 1989 that a new railway link was needed.

The ministry decided that the railway should run through the rural region of the Betuwe and a freight line was due to be completed before 1997. To implement this policy, the ministry set up the necessary procedures to determine the line's trajectory and its incorporation into the landscape. But while going through these procedures, the ministry encountered opposition from civilians and local authorities. In order to delay implementation, regional actors asked for additional studies to be carried out into the possible construction of an underground tunnel. Although the ministry indicated that this was not a realistic plan, the Second Chamber let itself be persuaded to investigate this option. This was the signal for other parties to present the Chamber with other new alternatives, such as the submersion of the railway line within a cutting. The involvement of parliament resulted in a considerable series of amendments and an increase in costs. While the first plans were expected to cost 4 billion Dutch guilders, subsequent calculations found that with the addition of the new line the project would have cost more than 9 million guilders. At the end of 1993 the project was approved by parliament. Decision-making was complicated, however, by the parliamentary elections of 1994. One supporter of the project left the cabinet and was replaced by a minister who opposed the project. To deal with this situation, the new cabinet appointed a Committee of Experts chaired by a member of the opposition. In January 1995 this Committee declared itself in favour, thus persuading the opposition to revise their point of view. In early 1997 all complaints were rejected by the Council of State. The construction works could begin.

## Application of the stream model: insights into how solutions, problems and politics come together

The first additional insight is that the need for a freight railway line had existed long before being placed on the cabinet's political agenda in 1989. In the early 1980s this idea had already been discussed in Rotterdam. Transport of goods to the German hinterland was only possible via road and inland waterways. Road transport was vulnerable due to environmental restraints, while any growth in water transport was questioned due to its rigid institutional nature. The attractive third solution, the construction of a freight railway line, however, was at that time incompatible with problems at the national level.

Years later, it was taken up again by the new enterprise responsible for freight transport by rails. This organisation resulted from the division of the Dutch Railway Company, a monopoly, into two separate companies, one for passengers and one for freight. The latter saw the railway line as a solution to its own unprofitable position. The line was defined as a prerequisite for the growth of freight transport by rail. However, the political argument for it was not made, and in 1988 the Transport Ministry turned down the proposal.

Suddenly in 1989 the ministry became interested in the solution, even though its characteristics had not changed. An explanation for this can be found within the ministry itself. It was preparing a strategic plan for transport investments in the next decade, and became aware in 1989 that a major key project was lacking in this plan, and other projects were faced with delays. A Ministerial Committee was set up which advised the minister to approve the Betuwe railway line. Due to budget deficits, financial problems remained. These were solved in two ways. First, it was assumed that it would be co-financed by private parties, and second, that exploitation of the line would be profitable. It was this combination of problems and solutions that convinced parliament in 1993. The policy was approved.

## *Application of the rounds model: additional insights into internal and external dynamics*

In the rounds model, attention is paid to streams of decisions taken by several actors. The following groups of actors can be distinguished: the Rotterdam Port Authority, the freight railway company NS Cargo, the Transport Ministry, parliament, local and national environmental groups, the German Railway Company, and the European and German governments. Five different rounds are distinguished. During the first round, which started in the beginning of the 1980s, supporters of the Rotterdam port called for an additional freight link to the hinterland, in addition to the existing roads and waterways. They initiated the process. The aim was to increase the amount of transport modalities that could be used. They were less interested in the use of rail as such, but rather in increasing the range of options. This idea was discussed locally and shelved after some time, partly due to the negative reaction of the Chamber of Commerce in Rotterdam. The first round was terminated for this reason, and it seemed as though the proposal had disappeared into a desk drawer for good.

A second round was started in 1987 by NS Cargo. It had recently split from its parent, the Dutch Railway Company, and was faced with a weak market position. To strengthen its position, it proposed to build a line specifically for freight transport. This had not been proposed in the past, for the reason that no powerful actor had been responsible thus far for freight transport by rail. In the former Dutch Railway Company freight had always been subordinate to passenger transport. With the birth of NS Cargo the railway line had obtained its own policy entrepreneur. However, NS Cargo did not have the legal or financial means to construct the railway line and began a lobbying process. Until 1989 the ministry showed no interest.

In that year, a third round of decision-making was begun in which the ministry now played a leading role. The line was placed high on the government's agenda and has held this position ever since. Decision-making was accelerated had already by the minister, and one year later a concrete route was proposed and the fourth round of decision-making had begun. In this round the ministry still played an important role, but was at times outclassed by Parliament. This stemmed directly from the role played by local and regional governments and environmental groups. At the beginning of the process, national environmental groups supported the choice in favour of transport by rail. Due to the speeding-up of decision-making, however, and a total lack of communication with local and regional governments, resistance grew quickly in 1992 and 1993, and national environmental groups felt compelled to withdraw their support. The Betuwe line became the Dutch example of a closed and autistic central government giving priority to the traditional economy (port development, transport and infrastructure) instead of the environment and quality of life, or a more modern type of economy (knowledge infrastructure, services). The ministry rejected all the alternatives presented by the local authorities and other groups in society. Parliament was more accommodating, however, and a range of amendments resulted, raising the cost to almost 10 billion guilders. The Betuwe line appeared to have been approved by the government.

The fifth round began with the parliamentary elections and the change in the coalition of governing parties, as has been described above. A high-level committee (the Hermans Committee) was created to provide independent advice about the Betuwe line. This committee advised in favour of the Betuwe line but found it difficult to formulate their advice. They received contradictory reports from consultancy firms, and various local and regional stakeholders tried to influence the committee. More interesting here is that under the surface of party-political manoeuvring, a lot of interaction was going on in terms of financing the project, exploiting the line when in operation and creating a European competing network of freight railway services. These decisions would be crucial to the success of the Betuwe line.

Several rounds of decision-making were yet to come. Decisions needed to be taken about financial support from private sources, exploitation of the line, harmonizing European working arrangements, and so on. These decisions would determine whether or not a parliamentary inquiry should be set up in the next century to investigate why so much public money had been invested in something thatwas a failure. Thus far, decision-making on this issue had already had two important unforeseen but desired results: the expected competition by the railway forced the inland waterways shipping sector to make institutional changes and adopt a more competitive approach. This had already led to an enormous increase in inland shipping. Second, freight transport by road was becoming ecologically more sound. Ironically, it was then argued that both these developments made rendered Betuwe railway line superfluous.

## *Application of the tracks model: additional insights into internal and external dynamics*

The tracks model enables us to analyse in more detail the composition of the various decisions marking the succession of the various rounds in the decision-making process.

Within the first round especially, the port authorities were convinced about the shortcomings of the existing railway's capacity. Their ambition to construct a railway was based upon empirical knowledge about the weaknesses of the other possibilities: road transport and inland shipping. This ambition matched that of the freight railway company perfectly.

However, for a long time the ministry and parliament did not recognize the urgency of the perceived problem. Only in 1989 was the Minister of Transport convinced of the necessity to develop better railway connections, but this was not based upon much factual evidence. The new 1980 cabinet (Christian Democrats and Socialists) decided to invest in sustainable economic growth and support the Betuwe line project. A breakthrough was came about by framing the Betuwe line in such a way that it was compatible with the policy of sustainable economic growth.

After two years of further investigation, the Dutch parliament hesitated to ratify the Planning Central Decision Procedure. A second opinion was sought and compensatory measures proposed to meet the wishes of local and regional stakeholders. Parliament only approved the Betuwe line after combining its main policy with a number of regional policies.

The Hermans Committee brought together much additional factual evidence but advised again in favour of the Betuwe line. Increasingly the line was framed as a long-term strategic investment and as the only viable alternative for the harmful environmental impact of the existing means of transport. This advice was an important building block for parliament to ratify the decision to start constructing the Betuwe line. Five years later, doubts arose about the short-term effectiveness of the Betuwe line, and it came to be regarded as a potential planning disaster.

*Table 23.2* Events in decision-making on the Betuwe line and a fourfold research result

| ***Empirical events*** | *Interpretations based on the phase model* | *Interpretations based on the stream model* | *Interpretations based on the rounds model* | *Interpretations based on the tracks model* |
|---|---|---|---|---|
| The Rotterdam Port Authority proposes a railway link to Germany (1985) | Irrelevant (Ministry did not respond to proposal) | Solution was unable to find a problem and sufficient participants | Start of first round; the port authority aims to increase the range of transport modalities | Based upon a strong interest to remain competitive, port authorities perceive hinterland connections as insufficient |
| New enterprise for railway freight transport adopts Betuwe railway line (1987) | Lobbying activity resulting in a ministerial committee in 1989 (still not relevant) | Problem of a lack of profit was combined with the solution of a new line | The start of second round of decision-making, aiming to create a viable freight train enterprise | Private ambitions are connected and stakeholders starts to work on a convincing factual underpinning and problem frame |
| A ministerial committee is set up to investigate the viability of the Betuwe line (1989/1990) | Minister begins decision-making by setting up a committee (starting point for analyses) | The department is faced with a lack of major key projects in its new strategic plan | Start of third round leading to the adoption of the project as part of the strategic plan of the ministry | Ambition of cabinet to invest in sustainable growth is connected to problem frame of Betuwe line coalition |
| The minister points out a concrete route (1992), starts Planning Central Decision Procedure and organizes popular participation | The official start of the Planning Central Decision Procedure (policy formation) | Choosing a concrete route was seen by the policy community as a solution to solve the problem of slow decision-making | Start of fourth round, aiming to speed up decision-making, but actually generating and activating opposition against project | The EIA and positive transport scenarios contribute to the problem frame that railway connections are the weak link |
| Parliament adopts proposal (1993) | Central decision is taken (policy adopted) | Coupling of problem, solution and participants | End of fourth round | Parliament accepts Betuwe line based upon second opinion and with compensatory measures |
| Parliamentary elections resulting in a new Cabinet (1994) | The central decision is reconsidered in an opaque political arena | Second coupling in which new participants introduce new policy definitions | Fifth round helps party to change position and used by societal groups to get additional proposal accepted | Hermans Committee decides to use data about existing capacity to advise in favour of Betuwe line. Parliament enforces additional compensatory measures |

*Table 23.2* (continued)

| ***Empirical events*** | *Interpretations based on the phase model* | *Interpretations based on the stream model* | *Interpretations based on the rounds model* | *Interpretations based on the tracks model* |
|---|---|---|---|---|
| The Administrative Court overrules all written objections (1997) | Official start of construction activities; the implementation really starts | Confirmation of the existing coupling between political, policy and problem stream | In sixth round, opponents activate potential coalition in business, criticizing added value of project | New factual evidence fuels framing of Betuwe line as potential planning disaster but is not combined with powerful ambitions that can alter new official frame in which Betuwe line is 'strategic choice for the long-term.' |
| The Cabinet decides not to build the northern branch of the Betuwe railway line (1999) | Partial policy termination due to new information | New linking of politics with alternative problems or solutions | In seventh round, minister is convinced by influential actors that public money is needed elsewhere. | New insights in the added value of the northern branch and local resistance against it, contribute to the decision not to build this branch |

Source: Authors

There was also fierce regional resistance. All these considerations led to the decision not to go ahead with the construction of the northern branch.

## Conclusion

Decision-making has become increasingly complex during the past decades. There is a growing variety of relevant actors and definitions of problems and solutions. In this chapter the question of how to conceptualize decision-making in order to generate useful insights for the understanding of complex dynamics in decision-making processes has been answered. Four conceptual models were presented: the phase model; the stream model; the rounds model; and the tracks model. In the phase model, the focus is on decisions taken by a focal actor, targeting a specific problem. In the stream model, the focus is on the linking of three more or less independent streams, namely problems, solutions and politics. The rounds model focuses on the interaction between the various decisions taken by different actors. And finally, the tracks model clarifies how decisions are composed out of specific selections of facts, frames and ambitions, where the separate tracks evolve erratically due to internal and external dynamics. If we analyse reality from these four models, different images of reality are obtained, each of which provides a partial insight into reality.

Thanks to the use of the phase model, we now know a great deal about how a single actor defines policy in terms of problems and solutions, policy adoption, implementation and evaluation. Attention is paid to a focal actor, often the central government, and the way in which this central actor organizes its own policy processes. The phase model focuses mainly on the intended policy of this focal actor. This is both its strength and its weakness. The case study on the Betuwe railway line presents a national government that is dedicated to the project and was able to defend it successfully against outside attacks.

The stream model concerns the fragmentation of the decision-making world into problems, solutions and politics as separate streams. If these streams come together by chance, progress can be made. It is not the intended policy of one actor, but the links between the streams that are crucial. The case study shows that different problems were linked to the Betuwe line solution. The lack of alternative solutions was an important reason for this project being placed on the central government's agenda. New fundraising initiatives are still a threat to the project.

The rounds model focuses on the interaction between interdependent actors. Every new actor entering decision-making introduces new problems and solutions. Particularly on these points, the rounds model offers a number of additional possibilities to enhance insight into decision-making. By not just accepting that there are various actors, but also accepting that all these actors contribute to the decision-making process and can even influence the results of this process helps to explain the complexity and gain insight into interaction patterns which are used for governance of the network society. The model emphasizes that achieving satisfactory results depends not only upon decisions taken by individual actors, but to an increasing extent upon the interaction between decisions taken by several actors. By using the rounds model, the researcher can analyse the interactions between decisions. All actors involved in governance can benefit from these insights.

As a further elaboration of this model, the tracks model highlights the evolution of the content of decision-making within the various rounds. It focuses upon the question: what is exchanged in the various interactions between actors? By distinguishing between facts, frames and ambitions and by analysing the way they influence each other, we enrich our understanding of how the results of decision-making processes are formed out of the complex interaction between a variety of partial and sometimes partisan knowledge claims, subjective problem perceptions and competing or complementary interests. Because of the fact that it combines attention to development in actor ambitions with attention to knowledge dynamics and framing/learning processes, it goes one step beyond traditional models which normally focus on only one or two of these issues.

New insights on traces, tracks, time lines and process systems indicate the need for a model able to accommodate a wider perspective.

## Notes

1 This is an updated and extended version of Geert R. Teisman (2000) 'Models for research into decision-making processes: On phases, streams and decision-making rounds, *Public Administration* 78(4): 937–56.
2 In this article we will not deal with the question of evaluation.
3 Between 1991 and 1997 the project director wrote a book on the subject entitled *Slag om de Betuwe Route* (The Battle of the Betuwe Line) (Boom 1997).

## Bibliography


Anderson, J. 1979. *Public Policy Making*. New York: Praeger.

Altman, J.A. and E. Petkus. 1994. 'Towards a stakeholder-based policy process: an application of the social marketing perspective to environmental policy development', *Policy Sciences* 27: 37–51.

Anglund, S.M. 1999. 'Policy feedback: The comparison effect and small business procurement policy', *Policy Studies Journal* 27(1): 11–27.

Bache, I. and M.V. Flinders. 2004. *Multilevel Governance*. Oxford: Oxford University Press.

Boom, H. 1977. *Slag om de Betuwe Route*. Leuven: Balans.

Börzel, T.A. 1998. 'Organizing Babylon: On the different conceptions of policy networks', *Public Administration* 765: 253–73.

Bryson, J.M. and B.C. Crosby. 1992. *Leadership for the Common Good, Tackling Public Problems in a Shared-Power World*. San Francisco: Jossey-Bass.

Butler, R. 1991. *Designing Organizations: A Decision-making Perspective*. London: Routledge.

Cohen, M.D, J.G. March and J.P. Olsen. 1972. 'A garbage can model of organizational choice', *Administrative Science Quarterly* 17(1): 1–25.

Crozier, M. and E. Friedberg. 1980. *Actors and Systems: The Politics of Collective Action*. Chicago: University Press.

Duit, A. and V. Galaz. 2006. 'Governance and complexity: Emerging issues for governance theory', *Governance* 23(3): 11–35.

Dunleavy, P. and Gillian Peel (eds). 1990. *Developments in British Politics 3*. Basingstoke: Palgrave Macmillan.

Edelman, M. 1971. *The Symbolic Uses of Politics: Mass Arousal and Quiescence*. Chicago: Markham Publishers.

Feldman, Martha. 1989. *Order Without Design: Information Production and Policy Making*. 1st edn. Stanford, CA: Stanford University Press.

Fischer, F. 2003. *Reframing Public Policy: Discursive Politics and Deliberative Practices*. Oxford: Oxford University Press.

Gerrits, L. 2008. *The Gentle Art of Coevolution: A Complexity Theory Perspective on Decision Making over Estuaries in Germany, Belgium and the Netherlands*. Rotterdam: Erasmus University.

Hanf, K. and F.W. Scharpf (eds). 1978. *Interorganizational Policy Making: Limits to Co-ordination and Central Control*. London: Sage.

Haynes, Philip. 2008. 'Complexity theory and evaluation in public management', *Public Management Review* 10(3): 401–19.

Heclo, H. 1974. *Modern Social Politics in Britain and Sweden: From Relief to Income Maintenance*. New Haven, CT: Yale University Press.

Heritier, A., C. Knill and S. Mingers. 1996. *Ringing the Changes in Europe: Regulatory Competition and Redefinition of the State*. Berlin: De Gruyter.

Hoogerwerf, A. (ed.). [1982, 1985]1989. *Public Policy: An Introduction to the Policy Science (Overheidsbeleid: een inleiding in de beleidswetenschap)*, 2nd, 3rd, and 4th edns. Alphen a/d Rijn: Samsom Tjeenk Willink.

Jessop, B. 1995. 'The regulation approach, governance and post-Fordism', *Economy and Society* 24, 307–33.

Jones, G. 1975. 'Development of the Cabinet', in W. Thornhill (ed.) *The Modernisation of British Government*. London: Pitman.

Judge, D. 1993. *The Parliamentary State*. London: Sage.
Kingdon, J.W. 1984. *Agendas, Alternatives, and Public Policies*. Boston: Little, Brown.
Kickert, W., E.-H. Klijn and J. Koppenjan. 1997. *Managing Complex Networks*. London: Sage.
Koppenjan, J. 1984. *Management of Policy Processes (Management van de beleidsvorming)*. The Hague: Vuga.
Lindblom, Charles E. and Edward J. Woodhouse. 1992. *The Policy Making Process*, 3rd edn. Englewood Cliffs, NJ: Prentice Hall.
Mackintosh, J.P. 1977. *The Politics and Government of Britain*. London: Hutchinson.
March, J.G. 1988. *Decisions and Organisations*. Oxford: Blackwell.
—— and J.P. Olsen. [1976]1979. *Ambiguity and Choice in Organisations*, 1st and 2nd edns. Bergen: Universitetsforlaget.
Marin, B. and R. Mayntz (eds). 1991. *Policy Networks: Empirical Evidence and Theoretical Considerations*. Frankfurt: Campus Verlag.
Mintzberg, H. 1973. *The Nature of Managerial Work*. New York: Harper & Row.
—— 1976. 'Planning on the left side and managing on the right', *Harvard Business Review* 54: 49–58.
——, D. Raisinghani and A. Therot. 1976. 'The structure of unstructured decision processes', *Administrative Science Quarterly* 21(2): 246–75.
Morgan, G. 1997. *Images of Organisation*, 2nd edn. London: Sage.
Ostrom, E. 1990. *Governing the Commons: The Evolution of Institutions for Collective Action*. Cambridge: Cambridge University Press.
Quade, Edward S. 1972. *Analysis for Public Policy Decisions*. New York: Rand Corporation.
Rhodes, R.A.W. 1995. 'From prime ministerial power to core executive', in R.A.W. Rhodes and P. Dunleavy (eds) *Prime Minister, Cabinet and Core Executive*. London: Macmillan.
—— 1996a. 'Governing without governance: Order and change in British government', inaugural lecture, University of Newcastle, 18 April.
—— 1996b. 'The new governance: Governing without government', *Political Studies* 44: 652–67
——and P. Dunleavy (eds). 1995. *Prime Minister, Cabinet and Core Executive*. London: Macmillan.
Rittel, H.W.J. and M.M. Webber. 1973. 'Dilemmas in a general theory of planning', *Policy Sciences* 4: 155–69.
Rosenau, J. 1992. 'Governance, order and change in world politics', in J.N. Rosenau and E.O. Czempiel (eds) *Governance without Government*, Cambridge: Cambridge University Press.
Sabatier, P.A. 1988. 'An advocacy coalition framework of policy change and the role of policy-oriented learning therein', *Policy Sciences* 21(2–3): 129–68.
—— 1999. *Theories of the Policy Process*, Colorado: Westview Press.
Sato, H. 1999. 'The advocacy coalition framework and the policy process analysis: The case of smoking control in Japan', *Policy Studies Journal* 27(1): 28–44.
Scharpf, F. 1997. *Games Real Actors Play: Actor-centered Institutionalism in Policy Research*. Boulder, CO: Westview Press.
——, B. Reissert and F. Schnabel. 1978. 'Policy effectiveness and conflict avoidance', in Hanf, K. and F.W. Scharpf (eds) *Interorganizational Policy Making: Limits to Co-ordination and Central Control*. London: Sage.
Schön, D.A. and M. Rein. 1994. *Frame Reflection: Toward the Resolution of Intractable Policy Controversies*, New York: BasicBooks.
Smith, M.J. 1998. 'Reconceptualizing the British state: Theoretical and empirical challenges to central government', *Public Administration* 76(1): 45–72.
——, D. March and D. Richards. 1993. 'Central government departments and the policy process'. *Public Administration* 71: 567–94.
Strand, R. 2002. 'Complexity, ideology, and governance', *Emergence* 4(1–2): 164–83.
Teisman, G.R. [1992, 1995]1998. *Complex Decision-making, A Pluricentric View (Complexe Besluitvorming)*, 1st, 2nd, and 3rd edns. The Hague: Vuga.
—— 2000. 'Models for research into decision-making processes: On phases, streams and decision-making rounds', *Public Administration* 78(4): 937–56.
——with E.H. Klijn. 1997. 'Strategies and games in networks', in W. Kickert, E.H. Klijn and J. Koppenjan (eds) *Managing Complex Networks*. London: Sage, pp. 98–118.
——and E.H. Klijn. 2002. 'Partnership arrangements: Governmental rhetoric or governance schema?', *Public Administration Review* 62(2): 197–205.
——, A. van Buuren, and L. Gerrits. 2009. *Managing Complex Governance Systems, Dynamics, Self-Organization and Coevolution in Public Investments*. London: Routledge

Termeer, C. 1993. *Dynamics and Inertia in Manure Policy (Dynamiek en inertie in mestbeleid).* The Hague: Vuga.

van Bueren, E.M., E.H. Klijn, and J.F.M. Koppenjan. 2003. 'Dealing with wicked problems in networks: Analyzing an environmental debate from a network perspective', *Journal of Public Administration Research and Theory* 13(2): 193–212.

van Buuren, A. 2006. *Competent Decision-making. Making Multiple Knowledge for Spatial Development* (in Dutch), Boom/Lemma, Den Haag.

——and L. Gerrits. 2008. 'Decisions as dynamic equilibriums in erratic policy processes', *Public Management Review* 10(3): 281–399.

——, A. Gerrits, P. Marks. 2009. 'Public policy-making and the management of co-evolution', in Tiesman, G., van Buuren, A., Gerrits, L. (eds) *Managing Complex Governance Systems*, London: Routledge, 134–153.

van Herk, S., C. Zevenbergen, J. Rijke, and R. Ashley. 2011. 'Collaborative research to support transition towards integrating flood risk management in urban development', *Journal of Flood Risk Management* 4(4): 306–17.

Vickers, Sir Geoffrey. 1965. *The Art of Judgment: A Study of Policy Making.* New York: Basic Books.

Wagenaar, H. 2007. 'Governance, complexity, and democratic participation: How citizens and public officials harness the complexity of neighborhood decline', *The American Review of Public Administration* 37: 17–50.

24

# The garbage can model and the study of the policy-making process

*Gary Mucciaroni*

## Origins and description of the GCM

Kingdon imported the garbage can model (GCM) into political science and adapted it to study public policy-making from the seminal work of Cohen *et al.* (1972) who used the "garbage can" metaphor to describe decision-making in universities and other complex organizations. As Nikolaos Zahariadis (2007: 66) points out, the GCM "theorizes at the systemic level, and it incorporates an entire system or separate decision as the unit of analysis." Kingdon applied the GCM to the study of the federal government and conducted panel interviews with more than 240 participants in the policy-making process, primarily in the areas of transportation and health policies. Borrowing from Cohen *et al.*, Kingdon described the federal agenda-setting process as a mix of order and chaos, or "organized anarchy." The "can" is the set of more permanent and predictable features of the policy-making process, such as institutional arrangements and procedures that shape and structure behavior.

The main focus of the GCM, however, is on the "garbage" in the can because the items that reach the agenda at any given time arise out of the mix of contents in the can. The can's contents consist of three "streams"—"problems," "solutions" and "politics", which operate largely independent of one another. According to Kingdon (1984: 93), an issue reaches the agenda when "a problem is recognized, a solution is available, and the political climate makes the time right for change." Policy-makers and others recognize problems when social indicators, such as crime or unemployment rates, indicate that an undesirable condition is worsening or reaching a critical threshold, or, when a "focusing event"—a salient and usually dramatic episode or crisis—draws attention to the problem and lends it a sense of urgency. Solutions include "the gradual accumulation of knowledge and perspectives among specialists in any given area." Specialists generate and disseminate solutions, provide evidence and arguments in support of them that are intelligible to non-specialists, and help to package them into concrete proposals. "Politics" refers to the wide variety of actors and forces that constitute the political environment, including the "national mood," the organization and mobilization of interest groups and social movements, the partisan and ideological composition of Congress and the executive branch, and other aspects of the political context in which agendas are set.

The streams operate largely independently because different groups of people or forces control each of them. Problems come and go given changing conditions in the world, without regard for either the status of solutions that might address the problems or the state of the political context. Groups of experts and advocates conceive, develop and disseminate solutions over the long-term, without necessarily reacting to the immediacy of problems or the tenor of the political environment. And political change is governed by processes, like elections, budgeting, and the mobilization of interests that operate on their own schedules and trajectories.

An item (problem or solution) reaches the agenda (or is adopted) only when the three streams are aligned properly. Problem X or solution Y will not get on the agenda (or be chosen) unless the problem is recognized, a solution is considered to be available, and political conditions are conducive for giving the problem and solution serious attention. If any of these three elements is missing, the item will not get on the agenda (or the policy adopted). Problem recognition, solution availability and political opportunity, thus, each constitute necessary conditions for an item to reach the agenda (or a policy adoption).

At particular junctures, a policy entrepreneur with a commitment to a particular issue and the ability to draw attention to it, will couple a problem with a solution. Entrepreneurs wait for an auspicious time, such as after a dramatic focusing event and when Congress and the president are controlled by officials who are interested in addressing the issue. These "policy windows" often open unpredictably and only for a short while. Thus, entrepreneurs must act expeditiously and efficiently to get their pet item on the agenda (or get it adopted) before the window closes, when the political environment changes and attention shifts to other issues.

## Criticisms and limitations of the GCM

Scholars have pointed to a number of important problems and deficiencies with the GCM. In this section, we review several of these criticisms.

*Falsifiability*. The model, at least as a whole, is not falsifiable. Can we imagine a set of circumstances in which some condition in society was *not* considered a problem receiving serious consideration in government? Or, a situation in which an item got on the agenda (or a policy adopted) even though the political environment was *not* favorable to getting it on? Since the agenda, by definition, is composed of conditions that some key group of decision-makers considers "problems," it would be impossible for non-problematic conditions to get on the agenda. Since the political environment refers to those actors who are in power or who have influence over those in power, a problem or solution could not receive serious attention unless they permitted it. Non-falsifiability arises, as in most cases, because the model is formulated very broadly and ambiguously. One strategy for making the model more falsifiable would be to develop categories of problems, solutions and political contexts from which we could derive testable hypotheses about how *particular* kinds of problems and solutions reach the agenda given the existence of *particular* political conditions (Mucciaroni 1992: 463–5).

Bendor *et al.* (2001) have critiqued the original GCM developed by Cohen *et al.* (1972), arguing that the model is more like a metaphor than a model. As a result, many applications of the GCM "do little more than describe some parts of an organization as garbage cans … but it is not at all clear that they provide real … explanations." According to them, the GCM merely provides a scheme for describing and labeling phenomena without explaining them.

*Situational versus structural levels of analysis*. Before we can model agenda-setting, we need to be clear about what we are trying to explain related to agendas. It makes a great deal of difference whether we are asking why certain items reach the agenda at particular moments in time versus why certain items reach the agenda ever. The GCM is better at explaining *when* the agenda changes than explaining *how and why* the agenda changes. Much of the reason that the GCM is better at explaining the timing of agenda (or policy) change rather than give a full accounting of it, arises because the model conceptualizes constraints on agenda-setting (or decision-making) mainly at what I call the "situational" level of analysis—aspects of the policy-making environment that are relatively temporary and changeable. Problems (e.g. crime, airline safety) "get hot" and then cool off as attention drifts to other problems and new crises. Solutions (e.g. the "flat tax," "deregulation") snowball into fads but eventually turn stale and their popularity fades. Congressional majorities and presidential administrations come and go every two, four, or eight years; the "public mood" varies with the vagaries of the economy and other conditions. But political actors and forces that are more *permanent*, that *change slowly or hardly at all* from decade to decade, also shape agendas and decisions. It would be as much of a mistake to overlook the impact of these forces on agendas and policy decisions as it would be to ignore the impact of old age or genetics on human health.

One of kind of structural constraint is culture, political traditions and dominant ideologies. For example, the problems of anti-gay discrimination and poverty were off the agenda for many decades before they appeared in the 1960s in the case of poverty, and after 1970 in the case of gay rights. They were kept off the agenda by deeply ingrained, taken-for-granted beliefs that either nothing could be done about poverty or that it was the result of personal failings and that discrimination against gays was justified because they were "sick," "predators," or "sinners." Similarly, institutional arrangements hinder and facilitate problems and solutions from reaching the agenda. For example, during the Great Depression of the 1930s, policy-makers in some countries considered Keynesianism a plausible solution to the crisis while those in other nations did not. But whether Keynesian ideas became accepted partly depended upon which institutions had responsibility for making economic policy and whether institutions provided Keynesian economists with access to decision-makers (Hall 1989; Skocpol and Weir 1985). And some solutions have a bad "fit" with particular institutions. For example, regardless of the backgrounds of particular judges, or other relatively fluid conditions, solutions that do not fit into the logic of legal reasoning and the language of "rights" may not get a hearing or may be rejected.

Kingdon was aware of the importance of structural features of the policy-making process. He mentions, for example, that the budget process has particular procedures and timetables that constrain agenda-setting, and that American political culture filters out solutions that are incompatible with it before they can reach the agenda. The problem is that the GCM does not theorize structural constraints, leaving them largely outside its parameters. Because they are not incorporated in the model, the GCM is significantly incomplete. Admittedly, all models are incomplete, but these are large omissions in light of the GCM's theoretical ambitions.

*Lack of historical causality*. Much of what happens in the policy-making process, how it happens, and to whom, is in some fashion rooted in the past. The GCM neglects much of history because it focuses solely upon immediate or near-term changes in problems, solutions, and politics. Kingdon justifies overlooking historical explanations for agenda and policy change on the grounds that historical investigation would simply lead us down a fruitless path of "infinite regress": in searching for the relevant antecedent events and conditions that shaped the agenda, we would be compelled to search for the antecedents to the more proximate antecedents, and so forth, endlessly. Tracing historically relevant antecedents to explain later choices and conditions need not, of course, end up being a slippery slope into an unceasing quest for initial causes. If that were the case, historical studies would be impossible.

The lack of historical perspective contributes to the overall randomness of the GCM. Without examining antecedent choices and conditions that might have given rise to, or facilitated, a problem or solution from getting on the agenda, many items seem to appear and disappear unpredictably and suddenly. Problems may indeed "suddenly get hot" but the problems themselves and the reasons they come to be perceived as problems are rooted historically. For example, under the GCM, we might observe that unemployment rises sharply within a few months and that the public and policy-makers take notice. But whether we regard unemployment as a problem suitable for government attention, how high unemployment must be to be considered "unacceptably high," and why the rate went up, we can only understand adequately in historical perspective. Similarly, to understand why "supply-side tax cuts" became perceived as a plausible solution to unemployment or sluggish economic growth, one has to have some historical understanding of the evolution of economists' theories and opinions, in what sense American economists came to understand "Keynesianism," its rise and fall as a theory and policy prescription, and the lessons that economists and others drew from experiences with previous efforts to cut taxes. It is not enough to know that at a particular point in time Keynesianism came to be seen as a solution to a particular economic problem. We want to know *why and how* it became a viable solution.

Items often reach the agenda and come up for decision because past efforts to put them there have failed or never materialized. Or, a problem reached the agenda and a policy was adopted to address it, which in turn, gave rise to new problems that eventually gained agenda status. Scholars working from a historical perspective have developed a number of concepts to help us to understand history as a causal process. The development and dissemination of solutions, for example, is often done through learning and lesson-drawing, which occur over time (Heclo 1975; Rose 1991). Public policies are also often the product of "critical junctures," which produce distinct "legacies" that would not have occurred if the critical juncture had not occurred (Collier and Collier 1991). Alternatively, the legacies may be the result of "antecedent conditions" and "constant causes" that predated the hypothesized critical juncture and account for the legacy. Policymaking is also subject to path dependency. Political events and policy choices at one point in time often put nations and organizations on particular trajectories that close out or reduce the probability of making other choices in the future because the original events and choices create dominant frames, institutions and interests that become entrenched long after the conditions that established the path have ended (Pierson 2000).

The criticism that the GCM is insufficiently grounded in historical analysis would be less problematic if the model was considered exclusively a model of agenda-setting. Since an "agenda" is conventionally defined as consisting of those items that a government (or set of decision-makers in any complex organization) gives serious attention at a point in time, paying attention only to contemporary, immediate, situational factors is understandable. An organization's attention to particular problems is usually short-term and often intermittent. But if we extend the GCM beyond agenda-setting to policy *formulation and adoption,* as many scholars have done, we have a harder time justifying the lack of historical analysis and appreciation of structural constraints. Policy-making is more than attention-getting and a deeper understanding must go beyond situational factors.

*Randomness and the separation of the streams:* Probably the most frequent criticism of the GCM is that it portrays decision-making as overly chaotic and random. Even defenders and users of the GCM admit that the model "shares common ground with chaos theories in being attentive to complexity, in assuming a considerable amount of residual randomness, and in viewing systems as constantly evolving and not necessarily settling into equilibrium" (Zahariadis 2007: 66). The feature of the GCM that contributes most to the model's randomness is the assumption the loose and independent relationship exists among the three separate streams. While changes within each stream reflect purposive behavior and patterns, the core of the model—the simultaneous occurrence of a salient problem, available solution and favorable political conditions—gives rise to outcomes that are largely fortuitous and unpredictable. The coupling of the three streams is a purposive, non-random process, but it occurs *after* the alignment of the three streams. Kingdon

(1984: 93) stipulated that only "hints of connection" existed among the streams. But is the lack of connectedness among the streams justified? An alternative model would stress the importance of changes in one stream contributing to changes in the others and would trace out the interactions and interdependencies among the streams. Pursuing an approach in which the streams were more interconnected would reduce the currently high level of indeterminacy and randomness in the GCM and uncover a greater degree of behavior that is collaborative, purposive, and strategic. Indeed, those items that reach the agenda may be precisely those that exhibit stronger linkages and congruence among the streams, where advocates and their allies do not leave congruence to chance, but actively promote it. In this model, changes in one stream give rise to and reinforce changes in the others, increasing the probability that entrepreneurs will attempt to couple the streams and that their efforts will succeed.

Perhaps the closest links are those between solutions and politics. Solutions that reach the agenda are those that have a good fit with policy-makers' goals, such as reelection, influence, and promoting the adoption of "good" policy (Fenno 1973). Obviously, policy-makers choose solutions that have the best chance of promoting their goals. At the same time, experts and advocates craft and promote their favorite solutions with at least some attention to policy-makers' goals. The type of policy or program promoted, its specific provisions, the evidence and arguments mustered for it, how it is packaged and framed—all are geared toward building support, muting opposition, and persuading the undecided and ambivalent that the proposed course of action is desirable, or at least plausible. Since policy-makers' goals are usually often broad, and their views on how to achieve them are malleable, those who advocate on behalf of particular solutions have some room to persuade them.

Politics and problems are also closely connected. Perhaps the best-known example of this phenomenon is when incumbent politicians are ousted from office, or threatened with being outsted, when economic indicators, particularly the unemployment rate, worsen or fail to improve during a recession. Many less salient examples also exist. For example, when fuel prices rose sharply in the mid-1970s, businesses that shipped their goods by truck, including farmers, manufacturers and many other businesses, formed a coalition with liberal consumer groups to push for trucking deregulation (Robyn 1987: 96–7, 234–5). In other cases, previous policy choices create new problems or exacerbate existing ones that, in turn, create political opportunities for elected officials. For example, the creation of very generous tax loopholes in 1981 resulted in large revenue losses. By the mid-1980s, a bipartisan coalition emerged in favor of closing the loopholes and converting them into across-the-board rate cuts for taxpayers generally (Conlan *et al.* 1990). Republicans regained control of the House and made gains in the Senate in the 2010 elections because the combination of a devastating recession, war spending and growing entitlement spending created a "debt crisis" that allowed Republicans to push debt reduction as the central issue on the agenda after the election. In both cases, the perceived worsening of problems contributed to conditions that were conducive to getting the problems on the agenda.

Finally, problems and solutions are linked. The GCM rightly uncovered instances when, counterintuitively, experts developed solutions before they found the problems to which they were eventually applied. At the same time, experts often develop solutions with very clear problems in mind at the outset and their linkage of a solution to that particular problem often carries through the policy-making process. Both patterns are at work, perhaps often in the same proposal. For example, the original rationale that tax experts in the Treasury Department put forward the argument for reforming the tax code (by reducing the number of special provisions in the code reducing taxpayers' liability) was to increase the fairness of the income tax. Eventually, policy-makers and others took up reform to address other problems (the complexity of the code and economic inefficiency created by distorted market incentives), but the original problem that the experts were trying to address endured as a principal rationale for reform.

Problems and solutions are linked in more subtle ways as well. As problems get worse, plausible solutions become attractive and are more likely to gain agenda status. Solutions that might have a harder time getting political support (for any number of reasons) when a problem is perceived to be under control or imposing only modest costs, will have an easier time as the problem worsens and the expected windfall from applying the solution grows. In the tax reform example again, as the problems of unfairness, revenue loss, complexity and inefficiency grew, so did the attractiveness of closing the loopholes because the costs of the existing policy rose at the same time that the expected benefit from closing the loopholes also rose (in the form of lower tax rates, for example).

## Studies that have employed the GCM after Kingdon

As of June 25, 2011, Google Scholar registered 6,650 citations for Kingdon's *Agendas* book.[1] Many of the citations are from political science and policy studies as well as other disciplines, fields and professions. At the same time, according to Bendor *et al.* (2001), the GCM is not used extensively in political science research or in related disciplines. Indeed, the number of studies in public policy that actually use the GCM or test hypotheses derived from it is surprisingly small given the attention that Kingdon's book received and its status as a staple on public policy syllabi. Zahariadis (2007: 79) acknowledges that the GCM, or "multiple streams model," as he prefers to call it, "does appear to be an argument that many scholars quote but few explicitly use." Bendor *et al.* attribute the GCM's relative lack of use in empirical studies to weaknesses in the model that render it a poor theoretical guide for research. Zahariadis counters that the problem has more to do with "paradigmatic problems" that have plagued the model. Following Sabatier (1999), he suggests a number of reasons for why the GCM does not guide empirical research in policy studies more frequently: the model's principal proponent and popularizer—Kingdon—did not vigorously promote its usage; many people consider the GCM only relevant for understanding agenda-setting rather than policy formulation and adoption; and, researchers working on subnational levels of government identify the GCM with agenda-setting at the national level. These reasons are plausible. Kingdon retired from academe not that long after he published the second edition of his book. And, in confining the application of the GCM to the agenda-setting stage, Kingdon may have limited its perceived relevance given that conceptualizing the policy process as a set of distinct stages may be a useful heuristic device, but not very realistic.

The GCM has appeared prominently in a modest number of public policy studies that came after Kingdon's book was published. Most of these works have sought to broaden the applicability of the GCM (or elements of it), refine its central concepts, and use it to interpret case study findings. Zahariadis, for example, has sought to show how the GCM (or "multiple streams" model, as he prefers to call it) is useful for understanding policy-making outside the United States, specifically the privatization of public enterprises in Britain and France (1995) and Greek foreign policy (2005). An important aim of Zahariadis's (1995, 9) study of privatization was to extend the GCM beyond agenda-setting, to the entire process of policy formulation and decision-making. Zahariadis argues that Cohen, March and Olsen formulated the GCM originally to explain decision-making, not just agendas, and that agenda-setting, policy formulation and decision-making are integrally related. These arguments are sensible, but extending the GCM to the policy-making process as a whole makes it even harder to maintain the notion that problems, solution, and politics are largely separate until a final coupling. Once an item reaches the agenda, it is implausible to believe that the independence of streams remains relevant during policy formulation and decision-making. Unless we are trying to answer the narrow question of "why did policy-makers make any decision rather than none at all?" the GCM would find it difficult to explain why policy-makers decided on one specific policy and rejected others. Second, extending the GCM beyond agenda-setting does nothing to ameliorate other problems with the model, such as its failure to ground its explanations sufficiently in the historical and structural aspects of policy-making.

Framing his explanation in terms of the coming together of the three streams of the GCM, Zahariadis (1995) argues that Britain and France adopted privatization when the following conditions converged: (1) policy-makers perceived the solution—selling off state-owned enterprises—as technically feasible and compatible with their values; (2) social indicators revealed a problem—that government budgets were under stress and the public was resistant to new taxes; and (3) the occurrence of a key change in the political environment—the rise to power of political parties that were not identified with public enterprise and that possessed the ideological commitment and political capacity to work to end it. In some of cases, as Kingdon had found earlier, specialists developed the solution (privatization) before the specific problem for which it eventually was adopted had emerged.

In trying to account for Greek foreign policy-making over the span of five years on the issue of Macedonia, Zahariadis (2005) argues that the GCM is more useful than two other explanatory frameworks ("rational internationalism" and "two-level games"). The substance of Zahariadis's explanation focuses on the importance of policy elites' manipulation of emotive symbols and domestic politics on foreign policy decisions. If the manipulation of emotion and considerations of domestic politics are what matter in his explanation of Greed policy, then the need for the GCM in Zahariadis's account is not readily apparent. According to Zahariadis (2005: 172), "as multiple streams [i.e. GCM] hypotheses, domestic agendas make a big difference in the making of foreign policy." But what rationale exists for equating the GCM (or "multiple streams") with "domestic politics"? And again, how does the GCM contribute to an explanation that the variables "emotion" and "domestic politics" do not already contribute on their own? A compelling case that the GCM helps to explain Greek foreign policy would require showing how elements of the GCM are essential causal mechanisms that facilitate or shape the influence of emotion and domestic politics on foreign policy.

McLendon (2003) employed the GCM in his study of how the issue of higher education decentralization reached the agenda in the US states in the 1980s and 1990s. He compared the GCM with incremental and rational-comprehensive theories of policy-making to assess their usefulness for explaining how the issue reached the agenda and for elucidating which actors in the policy-making process exerted the most influence. Analyzing an eclectic mix of data, including 61 semi-structured interviews, from in-depth case studies of three states, McLendon found that agenda setting on this issue resembled the GCM far more than the other two models. Like Kingdon, McLendon found "clarity, order and pattern" within the structure of each stream, and at the same time, "elements of ambiguity, anarchy and unpredictability … in the specific coupling of problems, solutions and politics." He also found support for several of the features of the GCM as Kingdon formulated them: different streams of activity that exhibited a "surprising degree of independence" (though they were "not entirely unrelated"); "conflict over autonomy and control within the education policy domain" was weakly connected to the reasons that decentralization reached the agenda; the development of the decentralization solution occurred before, not in response to, the problem policy-makers eventually addressed; the rapid, non-incremental movement of the issue to the top of the agenda; and the significant role of policy entrepreneurs in helping to push the item on to the agenda.

Instead of employing the entire GCM, other studies have explored and elaborated upon particular elements of it. Birkland (1997: 2004) has clarified and developed the concept of "focusing events" and investigated under what empirical conditions focusing events help to push issues on to the agenda and lead to the adoption of new policies. In his study of natural disasters, oil spills, and nuclear accidents, Birkland (1997) stipulates that focusing events are harmful, unexpected, relatively rare, and affect large numbers of people who learn about them simultaneously. Focusing events favor groups (particularly relatively weak ones) that seek changes in public policy because the events provide valuable opportunities for the groups to point out problems with the status quo and relieve them of the task of convincing the mass media to pay attention to their issue. Not all focusing events lead to changes in the agenda or in policy. Birkland argues that certain characteristics of focusing events and of the political environment in which they occur help or hinder them from having an impact on policy. How much "focal power" an event has depends, first, upon the media attention that it receives. The level of media attention, in turn, depends upon the scope of the event (or, how many people it affects), its rarity, the size of the media market in which it occurs, and the visibility and tangibility of the damages that it produces. Focusing events also have greater impact if the policy domain is characterized by a high level of organization, whether the community of experts support change, and in domains with less opposition and polarization among advocacy coalitions. In a follow-up study, Birkland (2004) examined the impact of the September 11 attacks on the United States He hypothesized that highly significant focusing events like 9/11—in which the level of damage, potential future damage, and media attention were greater than typical focusing events—would lead to windows of opportunity that were kept open much longer and would influence a broader set of policy areas, initiatives, and agencies.

Finally, a few studies have tried to test hypotheses derived from the GCM. Even though the GCM as a whole is not falsifiable, parts of it generate testable hypotheses. Robinson and Eller (2010) tested hypotheses related to one of the model's central and most contested features: the independence of the three streams. Robinson and Eller collected data from surveys of Texas school district superintendents related to participation in local, school district policy-making concerning violence prevention programs. They hypothesized that if the GCM is correct, we should observe different sets of participants involved in the problem and solution streams. Observing a participant in one stream should reduce the probability of finding the same participant in the other stream. Since Kingdon also suggested that special groups of experts dominate the solution stream, Robinson and Eller also tested the hypothesis that the solution stream would be dominated by elite participants rather than ordinary citizens and non-specialists. Contrary to the GCM, they found that participation in one stream *dramatically increased* the likelihood that a participant would participate in the other stream and that elite participation did not "crowd out" participation by "mass" participants (e.g. teachers and parents). One difference between Robinson and Eller's study and Kingdon's, of course, is that one focused at the local and the other at the federal level. Perhaps differences in policy-making at the two levels accounts for the different results. Obviously, much more research needs to be done to see if Robinson and Eller's results hold up at the local and state levels, in other policy areas and on other issues, and if they do, what might account for the differences found when we compare degree of independence of streams across levels of government.

## Conclusion

The GCM has been, and will continue to be, among a handful of approaches to the study of policy-making that all students in policy studies will learn about, discuss and use in their empirical work. Undoubtedly, the debate over its strengths and weaknesses, its promise and limitations for elucidating the real world of policy-making, will persist as well.

## Note

1 http://scholar.google.com/scholar?q=kingdon&hl=en&btnG=Search&as_sdt=1%2C39&as_sdtp=on

## Bibliography


Bendor, Jonathan, Terry M. Moe, and Kenneth W. Shotts. 2001. 'Recycling the garbage can: An assessment of the research program', *American Political Science Review* 95(1) (March): 169–90.

Birkland, Thomas A. 1997. *After Disaster: Agenda Setting, Public Policy, and Focusing Events*. Washington, DC: Georgetown University Press.

——. 2004. '"The world changed today": agenda-setting and policy change in the wake of the September 11 terrorist attacks', *The Review of Policy Research* 21 (2) (March): 179–200.

Cohen, Michael, James March and Johan Olsen. 1972. 'A garbage can model of organizational choice', *Administrative Science Quarterly* 17(March): 1–25.

Collier, Ruth Berins and David Collier. 1991. *Shaping the Political Arena: Critical Junctures, the Labor Movement and Regime Dynamics in Latin America*. Princeton, NJ: Princeton University Press.

Conlan, Timothy J. 1990. *Taxing Choices: The Politics of Tax Reform*. Washington, DC: Congressional Quarterly.

——, Margaret T. Wrightson and David R. Beam. 1990. *Taxing Choices: The Politics of Tax Reform*. Washington: CQ Press.

Fenno, Richard F. 1973. *Congressmen in Committees*. Boston: Little, Brown.

Hall, Peter. 1989. (ed.) *The Political Power of Economic Ideas: Keynesianism Across Nations*. Princeton, NJ: Princeton University Press.

Heclo, Hugh. 1975. *Modern Social Politics in Britain and Sweden*. New Haven, CT: Yale University Press.

Kingdon, John. 1984. *Agendas, Alternatives, and Public Policies*. Boston: Little, Brown.

McLendon, Michael K. 2003. 'Setting the governmental agenda for state decentralization of higher education', *The Journal of Higher Education* 74(5) (September/October): 479–515.

Mucciaroni, Gary. 1992. 'The garbage can model and the study of policy making: A critique', *Polity* 24(3) (Spring): 459–82.

Pierson, Paul. 2000. 'Increasing returns, path dependence, and the study of politics', *American Political Science Review* 94(2) (June): 251–67.

Robinson, Scott E. and Warren S. Eller. 2010. 'Participation in policy streams: Testing the separation of problems and solutions in subnational policy systems', *Policy Studies Journal* 382 (May): 199–216.

Robyn, Dorothy. 1987. *Braking the Special Interests*. Chicago: University of Chicago Press.

Rose, Richard. 1991. 'What is lesson drawing?', *Journal of Public Policy* 11(1): 3–30.

Sabatier, Paul A. 1999. *Theories of the Policy Process*. Boulder, CO: Westview Press, 117–66.

Skocpol, Theda and Weir, Margaret. 1985. 'State structures and the possibilities of "Keynesian" responses to the depression in Sweden, Britain and the United States', in P. Evans, D. Reuschemeyer and Theda Skocpol (eds). *Bringing the State back in*. Cambridge and New York: Cambridge University Press.

Zahariadis, Nikolaos. 1995. *Markets, States and Public Policy: Privatization in Britain and France*. Ann Arbor, MI: University of Michigan Press.

—— 2005. *Essence of Political Manipulation: Emotion, Institutions and Greek Foreign Policy*. New York: Peter Lang.

—— 2007. 'The multiple streams framework: Structure, limitations, prospects', in Paul A. Sabatier, *Theories of the Policy Process*. Boulder, CO: Westview Press, 65–92.

# Part VII

# Understanding the implementation process

# 25

# Bureaucracy and the policy process

*Ora-orn Poocharoen*

## Introduction

Bureaucracy is a concept that has been widely written about. Scholars in various fields of social sciences, including sociology, political science, economics, anthropology, history, public administration and public policy, have produced a vast amount of literature pertaining to almost every angle of bureaucracy one could ever imagine. This chapter focuses only on studies from the field of public administration and public policy. The aim is to provide a description of important debates, theories and frameworks that explain the relationship between bureaucracy and the public policy process. The chapter starts with definitions of the bureaucracy, followed by explanations of bureaucratic roles in policy-making and policy implementation. In the latter half of the chapter, the discussion focuses on the role of bureaucracy in the era of governance and the chapter ends with the topic of heterogeneity of bureaucrats in the present.

Every country has some form of bureaucratic apparatus to perform government functions, thus it is a subject of wide interest for scholars and practitioners who are involved with the public sector. The term originates from a cloth covering the desk of French officials in the eighteenth century called a 'bureau' (Niskanen 1973). In earlier works on public administration, scholars used the word bureau synonymously with bureaucracy (e.g. ibid.; Downs 1967). Since German sociologist Max Weber (1864–1920) wrote on the ideal type of bureaucracy, our understanding of the bureaucracy has evolved in various ways. The term has attracted different sentiments ranging from being powerful and effective to being slow and inefficient. The bureaucracy can be seen as the enforcer, the implementer, the administrator, the facilitator, the manager, or the mediator of government. We first turn to the original works on bureaucracy to explore its definitions.

## Definitions of bureaucracy

The word bureaucracy can be referred to in two ways. First, it refers to the bureaucracy as a form of organization, where there are structures, rules, resources and goals. The organization can be in any sector: public, private, non-profit or a combination of these. Second, it refers to the bureaucracy as administrative machinery that is part of the government. Its primary function is to execute the will of the state or in other words to implement public policies. It is worth noting that earlier scholars have identified the definition of bureaucracy to capture a spectrum of meanings that fall within the two categories of organizational form and as part of the government. An often-cited author is Albrow, who suggested seven definitions of bureaucracy: (1) bureaucracy as rational organization; (2) bureaucracy as organizational inefficiency; (3) bureaucracy as rule by officials; (4) bureaucracy as public administration; (5) bureaucracy as administration by officials; (6) bureaucracy as the organization; (7) bureaucracy as modern society (Albrow 1970). Definitions 1, 6 and 7 emphasize bureaucracy as an organizational form, whereas definitions 2, 3, 4 and 5 refer to bureaucracy as part of the government. When the word bureaucracy is used in everyday language, often it is a combination of these two definitions. In addition, sometimes the term bureaucracy is used synonymously with its agent, the bureaucrats. Typically, these are the people who work as civil servants in the public sector and who would be involved in public policy processes in various degrees. Next, we shall look at these two definitions in more detail.

## Bureaucracy as an organizational form

Organization theory is a subfield that cuts across many disciplines including public administration, business management and sociology. Organizations have various forms, structures, processes, cultures, goals and values. Bureaucracy is nothing but one of the organizational form. The subfield of organization theory provides rich research on the bureaucracy and bureaucratic behaviour. Examples include March and Herbert (1958), Blau and Scott (1962), Downs (1964), Hall and Quinn (1983), Wilson (1989), Scott (1992), Hall (1996), Christensen (2007) and Shafritz *et al.* (2010).

The classic definition of the bureaucracy as defined by Max Weber often forms the basic fundamental traits of public sector organizations. In his seminal work, Weber offers an explanation of the ideal type of bureaucracy that has six characteristics (1946).

There are fixed jurisdictional areas that are determined by rules that are laws or administrative regulations:

- There is hierarchy, where there is supervision of subordinates by supervisors.
- The management of the office is based upon written documents.
- There is office management.
- Full working capacity of the official is expected.
- The management of the office follows general rules that are stable and can be learned.

These characteristics were drawn from a study of various public organizations in Europe and non-Western civilizations, including Egypt, Rome, China and the Byzantine Empire. This ideal type describes the legal and rational system of authority that represents a modern bureaucracy. It is different from the traditional authority system that relies more on personal ties and the charismatic authority system that relies on strong leadership. Weber's work was translated into English only in 1940 and since has become the 'departure for all further analyses' of the bureaucracy (Shafritz and Hyde 2008).

This legal-rational foundation of the bureaucracy allows for institutions to gain and maintain expertise, power and legitimacy for governance overtime. Public organizations, whether they are ministries, bureaus, departments, or agencies, usually would be set up according to laws and would employ full-time professionals, who are categorized into different hierarchical ranks. The work of bureaucracies would be based on documentation, where records are kept and rules are followed. This form of organization or system of administration is also found in private companies, non-profit organizations, and international organizations where complex and large-scale administrative tasks take place. Kamenka provides a concise definition of bureaucracy that is applicable to all organizations and not just governmental organizations as 'a centrally directed, systematically organized and hierarchically structured staff devoted to the regular, routine and efficient carrying out of large-scale administrative tasks according to policies dictated by rulers or directors standing outside and above the bureaucracy' (Kamenka 1989: 157). Bureaucracy was and is still is, in some ways, understood to be the most efficient form of organizational arrangement and is inevitable in all societies. Elliot Jacques alluded to this when he wrote,

> [Bureaucracy] is one of the primary social institutions for any society which seeks the democratic enrichment and economic security which large-scale social, political, educational and production technologies seem at their best to be able to provide. The simple fact is that if we decide to proceed with the development of industrialized societies, then bureaucracies on a large scale are here to stay.
>
> *(1976: 13)*

## Bureaucracy as part of the government

This view of the bureaucracy equates all public sector organizations 'the bureaucracy'. Here, the bureaucracy is made up of public officials who are appointed through recruitment processes and not elected. They are in contrast to electoral institutions such as politicians, parliament, and the executive branch. The bureaucracy, as a legitimate actor of the state, has power to govern according to laws and rules. Governments define the scope and size of their bureaucracy differently. Some would include the military and judiciary, while others would not. In federal systems, the bureaucracy could refer to either national level or subnational levels of government agencies. Some scholars would use the term 'public bureaucracy' to emphasize that the focus is on the public sector. However, most of the time, writers do use 'bureaucracy' and 'public bureaucracy' synonymously and they usually mean bureaucracy in the public sector.

In conjunction with this definition, the bureaucracy is the institutional structure whereby the bureaucrats are the individuals within that structure to implement policy and enforce laws. Earlier, Downs wrote, 'In my analysis, the term "bureaucrat" is in no way derogatory, but because it is so universally regarded as an insult, I will use the more neutral term "official" to describe the type of person described above' (Downs 1964: 4). Fifty years on and the general feeling about the term have not changed. Due to connotations of inefficiencies and unresponsiveness, it is now more favourable to refer to bureaucrats as public managers. It gives the impression that the bureaucrat is not just someone who pushes paper and complies with standard operating procedures but rather someone who is entrepreneurial and innovative and who can manage complex situations and problems. Whether they are called bureaucrats, public officials, civil servants, administrators, or public managers they are all agents within the bureaucracy.

One of the major debates in the field of public administration is the premise that 'the will of the state' and 'the execution of that will' should and can be separated. This is known as the politics-administration dichotomy debate. Earlier scholars who have discussed this dichotomy include W. Wilson (1887), Goodnow (1900) and White (1926). It is worth noting that their works did not favour the dichotomy as many later claimed and that this debate has historical roots in the United States, where the foundation of the state lies in the separation of power between the executive, legislative and judicial branches of government (Svara 2001). This debate is closely linked to the policy-making and policy implementation discussion of whether in reality the two processes can be separated or not (e.g. Appleby 1949; Peters 1995). We can also argue in the normative sense of whether or not the two processes should be separated. These debates shape the normative direction of division of role between politicians and bureaucrats. The politicians are understood to be the designers of the will of the state, thus they have a clear role to make policies, while bureaucrats are to execute that will by professionally implementing policies using the bureaucratic machinery to achieve their objectives. Scholars have drawn extensively on the debate to analyse political-administrative arrangements in different countries. Examples of studies include Riper (1984), Rabin and Bowman (1984), Montjoy and Watson (1995), Dunn (1997) Svara (1998, 1999, 2001) and Rutgers (2001). While in practice most would agree that administrators do play important roles within the policy process and that the dichotomy does not hold true, this debate continues to serve as a theoretical starting point for refining and understanding the relationship between bureaucrats and politicians and the bureaucracy's role in the policy process.

In addition to the relationship between politics and administration, observation of the bureaucracy cannot be separated from the political system it operates in. Students of political science and public administration would notably agree that political system is one of the most important variables to explain decision-making processes, choices and outcomes of policy. Studies on the bureaucracy have pointed to the inherent tension between bureaucracy and democracy (Mosher 1968; Beetham 1987; Smith 1988; Gormley and Balla 2004; Goodsell 2004). Albrow suggests that this debate dates back to the nineteenth-century (Albrow 1970). Bureaucracy needs to have a strong capacity to be effective in administration but at the same time it needs to be controlled to ensure responsiveness to the public and higher authorities (Garvey 1995). Etzioni-Halevy argues that bureaucratic power generates a dilemma for democracy (1983). It poses a threat to democratic political structure. He also argues that democracy generates a dilemma for bureaucracy. Bureaucracy is expected to be independent and subservient to elected politicians at the same time. This rule is self-contradictory. Last, he argues that the dilemma of bureaucracy is an important source of political friction especially between senior bureaucrats and senior politicians. Many have used this debate as a point of departure and have either rebutted or supported these claims.

Some scholars see bureaucracy as not in conflict with democracy but as an important vehicle to push for better democratic governments, in addition to political parties, elections, and the legislatures (Thompson 1965). For example, Kim has empirically demonstrated that democratic control can and does go hand-in-hand with bureaucratic autonomy (2008). He emphasized how bureaucratic behaviour is influenced by multiple political institutions that have relationships with the public agency. Since the mid-1990s, scholars have begun to discuss the relationship between public bureaucracy and the use of performance management systems in the evolving democratic processes (e.g. Gormley and Balla 2004; Peters 2010). Performance systems can be seen as instruments to control the bureaucracy by electorates and citizens in democratic settings. Rather than focusing only on the bureaucracy, Meier points to the need to balance our focus on the electorates (1997). He argues that most problems in the United States stem from the inability of politicians to formulate good policies. These debates illustrate the ongoing need for students of political science and public administration to understand the two groups in relation to each other. In sum, bureaucracy continues to be an important component of democratic systems, despite inherent tensions between the two concepts. Needless to say, the bureaucracy has always been important for non-democratic systems especially in authoritarian and communist systems where the state has an overarching role in many aspects of citizens' lives. In general, bureaucracy in the twenty-first century is inevitably becoming more democratic as citizens continue to demand higher levels of accountability and responsiveness, regardless of the type of political system they are in.

As political systems and economic systems are intertwined, observation of the bureaucracy cannot be separated from the economic system it operates in. There are numerous studies of the relationship between bureaucracy and the market mechanism. There are three ways of viewing this relationship. One is to treat the bureaucracy as a system existing within a larger economic system. Weber's studies on the bureaucracy stemmed from his question of the consequences of modern capitalism. He infers that the capitalist system provided the best chance for preservation of individual freedom and creative leadership in a bureaucracy (Mommsen 1974: xv). Marxist schools of thought equally debated and discussed the role of the bureaucracy, specifically on the bureaucracy and class and implications for society as a whole (e.g. Chattopadhyay 1993; Burnham 1941; Westoby 1985). In this camp, bureaucracy presented the new elites with managerial and technical power that would dominate the working class (Westoby 1985). The second view sees the co-existence of the bureaucratic system and market mechanisms. Recent debates have extended the focus to observe the co-existence between market, bureaucratic and network mechanisms in public service delivery (e.g. Olsen 2006; Koliba 2011). This view does not treat the bureaucracy as working in a certain economic system but rather as a system operating side-by-side with other systems. The third view is to treat bureaucracy and the market as different mechanisms for organizational control or management (e.g. Ouchi 1980). Similarly, accountability systems, as a form of organizational control, can also be divided into market and bureaucratic or administrative frames, aside from the democratic frame (Koliba 2011).

Now that the two views of the definition of bureaucracy have been elaborated, next we will discuss the role of the bureaucracy in the policy process, which is an extension of this second definition that bureaucracy is part of government. From here onward I will use the term "bureaucracy" synonymously with the term 'public bureaucracy'.

## Role of the bureaucracy in the policy process

The bureaucracy plays a very important role in the entire policy process: setting agendas and formulating, implementing and evaluating policies. This understanding of the dominant role of the bureaucracy in the policy process is not new and has been recognized for many years by prominent scholars. Examples include *Our Wonderland of Bureaucracy* (Beck 1932) and *The Managerial Revolution* (Burnham 1941) as well as more recent works such as *Breaking through the Bureaucracy* (Barzelay 1992). In his work to introduce the concept of 'bureaucratic government', Peters writes, "It is by now almost trite to say that bureaucracy and administration are an increasingly significant – if not the most significant – feature of modern policy-making" (1981: 56). Peters identifies subsets of literature pertaining to bureaucracy and public administration. They are the positivist theorists that borrow economic rationality through the public choice approach to explain bureaucrats to be power-maximizing actors (Downs 1964, 1967). The other group of scholars, called descriptive theorists, explain bureaucrats' behaviour as political actors and not the non-political technicians stressed in the Weber's ideal-type bureaucracy. Bureaucracies are given wide latitude to include details of actual implementation of legislation and to spell out all the rules and guidelines that need to accompany the policy or law.

Peters reiterated in his often-cited book *The Politics of Bureaucracy* that administrative systems do influence policy outputs of the political system (1995). Bureaucracies are always either explicitly or implicitly included in theoretical discussions of the public policy process. Charles Lindblom's well-known incrementalism theory explains that due to standard operating procedures ingrained in the bureaucracy, there is always a tendency for governments to preserve the status quo or to change very minimally from the status quo. The bureaucracy is understood to be one of the main actors in other models of public policy whether it is the elite model, the group model or the institutionalist model. The traditional rational model of policy-making, by emphasizing objective and technical knowledge in decision-making is inevitably supporting the role of the bureaucracy (see Parsons 1995). Thus it is vital to understand the bureaucratic administration system alongside political, economic and social systems in order to understand public policy. Most public policy textbooks would not be complete without mentioning the role of the bureaucracy and bureaucrats in the policy process. See, for example, Wu *et al.* (2010), Howlett and Ramesh (2003), Parsons (1995), Considine (1994) and Gupta (2001).

There are several reasons why bureaucrats can and do influence policy processes at various stages. First, the policy process can only be divided in theory but not in practice. In practice, the process is often a mix of the policy stages because policies are constantly being changed or adjusted based on implementation and evaluation experiences. Second, because the bureaucracy often has expert and long-term institutional knowledge of public issues, it is often involved at the very early stage of agenda-setting. Sometimes it is the bureaucracy that initiates policies. A clear example is the bureaucracy's involvement in the national budget decision-making process. Line ministries are asked to submit a draft of their budget proposal each year. This often occurs without the direct involvement of ministers or politicians. Wildavsky has written extensively on this topic (e.g. Wildavsky 1979, 1986; Wildavsky *et al.* 2006) and this topic was extended to include assertions that bureaucrats tend to maximize their interests through the budget process (Blais and Dion 1991; Peters 1995).

In addition, bureaucrats usually stay in their posts longer than politicians. They have the opportunity to see through policies. They are sometimes known for taking a longer-term view of public problems. Furthermore, bureaucrats are recruited on the basis of their expertise and profession, while politicians are elected on popularity and big policy promises. The bureaucracy is often perceived to speak more creditably about the technical aspects of policies. This is a form of knowledge-based power that bureaucrats exercise. Finally, bureaucrats usually have access to more data and information regarding specific policies. By being the implementers of policies, bureaucrats have many opportunities to collect data and information that would be valuable for policy-making and evaluation. The level of influence that bureaucrats do have in the policy process is also determined by other factors, including historical legacies, governance structures or political systems, the Constitution or the most important laws. In one country, the level of influence can also change over time depending on the arrangement and preferences at different points in time. In sum, it has long been recognized that the bureaucracy plays an important role in all stages of the policy process. Next, we will focus on the policy-making process.

## Bureaucrats as policy-makers

Bureaucrats can and do greatly influence policy-making. They can be the source of ideas. They can be the advocate of ideas. They can take part formally and informally in the policy-making process. They can also be the sole actor or leader in the policy-making process.

Bureaucracy can directly and indirectly shape the discourse of public policies. Indirectly, during the policy formulation stage, bureaucrats can influence the discourse of broad policies through their communications with politicians and the wider public. After broad goals have been set, the bureaucracy plays an important role in outlining policy details through the design of specific programmes. It is precisely this that will largely influence the overall policy outcome and citizens' perceptions of the policy and the government. Peters suggests that there are soft and hard versions of agency ideologies (1995). Soft ideology refers to when ministers are being influenced by bureaucrats' preferences in order to maintain certain policies, that is to say they are the source of ideas and are indirectly influencing policy.

Hard ideology refers to when bureaucrats actively seek to alternate or initiate policies. This latter version sees bureaucracy as an active participant in the political arena of the policy process.

It accepts that bureaucrats can act similarly to pressure groups, namely they are the advocates of ideas and are directly influencing policy. This could take the form of lobbying, trying to influence discourse through media and possibly also through participating in protests. This is because bureaucrats have their own sets of ideologies and preferences. This view differs from seeing the bureaucracy as being politically neutral and acting as a buffer between the state and interest groups. A similar idea is found in the concept of representative bureaucracy, where bureaucracy is accepted as a political actor in the policy sphere and is expected to help shape public policies (Krislov 1974; Seldon 1997; Dolan and Rosenbloom 2003). To put it positively, bureaucrats can also be seen as policy entrepreneurs. In systems where the bureaucrat is stationed in one agency for their entire career, as is the case in the United States and Scandinavian countries, for example, they tend to be policy advocates because they hold such deep expertise and opinions on their policy area (Peters 1995). On the other hand, if bureaucrats are centrally recruited, and are rotated around various agencies, such as in France and the United Kingdom, they might be less attached to certain policy opinions (ibid.). This is in stark contrast to before the 1950s when bureaucrats were understood to discreetely shape policy behind the scenes (Svara 2001).

Furthermore, the bureaucracy sometimes even takes the leadership role with very little influence from other actors, including politicians (Peters 1995). This resonates with Mosher's idea of the 'professional state' where professionals in public agencies through their expertise and knowledge do not only generate new policy ideas but are the main actors to formulate the fine details of policies as well (Mosher 1968). In relation to seeing the bureaucracy as taking the leading role in specific policy areas, many scholars have pointed to the bureaucracy's critical role in the entire administration of developing countries. For example, scholars have associated the successful development of some Asian countries and regions with the idea of a strong state, namely strong bureaucracy. They include the so-called four tigers of Taiwan, South Korea, Singapore, and Hong Kong (for more on East Asia see, for example, Wade 1990; World Bank 1993; Henderson 2011). Japan is also known to have a strong bureaucracy with greater influence than politicians and which has dominated policy-making since World War II (Ramseyer and Rosenbluth 1993).

Bureaucracies that are core agencies, regulatory agencies and planning agencies are often in a position to influence policy-making and setting the policy direction for the country. The term 'super bureaucrat' depicts the prominent role of high-ranking bureaucrats in the policy process (Campbell and Szablowski 1979). These bureaucrats are usually in the central ministries or the peak policy agencies such as Thailand's National Economic and Social Development Board, Singapore's Economic Development Board, Taiwan's Council for Economic Planning and Development, Japan's Ministry of Economy, Trade and Industry, and Malaysia's Prime Minister's Office. Similarly in the area of public administrative reform policy, only a handful of key central agencies would be involved in the design of the policy. These agencies have been called 'system designers' (Olsen and Peters 1996). On the other hand, in some cases the line ministries might dominate policy-making. Mostly these are areas where great technical expertise is required. They are, for example, policies related to energy, health, transportation, food regulation, just to name a few. Examples of studies include the Medicare movement (Marmor 1973) and community mental health programmes (Foley 1975) in the United States and foreign policy-making (Ahn 1998) and telecommunication policy (Eiji 2001) in Japan.

In a bureaucracy, it is not only the bureaucrats who can influence policy-making. In presidential systems where there are political appointees in the bureaucracy, such as the United States and the Philippines, studies confirm that career and non-career administrators contribute significantly to policy-making (Aberbach *et al.* 1981; Rourke 1984; Dolan 2000). In parliamentarian systems, such as the United Kingdom, it is also known that officials whether selected by appointment with lifetime tenure or politically selected for the duration of a government, can also have significant influence on policy-making as long as they are part of the bureaucracy (e.g. Bevir and Rhodes 2006).

In the debate on the appropriate role of the bureaucracy in the policy process, some see that the bureaucracy can stabilize governance where the political party system is weak. In many countries, when the political executive is weak, the bureaucracy often gains more importance and strengthen its hold on policy decisions (Peters 1981: 68). For some developing countries in the early to middle stages of development, the bureaucracy often have control over policy directions of the country. For example, during the years 1932 to 1973 the bureaucrats in Thailand were considered to be elites who had overthrown the absolute monarchy. They led the government in an authoritarian fashion, setting the tone of a semi-democracy that still persists many years after (Bowornwathana 2011). In turn, bureaucracy can also dominate policy processes to the detriment of political institutions and actors. Heady calls this 'imbalance thesis' (2001). Similarly, Riggs has argued that bureaucracy is mostly made up of the ruling class that impedes the development of strong political systems (2001).

Naturally, this bureaucratic power in policy-making has never been a comfortable fact for politicians. Studies have shown how political leaders have intentionally excluded high-ranking bureaucrats from policy-making processes (Cole and Caputo 1979; Bevir and Rhodes 2006). Parliamentarians keep a check on the public bureaucracy by scrutinizing their policies and implementation in parliament debates (e.g. Ho 2000 on Singapore). The new public management (NPM) movement that originated in the Anglo-Saxon countries in the 1980s is an attempt to strengthen the checks on bureaucracies and bureaucratic power. On the contrary, when the relationship between bureaucrats and politicians becomes too cozy, it is labelled 'iron triangle' and that is when there is a monopoly of policy-making power among the politicians, the bureaucracy and industry or the interest groups. Some of these sectors include defence in the United States (Adams 1981) and agriculture in the European Union (Hix 1999). These relationships can easily lead to corruption and a conflict of interest for the government.

Another aspect of the bureaucracy that influences policy-making is structure. Bureaucratic structure can be both an independent and dependent variable in relation to policy. Policy can be a determinant to explain bureaucratic structures. Frequently we witness governments setting up new bureaucracies in order to take charge of new policies. These are usually new policies that existing agencies do not cover. For instance, they could be policies related to climate change, food security, crisis management, terrorism, non-traditional security and population or migration. Bureaucratic structure is a reflection of politics (West 1997). It shows how scarce resources are allocated. The structures are nothing but evidence of institutional choice and power in the public sector. However, bureaucratic structure can be a determinant of policy direction and policy choice. Examples include studies on bureaucratic structure and personality by Robert K. Merton (1957), Allison (1971) and Egeberg (1999). Bureaucratic structure determines the flow of information processing, which would influence the type and value of information that is filtered up and down the bureaucracy. Bureaucratic structure also dictates the dynamics of politics among bureaucracies. And scholars have long argued that policy decisions are dominated by the dynamics of bureaucratic politics (Allison and Zelikow 1999). Following Allison's (1971) seminal work on foreign policy other works have expanded our understanding of how bureaucratic politics govern policy processes (e.g. Peters 1995; Bowornwathana and Poocharoen 2010). There are many examples of when decisions on administrative reform policies are shaped by the struggle between key central agencies to maintain or gain more power during the reform and after the reform.

Bureaucracies can also indirectly influence domestic policy-making from the international arena. It is suggested that bureaucrats often take part in professional policy networks, where they pick up ideas and good practices and then try to implement those policies and practices to their own agency, community or government (Peters 1995). International organizations often provide platforms for such exchanges, such as the model of community of practice in the World Bank or Asian Development Bank. Many examples can be found in the EU especially in the standardization of various social services (ibid.). There are also studies that point to how domestic bureaucracies can influence policies made at the international level (Hopkins 1976). Lastly, aside from focusing on domestic bureaucracies, more and more attention is being focused on the role of international bureaucracies. In a highly globalized world, we cannot ignore the significance of international bureaucracies and their impact on global governance and domestic policy choices (e.g. Mouritzen 1990; Barnett and Finnemore 1999; Muldoon *et al.* 2010). In sum, international bureaucracies are also important actors in the policy-making process both domestically and internationally. Next we will discuss bureaucracy in the policy implementation process.

## Bureaucrats as policy implementers

The main function of the bureaucracy is to implement public policies, programmes and projects. In the process of implementation, the bureaucracy influences the direction of policy in several ways. Policies are often very broad and vague due to the complexity of most public policy problems. For example it is difficult for governments to have certain explicit policies on climate change issues, gender equality or poverty reduction because often the responsibility to solve these problems is diffused among many bureaucracies. There is no one bureaucracy to take ownership of these complex problems. Thus, during the implementation stage, depending on the level of discretionary power, different bureaucracies have room to interpret policies to fit their own views and maintain practicality. The bureaucracy also adjusts rules and instructions to suit local contexts. This process of interpretation is where intentionally or unintentionally bureaucrats can and do influence policies. Sometimes, the original intent of the policy, as set by policy-makers, is altered due to the bureaucrats' interpretation of the policy (Pressman and Wildavsky 1973). Also, during the implementation stage, as policies are being further defined and designed, bureaucracy can come up with bureaucratic standard operating procedures or process-oriented policies that can also affect the policy outcome. At this stage, politicians and other stakeholders might also intervene and influence how implementation processes are set (Furlong 1998).

Studies about street-level bureaucrats give a clear illustration of how bureaucracies influence policy outcomes at the implementation stage (Lipsky 1980). Street-level bureaucrats are those who have face-to-face communication with citizens. Examples include police, teachers, immigration officers, social workers and those who work in service delivery agencies such as birth and marriage registration or passport and driver's license issue. Street-level bureaucrats have to constantly interpret and reinterpret policy goals. At the same time, they often have individual agendas, expectations, values and capacity. Studies have found that street-level bureaucrats' lack of conformity to procedures and decision-trees set by top administration is a stable norm of policy implementation (Mashaw 1983; Mashaw and Marmor 1988). They often feel frustration due to the need to face ongoing conflict between responding to clients or citizens and the need to properly implement policies. Put positively, street-level bureaucrats' discretion can help policies to be more adaptive and enhance government's ability to respond to individual cases. On the other hand, street-level bureaucrats can also change the course of the policy entirely.

Aside from street-level bureaucrats, there are also studies that explain how mid-level bureaucrats also influence policies. In their study of mid-level civil servants in the United Kingdom Page and Jenkins identify three types of policy roles: (1) a production role in making policy drafts and documents; (2) a maintenance role in tending and managing policies; and (3) a service role in offering knowledge and skills to those involved in the policy process (2006).

Aside from large- and medium-sized states, some scholars have pointed to the uniqueness of bureaucracy of small island states. Similarly to many fragile states, these bureaucrats are often implementing not only the national policy but also policies directed by international donors (Baker 1992; Garcia-Zamor 2004). Often bureaucrats struggle to achieve policy goals set by international donors and international organizations because they are confronted with many challenges on the ground during the implementation stage.

During the policy monitoring and evaluation stage, bureaucrats often play the most important role in providing information to external evaluators, if the evaluation is not done in-house. As mentioned in the previous section, the bureaucracy has access to sensitive data and institutional information that outsiders do not have. Thus they have some control over the evaluation studies or reports of most policies and programmes. It is often difficult to determine the validity of evaluation reports when done in-house by the bureaucracy. Naturally they would be inclined to not publicize policy failures. Overall, there is limited scholarly work on the issues pertaining to bureaucracy and policy evaluation. In general, evaluation frameworks tend to focus less on who is doing it but rather on how to do it. This topic should be further expanded in the future.

In sum, we can see that the bureaucracy is very influential in the policy process. Bureaucrats can be seen as policy owners, policy advocates, policy managers, policy interpreters and policy technicians. Next we shall discuss the evolving role of bureaucracy in the era of governance.

## Bureaucracy and governance

Between the 1980s to 2000s, we witnessed the spread of the NPM movement across many countries. As bureaucracies grew in size and power over the years between the 1940s and the 1980s, the rhetoric of the need to curb bureaucratic power gained momentum. Many governments went through phases of downsizing the public sector, tightening control over bureaucracies, and introducing market-based competition for traditional public services. The discourse emphasized how bureaucracies were inefficient and too big. Proponents of such ideas came from public choice theorists (Niskanen 1974), New Institutional Economic theorists in New Zealand (Boston 1991), and New Right ideologies in the 1980s (Saint-Martin 2004; Pollitt and Bouckaert 2004). The book, *Reinventing Government* by Osborne and Gaebler (Osborne and Gaebler 1993), which made an impact on the United States reform movement, was widely read by practitioners of public administration and public policy in other countries.

The NPM movement highlighted that bureaucrats should only implement policies and be accountable to politicians and citizens for policy outcomes. Bureaucrats should not influence policy-making. The movement had a goal to change bureaucratic structure and culture to be more efficient and responsive to public interests (Barzelay 1992). Proponents of NPM used economic theory, incentive theories and market-driven decisions as a basis for solutions. A prime example of a tool that emerged was the signing of contracts between ministers and permanent secretaries to promise certain deliverables, such as in Australia and the United Kingdom. Another example was the separation of policy-making agencies from service delivery and production bureaucracies. Owing to NPM, some have pointed to the decline of bureaucratic power in the policy-making process (Wilson 2008). However, there are also a number of studies that explained how NPM was business as usual and that the bureaucracy's role had not diminished in any way (e.g. Cheung and Scott 2003).

Since the early 2000s, especially since 9/11 in the United States, scholars have referred less to the NPM paradigm and now refer more to the governance paradigm. The rapid process of globalization, the emergence and spread of the Internet and other communication media have changed the way that we understand and approach problems of governance. The meaning of governance can be broadly defined as 'structures and processes by which people in societies make decisions, set rules, and share power' (Folke *et al.* 2005: 444). Rhodes offers six approaches to the definition of the term: governance as corporate governance; governance as New Public Management; governance as 'good governance'; governance as international interdependence; governance as a socio-cybernetic system; and governance as networks (Rhodes 2000).

Despite the changes and reforms during the NPM era, in the era of governance, the bureaucracy continues to be an integral part of the policy process. Some argue that the bureaucracy is stronger than before and that there is a need to continue to build up bureaucratic capacity. Thus it is necessary to re-emphasize the bureaucracy in the study of policy processes (e.g. Howlett and Ramesh 2003; Krause and Meier 2005). In the governance paradigm, the role of the bureaucracy and the bureaucrats is understood to be different from before. Governance stresses the value of bureaucrats among other actors in creating public value and the bureaucracy as an important part of issue networks and service delivery networks. While most literature on public administration regards the evolution of the bureaucracy as a linear process, some have argued the contrary. Lynn argues that the traditional bureaucratic paradigm showed far more respect for law, politics, citizens and values than the NPM paradigm (Lynn 2001). Thus there is more resemblance between the traditional bureaucratic paradigm and the governance paradigm. The governance paradigm values the role of the bureaucracy, unlike the NPM paradigm, yet at the same time it is pushing the bureaucracy to improve and evolve further.

Within the governance paradigm the notion of networks and collaborations is prominent. There are now more studies on the bureaucracy and its relations and power in various types of networks. One example is the notion of policy networks. Policy networks refer to a group of various people or organizations who are connected or are held together by common interests in certain policy problems. Policy networks try to influence policy decisions (Marsh and Rhodes 1992; Marsh 1998). A bureaucracy is one actor in the complex web of actors in the society that make up policy networks. Effective bureaucracies would be able to manage and manoeuvre policy networks in the direction that is best for the general public. This is defined as network governance which is the act of designing, managing, coordinating strategies, structures and processes of inter-organizational relations in order to affect public policies (Baker 1992; Provan and Kenis 2007). Bureaucrats need to have a different set of skills to maneuver in this kind of context, whether it is to effectively take part in a policy network or to exercise network governance (Edelenbos and Klijin 2005).

Public managers are co-creators of public value, which in turn sets the direction for bureaucracies and public policies. Moore's concept of public value has gained momentum in the public sector and has implications on how we understand the role of the bureaucracy in the policy process (Moore 1995). As bureaucracies are working in a networked environment, they are consistently shaping public value through networks. Concepts that have gained attention include co-production and co-creation where the bureaucracy partners work with the private sector and non-profit organizations to provide public goods and services, and to set regulations for governance. These ideas fall under the rubrics of collaborative governance (e.g. Ansell and Gash 2008; O'Leary and Bingham 2009) and also sound governance (Farazmand 2004). All these frameworks have one common focus on partnership as a form of participatory governance. This shifting role of the bureaucracy will have implications on how it can influence the policy process. In one view, this could lead to a more restricted role for bureaucracies. This is due to the increased role and power of non-state actors in networks. On the other hand, bureaucracy might gain more power and control because of their continual advantage over public resources and the opportunity to shape public values through public policies.

In sum, the bureaucracy continues to be the centre of study no matter how paradigms have shifted in public administration, whether it is the traditional public administration, new public management, or governance paradigms (Koliba 2004; Jreisat 2012). Its role in the policy process will continue to change depending on the political, economic and social changes that each country goes through. For now, it continues to be one of the most important actors in all stages of the policy process.

## Future studies

To successfully understand this topic in greater depth, there need to be more studies of the different types of bureaucracy and of bureaucrats, in other words the 'heterogeneity of bureaucracy and bureaucrats'. Bureaucracies are currently not homogeneous. Many have little resemblance to Weber's original ideal type. We should compare different types of bureaucratic behaviour, structure and culture and their influences on policy processes. For example, they could be studies of comparisons between central and local bureaucracies, line -ministries versus central ministries, higher, middle and lower ranks of bureaucrats, developed and developing countries, and bureaucracies of different sectors such as health and education. The literature on decentralization has begun to focus on bureaucratic capacity but not so much on how local bureaucracy shapes policy at the local and national levels. Lastly the literature on multilevel governance has started to focus on the relationship between national and local bureaucracy with supra-national bureaucracy such as that of the EU. But there is much more room for research.

Another phenomenon worth noting is the expansion of semi-bureaucrats, in other words, those who are employed by the public sector but who are treated differently from a career civil servant or bureaucrat. Semi-bureaucrats are usually employed based on market-mechanisms. Examples of this group include contract employees, state enterprise employees, experts, professionals, advisors, consultants and ad hoc public managers. It is also important to understand how their role differs or is the same compared to the typical bureaucrat.

In the past, scholars could study one agency within a ministry and could claim that the study represented that entire bureaucracy. Today, uniqueness is the new norm. Each agency can be quite unique due to information technology, leadership style, organizational culture, and hierarchical arrangements of the organizations. Aside from the above mentioned semi-bureaucrats, many public agencies are frequently using more matrix approaches to management rather than relying solely on hierarchical control. These semi-bureaucracies or hybrid organizations have mixed management instruments between bureaucracy, the market and networks. They have a variety of structures for decision-making such as the use of task forces, inter-departmental committees, and ad hoc committees. Thus, in addition to understanding the semi-bureaucrats' roles, we should also understand how these new structures of the bureaucracy effect policy processes.

In sum, the Weberian model continues to be a reference point for any discussion on the bureaucracy and its role in the policy process. However, we have moved quite far from that starting point. Bureaucracies have achieved great success in some countries as well as failing miserably in others. Despite being understood as being rigid and hierarchical, they continue to evolve and adapt to changes in political, economic and social systems. In this era of governance we recognize the bureaucracy as public organizations and bureaucrats as public managers, who have to manoeuvre in the complex web of multiple actors in all stages of the policy process. bureaucracy has played an important, if not *the most* important role, in policy-making and policy implementation throughout the history of its existence and it will continue to do so.

## Bibliography

Aberbach, Joel D., Robert D. Putnam and Bert A. Rockman. 1981. *Bureaucrats and Politicians in Western Democracies*. Cambridge, MA: Harvard University Press.

Adams, Gordon. 1981. *The Iron Triangle: The Politics of Defence Contracting*. New York: Council on Economic Priorities.

Ahn, C.S. 1998. 'Inter-ministry coordination in Japan's foreign policy making', *Pacific Affairs* 72(1): 42–60.

Albrow, Martin. 1970. *Bureaucracy*. London: Pall Mall.

Allison, G. 1971. *Essence of Decision: Explaining the Cuban Missile Crisis*. Boston: Little Brown.

——and P. Zelikow. 1999. *Essence of Decision: Explaining the Cuban Missile Crisis*. New York: Longman.

Ansell, C. and A. Gash. 2008. 'Collaborative governance in theory and practice', *Journal of Public Administration in Research and Theory* 18(4): 543–71.

Appleby, Paul. *Policy and Administration*. 1949. Tuscaloosa, AL: University of Alabama Press.

Baker, R. 1992. *Public Administration in Small and Island States*. West Hartford, CT: Kumarian Press.

Barnett, Michael N. and Martha Finnemore. 1999. 'The politics, power, and pathologies of international organizations', *International Organization* 53: 699–732.

Barzelay, Michael. 1992. *Breaking Through Bureaucracy*. Berkeley, CA: University of California Press.

Beck, James M. 1932. *Our Wonderland of Bureaucracy: A Study of the Growth of Bureaucracy in the Federal Government, and Its Destructive Effect upon the Constitution*. New York: Macmillan.

Beetham, David. *Bureaucracy*. 1987. Milton Keynes: Open University Press.

Bevir, Mark and R.A.W. Rhodes. 2006. *Governance Stories*. Routledge: London.

Blais, Andre and Stephane Dion (eds). 1991. *The Budget-Maximizing Bureaucrat: Appraisal and Evidence*. University of Pittsburgh Press, Pittsburgh, PA.

Blau, Peter M and W. Richard Scott. 1962. *Formal Organizations: A Comparative Approach*. San Francisco: Chandler.

Boston, J. 1991. 'The theoretical underpinnings of public sector restructuring in New Zealand', in J. Boston, J. Martin, J. Pallot and P. Walsh (eds) *Reshaping the State: New Zealand's Bureaucratic Revolution*. Auckland: Oxford University Press,

Bowornwathana, Bidhya. 2011. 'History and political context of public administration in Thailand', in Evan Berman (ed.) *Public Administration in Southeast Asia: Thailand, Philippines, Malaysia, Hong Kong and Macau*. New York: CRC Press, Taylor & Francis, 29–52.

——and Ora-orn Poocharoen. 2010. 'Bureaucratic politics and administrative reform: Why politics matters', *Public Organization Review* 10: 303–21.

Burnham, James. 1941.*The Managerial Revolution*. New York: John Day.

Campbell, C. and G. Szablowski. 1979. *The Superbureaucrats: Structure and Behaviour in Central Agencies*. Toronto: Macmillan.

Chattopadhyay, Paresh. 1993. 'The (ex) Soviet economy: Towards a reassessment of contending theses', *Economic and Political Weekly* 28(5): 13–22.

Cheung, Anthony B.L. and Ian Scott. 2003. *Governance and Public Sector Reform in Asia: Paradigm Shifts or Business as Usual?* London and New York: RoutledgeCurzon.

Christensen, T. 2007. *Organization Theory and the Public Sector: Instrument, Culture and Myth*. London: Routledge.

Cole, Richard and David Caputo. 1979. 'Presidential control of the senior civil service', *American Political Science Review*, June: 399–413.

Considine, Mark. 1994. *Public Policy: A Critical Approach*. South Melbourne: Macmillan Education Australia Pty Ltd.

Dolan, Julie. 2000. 'The senior executive service: Gender, attitudes, and representative bureaucracy', *Journal of Public Administration Research and Theory* 10: 513–30.

——and David H. Rosenbloom. 2003. *Representative Bureaucracy: Classic Readings and Continuing Controversies*. New York: M.E. Sharpe.

Downs, Anthony. 1964. *Inside Bureaucracy*. Santa Monica, CA: RAND Corporation.

—— 1967. *Inside Bureaucracy*. Boston: Little, Brown.

Dunn, Delmer D. 1997. *Politics and Administration at the Top: Lessons from Down Under*. Pittsburgh, PA: University of Pittsburgh Press.

Edelenbos, J. and E.H. Klijin. 2005. 'Managing stakeholder involvement in decision-making: A comparative analysis of six interactive processes in the Netherlands', *Journal of Public Administration Research and Theory* 16: 417–46.

Egeberg, Morten. 1999. 'The impact of bureaucratic structure on policy-making', *Public Administration* 77: 155–70.

Eiji, Kawabata. 2001. 'Sanction power, jurisdiction, and economic policy-making: Explaining contemporary telecommunications policy in Japan', *Governance* 14(4): 399–427.

Etzioni-Halevy, E. 1983. *Bureaucracy and Democracy: A Political Dilemma*. London: Routledge and Kegan Paul.

Farazmand, Ali. 2004. *Sound Governance: Policy and Administrative Innovations*. New York: Greenwood Publishing Group.

Foley, Henry A. 1975. *Community Mental Heath Programs: The Formative Process*. Lexington, MA: D.C. Health.

Folke, C., T. Hahn, P. Olsson and J. Norberg. 2005. 'Adaptive governance of social-ecological systems', *Annual Review of Environment and Resources* 30: 441–73.

Furlong, F.R. 1998. 'Political influence on the bureaucracy: The bureaucracy speaks', *Journal of Public Administration Research and Theory* 8: 39–65.

Garcia-Zamor, Jean-Claude. 2004. 'The struggle of small bureaucracies to develop traditional ethical policies', in Ali Farazmand (ed.) *Sound Governance: Policy and Administratiive Innovations*. Westport, CT: Praeger, 290–308.

Garvey, Gerald. 1995. 'False promises: The NPR in historical perspective', in Donald F. Kettl and John J. DiIulio, Jr., *Inside the Reinvention Machine: Appraising Governmental Reform*. Washington, DC: The Brookings Institution, 87–106.

Goodnow, Frank J. 1900. *Politics and Administration: A Study in Government*. New York: Macmillan.

Goodsell, Charles T. 2004. *The Case for Bureaucracy: A Public Administration Polemic*. Washington, DC: CQ Press.

Gormley, William T. Jr. and Steven J. Balla. 2004. *Bureaucracy and Democracy: Accountability and Performance*. Washington, DC: CQ Press.

Gupta, Dipak K. 2001. *Analyzing Public Policy: Concepts, Tools, and Techniques*. Washington, DC: Congressional Quarterly Inc.

Hall, Richard H. 1996. *Organization: Structure, Processes and Outcomes*. Englewood Cliffs, NJ: Prentice Hall.

——and Robert E. Quinn. 1983. *Organization Theory and Public Policy*. Thousand Oaks, CA: Sage.

Heady, Ferrel. 2001. *Public Administration: A Comparative Perspective*. New York: Marcel Dekker.

Henderson, Jeffrey. 2011. *East Asian Transformation: On the Political Economy of Dynamism, Governance and Crisis*. London: Routledge.

Henry, J. 2006. 'Educating managers for post-bureaucracy: The role of the humanities', *Management Learning* 37: 267–81.

Hix, Simon. 1999. *The Political System of the European Union*. London: Macmillan.

Ho, Khai Leong. 2000. *The Politics of Policy Making in Singapore*. Oxford: Oxford University Press.

Hopkins, R.F. 1976. 'The "international role of "domestic" bureaucracy', *International Organization* 30(3): 405–32.

Howlett, Michael and M. Ramesh. 2003. *Studying Public Policy: Policy Cycles and Policy Subsystems*. Toronto: Oxford University Press.

Jacques, E. 1976. *A General Theory of Bureaucracy*. London: Heinemann.

Jreisat, Jamil E. 2012. *Globalism and Comparative Public Administration*. Boca Raton, FL: CRC Press.

Kamenka, Eugene. 1989. *Bureaucracy*. Oxford: Blackwell.

Kaufman, H. 1981. 'Fear of bureaucracy: A raging pandemic', *Public Administration Review* 41: 1–9.

Kim, Doo-Rae. 2008. 'Political control and bureaucratic autonomy revisited: A multi-institutional analysis of OSHA enforcement', *Journal of Public Administration Research and Theory* 18(1): 33–55.

Kjaer, Anne Mette. 2004. *Governance*. Oxford: Polity Press.

Koliba, C. 2004. 'Is service-learning contributing to the downsizing of American democracy? Learning our way out', *The Michigan Journal of Community Service Learning* Spring: 57–68.

—— 2011. 'Administrative strategies for a networked world: The educational imperative for inter-governmental relations in 2020', in K. Thurmaier and J. Meek (eds) *Network Governance: Implications for Intergovernmental Relations in 2020*. New York: Sage.

——, Jack W. Meek and Asim Zia. 2010. *Governance Networks in Public Administration and Public Policy*. New York: CRC Press.

Krause, George A. and Kenneth J. Meier. 2005. *Politics, Policy, and Organizations: Frontiers in the Scientific Study of Bureaucracy*. Ann Arbor, MI: University of Michigan Press.

Krislov, Samuel. 1974. *Representative Bureaucracy*. Englewood Cliffs, NJ: Prentice Hall.

Lipsky, Michael. 1980. *Street-Level Bureaucracy: Dilemmas of the Individual in Public Services*. New York; Russell Sage.

Lynn, Laurence E. Jr. 2001. 'The myth of the bureaucratic paradigm: What traditional public administration really stood for', *Public Administration Review* 61(2): 144–60.

March, James G and A. Simon Herbert. 1958. *Organisations*. New York: Wiley.

Marmor, Theodore R. 1973. *The Politics of Medicare*. Chicago: Aldine and Atherton.
Marsh, David. 1998. *Comparing Policy Networks*. Milton Keynes: Open University Press.
——and R.A.W. Rhodes. 1992. *Policy Networks in British Government*. Oxford: Clarendon Press.
Mashaw, Jerry. 1983. *Bureaucratic Justice: Managing Social Security Disability Claims*. New Haven, CT: Yale University Press.
——and T.R. Marmor. 1988. *Social Security: Beyond the Rhetoric of Crisis*. Princeton, NJ: Princeton University Press.
Meier, K.J. 1997. 'Bureaucracy and democracy: The case for less democracy and more bureaucracy', *Public Administration Review* 67(3): 193–99.
Merton, Robert K. 1957. *Bureaucratic Structure and Personality*. Glencoe, IL: Free Press.
Mommsen, Wolfgang J. 1974. *The Age of Bureaucracy: Perspectives on the Political Sociology of Max Weber*. Oxford: Blackwell.
Montjoy, Roberts S. and Douglas J. Watson. 1995. 'A case for reinterpreted dichotomy of politics and administration as a professional standard in council-manager government', *Public Administration Review* 55(3): 231–9.
Moore, Mark Harrison. 1995. *Creating Public Value: Strategic Management in Government*. Cambridge, MA: Harvard University Press.
Mosher, Frederick C. 1968. *Democracy and the Public Service*. Oxford University Press: New York.
Mouritzen, Hans. 1990. *The International Civil Service: A Study of Bureaucracy: International Organisations*. Aldershot: Dartmouth,
Muldoon, James P., Joann F. Aviel and Richard Reita. 2010. *The New Dynamics of Multilateralism: Diplomacy, International Organizations, and Global Governance*. Boulder, CO: Westview Press.
Niskanen, W.A. 1973. *Bureaucracy: Servant or Master? Lessons from America*. Washington, DC: The Institute of Economic Affairs.
—— 1974. *Bureaucracy*. Chicago: Aldine Press.
O'Leary, Rosemary and Lisa Blomgren Bingham. 2009. *The Collaborative Public Manager: New Ideas for the Twenty First Century*. Washington DC: Georgetown University Press.
Olsen, Johan P. 2006. 'Maybe it is time to rediscover bureaucracy', *Journal of Public Administration Research and Theory* 16(1): 1–24.
——and G. Peters. 1996. *Lessons from Experience*. Oslo: Scandinavian University Press,
Osborne, David and Ted Gaebler. 1993. *Reinventing Government: How the Entrepreneurial Spirit is Transforming the Public Sector*. New York: PLUME.
Ouchi, William G. 1980. 'Markets, bureaucracies, and clans', *Administrative Science Quarterly* 25: 129–41.
Page, C. and B. Jenkins. 2006. *Policy Bureaucracy: Government with a Cast of Thousands*. Oxford: Oxford University Press.
Parsons, D.W. 1995. *Public Policy: An Introduction to the Theory and Practice of Policy Analysis*. Cheltenham: Edward Elgar.
Parsons, Wayne. 1995. *Public Policy: An Introduction to the Theory and Practice of Policy Analysis*. Northampton, NH: Edward Elgar.
Peters, B.G. 1981. 'The problem of bureaucratic government', *The Journal of Politics* 43(1): 56.
—— 1995. *The Politics of Bureaucracy*, 4th edn. New York: Longman Publishers USA,
—— 2010. 'Bureaucracy and democracy in the modern state', *Public Administration Review* 70(4): 642–3.
——and John Pierre. 1998. 'Governance without government? Rethinking public administration', *Journal of Public Administration Reseach and Theory*: 223–43.
Pollitt, Christopher and Geert Bouckaert. 2004. *Public Management Reform: A Comparative Analysis*. Oxford: Oxford University Press,
Pressman, Jeffrey L and Aaron B. Wildavsky. 1973. *Implementation: How Great Expectations in Washington are Dashed in Oakland*. Berkeley: University of California Press,
Provan, Keith G and Patrick Kenis. 2007. 'Modes of network governance: structure, management, and effectiveness', *Journal of Public Administration Research and Theory* 18: 229–52.
Rabin, Jack and James S. Bowman. 1984. *Politics and Administration: Woodrow Wilson and Public Administration*. New York: Marcel Dekker.
Ramseyer, J.M and F.M. Rosenbluth. 1993. *Japan's Political Market Place*. Cambridge MA: Harvard University Press.
Rhodes, R.A.W. 2000. *Transforming British Government*. London: Macmillan,
Riggs, Fred W. 2001. 'Bureaucratic links between administration and politics', in Ali Farazmand (ed.) *Handbook of Comparative and Development Public Administration*. New York: Marcel Dekker.

Riper, Paul P Van. 1984. 'The politics–administration dichotomy: Concept or reality', in Jack Rabin and James S. Bowman (eds) *Politics and Administration: Woodrow Wilson and Public Administration*. New York: Marcel Dekker, 203–18.

Rourke, Francis E. 1984. *Bureaucracy, Politics and Public Policy*. Boston: Little, Brown.

Rutgers, Mark R. 2001. 'Splitting the universe: On the relevance of dichotomies for the study of public administration', *Public Administration Administration and Society* 33(1): 3–20.

Saint-Martin, Denis. 2004. *Building the New Managerialist State: Consultants and the Politics of Public Sector Reform in Britain, Canada and France*, 2nd edn. Oxford and New York: Oxford University Press.

Scott, W. Richard. 1992. *Organizations: Rational, Natural, and Open Systems*. Englewood Cliffs, NJ: Prentice Hall.

Seldon, Sally Coleman. 1997. *The Promise of Representative Bureaucracy: Diversity and Responsiveness in a Government Agency*. New York: M.E. Sharpe.

Shafritz, J.M. Jr. and A. Hyde. 2008. *Classics of Public Administration*, 6th edn. Boston: Wadsworth.

——, S. Ott and Y.S. Jang. 2010. *Classics of Organization Theory*. Boston: Wadsworth Cengage Learning.

Smith, B. 1988. *Bureaucracy and Political Power*. Brighton: Wheatsheaf.

Svara, James H. 1998. 'The politics-administration dichotomy model as aberration', *Public Administration Review* 58(1): 51–8.

—— 1999. 'Complementarity of politics and administration as a legitimate alternative to the dichotomy model', *Administration and Society* 30(6): 676–705.

—— 2001. 'The myth of the dichotomy: complementarity of politics and administration in the past and future of public administration', *Public Administration Review* 61(2) (March/April): 176–83.

Thompson, J.A. 1965. 'Bureaucracy in a democratic society', in R. Martin (ed.) *Public Administration and Democracy*. Syracuse, NY: Syracuse University Press, 210–12.

Wade, Robert. 1990. *Governing the Market: Economic Theory and the Role of Government in East Asian Industrialization*. Princeton, NJ: Princeton University Press,

Weber, Max. 1946. *Max Weber: Essays in Sociology*, H.H. Gerth and C. Wright Mills (ed. and trans.). London: Oxford University Press,

West, William F. 1997. 'Searching for a theory of bureaucratic structure', *Journal of Public Administration Research and Theory*: 591–614.

Westoby, Adam. 1985. 'Introduction', in Bruno Rizzi (ed.), Adam Westoby (trans.) *The Bureaucratization of the World: The First English Edition of the Underground Marxist Classic that Analyzed Class Exploitation in the USSR*. New York: Free Press, 1–33.

White, Leonard D. 1926. *Introduction to the Study of Public Administration*. New York: Macmillan.

Wildavsky, Aaron. 1979. *The Politics of the Budgetary Process*. Boston: Little, Brown.

—— 1986. *Budgeting: A Comparative Theory of Budgetary Processes*. New Brunswick, NJ: Transaction Publishers.

——, Brendon Swedlow and Joseph White. 2006. *Budgeting and Governing*, Brendon Swedlow (ed.). New Brunswick, NJ: Transaction Publishers

Wilson, James Q. 1989. *Bureaucracy: What Government Agencies Do and Why they Do it*. New York: Basic Books.

—— 2008. *American Government Brief Version*. Boston: Wadsworth.

Wilson, Woodrow. 1887. 'The study of administration', *The Academy of Political Science*: 197–222.

World Bank. 1993. *The East Asian Economic Miracle: Economic Growth and Public Policy*. New York: Oxford University Press,

Wu, Xun, Ling Hi Yan, Wen Sun Tung and Allen Lai. 2010. 'Public administration research', in *Reform and Transition in Public Administration Theory and Practice in Greater China: 1978–*. Hong Kong: University of Hong Kong.

# 26

# Disagreement and alternative dispute resolution in the policy process

*Boyd Fuller*

## Introduction

Disagreement is a natural feature of the policy process, and negotiation is one of the common processes for resolving it. Both are facts of life in the interdependent relationships among government and non-government actors involved in and impacted by the policy process. However, the degree and kind of disagreements can have very different impacts on the efficacy and outcomes of the policy process and its negotiations. Similarly, not all negotiation behaviors and processes are equally effective and they need to be chosen strategically to suit the context and kind of disagreement. Some negotiations are organized, visible, inclusive, and are managed using carefully constructed processes. In other cases, they can be disorganized, hidden, exclusive, and ad hoc. Whatever the case, where parties seek to cooperate, the quality of their negotiations and its contribution to public value can be improved by using the best knowledge from the alternative dispute resolution literature.

Studies on policy-making and the policy process tend to focus mostly on negotiations that are convened to find agreement among stakeholders who have varying interests and, where the policy has become the subject for significant disagreement among stakeholders, to resolve a dispute. As such, mediation and consensus building theory have received the most attention. Negotiation theory, however, provides much of the basis for them and so this chapter covers it too.

Negotiation theory starts with the premise that parties' publicly stated positions mask their needs and interests and that an effective negotiation must uncover the interests on all sides. After that, interests can be met creatively through a multiplicity of different possible solutions, which often also gain value through skillful trading across interests that the parties prioritize differently. More detail on negotiation theory is given in the next section.

Consensus building and mediation theory tell us about when parties can be brought together, by whom, for what purposes, and using what kind of processes. Getting the process right is important, and often challenging. In public policy settings, there are many processes and forums in which stakeholder representatives can pursue the goals of their organization, and thus it may be difficult to get stakeholders to authentically participate in negotiations until they are convinced that the other venues cannot produce a better solution. Even when stakeholders do send representatives to the negotiating table, it is often difficult to truly represent the constituencies, which are often large, divided, and thus inflexible. This inflexibility increases when one or more constituencies believe that fundamental values are at stake. Knowledge provides no assistance, because it is often uncertain and contested. These challenges and the ideas and practices in the consensus building literature that address these challenges are discussed below.

Finally, possible criteria for evaluating consensus building processes employed in the policy-making process, the shortcomings in the literature's current data and the trials facing those seeking to monitor and evaluate such processes in the future are summarized.

## Negotiation theory as a starting point

Alternative dispute resolution theories about negotiation, mediation, and consensus building touch upon all stages of the public policy process as long as there are interdependent parties who need to cooperate to achieve a solution. In this section, I introduce the fundamental building blocks of negotiation theory, which is the key building block for much of mediation and consensus building theory as well. Negotiation, mediation, and consensus building theory approach a similar problem, cooperation among parties with different interests, from slightly different perspectives. All are focused on the challenges to and opportunities for improving the outcomes of negotiations.

Negotiation theory focuses on the barriers, strategies and tools relevant to individual parties who are preparing for or participating in negotiations, and thus the ideas and practices proposed are evaluated according to what benefit they will bring one of the parties.[1] These parties can be an individual, an organization, a nation, or some kind of grouping of these as long as they seek to coordinate their actions together. However, the field generally assumes that parties can do better when they also help the other party(-ies) achieve results that are better than what the latter might achieve when there is no cooperation. Otherwise, their counterpart will seek to meet their interests elsewhere. (Fisher and Ury 1991)

Perhaps the most important building block of much of current negotiation theory is the separation of interests and positions, which in practice are often conflated by negotiators. Negotiation theory defines positions as the stated wants and solutions that one party seeks to get the other to accept. The underlying interests, on the other hand, are the wants and needs that motivate the positions negotiators take. So, for example, an organization may demand that certain best management practices for water management be required for farmers. That is their position. Their interests, on the other hand, may be to preserve an ecosystem or particular species, to gain political advantage in an upcoming election, or another want or need that can be fulfilled should their position be accepted by the other parties.

To be able to negotiate interests rather than positions, it is important that the negotiating parties also (a) identify the interests of their counterpart(s) in pre-negotiation research and in-negotiation discussions and (b) determine how each party, including themselves, prioritizes their interests. First, it is important to consider the interests of counterpart(s) because any idea we propose should meet their interests as well or they will not agree. Second, not all interests are equally important, and sometimes value can be gained when a negotiator agrees to a counterpart's proposal on one issue that impacts on less important interests as long as they get a more preferred option on another issue which touches more important interests.

Getting interests on the table is also important for problem definition. The purpose of a negotiation is, after all, to find a solution that meets the interests of the parties as effectively as possible. So, for example, in California, parties locked in a decades-long conflict about water allocation among agricultural and environmental uses were able to make progress when they redefined the problem. The conflict had for many years revolved around two contentious questions: (a) which universal best management practices should be used on farms throughout the state; and (b) and how much water could be saved by agricultural water users? The parties were able to engage in more productive negotiation when they redefined the problem by asking, simply, how can downstream environmental objectives be met in a way that allows farms to choose what means they employ for doing so? This definition touched more directly on the interests of the various parties (preservation of environmental systems, self-determination in managing farms and water, profit) and, once found, resulted in negotiations that reached an unexpected and welcome agreement.[2]

Once a negotiator clearly defines the interests of the parties to the negotiation, he or she must then identify different possible solutions for meeting his or her own interests effectively. Here, negotiation theory broadly distinguishes two kinds of solutions: options and alternatives. Options are the set of possible solutions that the negotiating party thinks (a) are beneficial to themselves and (b) also meet the interests of their counterparts in the negotiation. The negotiator is encouraged to prepare multiple options that can be combined to make deals possible; they must also be willing to brainstorm additional ones as they learn more about the interests of the other party(-ies). Often, value can be created on both sides if the right trades can be made, especially those based on differently prioritized interests, so that each side is trading something that they want less for something that they want more. Alternatives, on the other hand, are the set of possible solutions by which the party can meet its interests without the cooperation of their counterpart. The most attractive of these alternatives, or the best alternative to a negotiated agreement (BATNA), then becomes the minimum that a party will accept in the negotiation, because no party should accept an agreement that produces less value for them than what they could achieve elsewhere.

Interests, options, and alternatives are three elements of the Seven Elements Framework which was developed by the Harvard Negotiation Project.[3] The other elements are objective criteria, commitment, communication, and relationships. Objective criteria are external standards that parties agree to as the basis for a decision about how value will be divided among them.[4] Commitment is an important element in public policy and relates to the connection between the negotiators, the constituencies they represent, the broader institutions of governance, and the general public. Essentially, negotiators need to consider what authorization will be required for proposed deals to be implemented. Such authorization can come from the support of key individuals, but it may also require a change in regulation or law, the creation of a necessary organization, or some other change in the policy, rules, or another institution. The relationship element reminds negotiators that it is important to maintain and improve relationships with their counterparts and that this relationship building should be done in parallel with the substantive elements of the negotiation, rather than depending on its outcomes. Finally, the communication element is where a negotiator will consider what information will be shared and sought, and how he or she would like that process to proceed. Again, this is important in public policy settings where information must be managed among multiple, complex constituencies, the broader public, the media, and government decision-makers.

In the next section, this chapter introduces some of the challenges that make negotiation and consensus building in policy-making difficult.

## Why negotiations (and disagreements) in the policy process are more difficult

Negotiations in the policy processes are marked by several factors that can make the management of disagreement within them complex including challenges posed by managing the complexity and scale, representing complex or unorganized constituencies, stakeholders' contested knowledge, and divergent values, frames, and belief systems. I describe each in more detail in this section.

## *Complexity and scale*

As policies move through the policy process, discussions, debates, and negotiations occur in many forums, some concurrently and some sequentially. Policy-making interactions can occur, for example, in state and federal legislatures, courtrooms and administrative tribunals, the public media, global and local multi-stakeholder processes and, of course, various backroom negotiations. Each of these forums has its own rules and norms, includes different parties, and produces diverse kinds of outcomes.[5] More importantly for negotiation, these forums can restrict or encourage the participation of various stakeholders and other parties (e.g. experts and mediators). Such choices are often made to "set the table" by promoting or discouraging certain interests, ideas, and styles of deliberation (e.g. emotive vs. less emotive) as well as influencing what resources are brought to the table, how much and what information is shared (e.g. people are less likely to disclose sensitive information to parties they mistrust), and the methods by which the support of various constituencies be gained.

In addition, the visible processes are often not the only ones occurring nor are they always the most important. In rooms out of view, some parties may enter in negotiations that shape who gets standing, what issues are discussed, and other elements of the more official processes. Similarly, the bigger, more visible negotiations impact the backroom ones. These backroom negotiations may occur among fewer parties and exclude some stakeholders (de Sousa Briggs 2008), and there may be many smaller negotiations instead of one larger, multiparty one. In some cases, the convening of less visible processes is on purpose, providing space for exploring new ideas away from the inflexible gaze of warring constituencies (Martinez *et al.* 2000; Fuller 2009b, 2009c)

Keeping track of all the parties and processes can become overwhelming and so it is not a surprise that parties tend to reduce the complexity. Often they do so by forming coalitions organized around common positions and belief systems. However, while coalitions can reduce complexity, they also introduce some additional challenges. As coalitions form, they must negotiate what they stand for. Often, these negotiations are settled by difficult compromises on a common position that becomes inflexible. However, negotiation theory argues that negotiating from positions leads to unwise outcomes because of their inflexibility and because they hide the true wants and needs of the parties that could be solved in other ways more acceptable to their counterparts.

In two-party negotiations, skilled negotiators can build relationships and manage communication with their counterparts to get at the interests and look for creative options and trades to meet them concurrently with their own. However, as new ideas emerge from negotiations, each side must consider quickly the impact of these ideas on their interests. Individuals can do so quickly, but as the complexity of each entity increases, so does the time required to analyze the new ideas, particularly when the parties in the constituency need to reopen negotiations among themselves about what their joint response will be—e.g. accept, reject, modify for the other party's consideration.

## *Representing complex or unorganized constituencies*

The classic problem of divergent interests between principal and agent presents one well-known challenge.[6] Principal-agent or representative-constituency relationships are much more complex in public policy settings, however. First, constituencies are often too complex to be effectively characterized as a single entity. Instead, constituencies are often divided by their internal differences in interests, values, and frames—e.g. when the constituency is an alliance of multiple organized actors—or unorganized populations that have not yet formulated and articulated what they stand for. In both cases, negotiators of these constituencies will find it difficult to negotiate well. They may become inflexible, especially if their negotiating position is the result of a hard-won compromise among the factions of the constituency, who would naturally be reluctant to reopen their internal negotiations when the negotiators ask them to be more flexible.

Where constituencies are unorganized, it may be easy to ignore their interests and values at first. However, agreements can then be undermined if the unorganized feel that their interests and values have been ignored. Mansbridge (1996) notes that policy systems often go through cycles in which decisions are made which impact unorganized and uninterested groups, who then organize to change the policies, which then can impact other old and new parties, and the cycle repeats itself.

Of course, constituencies are not the only groups to which the negotiation and its parties are beholden. In the public realm, any deals must also respect the institutions of governance. Where there are sunshine laws which require transparency in public participation processes, for instance, then the meetings must be open to the public, and thus negotiators may play to their home crowd rather than seeking to make a potentially difficult deal. Whatever agreement is constructed must also be allowable given the laws, policies and regulations of the government(s) involved or there must be a plan to change the appropriate institution, perhaps along with a contingency plan should that change turn out to be impossible.

In the next two sections, this chapter covers the challenges that arise when facts are contested and stakeholders believe values are at stake.

## *Contested knowledge*

Knowledge is one of the pillars for problem definition and the formulation of solutions. When it is contested, identifying, developing, and deciding among multiple viable problem definitions and solutions can be difficult. And yet, without knowledge, policy-making is blind, both in what solution it chooses and also in what it learns from the implementation and evaluation of that solution.

Contested knowledge arises from apparently competing claims about what data and findings are correct. Knowledge can differ across groups for two kinds of reasons. The first kind relates to the different frames and practices that each group employs in creating, validating, and disseminating knowledge. The second kind occurs when parties choose which knowledge they share for strategic rather than factual reasons: lying, withholding, and re-interpretation are all possible activities here. I start with the first kind.

Parties holding different frames may ask different questions about the environment and hold to different facts and theories about how things work. Such disputes are hard to resolve in most policy disputes. Data is often incomplete, uncertain, and often associated with one side or the other. The problem is further exacerbated by how easily knowledge claims can be deconstructed in the different policy forums. Much knowledge relies on a set of imperfect practices that are nonetheless accepted within knowledge communities. The problem arises when such science enters other forums which have different methods for generating and validating knowledge. In the forums of public policy—legislatures, courtrooms, scientific advisory committees, and so on—it is easy to argue that the knowledge of other parties is invalid. The standing of different stakeholders as knowledge holders can be challenged. Assumptions and methodologies can be questioned. The amount of uncertainty and risk that is acceptable for decision-making can be contested. For example, local communities collect significant data, but the method of its collection (everyday practice and experience) and the form of its storage (often stories) is not considered valid by many scientific communities (Fischer 2000; Corburn 2005; Fuller 2009a). Those same communities, however, argue that much of expert science lacks the data that local communities have, and that they overly simplify the complex situations on the ground and use values and criteria for analyzing the meaning and impact of the data that do not reflect the values of the community. Furthermore, whosoever counts as an expert may be contested as well, and a person's standing is often crucial for the authority of his analysis in addition to whatever methods they use. Even the questions that the knowledge holders ask can be quite different, and thus the data that one side collects may be seen by another side as the invalid because its holder was asking the wrong question.

Furthermore, it would be naïve to neglect the strategic considerations behind contested knowledge. A party that feels under threat may construct false data and findings to protect its interests (Forester 2005). Given the degree of uncertainty in today's knowledge about the many complex systems being considered in public policy, such knowledge claims can be difficult to completely refute. While their authenticity may be called into question, the claimers can also easily undermine the knowledge claims of others. This again leaves policy analysts and makers with no one legitimate set of facts that they can use to make authoritative policy.

## Values, frames, and belief systems

Perception, interpretation, and the formulation of solutions are shaped by the lens through which we view the world. Schön and Rein (1994) and Lewicki *et al.* (2003) argue that many policy conflicts are driven by the divergence among actors' "frames," which they describe as normative/prescriptive stories that actors use to interpret the world, define problems, and choose actions. The frames that individuals, organizations, and coalitions use contain causal perceptions that link actions and impacts as well as values about right and wrong. Similarly, Sabatier and other students of the Advocacy Coalition Framework[7] argue that many long-term policy disputes are driven by the presence of two or more advocacy coalitions that are organized around divergent belief systems and who disagree about what should be done around a particular policy issue.

Conflicting values and frames pose several problems to effective negotiation. First, the different interpretations and meanings actors attribute to actions, words, and phenomena often lead to misunderstanding, which over time can lead to each side attributing hostile intentions to their counterparts. Even the most well-meaning actions by one party may antagonize the other(s). In some cases, leaders of one side may aggravate the situation by strategically misinterpreting the other's actions, since the creation and maintenance of a hostile enemy discourages the exploration of internal disagreements and differences.

Furthermore, the parties with divergent frames may define problems quite differently. Some might, for example, see that slums are an unsightly blight which will then lead them to think of removing the slums and placing its inhabitants elsewhere. Others might see slums as a place where poor people work as a community to generate resources for self-reliance and see the problem more as one of providing the right policy environment for that innovation to flourish. Often, the differences in stakeholders' stories of problem definition and appropriate solutions are missed by analysts and negotiators, who then attribute negative characteristics to the other side (unwilling to listen, not intelligent, aggressive) instead of understanding that the two sides are having two mostly independent conversations in which they argue about solutions (positions) without first clarifying what problem each side is talking about and what problem they should be solving as a group.

The problem is not only one of interpretation. When parties start speaking about values and rights, negotiation becomes even more difficult. Conflicts about values and rights are notoriously more difficult to resolve than interest-based disputes (Tribe *et al.* 1976; Lord 1979; Susskind and Field 1996; Fuller 2009b, 2009c). Once a party invokes one (or both), it becomes more difficult for them to consider solutions that are different from their public positions since no one wants to "compromise their values." This is especially true when the negotiators represent constituencies who have access to the meeting or its records. In these instances, negotiators tend to prefer tough language, inflexible positions, and disparaging language to maintain their reputation within their constituency. All of these, unsurprisingly, provoke the other side to negotiate in a similar fashion.

In public policy contexts, in which policy processes can extend over multiple years and even over a decade, these problems of framing become hardened as negotiators can fall into unhelpful routines and habits. In many cases, constituencies no longer believe that they have anything to gain from cooperating with the other side, and will punish representatives who start exploring those possibilities. Group polarization can occur, in which each side demonizes the other side, attributing the worst intentions to their actions while suppressing their own internal differences (Northrup 1989; Sunstein 2002). As hostility grows, the ability of each side to negotiate becomes more difficult as agreement is seen as a "deal with the devil" (Benjamin 1990; Mnookin 2010).

In the light of these challenges, it is not surprising that some authors propose that the parties need to increase their understanding of one another. Schön and Rein argue that policy deliberations should help the parties "put the other's shoes on,"[8] which means that each party can see the problems, solutions, and other elements of their discussion using the same frames or belief systems of their counterparts. In doing so, it is understood that the negotiating parties (or analysts) should be able to reframe the negotiation in such a way that the problems of their divergent belief systems—different and conflicting interpretations of communication and phenomena, problem definitions, and knowledge—will be resolved. What is not spelled out is how the parties use this shared understanding and how they will make their solutions acceptable to the constituencies who have not undergone this epiphany.

In the next section, I introduce and summarize consensus building and mediation theory, and show what ideas and recommendations they put forward to manage and move through these challenges.

## Consensus building and mediation theory

Consensus building and mediation theory relate to the convening and management of negotiation processes. In particular, they provide ideas, understandings, and guidance related to the challenges of and better approaches to designing processes, convening stakeholders, managing their negotiations, and promoting effective agreements. Both provide guidance about how the parties can approach the challenges described in the previous section. Consensus building theory focuses more on negotiations convened by actors other than the courts or other adjudicative bodies. However, for the purposes of this chapter, there is enough similarity between the two theories that I will hereafter refer to both as consensus building theory.

Negotiation theory is the building block for consensus building theory. Like negotiation theory, consensus building theory emphasizes interests instead of positions, the desirability of creating and investigating multiple options to meet interests, and so on. As a starting point, consensus building theory promotes certain steps as part of an effective strategy, which for the readers will seem mostly similar to the policy stages, save that evaluation is missing. I cover the evaluation of these processes in the next section. For consensus building, the recommended steps are[9] (with the equivalent policy stage in brackets):

- convening the relevant parties (agenda-setting);
- clarifying the rules and responsibilities for the group and its participants;
- deliberating to develop options and then packages of options that seek to meet the needs of the participating stakeholders as well as the public interest (policy formulation);
- making decisions that have the support of all or almost all the stakeholders (decision-making);
- implementing agreements and other commitments (implementation).

In the rest of this section, I describe the steps and highlight where they address the challenges described above.

## Convening—getting the problem and parties right

Convening in consensus building is about the iterative design of the consensus building process. Essential in convening are two tasks: getting the problem and parties right. Convening starts with identifying the key players, including both nongovernment and government actors. Some of these parties will need to participate in the proposed consensus building process. It often helps to have certain key agencies or players openly support the process—for example, a prominent leader might talk to certain people to gain their participation. Others may provide staff support, particular expertise, monetary resources, or just observation. (Carlson 1999)

To get the problem right and the right parties at the table, consensus building theory argues that a *conflict assessment* should be conducted. A conflict assessment occurs before the process is officially convened and is crucial both for process design, problem definition and for motivating stakeholders to attend. In practice, a conflict assessment is usually conducted by a neutral third party who is often but not always the mediator. The assessor's first task is to identify and interview potential stakeholders and their representatives. In these interviews, the conflict assessment has two basic tasks. The first is to gather information about the parties, including their interests, ideas for solutions, and their willingness to participate in the dialogue. The second task is to tell them, and answer questions, about the conflict assessment process and the proposed negotiation. The latter is a part informing and part trust-building task. It allows the stakeholders to develop more comfort about the process (Susskind and Thomas-Larmer 1999).

After the interviews, the conflict assessor should put together a report, usually without attribution, that summarizes what he or she has discovered about the parties and what process she suggests for their negotiation. In some cases, the assessor might also recommend that the negotiation should not proceed, especially if he or she believes that the parties are unlikely to reach agreement. This report is shared with the parties who are asked to provide feedback on it. Once it is completed, it will be handed over to the proposed convenor of the negotiations. Again, this feedback is not only intended to improve the document, but also to build trust with stakeholders. If they approve of the suggestions, they are more likely to attend when the negotiations are convened.

As an agenda-setting exercise, conflict assessment and the broader convening process is a proactive means of determining who the parties are and what issues should be discussed. Participation in a consensus building process is also voluntary and so the conflict assessor will seek some agenda of issues that attracts the interests of participants and decision-makers and will often seek an overarching framing of the issue that all sides agrees is a good start for the discussions. This reframing and agreement on the agenda is an important first step to dealing with problems of divergent frames and beliefs and in keeping constituencies apprised and supportive of the deliberations.

In some cases, for example, the conflict assessor may propose that stakeholders can be grouped into categories based on similar interests so that the common perspective can be spoken for by a few selected representatives. The process can also be set up other forums in which the representatives of large constituencies can meet with their selected representatives to debrief current developments in the consensus building group's emerging ideas for vetting and feedback.

While consensus building theory's ideas about convening and conflict assessment provide some traction on the challenges discussed above, implementing them in practice is no trivial task. For example, identifying the right stakeholders can be difficult when some of the interests are held by populations and communities who are unorganized (Mansbridge 1996; Laws 1999). Their members may not have realized that they do constitute a group or at least they may not have chosen a representative. Where an organization has chosen a representative, that person may not be the best choice for the negotiation because they are, for example, inflexible and unwilling to learn, poor negotiators, or unable to forge good working relationships with other participants. In other cases, some stakeholders may be reluctant to send a representative because they feel that they have little to gain—for example, because they distrust each other, believe that the convenor is unwilling or unable to translate their agreement into action, or feel that they can achieve their interests and protect their values more effectively in other policy forums.

## *Clarifying rules and responsibilities*

At the beginning of the process, the various parties should agree about the responsibilities of the group and the various participants (stakeholders' representatives, mediators, staff, experts, etc.). For example, they need to determine what purpose the group is supposed to achieve, what products it seeks to produce, what roles and responsibilities, the mediator, negotiating representatives, experts, and any other participating parties will take on, and so on. Ground rules will also have to be established. Some will cover what parties can and cannot do during the deliberations. Ground rules start with behavior at the table, but they can be extended to cover behavior away from it as well. Examples include whether parties will pursue their interests in other forums and whether and how the individual parties can share information with non-participants, including constituencies, other officials, the media, and so on.

Clarifying the responsibility of the group and its individuals is especially important when parties believe values and rights are at stake (Forester 1999). A relatively safe environment for dialogue and negotiation needs to be created when there is significant mistrust among the parties or about the process. By using rules to moderate the dialogue, and establishing norms of good listening, mediators can help to create the conditions needed where parties can explore each other's claims about values in order to test their genuineness and to acknowledge them as being legitimate. This inquiry and acknowledgment need not mean agreement.

Also, ground rules are important in terms of moderating how information is shared with others outside the group. Rules favoring transparency, for example, are common in some countries but while they have normative appeal, they may hamper communication and problem-solving in cases where the parties do not trust each other. Where constituencies distrust representatives who make overtures to the other side, it may make more sense for some of the negotiations to take place out of the public eye. During the less visible negotiations, the representatives can listen more carefully and explore some new ideas without fear of censure.

However, when this is done, there should be clear ground rules and a strategy for how information will be shared with constituencies, decision-makers, and the public (Martinez *et al.* 2000; Fuller 2009c).

## *Deliberating to find and package options*

To develop a solution, the parties need ideas that go beyond the initial positions that each bring to the table. These ideas, when combined, need to produce potential agreements that all parties see as being better than that which they could achieve in another forum (i.e. their best alternative to a negotiated agreement—BATNA). These ideas start as discrete solutions to different parts of the puzzle that the group is trying to solve. Some may provide value to all parties; others may benefit only some of the parties. This packaging is made more effective when parties prioritize among their interests, and then look for trade-offs in which each party gives up something less important in exchange for something more important. As parties move toward a solution, they will begin to package these ideas together more and more, with each party examining the emerging packages to determine whether their set of interests is being met more effectively in the proposed deal than in their best alternative.[10]

Often this packaging is done using single texts. Single texts—such as draft agreements, charts, and maps—can be used to synthesize and present certain understandings, draft ideas, and milestones during the process. They can be records created by the mediator that the parties agree clarify areas of emerging agreement and ongoing contention, including possible solutions, facts, and so on. Stakeholders can use draft agreements to organize their deliberation, by adding, subtracting, and modifying text in the single text until they can agree to what is stated there.

## *Making decisions*

In negotiations between two individuals, the decision is simply made by the parties at the table. In any other negotiations, decision-making becomes more complex, especially as the number of parties and constituencies increases. Public policy involves many stakeholders and so most negotiations will include more than two parties. Since not all these negotiations will require unanimity to make a decision, a decision rule must be agreed upon at the beginning of the negotiation. Such a decision rule could be simply 50 percent plus one or some kind of supra-majority such as 66 percent. It might also be a weighted majority. For example, the Kyoto Protocol decision rule required that at least 55 percent of the countries approve the deal and that the aggregate percentage of emissions represented by those countries must exceed 55 percent of the world's total emissions.

While the parties may make a decision at the table, the work of decision-making is not done. The transition to implementation often requires significant efforts to gain support from key members of constituencies and other parties who will be crucial to the decision's implementation. In international cases, the decision will likely have to be formally ratified, which requires an additional set of negotiations within the constituency.

## *Implementation*

Decision-making and implementation are in fact intertwined in consensus building. Decisions should not be made until the parties are fairly sure that they will get the support needed from decision-makers (legislators, community leaders, agency officials, etc.) who were not at the table. In well-managed processes, draft ideas and agreements will be shared with such leaders to get their feedback and seek their backing. Where success is unlikely, the negotiators should consider other options even if the parties agree the first idea is superior. Where success is possible, the parties then consider what additional mechanisms and responsibilities should be built into the recommendations to improve their implementation. For example, the parties might agree to lobby particular parties together to gain support for the recommendations.

Sometimes, the negotiations may also ignore various additional forums to test the emerging ideas with constituencies and the wider public. The city of Chelsea, Massachusetts, for instance, created a new city charter using a consensus building process in which developments were continually revealed to the public for their feedback and then support using radio and other media.

Often the convenor of a negotiation or consensus building process has the major role in implementing the recommendations. The negotiating groups themselves rarely have formal authority to make decisions. Instead, they make recommendations that they expect the convening actor to translate into an agenda, set of solutions, or a policy or program to be implemented as part of the policy process. In reality, the conveners may choose to follow only some or even none of the recommendations, though they put their legitimacy at peril when they do so. Or they may adopt them all but struggle to implement them in practice.

Finally, as the literature on public policy has also found, implementation brings about its different interpretations of the agreement, as well as new misunderstandings and disagreements. An effective agreement often includes provisions for how the parties will manage their disagreements and disputes during the implementation (Podziba 1999).

## Evaluating negotiations and mediations in the public sector

Negotiations that occur in policy processes can be both easy and very difficult to assess. At first brush, they are easy to evaluate because as long as the parties are satisfied, then the negotiations can be deemed to be a success. If efficiency is a concern, one could look at the interests of the different actors and see from a dispassionate viewpoint whether one or both of the parties could have done better without any party losing gains (Raiffa 1982; Raiffa *et al.* 2002).

However, scholars of the policy process can and should ask more demanding questions of such negotiations (Coglianese 2003). We ask that policy processes be efficient in time and resources, wise in the use of the best knowledge, and fair in how the process is conducted and how resources are allocated. In this light, Bingham (2003) proposes that there are three possible kinds of benefits from negotiations in the public sector: substantive, process, and relationships. *Substantive benefits* revolve around improved outcomes. One common claim is that the outcomes of negotiations are better than that achievable by each party without their agreement and cooperation (their BATNA). Similarly, some point to the creativity sparked by options, in which new ideas emerge from the deliberations among the participants. Proponents of public dispute resolution also argue that when parties do negotiate and their recommendations are implemented by the convening actor, stakeholders are more likely to support, or at least not actively oppose, the subsequent policy. This logic is also used to argue that the policies developed by such negotiations are better than those developed through other processes.

Process benefits include reduced time and resources to reach an implementable policy. A negotiation can also increase the perceived fairness of the process by providing opportunities for new actors to participate and by giving each actor an equal chance to present and advocate for their interests. A negotiation may also be considered more fair and wise when multiple forms of knowledge are brought to the table and when joint fact-finding allows the group as a whole to decide what facts they will accept.

Relationship benefits can include better personal relationships among the representatives who negotiated or between the groups who were represented. Groups can learn that the other side is reasonable even if they have come to different conclusions. They may share more information and thus be better informed. Future negotiations and other deliberative and policy-making processes may go more smoothly because the parties now understand one another better.

Unfortunately, the research on evaluating such processes is still in its infancy and faces several key challenges. Data can be hard to access because the group agreed to confidentiality. Many studies of negotiations in the public sector are individual, descriptive case studies rather than hypothesis testing, higher-*n* inquiries. These cases tend to be custom-designed to fit each context and they occur in a wide variety of settings, both of which makes them difficult to compare. The cases tackled through negotiation are sufficiently different from other cases in that it is difficult to compare the effectiveness of traditional policy-making processes with those supplemented by negotiation (Emerson *et al.* 2003).

In addition, many of the evaluations are written up by mediation practitioners, which raises the possibility of bias. Finally, negotiations convened in and around policy processes are not discrete phenomena. Even a process that fails to reach an agreement may produce information that improves the policy process or result in improved relationships, thus reducing the amount of conflict manifest in other stages of the policy process.

## Conclusions

Negotiation itself has always been a part of policy-making. However, the push in recent decades for more inclusive and science-based processes has brought negotiation out of the back halls and legislatures to include a wider group of people who set the agenda, seek inclusive and creative solutions, and make and implement agreements. Such negotiations can touch any part of the policy process. They may, for example, be used to set the agenda, to create ideas for policy formulation, to make recommendations that inform decisions, and to aid in the implementation of policies.

Negotiation and consensus building rely on the parties to share information and to be open to new ideas. To make the negotiations productive in public policy settings, much care must be taken to help the stakeholders to be willing and able to engage one another even when they feel that values are at stake or that they cannot trust the other parties. Such negotiations must be carefully convened, usually through an interactive conflict assessment that helps the convenor and mediator determine the agenda and process design and otherwise bring the parties together ready to talk about a solvable problem. For the negotiation to be credible and effective, it must be strategically linked to the ongoing policy-making process and to decision-makers outside government as well.

Knowledge is often contested and so mediators must help the parties to engage in joint fact-finding so that they have a common set of agreed-upon facts for their deliberations. Joint fact-finding does not necessarily result in one agreed-upon theory or interpretation of the data, but it is a common foundation for discussions about what is happening and what might happen if changes are made.

## Notes

1 This summary of negotiation theory draws upon several sources, including Fisher and Ury (1991), Lax and Sebenius (2006), and Raiffa (1982).

2 For more information on water conflicts in California and the challenges and opportunities of negotiating them, see Fuller (2009b, 2009c) and the special issue on the CALFED Bay Delta Program in the *Environmental Science and Policy Journal* 12(6).

3 See Fisher and Ury (1991) and the Program on Negotiation website: http://www.pon.harvard.edu.

4 For example, negotiators might refer to pollution standards in other areas with similar conditions and industries as a fair way of setting the standard for their own region.
5 Some outcomes are enforceable decisions, some provide input or analysis, and some have no real outcomes even as they try to increase the legitimacy of the process—for example, courtroom decisions have legal backing that encourages implementation while global agreements rely on national legislatures to ratify and enforce agreements.
6 Principles and agents' interests are not always aligned, and thus agents may act in ways that serve the agent's interests rather than the interests of the principle who hired them.
7 For more information about the Advocacy Coalition Framework, see Chapter 10 in this volume and Sabatier and Weible (2007).
8 See Schön and Rein (1994) and Rein and Schön (1996).
9 See Susskind (2005) and Susskind and Cruikshank (2006).
10 In fact, where parties, problems, and solutions are many and complex, negotiating groups often focus most of their efforts on developing, modifying, and make decisions by focusing mostly on packages, as opposed to the discrete trades often discussed and analyzed in the negotiation literature (Innes and Booher 1999, Fuller 2009c).

## Bibliography


Benjamin, M. 1990. *Splitting the Difference: Compromise and Integrity in Ethics and Politics*. Lawrence, KS: University Press of Kansas.

Bingham, G. 2003. 'Foreword', in R. O'Leary and L.B. Bingham (eds) *The Promise and Performance of Environmental Conflict Resolution*. Washington, DC: Resources for the Future.

Carlson, C. 1999. 'Convening', in L. Susskind, S. McKearnan and J. Thomas-Larmer (eds) *The Consensus Building Handbook: A Comprehensive Guide to Reaching Agreement*. Thousand Oaks, CA, Sage.

Coglianese, C. 2003. 'Is satisfaction enough? Evaluating public participation in regulatory policymaking', in R.O'Leary and L.B. Bingham (eds) *The Promise and Performance of Environmental Conflict Resolution*. Washington, DC: Resources for the Future.

Corburn, J. 2005. *Street Science: Community Knowledge and Environmental Health Justice*. Cambridge, MA: MIT Press.

de Sousa Briggs, X. 2008. *Democracy as Problem Solving: Civic Capacity in Communities Across the Globe*. Cambridge, MA: MIT Press.

Emerson, K., T. Nabatchi R. O'Leary and J. Stephens 2003. 'The challenges of environmental conflict resolution', in R. O'Leary and L.B. Bingham (eds) *The Promise and Performance of Environmental Conflict Resolution*. Washington, DC: Resources for the Future.

Fischer, F. 2000. *Citizens, Experts, and The Environment: The Politics of Local Knowledge*. Durham, NC: Duke University Press.

Fisher, R. and W. Ury. 1991. *Getting to Yes: Negotiating Agreement Without Giving In*. New York: Penguin Books.

Forester, J. 1999. 'Dealing with deep value differences', in L. Susskind, S. McKearnan and J. Thomas-Larmer (eds) *The Consensus Building Handbook: A Comprehensive Guide to Reaching Agreement*. Thousand Oaks, CA: Sage, 463–93.

—— 2005. 'Policy analysts can learn from mediators', in J.T. Schloz and B. Stiftel (eds) *Adaptive Governance and Water Conflict: New Institutions for Collaborative Planning*. Washington, DC: Resources for the Future, 150–63.

Fuller, B. 2009a. 'Local knowledge and consensus building: from access to impact', LKY School of Public Policy Working Papers, SPP09-08.

—— 2009b. *Moving Through Value Conflict: Consensus Building and Trading Zones for Resolving Water Disputes*. Wiesbaden: VDM Verlag Dr. Mueller e.K.

—— 2009c. 'Surprising cooperation despite apparently irreconcilable differences: Agricultural water use efficiency and CALFED', *Environmental Science and Policy* 12(6): 663–73.

Innes, J.E., Booher, D.E. 1999. 'Consensus building as role playing and bricolage: Towards a theory of collaborative planning', *Journal of the American Planning Association*, 65(1): 9–26.

Laws, D. 1999. 'Representation of stakeholding interests', in L. Susskind, S. McKearnan and J. Thomas-Larmer (eds) *The Consensus Building Handbook: A Comprehensive Guide to Reaching Agreement*. Thousand Oaks, CA: Sage, 241–85.

Lax, D.A. and J.K. Sebenius. 2006. *3-D Negotiation: Powerful Tools to Change the Game in your Most Important Deals*. Boston, MA: Harvard Business School Press.

Lewicki, R.J. and B. Gray. 2003. 'Framing of environmental disputes', in R.J. Lewicki, B. Gray and M. Elliott (eds) *Making Sense of Intractable Environmental Conflict: Concepts and Cases*. Washington, DC: Island Press.

Lord, W.B. 1979. 'Conflict in federal water resource planning', *Water Resources Bulletin* 15(5): 1226–35.

Mansbridge, J.J. 1996. 'Using power/fighting power: The polity', in S. Benhabib (ed.) *Democracy and Difference*. Princeton, NJ: Princeton University Press.

Martinez, J., L.E. Susskind, et al. 2000. 'Parallel informal negotiation: An alternative to second track diplomacy', *International Negotiation* 5(3): 569–86.

Mnookin, R. 2010. *Bargaining with the Devil: When to Negotiate, When to Fight*. New York, Simon and Schuster.

Northrup, T.A. 1989. 'The dynamic of identity in personal and social conflict', in L. Kriesberg, T. A. Northrup and S. J. Thorson (eds) *Intractable Conflicts and their Transformation*. Syracuse, NY: Syracuse University Press.

Podziba, S. 1999. '"Case 3". The Chelsea Charter consensus process', in L. Susskind, S. McKearnan and J. Thomas-Larmer (eds) *The Consensus Building Handbook: A Comprehensive Guide to Reaching Agreement*, Thousand Oaks, CA: Sage.

Raiffa, H. 1982. *The Art and Science of Negotiation*. Cambridge, MA: Belknap Press of Harvard University Press.

——, J. Richardson and David Metcalfe 2002. *Negotiation Analysis: The Science and Art of Collaborative Decision Making*. Cambridge, MA: Belknap Press of Harvard University Press.

Rein, M. and D. Schön. 1996. 'Frame-critical policy analysis and frame-reflective policy practice', *Knowledge and Policy: The International Journal of Knowledge Transfer and Utilization* 9(1): 85–104.

Sabatier, P.A. and C. Weible. 2007. 'The advocacy coalition framework: Innovations and clarifications', in P.A. Sabatier (ed.) *Theories of the Policy Process*. Boulder, CO, Westview Press.

Schön, D.A. and M. Rein. 1994. *Frame Reflection: Toward the Resolution of Intractable Policy Controversies*. New York: Basic Books.

Shafritz, Jay M., J. Steven Ott, and Yong Suk Jang. 2010. *Classics of Organization Theory*. Boulder, CO: Wadsworth Cengage Learning.

Sunstein, C.R. 2002. 'The law of group polarization', *Journal of Political Philosophy* 10(2): 175–95.

Susskind, L.E. 2005. 'Consensus building and ADR: Why they are not the same thing?', in M. Moffitt and R. Bordone (eds) *The Handbook of Dispute Resolution*. San Francisco, Jossey-Bass.

—— and P. Field. 1996. *Dealing with An Angry Public: The Mutual Gains Approach to Resolving Disputes*. New York: Free Press.

—— and J. Thomas-Larmer. 1999. 'Conducting a conflict assessment', in L. Susskind, S. McKearnan and J. Thomas-Larmer (eds) *The Consensus Building Handbook: A Comprehensive Guide to Reaching Agreement*. Thousand Oaks, CA: Sage.

——and J.L. Cruikshank. 2006. *Breaking Robert's Rules: The New Way to Run Your Meeting, Build Consensus, and Get Results*. New York: Oxford University Press.

Tribe, L.H., C.S. Schelling and John Voss 1976. *When Values Conflict: Essays on Environmental Analysis, Discourse, and Decision*. Cambridge, MA: Ballinger Publishing Company.

# 27

# Governance, networks and intergovernmental systems

*Robert Agranoff, Michael McGuire and Chris Silvia*

Governments today operate within systems of governance that include interacting governmental bodies and nongovernmental organizations (NGO). These interconnections have increased dramatically in recent decades because of increased intergovernmentalization and government externalization. The former refers to grant, regulatory, and related vehicles of connecting central and subnational governments and the latter to moving governmental functions and services delivery outside governments' boundaries through contracting, vouchers for goods and services, and related means of "privatization." This has led to the need to capture the essence of public activity as governance, "a mix of all kinds of governing efforts by all manner of socio-political actors, public as well as private; occurring between them at different levels, in different governing modes and orders" (Kooiman 2003: 3). Such interactive governance increasingly occurs within networks of government officials and NGO actors, that is "structures of interdependence involving multiple organizations or parts thereof, where one unit is not merely the formal subordinate of the others in some larger hierarchical arrangement" (O'Toole 1997: 45).

## Collaboration

In governance networks, the actors depend on the collaboration imperative, that is the actions of officials and managers crossing the boundaries of their organizations working in dyadic, triadic, or networked relationships that are transactional. These actions bring on the need for collaborative actions beyond cooperation, working jointly in some fashion, creating or discovering solutions within given constraints, for example knowledge, time, money, legal authority, or other resources. As such, "collaborative management is a concept that describes the process of facilitating and operating in multi-organizational arrangements to solve problems that cannot be solved, or solved easily, by single organizations" (Agranoff and McGuire 2003: 4). Collaborative activity among the actors within governance makes their home organizations more conductive, organizing its work for external as well as internal activity. A conductive organization is one "that continuously generates and renews the capabilities to achieve breakthrough performance by enhancing the quality and flow of knowledge and by calibrating its strategy, culture, structure and systems" externally (Saint-Onge and Armstrong 2004: 213).

## The transformation of intergovernmental relations

The era of governance networks has also transformed intergovernmental relations (IGR) beyond its traditional scope as involving "combinations of interdependencies and influences among public officials" working on financial, policy, and political issues (Krane and Wright 1998: 1168) to incorporate waves of collaborative operationalism external to governments as well as between them. Indeed, IGR has evolved through four distinct waves of development including the current network era (Agranoff 2010).

The first, law and politics, emerged with the building of integral nation-states, primarily in the eighteenth and nineteenth centuries, where legal distinctions of governmental isolation and "jurisdiction" held true. Generally, responsibilities were separated and isolated. The dual federalism doctrine in the United States held that the national government and the states were each sovereign in their respective spheres and that between them exist areas of activity in which neither can enter. While there is reasonable evidence that completely separate spheres never existed in practice (Elazar 1962), the legal distinction and intergovernmental norms of separation held for some time, despite the fact that by the mid-1800s modern communications, which required a series of local delivery units (postal units, roads, canals, railways) and cross-links, pushed jurisdictional separation to its limits.

This situation changed from the early twentieth century to roughly the 1960s when the welfare state ushered in the second epoch. It marked a time of growth and more professional central governments that also included an increasing interdependency that linked subnational and central governments (Skowronek 1982). In particular, the welfare state was very much a top-down effort that enhanced the fiscal and program strength of national governments everywhere (Loughlin 2007: 389). Most central social policies (welfare, social services, employment, economic development) were polity-wide because central governments were suspicious of universal local commitment, so national financing and programming were linked with local commitment (Ashford 1988: 18). Later in the era came newer social welfare programs, for example drug abuse, child and family abuse, mental disabilities, and new efforts in community development, which were less suited to central organizations, bringing on the need for "important intergovernmental adjustments" (ibid.: 19). The resulting impact was considerable jurisdiction overlap (Watts 1999: 38).

By the middle of the twentieth century governments began to recognize the gradual introduction of organized actors outside government as also involved in funding and programming, particularly in Western Europe and the Anglo-American countries. NGOs became agents and partners of the state (Rhodes 1997). Through some grants but predominantly by contracts, governments linked with nonprofit service agencies and for-profit vendors of services. In the case of nonprofits, they had been around for decades but the boundaries of the state expanded to include them in various forms of externalized direct services delivery, a sort of government "for hire" (Smith and Lipsky 1993: 5). For-profits have always been part of government procurement, and certain basic services like building security and road building were regularly contracted out, but now such direct government services as public health care, services for the disabled, vocational rehabilitation, mental health, substance abuse, and family violence, along with finance and accounting services and other management functions, are contracted out. Just as the welfare state philosophy once expanded the role and number of involved governments, beliefs in the primacy of market forces, reduction and importance of the public sector, deregulation of state controls, and abandonment of the principle of equality led to a prevailing political view of a more "minimalist" state, with less direct government intervention in the economy and society (Loughlin 2007: 390). "Market superiority" that could either provide for the needs of people or a market-model of government services that could provide greater efficiencies than by public operation prevailed as an attitude. This also was the era of the New Public Management (NPM), with heavy borrowing from the private sector with its benchmarking, performance targeting, competitive bidding, outsourcing, and the like, all of which reinforced IGR by government/NGO partnerships (Hood 1991). This led to new sets of alliances between governments at all levels and a host of public and private bodies. Thus, "the public administration problem has spread well beyond the borders of the government agency" (Salamon 1995: 2).

The fourth and currently developing IGR network era gradually emerged out of the previous era and became fully acknowledged in the first decade of the twenty-first century. It has been dubbed a world where everything is connected in networks (Castells 1996). Public agencies and NGOs now network for purposes of exchanging information, enhancing one another's capabilities, smoothing services interactions, and solving policy/program problems (Agranoff 2007). In some ways, IGR networking began as a parallel activity to contracting, where funders and their agents began to build contractor-government networks (Brown and Potoski 2004; Van Slyke 2007), building on prior networks of local government, business associations, and economic development agents who have worked among themselves at the community level for some four or five decades, and these entities have had extensive links with higher level governments in order to secure support to promote local economies (Agranoff and McGuire 2003; Eisinger 1988; McGuire 2002). The emergent set of intergovernmental networks—and what makes them different—is the way officials from the different levels of governments and NGOs representing the nonprofit sectors are challenged to sit down with one another *at the same table* to deal with uncertainties and discuss, explore, negotiate, and solve issues (Koppenjan and Klijn 2004; Radin *et al.* 1996).

## The network construct

While just one of a number of vehicles in the panorama of governance (Thompson 2003: 150, 237; Salamon 2002: 11), networks involve a cluster or complex of organizations connected to each other by resource dependencies and are distinguished from other clusters or complexes by breaks in the structure of resource dependencies (Rhodes and Marsh 1992). In order to broaden the discourse on networks (Thompson 2003: 9) into a potential theory in this area, it is important to understand "differentiation of governance capacity" when the potential role of networks is considered "to construct a more nuanced understanding of the relative contributions which these actions now make to the governance of society" (Peters 2000: 47, 50). This implies that both network opportunities and barriers are equally important to understanding any outcomes and process elements (Scharpf 1978: 346) in any set of "macro-level theories of the state" (Rhodes and Marsh 1992: 203).

To focus on governance networks requires the drawing of parameters around use of the term "network." As Rhodes (2003: 21) suggests, "network" is an everyday term used by consumers and managers (and perhaps politicians) to describe the web of relationships in which they are embedded, giving rise to different meanings that need to be captured. Here we focus on the construction of meanings given by government managers and their interlocutors as they work within organized entities that involve parts of organizations nonhierarchically (O'Toole 1997). As such, we are not directly focusing on the broader issue of "democratic network governance," that is, cross-sectoral and based in civil society involvement where issues of deliberation and citizen responsibility, as well as questions of equity, accountability, and democratic legitimacy to serve public purposes are at stake (Bogason and Toonen 1998; Skelcher 2004; Sorenson and Torfing 2007). Although we clearly realize that network management is a central part of public network governance and impacts it in many ways (for example, it could limit participation and representation), we choose here to focus more directly on managerial arrangements and behaviors that contribute to policy theory within larger issues of democratic participation and governance. We thus use the term "network" to refer to structures involving multiple nodes—agencies and organizations—with multiple linkages, ordinarily working on cross-boundary collaborative activities.

## Networks and their work

Some networks are constructs based more or less on forms of linkages and are intermittently interactive and cooperative, that have been identified as serendipitous, whereas others are goal-directed and are based on more regularized interactions (Kilduff and Tsai 2003: 91), that is the action of networking (Alter and Hage 1993). The latter can be either chartered or nonchartered in character. Both types of networks share certain characteristics: permanent status; regular formal meetings; a definable communication system; leaders and participants; taskforces or work groups; identifiable operating structures; identifiable partners; and some form of division of labor/task allocation. Chartered networks are formally established as organized entities. In the United States they are often established by intergovernmental agreement, registration as a 501c(3) nonprofit organization, by act or resolution of a state legislature, a governor's executive order, and/or through corporate registration with a state government representative, such as the secretary of state. Nonchartered networks have no such formal-legal status, but their continuing presence and operations, regular meetings, concrete problem-solving actions, websites, newsletters, and the like are testimony to their existence. Many longstanding networks are non-chartered. Nonchartered networks are often harder to locate in telephone directories or on websites than those that have been formalized, but those without chartered status prove to be equally viable bodies.

Networks need to be understood in the context of how they operate. Five basic characteristics of their functioning provide a context for understanding formation, operation, and value-adding. First, not all networks are alike; whereas some exchange information, some build partner capacity, some "blueprint" strategies and process interorganizational programming, and some make policy/program adjustments. Some do more than one or more. Second, networks are non-hierarchical but organized into collaborarchies that blend today's conductive bureaucracies with voluntary organization-like structures. The key is not the official leaders but their champions, vision-keepers, technical cores, and staff. They are mainly organized around work and working groups as communities of practice. Third, the most important function of these communities is to discover, organize, and engage in knowledge management (KM). The KM process binds the network as it approaches problems of a multi-organization, multijurisdictional orientation. Fourth, networks are overlays on the hierarchies of participating organizations. They influence but do not control home agency decisions. The core work of the public agency goes on but in an increasingly conductive manner. Fifth, networks do add public value. To varying degrees they help multiple organizations to engage in problem identification and information exchange, identify extant knowledge, adapt emergent technologies, engage in KM, build capacity, develop joint strategies and programs, and adjust policies and programs (Agranoff 2007).

## Governance networks and public policy

The first group of scholars to deal with the network concept in IGR were those who dealt with policy implementation (Marsh and Smith 2000). As IGR expanded through welfare state programs and beyond the problem became, as Sundquist (1969: 12) observes, "how to achieve goals that are established by the national government, through the actions of other governments." In most cases, he concludes, governments choose to rely "upon systems of mutual adjustment ... rather than through the exercise of hierarchical authority" (1969: 19). Implementation then began to focus on the interaction of actors down the line as they attempted to make programs work (Ingram 1977; Pressman 1975; Pressman and Wildavsky 1973; Williams 1980). The network of actors, particularly at the bottom rung of the chain of implementation, became a focal point of research (Elmore 1985; Hjern and Porter 1981; Lynn 1981). In one of the early studies of implementation by network, Scharpf concludes that:

> it is unlikely, if not impossible, that public policy of any significance could result from the choice process of any single unified actor. Policy formulation and implementation are inevitably the result of interactions among a plurality of separate actors with separate interests, goals, and strategies.
>
> *(1978: 347)*

As such, he concludes that research should go beyond the strategies of policy formulation and implementation but include the more structured and stable relations between organizations.

## Network formation

### *The policy implementation connection*

The formation of networks is, in many cases, driven organically by the simple need to combine resources in ways that facilitate the implementation of a program. Networks are also formed by legislation or are mandated by others. Hall and O'Toole (2000) examined the US institutional arrangements incorporated into the legislation enacted by the eighty-ninth and the one hundred and third Congresses. They found that the majority of significant new legislation prescribed the involvement of collaborative structures for policy implementation. Their findings

> demonstrate that the institutional settings in which public programs are placed, at least via national legislation, are multiorganizational and networked rather than unitary and unambiguously hierarchical. Most new and amended programs encounter implementation settings of the more complicated varieties—with intergovernmental and/or cross-sectoral involvement more the rule than the exception. The arrays for program execution also require significant and skilled public management, particularly because the extent of interunit coordination required for program success is often substantial ... The networked reality of today's public management, furthermore, is important but clearly not unprecedented.

Subsequent research by the authors showed that post-legislation rule-making by implementing federal agencies also led to collaborative administrative arrangements (Hall and O'Toole 2004).

Pressman and Wildavsky (1973) were among the first to discuss public policy in terms of shared administration, suggesting the networked nature of policy implementation. Based on an empirical investigation of the US Economic Development Administration's attempts in the 1960s to address unemployment of minorities in Oakland, California, their findings describe the multiplicity of participants and perspectives from all levels of government pursuing policy goals that in practice may be conflicting. The evidence from Europe is the same: collaborative structures used for implementing manpower training in Germany and Sweden in the 1970s were characterized at that time in terms of multiple power centers with reciprocal relationships, many suppliers of resources, overlapping and dynamic divisions of labor, diffused responsibility for actions, massive information exchanges among actors, and the need for information input from all actors (Hanf *et al.* 1978). More than three decades ago, Hjern and Porter (1981) described implementation structures that operate with representatives of different agencies and exercise considerable discretion in practice. Many policy studies in the 1980s revealed the extent of collaboration in public policy implementation (Hull with Hjern 1987; Mandell 1984; O'Toole 1985). There is thus a rich history of networked policy implementation.

## Activating networks

Activating a network for the purposes of policy planning and/or implementation requires a heavy dose of developmental activity on the part of some partners who act either as champions or promoters (or "vision keepers"). Exclusivity or limited involvement leads to information and support gaps, as well as lost potential in interagency adjustment, so network managers need to know who has the critical policy-making resources: money, technology, information, expertise, time, and other necessary commodities (Agranoff 2003). Even if networks are formed through mandated action, there is still the need to recruit constantly by enlisting necessary partners who possess particular resources, expertise, and support for the network's activities. All networks depend on one or a small number of champions not just to help establish the network, but also, perhaps most importantly, to maintain commitment among network partners.

Networks are based in at least four dimensions. First, all network structures have a technical core, or knowledge about "how to do it" (Agranoff 2007). For example, internal and external expertise is a mainstream source of technical knowledge. Most participants will ask staff scientists or specialists inside and outside governments, along with university-based researchers, to share their technological knowledge with the network. In environmental and natural resource networks, engineering knowledge that deals with flooding and floodplain concerns, water supply, water quality, agricultural use, and recreation and wildlife management are all at the forefront of participating agency needs. In local economic development, city administrators, development directors, and NGO development corporation executives work to revise development plans, requiring expertise in engineering and planning; they negotiate financing mechanisms with local business groups, financial institutions, and state and federal governments; and they handle issues of water capacity and waste water with the state environmental agency. The network activities become a technical basis of intergovernmental/interorganizational exchange.

Second, there is also a legal dimension that defines whether a particular networked action can be undertaken. Laws governing each entity affect the ability of any single organization to act. An added overlay is the set of legal norms governing the management activity, whether it is law determining the formal structure (e.g. task force, committee, coalition) or the general legal framework governing any project that a network might undertake. Control of operations may be achieved through the use of government regulations that constrain the actions of network partners, through the distribution of funds or manpower, or through regulations that stipulate the powers and responsibilities of certain actors or specify what conditions potential actors must meet before they can qualify to be members of a collaborative structure.

Third, financial feasibility is another important dimension of networks. "Can we afford it?" is a central question in any public undertaking. Perhaps the most contentious, difficult, but necessary element of networking is pooling financial resources. Such sharing or pooling is implicit in Barbara Gray's definition of collaboration in which she asserts that it is the pooling of appreciations and/or tangible resources, e.g., information, money, labor, and so on, by two or more stakeholders to solve a set of problems which neither can solve individually (Gray 1985). However, there is no magic formula for determining the extent to which public sector organizations and NGOs exchange, share, or pool resources.

The fourth important dimension of network management is political. The politics of activities between and among organizations and their managers permeate the managerial process. Public managers not only engage in politics within their own organizations, but also must strike political (in addition to operational) bargains with other partners. In many contexts, network management consists of conflict resolution using the important political skills of bargaining, negotiation, diplomacy, and consensus building (Gray 1989; Ingram 1977).

## Network operation

### *Building blocks*

Network management behaviors are employed to help to frame the structure and the norms and values of the network as a whole. Managers cannot draw up an organizational chart in a network as is done in single organization structures, but they do try to influence the roles that each participant may play at any given time and the perceptions one has about the common purpose of the network. Managers do this by facilitating agreement on leadership roles; helping to establish an identity and culture for the network; assisting in developing a working structure for the network (e.g. committees, network "assignments"); and altering the perceptions of participants to understand the unique characteristics of working with persons in contexts without organizational mechanisms based in authority relations.

Seeking support from external groups and stakeholders for collaborative operations has proven to be a major component of collaboration effectiveness. Those within the collaboration must foster the buy-in of key stakeholders, particularly those whose power will be relied upon to signal support of the collaborative throughout their home agency. Managing the external network environment thus is important for the collaborative public manager. Encouraging support from and keeping a collaborative network in good standing with the higher governmental authority ranked very high in an empirical study of network leadership (Silvia and McGuire 2010). Similarly, encouraging support from and keeping the network in good standing with stakeholders both inside and outside the government was viewed as being very significant. Such behavior helps to establish the legitimacy of the network (Milward and Provan 2006) and acts as a "mobilizer" to develop commitment and support for network processes from network participants and external stakeholders (McGuire 2002).

Managers must also employ behaviors intended to create an environment and enhance the conditions for favorable, productive interaction among network participants. One critical behavior of network management is to build relationships and interactions that result in achieving the network purpose. The strategies of each network participant and the outcomes of those strategies are influenced by the patterns of relations and interactions that have developed in the network. Such behaviors include facilitating and furthering interaction among participants, reducing complexity and uncertainty by promoting information exchange, and facilitating linkages among participants. Successful network management will thus achieve cooperation between actors while minimizing and removing informational and interactional blockages to the cooperation.

Klijn and Edelenbos (2008) draw a distinction between process design and management and institutional design for describing various network management strategies. Process design involves agreements regarding the nature of the interaction process and the ground rules for participating in the network. The authors assert that there is no standard, all-encompassing design type for networks; it is situational. Process management includes the direct, hands-on application of the behaviors and tasks discussed above. Institutional design, on the other hand, is indirect. Such design strategies are typically focused on changing the formal and informal rules that "influence, guide, and limit" the behavior of the network participants (2008: 207). The strategies include changing the network composition, influencing network outcomes, and affecting network interactions.

## Learning and network management

Public managers in network settings face a number of both constraints and opportunities, most of which exist due to the primacy of government in many such settings. Such actions are driven by the knowledge that develops as implementers work through the process and learn what works and what does not work. The public knowledge that is generated by the process is thus informed by the outcomes of networks. Knowledge is that major step beyond information; it provides the capacity to act (Sveiby 1997). It is the

> fluid mix of framed experience, values, contextual information, and expert insight that provides a framework for evaluating and incorporating new experiences and information … In organizations, it often becomes embedded not only in documents or repositories but also in organizational routines, practices, processes, and norms.
>
> *(Davenport and Prusak 2000: 5)*

The importance of learning together in networks to create knowledge is captured by the work of Koppenjan and Klijn (2004). Joint action by interaction is seen in part as

> searches wherein public and private parties from different organization (levels of) government and networks jointly learn about the nature of the problem, look at the possibility of doing something about it, and look at the characteristics of the strategic and institutional context within which the problem-solving develops.
>
> *(2004: 10)*

Cooperation, then, presupposes structured learning between actors: "It requires numerous skills, tacit knowledge of the network and negotiation skills since the adopted strategies are implemented in a situation where singular hierarchical relations are lacking" (Koppenjan and Klijn 2004: 11). Thus, learning in multi-actor situations is crucial.

Informal structures that develop around shared knowledge are namely communities of practice and the epistemic communities that they often lead to. The former are self-organizing systems that share the capacity to create and use knowledge through informal learning and mutual engagement (Wenger 2000). Most communities are self-organized and bring in new knowledge bearers when needed, from wherever they can be found. Maintenance of communities of practice requires efforts to keep different types of knowledge bearers in, by challenging busy people with solving important public problems, and by calling on their experience and know-how in an interdisciplinary manner. Epistemic community can be facilitated by mobilizing a multi-agency group of professionals from different disciplines because they often share common outlooks and similar solution orientations. They also tend to share causal beliefs, notions of validity, and a common policy experience. An epistemic community normally produces consensual knowledge. Epistemic communities also can be important knowledge sustainers, as they can have a disproportionate effect on organized learning and behavior. Bringing together these communities for enhanced deliberation is among the emergent networked tasks of public management.

## *Governance networks add value*

The ability to create or add value has long been a central concern of the public sector. As a result of public managers attempting to "discover, define, and produce public value" (Moore 1995: 20), the utilization of collaborative networks for public sector service delivery and policy implementation has increased notably over the last two decades. It is now quite common for governments at all levels to rely upon other governments, private sector actors, and non-profit organizations to plan, implement, and manage "government" programs and services (Silvia 2011). However, as Bardach (1998) concludes, the question is not whether networks exist, but rather, whether networks increase the public value beyond which the agency would have in the absence of the network.

It has been argued that the frequency of the establishment of networks and the sustained utilization of networked approaches in the public sector provides evidence that such organizational structures do add value (Cropper 1996; Howlett 2002; Thomson *et al.* 2008). Howlett (2002) found that in four policy sectors networks matter in policy change as ideas and interest are transmitted through policy subsystems. Nevertheless, collaboration is, after all, not easy. The presences and gravity of collaborative challenges, including time costs, the logistical issues, varying degrees of interorganizational and/or interpersonal trust, the integration of multiple organizational cultures, the sharing of control over resources, and the disparate goals and objectives held by the different collaborative partners, have caused some to dissuade parties from collaborating unless it is necessary (Huxham and Vangen, 2005). However, the inability of single organizations to solve the wicked problems they face often requires a collaborative approach. Thus, despite the challenges posed by collaboration, networked arrangements for addressing shared problems has "added important value to the public undertaking that undoubtedly would not have otherwise occurred" (Agranoff 2007: 4).

> To the network administrators, the rationale for investment in the network entails more than serving the collective public purpose, vaguely understood ... but also includes certain advantages the network can bring to their organization's mission and functioning and to the managers as professionals involved in public programs.
>
> *(Agranoff and Yildiz 2007: 337)*

Thus, this added value can be seen from the perspective of the individual collaborative partner, from the perspective of the participating organization, as a result of the network process, and as a result of network outcomes (Agranoff 2007, 2008; Agranoff and Yildiz 2007).

From the perspective of the individual collaborative partner, value is created through a number of different mechanisms. In his studies of 14 public management networks, Agranoff (2007, 2008) described five mechanisms through which individual collaborators benefit from their involvement in the network. The first relates to the knowledge gained and the skills learned through working with others. Second, networks are often interdisciplinary in nature. Thus, collaborators learn how to work with and learn from those from different organizations, backgrounds, and functional areas. In addition, the opportunity to work with and/or manage individuals from different organizations enhances the ability to manage and work within intergovernmental arenas is a third advantage. The fourth area for potential benefit for the individual is the increased networking opportunities. Working with representatives of other organizations allows network members to build relationships with and gain access to other entities and individuals. Finally, individuals perceive that networks add value to them personally as networked governance structures strengthen their public service motivation and provide them with additional opportunities for public service.

Policy design and implementation via a networked structure also provides a number of advantages to the organizations participating in the joint venture. The value added is realized by the participating organizations as they attempt to achieve collaborative advantage, or the synergy created as organizations collaborate (Huxham 1996; Huxham and Vangen 2005). Collaboration has been conceived of as a "strategy for increasing the value that a single organization is able to create on its own" (Kim 2010: 112) in part because such arrangements expand the capabilities and capacity of the individual organizations involved. By working together, organizations are able to increase their capacity to serve their constituents by accessing their collaborative partners' knowledge, information, connections, personnel, material, and monetary resources. In addition, the participating organizations also realize the value added via collaboration as risk is shared among all of the partners, as efficiencies are realized as networks are able to take advantage of economies of scale and sectoral differences, as the organizations are able to learn from each other, and as the delivery of services is coordinated (Cropper 1996; Huxham and Vangen 2005).

There is also value added as a result of the collaborative process. While not realized by any one person or organization, the benefits of the collaborative process are realized by the network as a whole and, more importantly, often felt by those for whom the network is intended to serve. If the "value" that the network is trying to create is the public value, then perhaps the different perspectives voiced while collaborating can help to determine what the public value is. This value creation may in essence be the product of the interorganizational, intersectoral, and interideological conversation aimed at problem identification and resolution between government agencies and its interlocutors. As Innes and Booher remind us, "a process that is inclusive, well informed, and comes close to achieving consensus is more likely to produce an implementable proposal than one lacking these qualities" (1999: 420). In the absence of the network, a siloed approach to value creation occurs, whereby individual organizations view the problem from their own, isolated perspective. Networked approaches to service provision and program implementation, on the other hand, can result in a process whereby the agencies involved engage in dialogues that they otherwise would not have, approach the issues from a less partisan perspective, create a synergy where individual members exchange ideas, and build communal knowledge to work toward a solution.

The added value resulting in improved collaborative outcomes is, generally speaking, the driver behind the formation of collaborative networks. Bardach (1998: 8) defined collaboration as any joint activity by multiple entities "that is intended to increase public value by their working together rather than separately." Here, this public value refers to the outcomes produced by the collaborative efforts. Networks, in the course of addressing the problems for which they were formed to solve, generate collaboratively produced products, such as reports, publications, conferences, training programs, datasets, and so on, that can be used not only by the networks and its constituent members, but also by others outside the network and even outside the area served by the network. Collaboration within a networked governance structure also commonly results in changes to old programs and the formation of new ones. These jointly constructed and implemented service delivery programs are often more holistic and comprehensive in their approach. In the process of working with each other on the issue that brought them together, networks also often engage in spin-off projects as discussion between network members bring previously unaddressed or unrealized issues to the forefront.

## Conclusion

Networks are notable information age responses to the most difficult of policy and administrative problems but they are by no means replacing the authority of government as they share involvement with NGOs. First, while networks and the NGOs work with public agencies, influence policy and have a role in management, those organizations and agencies that comprise these networks work *with* governments as the latter continue to maintain some important abilities that guide public action. The agencies retain their authority under law. Second, while an interactive interdependency has emerged within networks crossing many boundaries, public agency-NGO organization connections seem to overlay the hierarchy rather than act as replacements for government action. Networks are not the exclusive mode of collaborative government-nongovernmental relations. Many of the more standard tools of government—for example, grants, loans, regulatory programs, insurance guarantees, and cooperative agreements—tie governments together and public agencies to NGOs without employing networks. Finally, not all governmental agency administrators are totally or to a high degree in the business of working in networks. With the exception of certain "boundary spanners" who spend full-time in cross-agency work, many administrators spend a small proportion of their total work time in collaborative activity, including participating in networks.

Networks have *not* eclipsed or displaced the power or centrality of government agencies. The empirical evidence is too mixed to support such a contention. Thus, despite the very broad range of network activity, in the United States it was found that the "ability [of nongovernmental actors] to influence the public agency domain is real but quite limited in scope ... accommodations are made, decisions are influenced, strategies are altered, resources are directed, intensive groups exert undue influence, and public responsibility is indirectly shared (Agranoff 2007: 219). The reality is that neither networks (or the for-profit and nonprofit partners within them) nor government agencies dominate, and in many cases the government agencies prove to be the key leaders within the networks.

## Bibliography


Agranoff, Robert. 1986. *Intergovernmental Management: Human Services Problem-Solving in Six Metropolitan Areas*. Albany, NY: SUNY Press.

—— 2003. *Leveraging Networks: A Guide for Public Managers Working across Organizations*. Arlington, VA: IBM Endowment for The Business of Government.

—— 2007. *Managing Within Networks: Adding Value to Public Organizations*. Washington, DC: Georgetown University Press.

—— 2008. 'Enhancing performance through public sector networks: Mobilizing human capital in communities of practice', *Public Performance & Management Review* 31(3): 320–47.

—— 2010. 'Towards an emergent theory of governance within IGR', in Edoardo Ongaro, Andrew Massey, Marc Holzer, and Ellen Wayenberg (eds) *Governance and Intergovernmental Relations in the European Union and the United States*. Cheltenham: Edward Elgar.

——and Michael McGuire. 2003. *Collaborative Public Management: New Strategies for Local Governments*. Washington, DC: Georgetown University Press.

——and Mete Yildiz. 2007. 'Decision making in public management networks', in Goktug Morcol (ed.) *Handbook of Decision Making*. New York: CRC, Taylor & Francis, 319–45.

Alter, Catherine and Jerald Hage. 1993. *Organizations Working Together*. Beverly Hills, CA: Sage.

Ashford, Douglas E. 1988. 'Decentralizing welfare states: Social policies and intergovernmental policies', in Bruno Dente and Francesco Kjellberg (eds) *The Dynamics of Institutional Change: Local Government Reorganization in Western Democracies*. London: Sage.

Bardach, Eugene. 1998. *Getting Agencies to Work Together*. Washington, DC: Brookings.

Bogason, Peter and Theo A.J. Toonen. 1998. 'Networks in public administration', *Public Administration* 76(Summer): 205–27.

Brown, Trevor L. and Matthew Potoski. 2004. 'Managing the public service market', *Public Administration Review* 64(6): 656–68.

Castells, Manuel. 1996. *The Rise of the Network Society*. Oxford: Blackwell.

Cropper, S. 1996. 'Collaborative working and the issue of sustainability', in C. Huxham (ed.) *Creating Collaborative Advantage*. London: Sage.

Davenport, Thomas H. and Laurance Prusak. 2000. *Working Knowledge: How Organizations Manage what they Know*. Cambridge, MA: Harvard Business School Press.
Eisinger, Peter K. 1988. *The Rise of the Entrepreneurial State*. Madison, WI: University of Wisconsin Press.
Elazar, Daniel J. 1962. *The American Partnership: Intergovernmental Cooperation in the Nineteenth Century United States*. Chicago: University of Chicago Press.
Elmore, Richard F. 1985. 'Forward and backward mapping: Reversible logic in the analysis of public policy', in Kenneth Hanf and Theo A.J. Toonen (eds) *Policy Implementation in Federal and Unitary Systems*. Dordrecht: Martinus Nijhoff Publishers.
Gray, Barbara. 1985. 'Conditions facilitating interorganizational collaboration', *Human Relations* 38: 911–36.
—— 1989. *Collaborating: Finding Common Ground for Multiparty Problems*. San Francisco: Jossey-Bass.
Hall, Thad E. and Laurence J. O'Toole. 2000. 'Structures for policy implementation: An analysis of national legislation, 1965–66 and 1993–94', *Administration and Society* 31(6): 667–86.
—— 2004. 'Shaping formal networks through the regulatory process', *Administration and Society* 36(2): 186–207.
Hanf, Kenneth, Benny Hjern and David O. Porter. 1978. 'Local networks of manpower training in the Federal Republic of Germany and Sweden', in Kenneth Hanf and Fritz W. Scharpf (eds) *Interorganizational Policy Making: Limits to Coordination and Central Control*. London: Sage.
Hjern, Benny and David O. Porter. 1981. 'Implementation structures: A new unit for administrative analysis', *Organizational Studies* 3: 211–37.
Hood, Christopher. 1991. 'A public management for all seasons?', *Public Administration* 69(1): 3–19.
Howlett, Michael. 2002. 'Do networks matter? Linking policy network structure to policy outcomes: evidence from four Canadian policy sectors 1990–2000', *Canadian Journal of Political Science* 35(2): 235–67.
Hull, Christopher J. with Benny Hjern. 1987. *Helping Small Firms Grow: An Implementation Approach*. London: Croom Helm.
Huxham, Chris. 1996. 'Collaboration and collaborative advantage', in C. Huxham (ed.) *Creating Collaborative Advantage*. Thousand Oaks, CA: Sage, 1–18.
——and Siv Vangen. 2005. *Managing to Collaborate: The Theory and Practice of Collaborative Advantage*. New York: Routledge.
Ingram, Helen. 1977. 'Policy implementation through bargaining: The case of federal grants-in-aid', *Public Policy* 25(4): 499–526.
Innes, Judith E. and David E. Booher. 1999. 'Consensus building and complex adaptive systems: A framework for evaluating collaborative planning', *Journal of the American Planning Association* 65(4), 412–23.
Kilduff, Martin and Wenpin Tsai. 2003. *Social Networks and Organizations*. Los Angeles, CA: Sage.
Kim, S. 2010. 'Collaborative leadership and local governance', in R. O'Leary, D.M. Van Slyke and S. Kim (eds) *The Future of Public Administration Around the World: The Minnowbrook Prespective*. Washington, DC: Georgetown University Press, 111–15.
Klijn, Erik-Hans and Jurian Edelenbos. 2008. 'Meta-governance as network management', in Eva Sorensen and Jacob Torfing (eds) *Theories of Democratic Network Governance*. London: Palgrave Macmillan, 199–214.
Kooiman, Jan. 2003. *Governing as Governance*. London: Sage.
Koppenjan, Joop F.M. and Erik-Hans Klijn. 2004. *Managing Uncertainties in Networks*. London: Routledge.
Krane, Dale and Deil S. Wright. 1998. 'Intergovernmental relations', in *International Encyclopedia of Public Policy and Administration*. Boulder, CO: Westview Press, 1168–70.
Loughlin, John. 2007. 'Reconfiguring the state: Trends in territorial governance in European States', *Regional and Federal Studies* 17(4): 385–404.
Lynn, Lawrence E. 1981. *Managing the Public's Business: The Job of the Government Executive*. New York: Basic Books.
McGuire, Michael. 2002. 'Managing networks: Propositions on what managers do and why they do it', *Public Administration Review* 62(5): 426–33.
——and Robert Agranoff. 2010. 'Networking in the shadow of bureaucracy', in Robert F. Durant (ed.) *The Oxford Handbook of American Bureaucracy*. New York: Oxford University Press.
Mandell, Myrna P. 1984. 'Application of network analysis to the implementation of a complex project', *Human Relations* 37(8): 659–79.
Marsh, David and Martin Smith. 2000. 'Understanding policy networks: Towards a dialectical approach', *Political Studies* 48(1): 4–21.
Milward, H. Brinton and Keith G. Provan. 2006. *A Manager's Guide to Choosing and Using Collaborative Networks*. Arlington, VA: IBM Center for the Business of Government.

Moore, Mark H. 1995. *Creating Public Value: Strategic Management in Government*. Cambridge, MA: Harvard University Press.

O'Toole, Laurence J. 1985. 'Diffusion of responsibility: An interorganizational analysis', in Kenneth Hanf and Theo. A.J. Toonen (eds) *Policy Implementation in Federal and Unitary Systems* . Dordrecht: Martinus Nijhoff, 201–25.

—— 1997. 'Treating networks seriously: Practical and research-based agenda in public administration', *Public Administration Review* 57(1): 45–52.

Peters, B. Guy. 2000. 'Policy instruments and public management: Bridging the gaps', *Journal of Public Administration Research and Theory: J-PART* 10(1): 35–47.

—— 2002. 'Globalization, institutions, governance', in B. Guy Peters and Donald J. Savoie (eds) *Governance in the Twenty-First Century: Revitalizing the Public Service*. Montreal: McGill-Queen's University Press.

Pressman, Jeffrey L. 1975. *Federal Programs and City Politics: The Dynamics of the Aid Process in Oakland*. Berkeley, CA: University of California Press.

——L. and Aaron Wildavsky. 1973. *Implementation*. Berkeley, CA: University of California Press.

Radin, Beryl A., Robert Agranoff, C. Gregory Buntz, Ann O'M. Bowman, Barbara Romzek and Robert Wilson. 1996. *New Governance for Rural America: Creating Intergovernmental Partnerships*. Lawrence, KS: University of Kansas Press.

Rhodes, R.A.W. 1997. *Understanding Governance: Policy Networks, Governance, Reflexivity and Accountability*. Buckingham: Open University Press.

—— 2003. 'Putting people back into networks', in Arie Salminen (ed.) *Governing Networks*. Amsterdam: IOS Press.

——and David Marsh. 1992. 'New directions in the study of policy networks', *European Journal of Political Research* 21(2): 181–205.

Saint-Onge, Hubert and Charles Armstrong. 2004. *The Conductive Organization*. Amsterdam: Elsevier.

Salamon, Lester M. 1995. *Partners in Public Service*. Baltimore, MD: Johns Hopkins University Press.

—— 2002. 'The new governance and the tools of public action', in Lester M. Salamon (ed.) *The Tools of Government*. New York: Oxford.

Scharpf, Fritz W. 1978. 'Interorganizational policy studies: Issues, concepts, and perspectives', in Kenneth Hanf and Fritz W. Scharpf (eds) *Interorganizational Policy Making*. London: Sage.

Silvia, Chris 2011. 'Collaborative governance concepts for successful network leadership', *State and Local Government Review* 43(1), 66–71.

——and Michael McGuire. 2010. 'Leading public sector networks: An empirical examination of integrative leadership behaviors', *The Leadership Quarterly* 21(2): 264–77.

Skelcher, Chris. 2004. 'The new governance of communities', in Gerry Stoker and David Wilson (eds) *British Local Government into the 21st Century*. Basingstoke: Palgrave Macmillan.

Skowronek, Stephen. 1982. *Building a New American State: The Expansion of National Administrative Capacities, 1877–1920*. Cambridge: Cambridge University Press.

Smith, Steven R. and Michael Lipsky. 1993. *Nonprofits for Hire: The Welfare State in the Age of Contracting*. Cambridge, MA: Harvard University Press.

Sorenson, Eva and Jacob Torfing. 2007. 'Theoretical approaches to democratic network governance', in Eva Sorenson and Jacob Torfing (eds) *Theories of Democratic Network Governance*. London: Palgrave Macmillan.

Sundquist, James L. 1969. *Making Federalism Work*. Washington, DC: Brookings.

Sveiby, K.-E. 1997. *The New Organisational Wealth: Managing and Measuring Knowledge-Based Assets*. San Francisco: Berrett-Koehler.

Thompson, Grahame F. 2003. *Between Markets and Hierarchies: The Logic and Limits of Network Forms of Organization*. Oxford: Oxford University Press.

Thomson, A.M., James L. Perry, and T.K. Miller 2008. 'Linking collaboration processes and outcomes', in L.B. Bingham and R. O'Leary (eds) *Big Ideas in Collaborative Public Management*. Amonk, NY: M.E. Sharpe, 97–120.

Van Slyke, David. 2007. 'Agents or stewards: Government nonprofit social service contracting relationships', *Journal of Public Administration Research and Theory* 17(2): 157–87.

Watts, Ronald L. 1999. *Comparing Federal Systems in the 1990s*, 2nd edn. Kingston: Institute of Intergovernmental Relations, Queen's University.

Wenger, E. 2000. 'Communities of practice: The key to knowledge strategy', in E.L. Lesser, M. A. Fontaine and J.A. Slusher (eds) *Knowledge and Communities*. Boston: Butterworth-Heinemann.

Williams, Walter W. 1980. *Government by Agency: Administering Grants-in-Aid Programs*. New York: Academic Press.

# 28

# Development management and policy implementation

## Relevance beyond the global South

*Derick W. Brinkerhoff and Jennifer M. Brinkerhoff*

As a subset of the discipline of public administration, development management (also referred to as development administration) has traditionally concentrated on the organizational and managerial problems confronting the countries of the global South. Development management has been long associated with international foreign assistance, and debates regarding what it is, how to do it, and what it achieves are frequently embedded within larger arguments about foreign policy, development assistance, and power imbalances between the global North and South. Reflecting this association, development management is often distinguished as concerning the implementation of donor-funded policies, programs, and projects intended to promote socio-economic development in low-income countries. Development management has been swept by the same tides that have shaped foreign assistance over the decades since the post-World War II era, and that have revisited notions of development and what is needed to make it happen (Brinkerhoff 2008).

Some analysts distinguish between management of development—referring to the management of the "mechanics" of foreign aid procedures, programs, and projects—and management for development, which addresses the underlying substance of development as a transformational process that improves the well-being of citizens in poor countries (see Thomas 1999). Yet this distinction can be difficult to maintain. Donor countries pursue a wide variety of foreign policy objectives under the broad rubric of foreign assistance. The publicly espoused aim of most donor foreign assistance is to contribute to development in recipient countries. Thus, official development policy statements reflect an assumption that management of the development projects and programs that are designed to implement those policies is tantamount to, or at least aspires to be, management for development. As numerous critical studies of foreign assistance reveal, however, donor countries use foreign aid in the service of political, diplomatic, economic, humanitarian, and security aims that may sideline or subvert development. Further, the modalities of delivering foreign assistance are accused of contributing to these perverse impacts (see Easterly 2006; Picard and Buss 2009). Radical critiques of development management tar the discipline with the same antidevelopment brush (see Dar and Cooke 2008).

This chapter opens by briefly reviewing the range of perspectives on development management. The discussion is framed around our model of development management, which defines the discipline in terms of institutional agendas, tools, values, and processes (Brinkerhoff and Brinkerhoff 2006). We explicitly recognize the complexities, trade-offs, and tensions inherent in the foreign assistance policy environment where many development managers operate. We then turn to policy implementation and examine what the development management discipline has to say about how managers can transform policy reform intent into outcomes.

## Perspectives on development management

Defining development management remains problematic for several reasons. We have already noted the difficulty of separating it from its foreign assistance policy environment. Second is the question of what development is. Third is what, then, is being managed. Fourth is the issue of what we mean by management. The answers to these questions have occupied theorists and practitioners for decades, so we can only touch on them in the most cursory manner here.

Regarding the development question, the predominant view is informed by modernization theory, which (to oversimplify) posits that development is a process that moves countries and their citizens progressively along a path to Western-style liberal economies and democratic governance. Modernization involves societal transformations from rural to urban, ascriptive/personalistic roles to merit/position-based ones, impoverished to wealthier, low levels of health and education to higher ones, and so on. Besides these material advances ("having more"), development is widely seen as "being more"; that is, enhancing capacities, fulfilling potentials, expanding freedoms, and exercising rights (e.g. Sen 1999). In a much-cited shorthand, the end-state toward which this modernizing development path leads is "Denmark," that is, a stable, prosperous, and well-managed liberal democracy (Pritchett and Woolcock 2004).

As the dichotomy between developed and developing countries has become less distinct, and as a middle range of countries such as China, India, and Brazil has emerged, the modernization paradigm has been increasingly recognized as an artifact of outdated thinking. There are multiple paths to development, and issues of politics—contestation for power and patronage among elites—and of identity—how people define themselves relative to language, religion, family, and culture—figure strongly in determining what those paths are and where they lead. The innate superiority of Western-style modernization has been increasingly questioned, particularly in light of the global economic crisis, climate change, and the perceived failure of the United States and its allies to achieve quick success in rebuilding Iraq and Afghanistan.

As for the third question, whether these twin transformations of "having and being more" can be managed depends upon the conception of change that underlies them. Donor approaches to development, implicitly and explicitly, reflect the idea that societal change is both amenable to planning and intentional direction, and can be usefully guided and supported by external actors. The alternative view is that change is historically and institutionally embedded in a given society's individual trajectory, and is in essence emergent and not easily subject to manipulation. Management is only possible, at best, at the margins, and is not accessible to outsiders except in the most superficial ways. The experience of the international community in fragile and post-conflict states, such as Liberia, Afghanistan, and Iraq, has provided traction for this standpoint.

Regarding what is management in the international development context, in line with the modernization paradigm, early answers focused on the technical tasks associated with Weberian bureaucracies; for example, the classic public administration tasks encapsulated in the acronym, POSDCORB (planning, organizing, staffing, directing, coordinating, reporting, and budgeting), coined in 1937 by Luther Gulick and Lyndall Urwick, and on designing and operating the organizational systems to enable managers to carry them out (see the overview in Esman 1991). Later conceptions of management were, and remain, heavily influenced by the New Public

Management (NPM), again drawing on models from industrialized countries and transferring them to developing societies (see Brinkerhoff 2008). In the donor-funded international development arena, the tools and techniques of data gathering, project/program design (e.g. the Logical Framework), and monitoring and evaluation are well recognized defining features of management.

With the replacement of modernization's single path to development by what Woolcock (2009) terms "multiple modernities" and the focus on development as an indigenous, emergent phenomenon, management has expanded beyond administrative technologies and routines, to address reform, change processes, participation, learning, and local adaptation. Fowler (1997), writing about nongovernmental organizations engaged in international development, talks about management as "striking a balance" between the demands of donor-driven technocratic procedures and requirements, and the rights and needs of the poor and marginalized. In another example of an expanded conception of management, Andrews *et al.* (2010) consider leadership for change management as paramount, and see the leader's role as creating space where change can happen.

## A multidimensional definition of development management

As the above brief review demonstrates, a single, agreed-upon definition of development management would be difficult to come up with, and in fact, this is the case. Previously, we have sought to clarify the meaning of development management by characterizing it as encompassing four dimensions: a means to institutional agendas; a set of values; a planning and management toolkit; and processes that both support the agency of development actors and reconcile competing interests (Brinkerhoff and Brinkerhoff 2006).

### A means to institutional agendas

While donor agendas may predominate, due to their associated funding, they exist alongside those of national and local public officials, citizen groups, and private sector actors. Each of these interest groups may apply development management tools and processes to enact their particular values and further their particular agendas. Thus development management is not restricted solely to donor-designed and -funded initiatives. This is a particularly important observation when considering how development management relates to policy implementation.

### A set of values

With the expanded notions of what constitutes development and the inclusion of identity in its definition, the values dimension of development management becomes especially salient. Values associated with development management include empowerment, participation, a focus on the poor and disadvantaged, self-determination (commonly operationalized as "country ownership"), and, more recently, sustainability. Responsiveness to the needs and desires of recipient country governments and their citizens also requires respect for and incorporation of national values, culture, and identity. These increasingly overlap with aspirations encompassed in liberal values such as human rights and basic freedoms (e.g. speech, assembly, religion).

### Planning and management toolkit

Development management as a toolkit incorporates all of the basic tools supportive of public policy and public administration, as well as those more specifically designed to support development processes. These include analytic tools drawn from political science and human behavior, as well as management tools deriving from strategic management, budgeting, and evaluation. Tools, in and of themselves, are value-neutral instruments. Through their application in the service of particular institutional agendas and values, however, they lose their neutrality.

### *Processes*

The results of the application of management tools depend largely on the processes through which they are applied. That is, tools may be selected and modified to support particular agendas and values, but it is in their application that values, in particular, will be made manifest. Thus, the process dimension of development management self-consciously considers the politics of competing values and agendas and power differentials. The process dimension is specifically structured to bring into consideration the desires, needs, and values of those affected by development plans, programs, and investments.

## Development management debates

Because of the complexities in defining development, management, and development management, there are competing perspectives on the discipline. Our multidimensional framework recognizes these complexities, and seeks to capture the tensions and disconnects among them. The key disconnect is between development management as a means to implement institutional agendas and the other three dimensions. Our view is that through a commitment to pro-poor and empowerment values, and the application of participatory processes and interest mediation, this disconnect does not necessarily undermine the possibilities for achieving positive policy outcomes. Development management can serve the aims and intents of reformers and activists. Donor practices and procedures are not always the straitjacket that critics perceive them to be (Brinkerhoff and Ingle 1989).

This view places us in the reformist camp, which recognizes the political realities of foreign assistance, globalization, and national politics, and the limitations of externally supported socio-economic change. The reformist outlook critiques development management in practice, while still believing in its actual and potential contributions to desired development outcomes. The radicalist/rejectionist camp, on the other hand, holds that development management is so intimately connected with neocolonialist power relations and "managerialist" control that actions taken by development managers are invariably detrimental to the interests of developing countries, and particularly of the poor residing in those countries (see Gulrajani 2010; Mowles 2010). Table 28.1 illustrates these two competing perspectives on development management using our four development management dimensions.

For each of the dimensions of development management, the radicalist/rejectionist perspective focuses on their oppressive nature, and their contributions to reinforcing political and bureaucratic power imbalances and inequalities. The history of foreign assistance confirms that "bad things" have indeed been done in the name of international development, and that technocratic managerial hubris has been a contributing factor. We argue, however, that the conclusion to be drawn is not to throw the management "baby" out with the development "bathwater," but precisely to apply development management in the service of those actors who seek to confront the ills identified by the radicalist/rejectionist finger pointers.

We are not alone in making this argument. The results of a survey of development management scholars and practitioners reinforces the activist orientation in favor of empowering local actors to pursue country-led development strategies and objectives, and of seeking to

*Table 28.1* Competing perspectives on development management

| *Development Management Dimensions* | *Reformist perspective* | *Radicalist/rejectionist perspective* |
|---|---|---|
| Institutional agenda | Equitable growth, MDGs, good governance, rights-based approaches, enhanced capacities | Neo-colonialist replication of Northern dominance over the global South |
| Values | Bottom-up empowerment, pro-poor, pluralism, country ownership | Top-down imposition of Western paradigms and universal performance metrics |
| Tools | Responsive planning and management for efficiency and effectiveness | Technocratic, managerialist instruments of control |
| Process | Participation, agency, social accountability | Co-optation, lip-service to disguise power imbalances |

Source: Authors

influence donor agency practices and procedures to correct power imbalances (Brinkerhoff and Brinkerhoff 2010). Gulrajani (2010) elaborates the contours of "non-managerialist" development management, and both Mowles (2010) and Abbott *et al.* (2007) stress the role of joint learning, values, negotiation, and adaptation in dealing with the power imbalances inherent in development and its emergent, unpredictable nature.

We see some encouraging signs of changes. For example, current foreign assistance policies (e.g. the Organisation for Economic Co-operation and Development's Paris Principles that stress country ownership and alignment with indigenous systems) and practices (e.g. cash-on-delivery aid, and budget transfers) are reshaping the management environment for development, placing more emphasis on the role of country actors as development managers. While the Paris Principles have been criticized in some quarters as largely rhetoric, nonetheless there have been some operational changes on the ground in response to them. For example, in Liberia's health sector, the health minister has gotten buy-in from a range of international donors for his sector plan, and the donors have committed to a pooled funding arrangement where the minister retains control over the funds in the implementation of the programs that they support.

## Development management and policy implementation

The evolutionary trajectory of scholarship and practice related to the policy process and policy implementation in the global South closely tracks that of development management. The resulting confluence provides the rationale for development management's relevance in implementing policy. Three parallels are pertinent to the discussion here. First is the source of policy concepts, models, analytic tools, and practical advice. The policy literature has originated largely in industrialized countries, principally the US and the UK, which raises the same transferability issue that development management has debated. The evolution in both literatures has been a gradual recognition of the fallacies of institutional isomorphism and of the need for contextual understanding and adaptation to individual circumstances.

Second, very similar to thinking about development planning, where the transformation of plans into actions and results was given short shrift, the classic policy literature's stages heuristic treated implementation as (a) a separate step in the policy process, and (b) a "black box" that faithfully translates policy objectives into outcomes. Pressman and Wildavsky's classic book (1973) started to unpack the black box, and helped to launch the US policy implementation literature. Within a few years, international donors discovered and debated the implementation and sustainability gaps in development projects and programs.

The third parallel is the eventual acknowledgment that, while the technical content of policies is important to achieving desired policy outcomes, their implementation is strongly influenced by bureaucratic and political factors. Having the right policy is not sufficient, and in fact what may be technically optimal ("right') is in many cases likely to be bureaucratically and/or politically infeasible (e.g. Mazmanian and Sabatier 1989). This realization gave rise to the literature on policy advocacy, coalitions, and networks. In the international development arena, the mismatch between technical and politico-bureaucratic factors became increasingly clear during the period beginning in the 1980s when the World Bank and the International Monetary Fund were pursuing structural adjustment policies and encountering problems. Development management scholars and practitioners focused on these factors as well (Grindle and Thomas 1991; Brinkerhoff and Crosby 2002; Brinkerhoff 2008).

## Framing international development policy implementation

The focus on the policy implementation gap revealed some important features that distinguish implementing policies from project and program management. The following discussion draws upon Brinkerhoff and Crosby (2002), whose book encapsulates the findings of an extensive applied research effort on policy implementation in developing countries.

- *Policy implementation is not a linear, coherent process.* With policy implementation, change is often multidirectional, fragmented, frequently interrupted, and unpredictable. How to sequence actions, what to pay attention to, and who to include can be hard to determine, and can vary over the life of the policy change process.
- *Most policies require the concerted actions of multiple agencies and groups.* Even if one of them is nominally the lead agency, in reality no individual entity is "in charge" of policy implementation. Authority and responsibility are dispersed among the actors involved.
- *Policy implementation is often highly political.* Policies usually involve the imposition of costs on some societal groups as well offering advantages to others, which creates winners and losers, and makes reforms highly contentious. Current policy equilibriums favor the powerful that benefit from them; these actors are usually well positioned to defend the status quo and resist change.
- *The resources required to implement policies may not be readily available.* Projects and programs have dedicated budgets, but policies—particularly at the start of a reform—often lack the resources needed for implementation. Making progress means lobbying for new funding, identifying existing sources of implementation support, and negotiating for resource reallocation.

In response to these identified characteristics of policy implementation and building on the policy implementation literature, plus action research and technical assistance in approximately 30 countries, Brinkerhoff and Crosby (2002) developed a framework that parses implementation into six roughly sequential tasks. These are posited as an iterative succession through which managers need to cycle repeatedly during the life of a given reform:

1 *Creating legitimacy*, getting the policy accepted as important, desirable, and worth achieving, is the first implementation task. Legitimization means getting buy-in from the right people in the country to push the reform process forward. An important outcome of this

task is the emergence of a policy champion (an individual or group who believes in the policy) to take on leadership for the subsequent implementation tasks.

2 *Building constituencies*, or gaining active support for a proposed policy from groups that see the reform as desirable or beneficial, is the second implementation task. This support needs to translate into commitment to take actions that will help to achieve the policy's objectives. As well as establishing coalitions of supporters, constituency building seeks to reduce or deflect the opposition of groups that see the proposed reform as harmful or threatening. This task must often be pursued throughout implementation to assure ongoing support and to resist derailment.
3 *Accumulating resources* means ensuring that present and future budgets and human resource allocations are sufficient to support implementation requirements. Accomplishing this task can involve, for example: lobbying constituencies to contribute resources, negotiating with ministries for budget line-item funding, designing new resource allocation systems, and/or setting up public-private partnerships.
4 *Modifying organizational structures* is the fourth policy implementation task. This entails adjusting the objectives, procedures, systems, and structures of the agencies responsible for policy implementation. Sometimes this task can also include establishing new organizations to coordinate the various entities with a role in implementation.
5 *Mobilizing resources and actions* builds upon the favorable constituencies assembled for the policy (Task 2) and marshals their commitment and resources (Task 3) to engage in concrete efforts to make change happen. Its focus is on identifying, activating, and pursuing action strategies. It brings together mobilized constituencies and resources, and within the organizational structures created, develops and carries out the steps necessary to translate intent into results.
6 *Monitoring impact*, or setting up systems to monitor implementation progress, is the final policy implementation task. Monitoring systems not only alert decision-makers to implementation snags, but also inform them of the intended and unintended impacts of implementation efforts.

## Managing policy implementation

Brinkerhoff and Crosby argue that each of these tasks calls for explicit managerial attention, and that failure to do so is a major contributor to the slippage between policy intents and implemented outcomes. Development management's dimensions are visible in each of the implementation tasks, though one particular dimension may be more significant to some tasks than others. Institutional agendas and values, for example, come to the fore in the legitimization task. If disagreements around these are not sufficiently resolved, they complicate or may even preclude the constituency building and resource accumulation necessary to policy implementation.

Managing each of the tasks necessarily confronts competing institutional agendas and values whose effective resolution most often occurs through process interventions aimed at reaching agreement and specifying shared objectives. Where top-down decision-making is prevalent, two outcomes are likely: first, agreements and objectives may lack the broad buy-in necessary for effective implementation follow-through, and/or second, agreements and objectives may need to be revisited later in the implementation task sequence, resulting at best in delays or, at worst, an impasse. An important consideration for development managers is expanding access to decision-making, reflected in sensitivity to which stakeholders gain a "seat at the table" and whose priorities and purposes are ultimately served. Today's development policy emphasis on the Millennium Development Goals and poverty alleviation highlights equity, representativeness, and responsiveness.

Development managers use a variety of diagnostic and analytic tools to pursue the policy implementation cycle. They assess constituency preferences, identify organizational and political constraints, flag points of agreement/disagreement, develop work plans, and so on (e.g. using stakeholder mapping, strengths-weaknesses-opportunities-threats (SWOT) analysis, responsibility charts, etc.). In keeping with the values of empowerment and ownership, development managers apply the tools through participatory processes (see, for example, Blackburn and Holland 1998). Participation, as both a value and a management process, is a core feature of development management.

Participation in policy implementation, however, becomes problematic in the particular context of developing countries, with their varying degrees of dependence upon international donors for resources, policy advice, and technical assistance, where external actors play a major role by virtue of their ability to drive policy agendas and the resources they command. This feature brings us back to the radicalist/rejectionist critique discussed above, which holds that managing policy implementation under these conditions replicates existing international power relations, reinforces the dominance of the industrialized West, and is antithetical to the interests of recipient countries and their poorest populations. Our reformist perspective characterizes the elements of this critique as risks rather than certainties, and argues that the risks can be mitigated through attention to our development management dimensions during policy implementation to increase the chances that:

- policies incorporate institutional agendas that balance donor and country interests, including those of poor and marginalized citizens;
- the values policies enact reflect national values and identities;
- management tools serve to support responsiveness to country-driven policy priorities as well as donor accountability;
- processes of engagement facilitate putting local actors in the driver's seat and building their capacities.

The predominant influence of donor-driven development policy design and implementation makes such risk-mitigating efforts challenging to say the least. As Mowles (2010: 156) observes, "Strategic planning, log frames, and ideas of transformational management are so ubiquitous that it would be impossible to proceed without engaging with them." The trick for development managers is to employ the tools and the language of the dominant discourse to recalibrate the power distributions among the actors involved. These distributions are not simply between donors and country/local actors, but among local interest groups as well. Which local actors, for example, should gain access to the driver's seat? Experience shows that in many countries the more powerful and better-off groups tend to occupy the available societal space in ways that preclude change (see Andrews *et al.* 2010). Policies intended to be pro-poor are likely to be watered down so as to include some benefits for the better-off, and/or to have those benefits diverted away from the poor during implementation (see Gillespie *et al.* 1996). The dilemma is not just a matter of striking a balance between the power and interests of donors and local actors, but in reconciling the "multiple modernities" and associated interests of a broad range of local actors.

## Conclusion

Our starting point for this chapter was a characterization of development management as geographically bounded through its association with the poor countries of the global South, and operationally circumscribed through its connection to foreign assistance and international donor practices. Yet, poverty, social exclusion, pandemic diseases, food insecurity, political instability, and debt crises are recognized as affecting all countries to varying degrees. Policies and programs to address these issues no longer distinguish the developed from the developing world, leading to what some consider a convergence between the global North and South (see Mosley and Dowler 2003). The implication for development management is that its relevance is no longer geographically restricted; and its tools, processes, and values, and its explicit attention to whose agendas policy implementation serves render it broadly applicable beyond the international donor-funded realm.

In this sense, we see development management as having come full circle. From its birth as a subdiscipline of US/UK-based public administration, and drawing from that body of scholarship and practice to application in developing countries, it now offers experience, tools, and lessons that can inform poverty-focused change management and policy implementation in countries in the global North. As industrialized countries have increasingly turned to the non-profit and private sectors for social services through contracting out, the dynamics of the design and financing of those services more closely resemble the donor-funded international development arena of projects and programs than meets the eye.

## Bibliography

Abbott, D., S. Brown, and G. Wilson. 2007. 'Development management as reflective practice', *Journal of International Development* 19(2): 187–203.

Andrews, M., J. McConnell and A. Wescott. 2010. *Development as Leadership-led Change: A Report for the Global Leadership Initiative*. Washington, DC: World Bank.

Blackburn, J. and J. Holland (eds) 1998. *Who Changes? Institutionalizing Participation in Development*. London: Intermediate Technology Publications.

Brinkerhoff, D.W. 2008. 'The state and international development management: Shifting tides, changing boundaries, and future directions', *Public Administration Review* 68(6): 985–1002.

—— and M. Ingle. 1989. 'Integrating blueprint and process: A structured flexibility approach to development management', *Public Administration and Development* 9(4): 487–503.

—— and B.L. Crosby. 2002. *Managing Policy Reform: Concepts and Tools for Decision-Makers in Developing and Transitioning Countries*. Bloomfield, CT: Kumarian Press.

—— and J.M. Brinkerhoff. 2006. 'International development management in a globalized world', in E. Otenyo and N. Lind (eds) *Comparative Public Administration: The Essential Readings*. Amsterdam and Oxford: Elsevier Press, 831–63.

Brinkerhoff, J.M. and D.W. Brinkerhoff. 2010. 'International development management: A northern perspective', *Public Administration and Development* 30(2): 102–15.

Dar, S. and B. Cooke (eds) 2008. *The New Development Management: Critiquing the Dual Modernization*. London: Zed Books.

Easterly, W. 2006. *The White Man's Burden: Why the West's Efforts to Aid the Rest Have Done So Much Ill and So Little Good*. New York: Penguin Press.

Esman, M. 1991. *Management Dimensions of Development: Perspectives and Strategies*. West Hartford, CT: Kumarian Press.

Fowler, A. 1997. *Striking a Balance: A Guide to Enhancing the Effectiveness of Non-Governmental Organizations in International Development*. London: Earthscan Publications.

Gillespie, P., M. Girgis, and P. Mayer. 1996. '"This great evil": Anticipating political obstacles to development', *Public Administration and Development* 16(5): 431–53.

Grindle, M.S. and J.W. Thomas. 1991. *Public Choices and Policy Change: The Political Economy of Reform in Developing Countries*. Baltimore, MD: Johns Hopkins University Press.

Gulrajani, N. 2010. 'New vistas for development management: Examining radical-reformist possibilities and potential', *Public Administration and Development* 30(2): 124–36.

Mazmanian, D.A. and P.A. Sabatier. 1989. *Implementation and Public Policy*. Lanham, MD: University Press of America.

Mosley, P. and E. Dowler (eds) 2003. *Poverty and Social Exclusion in North and South: Essays on Social Policy and Global Poverty Reduction*. London: Routledge.

Mowles, C. 2010. 'Post-foundational development management: Power, politics and complexity', *Public Administration and Development* 30(2): 136–49.

Picard, L.A. and T.F. Buss. 2009. *A Fragile Balance: Re-examining the History of Foreign Aid, Security, and Diplomacy*. Sterling, VA: Kumarian Press.

Pressman. J.L. and A.B. Wildavsky. 1973. *Implementation*. Berkeley, CA: University of California Press.

Pritchett, L. and M. Woolcock. 2004. 'Solutions when *the* solution is the problem: Arraying the disarray in development', *World Development* 32(2): 191–212.

Sen, A. 1999. *Development as Freedom*. New York: Random House.

Thomas, A. 1999. 'What makes good development management?' *Development in Practice* 9(1–2): 9–17.

Woolcock, M. 2009. 'The next 10 years in development studies: From modernization to multiple modernities, in theory and practice', *European Journal of Development Research* 21(1): 4–9.

# Part VIII

# Understanding the evaluation process

# 29
# Six models of evaluation

*Evert Vedung*

## Evaluation defined

Evaluation is an activity aimed at distinguishing the precious from the worthless, the acceptable from the unacceptable, the beneficial from the detrimental. In present-day public sector management, however, evaluation has acquired more specific and narrow meanings. Here, evaluation is a mechanism for monitoring, systematizing, and grading ongoing or just finished government interventions (organizations, policies, programs, projects, activities, their effects, and the processes preceding these effects, perceptions of intervention content included) so that public officials and other stakeholders in their future-oriented work will be able to act as responsibly, creatively, equitably and economically as possible. In this chapter, the following minimal definition of evaluation will be adopted:

> Evaluation is careful assessment of the merit, worth, and value of organization, content, administration, output, and effects of ongoing or finished government interventions, which is intended to play a role in future, practical action situations.

## Merit criteria that evaluations use

In order to perform evaluation, descriptions, however exact, of the phenomena to be assessed are not enough: evaluators also need criteria of merit, worth and value.

Suppose that a municipal anti-smoking campaign targeted at secondary school students adopts as its goal that 5 percent of smoking students shall quit smoking within three months after the completion of the campaign. In addition, suppose that an evaluation is launched four months after the end of the campaign to find out whether the campaign did achieve its own goals. In this case, the merit criterion is the campaign's own goal: 5 percent of the smoking students shall quit smoking within three months after the completion of the campaign. An evaluation model taking goals as evaluative criteria is using the goal-attainment model.

The evaluation models included in this chapter are the most important ones in the field. A taxonomy is presented below:

1 goal-attainment model;
2 side-effects model;

3 relevance model;
4 client-oriented model;
5 stakeholder model;
6 collegial models: peer review, self-evaluation.

Evaluation models organized according to their criteria of merit constitute a fairly varied group. In addition to the standard goal-attainment model, the taxonomy embraces the side-effects model, the relevance model, the client-oriented model, the stakeholder model, and collegial models combining peer review with self-evaluation.[1]

One obvious set of models will not be covered here: economic models. In addition to substantive values, economic models focus on cost aspects of public interventions. The two basic variants among economic models are the productivity and the efficiency models. Efficiency models are divided into cost-effectiveness and cost-benefit. However, for reasons of space they are excluded from this chapter.

A different possibility would be to organize the survey according to methodology to be used in ascertaining intervention effects. This methods-driven point of view is pursued by the present movement for evidence-based policy and public administration. Models are ordered according to strength of designs for impact assessment (experiments, quasi-experiments, time-series, process tracing, etc). I have not chosen this option either.

Another significant dimension is subject matter to be appraised. Since the focus here will be on public sector interventions, subject matters are commonly divided into intervention results and intervention processes. Intervention results mean outcome effects, i.e. those consequences that the intervention, at least to some extent, directly or indirectly has produced in society or nature. In addition to members of the target group actually reached, results include target group responses to the intervention in terms of, e.g. attitudes, factual and valuational utterances, and actions suggested or actually taken. Intervention processes usually include procedures and practices preceding results, occurring in implementation between intervention adoption and intervention results. Naturally, processes do not include targets reached, target responses and consequences beyond those responses, because all that is included in intervention results.

There are many other possible dimensions that might be used to classify models. Data assembly methods is one (documentary, interrogatory or observational methods). Here, these possible dimensions will be discussed now and then under each evaluation model but they are not used to classify them.

My review will treat the models in the order shown above.

## Goal-attainment model (effectiveness model)

An approach on long standing is goal-achievement evaluation, also known as goal-attainment evaluation and effectiveness evaluation. The two basic ingredients of goal achievement evaluation are goal-attainment measurement and intervention impact assessment. In *goal-attainment measurement* the key question is: are the results in accord with intervention goals? And the *impact assessment* issue can be formulated thus: are the results produced by the intervention?

Goal-attainment evaluation is a paragon of simplicity and lucidity. Its first step involves identifying the intervention goals, teasing out their actual meaning and rank order, turning them into measurable objectives, and determining to what extent they are realized in practice. The second step implies ascertaining the degree to which the intervention has promoted or dampened goal realization. The plain anatomy of the goal-attainment model is outlined in Figure 29.1.

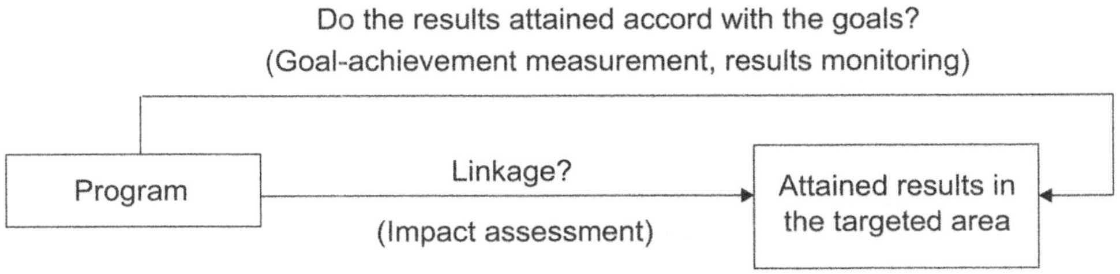

Do the results attained accord with the goals?
(Goal-achievement measurement, results monitoring)

Program → Linkage? (Impact assessment) → Attained results in the targeted area

*Figure 29.1* Goal-attainment model

## *The strength and shortcomings of the goal-attainment model*

In earlier literature, public sector evaluation *was* goal-attainment appraisal, period. Since then, however, quite a few other merit criteria have been suggested and used. There are, however, several worthwhile reasons in favor of goal-attainment assessment of public sector interventions. The argument from representative democracy is one.[2]

In a democracy, all power belongs to the people. Yet, due to lack of competence and time, the people cannot make all the complicated decisions concerning the well-being of citizens. The people do not have time to participate in hundreds of thousands of decisions. And they do not have the necessary competence to make wise decisions on, for instance, placement of patients in line for surgery, or day-to-day care for ailing senior citizens in public sector homes for the elderly. For these reasons, the citizenry must elect political representatives to make the decisions for them. But representatives in political assemblies do not have the time or competence to make all decisions. They must delegate their power to governments to make decisions for them. But governments do not have time and the specific knowledge necessary, so they in turn have to delegate to civil servants and professionals to take decisions, and so on. The public sector is made up of long chains of principal-agent relationships.

If an agency adopts a program in order to reach some goals, these goals derive their legitimacy from the fact that the agency's decision-making authority has been delegated to it by the government and that the government, in turn, has received its authority to do so from parliament, and parliament, in turn, from the people. It is a merit of the goal-attainment model that it recognizes this democratic aspect of public sector goals.

In sum, the goal-attainment model scores an important point with respect to its tilt toward representative democracy and the parliamentary chain of control. On the other hand, the goal-attainment model also suffers from persistent shortcomings. The most significant general reasons against the goal-attainment model are the haziness argument, and the unintended side-effects argument.

The *haziness argument* maintains that intervention goals are deficient as criteria of merit due to their obscurity. There are two kinds of goal obscurity: goal indeterminateness and goal catalogs. Occasionally, programs are based on *indeterminate goals*. Particular goals may be *ambiguous* and carry two or more meanings. Yet ambiguity in this sense of dual meanings is exceptional in policy and administrative language, and barely bothers evaluators. More uncertainty is caused by *vagueness*. A goal is vague if it does not delineate clearly cases where it is or is not applicable. The outer border delimiting the extension of a vague word is so fuzzy that within a certain range it is impossible to know what is included in the extension and what is not. Rampant in political rhetoric, vagueness is one favorite expedient to settle political conflicts through semantic formulas without really resolving them.

The second major obscurity is produced by *goal catalogs*. Most large social reforms contain impressive directories of diverse goals. While a single goal may be hailed as the major one, it is often maintained that this one must be balanced against all the others, maybe including potentially conflicting ones. But the necessary trade-offs between the several goals are not indicated, which makes it impossible to elicit from such lists of goals one distinct, transparent, expected outcome. Thus, program goals do not offer any safe guidance for continued data assembly. They are neither specific nor lucid enough to be usable as value criteria against which to measure intervention successes and failures.

The goal-haziness argument reveals an important misfit between the requirements of the goal-attainment model and the way public policies, programs, and activities are often composed. If elected officials and program planners have not specified individual goals into measurable objectives, and if they have not balanced the various stated goals into one global outcome or output measure, the goal-attainment evaluator cannot summarize her findings into a completely value-neutral evaluative judgment. She can do so only after she has clarified the goals and prioritized among them in a fashion that will cast doubts on the objectivity of the whole enterprise.

The second general counter-argument, about *unintended side-effects*, is in my view the crucial one. Public sector interventions, in social security and social work for instance, invariably lead to consequences which were not foreseen in the original decision situation. Were the evaluators to confine themselves to ascertaining the achievement of premeditated goals, the search for serendipitous results or unanticipated side-effects outside the goal area would not be included in the evaluation process. The evaluation findings would exhibit a tunnel vision of events, and produce a biased, if not fundamentally wrong, picture of what the intervention has attained. In all likelihood, a program generating some interesting spin-off effects must be better than a program producing several undesirable spillovers.

In sum, the major strength of the goal-attainment model is grounded in the theory of representative democracy. Yet, it has problems with hazy goals and goal catalogs, pervasive as we all know in public policy. The most compelling rebuttal, however, emanates from the model's blindness to side-effects.

At this point, I would like to present a model that expressly considers the weighty side-effects argument, while retaining the fundamental goal-orientation of the goal-attainment model: the side-effects model.

## Side-effects model

The side-effects model implies a widening of the *subject-matter* of the goal-attainment model in the sense that search for results in the target area is supplemented by search outside the target area for side-effects. The underlying idea is that public interventions may produce other things than intended results which, in turn, constitute reasons for new interventions. Interventions beget interventions.

The role of heat pumps in Swedish energy production is an illustrative case of a solution turned into a problem in need of a solution. From the 1970s, government subsidies were disembursed for the installation of heat pumps for the retrieval of the enormous amounts of waste energy produced by the paper and pulp industry along the northern coast of the Gulf of Bothnia as a solution to the oil and nuclear power problem. The rapid dissemination of heat pumps was a consequence of government subsidization. After some years, it was discovered that the heating medium, CFCs (freons), in the heat pumps might leak into the atmosphere and, over time, damage the stratospheric ozone layer protecting the earth from dangerous ultraviolet radiation. A small part of this damage can be regarded as an unforeseen and unintended side effect of Swedish government support of heat pumps. From the mid-1980s, the heat pumps turned into an environmental problem that needed to be solved politically.

From the interventionist point of view, a side effect can be defined as at least a partial consequence of the intervention, which cannot be included among the desired main effects. Main effects are those actual, expected and wanted consequences, which at least are partly produced by the intervention. Side-effects can be *unanticipated* but also *anticipated* and considered in calculations preceding decisions to adopt policies. They may be beneficial as well as detrimental.

Public interventions may also create *perverse effects*. Perverse effects run exactly counter to the very intentions of the intervention instigators. Since these impacts occur in the target area, they are not side-effects. Neither are they main effects, since they are not coveted by the policy instigators. Perverse effects are also different from *null effects*. Null effects mean that interventions produce no impacts at all on their targeted areas. In the perverse effects case, consequences are produced but entirely contrary to the ones intended.

Since perverse effects and null effects occur in the targeted areas, the goal-attainment model with all its attention directed at what happens in these particular fields has no problem with handling them. But this also means that the model cannot discover and ascertain side-effects because they fall outside the targeted sectors. This task is left to the side-effects model.

Evaluators and policy-makers should pay attention to side-effects because by-products, whether detrimental or beneficial, are crucial factors in every inclusive judgment of the operation of an intervention. Should it turn out that side-effects, which have been known, discussed, and positively valued in advance, have not materialized in spite of the fact that the program has been on the books for the intended period of time, this ought to have consequences for any appraisal of it.

If the totality of effects of a government intervention inside and outside its targeted area were to be investigated, the structure of the evaluation on the outcome side might be as shown in Figure 29.2.

I strongly commend side-effects to goal-attainment evaluation. Indeed, the major rationale for doing public sector evaluation in the first place is that state actions to some extent are unpredictable and regularly result in side-effects not originally foreseen. It is an important duty of evaluation to map and assess the worth of these side-effects.

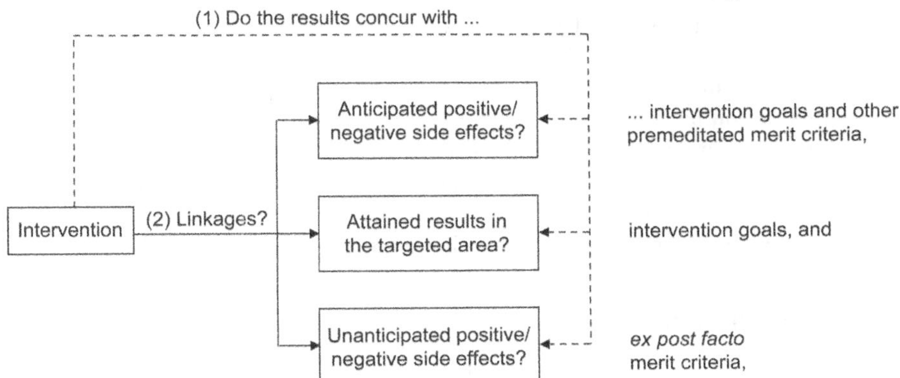


*Figure 29.2* Side-effects model with specified pigeonholes for side-effects

Also, in terms of merit criteria, the side-effects model engenders an extension of goal-attainment in that intervention goals stated in advance are supplemented with merit criteria for side-effects. If some effects are not foreseen, the criteria and standards for judging merits and demerits of these effects are not pre-specified either. Therefore, pre-specified goals are insufficient as instruments of judging unanticipated side-effects is concerned. A feasible solution is the following. Aside from mapping the main effect and comparing it with the pre-specified goals, the evaluator may also chart the side-effects but leave it to the commissioners and other users of the evaluation to ascertain their value and carry out the overall, global assessment of the program *ex post facto*. Attention to unanticipated side effects forces evaluators to use other merit criteria than initially incorporated into the intervention.

## Relevance model

In the relevance model, solving the underlying problem is the merit criterion against which the worth of the intervention is assessed. Is the intervention bearing on, connected with or pertinent to the solution to or at least the alleviation of the problematic matter in hand? If all or part of the problem has been solved by the intervention, the intervention is successful; if not, it is a failure (more in Vedung 2009: 116ff.).

The underlying problem is a complex criterion. Which underlying problem is at stake? As a first cut, the answer is the problem embedded in the intervention, namely the problematic situation that the intervention purports to attack. But of course there are others, to be omitted in this brief overview.

To be relevant, what does it mean? Pertinent to the problematic matter in hand would be one reasonable clarification. Yet, pertinence is not enough. To some degree, a relevant intervention must also be adequate, useful, sufficient and proper for the task at hand.

What should be relevant to the underlying problem? The intervention, of course, or more properly its agreed-upon goals and policy instruments. These relevance issues can be explored early on, that is once the intervention is adopted but not yet implemented, by reference to scientific findings and tested experience. Another possibility would be outputs. A third would be intervention effects obtained out there in the community. Effect relevance should be studied when the intervention has been implemented and in operation for some time. Are the impacts then achieved relevant to the solving of the problem that the intervention is supposed to attack?

Effect relevance seems very close, if not similar, to goal achievement (effectiveness). Yet, they are different. The change in the state of affairs referred to by a goal need not be identical to a change in the underlying problem. The goal of an information campaign may be to reduce purchases of alcoholic beverages while the underlying problem is to reduce prevalence of alcohol-related illnesses. But purchases may be down while alcohol-related illnesses are up due to increased purchases abroad or on international flights.

Here we leave the models using merit criteria derived from the intervention as such: the goal-attainment, the side effects and the relevance model. Now we will address *actor models*. Specific to actor models is that their evaluative criteria are taken from the agents concerned. We will discuss the client-oriented model, the stakeholder model and the collegial model.

## Client-oriented model

The client-oriented model allows members of the intervention's target group to perform the evaluation on the basis of their own merit criteria. Issues at stake are whether the public intervention (1) in terms of its content, (2) during the process up to its delivery, (3) in the delivery proper, (4) as regards client responses, or (5) through its eventual outcome effects achieves the quality that clients deem reasonable, or require or want to see. Clients are asked to pass judgment on service accessibility (process up to points of delivery), scope and quality of service provision, or service effects on the recipients themselves (impact at outcome level). As merit criteria, the client-oriented model may use participant desires, wishes, requests, demands, goals, concerns, expectations, and so on.[3]

The term *client* denotes the recipients of public interventions. Prisoners in jails, pupils of public schools, patients in county hospitals, elderly people receiving municipal home care, book-borrowers in municipal libraries and passengers on municipal buses and trains are examples of clients (addressees, participants, targets, consumers).

Several approaches might be considered client-oriented. Think about a contrived example concerning client satisfaction with public-sector services. During 2006 60 percent of parents in the city of Helsinki, Finland, were satisfied with the daycare that their children received in municipal daycare centers. Two years later, the number had dropped to 50 percent. In January 2009 members of the city council expressed concerns about the unexpected plunge. The council unanimously decided to set 75 percent parent satisfaction as the goal to be achieved in 2011. In 2012 a new study demonstrated that in 2011 65 percent of the parents were satisfied. Admittedly, both the 2008 and the 2012 studies are client-oriented. Are they client-oriented evaluations? The answer is yes. User satisfaction is a client-oriented value criterion. Interestingly, the 2012 study might be considered a goal-attainment evaluation as well, since 75 percent parent satisfaction was a goal set by the city council.

There are more advanced forms of client-oriented evaluation where clients are much more implicated. Let me reason from the case where the evaluation is first, commissioned by the administrators, and second, planned to involve the service users much more than merely asking them in a questionnaire about their service satisfaction. In this case, the clients themselves are encouraged to select the aspects of the intervention, its implementation and outcomes on which to pass judgments. For instance, clients may judge intervention output, service availability, service quality, or even service process and service administration. Is the core service tailored to meet the demands of the clients? Are the encounters of the clients with the service employees respectful? These are two questions that might be answered by the service users in their self-reports. The clients may also choose to raise the causal issue, that is, estimate intervention impacts on themselves or on the client community in general.

Currently, the client-oriented evaluation model is employed in numerous contexts such as nursing homes for the elderly, public housing, mental health, public utilities, recreation, and physical health services, where clientele participation is crucial to the operation of the services. Client-oriented models are used to evaluate library services, arts, zoos, and museums. It is a favorite with educators. At universities, students are routinely requested to share their opinions of courses, reading lists and lectures. They are asked to rate their teachers' abilities to organize the course contents, to stimulate and promote altercations, to stir student motivation and critical thinking, and to show concern and enthusiasm for the students.

### *Pros and cons of client-oriented evaluation*

Client-oriented evaluation is justified in several ways. Some philosophers ground it in political ideologies engendering that public administration produces goods and services for customers in the market place. They claim that customer pressures expressed through attitudes and suggestions for improvement via evaluations toward service providers, service management and decision-makers will lead to improvement of not only the core service, but also of service processes, service delivery, service effects, and customer satisfaction. Through client-oriented evaluation, public services will become more clearly geared toward the wishes and expectations of the users.

Yet, the customer parallel cannot be pushed too far, since the client notion includes participatory and deliberative aspects. The participatory feature suggests that clients are also citizens who may voice their complaints and desires to the evaluators and service providers, and to some extent influence and take responsibility for service content. The deliberative feature engenders a discursive, reasoning, and learning-through-dialogue countenance, which may educate service providers to pay heed to client concerns and clients to become better citizens: the consumer as citizen rather than the consumer as customer.[4]

Client-oriented evaluation may increase the legitimacy of the intervention. If clients are asked for their opinions and have some influence on intervention formation, processes and outputs, their acceptance of the system will probably increase. In addition, client-oriented evaluation may foster effectiveness and efficiency because concentration on clients may force service providers and managers to do away with many preoccupations besides providing good services.

But evaluators must be aware of the tendency of the clientele to exaggerate complaints in order to get more service. Clients may also nurture fiscal illusions. Greater client involvement in evaluation may surrender power to groups with narrow vested interests.

The client-propelled model may supplement the previously presented approaches, since it poses other problems. The requirement that the civil service must be responsive to client concerns is sound, but within limits. It can never take precedence over the requisite that front-line operators should follow the directives of their hierarchical administrative superiors, and indirectly political bodies like parliament, the municipal council, and, ultimately, the citizens as a collectivity, whose votes have determined the composition and general policy direction of these bodies. The elderly in a community who enjoy municipal social home aid cannot take decisions that run counter to the rules of the agents and principals in the representative chain of control. They cannot unilaterally lower the service fees, for instance. Evaluation models grounded in representative democracy must take precedence over client-oriented models. Client criteria are reasonable to use, but within limits; they must be balanced against other criteria like goal-attainment and professional norms for service excellence.

## Stakeholder model

In stakeholder evaluation claims, concerns and issues of the various affected actors serve as merit criteria when interventions—their contents, processes, outputs, outcomes, and organization—are assessed and evaluated (Vedung 1998: 73ff.). Stakeholders might be defined as groups or individual actors that have some interest vested in the intervention to be evaluated or its outcome effects. Interest may be measured in terms of money, status, power, face, opportunity or other coin, and may be large or small, as constructed by the groups in question (Guba and Lincoln 1989: 51). This is quite different from using prefixed objectives as merit criteria, as in goal-attainment evaluation. Stakeholder evaluation, however, does resemble the client-oriented model, the major difference being one of scope: while the client-driven model is basically concerned with one group of affected interests, the stakeholder model is geared to all of them.

An overview of conceivable stakeholders in local social welfare interventions is presented in Figure 29.3.

Stakeholder evaluation can proceed in different ways. The stakeholders may constitute themselves as the evaluation team and carry out the evaluation. The evaluation may also be conducted by particular evaluators, who elicit the views of the stakeholders. In the sequel, I shall reason from the case that stakeholder evaluation is carried out by particular evaluators.

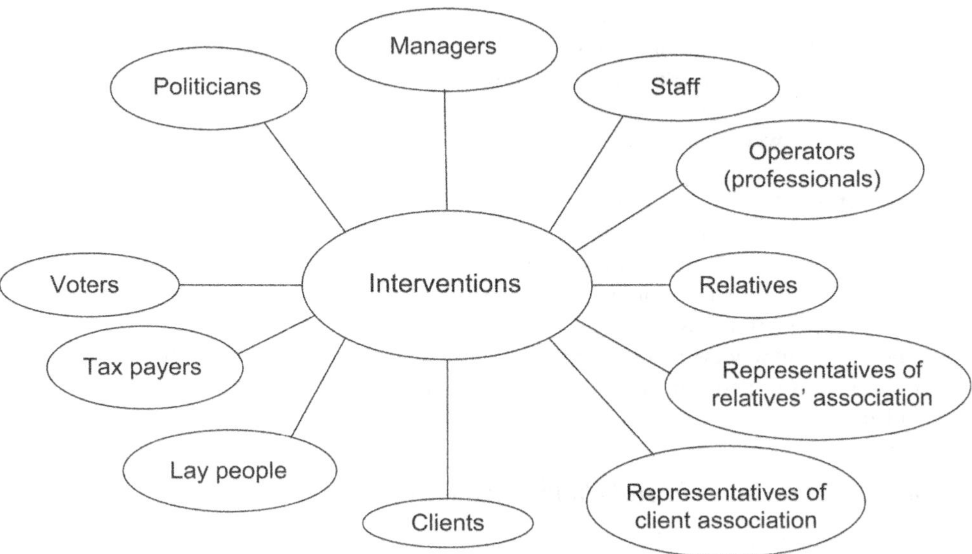


*Figure 29.3* Potential stakeholders in local social welfare interventions

Stakeholder-based evaluation starts by evaluator mapping the major groups who are involved or thought to have an interest in the content, execution, results, and organization of the intervention. The evaluator identifies the people who initiated, hammered out, funded, and adopted the intervention, that is basically the politicians. She identifies those who are charged with its implementation: senior, middle, and junior managers, staff, and front-line operators, who actually deliver intervention output. She singles out the intervention's primary clients and the clients' associations. She identifies relatives and relatives' associations. She may also include lay people. And she searches for those who know that they have a stake in the intervention but prefer to keep a low profile and those who are unaware of the stake they hold.

Advocates of stakeholder models nurture a strong penchant for qualitative, interactive data assembly methodology. The evaluator must talk to the stakeholders to elicit their narrative histories and observational data, which in turn should be allowed to affect the evaluator's next step in the search procedure. After a while, she might discover both the purported and the genuine aims of the intervention, and what concerns various stakeholders nurture regarding it. With time, the evaluator gets more involved and can start to determine which dimensions and concerns of the stakeholders should be included in the study. Only then can she take a stand on what the outline of the evaluation should be.

It is typical for the stakeholder model that the evaluator is permitted to search rather extensively for the dimensions and the crucial concerns on these dimensions. The idea is that the evaluator must be responsive to the issues and concerns of the affected people and let these govern the next step in the investigatory enterprise. Through interactive communication she is supposed to find out which stakeholder dimensions and concerns are to be taken seriously and probed more deeply. The evaluation design will be gradually determined. Stakeholder evaluation is *responsive evaluation*.

To elicit final data on stakeholder concerns, advocates of stakeholder models prefer stakeholder self-observation and sustained interviewing to questionnaires, documentary methods, and evaluator observation. In-depth interviewing of individual targets is one favored technique. In social service and social work, distribution of self-report instruments that clients, parents, relatives and other stakeholder networks can easily complete themselves is used. In some cases, client-oriented evaluators endorse *focus group interviewing* which allows for *group deliberations* among the participants and between the participants and the evaluator. The evaluator tries to create forums of debate to promote deliberative richness. This will support the development of new ideas, service concepts, solutions, and technologies. It might also, as a side-effect, educate participants to become better citizens in the future.

After data are amassed and processed, the reporting of findings, which might vary from one stakeholder to another, will commence. The key word seems to be "portrayals," that is, information-rich characterizations using pictures, anecdotes, thick descriptions, and quotes. The comprehensive holistic view mediated through a portrait is important. Normally, several criteria of merit, standards of performance on these criteria and several comprehensive assessments will be included.

## *Upsides and downsides of stakeholder evaluation*

Stakeholder models have *several advantages* of which four will be mentioned here.

The *democratic arguments* for the stakeholder model depart from participative and deliberative points of view. True, democracy means that citizens in general elections vote for competing elites that are supposed to make decisions on their behalf (*representative democracy*). Yet, the citizenry should also be able to partake in final public decision-making between elections (*participative democracy*). Furthermore, discussion, dialogue and debate are also important democratic values because they help people to form and refine their beliefs and preferences (*deliberative democracy*). The stakeholder model satisfies these participative and deliberative values somewhat more than the goal-achievement and the side-effects models.

According to the *knowledge argument*, avoiding intervention insights, which those involved indubitably have, would be foolish of evaluators. Stakeholders nurture convictions about inadvertent side-effects, sophisticated implementation barriers, and outright cheating which may furnish evaluators with ideas about topics for further investigation. Since stakeholder-orientation will bring up more aspects of the subject-matter for discussion, the quality of the evaluation findings will increase. All in all, it is easy to agree with the recommendation that almost every evaluation ought to begin with the determination of relevant actors and rounds of interactive data assembly.

Findings from goal-attainment and side-effects evaluations, carried out with quantitative methodology and with no interactive involvement of stakeholders, seem have little impact. The stakeholder approach increases the chances that issues of genuine interest to concerned parties will be addressed. It brings to light information that meets the real requirements of the different stakeholders, thereby enhancing the probability that the findings actually will be put to use. This is the *utilization argument* in support of stakeholder evaluation.

Finally, the stakeholder models might promote *compromises*, and forestall political struggle. Stakeholder assemblies are consensus-building mechanisms. They are vehicles for shaping agreement on the results of earlier efforts, and most importantly, proposals for future action. Consensus building and the rendition of legitimacy to fundamental decisions are considered great advantages of stakeholder evaluation.

There are also obvious *drawbacks* with stakeholder models. Stakeholder evaluations are *inordinately impractical and resource-demanding*, since several stakeholding constituencies must be contacted and nurtured.

Stakeholder models are *fuzzy*. They provide no authoritative answer to the question of who the stakeholders are. Furthermore, all the stakeholding audiences, however selected, are treated as equals. But in a representative democracy, elected politicians must carry more weight than administrators or experts and even clients on the substantive matters under consideration. The stakeholder model embodies *no priorities among the stakeholders*. Like client-oriented evaluation, stakeholder evaluation must work within the frames fixed by representative democracy.

While hazy in its contours, impractical and resource-demanding, the stakeholder model carries some important merits. Utilization and compromise arguments speak in its favor. Another strong reason for it is the knowledge argument: it can be used as a search strategy at the start of the evaluation in order to get a quick and provisional grasp of the meaning, implementation and outcome of the intervention.

Finally, a case from deliberative and participatory democracy can be made for stakeholder models. Through the use of the stakeholder approach, affected interests can deliberate public affairs and learn to become better citizens in the future. They can participate and influence the final outcome. On the other hand, this must take place within the confines set by representative democracy.

## Collegial models: peer review, self-evaluation and combinations thereof

Collegial evaluation models imply that personnel of the pertinent agency are entrusted to evaluate the performance of their colleagues in some other agency or branch of the public sector using their own professional criteria of merit and standards of quality.

The most celebrated collegial model is the *peer review approach*, in which the evaluation is conducted by an external collegium, which by definition is an assembly of professional equals. Ideally, these equals should be somewhat better in their area of expertise than the colleagues they are invited to assess. In this way, lawyers evaluate lawyers, scientists scientists, surgeons surgeons, nurses nurses, and so on.

*Self-evaluation* is another form. Then, the professional herself evaluates her own performance or professionals in an organization together evaluate their organization's performance. Often self-evaluation is combined with external peer review.

Collegial models are constantly used in evaluation of research and higher education. They are very much based upon dialogue, discussion and deliberation. The procedure usually starts with self-evaluation. The professionals to be evaluated carry out an appraisal of their own performance, of their research project, education program, or university department. They discuss strengths, weaknesses, opportunities and threats (the so-called SWOT scheme). Then, external renowned scientists and educators of the particular field are assigned to assess the quality and relevance of evaluatee work. These peers base their preliminary assessment on the written self-evaluation and site visits with dialogues. Then evaluatees are given the opportunity to comment on the evaluators' reports before they are finalized; all in all, the evaluators listen to the evaluatees and solicit their opinions.

We might wonder what collegial models have to do with public sector evaluation. These models seem kilometers away from the arena of policy-making and program enactment. The answer is embodied in the principle of the profession-driven public sector. In some areas of public life, goals are so complex and techniques so difficult that political officials have found it wise to leave the shaping and debating of them to well-educated professionals. Architects, judges, professors, doctors, veterinarians, and engineers would be cases in point. Hence, it is also considered natural to delegate *ex post* evaluation to the professions. But since these professionals work in the public sector, peer review must be regarded as an evaluation model on a par with the other models used in public life.

Let me illustrate this evaluation prototype with the Swedish National Agency for Higher Education former strategy for evaluation of research and education at the state universities in Sweden. The agency once instituted the following ten-steps evaluation policy:

1 The Board adopts a comprehensive evaluation policy: during the upcoming six-year period, all universities and colleges in the country will be evaluated on a rotational basis.
2 The Board decides in broad terms about groups of evaluations: e.g. research in all the university departments of social work will be evaluated next year.
3 For every particular evaluation, the Board appoints a project manager (project group) within the agency and a number of qualified external evaluators who receive introductory information.
4 Each department of social work performs a self-evaluation departing from the national agency's special requirements. An important feature of these requirements is that evaluation items ought to be placed under three headings: (i) preconditions for research, (ii) research processes, and (iii) research findings. The self-evaluations follow the SWOT scheme, i.e. strengths, weaknesses, opportunities, and threats.
5 The external experts familiarize themselves with the subject-matter by consulting self-evaluations, research reports, CVs and other relevant materials from the departments to be evaluated.
6 External assessments are carried out through site visits. In all, evaluatees, researchers and research groups make presentations for and participate in discussions with the external assessors. The expert panels are confronted face-to-face with the evaluated researchers. The experts observe, listen, ask questions, discuss and take notes.
7 The external assessors compile preliminary assessments for each department, to which the departments in question are asked to respond.
8 A final report is prepared by the external evaluators, and the project manager formulates a final assessment on the basis of which the National Agency Board decides on measures such as cancelation of examination rights.
9 Follow-up conferences are arranged, where each department is informed about the particular assessments performed by the external reviewers.
10 One year later, the Board carries out a follow-up to verify that recommended measures are taken.

Central to collegial evaluation is selection and application of evaluative criteria and standards for estimating the quality of preconditions, processes and findings. For this, the professionals themselves are particularly suitable, because these assessments require specialist knowledge. In addition, quality criteria are complex by being associated with specific methodological approaches. Furthermore, due to knowledge growth, yardsticks as well as professional approaches are continually changing in the disciplines. Add to this that quality criteria are often communicated orally only in the relevant professions as tacit knowledge. This tacit knowledge must be brought forward through penetrating dialogues among groups of colleagues.

A second strength is that site visits are short and therefore inexpensive. On the other hand, the evaluation may still become expensive through consultant fees, travel expenses, and because it takes time to complete the final report.

One weakness with short site visits and self-evaluations is that evaluatees may be tempted to show up facades and erect Potemkin villages.

Collegial models frequently produce shaky results. Matched panels use widely different merit criteria and performance standards and reach miscellaneous conclusions. However, in technically complex fields, collegial evaluation is probably the finest method available to judge the quality of what is produced.

## Final note on choice among the six evaluation models

This chapter has provided a broad overview of the evaluation landscape from a narrow but manageable perspective. Since evaluation is a normative, value-laden enterprise, I have organized the survey by merit criteria used in various evaluation models. Six such models have been reconstructed. An evaluation model is as a template based on one, two, three and even more dimensions indicating in a general way how an evaluation can be done

As an innovation in 1950s and 1960s evaluation was equated with the goal-attainment model. Owing to sharp criticism, this model was pushed into the background in the discourse, but hardly in practice. Since 1980, however, it has experienced a renaissance in the discussion, partly as a feature of so-called performance management. In addition, thanks to the so-called evidence-based wave that presently dominates the evaluation discourse, the goal-attainment model (sometimes under the designation effectiveness evaluation) has become even more important.

The major downside of goal-attainment evaluation is its inability to take account of unforeseen side effects. For this reason the side-effect model is recommended. The side-effects model is the goal-attainment model expanded into (1) an all-effects model using (2) merit criteria articulated expost in addition to pre-ordained goals.

In contrast with the goal-attainment model, the relevance model uses solution of underlying problems as merit criterion. This approach provides evaluators with a critical edge in allowing them to question the goals in case the intervention achieves its goals without solving the problem.

The stakeholder model has become popular particularly since 1970. Since full objectivity is impossible to reach in evaluative work, its proponents argue that providing multiple images of reality from different perspectives is an appropriate approach.

Collegial models take the quality criteria of one group of stakeholders—the relevant professionals—as their bases for assessment. These criteria are difficult to grasp, constantly changing and often embedded into the professions as tacit knowledge. A collegial evaluation starts with the evaluatees performing a self-assessment followed by an external evaluation carried out by independent highly qualified colleagues. The collegial models are assumed to capture and appreciate complex qualities of difficult policy areas like surgery, engineering, basic research, and so on.

Since about 1980 client-oriented evaluation has come to the fore especially within health care, culture, transportation, services and education. The philosophy is that the citizen is a customer whose needs should be considered so that public services become more accustomed to client wishes. Indirectly this also increases the efficiency and legitimacy of the system.

The client-oriented model may conflict with the goal-attainment, side effects and relevance models, all of which derive their legitimacy from representative democracy. Since representative democracy is the basic form of government in Western nations, the client model as well as the stakeholder model must work within the limits set by the representative system. In this way the information produced by the client model may supplement information produced by the other models.

Each evaluation model provides partial perspectives and answers only. For this reason, combinations of several models are commended.

## Notes

1 Besides a new text on the relevance model, the chapter is an abbreviated and reworked version of Chapter 4 in my book *Public Policy and Program Evaluation* (New Brunswick, NJ: Transaction Publishers,

paperback 2009 (1998), www.transactionpub.com/cgi_bin/transactionpublishers.storefront). For footnotes, see this book.

2 Several other reasons for and against are presented in Vedung [1998]2009: 40ff.

3 Actually, there is also a school of thought which uses client *needs* as a point of departure for client-oriented evaluation. To simplify I have avoided the needs issue here.

4 My extensive experience as an evaluation instructor has taught me to emphasize the difference between intervention clients (intervention participants, addressees) and evaluation clients (evaluation users). The evaluation client is the person, group, or agency that has commissioned the evaluation of an intervention or is supposed to use its findings, whereas the intervention client is the intended or actual recipient of the intervention.

## Bibliography


Bardach, Eugene. 2011. *A Practical Guide for Policy Analysis: The Eightfold Path to More Effective Problem Solving*. Washington, DC: CQ Press.

Guba, Egon G. and Yvonna S. Lincoln. 1989. *Fourth Generation Evaluation*, 1st edn. Thousand Oaks, CA: Sage.

Hansen, Hanne Foss. 2005. 'Choosing evaluation models: A discussion on evaluation design', *Evaluation* 11(4): 447–62.

Hansen, Morten Balle and Evert Vedung. 2010. 'Theory-based stakeholder evaluation', *American Journal of Evaluation* 31(3): 295–313. Available at: http://evi.sagepub.com/content/16/3/263.full.pdf+html

Preskill, Hallie and Darlene Russ-Eft. 2004. *Building Evaluation Capacity: 72 Activities for Teaching and Training*. Thousand Oaks, CA: Sage.

Rossi, Peter E., Mark W. Lipsey and Howard E. Freeman. 2004. *Evaluation: A Systematic Approach*, 7th edn. Thousand Oaks, CA: Sage.

Russ-Eft, Darlene and Hallie Preskill. 2009. *Evaluation in Organizations: A Systematic Approach to Enhancing Learning, Performance, and Change*, 2nd edn. New York: Basic Books.

Stufflebeam, Daniel L. 2000. 'Foundational models for 21st century program evaluation', in Daniel L. Stufflebeam, George F. Madaus and Thomas Kellaghan (eds) *Evaluation Models: Viewpoints on Educational and Human Services Evaluation*. Boston: Kluwer Academic Publishers, 33–84.

Vedung, Evert. [1998]2009. *Public Policy and Program Evaluation*. New Brunswick: NJ: Transaction Publishers. Available at: www.transactionpub.com/cgi_bin/transactionpublishers.storefront.

——. 2010. 'Four waves of evaluation', *Evaluation* 16(3): 263–77. Available at: http://evi.sagepub.com/content/16/3/263.full.pdf+html

Wholey, Joseph S., Harry P. Hatry and Kathryn E. Newcomer. 2010. *Handbook of Practical Program Evaluation*. 3rd edn. San Francisco, CA: Jossey-Bass.

# 30

# Policy feedback and learning

*Patrik Marier*

## Introduction

This chapter tackles two subfields that have recently grown in importance in the analysis of public policy: policy feedback and policy learning. While policy learning is a potential outcome resulting from policy feedback, the latter is not essential for learning to occur. In fact, relative to the well-focused literature on policy feedback, this chapter illustrates that the literature on policy learning is extremely diverse and encapsulates a myriad of concepts, actors, and learning mechanisms. This chapter is divided into two sections. The first defines, analyzes and explains how policy feedback and policy learning are employed in the study of public policy. The second section discusses the mechanisms and tools that facilitate or impede policy learning, with a particular attention given to commissions.

### *What is policy feedback and policy learning?*

This section discusses both subfields and how they matter when it comes to evaluating policy and fostering or hindering policy change. Each subfield is defined, analyzed and explained via these lenses. Special attention is put onto the different epistemological roots associated with these concepts and how this impacts the analysis of public policy.

### *Policy feedback*

Nearing the end of her high school life, Isabelle must decide what subject she will study as a senior. Should she follow in the footstep of her parents and study chemistry or pursue her dreams of becoming a historian? She opts for the later and selects a wide range of social science courses rather than studying chemistry and physics. According to students of policy feedbacks, Isabelle has made a crucial decision on her future. If she pursues this path in university, she might end up being a history professor at a high school or university in the future. Like so many students, however, she could change her mind. The literature on policy feedback would stress that this outcome would be far more likely during her first year of university than after completing her graduate studies in history. The costs of reversing back to chemistry increase every year while she remains on the history path. Expressed differently, a decision taken at $t_1$ alters the calculus for options at $t_2$, which becomes more and more entrenched further in time.

This is, in a nutshell, the logic underpinning policy feedbacks. It explains why we continue to employ a QWERTY keyboard instead of the vastly superior Dvorak model (David 1985) and, more controversially, why Americans do not have a universal health system (Hacker 2002). Each action building on a prior policy decision, akin to Isabelle following more history courses, generates positive feedback because it strengthens the importance and value of earlier decisions and, as importantly, increases significantly the cost of reversal. Economists refer to this as "increasing returns" (Pierson 2000; Arthur 1994), while similar phenomena have been discussed in policy studies under the umbrella of policy succession (Hogwood and Peters 1982) and policy inheritance (Rose 1990).

In political science, policy feedback owes its origin to the argument that "policies create politics" (Lowi 1969; Schattschneider 1935) and the historical institutionalism school (Pierson 1993). Policy feedbacks are also more common than in economics for multiple reasons (see Pierson 2004 for an in-depth discussion). First, policy reversal is more difficult to enact with political institutions than markets where underperforming firms and products are replaced by new firms and/or products. Consumers can choose the product or service they desire while public goods tend to be compulsory and exhibit non-excludability (ibid.: 30–1). Second, public policies tend to empower beneficiaries resulting in the creation of interest groups to safeguard these new benefits (Skocpol 1992). Interest groups are particularly important in political science since citizens, contrary to consumers, are engaged infrequently with the political system (Pierson 2004). Third, new policies often result in the creation of bureaucratic organization whose very existence is tied in to the success and expansion of specific programs (Derthick 1979). This results in policy professionals highly committed to protecting their program (Ross 2000: 18). Finally, studies have demonstrated that voters are more likely to remember negative experiences such as cutbacks than positive news like the creation of a program (Weaver 1986)

With the past playing such a predominant role, particular attention is given to the initial adoption of policies, formative moments (Rothstein 1992), and critical junctures (Collier and Collier 1991), which represent exceptional moments where opportunities arise to challenge pre-existing policy legacies. Although the concept of critical junctures seems reminiscent of Kingdon's (2003) "window of opportunity," these moments are far more exceptional and infrequent than what students of agenda-setting suggest (Hacker 2002) since they tend to require events such as wars, regime changes, or major economic recessions.

Central to the study of policy feedback is the concept of path dependence, which is defined succinctly by Hacker as being "developmental trajectories that are inherently difficult to reverse" (2002; 54; see also Kay in this volume). According to Pierson (2004: 44), there are four key features associated with path dependence processes. First, multiple outcomes are possible at the initial stage. This is where an actual path is created. Many comparative studies begin with a similar critical juncture and explain divergent outcomeS as a result of having opted for different paths. For example, Weir and Skocpol highlight that the lack of a cross-alliance between the labor and agrarian movements in the US explains why the Swedish Social Democratic party, built upon such a cross-alliance, has been much more successful in implementing a generous and encompassing social agenda (Weir and Skocpol 1985). Second, the starting point for a path may be a relatively minor event. In his study of the American welfare state, Hacker points to a 1974 last-minute amendment to the Employee Retirement Income Security Act (ERISA) bill that is at the origin of a weakening of employers' pension plans (2004: 254–5). Third, when an event occurs *and* in which sequence events occur matter greatly. This is because earlier events are far more important than those occurring at a later date. For example, countries who succeeded in introducing a value-added tax during the golden age of the welfare state have been able to diversify their source of revenue and obtained better protection against retrenchment (Kato 2003). Fourth, once a process is well established, the policy output is likely to remain quite stable and very resistant to change. In the comparative welfare state literature, multiple debates in the past 20 years have actually been focused on whether or not the welfare state is an "immovable object" (Pierson 1998).

In policy studies, the logic of policy feedback and the concept of path dependence have enjoyed tremendous appeal to explain the evolution and strong stability of many social policies such as pay-as-you-go pension programs. The adoption of social security during the great depression has actually been utilized to describe and compare six streams of policy feedback (Béland 2010). Policy feedback from social security has resulted in the creation of future beneficiaries who are now well organized within the AARP (Pierson 1994), in the mobilization of the electorate (Campbell 2003) and in the expansion of the social security administration, which has played a key role in promoting and expanding the program (Derthick 1979). Other important elements point to its stability. Potential reformers not only have to tackle the mobilized beneficiaries and the Social Security Association, but also issues related to the so-called double payment problem. After years of contributions, there is a strong sense of entitlement embedded with current and past contributors. With past contributions utilized to provide pension benefits to the previous generation, the introduction of privately funded pension plans requires contributions to be made to both public schemes—to honor prior commitments—and private schemes to build up assets in the funded scheme (Myles and Pierson 2001). The American political institutions, riddled with veto points, also makes it extremely difficult to build a coalition to reform social security (Pierson, 1994).

More recently, the literature has evolved by stressing that a distinction should be made between positive and negative policy feedback. The later stresses the "the consequences of policies that tend to undermine rather than reinforce the political, fiscal, or social sustainability of a particular set of policies" (Weaver 2010: 137). Although not identified as such by many authors, negative policy feedback constitutes a strong impetus for policy learning (see the section below). For example, the adoption of monetarism in the UK, which is presented as a case of learning leading to a paradigm shift (Hall 1993) has also been conceived as a response to negative policy feedback associated with Keynesianism (Pemberton 2000; Greener 2001). Another interesting development in the literature on policy feedback has been linked to policy instruments and policy change. For example, Hacker (2004) develops four kinds of policy change (drift, conversion, layering, and revision) depending on the number of veto players in the political arena and the level of policy discretion coupled with its support coalitions. These policy changes are associated with a different use of policy instruments.

Critics of policy feedback have emphasized two key points. First, with an underlying assumption that policies create politics, the latter is marginalized. While the political orientation of policy actors may matter when a policy is created, the importance of partisanship decreases to the point where political leadership, and conflict, no longer plays a vital role once a policy or policy constellation has matured (Ross 2000; Korpi and Palme 2003; Peters *et al.* 2005). Second, and reminiscent of previous debates surrounding incrementalism, the policy feedback literature has difficulties accounting for change. Incremental change, which can accumulate and represent a substantial policy departure, remains largely ignored (Hinrichs and Kangas 2003; Djelic and Quack 2007; Kay 2005). Most of the attention is given to patterns of persistence and institutionalization, which is often reflected in the selection of cases (Peters *et al.* 2005). The special attention given to pension policy is a case in point. With high sunk costs, long term commitments, well-established pension agencies and a growing cohort of politically active beneficiaries, it possesses the core attributes to justify the claims of policy feedback arguments.

## Policy learning

The analysis of learning has preoccupied researchers in a wide variety of disciplines such as psychology, education, economics, sociology and business. As a result, it is not surprising to notice that there are multiple conceptualizations and foci surrounding policy learning (Bennett and Howlett 1992; Dolowitz and Marsh 2000; Marsh and Sharman 2009; Braun and Gilardi 2006; Radaelli 1995; Evans and Davies 1999). Nonetheless, a common point of departure in public policy is to define policy learning as "a process of updating beliefs about key components of policy" (Radaelli 2009: 1146–7). This definition encapsulates all kinds of knowledge that can be acquired by various learning mechanisms, which reflects the eclectic environment of policy-makers. In this brief overview of policy learning, the focus is primarily on studies that employ the following concepts: lesson-drawing, social learning, organizational learning, policy transfer, emulation, adaptation, and policy diffusion.

Despite the diversity surrounding policy learning, there are core elements unifying the literature that also distinguishes it from other public policy writings. First, there is a prevalence on the importance of knowledge within the policy-making process at the expense of other factors such as politics, institutions, values, or agendas (Radaelli 1995). As stressed by Heclo in his classical study of social policy-making in Sweden and the UK, "politics finds its sources not only in power but also in uncertainty … policy-making is a form of collective puzzlement on society's behalf; it entails both deciding and knowing" (1974: 304–5). As such, there is an underlying assumption that policy-makers can draw lessons—good and bad—from a variety of sources to replace or improve public policies and programs (Rose 1991). Borrowing originally from the diffusion of technological discoveries, the literature on policy diffusion assumes that good innovations travel and it tends to focus on the determinants that facilitate or impede diffusion and the actual rate of diffusion with the so-called S-shape pattern (Walker 1969; Berry and Berry 2007; Weyland 2007).

Second, an underlying assumption in the literature is that learning must occur without coercion (Freeman 2006), although this is not embraced in some studies on policy diffusion and transfer where learning is not a precondition to the adoption of a policy by a host country (Dolowitz and Marsh 1996). Thus, learning is a co-operative undertaking, albeit sometime highly competitive (Dunlop and James 2007). While there are different forms of learning in public policy, like social learning (Heclo 1974; Hall 1993), organizational learning (Hedberg 1981; Levitt and March 1988; March 1991) and even political learning (May 1992), a core assumption remains that there is an exchange of information between various actors, organizations, and governments resulting in valuable lessons. As in the classroom, neither the importer nor the exporter of lessons is passive and both parties engage in meaningful exchanges for learning to be successful. There are varying degrees of engagements and this results in a broad theoretical and empirical focus stressing multiple facets of this exchange such as the underlying conditions pushing a group, organization, or country to seek out a lesson (Rose 1991; Bennett 1997; Bennett 1991), the mechanism or underlying structural conditions favoring the transfer or diffusion of a lesson (Walker 1969; Berry and Berry 2007; Shipan and Volden 2008), and the motivations of the exporter of lessons (Orenstein 2008; Brooks 2004).

Third, although rarely expressed so explicitly, policy learning assumes that the knowledge acquired is fungible (Rose 1993: Chapter 6) and easily accessible (Bennett 1991: 51). Beyond its intrinsic appeal, policy learning involves the translation of a lesson into practice and it is important "to distinguish between the knowledge of a (foreign) program, the utilization of that knowledge and the adoption of the same program" (Bennett 1991). A number of contributions have expanded the boundaries of knowledge utilization recently with, for example, contributions on the use of second-hand experience (Barzelay 2007) and on the importance of symbolic knowledge utilization where knowledge serves the purpose of increasing the legitimacy of an organization rather than improve its performance (Boswell 2008). Adaptation remains particularly important if one is concerned with policy transfer and diffusion. For example, the success of the World Bank in pension policy is largely attributed to the development of a model that was highly permutable resulting in its adoption in a high number of countries (Orenstein 2008).

Beyond traditional institutional barriers, the type of policy instruments matters greatly when it comes to exporting a lesson or policy in another jurisdiction. Contrary to programs with strong policy feedbacks, like national health care services, regulations are highly fungible. In an analysis of policy diffusion between Sweden and Finland, Karvonen (1981) emphasizes that the most identical policies adopted from Finnish authorities are regulations and that policy diffusion in the United States are facilitated by their strong preferences for regulations.

The fourth commonality is the broad acknowledgment that not all information is of equal value or weight in the learning process. This can be as a result of the quality of the information or simply because of the standing of the individual or group communicating the information, such as experts in an epistemic community (Haas 1992; Ruggie 1975). There is also evidence suggesting that the political orientation of a government matters. For example, right-wing governments are more likely to acquire information and learn from other right-wing governments in the American states (Robertson 1991). Gilardi (2010) goes further by demonstrating a differentiation in what is being studied with right-wing governments focusing on policy information related to their re-election and left-wing governments preoccupied mostly by policy effects.

Organizational learning provides another interesting example of how a certain kind of information dominates the learning process. Within organizations, lessons from previous experiences are deeper than those originating from practice. These are rooted in history, where previous experiences—and the interpretation of these experiences—shape a collective memory (Levitt and March 1988). This has a dual impact; it can ensure that failed alternatives are not attempted again but it can also prevent policy alternatives to emerge.

Finally, there is an underlying assumption that learning leads, at the very least, to a policy reassessment, but often in policy change. In the case of policy diffusion, this also takes the form of convergence, as more and more jurisdictions adapt an innovation (but see Radaelli 2004). An extensive search for lessons is often triggered when the status quo is no longer an option (Rose 1991: 10). The importance of knowledge is important for both problem recognition and the development of an alternative. In ways reminiscent of the policy entrepreneur in Kingdon (2003), groups empowered by their expertise often seek to demonstrate the failing of a policy arrangement while actively promoting a solution. These actors can be endogenous or external to the jurisdictions receiving the lesson and they include civil servants (Hall 1993; Heclo 1974; Etheredge and Short 1983), elected officials (Grossback *et al.* 2004; Gilardi, 2010; Marier 2008), policy entrepreneurs (Mintrom 1997), policy networks (Coleman *et al.* 1997; Haas 1990; Evans and Davies 1999), international organizations (Cao 2009; Orenstein 2008), economists (Markoff and Montecinos 1993), and public inquiries (Bradford 1998; Inwood 2005; Marier 2009).

Policy learning also occurs during the normal operations of government (Etheredge and Short 1983), which often results in incremental change. Bureaucrats learn from the policy itself and make adjustments to improve it (Heclo 1974; Lindblom 1959). Within this context, learning often results in change of the first and second order, which consists of fine-tuning previous policies and attempting to use new instruments to achieve policy goals (Hall 1993). The long-term effects of "learning by doing" may result in a "competency trap" where most learning happens while exploiting current practices at the expense of exploring better or more efficient alternatives (March 1991). It is far easier to improve what has been used rather than assimilate new learning. However, the more one invests in improving current practices, the less likely is an organization willing to adopt better alternatives especially if the implementation costs are substantial. The end result is the persistent use of sub-optimal procedures (Levitt and March, 1988).

Interestingly, the inability of a public administration to absorb, gather, and analyze lessons can be at the origin of a diffusion or transfer. This can be as a result of past policy failures, limited policy capacity or lack of time. In her comparative study of Estonia and Latvia, Tavits (2003) demonstrates that Latvia embraced the Swedish pension reform because its public administration did not have the capacity and confidence from the public to enact its own, following past economic policy failures while Estonian authorities had high confidence in the ability of their civil servant to devise a good pension system of their own. The adoption of Western policies in Meiji Japan occurred because there was an urgent need to develop policies quickly (Westney, 1987). In his analysis of pension privatization diffusion in Latin America, Weyland (2005) argues that the newfound knowledge does not even have to be well anchored within the policy elites. The perception of a highly successful policy in a neighboring jurisdiction may be sufficient to trigger its widespread adoption because of the cognitive heuristics utilized by most policy-makers.

Three important criticisms of the literature on policy learning concerns its diversity, issues related to the so-called Galton's problem and the marginalization of politics. First, the multiplicity of concepts related to learning and divergence related to the independent and dependent variables continue to plague the literature (Eyestone 1977; James and Lodge 2003). The ways in which a policy or lesson is defined is crucial. A closer inspection of programs and instruments can reveal that a diffusion process is no longer present because an adopted policy bears little resemblance to the one enacted by leaders (Clark 1985). Underpinning these debates is the continuous divide between qualitative and quantitative studies (Marsh and Sharman 2009). The quantitative corpus relies on event history analyses to study the diffusion of a policy innovation (Collier and Messick 1975; Walker 1969; Berry and Berry 2007). The theoretical knowledge and techniques originating from these studies have also been applied to study the diffusion of policies across nations such as the liberalization of the economy (Simmons and Elkins 2004), the privatization of pensions (Brooks 2005), and hospital financing (Gilardi *et al.* 2009). As such, most of these studies are interested primarily in explaining what characteristics account for the adoption of a lesson or innovation from another jurisdiction. According to Howlett and Rayner, in spite of improved quantitative techniques, confusion remains with regards to what is changing and what is being diffused (2008: 387) with Rose expressing disbelief about the lack of attention given to the content of the programs diffused (1993: 25).

The body of work relying primarily on qualitative research designs and comparative case studies has focused mostly on lesson-drawing (Rose 1991), transfers (Dolowitz and Marsh 2000; Radaelli 2000), emulation (Westney 1987) and adoption (Bennett 1997) of policies, programs and/or instruments across jurisdictions. Contrary to studies on diffusion, these contributions pay closer attention to the decision-making process, the relationship between the actors involved and the motivations that push a state to learn from abroad. However, as in the case of policy diffusion, there is also a lack of communality among these studies concerning the conceptualization of learning, the dependent and independent variables. The later is quite important since few studies have stressed that learning from abroad should be considered as an independent variable to explain policy change.

Second, Galton's problem where the motivations and sources behind the adoption of a policy can be endogenous rather than from an independent lesson remains an important issues in policy learning, but particularly in policy diffusion where the adoption of an innovation from an external source is the primary element under investigation (Braun and Gilardi 2006). There is a need to demonstrate that a policy change—or a very different kind of policy change—could not have occurred without the presence of learning (Bennett and Howlett 1992: 290) or the presence of a leader in policy diffusion. In a policy environment where information is easily available, this is increasingly problematic and difficult to disentangle. Thus, the distinction becomes much more of an issue related to whether knowledge from another source is being utilized or not and in conjunction with what other sources of knowledge. There are still a lot of improvements needed to understand how governments are learning from one another (Grossback *et al.* 2004).

Third, as in policy feedback, critics have mentioned the marginalization of politics. For example, the epistemic community approach overstates the importance of uncertainty and knowledge and the ability of policy-makers to act without the help of experts (Dunlop 2009). Politicians have multiple tools at their disposal to counter or minimize the influence of an epistemic community or network of experts, such as adding experts from another field in consultative bodies and empowering the expertise that closely resembles their own policy preferences. The ability to navigate throughout the policy process is also an important form of knowledge that is often ignored; this form of knowledge is possessed primarily by politicians. In a nutshell, the translation of learning into policy remains a highly political affair. A potent combination to enact policy change includes the expertise in both knowledge and process (Marier 2008) or at least connections to both kinds of experts (Mintrom 1997).

## Defeating the policy feedback and policy learning barriers—the role of commissions[1]

Both policy feedback and policy learning tend to underscore the capacity to enact policy change. While these limitations are more obvious in the case of policy feedback, policy learning also faces important hurdles such as the institutionalization of professional groups who often define who is an expert if not expertise itself (Abbott 1988; Eisner 1993), a bias towards learning from experience in organizations (Levitt and March 1988), and the traditional political barriers associated with the policy-making process such as veto players (Tsebelis, 2002) and veto points (Immergut 1992). This also includes the organizational structure of government, which is not a monolithic institution but rather a collection of various agencies and departments with their own organizational culture and operating procedures. Once a practice has been adopted among various departments and agencies to handle a specific policy issue, exceptional circumstances are necessary to alter this relationship.

In order to foster policy learning in this environment and shift discussions away from those engendered by policy feedbacks, governments may employ other sources of knowledge, such as the open method of coordination in the case of the European Union (de la Porte and Nanz 2004; Jacobsson 2004; Kerber and Eckardt 2007; Nedergaard 2006), think tanks (Weaver 1989; Stone and Garnett 1998), and commission of inquiries. This section focuses on the latter.

### *Commission of inquiries—expanding the learning potential of government*

The creation of a commission, defined as "a body to which some task has been referred or committed by some person or body" (Wheare 1955: 6), by a government can result in a transformation of the policy landscape if it is set up to encourage policy learning. There are multiple objectives associated with the creation of a commission that actually runs counter to fostering a learning environment. A government may actually want to delay a discussion on a controversial subject (ibid.: 91–2), to drum up support for its own projects (Bulmer, 1983), or even to avoid blame in the enactment of unpopular measures. Commissions are more potent when they are created to fulfill learning objectives such as enhancing knowledge, facilitating political compromise and educating the general population (Marier 2009). First, a key underlying theme in the policy learning literature is the search to curb the level of uncertainty in public policy. Contrary to what is available within individual ministries under normal circumstances, commissions possess the resources and the time to perform an in-depth assessment of policies (Olsen 1983; Bradford 1998). In a nutshell, they operate in a privileged environment, away from the traditional bureaucracy, allowing them to explore and innovate (Sheriff 1983). As a result, commissions have the capacity to tackle complex issues and relationships within the policy space and provide recommendations to resolve ongoing problems (Bulmer 1993).

With these assets, commissions can play a critical role in facilitating learning to improve all forms of policy knowledge. This goes beyond policy prescriptions since the ideas and paradigms they promote can remain in public debates for years (Jenson 1994). An excellent example is the McDonald Commission, which altered profoundly the economic policy goals of the Canadian government. Prior to its creation, only "a small number of senior government bureaucrats, a fraction of the business community, and mainstream economists" supported a continental economic strategy in Canada (Inwood 2005: 309). The McDonald Commission led Canadian authorities to embrace free trade with the United States and abandon a long-standing national approach to economic development, which facilitated a paradigm shift (ibid.).

The second learning objective of a commission is to facilitate the negotiation of a political compromise surrounding a controversial issue. Some political institutions, such as the Joint Committees in the United States, perform this role to a certain extent. However, commissions are notorious for granting a voice to multiple groups beyond organized political parties and for having far more latitude with regard to the elements under discussions. The presence of strong parliamentary commissions in Norway and Sweden, where experts and politicians interact, have represented an important forum to generate compromises among political parties, labor unions and employers' associations (Heclo 1974; Premfors 1983; Olsen 1983). As such, a government may want to utilize a commission to test the feasibility of an idea that requires more analysis and see whether it can be supported by other key stakeholders (Bulmer 1983). A recent example of a commission created with the purpose of facilitating the acquisition of knowledge and securing a political compromise is the Swedish working group on pensions, which was composed primarily of politicians and experts drawn from the civil service (Marier 2008).

Third, commissions can be established to educate the public about controversial policy issues, such as the use of nuclear energy. Commissions are utilized to debunk beliefs and advertise recent research in the policy area under study (Chapman 1973: 184). In these instances, a successful commission alters the policy discourse by marginalizing prior beliefs and reassessing problems and solutions (Inwood 2005).

## *The policy impact of commission*

A commission has the capacity to expand significantly the knowledge possessed by public authorities. However, the learning experience itself does not guarantee a transformation of public policies. It is important to distinguish between the acquisition of knowledge and the actual impact of a commission on policy. A lot of learning can take place and the commission may have no policy impact. Many variables are involved in the translation of the knowledge acquired during the workings of a commission into a new policy beyond the institutional barriers generated by political systems. The first key hurdle is the simple fact that commissions' recommendations are usually nonbinding. Political authorities have the ability to dismiss or ignore the findings of a commission. That being said, it is important to note that recommendations from commissions may be difficult to ignore since they can set policy discussions moving forward

(Bulmer 1983: 663), especially if there is unanimous support among commission members (Park 1972) and stakeholder groups.

Second, the ability of a commission to reshape the policy space is constrained by the terms of reference. For example, the influence of a commission will likely be stronger if a government asks for measures to reform a policy rather than providing an assessment. The terms of reference represent an important tool possessed by government to steer discussions, but there is no guarantee that commission's recommendations will please a government since the workings of a commission can diverge significantly from government's expectations resulting in unexpected findings and recommendations (Jenson 1994: 54).

Finally, the number of individuals involved in a commission and their respective affiliations plays an important role in determining whether the solutions proposed will have broad appeal and whether the commission will have the capacity to challenge existing policies. Based on the literature on veto players (Tsebelis 2002), a commission with a very large membership representing very divergent interests is unlikely to yield recommendations that have far-reaching consequences on current policies. In fact, it is more likely that they would produce a report with a lot of dissension and minority opinions. Therefore, commissions with a small membership are preferable, if the goal is to stimulate learning and bring about policy recommendations that differ from current practices. Who is selected in these commissions matters greatly. Governments can select members who are clearly identified with a policy position or associated with the government. However, such commissions are unlikely to generate the kind of recommendations that would obtain broad political support and succeed in altering the point of view of key political players. The most potent commissions, in terms of having the highest likelihood of generation recommendations that could potentially alter the policy landscape, tend to be the ones with a small independent membership composed of recognized experts in the field.

A good example of a recent commission that features all three elements stated above is the latest British Pension Commission. The three members were not linked to any political party; they included an individual with ties to the business sector, one with union ties and a university professor. As a result, they had broad political support for their activities. They worked closely with governmental officials to generate an exhaustive assessment of British pension policy and clear policy directions to resolve its shortcomings. Many of their recommendations were implemented (Marier 2009).

## Conclusion

As demonstrated in this chapter, there is a rich and burgeoning literature on policy feedback and policy learning. The former has generated multiple studies to explain why policy reform remains so difficult once a policy or program has been put in place. The emerging literature on negative policy feedback brings hope that the literature will slowly shy away from focusing primarily on stability of policy structures (Weaver 2010). The literature on policy learning is highly diversified, but remains committed to few core elements such as the importance of knowledge in public policy, the acquisition of knowledge and how individuals and/or organizations learn. Recent efforts to categorize the literature (Dunlop and Radaelli 2011) and engage in dialogues to clarify concepts, variables and expectations (Marsh and Sharman 2009) are promising since the eclectic nature of the literature is both its primary asset and weakness.

Policy feedback and policy learning actually have a lot in common when it comes to describing the process within which governmental authorities learn from the enactment of policies and programs and make incremental adjustments as a result. Within the policy learning literature, organizational learning is consistent with the literature on positive feedback where self-reinforcing mechanisms entrench programs further at the expense of competing policy proposal. However, the literature on policy learning assumes that learning can be much broader and emphasizes policy change while policy feedback stresses mostly the lack of change.

Many of the references discussed in this chapter refer to pension policy because this policy area illustrates well the differences between policy feedback and policy learning. On one hand, there is a wealth of contributions related to the lack of reforms in the pension systems of advanced industrialized countries. Learning is extremely limited and policy feedbacks are responsible for the limited reforms or the status quo. Pensions represent the case by excellence for policy feedback with high sunk costs, large upcoming cohorts of beneficiaries, and broad popular appeal. On the other hand, the literature on policy learning, and particularly contributions on policy diffusion, has emphasized rapid change and the adoption of pension privatization in a growing number of countries, often spearheaded by international forces. However, these patterns of diffusion do not apply to advanced industrialized countries (Brooks 2005). One would be led to conclude that policy learning remains marginal when there are strong policy feedback effects. However, as demonstrated in the later part of this chapter, the creation of commissions is one of the tools that can be utilized by policy-makers to enhance learning beyond the incremental options generated by the interpretation of actors involved in managing public programs, which are strongly associated with policy feedback.

The marginalization of politics and the measurement of policy change remain two core issues within both the policy feedback and policy learning literature. First, very few contributions have truly integrated traditional political variables, such as the political orientation of a government, within their contributions on learning (but see Gilardi *et al.* 2009; Robertson 1991) and policy feedback. The interpretation of a lesson or policy feedback is highly political and who is in power should matter. For a broader appeal in political science, some notions of political leadership, choice and interest need to be included in both cases moving forward (for policy feedback see Ross 2000). Second, a recurring problem in policy studies is to measure change. The literature on policy feedback has brought back discussions akin to those that were prevalent in debates surrounding incrementalism (Dempster and Wildavsky 1979) while some contributions in policy learning have overemphasized the place of learning and/or the extent to which lessons from abroad are truly exported (Clark 1985; Howlett and Rayner 2008). These issues are unlikely to find a satisfying resolution, but a better acknowledgment of these issues would go a long way to foster a genuine dialogue among researchers in both policy feedback and policy learning.

## Note

1 This section draws from Marier (2009).

## Bibliography


Abbott, A. 1988. *The System of Professions: An Essay on the Division of Expert Labor.* Chicago, IL: University of Chicago Press.

Arthur, W.B. 1994. *Increasing Returns and Path Dependence in the Economy.* Ann Arbor, MI: University of Michigan Press.

Barzelay, M. 2007. 'Learning from second-hand experience: Methodology for extrapolation-oriented case research', *Governance* 20: 521–43.

Béland, D. 2010. 'Reconsidering policy feedback: How policies affect politics', *Administration and Society* 42: 568–90.

Bennett, C.J. 1991. 'How states utilize foreign evidence', *Journal of Public Policy* 11: 31–54.

—— 1997. 'Understanding ripple effects: the cross-national adoption of policy instruments for bureaucratic accountability', *Governance: An International Journal of Policy and Administration* 10: 213–33.

—— and M. Howlett. 1992. 'The lessons of learning: Reconciling theories of policy learning', *Policy Sciences* 25: 275–94.

Berry, F.S. and W.D. Berry. 2007. 'Innovation and diffusion models in policy research', in P.A. Sabatier (ed.) *Theories of the Policy Process,* 2nd edn. Boulder, CO: Westview Press.

Boswell, C. 2008. 'The political functions of expert knowledge: Knowledge and legitimation in European Union immigration policy', *Journal of European Public Policy* 15: 471–88.

Bradford, N. 1998. *Commissioning Ideas: Canadian National Policy Innovation in Comparative Perspective,* Toronto: Oxford University Press.

Braun, D. and F. Gilardi. 2006. 'Taking "Galton's problem" seriously: Towards a theory of policy diffusion', *Journal of Theoretical Politics* 18: 298–322.

Brooks, S.M. 2004. 'What was the role of international financial institutions in the diffusion of social security reform in Latin America?', in K. Weyland (ed.) *Learning from Foreign Models in Latin American Policy Reform.* Washington, DC: Woodrow Wilson Center Press.

—— 2005. 'Interdependent and domestic foundations of policy change: the diffusion of pension privatization around the world', *International Studies Quarterly* 49: 273–94.

Bulmer, M. 1983. 'Introduction: commissions as instruments for policy research', *American Behavioral Scientist* 26: 559–67.

—— 1993. 'The Royal Commission and departmental committee in the British policy-making process', in B.G. Peters and A. Barker (eds) *Advising West European Governments: Inquiries, Expertise and Public Policy.* Edinburgh: Edinburgh University Press.

Campbell, A.L. 2003. *How Policies Make Citizens: Senior Political Activism and the American Welfare State.* Princeton, NJ: Princeton University Press.

Cao, X. 2009. 'Networks of intergovernmental organizations and convergence in domestic economic Policies', *International Studies Quarterly* 53: 1095–130.

Chapman, R.A. 1973. 'Commissions in policy-making', in R.A. Chapman (ed.) *The Role of Commissions in Policy-Making.* London: George Allen and Unwin.

Clark, J. 1985. 'Policy diffusion and program scope: research directions', *Publius* 15: 61–70.

Coleman, W.D., G.D. Skogstad and M.M. Atkinson. 1997. 'Paradigm shifts and policy networks: cumulative change in agriculture', *Journal of Public Policy* 16: 273–301.

Collier, D. and R.E. Messick. 1975. 'Prerequisites versus diffusion: Testing alternative explanations of social security adoption', *The American Political Science Review* 69: 1299–315.

—— and D. Collier. 1991. *Shaping the Political Arena: Critical Junctures, the Labor Movement, and Regime Dynamics in Latin America.* Princeton, NJ: Princeton University Press.

David, P.A. 1985. 'Clio and the economics of QWERTY', *American Economic Review* 75: 332–7.

de la Porte, C. and P. Nanz. 2004. 'The OMC: A deliberative-democratic mode of governance? The cases of employment and pensions', *Journal of European Public Policy* 11: 267–88.

Dempster, M. and A. Wildavsky. 1979. 'On change, or there is no magic size for an increment?', *Political Studies* 27: 371–89.

Derthick, M. 1979. *Policymaking for Social Security.* Washington, DC: Brookings Institution.

Djelic, M.-L. and S. Quack. 2007. 'Overcoming path dependency: Path generation in open systems', *Theory and Society* 36: 161–86.

Dolowitz, D. and D. Marsh. 1996. 'Who learns what from whom: A review of the policy transfer literature', *Political Studies* 44: 343–57.

—— and D. Marsh. 2000. 'Learning from abroad: The role of policy transfer in contemporary policy-making', *Governance* 13: 5–24.

Dunlop, C.A. 2009. 'Policy transfer as learning: Capturing variation in what decision-makers learn from epistemic communities', *Policy Studies* 30: 289–311.

—— and O. James. 2007. 'Principal-agent modelling and learning: The European Commission, experts and agricultural hormone growth promoters', *Public Policy and Administration* 22: 403–22.

—— and C.M. Radaelli. 2011. 'Systematizing policy learning: From monoliths to dimensions', European Consortium for Political Research, Joint Session Workshop, St. Gallen.

Eisner, M.A. 1993. 'Bureaucratic professionalization and the limits of the political control thesis: The case of the federal trade commission', *Governance* 6: 127–53.

Etheredge, L.S. and J. Short. 1983. 'Thinking about government learning', *Journal of Management Studies* 20: 41–58.

Evans, M. and J. Davies. 1999. 'Understanding policy transfer: A multi-level, multi-disciplinary perspective', *Public Administration* 77: 361–85.

Eyestone, R. 1977. 'Confusion, diffusion, and innovation', *American Political Science Review* 71: 441–7.

Freeman, R. 2006. 'Learning in public policy', in M. Moran, M. Rein and R.E. Goodin (eds) *The Oxford Handbook of Public Policy*. Oxford: Oxford University Press.

Gilardi, F. 2010. 'Who learns from what in policy diffusion processes?', *American Journal of Political Science* 54: 650–66.

——, K. Fuglister and S. Luyet. 2009. 'Learning from others: The diffusion of hospital financing reforms in OECD countries', *Comparative Political Studies* 42: 549–73.

Greener, I. 2001. 'Social learning and macroeconomic policy in Britain', *Journal of Public Policy* 21: 133–52.

Grossback, L.J., S. Nicholson-Crotty and D.A.M. Peterson. 2004. 'Ideology and learning in policy diffusion', *American Politics Research* 32: 521–45.

Haas, P.M. 1990. *Saving the Mediterranean: The Politics of International Environmental Cooperation*. New York, Columbia University Press.

—— 1992. 'Introduction: Epistemic communities and international policy coordination', *International Organization* 46: 1–35.

Hacker, J.S. 2002. *The Divided Welfare State*. Cambridge, Cambridge University Press.

—— 2004. 'Privatizing risk without privatizing the welfare state: The hidden politics of social policy retrenchment in the United States', *American Political Science Review* 98: 243–60.

Hall, P.A. 1993. 'Policy paradigms, social learning, and the state: The case of economy policymaking in Britain', *Comparative Politics* 25: 275–96.

Heclo, H. 1974. *Modern Social Politics in Britain and Sweden*. New Haven, CT: Yale University Press.

Hedberg, B. 1981. 'How organizations learn and unlearn', in P.C. Nystrom and W.H. Starbuck (eds) *Handbook of Organizational Design*. Oxford: Oxford University Press.

Hinrichs, K. and O. Kangas. 2003. 'When is a change big enough to be a system shift? Small system-shifting changes in German and Finnish pension policies', *Social Policy and Administration* 37: 573–91.

Hogwood, B.W. and B.G. Peters. 1982. 'The dynamics of policy change', *Policy Sciences* 14: 225–45.

Howlett, M. and J. Rayner. 2008. 'Third generation policy diffusion studies and the analysis of policy mixes: Two steps forward and one step back?', *Journal of Comparative Policy Analysis* 10: 385–402.

Immergut, E.M. 1992. *Health Politics: Interests and Institutions in Western Europe*. Cambridge Cambridge University Press

Inwood, G.J. 2005. *Continentalizing Canada: The Politics and Legacy of the Macdonald Royal Commission*. Toronto, University of Toronto Press.

Jacobsson, K. 2004. 'Soft regulation and the subtle transformation of states: The case of EU employment policy', *Journal of European Social Policy* 14: 355–70.

James, O. and M. Lodge. 2003. 'The limitations of "policy transfer" and "lesson drawing" for public policy research', *Political Studies Review* 1: 179–93.

Jenson, J. 1994. 'Commissioning ideas: Representation and Royal Commissions', in S.D. Phillips, (ed.) *How Ottawa Spends 1994–1995: Making Change*. Ottawa: Carleton University Press.

Karvonen, L. 1981. 'Semi-domestic politics: Policy diffusion from Sweden to Finland', *Cooperation and Conflict* 16: 91–107.

Kato, J. 2003. *Regressive Taxation and the Welfare State: Path Dependence and Policy Formation*. Cambridge Cambridge University Press.

Kay, A. 2005. 'A critique of the use of path dependency in policy studies', *Public Administration* 83: 553–71.

Kerber, W. and M. Eckardt. 2007. 'Policy learning in Europe: The open method of co-ordination and laboratory federalism', *Journal of European Public Policy* 14: 227–47.

Kingdon, J.W. 2003. *Agendas, Alternatives, and Public Policies*. New York, Longman.

Korpi, W. and J. Palme. 2003. 'New politics and class politics in the context of austerity and globalization: Welfare state regress in 18 countries', *American Political Science Review* 97: 425–46.

Levitt, B. and J.G. March. 1988. 'Organizational learning', *Annual Review of Sociology* 14: 319–40.

Lindblom, C.E. 1959. 'The science of "muddling through"', *Public Administration Review* 19: 79–88.

Lowi, T.J. 1969. 'The new public philosophy: interest group liberalism', *The End of Liberalism: Ideology, Policy, and the Crisis of Public Authority*. New York: Norton.

March, J.G. 1991. 'Exploration and exploitation in organizational learning', *Organization Science* 2: 71–87.

Marier, P. 2008. 'Empowering epistemic communities: Specialised politicians, policy experts and policy reform', *West European Politics* 31: 513–33.

—— 2009. 'The power of institutionalized learning: The uses and practices of commissions to generate policy change', *Journal of European Public Policy* 16: 1204– 23.

Markoff, J. and V. Montecinos. 1993. 'The ubiquitous rise of economists', *Journal of Public Policy* 13: 37–68.

Marsh, D. and J.C. Sharman. 2009. 'Policy diffusion and policy transfer', *Policy Studies* 30: 269–88.

May, P.J. 1992. 'Policy learning and failure', *Journal of Public Policy* 12: 331–54.

Mintrom, M. 1997. 'Policy entrepreneurs and the diffusion of innovation', *American Journal of Political Science* 41: 738–70.

Myles, J. and P. Pierson. 2001. 'The political economy of pension reform', in P. Pierson (ed.) *The New Politics of the Welfare State*. Oxford: Oxford University Press.

Nedergaard, P. 2006. 'Which countries learn from which? A comparative analysis of the direction of mutual learning processes within the open method of coordination committees of the European Union and among the Nordic countries', *Cooperation and Conflict* 41: 422–42.

Olsen, J.P. 1983. *Organized Democracy: Political Institutions in a Welfare State: The Case of Norway*. Bergen: Universitetsforlaget.

Orenstein, M.A. 2008. *Privatizing Pensions: The Transnational Campaign for Social Security Reform*. Princeton, NJ: Princeton University Press.

Park, Y.H. 1972. 'The government advisory commission system in Japan', *Journal of Comparative Administration* 3: 435–67.

Pemberton, H. 2000. 'Policy networks and policy learning: UK economic policy in the 1960s and 1970s', *Public Administration* 78: 771–92.

Peters, B.G., J. Pierre and D.S. King. 2005. 'The politics of path dependency: Political conflict in historical institutionalism', *The Journal of Politics* 67: 1275–300.

Pierson, P. 1993. 'When effect becomes cause: Policy feedback and political change', *World Politics* 45: 595–628.

—— 1994. *Dismantling the Welfare State? Reagan, Thatcher, and the Politics of Retrenchment*. Cambridge: Cambridge University Press.

—— 1998. 'Irresistible forces, immovable objects: Post-industrial welfare states confront permanent austerity', *Journal of European Public Policy* 5: 539–60.

—— 2000. 'Increasing returns, path dependence, and the study of politics', *American Political Science Review* 94: 251–66.

—— 2004. *Politics in Time: History, Institutions, and Social Analysis*. Princeton, NJ: Princeton University Press.

Premfors, R. 1983. 'Governmental commissions in Sweden', *American Behavioral Scientist* 26: 623–42.

Radaelli, C.M. 1995. 'The role of knowledge in the policy process', *Journal of European Public Policy* 2: 159–83.

—— 2000. 'Policy transfer in the European Union: Institutional isomorphism as a source of legitimacy', *Governance* 13: 25–43.

—— 2004. 'The diffusion of regulatory impact analysis: Best practice of lesson-drawing?', *European Journal of Political Research* 43: 723–48.

—— 2009. 'Measuring policy learning: Regulatory impact assessment in Europe', *Journal of European Public Policy* 16: 1145–64.

Robertson, D.B. 1991. 'Political conflict and lesson-drawing', *Journal of Public Policy* 11: 55–78.

Rose, R. 1990. 'Inheritance before choice in public policy', *Journal of Theoretical Politics* 2: 263–91.

—— 1991. 'What is lesson-drawing?', *Journal of Public Policy* 11: 3–30.

—— 1993. *Lesson-Drawing in Public Policy: A Guide to Learning across Time and Space*. Chatham, NJ: Chatham House.

Ross, F. 2000. 'Interests and choice in the "Not quite so new" politics of welfare', *West European Politics* 23: 11–34.

Rothstein, B. 1992. 'Explaining Swedish corporatism: The formative moment', *Scandinavian Political Studies* 15: 173–91.

Ruggie, J.G. 1975. 'International responses to technology: Concepts and trends', *International Organization* 29: 557–83.

Schattschneider, E.E. 1935. *Politics, Pressures and the Tariff: A Study of Free Private Enterprise in Pressure Politics, As Shown in The 1929–1930 Revision of the Tariff*. New York: Prentice Hall.

Sheriff, P.E. 1983. 'An Anglo-American comparison: Does social science contribute effectively to the work of governmental commissions?', *American Behavioral Scientist* 26: 669–80.

Shipan, C.R. and C. Volden. 2008. 'The mechanisms of policy diffusion', *American Journal of Political Science* 52: 840–57.

Simmons, B.A. and Z. Elkins. 2004. 'The globalization of liberalization: Policy diffusion in the international political economy', *American Political Science Review* 98: 171–89.

Skocpol, T. 1992. *Protecting Soldiers and Mothers: The Political Origins of Social Policy in the United States*. Boston: Belknap Press.

Stone, D. and M. Garnett. 1998. 'Introduction: Think tanks, policy advice and governance', in D. Stone, A. Denham and M. Garnett (eds) *Think Tanks Across Nations*. Manchester: Manchester University Press.
Tavits, M. 2003. 'Policy learning and uncertainty: The case of pension reform in Estonia and Latvia', *The Policy Studies Journal* 31: 643–60.
Tsebelis, G. 2002. *Veto Players: How Political Institutions Work*. New York: Russell Sage Foundation.
Walker, J.L. 1969. 'The diffusion of innovations among the American states', *The American Political Science Review* 63: 880–99.
Weaver, K. 2010. 'Paths and forks or chutes and ladders? Negative feedbacks and policy regime change', *Journal of Public Policy* 30: 137–62.
Weaver, R.K. 1986. 'The politics of blame avoidance', *Journal of Public Policy* 6: 371–98.
—— 1989. 'The changing world of think tanks', *Political Science and Politics* 22: 563–79.
Weir, M. and T. Skocpol. 1985. 'State structures and the possibilities for Keynesian responses to the Great Depression in Sweden, Britain, and the United States', in P.B. Evans (ed.) *Bringing the State Back In*. Cambridge: Cambridge University Press.
Westney, D.E. 1987. *Imitation and Innovation: The Transfer of Western Organizational Patterns to Meiji Japan*. Cambridge, MA: Harvard University Press.
Weyland, K. 2005. 'Theories of policy diffusion: Lessons from Latin American pension reform', *World Politics* 57: 262–95.
—— 2007. *Bounded Rationality and Policy Diffusion*. Princeton, NJ: Princeton University Press.
Wheare, K.C. 1955. *Government by Committee*. Oxford, Oxford University Press.

# 31

# Randomized control trials

## What are they, why are they promoted as the gold standard for causal identification and what can they (not) tell us?

*David Fuente and Dale Whittington*

### Introduction

Over the past decade scholars, research practitioners, and donors have shown an increasing interest in using randomized control trials (RCTs) to evaluate the effectiveness of a wide range of social and infrastructure programs in developing countries. Much as in medicine where randomized control trials are standard practice, the policy community has turned to RCTs in response to increasing calls for evidence-based policy. As a result, quasi-experimental approaches to program evaluation have come under increasing scrutiny and been strongly criticized by advocates of RCTs. In fact, in some policy and scholarly circles the term RCT has become nearly synonymous with "rigorous" and has been hailed as the primary, if not sole, arbiter of "hard" evidence in the policy process.

The use of RCTs to assess social policy is not new. Fisher (1935) described the use of a randomized experimental design to evaluate the response of agricultural fields to a variety of inputs. In the 1980s labor economists used RCTs to assess the effectiveness of large-scale workforce training programs in the United States (e.g. Bloom *et al.* 1993; Doolittle and Traeger 1990; LaLonde 1986). Over the past decade, a new generation of development economists has adapted and expanded the tools developed by labor economists and applied them in novel ways to study the impact of a wide range of development programs, including de-worming (e.g. Miguel and Kremer 2004); educational interventions (e.g. Kremer 2003; Todd and Wolpin 2006); micro-finance (e.g. Banerjee *et al.* 2010; Giné *et al.* 2006); and point-of-use water treatment (e.g. Kremer *et al.* 2009; Ahuja *et al.* 2010). These advances are well reflected in the work of the Abdul Latif Jameel Poverty Action Laboratory (J-Pal)[1] based at MIT, with offices in Africa, Europe, Latin America, and South Asia as well as Innovations for Poverty Action.[2] These organizations have collectively executed dozens of RCTs in developing countries across the globe.

Proponents of RCTs often have been vocal critics of past approaches to formulating development policy and strong advocates for the broader use of RCTs to identify development interventions "that work." For example, Banerjee (2007) has accused the World Bank of "lazy thinking" for not ensuring that its policy advice to developing countries is supported by a strong (RCT) evidence base. Similarly, Duflo (2004) has called RCTs in development "an international public good" and been a strong advocate for the broader funding of RCTs by the international donor community.[3] While scholars at the forefront of the RCT resurgence have been a prominent voice in academic journals, they have also taken their message to nontechnical audiences in a series of books (e.g. Banerjee and Duflo 2011; Karlan and Appel 2011) and made spirited calls for the wider use of RCTs in the popular media (Banerjee 2006; Glennerster and Kremer 2011; Das *et al.* 2011).[4]

The recent surge in the use of RCTs to evaluate development programs has improved the practice of program evaluation and yielded important and interesting empirical results. At the same time it has spawned a vibrant debate about whether, as their advocates suggest, evidence from RCTs should occupy a privileged position in the hierarchy of knowledge used to shape public policy. This has rekindled old debates ignited by LaLonde (1986) about the relative merits of RCTs compared to other modes of social inquiry.[5] The most recent incarnation of the RCT debate has been primarily between economists and has occurred largely in professional meetings and on the pages of academic journals. Three prominent examples of this debate include the exchanges between Banerjee (2005), Bardhan (2005), Mookherjee (2005), Kanbur (2005), and Basu (2005) in the journal *Economic and Political Weekly*; Angrist and Pischke (2010); Heckman (2010) and Keane (2010) in the *Journal of Economic Literature*; and a separate exchange between Deaton (2010) and Imbens (2010).

To date, the debate among economists about the relative merits of RCTs has largely been technical in nature. As a result, the broader implications of the debate for policy scholars and development practitioners are often obscured. This chapter provides an overview of this debate and offers guidance to policy scholars on the circumstances in which RCTs can be most useful in policy research.

The current dialog about RCTs is often narrowly pitched as a debate between experimental and quasi-experimental approaches to program evaluation or structural and reduced form methods in economics. This chapter does not compare alternative approaches to program evaluation that are used in economics. Rather, we provide an overview of the arguments typically advanced for and against the use of RCTs in policy research. Because the arguments for RCTs are typically more familiar to policy professionals, the chapter spends more time highlighting factors that complicate claims of RCTs' superiority. We do this not to advocate for one form of program evaluation over another, but to provide policy professionals a more nuanced understanding of both the strengths and limitations of RCTs. Clearly, if a researcher is interested in estimating a causal impact of a particular intervention, and they have sufficient funding to conduct an experiment, they can wait a long time for results, and the intervention can be randomized (ethically and practically), it is hard to imagine a situation in which the researcher would choose a quasi-experimental research design rather than an RCT. However, there are many potentially interesting policy questions, types of interventions, and contexts in which a researcher or policymaker might need to use alternative approaches. This chapter provides researchers and policy-makers with a framework for thinking about what RCTs can and cannot contribute to important public policy debates.

The chapter is organized as follows. The second section presents the standard motivation for RCTs and discusses the core strength of RCTs in relation to other modes of program evaluation. Section three outlines the common critiques of RCTs and draws attention to the type of policy questions to which RCTs are well suited. Section four concludes with a discussion of factors researchers, policy-makers, and donors should consider when assessing whether or not RCTs can best advance their policy or research agenda.

## Randomized control trials: what are they, what can they tell us, and why are they promoted as the gold standard in causal identification?

Research and formal program evaluation that seeks to establish causal inference between a program intervention and observed outcomes faces the classical counterfactual problem—namely what the outcomes for program participants would have been without the program. For example, to identify a causal connection between the use of a particular point-of-use (PoU) water treatment technology in a sample of households and reduced incidence of diarrheal disease, one needs to know the number of episodes of diarrheal disease the same households would have experienced over the same time period in the absence of the program. Since in this example an individual household would have either used the PoU water treatment technology or not, the counterfactual required for causal inference is not observable. That is, we cannot simultaneously observe the same household both with and without the PoU technology. The fundamental challenge of program evaluation is to construct a close approximation of this unobservable counterfactual. This requires a control group, which in the absence of a program or treatment would have similar outcomes to the treatment group.

In order for the control group to represent a valid approximation of the counterfactual required to identify a causal relationship, the treatment and control groups must be sufficiently similar in both observable and unobservable ways. If this condition is not met, the researcher cannot determine whether the difference in observed outcomes between the treatment and control groups is attributable to the program intervention (treatment) or to preexisting differences between the two groups. In general, quasi-experimental research methods (e.g. propensity score matching, regression discontinuity design, etc.) seek to construct control groups using observable characteristics. RCTs, on the other hand, construct the counterfactual via randomization into a treatment group.

For example, suppose we are interested in understanding the impact of a particular PoU water treatment technology on diarrheal disease, measured by the number of episodes of diarrheal disease per person per month in a household.[6] Let $Y_iC$ be the number of episodes of diarrhea for a given household i per month in the absence of the PoU water treatment (the control group) and $Y_iT$ the episodes of diarrhea per month in the same household with water treatment (treatment group). To identify the causal impact of the PoU water treatment technology on diarrheal disease, we would want to measure the average impact of the PoU treatment technology on all households in the program, which can be written as follows:

$$E[Y_iT - Y_iC]^7 \tag{1}$$

However, we cannot observe household i both with ($Y_iT$) and without ($Y_iC$) the PoU treatment technology at the same time. One might try to study a large sample of households, half with the PoU treatment technology and half without it (each of these quantities is observable) and calculate the average number of episodes of diarrheal disease per person per month in each group. This would provide us the difference between the average number of episodes of diarrheal disease conditional on household i having the PoU treatment technology, $E[Y_iT \mid T]$, and the average number of episodes of diarrheal disease conditional on household i not having the PoU treatment technology, $E[Y_iC \mid C]$ represented in equation 2:

$$E[Y_iT|T] - E[Y_iC|C] \tag{2}$$

Ideally one would like information on what would have happened to households in the treatment group if they were not provided with the PoU treatment technology. Let $E[Y_iC \mid T]$ be the average number of episodes of diarrhea in households in the treatment group if they did not receive the PoU treatment technology. Simply adding and subtracting $E[Y_iC|T]$ from equation 2 this yields:

$$E[Y_iT|T] - E[Y_iC|T] - E[Y_iC|C] + E[Y_iC|T] \quad (3)$$

The second and fourth terms cancel out and therefore do not affect the equation. Because the expectation operator is linear, we can rewrite equation 3 as:

$$E[Y_iT - Y_iC|T] + [E[Y_iC|T] - E[Y_iC|C] \quad (4)$$

The first term of equation 4 is the treatment effect we are interested in measuring. In our example, it represents the average effect of the PoU water filter on households in the treatment group. The second term is selection bias[8]—namely preexisting or systematic differences between households in the treatment and control groups. However, recall that we do not observe $E[Y_iC|T]$ (households in the treatment group without the PoU water filter). Thus, it is difficult to determine the magnitude or sign of the selection bias and whether estimates of program impact reflect the true program impact, selection bias, or a combination of both. To get accurate estimates of the program's causal impact, researchers face the burden of either estimating the selection bias and correcting it, or arguing that selection bias does not exist.

With a large sample, if households are randomly assigned to treatment and control groups they will on average (in expectation) be identical with respect to their observable and unobservable characteristics. Thus, under ideal conditions, randomization addresses selection bias by ensuring that the treatment and control groups would have the same outcomes on average in the absence of the intervention. More formally, in theory randomization should ensure that the difference in average observed outcomes between the treatment and control groups equals the average of the difference between the observed outcome for households in the treatment group and what the outcome for those households would have been in the absence of treatment. Namely that:

$$E[Y_iT|T] - E[Y_iC|C] = E[Y_iT - Y_iC|T] \quad (5)$$

In our example, this implies that the treatment and control groups would experience the same number of cases of diarrheal disease on average without the PoU treatment technology, i.e. that the control group is a valid counterfactual for the treatment group.

Equation 5 provides information about the average effect of the treatment on households in the treatment group (often referred to as average treatment on the treated), but not about the potential impact of the treatment on households in the control group or about the potential impact on the population in general.[9] If the random assignment is executed correctly and if the research participants comply with their assignments, the average effect of treatment on households on the treatment group should equal the average effect of the treatment on households in the control group. Similarly, the estimate of program impact obtained from equation 5 will only be representative of the potential impact of the program on an individual randomly chosen from the general population if the study sample is representative of the larger population.

By construction, RCTs provide information on the average (mean) treatment effects of a program or intervention. They do not provide information on the impacts on specific individuals or on the general population. Rather, RCTs provide an estimate of the average impact of an intervention on a random person drawn from the study sample.

Under ideal conditions randomization addresses the problem of selection bias. Equation 4 states that selection bias is the average difference in outcomes between the treatment group and control group in the absence of the intervention. (Recall that the former is the unobservable counterfactual and the latter is the observed outcome for the control group.) Randomization removes selection bias by ensuring that any potential bias in the sample is evenly distributed between the treatment and control groups (Heckman and Smith 1995: 89).

RCTs provide information on the mean overall impact of a project or intervention after the program participants and perhaps broader context has dynamically adjusted to the impact. As noted by Duflo *et al.* (2008) this is distinct from the program impacts holding all else constant, which is required to estimate the welfare-theoretic consequences of a program.

Under ideal conditions, RCTs provide a means to cleanly estimate the causal impact of a particular treatment. However, they do not prima facie provide information about the causal mechanisms that link the treatment to the observed outcome.

## *Arguments for RCTs*

Based on the strong methodological results discussed above, proponents argue that RCTs should be viewed as the gold standard for identifying causal impact and given special consideration in the policy arena.[10] Indeed Banerjee (2006) states "[w]hen we talk of hard evidence, we will therefore have in mind evidence from a randomized experiment." Proponents highlight two main reasons why RCTs are superior to other modes of inquiry. First, they argue that RCTs have the strongest internal validity of any impact estimation method (Banerjee 2005; Angrist and Pischke 2010; Duflo *et al.* 2008). Second, they assert that RCTs are based on fewer and less complicated assumptions than other methods and produce "clean" estimates of average program impacts RCT (Banerjee and Duflo 2009; Duflo *et al.* 2008). Therefore, proponents claim that RCTs provide information about program impacts that are more accessible to the policy community than many quasi-experimental methods, which often employ complex econometric techniques and rely on untestable assumptions. Each of these arguments is considered below.

## *Strong internal validity*

Empirical results from program evaluations are generally judged on two criteria: internal validity and external validity. Internal validity refers to the degree to which one accurately measures the true program impact in the study population. External validity refers to the degree to which the findings of a study can be generalized to populations not explicitly included in the study, whether in the same or other geographical locations and cultural contexts. Proponents of randomized experiments suggest that RCTs provide the highest degree of internal validity of any impact estimation method (see Duflo *et al.* 2008 for a detailed discussion of the RCTs, quasi-experimental methods, and internal validity).

Under ideal conditions, randomization ensures that the treatment and control groups are identical on average with respect to both observable and unobservable characteristics. In contrast, because all aspects of the treatment and control groups are not observable, quasi-experimental methods cannot guarantee that the treatment and control groups are on average identical along both observable and unobservable dimensions. Therefore, unlike RCTs, quasi-experimental methods cannot *ex ante* eliminate selection bias and thus may yield estimates of program impact that are biased by preexisting or fundamental differences between the treatment and control groups.

### *Parsimony*

Proponents of RCTs also argue that RCTs are more parsimonious than quasi-experimental methods and thus are better suited to impact evaluation of public policy programs. They argue that because RCTs are based on fewer (and more plausible) assumptions than quasi-experimental methods and report average program impacts, they are more accessible to policy-makers who may lack the technical training to interpret the results of quasi-experimental studies or discern the quality of these results. Banerjee and Duflo state:

> most evaluations of social programs focus exclusively on the mean impact. In fact, one of the advantages of experimental results is their simplicity: They are easy to interpret because all you need to do is compare means, a fact that may encourage policy-makers to take the results more seriously.
>
> *(2009: 169)*[11]

Under ideal conditions, RCTs are in fact based on fewer assumptions than quasi-experimental methods. Unlike quasi-experimental methods, which rely upon untestable assumptions about the independence of the treatment and important factors (individual or contextual) that may influence treatment outcomes in the treatment and control groups (i.e. the presence of selection bias), RCTs rely on the apparently simple concept of randomization to address selection bias.

The arguments in support of RCTs are simple, intuitive, and powerful. This in part explains why RCTs have received renewed attention from both the academic and policy communities. Despite the compelling logic behind RCTs, there has been considerable debate regarding the relative merits of RCTs. The following section provides an overview of the critiques commonly levied against RCTs.

## Critiques of RCTs

Critics of the RCT paradigm typically do not argue that quasi-experimental methods or other modes of inquiry are theoretically better suited to answer questions related to causal inference than RCTs. Rather the critiques take two primary forms. First, critics of the RCT paradigm assert that due to a number of practical issues associated with implementing RCTs or any type of program evaluation, the ideal conditions from which RCTs derive their relative strength rarely hold. Critics therefore argue that despite the clear theoretical strengths of RCTs, they do not deserve a special place in the hierarchy of program evaluation methods. This argument is not unique to the application of RCTs to social and development policy. Discussing the relative merits of RCTs in the medical field, Kramer and Shapiro state, "[t]he model of methodological rigor represented by the RCT invites close scrutiny for any departures from the ideal" (1984: 2744).

Second, critics assert that even if the ideal conditions for an RCT can be approximated or even met in practice, RCTs are well suited to answer only a small subset of questions of potential interest to policy-makers and scholars. This section first considers common practical issues associated with the implementation of RCTs and the challenges these issues raise for RCTs and then turns to the scope of problems that RCTs are well suited to answer.

### *Practical considerations and departures from ideal conditions*

In the face of budgetary, cultural, and political constraints, researchers face the challenge of ensuring that the design and implementation of a program evaluation meet the conditions required for their methods to yield accurate, reliable results. Thus, researchers must pay attention to any ways the execution of their research design may deviate from the ideal in both anticipated and unanticipated ways. Because RCTs share this challenge with other modes of inquiry, critics claim that the practical difficulties associated with implementing RCTs undermine their relative strength over other methods used to identify causal effects. This sentiment is perhaps best reflected by Deaton who states that:

> Conducting good RCTs is exacting and often expensive, so that problems often arise that need to be dealt with by various econometric or statistical fixes. There is nothing wrong with such fixes in principle ... but their application takes us out of the world of ideal RCTs and back into the world of everyday econometrics and statistics. So that RCTs, although frequently useful, carry no special exemption from the routine statistical and substantive scrutiny that should be routinely applied to any empirical investigation.
>
> *(2010: 447)*

There are a number of issues that can potentially compromise the internal validity of RCTs, undermine their apparent simplicity, and limit their external validity. These include, but are not limited to: randomization bias, substitution bias, and treatment compliance; practical difficulties associated with the randomization process; limitations on sample size; and selection issues.[12]

### *Treatment Compliance, Substitution Bias, and Randomization Bias*

For RCTs to provide unbiased estimates of the average treatment effects, the following three conditions must hold: (1) individuals in the treatment group must comply with their assignment (treatment compliance); (2) randomization cannot alter participants' behavior (no randomization bias); and (3) the control group must comply with their assignment (no substitution bias). Violations of these assumptions complicate causal inference from randomized control trials.[13]

Let us first consider the issue of treatment compliance. While researchers clearly hope that individuals assigned to the treatment group will comply with their assignment—namely participate in the program or accept the experimental treatment—this cannot be taken for granted. Returning to our PoU water technology example from the second section, consider a situation in which a researcher is interested in identifying the impact of a PoU water filter on reducing incidence of diarrhea among poor households. Ideally the researcher randomly assigns households in the study area to a treatment and a control group. The researcher then provides the PoU water filter as well as a set of common user instructions to households in the treatment group, and tracks the number of episodes of diarrhea in each household in both the treatment and control groups over the duration of the study period.

There are numerous plausible reasons why households in the treatment group may not comply with their assignment. First, some households may find the PoU water filter inconvenient to use and decide not to use the filter or use it only rarely, perhaps when guests visit the house. Second, some households may not like the taste of the filtered water and again decide not to use the filter. Third, some of the households who like the taste of the filtered water and find it easy or acceptable to use, may simply not operate the filter correctly and thus continue to drink water that is effectively untreated.[14]

In each of the above examples, households will not be in compliance with their assignment to the treatment group and unadjusted estimates of program impact will be biased. Thus researchers must adjust their estimates using various statistical techniques to obtain unbiased estimates of the program outcome. Here, researchers can no longer estimate the average treatment effect, but must estimate intent to treat (ITT), treatment on treated (TOT), and local average treatment effects (LATE). As noted by Deaton (2010) above, in principle there is nothing wrong with using econometric techniques to correct such biases. However, when there is noncompliance among the treatment group, the experiment deviates from the ideal conditions from which RCTs derive their comparative strength.

Similarly, in order to obtain unbiased estimates of average treatment effects in an RCT, the process of randomization cannot, in theory, affect the behavior of individuals in the treatment and control groups (randomization bias). With respect to the treatment and control groups, this refers to the well-known threats of Hawthorne and John Henry effects,[15] respectively. Medical trials seek to eliminate the possibility of randomization bias through a double blind process where neither the researcher nor participants know their treatment status (Deaton 2010). However, this is often not possible in the context of policy-relevant RCTs or social experiments. Referring to Fischer's (1935) seminal presentation of the randomized experimental design in agricultural productivity research, Heckman (1992) quips that while plots of land do not respond to their treatment status, people do (quoted in Deaton 2010). In our hypothetical PoU water filter experiment, households who have consented to participate in the experiment will clearly know whether or not they have received a water filter.[16]

Closely related to John Henry effects, substitution bias presents a threat to the internal validity of RCTs. Substitution bias occurs when individuals assigned to the control group seek close or exact substitutes for the intervention delivered in the experiment to the treatment group. In the PoU example, households assigned to the control group may suspect that because some households are receiving PoU water filters, their water must be dirty. This may prompt some households in the control group to either purchase some form of water purification technology or begin to boil their water. If this occurs, the control group no longer reflects the counterfactual situation required for causal inference. As with noncompliance among households in the treatment group, substitute-seeking behavior by households in the control group will bias estimates of a program's average treatment effects. In the case of noncompliance among the control group, estimates of program effects will be biased downward (Heckman and Smith 1995).

Treatment compliance and randomization bias are well known to scholars and practitioners of program evaluation, and there are widely accepted means of addressing these issues. For example, in the presence of potential endogeniety caused by treatment noncompliance or randomization bias, the researcher can use the randomized assignment as an instrumental variable for treatment status in a regression to obtain an estimate of the Local Average Treatment Effect (LATE).[17] The estimate of the LATE provides a means of identifying a causal effect of a given treatment. However, when participants do not comply with their treatment assignments or the process of randomization influences participants' behavior, the experiment no longer complies with the ideal conditions from which it derives its strong internal validity relative to other modes of program evaluation. This presents challenges to both the parsimony and internal validity of RCTs. With regard to parsimony, Heckman and Smith suggest, "[i]n the presence of randomization bias, the meaning of an experimental impact estimate would be just as difficult to interpret honestly in front of a congressional committee as any non-experimental study" (1995: 93).

## *Selection issues in RCTs*

Researchers who seek to identify a causal relationship between a program and an observed outcome must also be aware of the threat from selection issues. In theory, the randomization process ensures that any bias between the treatment and control groups is averaged out. While this is technically correct, the randomization process removes selection bias among the individuals (households) who participate in the study. In order for the results of a RCT to be applicable to the broader population from which the study sample was drawn, the sample must be reflective of the broader target population of an intervention. Researchers cannot assume a priori that the sample of individuals who participate in a given study is representative of the broader target population.

Standard research ethics dictate that researchers must obtain informed consent from participants in a research study. Thus, it is plausible that some individuals in the broader target population may not consent to participating in an RCT. In the PoU water filter example, some households may be suspicious of a new technology or simply not want to be inconvenienced by repeated visits from a research team. These households may not consent to participating in the study. If this situation occurs, the researcher cannot guarantee that households that agree to participate in the study are representative of the broader target population of interest.[18] Indeed, in the context of medical trials, Kramer and Shapiro (1984) note that individuals are more likely to participate in observational (quasi-experimental) studies than in RCTs (in Heckman and Smith 1995).

In general, the researcher can check whether participants are similar to the broader population in terms of observable socioeconomic and demographic characteristics. However, the researcher cannot rule out the possibility that the two populations differ systematically in unobservable ways. This raises many of the same challenges for RCTs inherent in quasi-experimental research methods.

This type of selection issue will not necessarily be a concern for all RCTs. For example, policies or programs may target individuals who want to participate in a program. This type of intervention relies explicitly on voluntary participation and is quite common for a wide range of social policies. In these instances, an oversubscription research design, in which willing participants are assigned to the control group by a random denial or postponement of treatment, can yield unbiased estimates of the treatment effects on the target population of interest—namely those who are inclined to participate in a given program or seek a given treatment.

There is a second type of selection effect that has received relatively less attention in the literature: selection among the partner organization(s) who implement RCTs. Heckman and Smith (1995) provide a detailed discussion of this issue in the context of the Job Training Partnership Act (JTPA) in the United States, where there was a 90 percent refusal rate among potential implementing agencies who feared that randomizing service delivery would impact their performance benchmarks (see also Allcott and Mullainanthan (2011) and Deaton (2010) for a discussion of selection issues among implementing partners). In the context of social or development policy, researchers often work with a partner organization such as a nongovernmental organization (NGO) who will implement and administer the program or treatment under consideration. Potential implementation partners face a range of incentives that will influence whether or not they agree to participate in an RCT.

Additionally, for obvious reasons researchers typically would like to partner with agencies or organizations that are capable of delivering the program or treatment in a high quality manner and closely following the research protocol. As a result, in developing country contexts researchers often partner with prominent NGOs or government agencies under specific directive to participate in the RCT. Clearly an NGO or government agency that values highly such academic collaboration may not be representative of the broader population of agencies or organizations who might be called upon to implement a particular program. Therefore, the researcher cannot rule out the possibility that the estimated program impact is not related to particular characteristics of the implementation partner or how the program was implemented.

Another concern is that staff of an NGO that can deliver the intervention efficiently and effectively are likely to believe strongly in the effectiveness of the treatment, and may communicate this to participants. This type of implementation differs markedly from a double-blind design and threatens the internal validity of an experiment. In a recent working paper, Allcott and Mullainanthan (2011) show evidence of partner selection bias in two sets of well-regarded RCTs, one set examining the response of residential energy use to information on household consumption and one set exploring the impact of microfinance in developing countries.

In some instances, selection effects among implementation partners may not threaten the internal validity of estimates derived from RCTs. However, they do raise concerns about the external validity of some experimental findings—namely whether or not researchers or policy-makers could expect roughly the same result if the program was scaled from a pilot program implemented by a competent partner to a broader program implemented by partners of varying ability or quality (Deaton 2010; Rodrik 2008).

### *Heterogeneity: parsimony reconsidered*

Critics of RCTs also question the ability of policy-makers to understand the relative merits of experimental and quasi-experimental techniques. Heckman and Smith (1995) point out that a criterion of simplicity or parsimony would argue for simple before-and-after research designs (without randomization).

Critics of RCTs also claim that their proponents mistake apparent simplicity for real simplicity (Heckman and Smith 1995; Deaton 2010). In theory RCTs are based on a relatively simple set of assumptions. However, in practice, addressing the challenges associated with implementing RCTs and developing "robust" estimates of program impact are both complex and technical. As a result of this complexity, critics of RCTs claim that there is no a priori reason to believe that the assumptions and techniques employed to estimate program impacts from experimental studies are more plausible or less complex than those used in quasi-experimental studies.

The issues of treatment compliance and randomization bias discussed above provide examples of how practical challenges associated with implementing RCTs can compromise the types of inference one can draw from them. There two other important issues where this becomes apparent: (1) basic heteroscedasticity in the error term in the regression used to estimate program effects;[19] and (2) the use of baseline surveys and statistical controls to sharpen estimates of program impact and reduce the required sample size.

Under ideal conditions, one can estimate the impact of the program intervention from experimental data using the following simple model:

$$Y_i = \alpha + \beta T_i + \varepsilon_i \qquad (6)$$

Where Ti is a dummy variable that represents whether individual i was randomly assigned to the treatment group, randomization ensures that essential assumptions of the Gauss-Markov theorem are met, so one can develop an unbiased estimate of β by ordinary least squares (OLS). The parameter estimate of β is the program impact we seek to estimate (Duflo *et al.* 2006; Deaton 2010). Citing Fisher (1935), Deaton (2010) emphasizes that randomization plays two fundamental roles. First, randomization ensures that the mechanism governing selection into the treatment group is the same as the mechanism governing selection into the control group. This is what allows randomization to eliminate selection bias. Second, randomization provides "a probability law that enables us to judge whether the difference between the two groups is significant" (ibid. 442).

Thus, while randomization allows the researcher to obtain unbiased estimates of program impact (the parameter estimate for β from equation 6) using OLS, this does not necessarily imply that the parameter estimate is statistically significant, namely that one would reject the null hypothesis that there is no treatment effect (Ho: $\beta = 0$). This can only be established by statistical inference, which requires one to calculate the standard error of the parameter estimate of $\beta$.

In order for OLS to yield correct standard errors for parameter estimates, one must assume that the error term is homoscedastic—that each observation has equal variance for all factors not explicitly included in the model. As Deaton (2010) suggests, there is no a priori reason to believe that the treatment and control groups in the sample have equal variance or that the act of randomization itself did not affect the variance of each group. Thus, in order to have confidence that the statistical inference from the OLS regression is correct, one must either invoke the assumption of homoscedasticity or correct for heteroscedasticity. The latter can be accomplished using standard econometric techniques. However, critics of the wholesale promotion of RCTs claim that assuming homoscedasticity in the error term or correcting for heteroscedasticity using econometric techniques compromises the claim that RCTs are based on more plausible assumptions and are less technically complex than quasi-experimental methods.

Also, RCTs can require large sample sizes to obtain the statistical power needed to identify program treatment effects at a level convincing to policy-makers. This can be expensive. To reduce the required sample size and hence the cost of a RCT, researchers often conduct baseline surveys to obtain covariates to include in the regression equation used to estimate program treatment effects. The basic justification for this practice is that including covariates that are unrelated to the treatment but related to the outcome variable reduces the standard errors of the parameter estimates and thus reduces the required sample size (Deaton 2010; Duflo *et al.* 2008). The general form of the resulting regression equation is:

$$Y_i = \alpha + \beta 1 T_i + \gamma X_{ij} + \upsilon_i + \omega_{ij} \tag{7}$$

where $X_{ij}$ is a vector of individual and/or group control variables over individuals i and groups j, $\gamma$ is a vector of parameters associated with $X_{ij}$, and $\upsilon_i+\omega_{ij}$ represents the compound error term after controlling for $X_{ij}$.

Conducting baseline surveys and including covariates in the regression used to estimate average treatment effects raises two issues that complicate RCTs claim to parsimony. First, covariates must be specified *ex ante*. Otherwise, including covariates in the regression equation opens up the possibility of searching for a "good" specification after the RCT is implemented (Deaton, 2010; Duflo *et al.* 2008). This raises similar concerns as post-trial subgroup analysis.[20] Second, when treatment effects are heterogeneous across the study population, including covariates in the regression equation will yield consistent, but not unbiased, parameter estimates of the average treatment effect (Deaton 2010).[21] Biased yet consistent parameter estimates are typically not a concern in large samples. However, as Deaton notes, in small samples the bias may be substantial (ibid.: 444).

## Scope of questions RCTs are well suited to answer

Up to this point in the chapter, we have discussed the basic rationale for RCTs, the core arguments advanced by proponents of RCTs, and the various ways in which RCTs can deviate from ideal conditions in practice. Each of these topics, while important, examines RCTs on their own turf, that is in problem contexts that are conceivably well suited to them. As Imbens notes "conditional on the question, the methodological case for randomized experiments seems unassailable" (2010: 14). We now directly consider the scope of policy questions RCTs are well suited to answer. This issue is well recognized in the program evaluation literature, but has received relatively little attention in the current debate about the relative merits of RCTs or from policy analysts.

Even the most ardent advocates of RCTs acknowledge that experimental methods can be used to answer only a small subset of potentially important policy questions. Banerjee and Duflo state that, "we [must] not forget that there are a lot of important questions that randomized experiments cannot answer" (2009: 152). Critics of RCTs have decidedly stronger feelings about the value of RCTs in scholarly and policy discourse. Indeed Heckman and Smith state that "experimental data provide no answers to many of the questions of interest to program evaluators" (1995: 86). Similarly, Deaton argues:

> [t]he price for [the success of RCTs] is a focus that is too narrow to tell us "what works" in development, to design policy, or to advance scientific knowledge about development processes. Project evaluation using randomized controlled trials is unlikely to discover the elusive keys to development, nor to be the basis for a cumulative research program that might progressively lead to a better understanding of development.
>
> *(2010: 3)*

Policymakers and policy analysts need a clear, nuanced understanding of the scope of questions that RCTs are well suited to answer and the types of questions they cannot address. We highlight below a number of considerations about the type of questions RCTs can address.

### *Average impact vs. distributional concerns*

Policymakers are usually interested in the distribution of outcomes across the target population. Distributional impacts that might be of interest to policy-makers include but are surely not limited to: outcomes by income decile, percent of participants who experienced positive program outcomes, the median (rather than mean) program impact, and so on.[22] In many circumstances, a policymaker would not want to implement a program that bestowed large benefits on a small subset of the population while inflicting harm on the rest of the population. However, without additional assumptions, statistical adjustments, or a research design specifically targeted toward identifying program impacts on different groups, RCTs typically cannot provide insight into the distributional impacts of a policy or program (Heckman and Smith 1995; Heckman and Vytlacil 2001; Heckman 2010; Deaton 2010; and Rodrik 2008).

### *Causal mechanisms: why and how vs. whether and how much*

Under the most favorable conditions RCTs provide an accurate, reliable means of identifying the causal effect of a policy or program. RCTs can identify whether or not a program "works" (has positive outcomes for program participants) and provide an estimate of the magnitude of the treatment effect (how much). However, RCTs do not provide insight into how or why a program "works." That is, RCTs do not provide insight into the causal mechanisms that drive program outcomes among a certain population.[23] This is particularly problematic for Deaton who states:

> RCTs of "what works," even when done without error or contamination, are unlikely to be helpful for policy, or to move beyond the local, unless they tell us something about why the program worked, something to which they are often neither targeted nor well-suited.
>
> *(2010: 448).*

Policy-makers need to understand why a program works in a specific context or location in order to assess whether it is likely to work elsewhere.[24] In other words, they need some assurance of not only a program's internal validity, but also its external validity.

Similarly, RCTs do not provide information on why individuals might choose to participate in a particular program or accept a particular treatment. For programs that rely upon voluntary participation, policy-makers need to understand the factors that influence individuals' decisions about whether or not to opt into a voluntary program or use a particular technology. For example, in our example of a PoU water filter, policy-makers or donors may want insight into why households might agree, or continue, to use PoU water filters or be willing to pay for them.[25] RCTs cannot provide this information. However, these perspectives are essential for policy-makers or donors to assess whether or not a program to market or distribute water filters is likely to be effective in a particular context and, perhaps more importantly, identify ways in which they can increase the uptake and usage of the filter.

### *RCTs are only well suited to interventions that can be randomized*

Policy researchers can only use RCTs if the interventions of interest can be randomized. There are a number of types of development programs that are amenable to randomization. Examples include insecticide-treated bed nets, point-of-use water filters, improved cookstoves, financial products among microfinance customers, and so on. However, many types of policy interventions cannot be effectively randomized for practical or ethical reasons. Indeed Banerjee states, "there are times when randomized experiments are simply not feasible, such as in the case of exchange rate policy or central bank independence: it clearly makes no sense to assign countries' exchange rates at random as you might assign them flip charts" (2006: 8).

Let us again consider PoU water filters and their impact on diarrheal disease reduction. As a practical matter, researchers may be able to randomize the distribution of PoU water filters to communities and particular households within communities. Indeed, a researcher could distribute multiple types of PoU filters randomly among sample households to determine which type of filter is more effective in reducing the episodes of diarrhea per household per month in the study population. However, what if the researcher were interested in determining the effectiveness of large dams on economic growth? It is impossible to imagine a situation in which randomizing such large-scale infrastructure projects would be politically feasible or ethically appropriate.

This raises a broader issue. If RCTs are the gold standard for causal identification, how does a researcher or policy-maker compare two interventions when one intervention is relatively easy to randomize (e.g. PoU water filters) and another is much more difficult (e.g. piped and sewerage networks)? From a policy perspective it would not make sense to limit the policy choice set to interventions than can be randomized. However, it is not immediately clear on what basis one can compare two interventions if the effectiveness of the interventions cannot be determined by comparable or epistemologically acceptable methods.

### *Value in refining a single parameter*

RCTs can provide insight into the effectiveness of a particular intervention, i.e. whether or not an intervention "works" and to what degree. However, this is only one of numerous pieces of information a researcher needs to know to conduct meaningful policy analysis. For example, suppose a researcher was interested in conducting a benefit cost analysis of competing health interventions, including PoU water filters (e.g. Whittington *et al.* 2009 and Jeuland and

Whittington 2009). The researcher would need to calculate the economic value of the reductions in mortality and morbidity associated with the use of the water filter. To estimate the economic benefits of mortality reduction associated with a reduction in diarrheal disease due to the use of the PoU water filter the researcher could use the following equation from Whittington *et al.* (2012):

$$\text{Mortality Benefits} = \text{Pop}^{*}\text{I}^{*}\text{Eff}^{*}\text{CFR}^{*}\text{VSL} \tag{8}$$

Where Pop is the number of individuals in the target population, I is the incidence of diarrheal disease in the target population, Eff is the effectiveness of the PoU filter in reducing diarrheal disease, CFR is the case fatality rate for diarrheal disease in the target population, and VSL is the value of statistical life in the target population. Often little is known about the exact values of the following parameters for a given study location: I, Eff, CFR, and VSL. RCTs can provide insight into the effectiveness of PoU filters (Eff). However, in many instances researchers know the most about the effectiveness of a given intervention. They are far less certain about the values of I, CFR, and the VSL for the study population (Whittington *et al.* 2012). Because the mortality benefits are the product of the five parameters, the uncertainty about parameter values (or error) is multiplicative. Thus, there is limited value in spending time and resources refining a single parameter value—e.g. effectiveness—when the values of the other parameters are less well known or highly uncertain.

## *Categories of policy questions RCTs are well suited to answer*

Despite that fact that RCTs can provide strong internal validity for the identification of the causal effects of an intervention, they do not provide researchers information required to answer a number of questions of potential interest to policy-makers. Heckman (2010) provides a useful framework for thinking about the types of questions to which RCTs are well suited. Heckman (ibid.) states that there are three types of policy questions in which policy-makers might be interested. First, policy-makers might want to evaluate the impact of interventions that have been or will be implemented. Typically these types of interventions represent an incremental, or marginal, change from existing policies. Second, policy-makers might be interested in predicting the impacts of an intervention originally implemented in one context in another context.[26] Third, policy-makers might be interested in predicting the impact of an intervention that has never been experienced. This refers to policies that do not represent an incremental change from an existing policy context, e.g. interventions to mitigate climate change.

In general, RCTs are well suited to answer the first type of policy question—i.e. where the intervention has been implemented or represents an incremental change from the existing policy context. RCTs may also be useful in helping to predict the impact of policies implemented in one context where such a policy has not been implemented in the past. However, because RCTs do not prima facie have strong external validity, they do not have a comparative advantage over other methods with respect to their ability to answer this type of policy question (Heckman 2010). Similarly, RCTs do not provide information that can help predict the consequences of policies that that never been experienced.

We would add a fourth type of policy situation where RCTs provided limited value or insufficient information. RCTs do not provide insight into whether an intervention should be implemented in a given context nor how to choose between multiple interventions 'that work'. This is well reflected in Das *et al.* who state:

> [R]andomized control trials typically tell you what would happen if you were to intervene. For instance, what would happen if the government were to provide free access to water. [sic] Randomized control trials do not tell you whether you should intervene.
>
> *(2011)*

Whether or not to implement a particular policy or program is a normative question that is typically addressed through the lens of welfare economics and benefit-cost analysis. Evidence from RCTs can certainly contribute to such analysis but is not a substitute for it.

## Summary and conclusions

Faced with very real monetary, political, and temporal constraints, researchers and policy-makers should have a clear sense of the types of questions to which RCTs are well suited. In this chapter, we discuss a set of fairly simple questions that policy professionals can use as a guide to determine whether or not RCTs are well suited to their own research question or policy problem.

First, policy professionals must ask the basic question of whether they are interested in identifying the causal impact of a policy or program and estimating the magnitude of this impact. If not, RCTs will not be of use to them. If so, RCTs may provide a useful means of obtaining this information. Whether or not this is the case will depend on a number of other factors, which are addressed in the questions that follow.

Second, policy professionals must ask whether or not they are interested in identifying why or how a program works, namely the causal mechanism behind program outcomes. Understanding why or how a program works can provide policy professionals with a sense of whether or not a policy or intervention is likely to work in a population or setting that differs from the particular context of the study. Guided by theory, RCTs can be designed to explore competing hypotheses about causal mechanisms. However, they cannot provide this information without an explicit research design to do so and do not necessarily have a comparative advantage over other modes of social inquiry in this regard.

Third, the policy professional must ask whether or not the policy or intervention of interest can be randomized. As a practical matter only certain types of policies or interventions can be randomized. Recalling our water treatment example, it may be possible to randomize the distribution of PoU water filters but it is hard to imagine a situation where one could randomize the provision of large water resources infrastructure such as dams. Similar concerns arise for large regulatory initiatives designed to improve environmental quality (e.g. air quality). This highlights two important points. First, RCTs can only be used to evaluate interventions or policies that can be randomized. Second, policy professionals must think carefully about whether and to what degree their choice of research methodology constrains their policy or intervention choice set.

Fourth, the policy professional must determine when they need the information. To conduct an RCT, a researcher must identify a partner organization—typically an NGO or less often a government department—or build the programmatic infrastructure needed to deliver the intervention of interest. This can take a considerable amount of time. More importantly, the potential impacts of a social or environmental intervention are often not immediate. Thus, even if the researcher has an implementation partner, the results of the RCT may not be available for numerous years. If a policy professional needs information on program impacts immediately, RCTs will be of limited use. Fifth, policy-makers must consider whether the randomization for the treatment is ethically sound and political feasible.

This chapter discuses the traditional motivation for RCTs and provides policy professionals with a more nuanced sense of the commonly cited strengths of RCTs as well as their limitations.

We devoted substantial attention to the limitations of RCTs and how the practical difficulties associated with implementing them can cause RCTs to deviate from the ideal conditions from which they draw their relative strength. We have done this not to advocate other modes of program evaluation over RCTs, but to provide policy professionals with a richer sense of factors that can complicate the ability of RCTs to provide internally valid estimates of program impact.

Perhaps more importantly, this chapter encourages policy professionals to view RCTs in the broader context of the types of research that can inform public policy. Much of the current debate about RCTs implicitly assumes that policy professionals seek to identify a causal effect of a policy intervention or program. While this is certainly an important goal for policy research, it is not the only one. There are numerous other important questions that public policy research must answer, including whether or not a particular policy or program should be implemented.

## Acknowledgments

We would like to express our appreciation to Dr. Juan Robalino, Director of the Latin American and Caribbean Environmental Economics Program, for his comments and suggestions on a previous draft.

## Notes

1 http://www.povertyactionlab.org/
2 http://www.poverty-action.org/
3 The arguments in favor of RCTs are best reflected in Banerjee (2005), Banerjee and Duflo (2009), Duflo (2004), Duflo *et al.* (2008), and Angrist and Pischke (2010).
4 Readers interested in a review of the recent books by Banerjee and Duflo (2011) and Karlan and Appel (2011) should refer to Harrison (2011). The full discussion in the *Boston Review* can be found at: http://www.bostonreview.net/BR36.2/ndf_behavioral_economics_global_development.php
5 See Handa and Maluccio (2010) for a more recent comparison between experimental and quasi-experimental methods in the context of PROGRESSA.
6 A number of authors, including Duflo *et al.* (2008), Deaton (2010), and Heckman and Smith (1995) present similar discussions of causal inference in randomized control trials. We follow the notation in Duflo *et al.* (2008). Interested readers should refer to Morgan and Winship (2007) for a more detailed overview of the potential outcomes framework.
7 For nontechnical readers the expectation operator E[ ] can be thought of as a simple mean.
8 This is often referred to as omitted variable bias in the econometrics literature.
9 In other words, it is not clear that: $E[Y_iT \mid T]- E[Y_iC \mid C] = E[Y_iT-Y_iC \mid T] = E[Y_iT-Y_iC]$. To arrive at this general conclusion, one must invoke the Stable Unit Treatment Value Assumption developed in Angrist *et al.* (1996) (see Duflo *et al.* 2008), which states that "the potential outcomes of an individual are unrelated to the treatment status of any other individual" (p. 8). Interested readers should refer to Morgan and Winship (2007) for a more detailed discussion of the Stable Unit Treatment Value Assumption.
10 Cartwright (2010) calls into question whether any research method can be considered *the* gold standard at all.
11 It is important to note that comparing means is one identification strategy, which one could use with both observational and experimental data. One could also use a difference in difference identification strategy with RCT data.
12 Readers interested in a more in-depth discussion of these as well as other issues associated with the implementation of RCTs should refer to Deaton (2010), Rodrik (2008), Heckman and Smith (1995), Heckman (2010), Imbens and Wooldridge (2009), Imbens (2010), and Duflo *et al.* (2008).
13 If conditions 1 and 3 are violated by the majority of study participants, the study cannot be considered an RCT at all. However, "minor" deviations from conditions 1 and 3 are often experienced in real-life field situations. It is a matter of judgment as to how severe the violations need to be before one concluded that the implementation of an RCT protocol failed.

14 These issues are well recognized by scholars who work on this issue. As a result, they pay considerable attention to obtaining objective assessments of whether or not households are using the water filter, e.g. conducting tests for residual chlorine in stored water.
15 Hawthorne and John Henry effects threaten the internal validity of social experiments. Hawthorne effects refer to the fact that the act of participating in a study, or knowledge of being studied, often influences the behavior of individuals in the treatment group. (See Gillespie (1991) for a history of the term Hawthorne effect.) For example, an individual who has been randomly assigned to the treatment group in the hypothetical PoU water experiment scenario may feel fortunate to have been selected to participate in the program and may wash their hands more often to ensure that they obtain the maximum benefit from the filter. Alternatively, the individual might engage in improved hygiene practices to give the study team a good impression of them. In these instances, the treatment effect measured by researchers would include the co-benefits of hand washing and the PoU filter, not simply the PoU filter. Conversely, John Henry effects refer to a situation in which individuals in the control group change their behavior in response to the experiment or their treatment assignment (Zdep and Irvine 1970).
16 Note that this would also be an issue with a quasi-experimental research design.
17 For a detailed discussion of LATE see Imbens and Angrist (1994), Heckman (1996), Heckman (1999), Urzua and Heckman (2009), and Imbens (2010).
18 Recall that randomization addresses selection bias by ensuring that the treatment and control groups are similar on average along both observable and unobservable dimensions. In this situation, even if the researcher can confirm that treatment and control groups are similar in observable ways, she cannot rule out the possibility that those who agree to participate in the study are different from those who refuse to participate in unobservable ways.
19 This issue will also be present in quasi-experimental studies and thus should not be interpreted as a problem with RCTs relative to other modes of research design. We raise the issue here simply to highlight a level of complexity that is typically overlooked in discussion about RCTs.
20 Recognizing the threat to the internal validity, proponents of RCTs have openly supported calls for a RCT registry where experiments would be registered *ex ante* along with proposed subgroups for analysis and model specification.
21 See Deaton (2010) for a summary of this issue and Freedman (2008) for a more detailed treatment.
22 See Deaton (2010) for an overview of distributional program impacts and Heckman and Smith (1995) for a more extensive treatment of this issue.
23 Contrary to the common complaint that RCTs are atheoretical (e.g. Bardhan 2005; Basu 2005; Mookherjee 2005) well-designed RCTs can be used to test hypotheses about competing causal mechanisms. Deaton (2010) holds up Duflo *et al.* (2009), Bertrand *et al.* (2010), Giné *et al.* (2010), and Karlan and Zinman (2008) as exemplary uses of RCTs to advance economic theory.
24 Pawson and Tilley (1997) present an interesting call for what they term "realistic evaluation" that explicitly examines the interaction between context and mechanisms in program outcomes.
25 See Whittington *et al.* (2012) for a discussion of how uptake and usage can affect the economic attractiveness of a variety of interventions.
26 This is referred to as "benefit transfer" in the environmental economics literature.

## Bibliography

Ahuja, A., M. Kremer and A.P. Zwane. 2010. 'Providing safe water: Evidence from randomized evaluations', unpublished working paper. Available at: http://www.economics.harvard.edu/faculty/kremer/files/ARRE_CLEAN_2010_04_14.pdf

Allcott, H. and S. Mullainanthan. 2011. 'External validity and partner selection', unpublished working paper.

Angrist, J. and J.S. Pischke. 2010. 'The credibility revolution in empirical economics: How better research design is taking the con out of econometrics', *Journal of Economic Perspectives* 24(2): 3–30.

——, G. W. Imbens, and D.B. Rubin. 1996. 'Identification of causal effects using instrumental variables', *Journal of the American Statistical Association* 91(434): 444–55.

Banerjee, A.V. 2005. '"New development economics" and the challenge to theory', *Economic and Political Weekly*: 4340–4.

—— 2006. 'Making aid work: how to fight global poverty – effectively', *Boston Review* 31(4): 7–9.

—— 2007. *Making Aid Work.* Cambridge, MA: MIT Press.

——and E. Duflo. 2009. 'The experimental approach to development economics', *Annual Review of Economics* 1: 151–78.

——and E. Duflo. 2011. *Poor Economics: A Radical Rethinking of the Way to Fight Global Poverty*. Cambridge, MA: Public Affairs.

——, E. Duflo, R. Glennerster and C. Kinnan. 2010. 'The miracle of microfinance? Evidence from a randomized evaluation', J-PAL Working Paper.

Bardhan, P. 2005. 'Theory or empirics in development economics', *Economic and Political Weekly* 40(40): 4333–5.

Basu, K. 2005. 'New empirical development economics: Remarks on its philosophical foundations', *Economic and Political Weekly* 40(40): 4336–9.

Bertrand, M., D. Karlan, S. Mullainathan, E. Shafir and J. Zinman. 2010. 'What's advertising content worth? Evidence from a consumer credit marketing field experiment', *The Quarterly Journal of Economics* 125(1): 263.

Bloom, H., L. Orr, G. Cave, S. Bell and F. Doolittle. 1993. '*The National JTPA Study: Title IIA Impacts on Earnings and Employment at 18 Months*', Bethesda, MD: Abt Associates.

Cartwright, N. 2010. 'What are randomized trials good for?', *Philosophical Studies* 147(1), 59–70.

Das, J., D. Shantayana and S. Hammer. 2011. 'Lost in translation', *Boston Review*. Available at: http://www.bostonreview.net/BR36.2/devarajan_das_hammer_behavioral_economics_global_development.php

Deaton, A. 2010. 'Instruments, randomization, and learning about development'. *Journal of Economic Literature* 48(2): 424–55.

Doolittle, F. and L. Traeger. 1990. *Implementing the National JTPA Study*. New York: Manpower Demonstration Research Corporation.

Duflo, E. 2004. 'Scaling up evaluation', Annual World Bank Conference on Development Economics.

——, Pascaline Dupas, Michael Kremer, and Samuel Sinei. 2006. 'Education and HIV/AIDS prevention: Evidence from a randomized evaluation in western Kenya," working paper, MIT.

——, R. Glennerster and M. Kremer. 2008. 'Using randomization in development economics research: A toolkit', *Handbook of Development Economics* 4: 3895–962.

——, M. Greenstone and R. Hanna. 2008. 'Cooking stoves, indoor air pollution and respiratory health in rural Orissa', *Economic and Political Weekly* 43(2): 71–6. Available at: http://web.mit.edu/ceepr/www/publications/reprints/Reprint_205_WC.pdf

——, M. Kremer and J. Robinson. 2009. 'Nudging farmers to use fertilizer: Evidence from Kenya', NBER Working Paper, 15131.

Fisher, Ronald A. 1935 (1960). *The Design of Experiments*. 8th edn. New York: Hafner.

Freedman, D.A. 2008. 'On regression adjustments to experimental data', *Advances in Applied Mathematics* 40 (2): 180–93.

Gillespie, Richard. 1991. *Manufacturing Knowledge: A History of the Hawthorne Experiments*. Cambridge: Cambridge University Press.

Giné, X., T. Harigaya (IPA), D.S. Karlan and B. Nguyen. 2006. 'Evaluating microfinance program innovation with randomized control trials: an example from group versus individual lending', *Asian Development Bank Economics and Research Department Technical Note Series* 16.

——, D. Karlan and J. Zinman. 2010. 'Put your money where your butt is: A commitment contract for smoking cessation', *American Economic Journal: Applied Economics* 2(4): 213–35.

Glennerster, R. and M. Kremer. 2011. 'Small changes, big results', *Boston Review*. Available at: http://bostonreview.net/BR36.2/ndf_behavioral_economics_global_development.php

Handa, S. and J. Maluccio. 2010. 'Matching the gold standard: comparing experimental and non-experimental evaluation techniques for a geographically targeted program', *Economic Development and Cultural Change* 58(3): 415–47.

Harrison, G.W. 2011. 'Randomization and its discontents', *Journal of African Economies* 20(4): 626–52.

Heckman, J.J. 1992. 'Randomization and social policy evaluation', in C.F. Manski and I. Garfinkel (eds) *Evaluating Welfare and Training Programs*. Cambridge, MA and London: Harvard University Press, 201–30.

—— 1996. 'Randomization as an instrumental variable', *The Review of Economics and Statistics* 78(2): 336–41.

—— 1999. 'Instrumental variables: response to Angrist and Imbens', *The Journal of Human Resources* 34(4): 828–37.

—— 2010. 'Building bridges between structural and program evaluation approaches to evaluating policy', *Journal of Economic Literature* 48(2): 356–98.

——and J.A. Smith. 1995. 'Assessing the case for social experiments', *The Journal of Economic Perspectives* 9(2): 85–110.

——and E. Vytlacil. 2001. 'Policy-relevant treatment effects', *American Economic Review* 91(2): 107–11.

Imbens, G.W. 2010. 'Better LATE than nothing: Some comments on Deaton (2009) and Heckman and Urzua (2009)', *Journal of Economic Literature* 48(2): 399–423.

——and J.D. Angrist. 1994. 'Identification and estimation of local average treatment effects', *Econometrica* 62(2): 467–75.

——and J.M. Wooldridge. 2009. 'Recent developments in the econometrics of program evaluation', *Journal of Economic Literature* 47(1): 5–86.

Jeuland, M. and D. Whittington. 2009. 'Cost-benefit comparisons of investments in improved water supply and cholera vaccination programs', *Vaccine* 27(23): 3109–20.

Kanbur, R. 2005. 'Goldilocks development economics: Not too theoretical, not too empirical, but watch out for the bears!', *Economic and Political Weekly* 40(40): 4344–6.

Karlan, D.S. and J. Zinman. 2008. 'Credit elasticities in less-developed economies: Implications for microfinance', *The American Economic Review* 98(3): 1040–68.

——and J. Appel. 2011. *More than Good Intentions: How a New Economics Is Helping to Solve Global Poverty*. New York: Penguin.

Keane, M.P. 2010. 'A structural perspective on the experimentalist school', *The Journal of Economic Perspectives* 24(2): 47–58.

Kramer, M.S. and S.H. Shapiro. 1984. 'Scientific challenges in the application of randomized trials', *JAMA: The Journal of the American Medical Association* 252(19): 2739–45.

Kremer, M. 2003. 'Randomized evaluations of educational programs in developing countries: Some lessons', *The American Economic Review* 93(2): 102–6.

——, E. Miguel, S. Mullainathan, C. Null and Alix Peterson Zwane. 2009. 'Making water safe: price, persuasion, peers, promoters, or product design?', unpublished working paper. Available at: http://ase.tufts.edu/econ/events/neudcDocs/SaturdaySession/Session17/MKremerMakingWaterSafePricePersuasion.pdf

LaLonde, R.J. 1986. 'Evaluating the econometric evaluations of training programs with experimental data', *The American Economic Review* 76(4): 604–20.

Miguel, E. and M. Kremer. 2004. 'Worms: Identifying impacts on education and health in the presence of treatment externalities', *Econometrica* 72(1): 159–217.

Mookherjee, D. 2005. 'Is there too little theory in development economics today?', *Economic and Political Weekly* 40(40): 4328–33.

Morgan, S.L. and C. Winship. 2007. *Counterfactuals and Causal Inference: Methods and Principles for Social Research*. Cambridge: Cambridge University Press.

Pawson, R. and N. Tilley. 1997. *Realistic Evaluation*, illustrated, reprint edn. London: Sage.

Rodrik, D. 2008. 'The new development economics: We shall experiment, but how shall we learn?' Faculty Research Working Papers Series, RWP08-055.

Todd, P.E., and K.I. Wolpin. 2006. 'Assessing the impact of a school subsidy program in Mexico: Using a social experiment to validate a dynamic behavioral model of child schooling and fertility', *The American Economic Review* 96(5): 1384–417.

Urzua, S. and J.J. Heckman. 2009. 'Comparing IV with structural models: What simple IV can and cannot identify', NBER Working Paper 14706.

Whittington, D., W.M. Hanemann, C. Sadoff and M. Jeuland. 2009. 'The challenge of improving water and sanitation services in less developed countries', *Foundations and Trends in Microeconomics* 4(6–7), 469–609.

——, M. Jeuland, K. Barker and Y. Yuen. 2012. 'Setting priorities, targeting subsidies among water, sanitation, and health interventions in developing countries', *World Development* (under review).

Zdep, S.M. and S.H. Irvine.1970. 'A reverse Hawthorne effect in educational evaluation', *Journal of School Psychology* 8: 89–95.

# 32

# Policy evaluation and public participation

*Carolyn M. Hendriks*

## Introduction

This chapter is concerned with the methods and challenges of evaluating policies through the participation of affected publics. For this purpose, policy evaluation is understood as an act of judgment about the performance of a particular policy process, department or program based on its desirability, worth, or value. Evaluation is the phase of the policy process where there is ideally an explicit opportunity for learning, reflection and improvement. It represents the moment where the policy cycle ends but also restarts (Althaus *et al.* 2007). For the most part, this chapter focuses on policy evaluation as a retrospective (*ex post*) exercise where past decisions and programs are formally assessed. Evaluations of this kind might be legally required, or they might be stimulated by a budget or planning process. In some cases evaluations are triggered by specific policy events, such as a perceived policy fiasco or change in political leadership (Bovens *et al.* 2006).

The dominant approach to policy evaluation has been inspired by a rationalistic or traditional model of policy analysis (Bovens *et al.* 2006). Evaluation of this kind typically sets out to determine the facts at hand using predetermined evaluation criteria, and attempts to keep values and ultimately politics out of the equation. In other words, the goal is to assess whether a program or policy achieved its set objectives (is it effective?), whether it is the best way to achieve these objectives (is it efficient?) and whether the policy or program is relevant under current conditions (is it appropriate?) (Althaus *et al.* 2007). Formal evaluations of this kind often proceed with an independent body (for example, an audit office, an ombudsman, a consultant and so on) establishing the scope of the evaluation, determining the assessment criteria (for example, cost-effectiveness), then collecting relevant data (often focused on the operation and implementation of the policy or program), and finally making an objective assessment and recommendations. The inherent assumption with this more traditional approach to policy evaluation is that the criteria used are appropriate and measurable, and that the conclusions drawn will be definitive and uncontroversial.

However, in practice, this kind of systematic and rational assessment of a policy program is rare (Bovens *et al.* 2006; O'Faircheallaigh 2002). Indeed, policy practice is littered with examples that demonstrate how policy evaluation is far from value neutral and apolitical. Different policy actors will almost always hold competing views on what constitutes policy success and failure, how it might be judged and what lessons the results imply. This makes evaluation an inevitably controversial and indeed political process, one that often generates more conflict and contestation than any other stage of the policy process. Even the most low profile and seemingly uncontroversial policy programs can become political battle grounds when an evaluation process commences because it triggers a host of questions about how funding is allocated and spent, who wins and loses, who is accountable and responsible, and it also opens up possibilities for reframing debates (Bovens *et al.* 2006).

Given the inherent political nature of policy evaluation in contemporary societies, its practice is best understood as a process that seeks to reflect the plurality of perspectives on any given policy or program. According to Majone (1989: 183) the imperative is thus "less to develop 'objective' measures of outcomes—the traditional aim of evaluation research—than to facilitate a wide ranging dialogue among advocates of different criteria." In other words, the evaluative task involves recognizing the multiplicity of criteria and perspectives on a given issue and helping to "contribute to a shared understanding of the various critical perspectives and of their different functions in the process of public deliberation" (1989: 170). This more participatory approach to policy evaluation requires that policy analysts (such as independent evaluators and public managers) elicit multiple perspectives. In practice, this involves going well beyond engaging diverse experts and elites, or conducting a simple client satisfaction survey. Ideally participatory policy evaluation involves engaging a diversity of actors that affect, and are affected by, a policy or program in the process of evaluation.

The perspective offered in this chapter sits within this participatory or argumentative tradition of policy evaluation. It views the assessment of any policy performance or program as something shaped by the underlying assumptions and values of the evaluation process, and those interpreting the evidence (Fischer and Forester 1993; Majone 1989). The argumentative approach to policy evaluation takes seriously the role of values in shaping and determining the worth of a policy program (Stewart 2009a). In other words, policy evaluation involves a process of judgment that is inherently subjective; it is influenced by numerous factors such as who is doing the evaluation, the scope of evaluation, the evaluative criteria used, and the way material is interpreted.

Participation is not a particularly well-understood or articulated theme in the literature on policy evaluation. This is despite the growing interest in, and practice with, more participatory and deliberative forms of governing. One reason for this could be that participation is typically framed as an activity that occurs at the front end of the policy process, for example during agenda-setting, policy design, and occasionally in decision-making. Yet participation is playing an expanding role in policy evaluation particularly with the push to create "public value," and the broader trend toward more participatory forms of governing.

In this chapter I consider *ex post* policy evaluation in light of various themes emerging from the practice and theory of participatory governance. I focus particularly on how multiple perspectives might be brought into the policy evaluation process, and the challenges and politics of doing so. Consideration is given to both conventional methods of public involvement in policy evaluation such as citizens' surveys and public hearings, as well as more inclusive and deliberative forms of citizen engagement. The chapter concludes by discussing some of the particular challenges of engaging the public in retrospective policy evaluation.

## The role of participation in policy evaluation

The idea of participation is not new in discussions on policy evaluation. Indeed, some scholars have identified participation as a central part of the evaluation process. For example, Guba and

Lincoln (1989), view evaluation as a process of encouraging consensus among various stakeholders. In their methodology (referred to as "fourth generation evaluation"), stakeholders engage in a collaborative process, and are empowered to develop and negotiate joint recommendations. Participation also features as a theme in the work of post-positivist scholars interested in expanding the argumentative basis for policy analysis (Fischer 1995; Forester 1999; Hajer and Wagenaar 2003b; Majone 1989). Here the emphasis is on policy analysts not so much "solving" a particular problem or finding its "truth," but in creating interactive settings where policy arguments and evidence can be exposed to public deliberation. More recently, scholars have argued that interactive or deliberative forms of policy analysis are essential for making practical judgments in contexts where governance increasingly involves a complex networks of actors, deep-value pluralism and radical uncertainty (Hajer and Wagenaar 2003a). Participation thus becomes central to the tasks of evaluating how policies work, and how they might be improved. As Hajer and Wagenaar put it: "Whatever knowledge we possess must be assessed for its relevance and usefulness in interaction with the concrete situation at hand, *and* that this ongoing process of assessment occurs in situations of intense social interaction" (2003a: 24, emphasis in the original).

Some themes on participatory evaluation have also emerged from the field of public management. The push here has been to bring more "client focus" to the monitoring and assessment of service delivery through consumer involvement. Participation in this context is about improving knowledge on client needs, increased transparency and improved accountability for services (Goetz and Gaventa 2001). Some of these imperatives have been promoted under the banner of certain managerial discourses, such as New Public Management (NPM), which emphasizes the importance of service providers satisfying the needs and desires of their clients and consumers (much like customers in the private sector). NPM has promoted passive and one-way forms of participation, such as satisfaction surveys, that encourage respondents to think as consumers rather than as citizens (Howard 2010; Parkinson 2004)—a theme I return to later.

"Participation" has also surfaced in recent academic and practitioner discussions on the importance of "public value" in public sector management. Public value is a concept that continues to evolve (see Alford and O'Flynn 2009; Jørgensen and Bozeman 2007) but in broad terms it refers to *what* the public values (Benington 2009; Horner *et al.* 2006). The idea of public value emerged in the US as a construct to help public managers make sense of their policy tasks and to encourage them to be more responsive to their public constituents (Moore, 1995). The notion of "public value" has gained interest in other Western democracies, such as the United Kingdom, where it is seen as a kind of corrective response to the managerial discourse of NPM (Horner *et al.* 2006). In contrast to NPM, the concept of public value does not conflate the views and preferences of consumers and citizens, and in doing so it encourages public managers to listen to the voices of different publics. While some of the literature on public value celebrates public participation, little detail is given on who should participate in the policy process and how.

Participation has also surfaced in recent discussions on performance management in the public sector. Measuring the performance of a program, department, or government is an important component of policy evaluation—though the roots of evaluation research and performance management are different (see Blalock 1999). Performance management is typically aimed at ensuring that public agencies are doing their job in an efficient and productive manner. This is as much about promoting public accountability as it is about ensuring that governments are effective service deliverers. Typically performance measures are quantitative, for example, drawn from budget data or from output measurements such as the units and standard of services provided (Holzer and Kloby 2005b).

More recently, there has been a call to include citizens directly in the assessment and measurement of government performance. Advocates argue that citizens can help to develop socially relevant measures as well as provide assistance with data collection and service design (Callahan 2000; Ho 2005). Some go further and argue that citizen-led performance management can promote accountability, and strengthen democracy by fostering trust and social capital (Halachimi and Holzer 2010). However, like discussions on public value, there has been limited discussion on the practicalities and politics of engaging citizens in the policy process. This may change as the practice of citizen engagement in performance management expands. Already in the United States hundreds of performance projects have been conducted where citizens have been asked for their feedback on services, or involved in developing performance measures. In most cases participation appears to involve relatively non-interactive methods such as customer surveys (e.g. Heikkila and Isett 2007; Holzer and Kloby 2005a, 2005b).

The discussion above reveals that the arguments for greater public participation in policy evaluation are mostly couched in epistemic terms. By engaging different publics in the evaluation process, we gain access to new information, alternative knowledge, and values. While this may be the case, this particular framing of public involvement bypasses a host of democratic and managerial reasons why participation is becoming such a central theme in contemporary governance.

## Broader drivers for public participation in policy

One of the most significant drivers for participation in public policy is a desire to democratize the policy process and public services. On one level this is coming from increased demands from different publics to contribute to decisions, services, or policies that they use, fund or support. Yet on another level there has been a push by some scholars and international bodies such as the Organisation for Economic Co-operation and Development (OECD) to address some of the democratic deficits in the policy process by giving communities the opportunity to participate in decisions that affect them (Dryzek 2000; Fung 2006b; OECD 2001). When communities are excluded from contributing to decision-making processes, they are left frustrated and angry, and question the fairness and authority of the "imposed decision" (Renn *et al.* 1995). In other words they may not accept the legitimacy of the decision, and consent to necessary behavioral or funding changes (Parkinson 2006). Others point to a host of other moral reasons why the public should have greater say in the policy process. For example, some argue that active citizen involvement in public policy (especially over the long term) can promote more equitable outcomes and address systemic inequalities in communities (Schneider and Ingram 1997). Participation is also said to promote more transparent decision-making, and thereby improve trust in public institutions and citizenship more broadly (Putnam 1993). These normative arguments are all relevant to policy evaluation.

Participation has also become a key managerial and administrative theme for many governments around the world (see OECD 2009). At a minimum, participation may be a necessary administrative requirement, for example, to fulfill certain legal requirements, such as an Environmental Impact Statement. Alternatively, a participatory process might be conducted to help prevent or resolve a conflict. For example, since the 1970s consultation exercises have been used by governments as a means to prevent protest politics and restore "trust" in political institutions. A related motive here is to use participation to help share the responsibility for policy outcomes (including successes and failures) (Head 2007).

Public participation is increasingly advocated as a means to improve the managerial efficiency, service delivery and accountability of government agencies—as discussed above. There has also been increased recognition that the task of governing is not something that governments do alone—it requires working with multiple interdependent actors (Wanna, 2009). Participation promises to improve the problem-solving capacity of governments and other organizations.

When different actors work together on problems, they have the opportunity to share knowledge and resources, which can improve the efficiency of public programs and services (Kickert *et al.* 1997; Kooiman 1993). Participatory and collaborative approaches also present decision-makers with an alternative approach to dealing with the complexities and uncertainties of modern policy issues (Koppenjan and Klijn 2004).

More ambitious managers and administrators might utilize public participation to catalyze change, or to shift the nature of the debate. For example, they might turn to more deliberative processes in order to expand discussion on a controversial policy issue beyond symbols and narrow interests (e.g. Carson *et al.* 2002; Einsiedel *et al.* 2001; Niemeyer 2004).[1] Public administrators might also seek to overcome some of the limitations of conventional modes of community involvement (such as opinion polls and pressure group politics), by experimenting with new participatory processes (Hendriks 2002; Reddel and Woolcock 2003).

## Who participates in policy evaluation, and how?

It would be a mistake to interpret participatory policy evaluation as a process in which relevant experts work together to reach a consensus on the "effectivenes" of a policy or program. What this approach bypasses is the important democratic argument underlying participatory policy evaluation; that the evaluative process (and its outcome) is legitimate to the extent that it engages those who might be affected by the policy in a process of informed public deliberation (Dryzek 2000).

One common way to include potentially affected populations in policy evaluation is to target "stakeholder" groups (e.g. Guba and Lincoln 1989). This term is typically reserved for identifiable groups or organizations that have expressed an interest in a policy issue, program, or proposal. Stakeholders might also be entities that have useful knowledge or perspectives, or the power and resources to block or promote policy change. Stakeholder engagement of this kind carries many of the democratic dangers associated with interest group pluralism—most notably that it tends to privilege institutionalized, well-organized and well-funded interests (Lowi 1969; Olson 1965). In practice, stakeholder forms of participation tend to restrict debate to a select group of elites and policy entrepreneurs (Curtain 2006; Hunold and Young 1998).

To address this mobilization bias, some scholars stress the importance of policy analysts listening to a diversity of voices including the under-represented and marginalized (Dryzek 2010; Fischer 2000; Forester 1999). A similar idea is promoted by those working from the perspective of public value who explicitly stress the need for broader public input beyond special interest groups and experts. For example, Horner *et al.* (2006: 19) argue that the goal should be "about placing individuals as citizens centre stage of decision-making so that public resources best serve the public's needs and not the self-interest of public managers, professionals or the interest of one particular group of citizens." Other scholars have been motivated to make emerging forms of network governance (which typically involve public, private, and nongovernment representatives) more inclusive of everyday citizens (Bingham *et al.* 2005; Hendriks 2008).

Clearly for any given policy issue or program there is a variety of relevant communities and groups. These publics will be constituted by the particular focus of the evaluation process, as is the case with all participatory projects (Barnes *et al.*, 2003). It can be useful to think about how different categories of "publics" might be called upon to contribute to different stages of the evaluation process. Such categories might include (adapted from Salter, 2007):

1 interest groups (including powerful and marginalized groups);
2 specific communities (particular socio-economic, user or disaffected groups);

3 elite stakeholders (businesses, experts, think tanks, consultants);
4 broader public (lay public, "users", taxpayers); and
5 government officials and departments.

The question of how these various publics might practically engage in policy evaluation is less straightforward. There is no shortage of participatory mechanisms available for engaging different kinds of publics in policy issues (Fung 2006a; Gastil and Levine 2005; Roberts 2004; Smith 2009). Participatory methods are often categorized in terms of a ladder or spectrum of public participation where mechanisms vary in purpose ranging from informing (for example, open days, websites and education campaigns) through to feedback and consultation (for example, surveys, focus groups, and public hearings), through to more interactive and collaborative processes (for example, advisory committees, citizens' juries and partnerships) (see Head 2007; IAP2 2007). In practice, the most common approach to public involvement in policy evaluation is to invite feedback or comments from the public, for example through surveys, focus groups, submissions, and public hearings. In most of these processes, participation is not particularly interactive and the scope for broader public input is limited. In some cases participatory processes are attached to more formal evaluation processes involving experts, such as advisory committees and inquiries (see Marier: Chapter 30).

In the following sections, I discuss two traditional modes of eliciting public input that are particularly prevalent in policy evaluation—satisfaction surveys and public meetings. I then take a brief look at some of the more innovative approaches to public involvement that emphasize inclusion and public deliberation. To be clear, my purpose here is not to provide a comprehensive survey of different participatory mechanisms, but rather to get a taste of their diversity, and discuss some of the broader policy and political issues that their use in policy evaluation raises.

## Citizen surveys

Citizen- or client-focused surveys constitute a common means to seek feedback on the performance of policy program, department, or initiative. There are different varieties but the most common format is a satisfaction survey that uses standard survey research methodology where participants are selected using random sampling and contacted either by mail or phone. In some cases, citizen satisfaction might be explored using more interactive methods such as focus groups.

Satisfaction surveys are not particularly new to public administration but their popularity has increased since the 1990s with the greater focus on customer-centered service delivery (Osborne and Gaebler 1992). In this sense, surveys are seen as a way for public managers to gain insight into how to improve their services to better meet the needs of their clients and customers (Kelly 2005). Satisfaction surveys also sit well with the discourse on more "evidence-based" policy-making because they produce "evidence" from a technique largely viewed as methodologically rigorous (Howard 2010).

There has also been a trend toward using citizen surveys as a benchmarking tool to track how citizens' satisfaction levels with public services change over time. In this respect Canada's *Citizens First* survey has become a particularly influential model that has been replicated around the world, providing public managers with data on program effectiveness and citizen demands.[2] Since 1998 Canadian governments have sought the opinions of thousands of citizens on public services in biennial surveys (for a critical perspective, see Howard 2010).

Satisfaction surveys are an attractive and popular tool for bringing the public into policy evaluation. They provide a quick barometer of users and their expectations of public services. However, such surveys represent shallow forms of citizen input, and are a long way from the kind of participatory or deliberative evaluation that some advocate (e.g. Majone 1989). A central problem is that citizens are given a narrow and passive role as a consumer; it also not always clear who these consumers are, and how to find them (Howard 2010). Evaluation surveys of this kind also focus respondents on questions about whether they are satisfied with a particular service, but not about broader issues such as their expectations for what the public service should do, how services should be delivered/provided and who should use them (Horner *et al.* 2006).

The data from citizen surveys has often been used to inform education campaigns rather than as a useful external measure of performance. So, for example, where citizens' level of satisfaction with a service is much lower than the "objective" administrative performance data—a common response by public managers is to better inform citizens on quality of services (Kelly and Swindell 2002). More problematic is that satisfaction surveys assume that "personal experience and indeed self-interest is the sole determinant of a user's evaluation of a service" (Horner *et al.*, 2006, p. 20). As a result they can unintentionally encourage particular public sector reforms that are focused on customer service delivery, such as the expansion of consumer choice and the increasing use of private sector providers (Howard 2010).

## Public meetings and hearings

Another prolific form of public involvement used in policy evaluation is the public meeting. In a typical public meeting, citizens and affected groups are invited to an open gathering to provide feedback on a specific policy issue, project, or proposal. Usually participation is open to anyone to attend, and the entire proceedings are ostensibly "public"—though size typically limits numbers (Snider 2003). Meetings vary in their formality, but the general structure involves a public audience facing a panel of experts and officials, who may deliver a formal or technical presentation. Following this, most public meetings allow members of the public to stand up and briefly voice their opinion. Dialogue is typically discouraged both between citizens, as well as between citizens and officials (Adams 2004).

Some public meetings might be part of a formal policy evaluation process such as a public inquiry. In such cases, public meetings that are legally required are referred to as public hearings. In some countries such as Canada, public hearings are a regular part of formal public inquiries (see Chapter 30). But as Salter (2007) points out hearings vary considerably depending on how the public is constituted. Some public hearings call on stakeholder representatives to engage in a process of interest negotiation, while others invite general members of the public to give personal testimonies or offer community expertise.

Public meetings remain a popular and often mandated form of public involvement in many Western democracies (Baker *et al.* 2005; McComas 2001; Snider 2003). Their practice is also increasing in more authoritarian contexts such as China (Zhong and Mol 2008). A recent variety in the UK and Australia is the use of community cabinets where ministers visit different locations in their jurisdictions to take questions from the community (Marsh *et al.* 2010; Reddel and Woolcock 2003).

Despite their prolific use, public meetings do not enjoy a good reputation (Heberlein 1976; Kathelene and Martin 1991). The primary criticism of public hearings is that citizens rarely influence policy decisions. They are often performed as a minimalist mode of participation where the focus is on transferring information to citizens rather than consideration of input from the public. In many cases, meetings are timed too late in the decision-making process where there is little room to take citizens' concerns or ideas into account. For this reason, public meetings are often experienced as forums for community venting, or opportunities for proponents to announce and defend policies (King *et al.* 1998: 322). Some argue that public meetings are hollow democratic rituals for manufacturing legitimacy (Topal 2009).

The participants of public meetings are also criticized on the grounds that they are unrepresentative of the broader community (Roberts 2004). A common observation is that meetings are typically occupied by people from organized interest groups; and the discussion dominated by the articulate and those with the most intense feelings (for an overview, see Williamson and Fung 2004).

Public meetings and hearings are also not particularly deliberative events. Much of their time is dedicated to technical presentations or speeches. Public input is typically restricted to short comment sessions in which there is limited or no opportunity for an exchange of arguments. Agendas are typically set in advance and the scope of discussion tightly controlled by the commissioning body. The structure of public meetings also tends to foster adversarial conditions. For example, contributors from the public typically stand at microphones at the front of the room facing officials with their backs to the other public participants (Williamson and Fung 2004).

While public meetings may not be a useful way for citizens to deliberate or directly influence policy decisions, some scholars argue that they provide an opportunity for citizens to perform a number of other political functions. Empirical research finds that public meetings enable citizens: (1) to send information and signals to decision-makers and the media; (2) to publically support or shame public officials; (3) to set the policy agenda; (4) to delay decisions; and (5) to form networks (Adams 2004). Unlike more structured consultative or deliberative forums (discussed below), public meetings are open events for anyone to attend, and therefore carry opportunities for citizens to employ advocacy tactics and political manoeuvring (Adams 2004). In this sense, public meetings fulfill an important democratic role in the policy system by encouraging public accountability and government responsiveness (Adams 2004; Snider 2003). Others speculate that public meetings might promote positive rituals that reaffirm civic values and encourage social cohesion (McComas *et al.* 2010).

Over the past decade, various improvements to public meetings have been proposed (e.g. see Baker *et al.* 2005), including incorporating more deliberative elements (McComas *et al.* 2010), linking them more closely to other forms of citizen engagement (Adams 2004), and utilizing new forms of information technology to make them more accessible, transparent, and publicly accountable (Snider 2003).

## Innovative forms of public engagement

Many of the limitations identified above with conventional approaches to public engagement have given rise to a host of innovative ways to involve different publics more deeply and meaningfully in policy issues. A particular emphasis of this innovation has been to diversify the kinds of participants that engage and their level of participation. I focus here on procedures that engage everyday citizens in a process of extensive public deliberation. Typically, the citizens' deliberations are independently facilitated, and informed by input from experts and other policy actors. The essence of the deliberative process is that the discussions and emerging recommendations are based on a thorough consideration of all the arguments in view of the public interest (Hendriks 2011).

The most popular deliberative process, particularly for local governments, is the citizens' jury, which typically brings together a panel of approximately 20 randomly selected citizens for several days to deliberate on a particular policy issue (Crosby and Nethercut 2005). Bigger events such as deliberative polls can engage hundreds of people in policy deliberations by combining small and large group discussions (Fishkin 2009). Even larger is the 21st Century Town Meeting model in which thousands of people can participate (often in multiple venues) with the aid of networked computers and polling key pads (Lukensmeyer *et al.* 2005). Participants work in small groups of around ten but are also collectively linked up to a central database for large-scale dialogues. Some innovative deliberative procedures, such as citizens' assemblies have been specifically designed to connect to formal institutions of representative democracy, such as parliaments and referenda (Warren and Pearse 2008).

Deliberative forms of public participation have been applied in most Western democracies on a range of issues including urban planning, energy, gene technology, health care, housing, nuclear waste, consumer protection, and indigenous affairs (Gastil and Levine 2005; Goodin and Dryzek 2006; Hajer 2005; Hendriks 2005; Johnson 2009; Parkinson 2004).

Notwithstanding the growth of deliberative governance, its practice faces some significant challenges. One of the key limitations with deliberative procedures to date is their lack of institutionalization. In practice surprisingly few deliberative projects are connected to, and have an impact on, existing governance arrangements (e.g. Goodin and Dryzek 2006). The most well-documented case is the British Columbia citizens' assembly which considered electoral reform (Warren and Pearse 2008). Limited institutionalization has implications for the sustainability of public deliberation because it relies on actors outside the state to instigate and fund projects (Williamson and Fung 2004). Indeed, the most innovative participatory projects (in terms of outreach and scale) in the United States, and in Australia have been instigated and funded by various non-state actors such as foundations, academics, entrepreneurs, think tanks and nongovernmental organizations (NGOs). But the promotion of public deliberation by non-state actors can be viewed as an important part of democratizing the policy process. Indeed these participatory projects represent "insisted spaces" used by non-state actors to build community capacity or evaluate projects or their own internal decision-making processes (Carson 2008).

Another important limitation of deliberative governance is that its practice does not typically extend into the realm of policy evaluation. To date most deliberative forms of public engagement have been used in the early stages of policy development, for example, to assist citizens to define policy problems and/or to develop future policy scenarios or prioritize policy options (Hartz-Karp 2005). Typically citizens have limited opportunity to deliberate on the effectiveness of a particular policy program and its implementation. Indeed, there are only a few documented cases where the deliberative process has given citizens the opportunity to not only set the policy agenda, but also to monitor and evaluate progress on proposed strategies or goals. For example, Fung (2003) describes a community policing project in Chicago in which there were extensive ongoing deliberations with opportunities for participants to review policies and recommend changes. A number of participatory budgeting projects have also provided opportunities for citizens to evaluate policy programs in the context of allocating and monitoring funds for local infrastructure and public services (Baiocchi 2005; Johnson 2009).

Innovative forms of public engagement have also taken place on the web in the form of e-governance. Governments are increasingly placing services online and encouraging citizens to provide feedback. Social media technologies such as Twitter and Facebook have opened up communication channels (though mostly one-way) for agencies to communicate with their constituents. Some departments now conduct web-based surveys, but these tend to replicate many of the problems with traditional surveys as discussed above (Robbins *et al.* 2008). For this reason there has been some experimentation with more interactive forms of online engagement where discussion is facilitated (Boner *et al.* 2005).

A growing number of government agencies have also been championing the application of collaborative web technologies (web 2.0) such as wikis and social networking platforms as a means to promote more open, accountable and responsive government (e.g. Government 2.0

Taskforce 2009). While these "crowd sourcing" approaches offer new interfaces for citizens to learn more about, and possibly engage in, government activities, there is the danger that they offer only a limited form of "e-engagement" among groups of like-minded people (Lubensky 2009).

The Internet offers a number of opportunities for expanding who engages in participatory processes, and how. Web technology has also been used effectively to complement face-to-face deliberative processes (Hartz-Karp 2005). Notwithstanding the potential of the Internet for enhancing public participation, its use to date in public agencies has been mostly about enhancing customer service as opposed to consultation and engagement (Dutil *et al.* 2007). Indeed the long-term danger, particularly for policy evaluation is that opportunities for public engagement are filled with shallow forms of e-governance that seek limited customer and client feedback rather than considered input from citizens.

## Pursuing participatory policy evaluation

The expansion of participatory governance over the past decade has gone largely unnoticed by the literature on policy evaluation. Instead the role of participation in evaluation has been construed in narrow terms through the lens of performance management where public engagement is limited to one-way modes of involvement, such as citizen satisfaction surveys.

Yet as this chapter has shown *ex post* policy evaluation can be greatly enriched by the application of more innovative forms of public participation. Processes that emphasize inclusion and deliberation can help to elicit important perspectives on policy programs and agencies, and expose relevant arguments, perspectives, and values to public scrutiny. Participation can also help public managers to negotiate the increasing complexity of policy issues by bringing those affected by policies into the evaluation process. Most importantly the inclusion of affected publics helps to secure the democratic legitimacy of an evaluative process and its outcomes.

Participation, however, poses a number of challenges for policy evaluation. First, drawing more voices into the evaluation process can intensify the politics of an evaluation program. While all forms of policy evaluation involve competing actors "framing, blaming and credit claiming" (Bovens *et al.* 2006: 323), opening the process up to more inclusive and deliberative forms of participation risks intensifying contestation. This is especially the case when participation is extended to everyday citizens, whose perspectives may not be considered valid or legitimate. Greater deliberation in policy evaluation is likely to be resisted by powerful actors who benefit from the status quo or those who are keen to keep issues out of the public spotlight (Hendriks 2002, 2011). It also needs to be recognized that not all services and issues are amenable to direct citizen engagement and participation. Fair and open dialogue will be difficult in those contexts where there is a sense of policy failure, crisis or declining trust (Bovens *et al.* 2006).

The second challenge concerns the common criticism that public participation is too often tokenistic and unsustainable. Many participatory efforts represent one-off projects that are poorly integrated into existing governance arrangements and institutions (Williamson and Fung 2004). Evaluation processes are especially vulnerable in this respect because they are often outsourced to independent bodies. Moreover, it is not uncommon for the one agency or policy to be evaluated multiple times resulting in piecemeal and disconnected recommendations (Bovens *et al.* 2006). The challenge with any participatory evaluation is to ensure that it is connected to other forms of evaluation and the broader institutions of governance. It is also important that any participatory evaluation is situated in an overall strategy for public engagement that targets a range of policy actors using different processes.

Third, participation can generate tensions and complexities for public managers. One core challenge is trying to reconcile the public's desire for greater involvement while at the same time attempting to be an authoritative voice or decision-maker (Yang and Callahan 2007). Public managers also face constraints within their organizations, for example they are often unable to choose the way they engage with the community, since "the mandate and powers of their agency shape purpose and practice" (Stewart 2009b: 49). As a result, many participatory activities are outsourced to private consultants, which has implications for public sector accountability (see Speers 2007) and the sustainability of public engagement more generally (see Hendriks and Carson 2008; Williamson and Fung 2004). The broader challenge here is that participatory policy evaluation requires a shift in the way bureaucracies authorize, manage and demonstrate accountability (Goetz and Gaventa 2001).

Participation also requires public managers to accommodate alternative forms of knowledge that typically do not sit well alongside more traditional evaluation approaches which produce quantitative data with seemingly "definitive" results. Ultimately, the outputs from any evaluation process involving participation must compete with the findings emerging from other more traditional forms of policy evaluation. In the process of judging different arguments, the validity of citizens' preferences can often be called into question, and labeled as too impressionistic, irrational, or idiosyncratic (Hendriks 2011; Yang and Callahan 2007). The challenge for public managers is to ensure that citizens' input into an evaluation process receives equal consideration alongside the perspectives of elites and lobby groups.

In order to tackle these and other challenges, the field of public administration needs to better equip its practitioners with skills for undertaking participatory forms of governance (Bingham *et al.* 2005; OECD 2001). New skills and incentive structures are required to help practitioners expand their participatory efforts in evaluation beyond citizen surveys towards more inclusive and deliberative approaches. Skills are also needed to not only manage and conduct participation, but also to effectively communicate its limits and constraints. As Stewart suggests (2009b: 49): "Engagement is about understanding where people are coming from and making sure they know which of their concerns might (or might not) be affected as a result of their participation."

Deepening the role of participation in policy evaluation offers an important opportunity to democratize the policy process. After all evaluation is the stage where the effectiveness of policy programs are assessed, and the site where new ideas and agendas are formed. Thus widening and deepening public involvement in the policy evaluation process will enrich the conclusions reached, and ultimately their legitimacy.

## Notes

1 By "deliberative" here I mean an interactive form of communication in which participants provide reasons for their positions, listen to the arguments of others, and are open to changing their position in view of the better argument (Dryzek 2000).

2 For more, see Institute for Citizen Centre Service (ICCS), available at: http://www.iccs-isac.org/en/cf/

## Bibliography


Adams, B. 2004. 'Public meetings and the democratic process', *Public Administration Review* 64(1): 43–54.

Alford, J. and J. O'Flynn. 2009. 'Making sense of public value: Concepts, critques and emergent meanings', *International Journal of Public Administration* 32(3): 171–91.

Althaus, C., P. Bridgman and G. Davis. 2007. *The Australian Policy Handbook*. Crows Nest: Allen and Unwin.

Baiocchi, G. 2005. *Militants and Citizens: The Politics of Participatory Democracy in Porto Alegre*. Stanford, CA: Stanford University Press.

Baker, W.H., H.L. Addams and B. Davis. 2005. 'Critical factors for enhancing municipal public hearings', *Public Administration Review* 65(4): 490–9.

Barnes, M., J. Newman, A. Knops and H. Sullivan. 2003. 'Constituting "the public" in public participation', *Public Administration* 81(2): 379–99.

Benington, J. 2009. 'Creating the public in order to create public value?', *International Journal of Public Administration* 32(2): 232–49.

Bingham, L.B., T. Nabatchi and R.O. Leary. 2005. 'The new governance: Practices and processes for stakeholder and citizen participation in the work of government', *Public Administration Review* 65(5): 547.

Blalock, A.B. 1999. 'Evaluation reseach and the performance management movement: From estrangement to useful integration?', *Evaluation* 5(2): 117–49.

Boner, P.A., R. Carlitz, R. Gunn, L.E. Maak and C.A. Ratliff. 2005. 'Bringing the public and government together through online dialogues', in J. Gastil and P. Levine (eds) *The Deliberative Democracy Handbook: Strategies for Effective Civic Engagement in the 21st Century*. San Francisco: Jossey-Bass, 141–53.

Bovens, M., P. 't Hart and S. Kuipers. 2006. 'The politics of policy evaluation', in M. Moran, M. Rein and R.E. Goodin (eds) *The Oxford Handbook of Public Policy*. Oxford: Oxford University Press, 319–35.

Callahan, K. 2000. 'Performance measurement and citizen participation', in M. Holzer and S. Lee (eds) *Public Productivity Handbook*, 2nd edn. New York: Marcel Dekker.

Carson, L. 2008. 'Creating democratic surplus through citizens' assemblies', *Journal of Public Deliberation* 4(1): Article 5. Available at: http://services.bepress.com/jpd/vol4/iss1/art5/

——, S. White, C. Hendriks and J. Palmer. 2002. 'Community consultation in environmental policy making', *The Drawing Board: An Australian Review of Public Affairs* 3(1): 1–13.

Crosby, N. and D. Nethercut. 2005. 'Citizens juries: Creating a trustworthy voice of the people', in J. Gastil and P. Levine (eds) *The Deliberative Democracy Handbook: Strategies for Effective Civic Engagement in the Twenty-First Century*. San Francisco: Jossey Bass, 111–19.

Curtain, R. 2006. 'Engaging citizens to solve major public challenges', in H.K. Colebatch (ed.) *Beyond the Policy Cycle: The Policy Process in Australia*. Crows Nest: Allen and Unwin, 121–42.

Dryzek, J.S. 2000. *Deliberative Democracy and Beyond: Liberals, Critics, Contestations*. Oxford: Oxford University Press.

—— 2010. *Foundations and Frontiers of Deliberative Governance*. Oxford: Oxford University Press.

Dutil, P.A., C. Howard, J. Langford and J. Roy. 2007. 'Rethinking government-public relationships in a digital world', *Journal of Information Technology and Politics* 4(1): 77–90.

Einsiedel, E.F., E. Jelsøe and T. Breck, T. 2001. 'Publics at the technology table: The Australian, Canadian and Danish Consensus Conferences on Food Biotechnology', *Public Understanding of Science* 10(1): 83–98.

Fischer, F. 1995. *Evaluating Public Policy*. Chicago: Nelson Hall.

—— 2000. *Citizens, Experts, and the Environment*. Durham, NC: Duke University.

—— and J. Forester (eds). 1993. *The Argumentative Turn in Policy Analysis and Planning*. Durham, NC: Duke University Press.

Fishkin, J. 2009. *When the People Speak: Deliberative Democracy and Public Consultation*. Oxford: Oxford University Press.

Forester, J. 1999. *The Deliberative Practitioner: Encouraging Participatory Planning Processes*. Cambridge, MA: The MIT Press.

Fung, A. 2003. 'Deliberative democracy, Chicago style: Grass-roots governance in policing and public education', in A. Fung and E.O. Wright (eds) *Deepening Democracy: Institutional Innovation in Empowered Participatory Governance*. London: Verso, 111–43.

—— 2006a. 'Varieties of participation in complex governance', *Public Administration Review* 66(1) (supplementary): 66–75.

—— 2006b. 'Democratising the policy process', in M. Moran, M. Rein and R.E. Goodin (eds) *The Oxford Handbook of Public Policy*. Oxford: Oxford University Press, 669–85.

Gastil, J. and P. Levine. (eds). 2005. *The Deliberative Democracy Handbook: Strategies for Effective Civic Engagement in the Twenty-First Century*. San Francisco: Jossey-Bass.

Goetz, A.M. and J. Gaventa. 2001. *Bringing Citizen Voice and Client Focus into Service Delivery*, IDS Working Paper 138. Brighton: Institute of Development Studies.

Goodin, R.E. and J. Dryzek. 2006. 'Deliberative impacts: The macro-political uptake of mini-publics', *Politics and Society* 34(2): 219–44.

Government 2.0 Taskforce. 2009. *Engage: Getting on with Government 2.0*. Canberra: Commonwealth of Australia.

Guba, E.G. and V.S. Lincoln. 1989. *Fourth Generation Policy Evaluation*. Newbury Park, CA: Sage.

Hajer, M. 2005. 'Rebuilding Ground Zero. The politics of performance', *Planning Theory and Practice* 6(4): 445–64.

—— and H. Wagenaar. 2003a. 'Introduction', in M. Hajer and H. Wagenaar (eds) *Deliberative Policy Analysis: Understanding Governance in the Network Society*. Cambridge: Cambridge University Press, pp. 1–30.

—— and H. Wagenaar. (eds). 2003b. *Deliberative Policy Analysis: Understanding Governance in the Network Society*. Cambridge: Cambridge University Press.

Halachimi, A. and M. Holzer. 2010. 'Citizen participation and performance measurement: Operationalising democracy through better accountability', *Public Administration Quarterly* 34(3): 378–99.

Hartz-Karp, J. 2005. 'A case study in deliberative democracy: Dialogue with the city', *Journal of Public Deliberation* 1(1): Article 6. Available at: http://services.bepress.com/jpd/vol1/iss1/art6.

Head, B. 2007. 'Community engagement: Participation on whose terms?', *Australian Journal of Political Science* 42(3): 441–54.

Heberlein, T.A. 1976. 'Some observations on alternative mechanisms for public involvement: The hearing, the public opinion poll, the workshop and the quasi-experiment', *Natural Resources Journal* 16: 197–212.

Heikkila, T. and K.R. Isett. 2007. 'Citizen involvement and performance management in special-purpose governments', *Public Administration Review* 67(2): 238.

Hendriks, C.M. 2002. 'Institutions of deliberative democratic processes and interest groups: Roles, tensions and incentives', *Australian Journal of Public Administration* 61(1): 64–75.

—— 2005. 'Participatory storylines and their impact on deliberative forums', *Policy Sciences* 38(4): 1–20.

—— 2008. 'On inclusion and network governance: the democratic disconnect of Dutch energy transitions', *Public Administration* 86(4): 1009–31.

—— 2011. *The Politics of Public Deliberation: Citizen Engagement and Interest Advocacy*. London: Palgrave Macmillan.

—— and L. Carson. 2008. 'Can the market help the forum? Negotiating the commercialization of deliberative democracy', *Policy Sciences* 41(4): 293–313.

Ho, A.T. 2005. 'Citizen participation in performance management', in R.C. Box (ed.) *Democracy and Public Administration*. Armonk, NY: M.E. Sharpe.

Holzer, M. and K. Kloby. 2005a. 'Sustaining citizen-driven performance improvement: models for adoption and issues of sustainability', *The Innovation Journal: The Public Sector Innovation Journal* 10: 1–20.

—— and K. Kloby. 2005b. 'Public performance measurement: An assessment of the state-of-the-art and models for citizen participation', *International Journal of Productivity and Performnce Management* 54(7): 517–32.

Horner, L., R. Lekhi and R. Blaug. 2006. *Deliberative Democracy and the Role of Public Managers*. London: The Work Foundation.

Howard, C. 2010. 'Are we being served? A critical perspective on Canada's Citizens First satisfaction surveys', *International Review of Administrative Sciences* 76: 65–83.

Hunold, C. and I.M. Young. 1998. 'Justice, democracy and hazardous siting', *Political Studies*, 46(1): 82–95.

IAP2. 2007. 'IAP2 Spectrum of public participaton' (International Association for Public Participation (IAP2). Available at: http://iap2.org/associations/4748/files/IAP2 Spectrum_vertical.pdf (accessed 6 January 2009).

Johnson, G.F. 2009. 'Deliberative democratic practices in Canada: An analysis of institutional empowerment in three cases', *Canadian Journal of Political Science* 42(3): 679–703.

Jørgensen, T.B. and B. Bozeman. 2007. 'Public values: An inventory', *Administration and Society* 39(3): 354–81.

Kathelene, L. and J. Martin. 1991. 'Enhancing citizen participation: Panel designs, perspectives and policy formulation', *Policy Analysis and Management* 10(1): 46–63.

Kelly, J.M. 2005. 'The dilemma of the unsatisfied customer in a market model of public administration', *Public Administration Review* 65(1): 76.

—— and D. Swindell. 2002. 'A multiple-indicator approach to municipal service evaluation: Correlating performance measurement and citizen satisfaction across jurisdictions', *Public Administration Review* 62(5): 610.

Kickert, W.J.M., E.-H. Klijn and J.F.M. Koppenjan. (eds). 1997. *Managing Complex Networks: Strategies for the Public Sector*. London: Sage.

King, C.S., K.M. Feltey and B.O.N. Susel. 1998. 'The question of participation: Toward authentic public participation in public administration', *Public Administration Review* 58(4): 317–26.

Kooiman, J. (ed.). 1993. *Modern Governance: New Government: Society Interactions*. London: Sage.

Koppenjan, J. and E.-H. Klijn. 2004. *Managing Uncertainties in Networks: A Network Approach to Problem Solving and Decision Making*. London: Routledge.

Lowi, T.J. 1969. *The End of Liberalism: The Second Republic of the United States*, 2nd edn. New York: Norton.

Lubensky, R. 2009. Submission to Government 2.0 Taskforce (Canberra). Available at: http://gov2.net.au/submissions/ron-lubensky/.

Lukensmeyer, C.J., J. Goldman and S. Brigham. 2005. 'A town meeting for the twenty-first century', in J. Gastil and P. Levine (eds) *The Deliberative Democracy Handbook: Strategies for Effective Civic Engagement in the 21st Century*. San Francisco: Jossey-Bass, 154–63.

McComas, K.A. 2001. 'Theory and practice of public meetings', *Communication Theory* 11(1): 36–55.

——, J.C. Besley and L.W. Black. 2010. 'The rituals of public meetings', *Public Administration Review* 70(1): 122–30.

Majone, G. 1989. *Evidence, Argument and Persuassion in the Policy Process*. New Haven, CT: Yale University Press.

Marsh, D., C. Lewis and P. Fawcett. 2010. 'Citizen-centred policy making under Rudd: Network governance in the shadow of heirarchy?', in C. Aulich and M. Evans (eds) *The Rudd Government: Australian Commonwealth Government 2007–2010*. Canberra: ANU E-press, 143–60.

Moore, M. 1995. *Creating Public Value: Strategic Management in Government*. Cambridge, MA: Harvard University Press.

Niemeyer, S. 2004. 'Deliberation in the wilderness: Displacing symbolic politics', *Environmental Politics* 13(2): 347–72.

O'Faircheallaigh, C. 2002. *A New Approach to Policy Evaluation: Mining and Indigenous People*. Aldershot: Ashgate.

OECD. 2001. *Citizens as Partners: Information, Consultation and Public Participation*. Paris: OECD.

—— 2009. *Focus on Citizens: Public Engagement for Better Policy and Services*. Paris: OECD.

Olson, M. 1965. *The Logic of Collective Action: Public Goods and the Theory of Groups*. Cambridge, MA: Harvard University Press.

Osborne, D. and T. Gaebler. 1992. *Reinventing Government*. New York: Plume.

Parkinson, J. 2004. 'Why deliberate? The encounter between deliberation and new public managers', *Public Administration* 82(2): 377–95.

—— 2006. *Deliberating in the Real World: Problems of Legitimacy in Deliberative Democracy*. Oxford Oxford University Press.

Putnam, R.D. 1993. *Making Democracy Work: Civic Traditions in Modern Italy*. Princeton, NJ: Princeton University Press.

Reddel, T. and G. Woolcock. 2003. 'From consultation to participatory governance? A critical review of citizen engagement strategies in Queensland', *Australian Journal of Public Administration* 63(3): 75–87.

Renn, O., T. Webler and P. Wiedemann (eds). 1995. *Fairness and Competence in Citizen Participation*. Dordrecht: Kluwer.

Robbins, M.D., B. Simonsen and B. Feldman. 2008. 'Citizens and resource allocation: Improving decision making with interactive web-based citizen participation', *Public Administration Review* 68(3): 564.

Roberts, N. 2004. 'Public deliberation in an age of direct citizen participation', *American Review of Public Administration* 34(4): 315–53.

Salter, L. 2007. 'The public of public inquiries', in L. Dobuzinskis, M. Howlett and D. Laycock (eds) *Policy Analysis in Canada*. Toronto: University of Toronto, 291–314.

Schneider, A.L. and H. Ingram. 1997. *Policy Design for Democracy*. Lawrence, KS: University of Kansas.

Smith, G. 2009. *Democratic Innovations: Designing Institutions for Citizen Participation*. Cambridge: Cambridge University Press.

Snider, J.H. 2003. 'Should the public meeting enter the information age?', *National Civic Review*, 92(3): 20–9.

Speers, K. 2007. 'The invisible private sector: Consultants and public policy in Canada', in L. Dobuzinskis, M. Howlett and D. Laycock (eds) *Policy Analysis in Canada*. Toronto: University of Toronto, 399–422.

Stewart, J. 2009a. *Public Policy Values*. London: Palgrave Macmillan.

—— 2009b. *The Dilemmas of Engagement: The Role of Consultation in Governance*. Canberra: Australian New Zealand School of Government and ANU E-Press. Available at: http://epress.anu.edu.au/dilemmas_citation.html.

Topal, C. 2009. 'The construction of general public interest: Risk, legitimacy and power in a public hearing', *Organization Studies* 30(2–3): 277–300.

Wanna, J. 2009. 'Collaborative government: Meanings, dimension, drivers and outcomes', in J. O'Flynn and J. Wanna (eds) *Collaborative Governance: A New Era of Public Policy in Australia?* Canberra: ANU EPress, 3–12. Available at http://epress.anu.edu.au/anzsog/collab_gov/pdf/whole_book.pdf

Warren, M. and H. Pearse. (eds). 2008. *Designing Deliberative Democracy: The British Columbia Citizens' Assembly*. Cambridge: Cambridge University Press.

Williamson, A. and A. Fung. 2004. 'Public deliberation: Where we are and where can we go?', *National Civic Review*, winter.

Yang, K. and K. Callahan. 2007. 'Citizen involvement efforts and bureaucratic responsiveness: Participatory values, stakeholder pressures, and administrative practicality', *Public Administrative Review* March/April: 249–64.

Zhong, L.J. and A.P.J. Mol. 2008. 'Participatory environmental governance in China: Public hearings on urban water tariff setting', *Journal of Environmental Management* 88(4): 899–913.

# Part IX

## Policy dynamics

### Patterns of stability and change

# 33

# Policy dynamics and change

## The never-ending puzzle

*Giliberto Capano*

## Understanding policy change in order to grasp policy dynamics

Public policy is a dynamic phenomenon. This means not only that policies are intrinsically processual, but also that as a whole they are not the simple sum of their individual parts (stages, actors, institutions, time, instruments, etc); at the same time their parts are variously interlinked via a dense web of interconnections, the nature, dynamics and effects of which should not be taken for granted. The world of policy dynamics is an incredibly fascinating puzzle of which scholars are constantly striving to discover the basic elements and reliable, regular patterns. It is precisely because of their dynamic nature that policies may appear at one and the same time both stable and changing. However, stability and change are a product of observers' viewpoints. They depend on which analytical categories are used, and on what observers are actually looking for. The same element of dynamics, or the same time span, in the historical development of a policy may appear either stable or characterized by significant changes. The different theoretical perspectives cannot, however, hide the dynamic nature of public policy, and the difficulties encountered in trying to explain its underlying features. Moreover, those scholars who assume that policies are characterized by long periods of stability have to admit that in the end these same policies change, possibly in a dramatic, radical manner, and they often struggle to explain such structural movements. On the other hand, those who assume that the dynamic character of policy means that it continuously changes, albeit from another point of view, have to deal with a complex, multifaceted, evasive set of questions.

The truth is that in order to understand policy dynamics, the analytical focus has to be directed towards change. As Heraclitus stated, "everything flows": change is a feature of human development, and also of social and political phenomena. The same is true of public policies: they are "moving events, routines, strategies, and adaptations" (Heclo 1972: 83). In the policy field, as in politics, change is the norm (Lewis and Steinmo 2010), so to say that "all policy is policy change" (Hogwood and Peters 1983) is not a provocation or a symbolic metaphor, but an inexorable fact.

Change is the normal status of policy-making, whereas stability is simply contingent upon human agency (through rules, institutions, social norms, ideas, etc.) striving to control environmental uncertainty (Blyth 2011). However, this collective effort is not always coherent, and is very often conflictual (because different actors have different ideas about what constitutes stability), and thus the stability of public policy is simple a partial, static point of equilibrium in policy dynamics. From this point of view, studying policy dynamics means developing, from both theoretical and empirical points of view, patterns of policy change over time.

All theoretical attempts made to explain the puzzle of policy change have to deal with certain fundamental issues which may be summarized as follows.

First of all, there is a set of basic questions. What has really changed? How do policies change? When do they change? Why do they change? (Capano 2009). These questions focus on the fundamental elements that every scholar interested in solving the puzzle of policy dynamics has to face up to, namely: (1) the definition of what change is at stake (the dependent variable problem); (2) an understanding of how policy change develops (the logic of change direction); (3) the explanation of why policy change occurs (the causality problem); and (4) the reasons for the timing of change.

Second, all efforts to explain policy have to identify its fundamental causal mechanisms (also perceived as the drivers, generators, motors of change).

Third, all theoretical frameworks have to deal with the problem of the role of agency in policy change (are actors really agents of change, or are they simply tools in the hands of structural factors?).

The most important frameworks present in studies of policy dynamics—including the Advocacy Coalition Framework (ACF) (Sabatier and Jenkins-Smith 1993; Sabatier and Weible 2007), the Punctuated Equilibrium Framework (PEF) (Baumgartner and Jones 2002, 2009; Baumgartner *et al.* 2009), the Multiple Stream Approach (MSA) (Kingdon 1984; Zahariadis 2003), the Path Dependence Framework (PDF) (Mahoney 2000; Pierson 2000, 2004), the Policy Generations Framework (PGF) (de Vries 2005, 2010), as well as neoinstitutionalist theories (both from the historical perspective (Streeck and Thelen 2005; Mahoney and Thelen 2010) and from the rational perspective (Ostrom 1990, 2005), have all proffered different sets of answers to the above-mentioned issues.

## The basic questions

### *The dependent variable problem*

The study of the content of policy change is a puzzle within a puzzle, since very often the object of analysis is presented in an ambiguous, unclear manner. Policies are not only dynamic, but are also composed of different elements (actors, goals, instruments, strategies, laws, plans, paradigms, preferences); furthermore, from a structural point of view, policies are multilevel processes (health policy ranges from the state level to the individual level, via an intermediate political-institutional level). So when policy change is the dependent variable, we need to clarify exactly "what" dimension of policy is under scrutiny, and "where" this is situated in the institutional arrangement. The "what" question represents the real cornerstone of all attempts to analyze policy change (although the "where" question may still be important). The "what" question is not a problem for mainstream political science, whereas policy change is simply the output of the political process. However, this perspective (which can help us to understand, for example, the content of policy decisions at the legislative level) is somewhat limited, and is not useful to those who believe in the dynamic, processual, and multilevel nature of policy-making. For policy scholars studying policy as political scientists, policy is not simply an output of the political process but is the political process itself. So, in order to resolve the question, the complex composition of policies should be disaggregated for analytical purposes (Howlett and Cashore 2009).

It is clear that this analytical disaggregation is a researcher's decision. It depends on the definition attributed to policy, and on the scientific goals of the investigation. Policy literature since the end of the 1980s has witnessed various definitions of the different components of policy, and thus of policy change, starting with the idea of tripartition, submitted by Sabatier (1988), based on the distinction between technical aspects, policy strategies, and deep policies values. Peter Hall (1993) echoed this tripartition idea, albeit from a different theoretical perspective. Cashore and Howlett (2007) proposed a sixfold taxonomy of policy elements, based on the separation between ends and goals, and the tri-cotomization of the level of abstraction through which ends and means can be dealt with (high level abstraction, program level operationalization and specific on-the-ground measures). However, none of these examples is exhaustive, since the disaggregation of the components of policies, and thus of the possible dependent variable in the case of the analysis of policy change, is based on the specific definition of what policy is, as there could be several potential lists of the constitutive components of policies. What is important here, nevertheless, is that research attempts to clearly define which dimension, aspect or element of policy is the real object of its analysis.

The game being played out here is not a simple one: due to the constitutive multidimensional nature of policies, their dynamic nature, and the unclear character of their horizontal and vertical borders, the problem of identifying the dependent variable in policy change is highly demanding, and one that needs to be dealt with while avoiding any form of reductionism. You can choose to study policy change in a specific sector by focusing on changes in instruments, or in the legislative content of policies, or in the role of policy actors; however, it is theoretically and methodologically wrong to assume that the chosen aspect perfectly represents the overall trend in that policy sector. Thus a strictly epistemological consciousness is required in order to accept that the choice of dependent variable—the way in which policy change is operationalized—does not perfectly fit with the observed general developments of policy dynamics, whereas it can help to explain a part thereof. The possible implications of the ways in which these partially explained changes can influence the rest of the dynamics in question, are a matter for further research.

## *The logic of direction problem*

The "how" problem focuses on the directionality of policy change (Nisbet 1972; Baumgartner and Jones 2002; Cashore and Howlett 2007). Policy change can be incremental or radical; linear (a coherent development of the past) or nonlinear (when a change represents a break with the past, creating a completely new situation); reversible or irreversible (Capano 2009). Obviously, these dimensions of the "how" problem are not objective, but are the researcher's intellectual construct. "How" policies change is another puzzle within a puzzle, the solution of which lies with the researcher, that is, it depends on his/her epistemological and theoretical choices. However, what needs to be underlined here is that there are no strict relations between these three dimensions of the question of "how" policy changes. For example, even though one would think of linearity as being linked with incremental dynamics, studies show that incremental processes can lead to radical, apparently irreversible, changes in the medium-/long-term nonlinear output (as all historical-institutionalist studies have shown; see Mahoney and Thelen 2010 for all).

However, at the same time, linearity and incrementalism are not logically connected with irreversible outputs (as the renewed role of governments in addressing the economy following the financial crisis of 2008 clearly shows). The same reasoning can be adopted with regard to the possible links between radical change and its irreversibility. As the PEF and PGF have shown, the punctuated developments of policy dynamics (radical changes following long periods of stability) are not necessarily irreversible, and are very often characterized by oscillation between policy choices (but against this conclusion are those historical neoinstitutionalists who adopt a path-dependent perspective). It is clear here that the temporal dimension is essential if we are to establish whether a change is linear, radical, or irreversible. However, as we shall see "tempo" is a key factor in policy dynamics and change. It is clear that a change may seem incremental if the period of time in question is very brief, whereas it can appear radical if the time span is increased. The temporal dimension makes the difference in the perception of "how" policies change. However, once again what matters is the researcher's choice: the temporal aspect of the considered change is clearly at his/her discretion. From this point of view, all debate between the incrementalist and radical perspectives, vis-à-vis policy change (as well as political change), yields very little. Given that "everything flows" in policy dynamics, in the long run everything changes radically, albeit through an incremental process. At the same time, a radical change in time t1 can open the door to the reestablishment of old policy features in time t2. From this point of view, the "how" of policy change should be contextualized from both the structural and the diachronic perspective. It is intrinsically contingent and related to the specific context in which change occurs.

## The causality problem

Why do policies change, and why do they change in a given manner? In order to answer the third fundamental question when dealing with the puzzle of policy dynamics, account must be taken of the structural complexity of policy. In fact, policy is a process, and thus the dependant variable chosen to operationalize policy change, is embedded in a flux of interrelated factors (actors, institutions, interests, routines) which influence each other; since it is a process, policy develops over time, so the same dependent variable may be affected by different factors at different times; since policy does not exist in a vacuum, but is firmly situated within a specific environment (with specific political, social, economic characteristics) there are many potential independent and intervenient variables which could influence policy change (Capano and Howlett 2009b). This structural complexity of policy dynamics cannot be understood by pursuing oversimplifications or general theories. In fact there is not only one possible way by which policies change, and there are several different possible explanations of such change. Nevertheless, recent research may help to clarify our explanations of policy change.

First of all, the complexity of policy dynamics (and the highly intricate interdependence of its components) is a structural factor inviting scholars to abandon their exogenous-driven explanations. External factors matter, obviously, but they do not directly determine policy change. Environmental changes can be facilitators or triggers of change, but the "what change" and "how policy changes" conundrums depend on the internal characteristics of the policy field affected by the external *stimuli*. So all the "external shock" hypotheses should be put aside when studying policy change. This is a real problem for the more commonly adopted explanatory frameworks: it is particularly true for the ACF and for the PEF, which assume the fundamental role of external perturbations, events, and changes in determining policy change. However, the relevance of internal dynamics as a reaction (not only in an adaptive way) to environmental pressures, has been pointed out on several occasions in the past (Mahwinney 1993; Capano 1996), and empirically proven in recent years by research in various different policy fields (Capano and Howlett 2009a; Williams 2009), while also being admitted by those scholars who have done relevant research following the ACF (Weible *et al.* 2009). So the explanation of policy change should be integrative, by ordering relations between external and internal dynamics. Thus the "why" of policy change can be externally influenced, although the final word rests with internal characteristics and developments.

Second, due to the complexity of policy dynamics, the relationship between cause and effect is extremely problematic, and strictly linked to context, timing, and contingency. So policy change is unforeseeable: small movements can lead to large-scale change, while important events may have extremely limited effects.

Third, and most importantly, due to its complexity, the "why" question cannot be answered from a linear, causal perspective. Explaining policy change cannot be done by searching for net causal effects, that is, by assuming simple and linear causal relations between independent and dependent variables. Policy change is a matter of combinatorial causes (Ragin 2006), and due to its complexity, the same policy change can be caused by different combinations of causes or of causal mechanisms present at any given moment (Jervis 1997). It would seem that Aaron Wildavsky (1979) was right when he invited scholars to consider policy as its own cause, because its complexity means that its specific configuration (its contextual pattern of behavior and interactions) matters in the policy change process. Furthermore, policy configuration is stable but not static, due to its continual adjustments caused by both its internal and external interactions.

So in order to explain "why" policies change, the researcher has to resolve a moving puzzle: the dependent variable is constantly moving within a context (the configuration of the policy) that is stable, but not static.

## *The temporal problem*

For too long, policies have been considered as historical phenomena. However, policy dynamics represent a process, meaning a sequence of events, actions, interactions, outputs and outcomes over the course of time. The temporal dimension of policy change has been rediscovered thanks to the historical-neoinstitutionalism and path-dependent perspectives, although both approaches are based on a traditional perception of the temporal dimension of policies as another way of representing historical time.

However, there are other dimensions of "time" involving policy dynamics and change. Following the theoretical proposals of Barbara Adam (2004), these different dimensions of temporality constitute the *timescape* of policy change. Time frame, timing, temporality, tempo, duration, and sequence are the most relevant dimensions of the intrinsic temporality of policy dynamics and change. The *time frame* is the period of time of policy dynamics that is analyzed when studying changes in said policy dynamics. The ACF, for example, suggests that the study of policy change should focus on a period of at least ten years of the policy dynamics, because changes need time to develop and emerge. The time frame chosen by the researcher has a deep impact on the explanatory effort. In fact, the longer the period analyzed, the greater the likelihood that the status of the dependant variable changes, becoming an independent or intervenient variable Furthermore, it is clear that the time frame also affects the evaluation of "how" policy has changed: what seems to be incremental in the short run could become radical in the long run, and vice versa. The *timing* of policy dynamics and change focuses on the synchronization between policy dynamics and the external environment. For example, there could be a temporal misalignment between the debate over possible changes inside and outside the policy domain (i.e. in the public's opinion or in the political system). From this point of view, timing is also the temporal dimension of the "policy windows" (Kingdon 1984), which can be conceived as the perfect overlapping of the timing of different dynamics (the political and policy ones). *Temporality* represents the directionality of time: it can be linear or cyclical. It is linear when "that time returns no more," indicating the irreversibility of the change in question. It is cyclical when "that time finally returns," thus representing the reversibility of change. The *tempo* dimension accounts for the intensity and the density, and thus the speed, of the dynamics, and therefore of the achieved change. A high tempo means that the change in a specific policy time frame has been very fast, and that time has been utilized intensely. *Duration* is the dimension through which policy dynamics develop, and the time required to achieve policy change.

The *sequence* is the order of succession through which policy dynamics develops, and policy scholars have specifically focused on this temporal dimension of public policy in their analytical efforts to take account of the path dependency influence on policy trajectories (see Adrian Kay in this volume) and to explain the policy sequence through the process tracing (see Carsten Daugbjerg in this volume). There are two ways of conceiving the temporal sequence of the policy dynamics and change (Howlett 2009). The first one, following the path dependence approach, is characterized by turning points, that is, critical junctures at which policy change occurs—very often due to contingent events—and long periods of inertia. This type of sequence represents the historical trajectory of policy dynamics, characterized by periods of momentum in which changes occur. It is a kind of linear succession between changes which are intended as irreversible, and produced substantially by external shocks or by the incapacity of current policy (and its inertial character) to adapt to external transformations. In this version, the sequence seems to be external to policy dynamics and change. The second type of sequence, suggested by Haydu (1998), is conceived as a kind of "dialectical" confrontation over time between contrasting solutions to recurring problems. From this point of view, the temporal sequence of policy dynamics and change is an ongoing battle between solutions to the same problems, in which the temporary winner is the result of contingent factors which are not random, as in the path-dependent sequence, but the product of agency (actors pursuing their own interests or ideas). So the logic of this sequence is based on reversible changes. This way of defining the sequence considers the succession of events as an "internal," intrinsic process of policy dynamics and change. Conceived in this way, the temporal sequence is another way of emphasizing the potential that endogenous factors have to forcibly influence policy change.

This deconstruction of time in policy dynamics and change considerably helps our understanding of how important the choice of time dimension is when analyzing and accounting for policy change. For example, were one to decide to focus on a time frame of one year, during which a new legislative reform has been adopted, the result would be a change characterized by high tempo (high density and speed), right timing and linear temporality. However, were this time frame extended to 20 years, the researcher may discover, for example, that ten years later the new law has been reversed (cyclical temporality) or its implementation has been slow and ineffective (low tempo) and characterized by a contingent, and so nondecisive, overlapping between the policy timing and the external one (Loomis 1994; Pollit 2008). The concept of time, then, should be taken seriously by policy scholars, especially by those involved both in better developing the sequential nature of policy dynamics and in designing fine-grained frameworks of policy trajectories, while it should be pointed out here that the most highly reputed theoretical frameworks give only limited importance to it. The PDF simply adopts the first type of temporal sequence, while the ACF takes the time frame dimension into consideration, since longitudinal analysis is at the basis of the analytical logic of those advancing the latter. The PGF assumes the second type of sequence. In the case of the MSA, only timing is a relevant dimension of temporality. Finally the IAD seems to be uninterested in the temporal dimension of policy-making altogether.

## Causal mechanisms of policy change

Explaining policy change is a frustrating activity for those who do not adopt a covering-law legal perspective of explanation. If the search for linear causality is abandoned, as I have proposed above, the explanatory enterprise becomes very complex, and basically never-ending. It is no coincidence that many theoretical frameworks have been proposed in the policy literature to explain policy change, and that they are all complex designs of multiple interconnected factors. Combinatory causality, that is, the search for the interconnected mechanisms whereby change occurs, characterize all of them. There is not sufficient space here to portray their fundamental characteristics, and as such they are well-known to the policy scholars. Multiple Stream Approach, Punctuated Equilibrium Framework, Advocacy Coalition Framework, Policy Generation Framework, Path Dependence approaches and Institutional Analysis and Development Framework have for a long time been part of policy scholars' toolkit. They are all different from each other, although they have certain characteristics in common: they all assume the processual nature of policy dynamics, that is, that policy change occurs through a specific process; they analyze episodes that are continuous streams of social and political life (Tilly 2001), and they try to grasp the most relevant factors which influence change. To be more precise, all these frameworks try to define the most relevant causal mechanisms of policy change.

Causal mechanisms are "portable concepts that describe how causation occur" (Falleti and Lynch 2009: 1148). As Tilly points out, mechanisms "form a delimited class of events that change relations among specified sets of elements in identical or closely similar ways over a variety of situations" (2001: 25–6). Mechanisms constitute the links between input and outputs, between external shocks and policy change, between internal policy development and subsequent changes. As Falleti and Lynch point out: "Mechanisms tell us how things happen: how actors relate, how individuals come to believe what they do or what the draw from past experience, how policies and institutions endure or change." (2009: 1147). So, focusing on mechanisms means searching for the "the pathway or process by which an effect is produced or a purpose is accomplished" (Gerring 2008: 178).

The concept of causal mechanisms is more precise than that of drivers or factors. It assumes that a potential driver or factor of change is exactly the means by which causes produce effects. A causal mechanism means that a factor or a driver, thanks to its action, produces certain outcomes. Another property of mechanisms is that they do not produce effects in a determinist way; their outcomes are influenced by the context. This is because the same causal mechanism can produce different effects in different contexts, and the same effects can be produced by different causal mechanisms.

Assuming a *mechanismic* perspective leads scholars to choose the most relevant causal mechanisms from among all potential factors, thus simplifying the possible theoretical framework.

Seen from this point of view, all of the most commonly used theoretical frameworks for explaining policy change have clearly some specific factors handled as causal mechanisms. The ACF, for example, has particularly emphasized actors' beliefs and learning; the path dependence approaches and certain versions of historical-institutionalism have focused on critical junctures and increasing returns; other streams of neoinstitutionalist thought have placed the emphasis on policy drift, conversion, layering, and replacement; the PEF and the PGF have given importance to the shifting of attention and on the flux of new information. The PEF (in an initial version) also emphasized the role of multiple institutional venues, which were later perceived as 'institutional frictions'. The IAD approach has focused on institutional arrangements. The MSA has emphasized the relevance of policy windows and policy entrepreneurs. Furthermore, all of the aforementioned frameworks and theories pay attention, albeit to different degrees, to the role of ideas and institutions as significant causal mechanisms.

So from this point of view, the variety of theoretical frameworks designed to explain policy change reflects different choices with regard to what are considered the most significant causal mechanisms in play within policy-making. They vary also regarding another causal mechanism, time, as I have shown above.

There are some positives to reasoning in terms of a *mechanismic* perspective when trying to explain policy change. The first one is that this approach takes due account of a chosen set of potential causal mechanisms, handling them in a more comfortable way, thus avoiding the risk of overestimation (for example, globalization is clearly a causal mechanism influencing many national policy fields, but should be considered together with other specific causal mechanisms which vary from one country to the next, according to the specific national context).

The second one is that the *mechanismic* approach to explanation perfectly fits with the processual nature of change: finding causal mechanisms means, in fact, reconstructing the diachronic dynamics leading to change.

The third one is that, through a comparative analysis, this approach provides us with a better understanding of which contextual factors favor the effectiveness of specific causal mechanisms (policy learning does not work in the same way in different countries and in different policy fields; new information do not have the same effects in different countries or in different policy fields).

Fourth, the search for causal mechanisms could be the best way of dealing with the structural, multilevel nature of policy dynamics and change. In fact the multi-institutional arrangements of public policy means that different causal mechanisms can work in the same policy field, but because every institutional layer represents a different context, changes are not only of different types, according to the diversity of the layer, but are also based on different sets of causal mechanisms. The same mechanism may work in different ways, depending on the specific level at which the change is occurring (learning at the legislative stage is somewhat different from, and works in a different way from, learning at the micro level, where the change has not only to be approved but also to be implemented).

Fifth, causal mechanisms can also help us to understand how agency and structure actually interact and matter in determining policy change (for example, whether the effect of new information alters the behavior of actors because of structural conditions, or because of the rational will of policy actors).

Sixth, focusing on causal mechanisms could be very fruitful when performing comparative processual analyses, by reconstructing policy trajectories and sequences. In fact, the majority of current theoretical frameworks are not very helpful when it comes to comparing policies or countries, since they contain too many factors and elements (especially the ACF and IAD, whereas PEF is more interested in analyzing policy change as a sequence of discrete decisions). This is not a call for theoretical parsimony, which would be an impossible mission when analyzing policy change, but simply for more affordable theoretically oriented research, in which the comparative perspective constitutes an ineludible methodological tool.

So, by focusing on sets of causal mechanisms, the study of policy change could be more manageable and better suited to the accumulation of knowledge. At the same time, the adoption of a mechanismic perspective seems to be very much in keeping both with the trajectory and the sequence of policy dynamics and with the intrinsic processual nature of policy change. By working on sets of causal mechanisms, the interaction and effects of which develop over time, it is possible to investigate and order the possible patterns (that is, trajectories and sequences) of policy dynamics and change.

One final point which deserves to be mentioned here is that the present plethora of studies of policy change by policy scholars contains certain potential causal mechanisms which have not been taken into due consideration, or which have been afforded marginal importance. In fact, the theoretical frameworks proposed in an attempt to explain policy change, have paid considerable attention to causal mechanisms such as learning, policy legacy, lock-in effects, feedback, information, rules, ideas, and institutional arrangements, and so on, but have given little importance to other possible factors which could play a relevant role as causal mechanisms in policy change, such as leadership, the features of political systems, and interest groups. These factors are basically absent from policy change research, perhaps because they belong to the mainstream of political science, and are thus considered to be the conceptual tools of policy scholars' "rivals." I think that this gap should be filled, because policy change is replete with leaders trying to lead processes (that is, to resist or to address change) at all institutional levels; parties, politicians, bureaucrats and governments which are all constantly involved in policy dynamics; interests groups which, day by day, attempt to maintain or change their status and rewards within the dynamics of policy change (for example, how much of the comparative difference in welfare reforms is due to the national structure of interests groups?).

Thus, broadening the perspective of the potential causal mechanisms, by taking in the theoretical toolbox of policy scholars and the abovementioned three causal mechanisms, is a necessary step toward improving the quality of research into policy change.

## The puzzle and the agents

The dynamics and characteristics of change may vary, depending on the country in question, the chosen policy field, the content at stake, the institutional level, and the historical period. What definitely does not vary is the central role of agency in influencing such change. Policies are made by actors, not by structural conditions, ideas, institutions, political parties, or interest groups. (Lundquist 1980). Policy actors are those who act in the policy arena, during all phases of the policy-making process. They are the ones who learn, who receive new information on policy problems, and who interpret such problems. They are the ones whose attention shifts diachronically. They are the ones who pursue their own interests and ideas. They are the ones who determine the internal temporal dimensions of policy change and dynamics. They are the ones who, through their daily behavior (consisting of decisions and nondecisions, interactions, learning, search for solutions) determine the persistence of, or change in, policy dynamics. Obviously they are strongly influenced and guided by the context, that is, by institutions, social norms, and patterns of institutionalized roles. However, in the end, actual decisions are the results of their own will—their constrained will—but nevertheless their will. Policy actors are the ones who, take causal mechanisms and make them work within the reality of policy-making. Policy actors are those who determine how policy changes. They do so both for incremental and radical changes (Wilsford 2010).

In fact, even in an apparently static situation, the actors' decision to choose Y instead of X (for example, to eliminate a specific policy instrument, or to adopt another in its place) can make a difference because this incremental choice could alter the policy configurations, inducing other actors to change their behavior by creating a slow, but clear, cascade of effects. Although Y or X are limited alternatives permitted by the present equilibrium, and by the strong institutionalized constraints on actors, their choice is not determined by the context but depends on the will and the actions of policy-makers. Why do policy actors opt for Y rather than X in a similar context, given their similar preferences and boundaries? The question may be a small one, but small decisions in similar contexts may lead to changes in policy trajectory and sequence in the medium and long term.

Policy actors are also those responsible for deciding what can be done at critical junctures in time and at turning points, precisely when existing boundaries and contextualized constraints become minimized. In such contingent situations, when a new trajectory can be chosen or the policy sequence can be redirected, it is precisely the policy actors and their coalitions who decide what the new path to be taken is going to be, and what the contents of radical change shall consist of. Policy actors are the ones who constantly interpret contingencies, and take responsibility for deciding whether there are any opportunities for change, and they sometimes act so as to create the conditions for change.

Policy dynamics is an abstract concept constantly fed by the real actions of policy actors. Such policy actors may behave as leaders, entrepreneurs, interest-driven politicians, old-fashioned bureaucrats, and so on, but they nevertheless constitute the core of policy dynamics and its sequence, and thanks to their actions and interactions, policy dynamics survive and policy change occurs.

It is precisely due to this agency role that the theoretical efforts made to order policy dynamics and to understand policy change constitute a never-ending puzzle. We constantly try to confine agency within patterns of regular behavior (institutional arrangements, arenas, networks, etc.), but very often it evades our theoretical restraints, and thus the search for the solution to the puzzle continues.

## Bibliography


Adam, Barbara. 2004. *Time*. Cambridge: Polity Press.

Baumgartner, Frank R. and Bryan D. Jones (eds). 2002. *Policy Dynamics*. Chicago: University of Chicago Press.

——and Bryan D. Jones. 2009. *Agendas and Instability in American Politics*, 2nd edn. Chicago: University of Chicago Press.

——, Christian Breunig, Christoffer Green-Pedersen, Bryan D. Jones, Peter B. Mortensen, Michiel Nuytemans and Stefaan Walgrave. 2009. 'Punctuated equilibrium in comparative perspective', *American Journal of Political Science* 53(3): 603–20.

Blyth, Mark. 2011. 'Ideas, uncertainty, and evolution', in Daniel Beland and Robert Henry Cox (eds) *Ideas and Politics in Social Science Research*. Oxford: Oxford University Press, 83–101.

Capano, Giliberto. 1996. 'Political science and the comparative study of policy change in higher education: Theorico-methodological notes from a policy perspective', *Higher Education* 31(3): 263–82.

—— 2009. 'Understanding policy change as an epistemological and theoretical problem', *Journal of Comparative Policy Analysis* 1(1): 7–31.

——and Michael Howlett (eds). 2009a. *European and North American Policy Change. Drivers and Dynamics*. London: Routledge.

——and Michael Howlett. 2009b. 'Conclusion: A research agenda for policy dynamics', in Giliberto Capano and Michael Howlett (eds) *European and North American Policy Change. Drivers and Dynamics*. London: Routledge, 215–31.

Cashore, Benjamin and Michael Howlett. 2007. 'Punctuating which equilibrium? Understanding thermostatic policy dynamics in Pacific Northwest forestry', *American Journal of Political Science* 51(3): 532–51.

de Vries, Michiel S. 2005. 'Generations of interactive policy-making in the Netherlands', *International Review of Administrative Sciences* 71(4): 577–91.

—— 2010. *The Importance of Neglect in Policy-Making*. London: Macmillan.

Falleti, Tulia and Julia Lynch. 2009. 'Context and causal mechanisms in political analysis', *Comparative Political Studies* 42(9): 1143–66.

Gerring, John. 2008. 'The mechanismic worldview: Thinking inside the box', *British Journal of Political Science* 38(1): 161–79.

Hall, Peter. 1993. 'Policy paradigms, social learning, and the state: The case of economic policymaking in Britain', *Comparative Politics* 25(3): 275–96.

Haydu, Jeffrey. 1988. 'Making use of the past: Time periods as cases to compare and as sequences of problem solving', *The American Journal of Sociology* 104(2): 339–71.

Heclo, Hugh. 1972. 'Review article: Policy analysis', *British Journal of Political Science* 2(1): 83–108.

Hogwood, Peter W. and Guy B. Peters. 1983. *Policy Dynamics*. New York: St. Martin's Press.

Howlett, Michael. 2009. 'Process sequencing policy dynamics: Beyond homeostasis and path dependency', *Journal of Public Policy* 29(3): 241–62.

——and Ben Cashore. 2009. 'The dependent variable problem in the study of policy change: Understanding policy change as a methodological problem', *Journal of Comparative Policy Analysis* 1(1): 33–46.

Kingdon, John W. 1984. *Agendas, Alternatives, and Public Policies*. Boston: Little, Brown.

Jervis, Robert. 1997. *System Effects: Complexity in Political and Social Life*. Princeton, NJ: Princeton University Press.

Lewis, Orion and Sven Steinmo. 2010. 'Taking evolution seriously in political science', *Theory in Biosciences* 129 (2–3): 235–45.

Loomis, Burdett A. 1994. *Time, Politics, and Policies: A Legislative Year*. Lawrence, KS: University Press of Kansas.

Lundquist, Lennart. 1980. *The Hare and the Tortoise: Clean Air Policies in the United States and Sweden*. Ann Arbor, MI: University of Michigan Press.

Mahoney, James. 2000. 'Path dependence in historical sociology', *Theory and Society* 29(4): 507–48.

——and Kathleen Thelen (eds). 2010. *Explaining Institutional Change*. Cambridge: Cambridge University Press.

Mawhinney, Hanne B. 1993. 'An advocacy coalition approach to change in Canadian education', in Paul Sabatier and Henk Jenkins-Smith (eds) *Policy Change and Learning*. Boulder, CO: Westview Press, 59–81.

Nisbet, Robert. 1972. 'Introduction: The problem of social change', in Robert Nisbet (ed.) *Social Change*. New York: Harper and Row, 1–45.

Ostrom, Elinor. 1990. *Governing the Commons*. Cambridge: Cambridge University Press.

—— 2005. *Understanding Institutional Diversity*. Princeton, NJ: Princeton University Press.

Pierson, Paul. 2000. 'Increasing returns, path dependence, and the study of politics', *American Political Science Review* 94(2): 251–67.

—— 2004. *Politics in Time: History, Institutions, and Social Analysis*. Princeton, NJ: Princeton University Press.

Pollitt, Christopher. 2008. *Time, Policy, Management*. Oxford, Oxford University Press.

Ragin, Charles. 2006. 'How to lure analytic social science out of the doldrums: Some lessons from comparative research', *International Sociology* 21(5): 633–46.

Sabatier, Paul. 1988. 'An advocacy coalition framework of policy change and the role of policy oriented learning therein', *Policy Science* 21(2–3): 129–68.

——and Henk Jenkins-Smith (eds) 1993. *Policy Change and Learning. An Advocacy Coalition Approach*. Boulder, CO: Westview Press.

——and Christopher Weible. 2007. 'The advocacy coalition framework: Innovations and clarifications', in Paul A. Sabatier (ed.), *Theories of the Policy Process*, 2nd edn. Boulder, CO: Westview Press, 189–220.

Streeck, Wolfgang, and Kathleen Thelen (eds). 2005. *Beyond Continuity: Institutional Change in Advanced Political Economies*. Oxford: Oxford University Press.

Tilly, Charles. 2001. 'Mechanisms in political processes', *Annual Review of Political Science* 4: 21–41.

Weible, Christopher, Paul Sabatier and Kelly McQueen. 2009. 'Themes and variations: Taking stock of the advocacy coalition framework', *Policy Studies Journal* 37(1): 121–40.

Wildavsky, Aaron. 1979. *Speaking Truth to Power: The Art and Craft of Policy Analysis*. Boston: Little, Brown.

Williams, Russell A. 2009. 'Exogenous shocks in subsystem adjustment and policy change: The credit crunch and Canadian banking regulation', *Journal of Public Policy* 29(1): 29–53.

Wilsford, David. 2010. 'The logic of policy change: Structure and agency in political life', *Journal of Health Politics, Policy and Law* 35(4): 663–80.

Zahariadis, Nikolaos. 2003. *Ambiguity and Choice in Public Policy*. Washington, DC: Georgetown University Press.

34

# Policy trajectories and legacies

## Path dependency revisited

*Adrian Kay*

The emergence of a 'new' institutionalism across the social sciences has coincided with the increased interest in temporality, change and history in social and political analysis. Institutions are structures that endure, have a history and can be used to link temporally events and processes. The concept of path dependency has been used within policy studies and political science almost exclusively within a broad institutionalist framework. It is institutions that are path dependent; as Raadschelders (1998: 569) states: 'whatever the discipline ... contemporary neo-institutional analysis has one feature in common: the notion of path dependency'. The widespread and cross-disciplinary use of path dependency for the analysis of institutional 'stickiness' makes the concept an obvious starting point for the examination of policy trajectories and legacies. Indeed, the concept appeals as a label for the simplest of policy dynamics: that past policy decisions act as an institution-like constraint on the options available to current policy-makers; or to use the language of dynamics, past policy decisions act to circumscribe or foreclose parts of policy space.

This chapter revisits path dependency in light of its appeal as a means of understanding the process and logic of policy trajectories and legacies, with a particular focus on the refinement of the concept in response to complaints of determinism and an inability to accommodate change.

A process is path dependent if initial moves in one direction elicit further moves in that same direction; in other words the order in which things happen affects how they happen; the trajectory of change up to a certain point *constrains* the trajectory after that point. As Douglass North puts it, path dependency is a process that constrains future choice sets:

> At every step along the way there are choices – political and economic – that provide ... real alternatives. Path dependence is a way to narrow conceptually the choice set and link decision-making through time. It is not a story of inevitability in which the past neatly predicts the future.
>
> *(1990: 98–9)*

The reference to choice sets and decision-making reveals the origins of the concept in economics. Indeed, path dependency is problematic for that discipline because it implies that decentralised interactions between economically rational actors do not necessarily lead to efficient outcomes; indeed, inefficient equilibria may be recognised as such but still persist.

The concept of path dependency is not a framework or theory or model in the terms of Ostrom (1999: 39–41): it does not provide a general list of variables that can be used to organise 'diagnostic and prescriptive inquiry' nor does it provide hypotheses about specific links between variables or particular parameters of those links. Instead, path dependency is an empirical category, an organising concept or metaphor which can be used to label a certain type of temporal process. As Hall and Taylor put it:

> they [historical institutionalists] have been strong proponents of an image of social causation that is path dependent in the sense that it rejects the traditional postulate that the same operative forces will generate the same results everywhere in favour of the view that the effect of such forces will be mediated by the contextual features of a given situation often inherited from the past.
>
> *(1996: 941)*

The application of this organising concept or metaphor to a phenomenon is only the beginning of a form of explanation. Although it asserts a relationship between the sequence of early events and the probability of later events, the concept of path dependency does not per se provide necessary or sufficient conditions to understand or explain that which it labels: path dependent processes, even when identified, require theorising; it is the mechanisms that connect decisions or actions across time that explain a path-dependent process.

Although both refer to mid-range phenomena, 'policy' and 'institution' are not synonyms. Within the policy system, there are various structures at different scales which act as institutions in shaping agents' decision-making in the formulation, enactment and implementation of policy. These are not reducible to individual level agents or single elements in the policy process. Examples of policy institutions are budget rules, policy networks, shared mental maps as well as the standard operating procedures for policy-making in government departments and agencies. Most importantly in terms of understanding policy development as path dependent, past policy decisions are institutions in terms of current policy decisions: they can act as structures that can limit or shape current policy options.

The question of what about a policy is path dependent does not admit a single, conclusive answer; rather it remains an open question for scholars applying the concept with theoretical and empirical corollaries. If the policy whole or system is path dependent, there may be several potential underlying mechanisms operating, independently or in combinations. This property of 'multiple realisability' has theoretical implications in terms of the micro foundations of path dependency and the spatial and temporal scales of policy analysis. It is necessary when using the concept, either theoretically or empirically, to be clear about the perspective being adopted. The development of a policy may be labelled path dependent over some period, but the various mechanisms that underlie that process remain unclear unless a more fine-grained perspective is adopted. Without micro foundations, the value of the concept in making sense of policy trajectories is doubtful. Indeed, path-dependent processes may coexist with other types of processes *within* policy systems. This is important in order to avoid the imputation that path dependency is simply a fashionable neologism for the notion that 'history matters'. An adequately fine-grained perspective is essential in using path dependency analytically; when policies or elements of policies are seen as strongly interrelated or where our analytical lens shows policy institutions as deeply interwoven then a much clearer sense of the mechanisms that underlie path-dependent processes is gained.

The first section of the chapter considers the application of path dependency to the analysis of policy development and its potential advantages in understanding the dynamics of that development. The next section considers several criticisms of the concept: that it lacks a convincing account of decision-making over time, both of the accumulation of constraints and context bound rationality; it is incapable of dealing with policy change; and it lacks a clear normative focus. In the final section, I argue that despite its theoretical underdevelopment and relatively limited number of successful empirical applications, the concept of path dependency does have potential utility in the field of policy studies in terms of understanding why policies might be difficult to reform and also why they may tend to become more complex over time.

## Benefits of path dependency for understanding policy trajectories and legacies

Path dependency is an appealing concept for understanding public policy development; it provides a label for the observations and intuitions that policies, once established, can be difficult to change or reform. Early and influential examples of the use of path dependency for understanding policy development include health care policy in the US (Hacker 1998, 2002; Wilsford 1994) and the UK (Greener 2002); the reform of housing benefit in the UK (Kemp 2001); to UK pension policy (Pemberton 2003); and the Common Agricultural Policy (CAP) of the European Union (Kay 2003).

Path dependency encapsulates the insight that policy decisions accumulate over time; a process of accretion can occur in a policy area that restricts options for future policy-makers. In this sense, path dependency arguments can 'provide an important caution against a too easy conclusion of the inevitability, 'naturalness', or functionality of observed outcomes' (Pierson 2000a: 252). For example, Pemberton (2003) argues that the pensions 'crisis' in the UK is not primarily demographic but rather due to a low savings rate; further, this low rate is a function of the path dependency and increasing complexity of pension policy. The system of pension provision in the UK has shifted over the last 25 years from one dominated by state provision to one in which the state pension plays a residual welfare role. Despite this large change at the policy system level, there is evidence of path dependency in particular policy subsystems. In the case of UK pensions, policy subsystems exist around specific pension schemes. An individual contract established under a particular pension scheme at a particular time is costly to change: there are large sunk costs; increasing returns associated with rising numbers of contributors and pensioners in a particular scheme; further, there may be significant learning effects. All of these factors contribute to significant switching costs for the abolition of one scheme and the transferring of that set of individual contracts into a superseding scheme. Particular schemes are 'locked in' for particular individuals. Nonetheless, pension reform has been possible but change has come in the form of the addition of new schemes or elements to the system. This amounts not to a single, path dependent policy trajectory but rather to a widening array of 'locked in' subsystems over time. This accretion of new subsystems or schemes has led to the increasing complexity of the overall system of pensions and raised questions of effectiveness at a policy 'whole' level. Kemp (2001) reports similar dynamics with regard to housing benefit policy in the UK.

Path dependency can help separate not just different *orders* of policy change as in Hall (1993), but different *rates* of policy change. One of the foundations of dynamic policy analysis is the assumption that there are a multitude of temporal scales immanent in any system. Therefore, within a policy system, there may be some elements that are path dependent, and others that are not. Further, there may be a relationship between the different processes at different speeds. Later in the chapter, I develop the point that it is the combinations of institutions and policies that provide the important mechanisms underlying path dependency but also create the potential for strategic action and policy innovation by agents.

The concept of path dependency has the additional advantage of flexibility for policy scholars. In particular, because the concept does not contain within it a fixed temporal or spatial scale of analysis, the insights of path dependency can often complement rather than rival other accounts of policy change. Social housing in the UK is an example of where path dependency can hold at the subsystem level with interesting consequences, but where the policy system as a whole has changed profoundly. Since the mid-1970s there has been a series of failed initiatives by central government to directly control the rents charged in the social housing sector and ensure equity between local authorities and housing associations. This particular element of social housing policy is path dependent; each local authority has an established policy for rent calculation, often determined by initial decisions made in the immediate post-war era. That these have proved resistant to central control or influence significantly constrains the ability of central government to pursue some of its objectives for social housing. However, during the same period as this path-dependent process there has been a clear shift in the social housing policy paradigm as home ownership increased substantially, notably through the central government's 'right to buy' scheme introduced in the early 1980s that allowed local authority tenants to buy their own home.

## Problems of path dependency for understanding policy trajectories and legacies

### *Accounts of decision-making over time*

The criticism that the concept of path dependency lacks explanatory power is well expressed by Raadschelders:

> it is only by virtue of retrospect that we are aware of stages or paths of development. 'Path dependency' refers to a string of related events: causality in retrospect. The concept does not come even close to pinpointing a mechanism or the mechanisms that propel social change.
>
> *(1998: 576)*

The quotation contains two criticisms. The first is that the concept cannot be used for current or future phenomena. This is, of course, not a singular feature of path dependency but common to all concepts that are useful for structuring retrospective, 'thick' historical descriptions to support narrative explanations in the social sciences. Indeed, as discussed in the previous two chapters, a dynamic perspective reveals that this is not an appropriate standard for considering the utility of different concepts, theories or metaphors.

The more important criticism is that even if one accepts path dependency as intuitively appealing, it is unlikely to be convincing analytically because the notion does not provide any fine-grained mechanisms that might provide necessary and sufficient conditions for the process observed. The challenge for the use of path dependency in the study of policy trajectories is the uncovering of mechanisms that can help make sense of a path dependent process. One influential strand of the literature on path dependency has worked on the micro foundations of the concept using insights from new institutional economics. Much of this literature proceeds by analogy from technological development to institutional development. In simple terms, imagine two technologies, A and B, both of which are subject to increasing returns but there is uncertainty over the rate of increasing returns. Initial adoptions of one technology, say B, which may occur for a number of small or chance reasons, beget further adoptions of B in the market because of increasing returns namely it becomes cheaper for future firms to adopt technology B rather than A. The interesting results from the models built on these assumptions (for economists at least) are that you might get inefficient technologies adopted by markets. The normative implications of this borrowing from economics are considered in more detail later.

Arthur (1994) states the circumstances in which path dependence as an increasing returns process is likely: the presence of large fixed (and sunk) costs; network effects; learning effects; and adaptive expectations. As noted, these factors have been used at a macro, constitutional level to make arguments about path dependency in institutional development (North 1990; Pierson 2000a, 2000b, 2000c). Within this list of sources of increasing returns, it is useful to distinguish between those factors that relate to the internal efficiency of firms – large fixed costs leading to declining average costs as production increases and learning effects – from those that are external to the firm, in particular, network effects. The distinction is important because later in the chapter, path dependency is discussed in terms of the increasing returns involved in *combinations* of institutions and policies rather than increasing returns as a property of the internal operations of firms. This complements the insistence on a fine-grained perspective of policy systems developed in this chapter.

A focus on increasing returns is only a partial interpretation of the economics of path dependency. Increasing returns are sufficient but not necessary for path dependency. As Arrow (2000) points out, the existence of significant sunk costs along with sequencing arguments can support many of the path dependency narratives of technological change. Although he does not use the concept of path dependency, Arthur Stinchcombe's (1968: Chapter 5) celebrated work on constructing theories of historical causation emphasises the central importance of sunk costs. I submit that any decision that is difficult to reverse and which has enduring and ongoing effects can be said to have initiated a path-dependent process; and work on path-dependent processes should not focus exclusively on increasing returns processes and it is moot whether they should privilege this mechanism-type over other sources of path dependency.

Contrarily, Schwarz (2004) argues that the combination of initial, small and contingent steps with increasing returns defines a path dependent process; if there was an large initial cause that had significant and enduring effect on the subsequent process then this historical cause would be salient in any explanation of the process. The process would no longer be *path* dependent but rather, as a policy dynamic, be better characterised as the temporal unravelling of the consequences of some initial event. In a similar vein, Page (2006) introduces the idea of *phat* dependence to refer to cases where it is the distribution rather than the precise sequence of early events that is important in shaping later events. Both these insights are noteworthy in highlighting the need for future scholarly work in cataloguing and explaining different types of path dependency and its relationship to other policy dynamics such as process sequencing (see Daugbjerg in this volume). However, for the sake of expositional clarity this chapter remains with the definition of path dependency as a general metaphor for sticky policy or institutional processes.

A number of non-increasing returns mechanisms have been suggested as underlying path dependency in policy development: the effect of policy on interest groups as when policies constrain some groups and enable others (Pierson 2000a); self-reinforcing mechanisms where policies involve investment or disinvestments in administrative infrastructure which transforms governmental capacity and the set of possible future policies that may be enacted (Skocpol 1992); policies that involve the establishment of formal or informal contracts with individuals (Pemberton 2003; Kay 2003; Kemp 2001) which are costly to change. Further, there are network effects to *types* of contracts rather than the number of signatories. Once a contract is established, the transaction costs of agreeing another contract of that type in that area of public policy will be considerably lower than any alternative contract.

All these policy-specific mechanisms are based on definite, conscious choices, which have the foreseeable consequence of high future switching costs; none relies on an increasing returns process. Nevertheless, there are examples that suggest that increasing returns processes can occur in policy development. In the structural reforms of the primary care sector in the UK after 1997, a series of primary care models were piloted. By a series of chance factors, a particular primary care trust model quickly became popular. This model subsequently became the government's template for all future combinations of primary care organisations. There was no particular feature to this model to recommend it over any of the others that were piloted between 1997 and 2000; instead it was the case that this model was adopted early in the government's reform process, which made it considerably easier (or cheaper) for subsequent primary care groups to use it, and with such a momentum became the template adopted by the government for all primary care agglomerations. At a general level, all metaphors of policy ideas or proposals emerging from the 'policy soup' or 'garbage can' share a notion of a market place of ideas; analogous to a market system, ideas compete for attention and influence. Where the market structure produces increasing returns, policy ideas can succeed into proposals and eventual enactment by an initial series of small, contingent steps as early adopters of an idea increase the return to future adopters.

Any borrowing from microeconomics, including the idea of increasing returns, inevitably situates the agent in terms of responding to the costs and benefits of different options in a manner consistent with straightforward parametric rationality. The assumption of this type of rationality serves certain purposes in formal economic modelling, but to use it in more informal, intuitive and post-positivist accounts of path dependency in public policy is problematic (Hay 2004). One response is to use the notion of context-bound rationality in an account of decision-making in a path dependent process. Nooteboom (1997) describes the manner in which markets lock in to certain technologies in similar terms to how philosophers of science characterise the entrenchment of scientific theories. Both can be path dependent. He cites Kuhn's famous account of how scientific theories develop according to paradigms, a set of tacit and unarticulated guiding assumptions, rather than the standard conceptions of 'pure' rationality at the heart of a scientific approach. Further, just as the Kuhnian model challenges the conception of scientific activity approximating to certain canons' rationality, so will any parallel model applied to the economic case. Hall's (1993) widely cited notion of a policy paradigm exemplifies this insight in policy studies: a policy paradigm is an interpretative framework that operates in the policy-making process; specifically, it refers to the ideas and standards that specify the goals, instruments and the very nature of a policy issue.

In these terms, the mechanism that underlies path dependency in the policy process is a form of context-bound rationality among policy actors. The current path dependency literature is mostly developed around the following two claims: (1) that the analogy from economics to institutions can be extended to policy, and (2) that microeconomics can be borrowed as the micro foundations of path dependency in policy development. Importantly, these claims require a rational choice actor making the decisions. The assumption of this type of rationality is a strict corollary of claims (1) and (2). This is potentially problematic for policy studies; in particular, those parts of contemporary public policy theory that have begun to move away from a reliance on the simple postulates of instrumental rationality to a more nuanced and contextualised views of rationality.

## *Policy change and stability*

At the heart of any account of path dependency is stability: observations of change challenge the notion. This is a common criticism of the historical institutionalist school, 'in its emphasis upon path dependence and historical legacies it is rather better at explaining stability than change' (Hay 2002:15). Thelen (1999) argues that path dependency is simultaneously overly sensitive to initial conditions and too deterministic and mechanical with respect to subsequent policy development.

In terms of policy studies, one possible counterargument is based on the interpretation of stability in path dependency. Specifically, the notion does allow policy change; policy legacies *constrain* rather than *determine* current policy. Policy does change but within a particular set of possibilities, and thus the policy may be said to exhibit stability. There are two main implications of the constrained change argument. The first is that these bounded possibility sets may be large or paths wide; and, the wider they are, the less the notion of path dependency can account for current policy development. In alternative terms, the weaker is the 'echo' of past policy developments in the present and the more other concepts, framework and theories are required.

The notion of policy direction may assist constrained change accounts of policy development. A stable policy path when projected into policy space may well imply significant *cumulative* policy change over time or in other terms, a significant distance from the initial position in policy space and time. Rose and Davies (1994) show the importance of compounding effects as small, incremental and constrained changes in annual budget allocations can accumulate to significant policy shifts over a period of a decade or more. Further, a change in direction may appear at one distance a small perturbation but by shifting the direction of the policy may turn out in retrospect to have been a critical juncture and a problem for the validity of path dependency as a description.

Nonetheless, the limitations of path dependency as a conception of policy change have been highlighted in empirical applications in public policy: for example, Kemp (2001) with respect to housing benefit reform in the UK; Pemberton (2003) with regard to pensions; Greener (2002) on the NHS. Each of these studies finds path dependency in policy development alongside some policy change. They consider change as a reaction to the unintended consequences or side effects of policy, or from pressure for reform due to exogenous shifts in the wider policy environment, for example where the distribution of power between interested groups has changed. Once a dualism between policy stability and policy change is established, the notion of path dependency is only useful for accounting for the former; indeed the purpose of the concept is to aid understanding of policy stickiness and why actors do not change policy across time.

However, the dualism between stability and change can be avoided by considering the sedimentation of policy decisions or the growing complexity of policy space that is implied by the notion of path dependency. The dynamics of policy subsystem accumulation are theoretically underdeveloped but are important for the use of path dependency in policy narratives. The development of UK pharmaceutical policy since the 1980s is an example of new policies being added on as a 'patch' or 'fix' to satisfy pressure to mitigate the consequences of the original policy. Relatively high prices for medicines were agreed by the government to reward innovation by the industry under the Pharmaceutical Price Regulation Scheme (PPRS), and this contributed to the rapid increases in public expenditure on medicines observed since the late 1980s. The PPRS remains unchanged and potentially path dependent but its budgetary consequences have precipitated a series of new policies aimed at controlling the demand for medicines in the NHS e.g. cash-limited prescribing budgets. The path dependency of particular policy subsystems is a contributory factor in the explanation of the accumulation of these policy patches and the growing complexity of the policy system, with potential consequences for the overall coherence and effectiveness of policy.

To reprise, a key issue when using the concept of path dependency is the granularity of the perspective. Much of the work within the historical institutionalist literature uses the concept at a macro perspective in which there is a single whole, that allows for discussion of an 'institutional setting' or a 'policy'. The path then refers to the trajectory for that composite variable, the direction of which is reinforced after early moves in the sequence. While this is valid for some narratives, from a more fine-grained perspective the issue is which elements of that composite system are fixed or locked-in, and which are capable of being reformed. Further, within the policy space occupied by the composite whole there may be potential for the introduction of new institutions or policy subsystems.

In more fine-grained analysis, increasing returns processes operate at the level of sequences of institutional or policy choices: once an initial policy framework is established, there are strong increasing returns involved in the choice of new, supplementary policies within that framework. That is, an increasing returns process explains policy change *qua* the introduction of new, supplementary policies. As North (1990: 95) states, it is 'the interdependent web of an institutional matrix that produces massive increasing returns'. This view of increasing returns helps to avoid too sharp a distinction between stability and change, as seen in on-path versus off-path change or where stability is followed by a path-breaking juncture, and the introduction of a new institutional or policy setting. At a more fine-grained perspective, institutions exist in combinations: they are interdependent, with necessary and contingent relationships. Thelen describes examples where institutional lock-in is combined with elements of institutional innovation that can push the overall trajectory of policy and politics in a different direction; indeed 'to understand how institutions evolve, it may be more fruitful to aim for a more fine-grained analysis that seeks to identify what aspects of a specific institutional configuration are (or are not) negotiable and under what conditions' (2003: 233).

In an important recent work pushing the concept path dependency beyond simply the understanding of continuity, Crouch and Farrell (2004) consider how actors cope with exogenous changes in their environment. At some point, the once reliably successful path no longer works, and even though policy actors know this, they find it extremely difficult to change. Simple path dependency has the actor trapped—in a strict sense the concept does not admit any other possibility; however, a more nuanced account would look at how the perceived failure of a habitual path may lead to the search for alternatives, but where that search process is itself path dependent.

The relatively informal models offered by Crouch and Farrell (2004) are designed to address the apparent determinism of path dependency once a path is selected. Change is explicitly modelled as the intentional adaptation of agents to exogenous, environmental shifts. The emphasis is on the ability of agents to reactivate redundant institutions, or convert existing institutions to different purposes, or borrow wholly new institutions from elsewhere to tackle exigencies.

This opens up an alternative theoretical line on the problem of policy change in historical institutionalist theory: instead of insisting on a strict dualism between stability and change, policy systems may be adapted to new circumstances through a gradual process of layering and conversion rather than through periods of drastic and rapid change (Streeck and Thelen 2005; Ackrill and Kay 2006). Layering and conversion are important causal mechanisms in a nascent non-determinist institutional analysis of policy change (Campbell 2004; Crouch 2005, 2007). Recognising that institutions shape the desires, motives and preferences of individual and group actors, layering refers to the adding of new preferences onto an existing set of institutionally shaped policy preferences. Such appending of new elements can lead to dysfunctionality and incoherence in the policy system and set off path-changing dynamics. In the conversion mechanism, agents develop new policy preferences from outside the institutionalised policy system, and convert inherited institutions toward these novel goals and functions. There is a significant empirical gap in the comparative public policy literature that explores the explanatory power of the policy layering and conversion mechanisms.

One implication of conversion and layering is that at the level of the composite whole, policy systems cease to embody a simple unique logic, but rather a complex bundle of different policy logics, ideas and interests. Some of these may be dormant, unused or 'forgotten' for periods but are capable of being reactivated by strategic action by agent in response to exogenous environmental shifts.

The reassertion of the capacity of agents situated within path dependent processes with increasing returns to act to change the direction of the path in response to shifts in their environment is important. Inheritance and policy legacies are not as hard or fixed or as determined as some of the simple path dependency analysis may suggest; or more accurately, increasing returns processes in economics typically assume a static environment whereas changes in that environment can attenuate (or amplify) feedback processes. In providing a set of mechanisms that may help to structure a narrative in terms of transitions *between* paths, Crouch and Farrell (2004) provide a service to the analysis of policy dynamics. This can complement the emphasis on inter-policy and inter-institutional relationships, in particular combinational effects, which imply that policy development proceeds in a more subtle way than the two-speed view of policy development.

## Normative aspects of the term

One of the consequences of constructing the explanatory foundations of path dependency in public policy by analogy from the economics of technological development is to 'import' the normative result that inefficiencies can persist in path dependent processes. This is a powerful result for neoclassical economics: certain historical factors can ensure that inefficiencies occur and markets do not eliminate these over time. Efficiency is understood here as social efficiency namely a situation where both technical and allocative efficiency hold. The strength of this normative result depends on the judgement as to whether the inefficiency could have been foreseen at some point in the initial stages in the path dependency process and corrected; and second, whether the inefficiency remains remediable, namely that a Pareto improvement can be identified and is achievable from the current situation.

For some writers the question of whether path dependency implies the persistence of inefficient institutions is an open and empirical question (e.g. Hay and Wincott 1998); for others path dependency is more clearly something which inhibits the introduction of 'better' or perhaps more rational policy or organisational form (e.g. Greener 2002). Overall, the normative implications of path dependency are less pressing for scholars outside the boundaries of neo-classical economics; it is generally accepted that inefficient policies or institutions may persist. However, it is a much stronger claim that policies in a path dependent process are *necessarily* inefficient, or alternatively, contained within the concept is the imputation of inefficiency. The claim is strong at a theoretical level as the concept would require significant elaboration in terms of both policy design and the pressures that sustain path dependent and inefficient policy. There is also the problem of indeterminism: path dependency emphasises that policy paths are unique and arrived at by a series of small and contingent moves. As such, it is difficult to say that there exists another path that could have been arrived at which is more efficient and without such a relevant counterfactual it is difficult to accept the imputation of inefficiency.

At an empirical level, the claim that policies are necessarily inefficient is also strong. Developments in performance measurement in the public sector that might allow arguments that, for example, health care or education policy are better in one system than another. Despite this, it is difficult to assert, within a particular political system, that there exist policy options which represent a welfare improvement over the current policy (net of switching costs and increased transaction costs) and there is widespread recognition of this by policy actors. Without these two conditions holding, the normative implications of path dependency in terms of public policy are attenuated. Nonetheless empirical works on path dependency in policy development seem willing to impute inefficiency to some degree (Pemberton 2003; Kay 2003; Greener 2002; Kemp 2001; Wilsford 1994). This often not so stark as labelling policies in terms of efficiency and certainly involves no quantitative analysis; however, it is not an over-interpretation of these works to tease out the implicit assumption that a policy would be 'better' without path-dependent processes acting as a barrier to effective reform.

## Conclusion

The rise of the broad school of historical institutionalism has been a salient trend in the social sciences over the last 20 years and its critical insights have recently been adapted for the more fine-grained concept of policy by recognising that clusters of governmental decisions, actions, and norms can – over time – form policy systems, reinforced by feedback mechanisms, which function as institutions. Historical institutional theory is becoming increasingly refined in its attention to historical causality and aims to explain different types of path dependency beyond the simple version where the inheritance of accumulated prior commitments limits substantially current options for policy-makers (Page 2006).

Historical institutionalism has often been judged as over-emphasising positive feedback processes and the sensitivity of institutional development to small effects at origin but under-emphasising the subsequent opportunity for endogenous change in the process of institutional reproduction over time (e.g. Hay 2002). It is perturbations occurring outside the institutionalised policy system, often characterised as societal or political upheaval or learning, that explain policy changes; without such exogenous shocks institutions tend to be stable.

In revisiting the concept of path dependency, this chapter has cast some light on a recent seam of work that provides a particular focus on the capacity of policy-makers, in the context of strong path dependent policy legacies, to innovate in response to novel demands from the external environment. However, there are two problems for the analysis of change within path dependent trajectories: (1) a theoretical one: it is unclear how much or which elements of a policy system must change to be regarded as a structural break in policy development, not just an insignificant, within path, fluctuation in policy history; and (2) an empirical one: comparative policy scholars have produced significant and important works on policy reform in response to various pressures, but there are few cases where different periods of reform have been matched neatly to salient structural breaks or punctuated equilibria in path-dependent trajectories.

## Bibliography

Ackrill, R.W. and A. Kay 2006. 'Historical institutionalism and the EU budget', *Journal of European Public Policy* 13(1): 113–33.

Arthur, W.B. 1994. *Increasing Returns and Path Dependence in the Economy*. Ann Arbor, MI: University of Michigan Press.

Arrow, K.J. 2000. 'Increasing returns: Historiographic issues and path dependence', *The European Journal of the History of Economic Thought* 7(1): 171–80.

Campbell, J.L. 2004. *Institutional Change and Globalization*. Princeton NJ: Princeton University Press.

Crouch, C. 2005. *Capitalist Diversity and Change*. New York: Oxford University Press.

—— 2007. 'How to "do" post-determinist institutional analysis', *Socio-economic Review* 5(3): 527–537.

—— and H. Farrell. 2004. 'Breaking the path of institutional development? Alternatives to the new determinism', *Rationality and Society* 16(1): 5–43.

Greener, I. 2002. 'Understanding NHS reform: The policy-transfer, social learning and path dependency perspectives', *Governance* 15(2): 161–83.

Hacker, J.S. 1998. 'The historical logic of National Health Insurance: Structure and sequence in the development of British, Canadian, and US medical policy', *Studies in American Political Development* 12: 57–130.
—— 2002. *The Divided Welfare State*. Cambridge: Cambridge University Press.
Hall, P.A. 1993. 'Policy paradigms, social learning, and the state', *Comparative Politics* 25(3): 275–96.
——and R.C.R. Taylor. 1996. 'Political science and the three new institutionalisms', *Political Studies* 44(4): 936–57.
Hay, C. 2002. *Political Analysis: A Critical Introduction*. Basingstoke: Palgrave Macmillan.
—— 2004. 'Theory, stylized heuristic or self-fulfilling prophecy? The status of rational choice theory in public administration', *Public Administration* 82(1): 39–62.
——and D. Wincott. 1998. 'Structure, agency and historical institutionalism', *Political Studies* 46(5): 951–7.
Kay, A. 2003. 'Path dependency and the CAP', *Journal of European Public Policy* 10(3): 405–21.
Kemp, P. 2001. 'Housing benefit and welfare state retrenchment in Britain', *Journal of Social Policy* 29(2): 263–79.
North, D.C. 1990. *Institutions, Institutional Change and Economic Performance*. Cambridge: Cambridge University Press.
Nooteboom, B. 1997. 'Path dependence of knowledge: Implications for the theory of the firm', in Lars Magnusson and Jan Ottosson (eds) *Evolutionary Economics and Path Dependence*. Cheltenham and Lyme, NH: Edward Elgar.
Ostrom, E. 1999. 'Institutional rational choice: An assessment of the institutional analysis and development framework', in Paul Sabatier (ed.) *Theories of the Policy Process*. Boulder, CO: Westview, 35–72.
Page, S. 2006. 'Path dependence', *Quarterly Journal of Political Science* 1(1): 87–115.
Pemberton, H. 2003. 'Lock-in or lock-out? Path dependency and British pensions', Annual Conference of the Political Studies Association, 17 April.
Pierson, P. 2000a. 'Increasing returns, path dependence, and the study of politics', *American Political Science Review* 94(2): 251–67.
—— 2000b. 'Not just what but when: Timing and sequencing in political processes', *Studies in American Political Development* 14(1): 72–92.
—— 2000c. 'The limits of design: Explaining institutional origins and change', *Governance* 13(4): 474–99.
Raadschelders, J.C.N. 1998. 'Evolution, institutional analysis and path dependency: An administrative-history perspective on fashionable approaches and concepts', *International Review of Administrative Sciences* 64(4): 565–82.
Rose, R. and P.L. Davies 1994. *Inheritance in Public Policy: Change Without Choice in Britain*. London: Yale University Press.
Schwarz, Herman 2004. 'Down the wrong path: Path dependence, increasing returns, and historical institutionalism'.Available at: http://www.people.virginia.edu/~hms2f/Path.pdf (accessed August 2011).
Skocpol, T. 1992. *Protecting Soldiers and Mothers: The Political Origins of Social Policy in the United States*. Cambridge: Belknap Press of Havard University Press.
Stinchcome, A.L. 1968. *Constructing Social Theories*. London: University of Chicago Press.
Streek, W. and K. Thelen 2005. 'Introduction: Institutional change in advanced political economies', in Wolfgang Streek and Kathleen Thelen (eds) *Beyond Continuity*. Oxford: Oxford University Press.
Thelen, K. 1999. 'Historical institutionalism in comparative politics', *Annual Review of Political Science* 2: 369–404.
—— 2003. 'How institutions evolve', in James Mahoney and Dietrich Rueschmeyer (eds) *Comparative Historical Analysis in the Social Sciences*. Cambridge: Cambridge University Press, 208–41.
Wilsford, D. 1994. 'Path dependency, or why history makes it difficult but not impossible to reform health care services in a big way', *Journal of Public Policy* 14: 251–83.

# 35
# Process sequencing

*Carsten Daugbjerg*

## Introduction[1]

Much policy research is undertaken within a restricted time perspective. In explaining policy decisions, many studies focus on the immediate, assuming that 'causes and outcomes … are both temporally contiguous and rapidly unfolding' (Pierson 2003: 178, see also Bulmer 2009). As Pierson (2003: 180) argues: 'There is … no reason to think that most political processes, or the most interesting ones, are necessarily best understood by invoking accounts with this kind of temporal structure'. A research strategy in public policy analysis focusing on the immediate may at best provide partial understanding of policy evolution since important dynamics which are rooted in past events may be missed. Hence, in the recent two decades or so, there has been a growing interest among policy analysts in policy development over time, in particular among historical institutionalists who have attempted to establish the reproduction mechanisms maintaining path dependent policy development (see Kay, this volume). An alternative, but related, approach to explaining policy evolution over time is process sequencing. It focuses on the temporal connections between policy events and attempts to establish how previous policy change enables and shapes subsequent policy changes. While analysis on path dependency focuses on the mechanisms retaining policy development within a particular path, allowing for bounded policy change, the sequencing approach concentrates on the way in which policy evolves without assuming that the policy direction resulting from a series of policy reforms would be predetermined by path dependency. Rather, it is an analytical approach to policy evolution in which fine-grained temporal analysis of the causal relations between policy events is the key to explaining policy evolution. The basic assumption in process sequencing is that an event in a policy sequence is both a reaction to an antecedent event and a cause of a subsequent one. Thus, policy outcomes feed back and become inputs in the policy process. In process sequencing, the analytical focus is on the structural constraints and opportunities embedded in previous policy events and the ability of reform advocates to overcome the constraints and utilise the opportunities in order to respond to challenges emerging from the broader policy context or from within the policy. Though each policy adjustment is unlikely to be radical, the sequence of adjustments may over time cumulatively amount to substantial policy change (Rose 1990: 264).

Process sequencing has only recently been suggested as an approach to analyse public policy evolution (Howlett and Rayner 2006). It is under-theorised and therefore the purpose of this chapter is to outline the approach and its basic concepts and an attempt is made to further develop the approach by identifying some of the causal mechanisms which link events in a policy sequence. It is suggested how learning and precedent are potentially important causal mechanisms connecting events in a policy sequence. Examples from the sequence of agricultural policy reforms in the European Union (EU) over two decades are used to highlight the analytical advantages of applying process sequencing in the study of policy evolution and reform.

## Path dependency and process sequencing: two distinct approaches to temporal analysis

Most recent dynamic analyses on policy change are based on the notion of punctuated equilibrium which describes policy development as characterised by relatively short moments of innovative change followed by extended periods of stability (Krasner 1984: 240–4). The notion of punctuated equilibrium has been widely accepted as a plausible model of policy evolution. For instance, though not explicitly positioning themselves in the historical institutionalist literature, but within the agenda-setting literature, Baumgartner and Jones (1993) apply the notion of punctuated equilibrium in explaining agenda stability over long periods of time and how punctuations interrupt and subsequently change the policy agenda. Similarly, the advocacy coalition framework developed by Sabatier (1988) and the policy network analysis school (Rhodes and Marsh 1992) also focus on explaining policy change from a not dissimilar perspective though the notion of punctuated equilibrium is not explicitly applied.

From a historical institutionalist perspective, radical institutional change is caused by exogenous shocks, creating a critical juncture which is generally understood as a 'contingent event … that was not expected to take place, given certain theoretical understandings of how causal processes work' (Mahoney 2000: 513). The concept of path dependency was used to explain the periods of stasis though it was not until a decade ago that more analytical emphasis was put on identifying the self-reinforcing reproduction mechanisms maintaining a particular path. Clearly, this improved our understanding of the phenomenon of path dependency (see Thelen 1999; Pierson 2000a; Mahoney 2000). This theoretical preoccupation with path dependency within the historical institutionalist literature left unanswered the question of what explains institutional/ policy change. The notion of path dependency does not enable policy changes which amounts to more than incrementalism to be explained. The statement by Thelen and Steinmo (1992: 15) that 'institutions explain everything until they explain nothing' still seems to apply. Therefore, the notion of path dependency has limitations in explaining policy evolution because policies are adjusted occasionally and such incremental adjustments may amount to substantial change over time. Further, some adjustments appearing insignificant at the time of their adoption may turn out to be an important catalyst for more comprehensive changes at a later stage. Thus, an important theoretical question in relation to policy change is whether a sequence of cumulative incremental policy changes can gradually lead to paradigm shift within a policy. There is a growing literature arguing that this may be possible (Coleman *et al.* 1997; Cashore and Howlett 2007; Daugbjerg and Swinbank 2009), in effect questioning the assumption of the punctuated equilibrium model that radical change occurs in critical junctures over relatively short time periods.

Indeed, some of the critique of path dependency originates from within the historical institutionalist literature. It has been questioned whether the notion of punctuated equilibrium is a valid metaphor for institutional and policy development, suggesting that 'there often seems to be too much continuity through putative breakpoints in history, but also often too much change beneath the surface of apparently stable formal institutional arrangements' (Thelen 2003: 211).

Among historical institutionalists, this scepticism towards the notion of punctuated equilibrium as the only model of institutional development has triggered a theoretical discussion on gradual institutional change which amounts to more than just minor adjustments. Thelen (2003) and her associates (Streeck and Thelen 2005; Mahoney and Thelen 2009) have engaged in efforts to develop analytical devices which can help identify various types of gradual institutional transformation and understand their causes and how the transformation process unfolds. Recent theoretical developments suggest that much gradual institutional transformation is driven from within the institution rather than by forces exogenous to the institution; however, institutional theory has had little to say on this thus far (Streeck and Thelen 2005: 19; Mahoney and Thelen 2010: 6–7). Though this discussion focuses on institutional development, it is also highly relevant for public policy evolution. Public policies can be considered institutions since they consist of a set of rules which facilitate or dictate certain actions and constrain or preclude others and influence 'the allocation of economic and political resources, modifying the costs and benefits associated with alternative political strategies, and consequently altering ensuing political development' (Pierson 1993: 596).

## Reactive sequencing and path dependency

A promising starting point for the development of analytical models enabling us to explain and understand gradual institutional and policy change is the notion of reactive sequencing. Reactive sequences 'are chains of temporally ordered and causally connected events' (Mahoney 2000: 509) and

> in a reactive sequence, each event in the sequence is both a reaction to antecedent events and a cause of subsequent events … In a reactive sequence, early events trigger subsequent development … by setting in motion a chain of tightly linked reactions and counterreactions.
>
> *(Mahoney 2000: 526, see also Pierson 2000b: 84)*

Earlier events cause the subsequent events, 'because they trigger a powerful response' (Pierson 2000: 85), thus producing an inherent logic in the chain of events. In other words, 'events in one period [are used] to explain outcomes in another' (Haydu 1998: 353). This type of sequencing has also been dubbed reiterated problem solving (Haydu 1998, 2010) or process sequencing (Howlett and Rayner 2006). While Haydu's discussion of reiterated problem solving tends to be more general and focusing on macro-political developments and the big steps in a historical trajectory, Howlett and Rayner's discussion is focused on its relevance for the policy sciences. Process sequencing focuses on the way in which policy events are causally connected in a policy sequence. Some of the events may seem insignificant at the time they happen, but may turn out to be significant events changing direction of policy or even reversing it. Therefore process sequencing requires fine-grained empirical analysis and a detailed understanding of the case under scrutiny. Since this chapter is focused on public policy issues, I shall refer to process sequencing in the balance of the chapter.

Mahoney (2000: 509) considers reactive sequencing as a type of path dependency because 'each step in the chain [of events] is "dependent" on prior steps'. This labelling of reactive sequencing as a type of path dependency is based on his extraction of three basic defining features of path dependent analysis. According to Mahoney (2000: 510–11), the analysis of path dependency is characterised, first, by the 'study of causal processes that are highly sensitive to events that take place in the early stages of an overall historical sequence'. Second, he argues that 'in a path dependent sequence, early historical events are contingent occurrences that cannot be explained on the basis of prior events or "initial conditions"'. Third, after the initial step, 'path dependent sequences are marked by relatively deterministic causal patterns'.

From a different perspective, Haydu (1998, 2010) and Howlett and Rayner (2006) make a clear distinction between path-dependent sequencing and process (or problem solving) sequencing. While the first defining feature of path dependency, as outlined by Mahoney, is unproblematic for these writings, the second and the third are not defining features for process (or problem solving) sequencing. As to the claim that the initial event in a sequence is contingent, scholars distinguishing sharply between the two approaches to temporal analysis have argued that 'outcomes at a given switch point are themselves products of the past rather than historical accidents' (Haydu 1998: 354). In their review of the public policy literature applying the punctuated equilibrium model, Howlett and Rayner (2006: 7) also reach the conclusion that the outcomes of policy switch points are 'outgrowths of earlier trajectories'.

The third feature of path dependency, deterministic causal patterns, is also a feature difficult to recognise in process sequencing and perhaps even in Mahoney's own portrayal of reactive sequencing. While there is agreement that events in a temporal sequence are causally connected and can be traced back to a historical juncture, process sequencing analysts do not recognise this historical legacy as deterministic for future developments (Howlett and Rayner 2006: 7). In path dependency, choices made at a critical juncture to a considerable extent lock in the trajectory of future choices (Pierson 2000a). In process sequencing, the overall direction of the trajectory is not conceived off as uni-directional (Howlett and Rayner 2006: 7–8, see also Sewell 1996: 263). Events are causally linked through reiterated problem solving and this may involve a change of direction. A particular trajectory is strengthened where the feedbacks from previous choices are positive. Where feedbacks are negative, the trajectory may change direction but not necessarily in the dramatic manner envisaged for critical junctures. Thus, as Jervis (1997: 129) argues in relation to policy evolution: 'although some … feedbacks are amplifying or dampening, in many other cases they force the policy in a different direction'. The possibility of counter-reactions caused by negative feedbacks weakens the argument, put forward by Mahoney, that the trajectory laid down by the initial events in a sequence determines future choices and thus maintain the path. A trajectory can only be retained in a particular direction when there are self-reinforcing reproduction mechanisms at work in a sequence. Such mechanisms are essential to the path dependency argument, but not to process sequencing. Though reactive sequencing, as outlined by Mahoney, 'involves reaction and counterreaction mechanisms that give an event chain an "inherent logic" in which one event "naturally" leads to another event' (Mahoney 2000: 511), the resultant sequence is not path dependent because there are no reproduction mechanisms to sustain the sequence on a particular path.

## Process sequencing in public policy

Process sequencing is particularly useful in public policy analysis (Howlett and Rayner 2006: 13–14). To understand policy development, the approach emphasises fine-grained temporal analysis of reactions and counter-reactions in a process of reiterated problem solving. The downside of process sequencing is its limited potential to generate theoretical statements on the way in which events in sequences are connected (Pierson 2000b: 84). In this section, the under-theorised nature of this approach to temporal analysis of policy is addressed and it is suggested how learning and precedent can become causal mechanisms connecting events in a policy sequence.

Connecting events causally in a sequence is an important challenge facing process sequencing analysis. In sequential analysis

> explanations should respect historical time by casting causal analysis in the form of sequenced events, with earlier happenings leading to and accounting for later ones. Explanations of this kind should, moreover, carefully specify the mechanisms through which causal influence is conveyed through time.
>
> *(Haydu 1998: 354)*

The theoretical challenge is to consider what connects policy events without violating the ability of the analytical approach to identify case-specific empirical details which are important for understanding the sequence of events under scrutiny.

## *Policy problems and policy actors*

In process sequencing, events are connected through a reiterated process of problem solving unfolding over longer periods of time (Haydu 1998: 349). Since most public policy formulation and implementation take place in sub-systems in which a limited number of actors are continuously and actively involved in decision-making and often in many day-to-day administrative decisions (e.g. Richardson and Jordan 1979; Rhodes and Marsh 1992; Baumgartner and Jones 1993; Sabatier 1988) it is analytically useful to distinguish between endogenously or exogenously problem dynamics. Problems are endogenously generated when they originate from within the subsystem. These may be unintended policy effects which threaten the core functions and thus viability of the policy. They need not necessarily affect political actors outside the subsystem but may often do so. An example of endogenously generated policy effects is recurring budgetary difficulties caused by the cost of implementing certain policy instruments. Exogenously generated problems emerge as a result of evolving broader policy contexts beyond the control of the policy subsystem. Developments in the broader policy context may challenge the policy and thus put pressure on the members or the subsystem to respond with policy changes. Exogenous problems can, for instance, be caused by the growing level of economic, cultural and political globalisation. An instance of the latter is the inclusion of agricultural trade on the negotiating agenda of Uruguay Round of the General Agreement on Tariffs and Trade (GATT) in the mid-1980s. As it became evident in 1990 that agricultural support and protection could not be sidelined in the Round, as had happened in earlier rounds, the trade impacts of the Common Agricultural Policy (CAP) became a new key policy problem which EU agricultural policy-makers had to address (Daugbjerg and Swinbank 2009).

An important theoretical challenge is to establish the conditions under which individual events in a policy sequence become both an outcome of previous policy decisions and developments and a cause of subsequent policy changes. Mahoney (2000: 511) refers to an 'inherent logic' and a 'natural' connection between events and thus puts forward a somewhat deterministic view on the driving forces behind a sequence. He tends to emphasise structure and devotes limited attention to the role of actors in connecting events. To establish the causal link between events in a policy sequence more attention must be paid to the way in which policy actors act within a policy structure and how they change it. Policy sequences 'are continually shaped and reshaped by the creativity and stubbornness of their human creators' (Sewell 1996: 272; see also Haydu 1998: 357, 2010: 32–3, 39–40). Therefore, on the one hand, theory on sequencing must leave room for agency when theorising about the causal connection between individual events in a sequence. On the other hand, since public policies are institutions, they constrain and facilitate certain actions over others. To have some independent impact on a policy sequence, actors must have capacity to reflect over the opportunities and constraints embodied in previous policy events when responding to policy problems.

Hay's (1995, 2002) concept of strategic learning spells out the potentials and limitations in actors' ability to reflect over the policy processes in which they are involved. While lacking complete information, political actors have some capacity to learn. As Hay (2002: 210) points out: 'given that actors are reflective, routinely monitoring the consequences of their action, we might expect their knowledge of the context to evolve over time'. However, since the broader and policy-specific context is complex and evolving, they are unlikely to reach a state of complete knowledge. Through their actions and the consequences of these, policy-makers learn, 'enhancing awareness of structures and the constraints/opportunities they impose, providing the basis from which subsequent strategy might be formulated and perhaps prove more successful' (1995: 201, see also 1998: 43). Learning is based on selective knowledge on the context within which strategic action is conducted. Since agents have incomplete information on the constraints and opportunities embodied in the settings within which they operate, they use 'more or less informed projections regarding the strategic motivations, intentions and likely actions of other significant players' (ibid.: 44). However, since the context is 'constantly evolving through the consequences (both intended and unintended) of strategic action' (ibid.: 43), cumulative learning may not necessarily result. There is no guarantee that actors draw the 'right' lessons from past experience; indeed, they may not even have the insight to judge which lessons are right and which ones are wrong (2002: 211). Thus, it is not the context as such which is the source of learning but actors' perceptions of the intended and unintended consequences of previous policy decisions which connect events in a sequence.

## *Policy feedback: learning and precedent*

The feedback from previous policy decisions is the key to establish how the actions of reflective policy actors create a link between antecedent and subsequent events in a policy sequence. Public policies produce various types of outcomes which feed back into the policy process and thus they become inputs into the policy process (Pierson 1993). Feedbacks affect the perceptions and actions of government officials and various types of stakeholders continuously and actively involved in policy formulation and implementation. These reflect over the feedback from policy implementation when attempting to understand whether the policy works as intended or whether it produces undesired unintended consequences (Lindblom 1959: 86).

As Heclo (1974: 305) pointed almost four decades ago, 'Governments not only "power" ... they also puzzle'. What he meant was that policy development was not only driven by powering, but also by attempts to learn from experience and adopt the best available solutions to policy problems. However, the two processes of powering and puzzling cannot easily be separated. Policy actors act within a structure which constrains certain actions and facilitates others. This structure may also facilitate and constrain which lessons are learned from policy experience and which are ignored. Since policy, as an institution, also reflects the outcome of past power struggles, learning may be constrained by powering (Roederer-Rynning and Daugbjerg 2010: 316–17).[2]

Policy-makers have to respond to policy problems emerging from an evolving broader policy context and to policy problems generated from within the policy itself. Though some policy problems can be ignored, at least for some time, others require action to maintain output legitimacy; that is, demonstrating to a broader universe of policy participants that policy can effectively address the problems with which it is confronted. The extent to which policy-makers are able to respond to the policy problems depends on their ability to reflect continuously over the opportunities and constraints embodied in the policy structure and develop strategies to address the challenges.

Each event in a policy sequence embodies a number of constraints and opportunities which policy actors can utilise to prevent or to facilitate further evolution of the policy; while previous events constrain certain policy responses, they provide opportunities for others. Prior events 'foster and shape the crises that prepare the ground for new solutions, and they influence the choices made by actors in response to those crises' (Haydu 2010: 36). Feedback process may reveal these constraints and opportunities to reflective and skilful reform advocates who want to change policy in particular directions and to those who desire the status quo and at the most willing to accept limited adjustments to address the most immediate policy problems. These perceived opportunities and constraints influence the power balance within the policy process by empowering some actors with particular interests and weaken others who hold differing views on the desired direction of policy evolution regardless of whether or not these views are motivated by power concerns or are outcomes of genuine learning processes.

As argued above, feedback involves an element of learning albeit constrained by the policy structure. In a larger policy complex, small-scale experiments with new policy solutions may be undertaken for more limited parts of the policy. Positive experiences with these can produce positive learning effects modifying entrenched perceptions of certain types of policy instruments among some policy-makers and thus create opportunities for extended and more intensive use of these. For instance, the 1992 reform of the CAP shows how positive experiences with new policy instruments can change preferences. The reform lowered the guaranteed minimum prices by a third and introduced annual direct compensatory payments. This switched a substantial share of farm support from indirect price support, in which subsidies to farmers were paid through artificially high consumer prices, to direct payments. The farm unions were strongly opposed to this change because it would make farm support look like social benefits (Daugbjerg 2009). However, 'the compensatory payments proved much more popular than anticipated in the farm community' (Moyer and Josling 2002: 194). Farmers learned that direct payments increased their income security and safeguarded them against drastic income losses from, for example, poor harvests (ibid.). Since the early 1990s, direct payments to farmers have been unquestioned and an integral and growing component of EU farm policy.

On the contrary, negative policy experiences may produce counter-reactions precluding the increased use of such instruments and perhaps even policy reversal. However, such learning effects may not materialise in policy change until the power balance shifts in favour of those interests desiring an effective response to the policy problems. For instance, surplus production emerged as a major problem in the EUs agricultural policy in the late 1970s and early 1980s. In the dairy sector, surplus production was effectively dealt with by introducing dairy quotas in 1984. In the arable sectors, the problem was not effectively addressed until 1992 when compulsory set-aside of arable farm land was introduced (Daugbjerg 2012). The 1992 reform of the main arable policy sectors demonstrates that negative feedback can change the power balance within a policy subsystem. Subsidised exports of EU surplus production had triggered the anger of the United States and other cereals exporting countries and therefore the EU was unable to avoid farm trade became an integral part of the GATT negotiating agenda (Daugbjerg and Swinbank 2009). This led to a shift in the power balance between the EU Commission and the Council of Agriculture Minsters in favour of former and eventually enabled substantial reform of the CAP (Coleman and Tangermann 1999).

Feedbacks may reveal policy inconsistencies which are counterproductive in relation to the objectives to be achieved within the policy field. Specific measures may pull policy in different directions and in some instances even neutralise the effects of each other. Such effects may be ignored, particularly in situations in which contradictory measures have been deliberately introduced to create or maintain a delicate balance between different groups of stakeholder with opposing interests. However, when these inconsistent measures start generating effects that threaten the core functions of the policy, and particularly when this amounts to a crisis, policy change becomes inevitable.

The most likely policy responses to learning feedbacks are those which are seen as representing the logical continuation of the direction set by the previous event in the policy sequence. In situations in which the distance between the existing policy design and the policy changes which from a rational perspective would be required to solve the problems is too large to be undertaken in one step for political reasons, policy change will tend to be gradual. In some, but more rare, situations the change of policy direction may be more abrupt and substantial. This tends to happen when contextual changes provoke a policy crisis and immediate response is needed. But even in these situations the policy response may grow out from the previous events in the policy sequence (Howlett and Rayner 2006: 7). Learning feedbacks from previous events in the policy sequence are most likely to impact on policy responses in situations in which the level of politicisation is low. As the level of politicisation increases, the less likely it is that learning will influence policy responses. Rather, policy-makers will exercise power to attempt moving policy in a particular direction when responding to policy problems and as a result learning processes might be sidelined (Pierson 1993: 617–18).

The causal connection to previous policy events in such politicised situations may be a new measure introduced in a previous reform to address a particular problem. This can be utilised to legitimise a full-scale use of the new measures within the policy even when it was originally aimed at a more marginal problem or was limited to solve a temporary problem. Policy-makers use precedent to legitimise policy change by claiming that the 'new' measures have indeed already been applied within the policy and that its extended use is a logical continuation of the direction of policy evolution previously set out. Reform advocates can, thus, construct precedent to support their interests in moving policy in a particular direction. Precedent can be a quite powerful political tool. Even though a new measure may be insignificant when introduced, or appear so, it may sow the seeds for a sequence of policy adjustment amounting to substantial change over time.

For instance, the introduction of the so-called Small Farmers Scheme in 2001 to simplify administrative procedures in EU agricultural policy demonstrates that a policy change aimed at addressing a relatively limited problem can form a powerful precedent for more comprehensive reform later on. The scheme offered farmers receiving less than €1,250 in direct aid payments annually to transform these payments into a single flat rate payment based on a historical reference period. The introduction of this scheme seemed insignificant at the time. However, it introduced a new form of direct aid payments to farmers. The direct payments introduced in 1992 required farmers to produce certain crops of keep particular types of livestock. The payments of the Small Farmers Scheme were not linked to production requirement and thus they were what is known in agricultural policy terminology as decoupled payments. They eventually spread to most of the commodity support schemes under the CAP in the 2003 policy reform. Simplification served as the precedent legitimising the proposal to apply the decoupled farm payment model, introduced in the Small Farmers Scheme, as the general support model in the CAP. As stated by the Commission: 'The Small Farmers Scheme represents an important *precedent* for reducing the administrative burden' (author's italics, Commission of the European Communities 2002: 10).

## Conclusion

In this chapter, process sequencing has been outlined and it has been argued that it is a distinct analytical approach to studying policy evolution. Though it shares a temporal approach to the study of policy-making with the path dependency approach, it is not based on the assumption that public policy evolution is predetermined by a particular path sustained by a set of self-reinforcing reproduction mechanisms. Rather, events in a policy sequence are connected by the attempts of policy actors to solve policy problems. As Haydu (2010: 36) points out: 'Thinking in terms of reiterated problem solving thus corrects the tendency of path dependency to make historical trajectories overdetermined, with outcomes increasingly locked in over time'. Policy events in a temporal sequence are casually linked by the feedbacks from previous events. These feedbacks disclose the constraints and opportunities for further reform to policy-makers. Though constrained by the policy structure, these actors utilise learning effects and precedent to generate support for policy changes. Thus, learning effects and precedent can provide causal link between antecedent and subsequent policy events in a sequence.

Process sequencing is theoretically underdeveloped in terms of specifying the factors linking antecedent and subsequent events in a policy sequence. In this chapter, some initial theoretical considerations have been presented, focusing on the role of learning and precedent as casual links between individual events in a policy sequence. It has also been emphasised that policy sequences are the outcomes of human action and therefore analysis of sequencing must focus on the interaction between structure and agency as policy-makers respond to policy problems.

Future research should concentrate on identifying other factors which potentially provide the causal connection between antecedent and subsequent policy event, specify how they privilege certain policy decisions and constrain others and explain how policy actors identify and conceive of the opportunities and constraints embodied in previous policy events. However, it is important not to over-theorise process sequencing. There is a risk that too much reliance on theory in identifying the causal mechanisms linking events in a sequence tempts analysts to downgrade fine-grained empirical analysis of the way in which events are actually connected. As Bearman *et al.* (1999, 508) caution: 'Theory involves denying data. Thin narrative accounts are the product of specific theories that direct the [analyst] to identify some events as salient and to deny others as not salient'. Thus, the further development of process sequencing as an analytical framework to studying policy evolution must balance between theory as an analytical tool to guide the search for the causal mechanisms on the one hand and an open-minded empirical approach to how events are casually connected in the specific case study on the other hand. Another but related challenge, not addressed in this chapter, is methodological. The challenge is to apply research methods which enable the scholar to establish the causal connection between policy events and avoid substituting causal analysis for accounts of a series of events which are temporally ordered but not explained. Process tracing is the most obvious research method to apply in process sequencing. The key focus of this research method is to develop tools which can help the scholar to establish whether events in a sequence are causally connected (Beach and Pedersen 2012).

## Notes

1 I would like to thank Darren Halpin, Adrian Kay and Rasmus Brun Pedersen for helpful comments on earlier versions.

2 See Pierson (1993: 614–19) and Bennett and Howlett (1992) for a discussion of the difficulties of applying the learning concept in empirical research.

## Bibliography

Baumgartner, Frank R. and Bryan D. Jones. 1993. *Agendas and Instability in American Politics*. Chicago: University of Chicago Press, 1–102.

Beach, Derek and Rasmus Brun Pedersen. 2012. *Process Tracing Methods: Guidelines and Foundations*, Ann Arbor: University of Michigan Press.

Bearman, Peter, Robert Faris and James Moody. 1999. 'Blocking the future: New solutions for old problems in historical science', *Social Science History* 23(4): 501–33.

Bennett, Colin J. and Michael Howlett. 1992. 'The lessons of learning: Reconciling theories of policy learning and policy change', *Policy Science* 25(3): 275–92.
Bulmer, Simon. 2009. '*Politics in Time* meets the politics of time: Historical institutionalism and EU timescape', *Journal of European Public Policy* 16(2): 307–24.
Cashore, B. and M. Howlett. 2007. 'Punctuating which equilibrium? Understanding thermostatic policy dynamics in Pacific Northwest forestry', *American Journal of Political Science* 51(3): 532–51.
Coleman, W.D. and S. Tangermann. 1999. 'The 1992 CAP reform, the Uruguay round and the commission', *Journal of Common Market Studies*: 37(3): 385–405.
——, G.D. Skogstad and M.M. Atkinson. 1997. 'Paradigm shifts and policy networks: Cumulative change in agriculture', *Journal of Public Policy* 16(3): 273–301.
Commission of the European Communities. 2002. *Communication from the Commission to the Council and the European Parliament. Mid-Term Review of the Common Agricultural Policy*, COM(2002)394, Brussels: CEC.
Daugbjerg, Carsten. 2009. 'Sequencing in public policy: The evolution of the CAP over a decade', *Journal of European Public Policy* 16(3): 395–411.
—— 2012. 'Globalization and internal policy dynamics in the reform of the Common Agricultural Policy', in Jeremy Richardson (ed.) *Constructing a Policy-making State? Policy Dynamics in the EU*, Oxford: Oxford University Press.
——and Alan Swinbank. 2009. *Ideas, Institutions and Trade: The WTO and the Curious Role of EU Farm Policy in Trade Liberalization*. Oxford: Oxford University Press.
Hay, Colin. 1995. 'Structure and agency', in D. Marsh and G. Stoker (eds) and *Methods of Political Science*. Basingstoke: Palgrave Macmillan.
—— 1998. 'The tangled webs we weave: The discourse, strategy and practice of networking', in David Marsh (ed.) *Comparing Policy Networks*. Buckingham: Open University Press, 33–51.
—— 2002. *Political Analysis: A Critical Introduction*. Basingstoke: Palgrave Macmillan.
Haydu, Jeffrey. 1998. 'Making use of the past: Time periods as cases to compare and as sequences of problem solving, *American Journal of Sociology* 1(2): 339–71.
—— 2010. 'Reversal of fortune: path dependency, problem solving, and temporal analysis', *Theory and Society* 39(1): 39–48.
Heclo, Hugh. 1974. *Modern Social Policy in Britain and Sweden*. New Haven, CT: Yale University Press.
Howlett, Michael and Jeremy Rayner. 2006. 'Understanding the historical turn in the policy sciences. A critique of stochastic, narrative, path dependency and process-sequencing models of policy-making over time', *Policy Sciences* 39(1): 1–18.
Jervis, R. 1997. *System Effects: Complexity in Political and Social Life*. Princeton, NJ: Princeton University Press.
Krasner, S.D. 1984. 'Approaches to the state: Alternative conceptions and historical dynamics', *Comparative Politics* 16(2): 223–46.
Lindblom, Charles E. 1959. 'The science of "muddling through"', *Public Administration Review* 19(2): 79–88.
Mahoney, J. 2000. 'Path dependence in historical sociology', *Theory and Society* 29(4): 507–48.
——and Kathleen Thelen. 2010. 'A theory of gradual institutional changed', in James Mahoney and Kathleen Thelen (eds) *Explaining Institutional Change: Ambiguity, Agency, and Power*. New York: Cambridge University Press.
Moyer, H.W. and T.E. Josling. 2002. *Agricultural Policy Reform: Politics and Policy Process in the EC and the US in the 1990s*. Aldershot: Ashgate.
Pierson, P. 1993. 'When effect becomes cause: Policy feedback and political change', *World Politics* 45(4): 595–628.
—— 2000a. 'Increasing returns, path dependence and the study of politics', *American Political Science Review* 94(2): 251–67.
—— 2000b. 'Not just what, but when: Timing and sequence in political processes', *Studies in American Political Development* 14 (spring): 72–92.
—— 2003. 'Big, slow moving, and … invisible: Macrosocial processes in the study of comparative politics', in J. Mahoney and D. Rueschemeyer (eds) *Comparative Historical Analysis in the Social Sciences*. Cambridge: Cambridge University Press, 177–207.
Rhodes, R.A.W and David Marsh. 1992. 'New directions in the study of policy networks', *European Journal of Political Research* 21(1–2): 181–202.
Richardson, J.J and A.G. Jordan. 1979. *Governing under Pressure: The Policy Process in a Post-Parliamentary Democracy*. Oxford: Robertson.
Roederer-Rynning, Christilla and Carsten Daugbjerg. 2010. 'Power, learning or path dependency? Investigating the roots of the European Food Safety Authority', *Public Administration* 88(2): 315–30.

Rose, R. 1990. 'Inheritance before choice in public policy', *Journal of Theoretical Politics* 2(3): 263–91.

Sabatier, Paul. 1988. 'An advocacy coalition framework of policy change and the role of policy-oriented learning therein', *Policy Sciences* 21(2): 129–68.

Sewell, William H. 1996. 'Three temporalities: Toward an eventful sociology', in Terence J. McDonald (ed.) *The Historic Turn in the Human Sciences*. Ann Arbor, MI: University of Michigan Press, 245–80.

Streeck, Wolfgang and Kathleen Thelen. 2005. 'Introduction: Institutional change in advanced political economies', in Wolfgang Streeck and Kathleen Thelen (eds) *Beyond Continuity: Institutional Change in Advanced Political Economies*. Oxford: Oxford University Press, 1–39.

Thelen, Kathleen. 1999. 'Historical institutionalism in comparative politics', *Annual Review of Political Science* 2: 369–404.

—— 2003. 'How institutionalism evolves: Insights from comparative historical analysis', in J. Mahoney and D. Rueschemeyer (eds) *Comparative Historical Analysis in the Social Sciences*, Cambridge: Cambridge University Press, 208–40.

—— and S. Steinmo. 1992. 'Historical institutionalism in comparative politics', in S. Steinmo, K. Thelen and F. Longstreth (eds) *Structuring Politics: Historical Institutionalism in Comparative Analysis*. Cambridge: Cambridge University Press, 1–32.

# 36

# Learning from success and failure?

*Allan McConnell*

## Introduction

A common sense view of the political world might expect policy-makers to seek success and avoid failure. Such assumptions are echoed in the public language of policy and political elites, from presidents and prime ministers to government ministers and senior officials. Stated success goals include building on what 'already works', as well as learning from mistakes when policies fail or disaster strikes.

To what extent do such assumptions and 'official' rhetoric accord with the realities of public policy? Perhaps surprisingly, the phenomenon of policy success has been given scant attention in the public policy literature (for exceptions, see Kerr 1976; Marsh and McConnell 2010; McConnell 2010a, 2010b). More has been written on aspects of failure, including policy fiascoes, crises and disasters, although the literature tends to concentrate on the management of acute episodes, rather than on long-term repercussions (see Hogwood and Peters 1985; Dunleavy 1995; Bovens and 't Hart 1996; Bovens *et al.* 2001; Birkland 2007; Boin *et al.* 2005). The purpose of this chapter is to build on the insights and implications of this relatively small group of literature (particularly that of McConnell 2010a, 2010b) in order to offer a more nuanced analysis of the simple assumption that policy-makers seek to cultivate success and avoid failure.

The chapter is structured as follows. First, it examines the innumerable methodological difficulties in conceiving of success and failure. Second, it deals with the issue of 'success as fact' vs. 'success as interpretation', and produces a working definition which allows us to conceive of success (and failure) as occurring in three realms: processes, programmes and politics. Third, it argues that by understanding the malleable, contested and multidimensional aspects of success, we are better placed to understand why the common sense logic of learning from success and failure has some validity, but not nearly as much as we might assume. Policymakers can certainly build on existing successes and learn from failures, but they may also tolerate, mask, risk, exploit and even cultivate failure.

## The methodological difficulties of ascertaining 'success' and 'failure'

Broadly speaking, public policy is whatever governments choose to do or choose not to do. We know from the literature on policy instruments (see e.g. Hood and Margetts 2007; Howlett

2010) that governments have many tools at their disposal, from laissez-faire to active provision of public services. They can refuse to intervene in industrial disputes, initiate anti-drink-driving campaigns, set regulatory standards for food hygiene, impose new taxes, build public hospitals, establish customs and immigration controls and send troops to foreign lands. What constitutes 'success' in making such policy choices? The issue is predictably contested and methodologically difficult, as it is with many phenomena within the political and social sciences.

*Differing perceptions:* put simply, is success a matter of fact or a matter of interpretation? Broadly speaking, there are two different tendencies – often implicit in the literature and reflecting broader trends within the policy sciences.

One tendency is interpretive or discursive, leaning heavily towards the assumption that success is in the 'eye of beholder' (see e.g. Bovens and 't Hart 1996; Fischer 1995, 2003). It is easy to see why such a position has some analytical validity. For example, in relation to the coalition interventions in Iraq or Afghanistan, it is likely that no amount of argument or evidence would persuade anti-war campaigners that the incursions were successful in bringing peace and stability to authoritarian regimes. It is also highly unlikely that animal rights activists would be persuaded that legislation permitting drug testing on animals was successful because of the benefits it provided in developing vaccines, drugs and treatments. The corollary of this tradition is that 'success' and 'failure' are little more than labels used by governments, commentators, the media and others, depending on their values, acceptance of government goals and the means of achieving them.

A counter-tendency is in the rational-scientific tradition, which leans heavily towards the assumption that policy outcomes are objective facts. Therefore, armed with the knowledge of government goals, we simply gather evidence which can be matched against these goals in order to ascertain an outcome of 'success' or 'failure' (see e.g. Gupta 2001; Davidson 2005). Again, it is easy to see some analytical worth in this tradition, because government can achieve broadly what it sets out to achieve, regardless of whether the goals and the outcomes are supported. No amount of differing perceptions, for example, can refute the fact that a public school was built, or that income taxes were levied and collected, or that NASA launched space shuttles into space, or that Saddam Hussein was deposed as president of Iraq. One implication of the rational-scientific tradition, therefore, is that, success and failure are matters of objectivity, with little or no room for perceptions of the merits or otherwise of a policy.

Overall, we are confronted with the real difficulty of how to conceive of success, when two such apparently diametrically opposed positions are evident. We will return to this issue shortly.

*Multiple benchmarks:* no definitive standards exist, by which we can judge success or failure. An examination of discourse surrounding policy success reveals a number of potential success measures. They are not mutually exclusive and they may complement or conflict, but they indicate substantial diversity.

- Implemented as intended e.g. public servants were efficient and effective in carrying out instructions.
- Original objectives were met e.g. target of 80 per cent of local property taxpayers, paying their bills online.
- Benefit was achieved for the target group(s) e.g. welfare payments to farmers.
- An improvement on a prior state of affairs e.g. unemployment has fallen by 2 per cent.
- Criteria have been met which have wide value in that policy domain e.g. efficiency in budgeting, adherence to risk management standards in continuity planning, secrecy in intelligence.
- The policy is supported by key interests e.g. citizens, key stakeholders, media.
- The policy is achieving more when compared to another jurisdiction e.g. one country doing better than another in dealing with the global financial crisis.

- Benefits outweigh the costs e.g. benefits of waging war on another regime, outweigh the human and financial costs.
- The policy is innovative e.g. using new technology to tackle online fraud.
- The policy complies with moral, ethical or legal standards e.g. adherence to principles of fairness; operates within the parameters of existing laws.

It seems, therefore, that success standards are malleable, to the point for example that a government and its supporters, can claim policy success, while its opponents can claim failure. A June 2010 Gallup poll on President Obama's management of the BP Gulf of Mexico oil spill, revealed a 56 per cent approval rating from Democrats and Democrat–leaners, but only 11 per cent approval from Republicans and Republican-leaners.

*Dealing with shortfalls, ambiguities and conflicts:* success isn't 'all or nothing' based on the achievement (or not) of a singular goal. Policy outcomes typically fall short of aspirations to varying degrees, If a government seeks to eliminate a 30 billion dollar budget deficit, many outcomes are possible, such as reductions to 28 billion, 20 billion, 10 billion and 5 billion. Yet there is no scientific line that can be drawn to demarcate success from failure. In all likelihood, government and its supporters will emphasise the importance of what has been achieved, while opponents and critics will highlight the shortfalls.

Furthermore, it is by no means certain that outcomes will be clear and unambiguous. Evidence may be lacking, stated goals may mask hidden agendas and success may produce unintended consequences. Indeed, one of the most common difficulties relates to the existence of multiple and conflicting goals where some are achieved and some not (indeed the achievement of one may be at the expense of another). For example, police resources focused heavily on crime investigation, may be at the expense of crime prevention. Similarly, a drive by schools to increase educational achievement, may conflict with a goal of increasing the number of pupils/ students from deprived backgrounds. In reality, therefore, policy outcomes are often messy, requiring judgement on the significance given to what has been achieved, weighed up against the failures and the grey areas in between.

*Success for whom*? Public policy, by its very nature of intervening (or not) to persuade, financially reward/penalise, regulate and provide, typically benefits some groups or interests by comparison with others, albeit that the broader rationale is articulated as being in the public interest. So, for example, the rights of smokers to smoke cigarettes, can be restricted in public places on the basis that doing so limits passive smoking and improves public health. Similarly, income tax payers who have no children, would be required to pay an increase in income tax that was levied specifically for the purpose of generating additional resources for schools. It is hard to escape the fact that a policy may be successful for those to whom it brings rights and rewards, but may not be conceived as such by those whose freedoms or resources are curtailed/reduced in order to achieve the broader goal.

*Variance over time:* it may be tempting to view policies as succeeding or failing, as though a snapshot is able to capture policy outcomes at an appropriate point in time. Yet, to continue the analogy, snapshots at different points in time might lead to different assessments. Apparent short-term failure may produce long-term success, such as the 'great planning disaster' of the Sydney Opera house (see Hall 1982) and its transformation into an iconic, revenue-raising tourist attraction. The opposite may be the case, where short-term success fades away to be replaced by conditions more likely to be considered as failure. The 2008–9 global financial crisis is a case in point, where light touch regulation and faith in the efficiency and self-corrective capacities of markets, has been viewed widely in hindsight as producing unsustainable levels of profitability. Analysing policy success needs to contend with the existence of multiple and perhaps contradictory outcomes over time.

*Isolating the policy effect:* political science is home to multiple methods and approaches (Hay 2002) and policy analysis is no different, including widely differing assumptions about how to evaluate outcomes (for contrasting positions see e.g. Fischer 1995; Davidson 2005). The very fact that multiple and conflicting assumptions exist, is a clue to the difficulties of explaining and assessing policies and their outcomes. If, for example, we wanted to assess the success of a government's anti-drugs advertisements, we would confront the fact that changes in drugs habits can be the product of many factors such as availability of supply, family pressures, peer influences, mass media stories and individual psychologies. We would either need to operationalise all the main variables and engage in rigorous statistical examination, or perhaps make a series of informed judgements, based on imperfect and perhaps conflicting evidence. In the policy sciences, it would be very difficult to reach a universal consensus on our ability to isolate the outcome of a policy.

There are no magical answers to these questions, or solutions to any of the other methodological difficulties. However, I would argue that rather than being deterred by such matters, there is an opportunity to gain insight from them.

## Moving forwards: the nature of policy success and policy failure

For heuristic purposes, we need to confront the issue of whether success is a 'fact' or an 'interpretation'. I would argue that to side purely with one or the other is to be analytically blind to important aspects of policy phenomena. A rational-scientific approach can never escape the existence of multiple interpretations and differing levels of support in plural societies. Equally, an interpretive approach can never escape the reality that governments can do broadly what they set out to do, regardless of whether the outcomes are perceived as successful. We need a conception of success that recognises and embraces both. Accordingly, I propose the following definition:

> A policy is successful if it achieves the goals that proponents set out to achieve and attracts no criticism of any significance and/or support is virtually universal.
>
> *(McConnell 2010b: 351)*

The key advantage of this definition is that it manages to combine more objective-oriented achievements, with perceptions of whether such achievements deserve the label of 'success', depending on popular and stakeholder support (explicit or implicit) for the means and ends. An example of success is the system of dams and dykes in the Netherlands, aimed at preventing about a quarter of the country's land mass being submerged by water, and universally supported among the populace. Many matters of low politics on non-controversial issues may also fall into this category, where government goals are achieved and there is no objection or criticism of any significance.

It is also possible to conceive of a spectrum of outcomes (see McConnell 2010a, 2010b) moving from durable or resilient success (where shortfalls in goal achievement are second best but tolerable and sustainable), to conflicted success (where achievements and support are finely balanced with failures and criticism), through to precarious successes (where failures and criticism outweigh some achievements and support) and finally to outright policy failure.

> A policy fails if it does not achieve the goals that proponents set out to achieve, and opposition is great and/or support is virtually non-existent.
>
> *(McConnell 2010: 357)*

Failures may generate high levels of media interest (such as the poll tax in the UK) or they may be contained within the realms of small policy subsystems, away from the glare of the media.

## Three realms of policy success

If we want to understand the dynamics of success and failure, a crucial step now needs to be taken in developing our understanding. What 'governments do' can usefully be split into three realms. Table 36.1 provides fine detail and hence the discussion here is confined to making the general point that governments can succeed and/or fail in each of these realms.

*Process:* among other things, governments define problems, appraise options, design instruments, engage with stakeholders and take decisions. Processes of policy formation involve strategies which, if they succeed, allow governments to preserve their goals and policy instruments, produce policy in a legitimate fashion, build sustainable coalitions, appear innovative and attract little or no criticism for the process of policy formation. For example, a range of processes from adherence to constitutional rules or norms, to utilising good practice in stakeholder engagement can form the basis of 'successful' and legitimate, coalition-building processes. If policy is about what governments do, they 'do process' and they may succeed and/or fail in this regard

*Programmes:* As we know, governments produce programmes, involving varying mixes of policy instruments. Regardless of the process of policy formation, we may judge programmes separately, to the extent of matching them against a number of possible indicators. They may be implemented in line with objectives, achieve desired outcomes (such as the switchover from analogue to digital television in Luxembourg, Finland and Sweden) create benefit for the target group(s), satisfy criteria valued highly in that policy domain (such as secrecy in the intelligence sector) and attract widespread support or at least no criticism/opposition of any significance. Governments 'do programmes' and they may succeed/and or fail in this realm.

*Politics:* the processes and programmes of governments also have political repercussions. They can boost political reputations and electoral prospects, ease the business of governing through agenda containment, contribute to desired policy trajectories, maintain broader governance agendas and help to galvanise political support behind these moves. An example is Australian Prime Minister Kevin Rudd's 2007 historic 'sorry' speech to aboriginal people for the forced removal of a

*Table 36.1* The three realms of policy success

| *Process success* | *Programme success* | *Political success* |
|---|---|---|
| Preserving government policy goals and instruments | Implementation in line with objectives | Enhancing electoral prospects or reputation of governments and leaders |
| Conferring legitimacy on the policy | Achievement of desired outcomes | Controlling policy agenda and easing the business of governing |
| Building a sustainable coalition | Creating benefit for a target group | Sustaining the broad values and direction of government |
| Symbolizing innovation and influence | Meets policy domain criteria | Opposition to political benefits for government is virtually non-existent and/or support is virtually universal |
| Opposition to process is virtually non-existent and/or support is virtually universal | Opposition to programme aims, values, and means of achieving them is virtually non-existent, and/or support is virtually universal | |

Source: Adapted from McConnell (2010b: Tables 1, 2 and 3)

'stolen generation' of children from their families. Governments 'do politics' and they may be more, or less, successful in doing so.

## Policy-making as the juggling of success and failure

There is no doubt that governments can learn from both successes and failures. Learning from success involves a form of positive feedback, where policies deemed successful are reproduced and expanded, such as the waves of privatisation of the late 1980s and 1990s. Learning from failure can be described as negative feedback, where a form of self-correction ensures that failures are addressed. Corrections may involve the fine-tuning of existing policies (through, for example, amended guidelines for front-line public housing officials), the replacement of existing policies with new ones (Australian gun law reforms after the 1996 Port Arthur massacre) or even a paradigm realignment which sets the agenda for reform (arguably, pre- and post-global financial crisis shifts in political elite attitudes to debt, regulation and the free market).

Yet an implication of the foregoing discussion of success and failure, is that governments may aspire to different 'successes'. Indeed, doing so may involve prioritising some over others, and using the malleable label of 'success' to help legitimise their choices and direction. Failure in some realms is often a precondition for success in others. Failures in some areas can be tolerated, masked, risked, exploited and even cultivated in the pursuit of success elsewhere.

### *Tolerating failure*

Public policy failures are everywhere. Judging how significant they are, may involve Wildavskian art rather than science. Nevertheless, some simple examples help to make broader points. Low level failures involve small shortfalls, for example 97 per cent of welfare claims processed within two weeks as opposed to a target of 98 per cent. There is no incentive to address such minor failures if broader programme successes are evident and not compromised by the failures.

Moderate or medium-level failures may also be tolerated on the grounds that, on balance, the programme successes are a price worth paying. The European Union's (EU) Common Agricultural Policy is a good example. It does achieve key goals such as EU self-sufficiency and raising the standards of farmers' incomes, but has generated considerable criticism and controversy because of its drain on the EU budget and production of huge surpluses. Supporters perceive it to be an EU 'flagship' policy while opponents portray it more as the *Titanic*.

Dealing with such failures may also compromise political success. For example, few are likely to disagree with a diagnosis of failure in relation to squalid high rise/tower blocks which are home for some of the poorest and most vulnerable people in society. Yet is not difficult to see why such failures may be tolerated, especially under conditions of economic stress and fiscal stringency. Costs of reform would need to come from other programmes, potentially jeopardising their success. Dealing with programmatic problems may also compromise political success. Exemplars are austerity measures, debt reduction programmes and efficiency drives. Japanese Prime Minister Hashimoto's efficiency drive in the banking sector in order to revive a struggling economy underestimated the adverse political effects and was a major factor in his defeat at the 1998 general election. In 2011 similar political pressures were brought to bear on governments in Greece, Spain and Ireland. The success of debt reduction programmes generates high risk of political failure, at least in terms of popular support for governments.

Even high-level failures may be tolerated, or at least there may be attempts to suppress them, if policy-makers consider that addressing the issues is likely to jeopardise programmatic and/or political success. One such example is arguably the Guantanamo Bay detention camp under the

Obama Administration, where innumerable ethical, human rights, legal and logistical problems continue, but closure of the camp may well jeopardise the success of the incarceration programme itself (what to do with approximately 170 potential terrorists when there is a lack of a strong evidence base to convict?) as well as jeopardising the political goals of the Obama Administration to fight terrorism in a climate where approximately six out of every ten voters in America, do not want the camp to be closed.

A more general point needs to be made. Policy problems vary in complexity, from simple well-structured problems and no clear solutions, to 'wicked issues' with multiple and complex causes, and absence of widely accepted and authoritative solutions (Head 2008; Hoppe 2010). Also, signals of failure are often vague and ambiguous, subject to multiple (mis)interpretations, leading to policy-makers processing information disproportionately – sometimes over- or under-reacting to signs of failure (Jones and Baumgartner 2005).

In sum, failures are often tolerated because to do otherwise would be to consume valuable agenda time, as well as engage in costly reforms with no guarantee that they will work. Political success in terms of easing the business of governing and keeping broader policy and paradigm values on track, is often at the expense of tolerating failures.

## Masking failure

It is not only that failures may be tolerated, but they may also be masked, intentionally or unintentionally, by the activities of policy-makers.

The use of political language can push failures, to the lower realms of political agendas. Edelman's (1977) famous dictum, 'words that succeed and policies that fail', was used to refer to political promises and reassurances which hid chronic inequalities, injustices and policy failure, especially in the area of social welfare. Deborah Stone (2002) provides a more detailed analysis of the ways in which metaphors, synecdoche and other linguistic devices, can be used to suppress policy problems. Phrases such as 'storm in a teacup' or 'freak events' can be used to dampen the salience of failures, while those that seek to elevate the issues can be labelled as 'trouble-makers' or even 'enemies of democracy'. Indeed, the argumentative turn in policy analysis (see e.g. Majone 1989; Fischer and Forester 1993: Hodgson and Irving 2007), illustrates the importance of argumentation and framing, with different interests battling to elevate and even dominate political discourse with their views.

Policymakers may also produce placebo policies (where there is a high symbolic content in terms of appearing to tackle the problem, with a low likelihood that they will do so, see McConnell 2010a). For example, Clarke (1999) in his work on contingency planning for crises and disasters, argues that plans are primarily of symbolic value ('we are prepared and in control') rather than operational value. Sharman (2011) in his detailed study of the regulation of money laundering, explores the rapid diffusion and copying of regulations as being 'politically successful policy failures'. They demonstrate 'political success' because they create the appearance of good governance, strong regulation and zero tolerance of money laundering, but outcomes are patchy at best and ineffective at worst, particularly in developing countries. For example, the small Pacific island of Nauru (population 11,000) has developed state-of-the-art anti-money laundering legislation but it has no financial sector of any kind – not even a bank or an ATM! Even institutional reforms and restructuring can have strong symbolic and 'feel good' elements, without necessarily minimising long-term, chronic problems. The creation of the Department of Homeland Security (DHS) in the United States symbolised an integrated response to the threat of terrorist attacks, but in reality has arguably done little to minimise the behaviour of actors in policy subsystems (May *et al.* 2009).

Often, when policies fail and/or when crisis and disaster strikes, inquiries are used in order to find out what went wrong and learn lessons for the future. We might expect them to reveal, rather than mask, failures and their causes. Yet as argued by recent literature on the politics of inquiries (Stanley and Manthorpe 2004; Kitts 2006; Prasser 2006; Birkland 2007; Boin *et al.* 2008), investigations may be steered away from examining potential causal factors, as a consequence of terms of reference, membership and funding. In essence, when failures occur, potential underlying causal factors may be insulated from investigation, in order protect the values and policies which sustain broader success trajectories. In 2005–6 when the privatised Australian Wheat Board Ltd was investigated by the Cole inquiry for paying 'kickbacks"to Saddam Hussein's regime in contravention of UN sanctions, the terms of reference did not encompass inter alia the minimalist regulatory regime emanating from the original privatisation, that may have helped explain why the company had freedom to engage in illicit financial activities (McConnell *et al.* 2008).

A related issue is blame games, involving the deflection of attention towards particular individuals, interests, institutions, technical and climatic/geophysical factors (see Weaver 1986; Hood 2011). The purpose in deflecting attention towards a particular actor or set of conditions, is also to deflect attention away from other factors. In other words, blame games may be an attempt to shore up the returns of policy success.

As Schattschneider (1960) and Bacharach and Bartatz (1970) argued convincingly many years ago, political systems develop a 'mobilization of bias' which is capable of filtering out grievances and failures. The masking of failure is the flip aside of dominant biases, geared towards particular aspirations of programmatic and political success.

## *Generating the risk of failure*

Policymakers cannot predict the future with absolute certainty. They can certainly engage in small policy trials, use *ex ante* evaluations and attempt to model outcomes, but there are always elements of uncertainty and contingency (Shapiro and Bedi 2007). All policy-making involves an element of judgement, sometimes instinctive and sometimes the product of careful scenario planning, in relation to the risks (May 2005; Althaus 2008). All policy processes carry some possibility of failure. To put this in the language of this chapter, attempts to achieve process success carry risks of programme and political failure (see McConnell 2010a). For example:

- log-rolling and horse trading carry the risk of differing interpretations at the implementation stage, actors not behaving as agreed, and changing socio-economic and political contexts rendering the agreements unworkable;
- evidence-based policy-making brings the risk of policy-making being informed by skewed or incorrect evidence, or being merely the legitimating basis for policy and political trajectories that bring strong contradictions;
- deliberation and stakeholder engagement can be little more than the legitimating framework for policy and political pathways, bringing the risk of inflated expectations which cannot be met;
- use of strong executive power to push through policies and legislation carries the risk of political backlash, as well as programmes lacking sufficient scrutiny to ensure effective implementation;
- policy transfers from other jurisdictions carry the risk of being uninformed, incomplete or inappropriate for the new policy context.

The list could be longer but the basic point is clear. Every strategic process strategy brings opportunities but also risks. What constitutes process success for policy-makers in producing their desired policies through constitutionally and quasi-constitutionally legitimate means, can carry the longer-term risk of producing programmes which fail to fulfil intended goals, while backfiring politically on government agendas and compromising its broader political goals and pathways. Failure is not inevitable but failure is often a prospect, to varying degrees and depending on the context such as the degree of politicisation surrounding the issue and likely levels of support/ opposition. Public policy-making and accepting the risk of failure go hand in hand.

## *Cultivating/creating/exploiting failure*

The logic of the policy cycle approach is that policy-making is driven by problems in search of solutions. However, as 'garbage can' theory indicates, the opposite may be the case. Policy can be driven by solutions in search of problems in order to justify an intended course of action. The literature on crisis and disaster makes similar points, that crisis conditions can be capitalised upon and even exploited in order to achieve longer-term programmes and political goals (Klein 2007; Boin *et al.* 2009). For example, often cited allegations include the existence of 'weapons of mass destruction' in Iraq as a means of legitimating the coalition invasion of Iraq in 2002, and asylum seekers throwing their children overboard a stricken vessel bound for Australian waters, in order to legitimate immigration reform. Crises can be an opportunity to boost political careers and demonstrate fitness for office. For example, the 2002 floods in Germany helped to provide the foundation for the invigoration of Chancellor Schröder, some six weeks before the federal election - helping his party to victory (Bytzek 2008). In the wake of the 9/11 attacks, George W. Bush's approval ratings soared to the highest in US polling history. As Rahm Emanuel, Barack Obama's Chief of Staff, stated: 'you never want a good crisis to go to waste' (*Washington Post*: 6 March 2009). Overall, therefore, 'failure' may be sought out and even cultivated, in order to pave the way for programme and political success.

## Conclusion

Conventional wisdom and governmental rhetoric lean heavily towards the promise that political and policy elites will build on successes and learn from failures. Leaving aside the issue that what constitutes learning is a value assumption, change and learning can certainly happen. However, it is far from an automatic or reflexive process. The nature of policy success is contested and riddled with methodological difficulties, requiring a value judgement in terms of attaching the label of 'success' to outcomes, depending on the salience given to achievements and the significance given to shortfalls and ambiguities. There is a degree of malleability in the way that policies can be framed, as successful or otherwise.

When we also factor in the existence of different forms of successes in the process, programme and political realms of policy, it is evident that failures – and lack of learning from them – are not only commonplace, but often necessary because they have been disregarded in the pursuit of longer-term success goals. Successful processes (such as a government rushing a bill through a legislature) in order to achieve its goal, may run the risk (conceived of as acceptable risk by policy-makers) of programme failure through ill-thought-out legislation, and even of political failure if the issue is high profile and politically partisan. Or, successful programmes, especially if they are ruthlessly efficient in achieving highly contested goals, may carry the risk of political failure. Alternatively, ineffective programmes tackling difficult and perhaps 'wicked issues', may be tolerated and even promoted, if it suits political success aspirations in maintaining control of agendas through the appearance of tackling problems. Colloquially, we might refer to this as 'good politics but bad policy'.

As indicated by the argument and analysis in this chapter, failures are not always abhorrent to policy-makers. Failures can be tolerated, masked, risked, cultivated and even exploited in order to pave the way for process, programme and political goals. Policymaking involves trade-offs and risk taking, juggling the hope of some successes, with the acceptance and even desirability of failure.

## Bibliography

Althaus, C. 2008. *Calculating Political Risk.* Sydney: University of New South Wales Press.

Bacharach, P. and M. Baratz. 1970. *Power and Poverty: Theory and Practice.* New York: Oxford University Press.

Birkland, T.A. 2007. *Lessons of Disaster: Policy Change after Catastrophic Events.* Washington, DC: Georgetown University Press.

Boin, A., A. McConnell and P. 't Hart eds. 2008. *Governing after Crisis: The Politics of Investigation, Accountability and Learning.* Cambridge, Cambridge University Press.

——, P. 't Hart and A. McConnell. 2009. 'Towards a theory of crisis exploitation: Political and policy impacts of framing contests and blame games', *Journal of European Public Policy* 16(1): 81–106.

——, P. 't Hart, E. Stern and B. Sundelius. 2005. *The Politics of Crisis Management: Public Leadership under Pressure.* Cambridge: Cambridge University Press.

Bovens, M.P. and P. 't Hart. 1996. *Understanding Policy Fiascoes.* New Brunswick, NJ: Transaction.

——, P. 't Hart, and B.G. Peters (eds). 2001. *Success and Failure in Public Governance: A Comparative Analysis.* Cheltenham: Edward Elgar.

Bytzek, E. 2008. 'Flood response and political survival: Gerhard Schröder and the 2002 Elbe floods in Germany', in A. Boin, A. McConnell and P. 't Hart (eds) *Governing after Crisis: The Politics of Investigation, Accountability and Learning.* Cambridge: Cambridge University Press, 85–113.

Clarke, L.B. 1999. *Mission Improbable: Using Fantasy Documents to Tame Disasters.* Chicago: University of Chicago Press.

Davidson, E.J. 2005. *Evaluation Methodology Basics: The Nuts and Bolts of Sound Evaluation.* Thousand Oaks, CA: Sage.

Dunleavy, P. 1995. 'Policy disasters: Explaining the UK's record', *Public Policy and Administration* 10(2): 52–70.

Edelman. 1977. *Political Language: Words that Succeed and Policies that Fail.* New York: Academic Press.

Fischer, F. 1995. *Evaluating Public Policy.* Chicago: Nelson-Hall Publishers.

—— 2003. *Reframing Public Policy: Discursive Politics and Deliberative Practices.* Oxford: Oxford University Press.

——and J. Forester. 1993. *The Argumentative Turn in Policy Analysis and Planning.* Durham, NC: Duke University Press.

Gupta, Dipak K. 2001. *Analyzing Public Policy: Concepts, Tools, and Techniques.* Washington, DC: Congressional Quarterly Inc.

Hall, P.G. 1982. *Great Planning Disasters.* Berkeley, CA, University of California Press.

Hay, C. 2002. *Political Analysis.* Basingstoke, Palgrave Macmillan.

Head, B.W. 2008. 'Wicked problems in public policy', *Public Policy* 3(2): 101–18.

Hodgson, S.M. and Z. Irving (eds). 2007. *Policy Reconsidered: Meanings, Politics and Practices.* Bristol: Policy Press.

Hood, C. 2011. *The Blame Game: Spin, Bureaucracy and Self-preservation in Government.* Princeton, NJ: Princeton University Press.

——and H.Z. Margetts. 2007. *The Tools of Government in the Digital Age.* Basingstoke: Palgrave Macmillan.

Hogwood, B.W. and B.G. Peters. 1985. *The Pathology of Public Policy.* Oxford: Clarendon Press.

Hoppe, R. 2010. *The Governance of Problems: Puzzling, Powering and Participation.* Bristol: Policy Press.

Howlett, M. 2010. *Designing Public Policies: Principles and Instruments.* New York: Routledge.

Jones, B.D. and F.R. Baumgartner. 2005. *The Politics of Attention: How Government Prioritizes Problems.* Chicago: University of Chicago Press.

Kerr, D.H. 1976. 'The logic of "policy" and successful policies", *Policy Sciences* 7(3): 351–63.

Kitts, K. 2006. *Presidential Commissions and National Security: The Politics of Damage Control.* Boulder, CO: Lynne Rienner.

Klein, N. 2007. *The Shock Doctrine: The Rise of Disaster Capitalism.* New York: Metropolitan Books and Henry Holt.

McConnell, A. 2010a. *Understanding Policy Success: Rethinking Public Policy*. Basingstoke: Palgrave Macmillan.
—— 2010b. 'Policy success, policy failure and grey areas in-between', *Journal of Public Policy*, 30(30): 345–62.
—— A.Gauja and L. Botterill. 2008. 'Policy fiascos, blame management and AWB limited: The Howard government's escape from the Iraq wheat scandal', *Australian Journal of Political Science* 43(4): 599-616.
Majone, G. 1989. *Evidence, Argument, and Persuasion in the Policy Process*. New Haven, CT: Yale University Press.
Marsh, D. and A. McConnell, A. 2010. 'Towards a framework for establishing policy success', *Public Administration* 88(2): 586–7.
May, P.J. 2005. 'Policy maps and political feasibility', in I. Geva-May (ed.) *Thinking Like a Policy Analyst: Policy Analysis as a Clinical Profession*. New York: Palgrave Macmillan, 127–51.
——, J. Sapotichne and S. Workman. 2009. 'Widespread policy disruption: Terrorism, public risks, and homeland security', *Policy Studies Journal* 37(2): 171–94.
Pawson, R. 2006. *Evidence-based Policy: A Realist Perspective*. London: Sage.
Prasser, S. 2006. *Royal Commissions and Public Inquiries in Australia*. Chatswood, NSW: LexisNexis Butterworths.
Schattschneider, Elmer Eric. 1960. *The Semisovereign People: A Realist's View of Democracy in America*. New York: Holt, Rinehart and Winston.
Schneider, A.L. and H. Ingram. 1997. *Policy Design for Democracy*. Lawrence, KS: University Press of Kansas.
Shapiro, I. and S. Bedi. (eds). 2007. *Political Contingency: Studying the Unexpected, the Accidental and the Unforeseen*. New York: New York University Press.
Sharman, J.C. 2011. *The Money Laundry: Regulating Global Finance in the Criminal Economy*. Ithaca, NY and London: Cornell University Press.
Stanley, N. and J. Manthorpe. 2004. *The Age of the Inquiry: Learning and Blaming in Health and Social Care*. London: Routledge.
Stone, D. 2002. *Policy Paradox: The Art of Political Decision Making*, 2nd edn. New York: W.W. Norton.
Weaver, R.K. 1986. 'The politics of blame avoidance', *Journal of Public Policy* 6(4): 371–98.

# Author index

# Subject index